Beyoncé

Raising Genius

By David Lee Brewer

Beyoncé: Raising Genius
Copyright © 2017 by David Lee Brewer
With a Foreword by Björn Teske, Berlin
For information address Tony Coles at Tony Coles Pr
http://www.tonycolespr.com

Book Design: Erik Kinting, Hamburg – www.buchlektorat.net
Cover Design: net-realizer GmbH & Co. KG, Nürnberg
Editor: Sandra Hyslop
Book Cover Design Credit: Ferdinand and Kristina Herrmann, Nürnberg
David Lee Brewer's photo credit: Devon Cass, NYC www.devoncass.com
Beyoncé's photo credit: The Tillman Estate
Photos not credited are furnished courtesy of the author:

David Lee Brewer
tony@tonycolespr.com

Publisher and printing:
CreateSpace

Thanks be to God

Not many of you should become teachers, my brothers, for you know that we who teach will be judged with greater strictness.

James 3:1

TABLE OF CONTENTS

Forward

I was born for the music business.

Early on I was surrounded by music. When I was five years old, my father, who was a music business executive in Hamburg, brought home the latest vinyl recorded singles and albums of the day – Elvis Presley, Lou Reed, David Bowie, Rick Springfield, and Eurythmics. For a young boy, this was exciting. At that time, music-lovers could either buy the record, or hear it on the radio or in bars and cafés on jukeboxes. Those were hardly options for a five-year-old, so my father's demos gave me a real head start in appreciating music. Several years later, I began learning how to make mix tapes of music from my father's 7-inch records and albums and from the best radio shows. There was no on-demand streaming, like there is today. Rather, we had to set our alarm clock to record the shows we wanted to hear, live from the radio. I will never forget buying my first very own singles, that first album, tickets for my first live concert. I must have asked my father a million questions, which he always answered patiently.

Today, as the managing director of my own company (bt'em entertainment management in Berlin), I have the honor of supporting music artists, bringing more than 20 years' experience in the music industry to the table. It is a huge responsibility to be part of the network that helps to bring a performer to the attention of the world and to success. I love my job, which is often likened to the profession of a jeweler who takes raw material and polishes it into a sparkling gem. I, too, take raw material – young, inexperienced artists – and guide them in shaping and polishing their talent into the unique jewel that they dream they can become. There is, however, a remarkable difference between my profession and the jeweler: real artists are never finished, and are driven to develop over the years, always reinventing themselves to maintain their polish.

In my career as a product manager, A & R executive, label manager, and managing director of my own agency, I have been responsible for the international exposure, A&R, and the complete marketing campaigns of many artists. The lengthy list includes N'Sync, Sweetbox, Guano Apes, Lou Bega, Germany's Pop Idol show, Yvonne Catterfeld, David Garrett, and one of Germany's most legendary artists, Udo Lindenberg. These musicians and a multitude of others have always asked me the same central question: How do I become famous as an artist and how do I turn my art into money? My reply, "You, yourself!" appears to be easy to understand, but implementing this directive is actually very complex. A star does not fall from the sky.

My colleagues and I face the difficult task of finding an outstanding artist from a huge talent pool. We look for someone who is authentic and passionate, capable of conveying emotions, who comes with an interesting story, and who has the fundamental and relevant stuff to become a star. Where is that hit record? Is there a second and third? Does the artist have the ability to record a whole album, and is he or she also convincing enough to make a second or third? If the answer to all these issues is Yes, then I sign them and thus begins the real work. And hard work it is. Still, we never know until all the factors come together. Everything is crucial.

Funnily enough, talent is not even the most important factor. Sometimes the artist's potential has not been developed, since he has not yet worked with the right people, or perhaps he has not even recognized his niche yet. It is therefore essential to aid the artist to develop a strong work ethic and to build upon the basic and core principles that must be there. In addition, an artist must learn to deal with the media. That "skill," or the lack thereof, will determine whether the artist is loved or rejected. How the artist maneuvers in that shark pool cannot be left to her own devices.

All these factors must be taught.

Until an artist gets signed by a label, he or she often travels the long and difficult road alone. They will need to be singer / instrumentalist, interpreter, songwriter, actor, entertainer, high-performance sportsman, photographer, social media specialist and, and, and – the list can be long. The best performing musician is the boss of his own small corporation – a 360-degree commitment to a 360-degree idea.

Today the model in the music business is what we call "360 Degrees." The goal is to offer the artist an extremely good and profitable complete service, the scope of which must be as flexible as possible. The development stage of the artist should be outlined in the contract. Who plays which role? Classical structures such as labels, publishing, concert agencies will continue to exist, but the focus is constantly shifting. By all accounts, a complete team is essential: music production, songwriters, coaches, a visionary and powerful A & R, marketing, promotion and sales force (still mostly only a few labels), concert agencies, and the most important, an experienced management that understands the artist, recognizes his or her visions and assists them while remaining a totally honest and sincere consultant. Everyone in the team must be able to say, "That's it!"

Not to be taken lightly, the infighting and goings-on of the personal network of the artist (parents, relatives, friends, etc.) can lead to unpleasant reactions – even dismissal – from the label. People of the personal network are crucial--positively crucial if they work in support of the professional network, and disastrously crucial if they work at cross purposes. The latter is, unfortunately, often the case.

The Marketing component closes the 360-degree circle. If the product and marketing staff fail to understand the artist and the concept – and if during the process, holes have been torn in the network – the artist is out. It's all about business: in artistic terms, "communication with the audience," and in industry terms, "creating a profitable sales bond between artist and audience."

Because my great love is developing the artists, I have felt fortunate to have met David Lee Brewer thirteen years ago and to have worked closely with him ever since. David, who with this book adds "author" to his many illustrious accomplishments, is an outstanding voice teacher and vocal coach, one of the best. He is also one of only a few vocal and music professionals who consider the artists in their entirety, who works with them as human beings, developing, supporting, and arming them for the hard fight that is the music business.

A true man of music, David understands the quality demanded by our industry – not only from an artistic standpoint, but also from the demands that the business makes on the artist. He respects the transaction between the music industry and its customers, and he knows how to instill that respect in the inexperienced artist. David's abilities are based in the rich experiences that he himself gathered both on and behind the stage as a highly regarded professional singer. Like no other, he has an immediate grasp of a new artist's capabilities and he works with extreme care to help each artist find the unique vocal identity that serves as their X-factor in the long term of his or her professional career.

David brings with him a wide spectrum of experience and he thinks internationally. Whether an R & B artist, rock artist, jazz singer, classical tenor, or percussionist: whoever wants vocal quality goes to David Lee Brewer. His musicality and his diversity connect the artists to their goals within minutes of their work together. I've seen it. No matter what topic you have, he's quick to get excited when he sees talent.

I admire and depend upon David's unique ability to translate calm and confidence to the artists, to focus them, and to create the atmosphere and chemistry that they need to do their best work. This translates into star performances, hit recordings, and enduring careers.

Reading this memoir, I have now learned that his method and principles come from a deep well of knowledge. Yes, it is a cautionary tale written about his work with Beyoncé and the creation of Destiny's Child. Even more important, David's book reveals the authenticity, passion, and wisdom that he brought to the lives of these young singers. I felt as though I had a front row seat in his studio, in rehearsals, and in recording sessions as he meticulously prepared the girls for their career. When he described their path to stardom, I knew that I could trust his account, because the hard labor, that "crucial network" I talked about, the highs and the lows, the successes and the pitfalls are completely accurate depictions of the world that people outside the music business rarely get to see.

The fact is that the voice teachers and the vocal coaches play a crucial role in laying the very foundation for artists' successes, and in maintaining the polish that can be so easily tarnished without constant care. Yet – and this is nothing new – their value to the performer remains largely unacknowledged. They are, in my opinion, true unsung heroes. When does an artist think to give his or her vocal coach public recognition? Far too rarely, I'd say. Performers may think to acknowledge their management and label staff, which is certainly deserved. But I would like to correct the bad habit here. David is *NOT* your ordinary voice teacher or vocal coach. His work culminates in millions of record sales all over the world. He has certainly earned a seat at my artists table.

Whenever I need a partner in supporting talent, I know where to look, sure that I can count on David Lee Brewer to take the rough raw material I sometimes find in the shadows and polish it into a high-quality diamond. Ours is a wonderful collaboration.

Björn Teske, bt'em – entertainment management
Berlin, March 2017

Prelude

There have been numerous attempts to pen the definitive story of what some have called Beyoncé's meteoric rise and Destiny's Child's history and subsequent break-up. At the peak of their fame at the turn of the century, Destiny's Child together with James Patrick Herman, wrote their own account of events in *Soul Survivors: The Official Autobiography of Destiny's Child*, published by Harper Entertainment, 2001. It obscures or omits many backstory details and anecdotes to which I was privy; however, I am mentioned, ever so briefly by Kelly Rowland.

Other more journalistic accounts such as Ian Gittin's *Destiny's Child*, published by Carlton Books, 2002; Kelly Kenyatta's *Yes, Yes, Yes: The Unauthorized Biography of Destiny's Child – A Tale of Destiny, Fame and Fortune*, for Busta Books, 2001; and Keith Rodway's *Destiny's Child: The Unauthorized Biography in Words and Pictures* by Independent Publishers Group, 2002, are told from a distance and do not mention me at all.

In Daryl Easlea's *Beyoncé: Crazy in Love: The Beyoncé Knowles Biography*, published by Omnibus Press, 2011, the author writes: "The group played countless shows supporting acts passing through Houston, and they became involved with vocal coach David Brewer, who gave Kelly, Beyoncé and LeToya vocal lessons. He stated in 2000 that he'd had greater influence over the girls than Mathew Knowles, developing their vocals." Destiny's Child didn't become involved with me, I co-founded them. But I can't blame Daryl Easlea, or any other author/journalist for their one-sided report of Beyoncé's idyllic life and wholesome rise. That's the way Mama Celestine wanted it.

Another writer, Anna Pointer, writes a beautiful biography of who Beyoncé became, citing all of her accomplishments. *Beyoncé: Running the World: The Biography*, published by Hannibal publishers 2014, mentions my involvement in Beyoncé's life and career, but by quoting words from my website – verbatim. And by 2015, J. Randy Taraborrelli writes what he calls the most comprehensive book about Beyoncé, ever. *Becoming Be-*

yoncé: The Untold Story, published by Hachette Book Group, which ignores my contributions altogether. He definitely knew who I was and what my significant contribution and influence had been. I definitely have my theory as to why I am left out of the most comprehensive book on Beyoncé's start and ultimate rise. The rise that had everything to do with me.

I find it most interesting that Mr. Taraborrelli chose to lie in his mini documentary film, (The Making of "Becoming Beyoncé" – A Mini Documentary), and for all the world to see and hear. He knew full well that he was airing an egregious misrepresentation of the facts in claiming that Kim Wood Sandusky was Beyoncé's first vocal teacher. The insult feels intentional. But why? Nevertheless, I've had enough.

Am 13.07.2014 19:51, schrieb cathy griffin:
Hi David:

I am a journalist working for bestselling biographer J. Randy Taraborrelli. He is writing a major biography on Beyonce to be published by Hachette Books in late 2015. http://www.hachettebookgroup.com/about/

Congratulations on all your many successes. We heartily read the few snippets we can find about you online about your work with Girl's Tyme and Destiny's Child. You had such an amazing and intimate relationship with them all and as their first and primary vocal coach.

We would so like to interview you about your being so very instrumental in the early days Beyonce's career. We know your memories are so rich regarding all the girls and their families.

You have a lot of unique perceptions and perspectives to share. We want to give you the credit and recognition you deserve. Randy has authored 14 New York Times bestsellers and thus, his books get attention. I left a message on your voice mail this morning.

I can be reached here and my cell is: ……….. If you would list some dates and times where I could have about 45 minutes of your time on the phone as I am in L.A., would much appreciate your courtesies. I work weekends and any time zone convenient for you.

Best!
  Cat Griffin
  On behalf of J. Randy Taraborrelli: www.jrandytaraborrelli.com
clgrif@…

* * * * *

Paul Burrell, the author of *A Royal Duty,* which chronicles his life and experiences with Princess Diana, once said in the press, "I never thought I would have to write this book – but then I never believed I would have to redress balance." This is my sentiment exactly, and it expresses only one of the reasons I am writing this book. The other reasons have to do with former manager Andretta "Ann" Tillman and the vicious deceit and greed she suffered at the hands of Celestine Knowles. Beyoncé and all the other girls were the daughters I never had, but for Ann they were her lifeline. We both knew and loved that they were honest and decent children, but dealing with serious family issues that no child should have to experience. Still, that's no excuse to deny her, or my many years of dedicated work.

I took on Beyoncé and the other girls, knowing that one day they would have to go out and conquer on their own. It was necessary to equip them and not cripple them. I breathed with them, and I cried with them. And I rejoiced with them as they set their emotions free and conquered their fears. I helped them to identify their feelings, listening to their dreams and nightmares – to the point where those dreams and nightmares became my own. And I guided their understanding of how to access and connect with their audience's emotions. Above all, I gave them tools they will need for life, both in their professional and their private lives. Yet, you, the reader, have never heard of me.

Beyoncé Knowles received the best of what I had to give as a teacher, mentor, protector and friend. She was trained better than most opera singers and deserves every accolade she has received. But now it's time for the truth, for my credit. I deserve it. God uses many people but blesses few. It's time Beyoncé Giselle Knowles remembers the reason why!

Again, there have been numerous attempts to pen the story of what they all call the meteoric rise and success of Beyoncé Giselle Knowles. *They* have all missed the mark. *They* weren't there. *They* don't know her, or the story. I'm delighted that **Beyoncé: Raising Genius** is not forced to follow the story that the family has orchestrated. It becomes the only definitive book that will ever be written about Beyoncé's rise, because only one person can recount what she learned to make her the phenomenon she became. I was determined to build 360-degree artists, and by all accounts I feel that I have been more than successful. **Beyoncé: Raising Genius** will also answer those questions that have gone unanswered, as well as ones the reader didn't even realize might need to be asked. Family is where things got interesting.

Dispelling the many widely believed myths surrounding Beyoncé's rise, I use captivating stories that no one else can or will tell, to reveal Beyoncé's parents' illusions of grandeur and self-serving delusions of superiority. In balanced and sensitive language – with humor and with compassion – I write about a teacher and his prodigy. A beautiful young, talented girl, Beyoncé was guided to superstardom at an incredible cost to herself and everyone around her.

Today, my disappointment is monumental.

And as I told the German press in 2016, *"It"* is bigger than selling records. *"It"* is bigger than your career. *"It"* is about truth….

So, here's to truth as I remember it, and more importantly – *significance*.

Part I

The Beginning

---

1. Learning about faith!

"God made you for music!"

For my three-year-old self, Grandmother's words were life changing. They were so powerful an affirmation that I could think of nothing else. I loved singing and dance, and my grandparents had everything to do with it.

My grandmother's voice was the first beautiful sound I remember hearing. Even now, I still get goosebumps when I think of her: singing, self-assured, standing at that big stove preparing one of her delicious meals, or baking a scrumptious cake. A tiny thing, Grandmother had a big voice – but then again, it could be that my small ears heard it that way. Nevertheless, it was impressive. Mixing a chocolate cake batter, she would cascade upward to high notes with the ease of a trilling bird, while I would stand by her side, eagerly listening and hanging on her every melisma and waiting for the moment when she'd give me the bowl and beaters to lick.

Sweet sounds, sweet flavors, sweet spirit: my Grandmother Evelyn.

* * * * *

I clearly remember my first music lessons with Grandmother. In the kitchen, a place where love and family come together, we'd spend time singing little melodies. She had a radio, just above the stove, and when I wasn't humming to one of those tunes, I was working over Grandmother's favorite repertoire, Gospel. She'd sing. I'd imitate. I was having fun like Christmas.

I don't remember the pop songs that came on the radio, the ones I lightly hummed to, probably because I never knew their words. But there was one song that I definitely remember. "Jesus loves me," the very first Gospel Song Grandmother taught me, would become an important staple in my own teaching. But before I'd grow up to teach it to others, I had a *few things to learn about interpretation.* That was what Grandmother said. I can see it as if were yesterday. Handing me the song's words, which she had written out clearly onto a piece of paper, Grandmother said, "Sing it back to me. With feeling."

I began, singing in my clear, little-boy voice, "Jesus loves me, this I know. For the Bible tells me so. Little ones to Him belong. They are weak but He is strong."

"Good, baby. Now I want you to take a close look at the words on the paper and sing it again," Grandmother said.

A little doubtful – after all, I already knew all the words of this song – I did what she asked. Looking down at the paper, which I had sort of ignored during my first rendition, I noticed the red markings that Grandmother had made on the paper. "These are the rules," she said, "and to sing this song right you have to follow them. Think of it like a puzzle." I liked puzzles.

Starting again, I saw that Grandmother had put a red exclamation point after the word "me" (Jesus loves me!) in the first line. That was the Who, the singer of the song, the teller of this important story. When I got to the next sentence, I saw that Grandmother had capitalized the T on the word "this" (This I know). A capitalized letter meant that the word should be sung with assurance, a certain stress. I had messed up.

"Can I start again, Grandmother?" I asked. She nodded her head. This time I sang out, accenting and stressing the words "me" and "this," just as Grandmother had taught me to do.

"Good, baby," she said, smiling.

I was on a roll, so I sang on: *"For* the *Bible Tells* me *So."* Capitalized first letters, again, meant assurance. Then I noticed another detail. If the first letter was also *slanted,* it meant, "Pay attention to a sudden switch in rhythm, from a smoother singing style to a more emphatic tone." I stopped. This time, I looked over the entire song text before beginning to sing again. I wanted to do it perfectly, for Grandmother. I saw that in the third phrase she had capitalized two initial letters, with slants, "*L*ittle ones to *H*im belong,' and in the last verse, the phrase "*T*hey are weak but *He Is Strong*" had *four capitalized and slanted letters*!

All right, David, she's smiling. Are you ready?

I was.

I started again. This time I sang confidently, translating Grandmother's red puzzle marks into heartfelt song. She beamed. Finally, I sang the last phrase of the opening verse, which I sang almost screaming it, I was so excited.

"Wonderful!!!" Grandmother shouted.

I stopped again, smiling like a Cheshire cat.

Then it was time for the chorus, my favorite part. I looked it over before beginning. Grandmother had written a comma after the word "Yes," and the "Y" was oversized. I remembered that this meant that the word exploded a bit with joy, and that it should be sung short, syllabic. I was also to take a clear breath after the comma. The J in Jesus was capitalized and there was an exclamation point after the word "me"! The triumphal last line had four capital letters that were slanted (*F*or the *B*ible *T*ells me *S*o).

Starting from the beginning, I successfully sang to the end – perfectly – prouder than a hound pup in his first flea.

I was having fun like Christmas.

* * * * *

Grandmother and Grandfather discovered my talent when they caught me singing and dancing to the 1965 Oscar Mayer Wiener 60-second commercial in front of their Admiral color television console. I had drifted off into my own special world, one where "magic lived," I told Grandmother. I hadn't noticed Grandfather Charles checking me out, looking over his spectacles from behind the *Omaha World-Herald* newspaper. Nor did I see that Grandmother Evelyn had been eyeing me from the kitchen. When I finished, she and Grandfather gave me a resounding round of applause.

It was then that Grandmother exclaimed, "You are going to be a singer one day, baby." Grandfather added, "If the boy is going to sing, he'll have to learn to dance."

So I did both.

Just like every young person who has been bitten by the showbiz bug, I could imagine nothing else from that day forward. I became the kid in a candy store. "Magical Saturday" is how I thought of lesson day with my grandparents. Those days, singing with Grandmother in what I called "the happy room," the kitchen, and dancing with Grandfather, in the living room, analyzing performances in old movies, couldn't come round fast enough.

Evelyn Childs-Sims had such high aspirations for me. Born in Topeka, Kansas, to John and Lula Childs, a teacher and aspiring pianist, Grandmother told me that her mother, Lula, had taught her everything she knew about music. Although she had passed before I could know her, Great-grandmother Lula, through Grandmother Evelyn, wielded significant power in my musical upbringing.

From her pictures, Great-grandmother appeared to be tall, thin, and strong. Her skin was smooth and her hair was coal black, long, and wavy. Family lore ascribed her physical appearance to her heritage of Blackfoot Indian and Spanish blood. But toward the end of her life she became sickly, and her behaviors frightened my then-young mother, Fern Sims.

"That ole lady would pinch my cheeks. She didn't know how to let go," Mama said.

Mama told me that Great-grandmother Lula couldn't talk because of "the stroke" and that she made strange, guttural utterances. Although Grandmother Evelyn had tried to explain what a "stroke" was, Mama had been too young to grasp the connections between Great-grandmother's odd behaviors and that traumatic event.

It wasn't just her inability to talk, the guttural sounds, or the pinching of her cheeks that frightened Mama. Great-grandmother's hands were scary and black. She had suffered that stroke while cooking, and at the same time she had an epileptic seizure. Falling forward toward the coal stove, she burned her hands badly on the front burners. The imprints of the stove's eyes were etched into her hands as though they had been carved there. She loved music and played the piano, but had to give it up after *the accident*, Grandmother said. She never played again and, as Mama put it, "She turned cold and mean after that accident."

But that wasn't the only grief she suffered. Great-grandmother Lula's daughter Fern had died at age eighteen of unknown causes. Grandmother Evelyn never got over her sister's death, and neither did Great-grandmother Lula, I understood. To honor her, Grandmother Evelyn named my mother for her deceased sister.

"So that's how you got your name, Mama?"

"Yes, baby. That's how Mama got her name," my mother answered.

Hearing all those stories was interesting, but not as interesting to me as my singing and dancing lessons with Grandmother and Grandfather. Grandmother was my first coach in musical interpretation. "You must feel what you sing." Grandmother would add, "If you don't feel it, your audience doesn't feel it." Again, she'd demonstrate. I'd imitate. Even then she would ask me why I had chosen a particular way of singing.

Phrasing was extremely important, Grandmother said, because it shows that you understand the song, and people who hear you sing it will understand it, too. "A person's understanding of phrasing determines their musical tastes." Taste was paramount. I would find myself, much later in life, repeating those very words as well, to my own students.

Grandmother Evelyn's father, Great-grandfather John Childs, was an elegant man whom I was fortunate to know in my childhood. Also small in stature, he had large hands. He always wore starched white shirts, a tie, creased pants with suspenders, and spectacles. His shoes were always polished and immaculate, with no scuff marks. He seemed very smart to me, and I rejoiced whenever he came to visit. Although he had lived in

Topeka when his daughter, my Grandmother Evelyn, was born, Great-grandfather now lived in New York, she said. I'd only heard of New York, from the movies that I watched with Grandfather. Sometimes I think now that I must have overwhelmed Great-grandfather with my thousands of questions during his short visits. If he minded, he never showed it.

Grandfather Charles Sims, too, taught me about music and performance. From his experience as a professional dancer, and now retired from a successful career in vaudeville, Grandfather opened my eyes to this new world. "Dancing is a whole lot more than moving your feet," Grandfather explained to me. "The hands are very important in dance, and so is what you do with your head and neck, the torso, and the hips."

Grandfather insisted that I learn to hear the music in silences. "Silence in performance is essential," he said repeatedly.

Taking me outside into the Nebraska winter one day – I was almost five years old – he instructed me to look up. "David, movement must be as smooth as that gentle smoke you see coming out of that chimney." That's how I remember it. And all these years later I still find myself studying how gentle hints of smok e waft upwards and then outwards from chimney stacks in winter. It is the perfect visual for understanding breath flow. It is also the perfect analogy for fluidity in movement. "You can hear rhythmic music in everything," Grandfather said. "Even water."

"Hoofing it," as Grandfather and his colleagues termed it, was essentially tap dance. It required you to jump around with a big smile on your face, like a minstrel. At first I felt that this type of the dance was silly and demeaning. Tactfully ignoring my turned-up nose, Grandfather convinced me of the beauty in that art form.

The wealth of films on television during my childhood documented the dancer's art, and on Magic Saturdays Grandfather and I would make a study of the dancing greats of the past. The Nicholas brothers, Fred Astaire and Gene Kelly, Shirley Temple, John W. Bubbles, Charles "Honi" Coles, Donald O'Connor, Rita Hayworth, Betty Grable, and Bill "Bojangles" Robinson, the most famous of them all, mesmerized me. I sat transfixed in front of the television, every Saturday without fail.

My favorite movie was "The Little Colonel," starring Bill "Bojangles" Robinson and a very young Shirley Temple. Over and over again, Grandfather and I would analyze my favorite scene, in which the elegant Bill "Bojangles" Robinson danced up and down the stairs while a tiny blond curly-haired Shirley Temple looked on, before joining in.

While Grandfather imitated Bojangles's complex dance moves, I would count off the rhythm, loudly. If I got the count wrong, Grandfather would fall about in laughter, plummeting to the floor. I remember thinking Grandfather's antics fun, and my jumping into his loving arms reassured me. He'd stand up and we'd begin again. I'd count, mess up, he'd fall, I'd jump on him – again. Eventually, I got it and when I did, I realized that dance, too, had its capital letters, slants, and commas.

Through his skillful demonstrations Grandfather taught me the grace, timing, and showmanship that good dancing requires. During those years I must have asked Grandfather, too, a million questions. He answered every one of them, patiently and clearly.

I didn't know it then, but those moments with my grandparents helped determine my comprehension of the arts on a greater scale. The lessons and conversations I had with them opened me up, freeing me for expression. My later studies with such sophisticated interpretation teachers as Sylvia Olden Lee would be well rooted in the rich, intuitive wisdom of Grandfather and Grandmother Sims's teachings in my childhood.

Which brings me to my next point. I was more than a little curious as a child, always trying to figure things out. Take my beloved grandfather, for instance. Charles Sims was said to have been born on May 14, 1900, on an Indian reservation in or near Harrisburg, Pennsylvania. My mother tells the story that he had thirteen brothers and sisters, and that he had a twin brother who had blond hair and blue eyes. She'd seen him, she said. Grandfather swore that she was mistaken, but Mama seemed sure she hadn't been.

Mama also told me that Grandfather had run away from his mother, a woman named Edith, when he was around thirteen years old; that prostitutes had rescued him from his life on the streets; that they had reared him in their brothel and had seen to his education and well-being.

"What's a brothel?" I asked.

"A whore house," Mama answered. Mama believed in honesty. Honesty was huge in our house. If we asked it, she answered it, and always candidly.

"Did the prostitutes become Grandfather's new mother?"

"Yes, baby," Mama answered. "Your grandfather had the love of many mothers. They sent him to school daily with clean clothes, food in his belly."

"Good," I remember saying.

Naturally, I asked my grandfather about what Mama had told me. He didn't deny one word of it, which led me to ponder why he'd denied his siblings. He told me, further, that the brothel had given birth to his vaudeville career.

"I learned to dance there," Grandfather told me.

Apparently, one of the clients, a tap dancer, taught Grandfather "the ole soft shoe," which started him on his way to becoming an elegant dancer, in the same style.

"He reminded me of Fred Astaire," Grandmother said of her husband.

Her comment gave me pause. I'd been dying to ask why Grandfather looked so pale. I'd seen Fred Astaire in those old movies. With his fair skin, he looked a lot like my grandfather, and nothing like me. I shouldn't have asked, but hey, I was a kid. I got away with bloody murder.

Grandmother had been hesitant about Charles Sims at first, she said. "I thought he was a white man." Somehow he managed to prove his Cherokee heritage to her, courted her, and held on to a marriage that lasted many decades.

Over the years all those puzzling questions rattling around in my little brain were answered. Ultimately, those were footnotes to the main text: Grandfather was Grandfather, and I adored him.

My grandmother, in particular, began prodding my mother and teachers to assist her in her campaign to make me into Mozart. Her insistence guided my interests, and along with my curiosity about family matters, I asked how I'd come to be born. How did my origins connect with a possible future as a singer? Slowly, Grandmother revealed to me the story of my birth, with Mama herself sometimes filling in essential details.

My grandparents, Evelyn and Charles Sims, were real socialites within the black community in Omaha. Grandfather, who worked for Omaha's first Cadillac dealership, "Rosen Novak," invested his earnings into the selling of "spirits" – alcohol. He did very well financially and took his place as a respected member of the general community. He also joined several clubs and organizations, including the Elks Lodge, the Iroquois Lodge, and the Brummell Club, while Grandmother worked in several charitable organizations. I'll never forget going to meetings with Grandmother. Through those meeting I was exposed to my first lessons in the importance of giving to others. I remember the sense of pride I felt when I learned that she had helped spearhead the committee that successfully introduced the Salvation Army's first Tree of Lights in North Omaha.

Determined to have a theatrical protégé, my grandfather enrolled my mother in ballet classes when she was four years old. Little Fern was too young for serious study, but having your child in ballet was perceived as a socially advantageous move, a status symbol. Furthermore, Grandfather thought his younger daughter should become familiar with structured movement as soon as possible, and indeed she did.

Little Fern was able to utilize her many years of dance training to become the lead majorette in the Iroquois Lodge Drum and Bugle Corps, of which Grandfather was president. At the age of twelve, Mama was the youngest ever to hold that coveted position.

David Lee Brewer was the lead drummer in that same drum and bugle corps, which was the most popular in Omaha. He was tall, dark, *and* handsome. He was suave. He could talk his way into and/or out of any situation. Today he would be considered a handsome "bad boy." Once, while on tour with the drum and bugle corps, he talked my mother into having sex with him. At fifteen she should have known better; she was, after all, Charles and Evelyn's daughter. But as I said, David Lee Brewer was good-looking and suave.

When my father sweet-talked, my mother listened. After it was over – the sex, that is – Fern thought, is that what sex is? "It was over so quickly and sticky." Ugh, she thought.

It was the first time Fern had ever had sex and she was caught: wet behind the ears, and scared after the doctor's announcement of her pregnancy. Instantaneously, three things happened: Grandmother cried, my Aunt Lee Lee scooped up Fern and carried her to safety, and Grandfather went looking for David Lee. Hearing the news of his impending fatherhood, Daddy tried to skip town.

"Your grandfather was just in time," Grandmother said, explaining how he'd chased Daddy down. Even though Fern had just disastrously ruined Grandfather's college plans for her, there was no way in hell she was going to embarrass the family. Grandfather handed Mr. Brewer a piece of paper bearing the date when he and Fern would wed, January 20, 1963, and threatened Daddy within an inch of his life if he didn't show up. He even called Daddy's mother, who insisted that her son would be on time for his wedding.

Nevertheless, "Your grandparents didn't like your father's family," Mama said to me years later.

"But why?" I asked. "Grandma Anna Laura was nice."

When I asked Grandmother Evelyn about my daddy's family, her grunted disapproval told me that my youthful character analysis was misplaced. "His family was scandalous," Grandmother said.

Although I knew her only in my childhood, my memories of daddy's mother are vivid. Grandma Anna Laura McCants-Dorsey was a tall woman with long red fingernails and beautiful hair. She was a card-loving gambling woman who could go a round or two with the best of them. To me she was a loving presence, always interested in our welfare. She smoked cigarettes like a chimney and – fascinating to us little kids – she never lost an ash. While engrossed in her card game, she'd talk animatedly with her cigarette hanging from the right corner of her mouth, dancing and jutting to and fro. As the cigarette burned down it produced ash, a long stream of ash. I can still see my brother and me staring at that phenomenon, waiting for it to fall from her cigarette. It never did.

Her second husband, Grandpa Fred, was a jolly old man who loved baseball. He let Grandma Anna Laura do whatever she wanted and he, too, showered us with affection. I can't remember ever eating as many chocolate chip cookies as I did then, visiting my paternal grandparents' home. Although Grandpa Fred was a responsible man who worked hard, and although Grandma Anna made sure that her son showed up at his own wedding, with bells on, the Simses never warmed to Daddy's parents.

At first, my father tried to ingratiate himself with Mama's parents. He figured out that learning his way around society folks would do the trick. This really interested him. For a moment there, Grandfather wanted to trust his new son-in-law. Grandmother Evelyn even got him a job in the place where she worked as a seamstress.

Unfortunately, Daddy had other things on his mind. On the 22nd of July, 1963, the day of my birth, Daddy went to jail for theft. He had learned how to move in the right circles, all right. In only a few months he had learned how to move right in to my grandparents' friends' homes and relieve them of their belongings. Scared, my mother gave birth to me, a 6 pound, 9-ounce baby boy, at 7:22 p.m., without her husband by her side.

Grandfather had set my parents up in their own apartment, which was supposed to be a nice start for their married life and their bouncing baby boy. However, despite the fact that Grandma Anna Laura had made David Lee show up for his wedding, neither she nor anyone else could make him spend time with us. Mama said that Daddy was never there. He had serious problems.

Mama tried being "Suzie homemaker." Everything, cooking included, was new for her. Once, she worked all day to cook dinner for my father, who came home and made himself a hot dog. Disrespectful of his new wife, he hated his new domestic responsibilities and his child. Soon Fern was pregnant again. In November 1964, my little brother, Darryl LaMar, was born. Daddy, however, couldn't pull himself away from his friends and his pool game long enough to go to the hospital. Grandfather sought him out and dragged him, kicking and screaming, to visit his wife and new son.

This time Mama was fed up. They soon divorced. The year was 1965. Shortly afterwards Daddy got carried off to prison for stealing. Mama always said, "Once a thief, always a thief." She hated a liar and a thief, she said repeatedly, as if she was trying to drill it into our heads. She even told us that if we ever stole anything, she'd leave us in the jail house. I believed her every word, and have never forgotten them, nor the fact that both sins were listed on Moses's tablets, which he threw down onto the people from Mt. Sinai, in the movie "The Ten Commandments." Mama made us watch that movie every year. She wasn't religious but a little hell, fire, and brimstone never hurt anybody…

For the next few years, my mother and brother and I lived in peace. But when I turned five, Mama sent me to live with her sister, Young Lee Clayter. There was a special school, which had a very special kindergarten teacher, in my aunt's neighborhood, and according to Young Lee, I just had to go there.

I will always have fond memories of kindergarten class at Lothrop Elementary School in Omaha, and of my wonderful teacher, Ms. Graham. Gentle and caring, Ms. Graham was a petite woman, even in the high heel pumps she wore every day. Her hair was an intense black color and wavy, and she always wore it in a bun. It was so perfect that I remember wondering if it was real. I moseyed right up to Ms. Graham's desk, with "that look," as she called it, and asked her, straight out. Shamelessly, I asked her a little of everything. (In later years I got my just reward when I got assigned to kindergarten during my student teaching, which made me appreciate Ms. Graham even more.)

When she removed her shoes during our active days in school, Ms. Graham walked around the room in her stocking feet on her tippy toes.

Children don't forget something like that. Her lessons in "getting along," her way of solving our childish disagreements, required us kindergarteners to talk things over. Standing face to face with our classmates, instead of struggling over the possession of a toy, we would discuss the issue. "Learn to share. There are others in the world besides you," she would prompt. She also reiterated, time and time again, the consequences of telling a lie, a lesson I thought everyone had already learned at home.

With some financial help from parents, Ms. Graham constructed her own special kindergarten classroom: a complete playground, with slides, jungle gyms, and sand boxes. Mama said that it was her intent to create the supportive and imaginative environment that she considered essential for children's development. And I'll never forget how she exerted complete control over the atmosphere of her "Wonderland," the title that was inscribed over the classroom's entry way.

My brother and I started to spend loads of time in the doting company of Grandfather and Grandmother Sims, as well as of Daddy's parents, who also had a two-bedroom home. Mama, still young and very attractive, was in college. There she met a man I didn't like, got pregnant, and nine months later, in January 1966, gave birth to my little sister, Donetta Lynn. Marrying David White was out of the question, Mama said. It had been only a year since her divorce from Daddy. "I'm not ready," she told Grandmother.

Thank God, I thought to myself.

And then, three years later, without warning, my world fell apart.

On January 19, 1969, in a civil service at the Omaha court house, Mama became Mrs. Roy Edward Kellogg, and life as I knew it was over.

My mother was in love.

Raising three children alone in her early 20s couldn't have been easy for Mama, and I feared that this was the reason she re-married almost four years after her divorce from Daddy. During those four years, with the help of my grandparents, there had no longer been anything that we kids wanted for – Mama just had to ask. Now she believed that she had found true love. Roy had swept her off her feet.

I did not like my new stepfather. Within the first few months of their marriage Roy began beating Mama. Hiding the pain and the evidence of his abuse became her focus. She hadn't had a clue that Roy would become violent and she certainly didn't want my grandparents to know. Mama had been reared in a loving environment and was at a loss to know how to cope with her new reality. The police might respond to domestic violence calls, but they would make an arrest only if the woman pressed charges, or if someone had died.

Despite fearing for her life, Mama never pressed charges, "I felt trapped," she told me many years later. I had heard her late-night whimpering, muffled by her own hands, as he delivered each one of those punches to her body. It was as if I myself was the one being beaten. With each blow Roy Edward Kellogg terrorized not only my mother, but all three of her children. It took all of her strength to effect a separation from Roy, who reluctantly moved back to his parents' home.

On a hot summer Friday morning in 1969, Roy's sister Carol (18) called our house at around 8:15 a.m. She told Mama that Roy had threatened to kill her and their sibling Jeanine (17). He had vowed to set their parents' house on fire with them in it. He was crazed, and they were terrified. Mama told the two girls to get out of that house and into a taxi, assuring them that she would pay the fare upon their arrival at our house. Mama then tried to contact Roy's mother at work. (His father would have been of no help. He too was abusive. An alcoholic, he not only beat his own wife, but he encouraged his son's warped ideas, insisting that he "be the man of his own castle.") When Carol and Jeanine arrived at our home, they called their brother Robert, who immediately showed up to take them to safety. According to police reports and the press, Robert was accompanied by his friend James Gill.

My little sister, Donetta Lynn, only three years old, was having breakfast in the kitchen, as usual, with her dolls. As my mother comforted Roy's sisters in the living room, Roy showed up on our doorstep. He had easily followed Carol and Jeanine to our home. Still angry, he continued his vehement threats, and his brother went outside to calm him down. Robert's friend James Gill then made the biggest mistake of his life.

Standing at the kitchen sink, Gill said to my mother, "Fern, can I have a glass of water?" Roy, overhearing the request through the open kitchen window, entered the house in a rage. He assumed that Gill was flirting with my mother and he wasn't going to stand for being disrespected; Fern was still his wife. Roy and Gill got into an argument and as Gill turned the glass up and began to drink, Roy drew out a gun and shot him in the neck. Gill ran out of the house, blood streaming from his artery through his fingers; Mama followed closely behind with Donetta. She met our neighbor Barbara Pointer, who upon hearing the gunshot had come running. The next door neighbor, Miss Pearl, called the police. According to newspaper reports it was 9:30 a.m.

My brother and I, four and six, still asleep upstairs, were awakened by that loud crack. I knew instinctively that it was gunfire. Used as I was to shepherding my siblings away from Roy's anger, I rose from my bed and gathered up my little brother. But, where was my little sister?

Barefoot and in pajamas, I told my brother to follow me, and with sleep in our eyes we headed downstairs. Just as I got to the bottom of the stairs, I met an adult heading my way. Roy?! I nearly jumped out of my skin. No, it was Mama. The sudden shock of her presence only increased when I saw that she was covered in blood – blood, she immediately reassured me, that was not hers. Quickly opening the front door, she told me and my brother to go to our neighbor's house. I must have inquired about my little sister, because I remember Mama's screaming at me, "Go! Go to Brenda's! She is OK."

The last image I saw before going out that door was my stepfather, Roy Edward Kellogg, gun in hand, pulling Mama back into the house by the hair as she tried to escape. I turned back to see if she was following and saw instead that her eyes were full of fear. I will never forget the look in her eyes. She smiled at me, and I thought it would be the last time I would ever lay eyes on her. That smile said, "I love you." It was frightening. I could hear police sirens and feel the hot Nebraska summer morning on my bare feet. Moments later it looked like something out of a movie. Police and SWAT were everywhere. I have never seen so many guns, positioned and ready to fire, neither before that time, nor since.

Negotiations for Roy's surrender led to his shooting at the officers, and minutes later the police fired tear gas bombs into our house. My mother was in that house, held hostage. Roy's sister Carol was eventually able to talk him down and he finally succumbed to the pressure. Mama was overcome by the tear gas. As the detectives questioned her, the emergency workers arrived. I ran back into our house just in time to see that Mama had fainted from shock.

My grandparents, having seen the incident – including Roy's surrender – on the television news, rushed to our aid. That was that. Our secret was out. The police carted Roy off to jail and Mama was taken to the hospital. I was worried about Mama, but Grandmother told me she'd be all right. I insisted on going with her to the hospital to see for myself. Grandfather took my little brother and sister home with him.

My Aunt Lee Lee, Mama's sister, met Grandmother and me at the hospital. I had begun to feel relief – something like happiness, that perhaps Roy was now out of our lives. After all, the police had put him in jail.

But James Gill had not died. I heard Aunt Lee Lee tell Grandmother, "Roy will have to be arraigned in a municipal court, but his lawyer might be able to get him out of jail on bail since the man he shot didn't die." Gill lived? What could this mean? What was "attempted murder"? Would Roy be back?

As Aunt Lee Lee finished her conversation with Grandmother and then the doctor, who wanted to keep Mama overnight for observation, a police officer arrived to take Mama's statement. It was during this process that I learned that my Aunt Lee Lee worked in the accounting department for the Omaha Police, and by the time I entered Nathan Hale Junior High School she had become the department director. When I had lived with her while attending kindergarten I'd had no idea whom she worked for. I just knew that every morning I went to school and she went to work. Now, at the hospital, she and that police officer greeted one another like old friends before he disappeared into the room where they were attending to my mother.

Mama recovered and was released, but I was still in shock. Thoughts of Roy's return began to surface. I was terrified of him.

Just as my aunt had predicted, his lawyer was able to get Roy out on bail – thanks to Roy's mother, who offered her house as collateral. Within weeks he was back on our doorstep.

This time Roy arrived late in the night with a couple of friends, all of them high. Still afraid of Roy, my mother reluctantly let them into the house, asking them to keep things quiet because of the three sleeping children. Their loud voices and Roy's abusive threats awakened me, and I crept downstairs. I peeked around the corner just in time to see my mother defending herself against Roy with the first weapon that came to hand: one of his own Seagrams Seven Crown Royal bottles. More than forty years later, that image, imprinted as a slow-motion movie, still plays and re-plays on the screen of my brain. My mother's arm comes up in an arc, lowers the bottle on Roy's head, the heavy glass shatters, the blood spurts, Roy's buddies call out Fern! Fern!, and I run for the telephone.

God answered my prayers that night. My sweet, small, God-fearing Grandmother showed the stuff she was made of.

Arriving to rescue us from Roy's rampage, Grandmother ordered Fern to gather up the children and get into the car. Roy, who had wrapped his bleeding head with a white towel, shouted at Grandmother, "Look at what your bitch daughter did to me! Look at my head! I'm bleeding! You have to take me to the hospital!"

Roy ran in front of the car as Grandmother started the engine to drive away with her daughter and grandchildren. As we cowered, wide-eyed, in the back seat, Grandmother shouted at Roy. "Stand aside!" When he belligerently held his ground, Grandmother put the car into drive and moved forward. He jumped fast, but not before she had side-swiped him, running over his foot. She had made her point. Grandmother drove her three astonished grandchildren to the safety of her home.

According to our neighbor, my mother's best friend, Barbara (our neighbor who had rescued my sister during that shooting ordeal), an ambulance arrived shortly thereafter to take Roy to the old Immanuel Hospital. After the doctors had finished stitching him up, they released him.

Roy then asked the on-duty security guard for a dollar to buy some cigarettes. I suspect he needed drug money. People trusted such requests back then, and for God's sake, what could possibly happen in the middle of a hospital emergency ward in 1970? When the guard reached into his wallet, Roy attacked the man with a knife and robbed him.

Once again the Omaha Police put Roy behind bars. This time, the charges of robbery, assault, and attempted murder got Roy "sent up" for a long time. Finally, we were free of him.

This time Mama filed for divorce from Roy without any pressure from her mother and father. She confessed to me what finally sent her over the edge: She arrived home from work one day to find Roy high and lasciviously dressing my little brother and me in dresses. Having completely repressed that incident, I don't remember any of those details. I would have given anything to get Roy to stop hitting my mother, and in that moment Mama realized that her continuing to enable Roy would have serious consequences for me and my brother. They divorced on November 10, 1970, and with the help of my grandparents, life returned to normal.

This violent period left indelible marks on all of us. Beyond the obvious negative reactions – my fears of physical abuse and of losing my mother – my interest in human behavior became acutely aroused. Already a curious child who wanted to know everything, I had seen and experienced some extremes of behavior that challenged my abilities to understand. My father's youthful stupidity was an easily read book compared to the complexities of Roy's problems. It would be years before my studies in psychology and my life experiences would give me the clues to understanding him.

Barely healing from the eighteen months with Roy, Mama faced the worst week of her life just four weeks after their divorce. She was working as a licensed practical nurse. While at daycare, my sister had taken ill. Donetta, then four and a half, had been complaining of headaches. After two days, she wasn't getting any better and had developed a fever. Mama put her in a cool bath to try and break the fever, but she was soon drenched in sweat again. I happened by my sister's room and saw that she was convulsing in her bed. I yelled to my mother, who within seconds reached the top of the stairs.

"Call 911!" she said. Seconds later she told me to hang up. There was no time. Donetta was seizing.

"David, get my purse and lock the door behind you. Darryl, come on," she said.

Mama placed my sister into the driver's seat of her Ford and sat on her. She screamed for me to hurry, which I did. Within minutes we were at children's hospital. Mother put the car in park, opened the door, scooped my sister up into her arms, and leaving the car, us, and the door open, entered the emergency entrance. Doctors took my sister, and I could see Mama talking to a doctor as they began to move down the hallway, out of sight. I turned the car off, having seen many times how it was done, and told my brother to follow me. I too, left the car door open.

My mama was falling apart. Seeing Darryl and me, she returned to some semblance of reality, but when the security officer started hassling her about her car, she screamed at him. Quickly apologizing, she asked the nurse to keep an eye on us and told me to sit with my brother in the waiting area. "Don't move. I will be right back."

When she returned from parking the car, she could see that we were upset and she tried to calm us. Just in that moment the doctor came into the waiting area and told my mother that they had given my sister medicine to stop any more swelling on the brain, which had caused her to seize.

"Brain swelling?" Mama repeated.

"Yes. Mrs. Brewer, I'm afraid your daughter has bacterial meningitis. We are admitting her to the hospital immediately." He directed Mama to a nurse's station to fill out paper work. Minutes later Aunt Lee Lee and Grandmother and Grandfather arrived. Mama had called them from the nurse's station. Grandmother greeted my mother and asked the nurse where the chapel was.

"Fern, you know what to do," she said.

If I knew Grandmother, she had already been praying.

My little sister was admitted into the ICU (intensive care unit) of Children's Hospital, very sick and fighting for her life. Mama slept at the hospital round the clock, and my brother and I were in Grandmother and

Grandfather's care. Not wanting to disturb our routine, they stayed with us at our own home.

At first Donetta did not improve, but she also failed to get worse. I found it difficult not to worry, and I was relieved that it was Christmas vacation time. I was already a conscientious little boy and knew that worrying simultaneously about my sister and schoolwork would have been almost too much for seven-year-old me.

For five days, no one gave us boys any information about Donetta. Then Aunt Lee Lee took us to the hospital to see Mama, hoping to cheer us all up. Coming out of the elevator on our way to the ICU waiting room area, I spotted Mama. She threw out her arms, welcoming us. We were happy to see her too, and hugged her tightly. Still, something didn't feel right.

Then I saw her – my sister. The doctor was leaving her room, and in the brief moment it took for the door to close I caught a glimpse. Donetta appeared to be asleep in a bed that was totally enclosed by transparent plastic. Her hair looked funny: white, as though frozen. But that was because she had been packed in ice, I later learned.

Mama saw me peering into my sister's room. Was my sister dead, I wondered? She wasn't moving. Upset by my anxiety, Mama asked my aunt to take us home. In that instant the doctor approached to speak with them. Seconds later, Mama burst into tears and collapsed. Aunt Lee Lee broke her fall.

The doctor had just told Mama that they had done all they could do for my sister.

"It is in God's hands now," he said.

As Mama wept uncontrollably, my Grandmother exited the elevator. No one had called her. Mother had only just gotten the news of my sister's plight. But Grandmother was there. She walked past us, not saying a word. She didn't even acknowledge that we were all standing there or that Mama was in tears. She simply walked towards my sister's room with single-minded focus. As she got to the door she encountered the nurse who had been administering some treatment to my sister.

The nurse attempted to bar Grandmother from going in, but then stepped back. Grandmother had not said a word. She simply entered the room and closed the door. While Mama was being attended by the nursing staff and the doctor, Aunt Lee Lee opened the door to Donetta's room. Grandmother told her emphatically to "get out." Then I heard the oh-so-familiar sound of my grandmother praying, ululating loudly and with great fervor. I think the whole floor could hear her. It was surreal. Mama suddenly calmed. Everything stopped in mid motion. When Grandmother finally exited the room, everyone breathed again.

"Fern, she will be all right. Go to her," Grandmother said. Mama entered Donetta's room and screamed. This time she cried tears of joy. The doctor and nurses came running. My sister was sitting up in her bed, alive and alert.

And I learned about faith.

2. Fine with Me

After witnessing the miraculous recovery of my sister against all the odds, I developed an anxious habit of questioning Grandmother about God. Mama was one of those people who had nothing against children learning about God but she was adamantly against forcing religion. However, she saw that I really wanted to know what Grandmother's "faith in God" was all about. Without reservation, Grandmother obliged me and my inquisitiveness, happy that her example had made such a strong impression on me. In addition to Magic Saturdays, Grandmother welcomed me to spend Sundays with her on a regular basis.

I loved going to church with Grandmother and singing in the choir. Like most black singers, my roots can be traced back to the church; for me it was Clair Memorial United Methodist in Omaha. Every Wednesday at 6:30 p.m. sharp, Grandmother's beautifully preserved blue and white 1956 Bel Air drove into our driveway to take me to the 7:00 p.m. choir rehears-

al. I don't think that I ever missed one. That would not have been acceptable to Grandmother.

Although I loved Gospel and singing in the church choir, I somehow
felt it would not be my path. But I did not discuss any alternatives. I simply did whatever my mother and grandparents wished.

My Omaha had finally become a wonderful place to be a child, a happy place, an idyllic Wizard of Oz fantasy place. My mother did everything, after Roy's departure, to make us kids feel safe, including taking us
to a family psychologist named Dr. Dunlop. I don't recall Dr. Dunlop's
first name, but I do remember his kindness, and the puppets.

After several months of weekly visits to Dr. Dunlop's office Roy's
reign was beginning to find its proper place. The nightmares were subsid-
ing. They were horrible. Night after night I awakened seeing my mother's
bloody face, and the haunting image of the whites of her eyes staring back
at me. But Mama was OK. I could feel safe. My brother and sister were
once again free to play in the streets until nightfall, and I could finally
enjoy singing and dancing again with my grandparents. My bed had finally become a place of rest.

* * * * *

Neighborhood friends and kids who always found their way to our house,
will tell you that my favorite game was playing school. I loved being the
teacher. While my brother and sister got fire trucks and dolls for Christmas, I got microscopes and books and a BIG chalkboard (one side blank
and the other side with the five-line musical staff useful for the music
theory lessons that my grandparents promoted at the behest of my clarinet
teacher, Otis Westbrook). I must say, my siblings also got educational
gifts, which they quickly tossed to the side. All these gifts thrilled me, and
in my spare time I read Mama's college books.

Once, when the baby sitter cancelled, my younger brother and sister
and I had to accompany Mama to her biology class at Creighton Universi-

ty in Omaha. I must have been ten years old, and definitely precocious. Mama gave us a real good talking to before getting out of the car, warning us to be on our best behavior. Accordingly, my brother and sister sat in the back of the class room as quiet as church mice. It didn't take long for me to become bored. So, I just moseyed on up front, seating myself smack dab in the middle of Mama's classmates.

Just as I had gotten settled, the professor asked a question about how trees and plants got oxygen. I raised my hand, and the students began to chuckle. The professor ignored me, the chuckling intensified, and my mother turned three shades of red. But I was insistent. Mama gave me "the look," but my hand still waved in the air. Finally, the professor decided to humor me. "Photosynthesis," I blurted out. Astonished, he said, "That is correct." I glanced nervously, and a little proudly, at my mother, whose color had returned.

When I was twelve years old, an age of great significance, I sang my first solo in church choir and was a hit. "Said I Wasn't Gonna Tell Nobody" was a radio favorite of Gospel enthusiasts at the time, and I gave it my all on that Sunday morning. Grandmother was the proudest I had ever seen her. Everyone in the church was complimentary and it was then that I realized that just maybe my grandparents knew what they were talking about. Grandmother kept up her campaign on my behalf, frequently calling the pastor, Reverend Young, on his home telephone, urging him to urge the choir director to allow me to sing further solos. I am sure Clair's former choir mistress, Ms. Rose Duncan's family, remember the calls that Reverend Young relayed in response to Grandmother's *urgings*.

My middle school years were largely uneventful, but when I was fourteen years old, my brother and I got ourselves into the newspapers. We were rising talents on the amateur tennis circuit in Omaha, and a newspaper article mentioned our court prowess, which brought our father out of hiding and back into our lives. I hadn't seen him since Mama divorced him in 1965. Now here he stood, chest inflated, and all proud. His boys were going to be tennis stars.

Although Daddy engaged my brother and me in long oratories about Arthur Ashe, Darryl made it clear that he dreamed of basketball stardom, not tennis. Suddenly, I become the focus of my father's grandiose ambition. He insisted on driving me in his big car to the Omaha Tennis Club, offering to pay for private tennis lessons, to the tune of almost $1,200.00. I couldn't believe it. He was willing to pay all that money, in 1978, for private tennis lessons and yet he hadn't given my mother even a penny in all our years. On the ride back home, I turned down his offer and confessed that music was my intended profession – more specifically, singing.

"Grandmother Sims is seeing to it," I said.

My father looked at me square in the eye and said, "Singing is for sissies."

I was devastated, and angry. It didn't matter that Grandma Anna Laura, his own mother, had bragged about my voice. She even tried encouraging him to have a listen to me sing before trying to force his will on me. However, Daddy was impervious to anyone's advice. He wanted an athlete, point blank period.

The fact that under Grandfather's strong influence I had also become a proficient dancer only intensified Daddy's impression of his sissified first-born. I couldn't wait to get out of his car. I loved tennis and still play today, but my first love would remain any- and everything artistic. Furthermore, in 1978-79 I was also developing a strong desire to become a psychiatrist. Helping others, the way Dr. Dunlop had helped me, seemed like a grand thing to do. My insatiable curiosity continued to feed my dreams.

Then something wonderful and completely unexpected happened. I was scouted at a local fashion show, held at Omaha's Westroads Shopping Mall. There, I met the lady who would represent me as a model.

Carol Bailey-Seldon was a gorgeous black American woman who had been a professional model in Europe and New York. After she married and settled down in Bellevue, a small city on the outskirts of Omaha, she remained active in professional modeling. She was a star. She appeared frequently in local advertisements, commercials, and the newspapers, I was fascinated by her. After seeing me in the fashion show she approached me.

40

"I've been watching you," she said. "There's something about the way you move across the floor."

I explained that I was a dancer.

"No, it's something else," she answered.

Hardly able to believe it, I ran home babbling all about it to Mama. "She was very encouraging and promised me that I could have a professional career. She said she would train and represent me," I said.

Carol spoke with my mother and clarified her intentions. Satisfied of Carol's professionalism, Mama drove me over to Bellevue for my first round of coachings. I learned so much from her and within six months of training I was indeed modeling professionally. Brands like Vidal Sassoon, and department store chains booked me regularly. I owe her so much. Everything I pass on to my singing students about posture and photo taking, about energy in the eyes, line in photography and selling product, came from Carol.

One particular fashion show proved unforgettable, and the memory of it gives me chills to this day. Carol had gotten me booked for a Ralph Lauren show to be held at a hot Omaha disco. It was the ideal setting for a fashion show, with a built-in stage and spacious walk ways for the runway portions of the show. After a successful rehearsal, the other models and I (ages 14-27) stepped onto the runway for the first show. I began to notice that every time I went out – especially in the swimsuit portion of the show – someone was photographing me.

I wondered whether Carol had arranged a private photographer or if she had invited a scout to see me; she often did that sort of thing. At the end of the first show, one of my colleagues told me that I had a visitor out front. What? I hadn't invited anyone. Prepared to go out to meet Carol's surprise guest, I got the shock of my life. The visitor – and mysterious photographer – stood there with a smile on his face. It was Roy Edward Kellogg, fresh out of prison. He had seen my face in a newspaper ad for the show.

Roy congratulated me, saying, "You turned out to be a beautiful boy." I stifled the fears I felt and thanked him for coming. I told him I needed to get backstage for notes before the second show. He said he understood and extended his hand. I responded politely, but when he released my hand, he stroked the inside of my palm with his middle finger (the finger used to suggest a certain obscenity; it was sexual). Nervous and revolted, I excused myself and disappeared backstage.

The next day, arriving home after school, I found Roy Edward Kellogg sitting on our couch. How did he know where we lived? Had he been spying on us? My little sister had let him into the house, which was against Mama's rule: no strangers in the house when she wasn't home. I immediately telephoned Grandmother. She had to get Roy out of our house before Mama got home. I was motivated partly by my ongoing fear that he and Mama would get back together, but I also knew that Donetta and I, right here and right now, would be helpless against him.

Grandmother was there within minutes. She must have broken every speed limit law, and just in the nick of time too; Mama walked in shortly thereafter. Neither Grandmother nor I ever mentioned the incident again. It had been eight years since I had laid eyes on Roy and seeing him again brought back every horrible memory I'd pushed down. Once again he disappeared from our lives.

By 1979, I was a student at Technical High School, Omaha's first public magnet and college prep school. It was there that I dreamed out loud about becoming a leading psychiatrist. Seeing Roy again had reawakened my interest in understanding human behavior. It became an obsession. In tandem with my high school studies in psychology, I continued reading widely and discovered the power that words had to teach and to heal. Yolanda Martin (my junior year English teacher) and Mary Lou Larson (the department chair and my senior year honors English teacher) challenged and encouraged me. I loved languages, including my own, English, and I loved the written word. "Maybe one day," I thought, "I'll write an important paper on abuse in the family." I learned many things from both Mrs. Martin and Ms. Larson, but what I remember most was their encouragement regarding my ability to tell the story – an ability that would intensify my understanding of interpretation in music. For her part, Grandmother would tolerate my half-formed speculations and thoughts about the psychological implications of just about everything, which I expressed to her in long and passionate monologues. Then she would remind me to get back to my music lessons, while Grandfather reminded that my dancing had become important. I had become a professional at the age of fifteen.

Early in my high school career I joined the high school theater troupe, and over the next three years I sang the Russian Soloist in *Fiddler on the Roof*, chorus in *South Pacific*, and the Scarecrow in *The Wiz*. James Eisenhardt, my theater instructor, was not the only teacher who recognized and encouraged my vocal and acting talent. The choir director, Mary Jean Johnson, insisted I join her ensemble after she heard my *Fiddler on the Roof* audition. Her successor, Mr. David Carlson, placed me in the Nebraska All-State music competition, vocal solo division. "You have the special talent to win," he said. Win I did. I sang Georg Friedrich Handel's "Where'er You Walk," and since then I have opened every one of my professional recitals with that beautiful air. Earmon Wilcher, my band teacher, gave me private lessons on the clarinet three times per week. My successes were beginning to prove, even to me, the wisdom of Grandmother's and Grandfather's assessments. But through a third teacher, Denise Arnold, with whom I studied French for three years, I would discover my true calling.

Ms. Arnold saw my performance in Technical High's production of *The Wiz*, and she thenceforth declared that I had "the stuff" opera careers are made of: Voice, Voice and more Voice. Mr. Eisenhardt (who impressed upon me the valuable lesson that mistakes are not forgiven in a performance) told me that he had chosen this musical as a vehicle to showcase my talents. Mama, and many of our neighbors, cheered me on every performance. Those performances, and the theater, had been such a humbling experience. It seemed that everybody saw the same thing in me: success in the arts. Tears would well up in my eyes every night as a fifteen-year-old Kathy Tyree, who played Dorothy, the female lead in *The Wiz*, sang her final number, "Home." Those words spoke to the warm feelings I had about home and her singing brought up memories associated with thank-fulness.

Ms. Arnold not only heard beauty in my voice, she also told me that she saw in me the intelligence, determination, talent for languages, and absolute discipline necessary for a career as an opera singer – her words. Convinced I had what it took, she offered to take anyone who wanted to go to see Opera Omaha's production of George Bizet's great opera *Carmen* at the Orpheum Theater.

Before going to the opera our class had studied the entire libretto and music, so I understood the story and knew what was going on. Still, I was fidgety during the performance, and Ms. Arnold didn't understand why. Becoming annoyed with my squirming about, she whispered to me, "David, what on earth are you doing?"

"I am looking for the microphones," I whispered, "but I don't see them. Where are they? I don't see them." Yes, we had used no microphones or amplification for our high school theater performances, but the high school auditorium was no match for this place. The huge Orpheum Theater seated more than 2,500 people.

Ms. Arnold leaned close to me. "There are no microphones. In opera the singers are required to use their natural voices. You have to learn to project your voice through natural means," she said. I was amazed. It sounded as though the singers were standing right next to me.

I had never heard such power coming from the human voice and I was more than intrigued. As someone who loved a challenge and sought perfection in all I did, I was convinced when Ms. Arnold explained that opera was the most intricate of all the art forms. I went home an excited sixteen-year-old.

I begged my mother to buy me an opera recording, and within a day she presented me with my very first recording, *Aida*. She had purchased that album because it had a black woman on the cover. Mama was all about finding experiences for me that would support my being proud of my blackness. She always said that black men were an endangered species and that strength in pride would be our saving grace. Singing on that recording were Leontyne Price and Grace Bumbry. I was enthralled, to say the least. Although I became a fan of both ladies and their voices, I was particularly drawn to Ms. Bumbry's singing and I dreamed of one day meeting her. She possessed one of the most honest sounds that I had ever heard.

Having always expected that I would sing Gospel music, Grandmother got the shock of her life when I eventually announced my chosen path: opera. The shock was ameliorated when she attended, on June 2, 1981, my high school graduation ceremony. Grandmother's prediction about my becoming a singer was being realized. We were all pleasantly surprised when it was announced that the winner of the Harry T. Burke scholarship, the Omaha Public Schools' most prestigious scholarship for music, was being given to Tech's own David Lee Brewer. Mama was so proud and I, in turn, was happy. That scholarship, along with the others I'd received, would help to defer costs of my undergraduate college studies at Langston University.

But before I would head off to university, Mama had to appear in court. My father, David Lee Brewer, Sr., was being sued as a dead-beat dad. Finally, someone was going to make him pay, I thought.

It may seem presumptuous of a teenaged son to diagnose his father, but according to my psychology text books, Mr. Brewer, Sr., exhibited all the characteristics of a narcissist. Every conversation was about him and what he wanted. He felt entitled, was never wrong, and he lacked empathy for others, which helped to explain why he had problems sustaining relationships. Although he'd fathered many children, he'd raised none of them. In addition, he was extremely unpredictable, often switching personas with the rapidity of a changing Dr. Jekyll to Mr. Hyde. He detested those who didn't recognize his wit or brilliance. He bragged relentlessly, demanded respect and always pretended to be more than he was. An expert of nothing, he would argue you down about any topic, shouting that he knew best. To make matters worse, he'd become a dogged alcoholic by the time I finished high school.

At any rate, the State of Nebraska had just begun enforcing the "dead-beat father" laws in the late 70s, early 80s. Mama told the Omaha Court she didn't need any help and requested that they "leave Mr. Brewer alone." But the State intended to force her hand. The case went to court. On the appointed day, a judge called Fern and David Lee Brewer, Sr., for questioning. Mama stood up alone and approached the bench. *Daddy* didn't budge. He sat in court reading the *Omaha World-Herald* newspaper. Once again the Judge called out his name. No response. The Judge asked Mama if her ex-husband was in the court room, to which she replied, "Yes, Your Honor, he is the one reading the newspaper."

"Excuse me sir, are you David Lee Brewer Sr.?" *Daddy* did not answer. The Judge called out *Daddy's* name again. Still no reply.

"Excuse me sir," said the Judge. "You, with the newspaper. Are you David Lee Brewer, Sr.?"

Daddy looked at him over the upper right corner of the *World-Herald* page.

"No, I am not," he answered. *Daddy* had become a member of the Muslim faith and had changed his legal name to Dahud Mohammad, something in keeping with his newly found religion. He claimed freedom from society's rules (such as child support). For some mysterious reason, the judge upheld his claim. When I heard the judge's decision, I was floored. Who goes to such lengths to deny their children?

As Fern Brewer had expected, she would continue to pay all the bills for raising their children. Nonetheless, with help from Grandmother and Grandfather, and scholarship assistance for my tuition, Mama began preparing her first fledgling to leave the nest. She was worried, yet proud.

* * * * *

During my senior year I had my very first disagreement with Mama.

I remember it as if it were yesterday. Having called it quits with my girlfriend Sophia Coles, I then met a male friend who aroused feelings in me that I could no longer ignore. Things would never be quite the same again.

Jerry Gills was hot. Ten years older than my sixteen-year-old self, he had just gotten out of the army. In the words of the singer CeCe Peniston, Jerry Gills had brown cocoa skin and curly black hair and his stare pierced my very being. I could think of nothing else. His remains the most significant kiss of my life. I had never felt like this. My insides shook and I was both confused and overjoyed, all at the same time. I didn't know what I was going to do, but denying my feelings seemed no longer an option.

It was Sunday, the day Mama cooked the family meal, the day my siblings and I were required to have dinner together. Mama was in the kitchen cutting carrots for the cake she was preparing for dessert. I don't know what I was thinking, but I chose that moment for outing myself. Dumb.

I hopped up to sit on our kitchen counter and blurted out, "Mama, I think I am bisexual." Without looking up from her mixing bowl, she said, "No, you're not."

"Yes, I believe that I am," I said.

This time, looking me in the eye, she said, "You're young. I am sure you are just going through one of your crazy phases."

"Maybe. But I don't think so. I met someone."

"Go on," she said.

"His name is Jerry, and I think you'd like him."

Her stare said otherwise. Mama had always told us kids that we could come to her and discuss anything, that nothing was so terrible that she'd abandon us in our time of need. But it was becoming painfully obvious that my timing was off.

"When did you meet this….person?" She could not say his name.

"About two weeks ago."

"There now, you see. You haven't known…. this person long enough to know how you feel."

"Mama, I know how I feel. And, I am sorry that I brought it up." I was beyond agitated.

I walked away from our conversation realizing that my father wasn't the only one who had a problem with the complete me. What about the ten commandments, I thought. Was it not a good thing that I told the truth?

Later that evening Mama asked me if I'd had sex. I didn't answer. She then asked if I would do her a favor. "Will you go to the doctor?"

I knew that the doctor was not going to find anything. I had not had any sex, but I still refused to satisfy her curiosity. "Of course I will go to the doctor."

The next day at school I told my best friend, Tracey Hebron, that my mother was "trippin" (slang of the day for being unreasonable). When I explained what had taken place, Tracey said, "Whoa, that took balls. Good for you!" And then she asked what I was going to do.

"I'm gonna check out of school early today and go to the doctor. I want to put this all behind me and go on with my life and plans." I was on a quest for peace. Honesty seemed like a sure fire way of getting to it.

Mama was on time to pick me up. Expecting to drive to Dr. Bicker's, our family physician, I noticed that we were going a different way.

"Has Dr. Bicker's office moved?" I asked.

Mama did not reply. Then it hit me. We were going to Dr. Dunlop, our family psychologist. I didn't know how to feel about what I knew was coming, but I knew better than to voice my opinion at that moment. I sat quietly in my mother's Cadillac de Ville and when we arrived, Mama and I got out of the car without a word. We walked into the office and Dr. Dunlop's nurse announced me.

With my back straight, I entered that office that I'd known from my childhood. Prepared for anything, I remember noticing how old Dr. Dunlop had gotten since the last time I'd seen him, seven years ago.

"So, David, how have you been?" he asked.

"Great! Just great!"

"Your mother tells me that you have 'decided' to be gay."

Baffled, I said, "Uh – Dr. Dunlop, can one decide to be gay?" He smiled. His non-response was all the answer I needed. He then went on to explain the dangers of homosexuality (being harassed, beaten up, discriminated against, and ridiculed). In response, I laughed.

"Dr. Dunlop, have you forgotten that I am a black boy in America? I couldn't imagine that anyone's sexuality could be more painful than that."

Dr. Dunlop lowered his pale face and head. When he lifted it again he changed the subject.

"So, what do you have planned for your life?" he asked.

"First, I am going to get out of Omaha. I want adventure – to see the world." I told him that I was going to become an opera singer, perform internationally, teach, and eventually live in Europe. Dr. Dunlop asked how I planned to achieve all this. I spelled out for him my well-laid plans, step for step. I had charted the course of my future to the second and knew exactly what I wanted. *"Nothing,"* I declared, *"will take me off track –* certainly not bi-sexuality, or homosexuality, for that matter."

He asked about my grades. I told him about all the scholarships I'd been offered and that I was graduating number 21 in my class of 350 plus. "And that was without much studying," I boasted. I also told him about dancing professionally and about my new-found modeling career. "I have talent and I will have a wonderful life," I said confidently.

Dr. Dunlop then returned to the topic of my visit, the reason why I was there. I stopped him and assured him that I would be OK. "Nobody is going to break me. I am quite accustomed to name calling. That sort of thing doesn't bother me." Seconds later our interview was over.

Dr. Dunlop called Mama in and asked me to sit in the waiting area. When Mama emerged from his office she was crying so hard I don't know how we made it home.

Mama didn't say a word for three days. My brother and sister noticed the cold atmosphere in the house but didn't dare pry. I could imagine that my shocking news troubled Mama but I didn't think it would be this bad. When I tried to make small talk all I got from her was a half-baked smile. And then she called me into her room and told me that she didn't like my life choice, at all, but that she loved me. Grateful for at least her love, I still felt offended. "I can move out if you'd prefer," I said. "That won't be necessary, David," she answered.

It took several years for her to tell me what Dr. Dunlop had said that had so upset her. "Fern, you have done a magnificent job. David is self-assured, knows what he wants, and he knows how he is going to get there.

You may not like what he has chosen to do with his life, but if you insist on your point of view, you could lose him. All that you have worked for where he is concerned could turn on you. Is it worth it?"

I should have been grateful, but I wasn't. Dr. Dunlop, and my mother included, would never have to live my life. They couldn't protect me. Fern had raised no fool. And she sure hadn't raised a punk. I could take care of myself. But in typical David fashion, I said nothing. We never discussed the subject again. I've since learned to be OK with that – *grateful even* – I was fine with me! As far as I know, a person's sexuality never made it onto God's top ten commandment list.

Nevertheless, it was 1981. I was seventeen years old and had adopted my "Don't dream your life, live your dream" philosophy, which has guided me – and through me, my students. Self-worth is everything.
I respected me, even if the world wouldn't be so kind.

* * * * *

Mama said I was *lost*. So, it was decided that I would attend a historically black college or university [HBCU].

"No problem," I said. "Fisk University has an excellent music program."

"Nope," Mama answered.

I suggested Howard University.

Again, Mama said "Nope."

"Well, what about Tuskegee, Morehouse, or even Morgan State…"

"Nope, Nope and Nope," Mama answered. Mama knew of all those *fine* institutions but maintained that I needed grounding. "There is no way I'm going to send you to a school where you'd be in danger of not learning to see people for who they are, and without judging them."

So, Langston University it was.

My childhood friend from the neighborhood, Donald Jackson, had recently returned from a black college campus tour with the Omaha chapter of the NAACP. According to Donald, Langston was the place to be. "The students are right up your alley," he said. He told stories of well-dressed black folks who had a real sense for quality. Much more subdued than I was, in every aspect, Donald knew my tastes in just about everything. "Langston sounds perfect," Mama said. The fact that she'd never heard of it pleased her immensely. Only one thing. After having done a bit of research on my own, I discovered that Donald hadn't gotten an accurate account of day-to-day life at Langston. He'd visited the campus during homecoming. I started to panic. "My God, what am I agreeing to," I said, adding my own flare for the dramatic.

"Don't be so negative," Mama said. "Give it a chance."

I did some research and discovered that Oklahoma colleges knew a thing or two about singing. The state had produced many successful opera talents. Only Texas equaled that record. So, I boarded a bus and set off for my new life, in Oklahoma. I was going to be an opera singer if it killed me.

If you didn't own a car, taking the Greyhound bus was the only transport to "the school on the hill," Oklahoma's only predominately black university. For the more than twenty-hour trip from Omaha I had chosen to wear a green Camp Beverly Hills tee shirt and Levi jeans worn in the knee, all the rage in my world. My hair was chemically straightened (due to my work as a hair model), and coiffed to perfection. On my feet I wore moccasins. White socks and moccasins. What black boy, anywhere, wore moccasins? I had accessorized the bizarre wardrobe in imitation of Richard Gere, my favorite actor, whose film *American Gigolo* I had recently added to my desert-island list of life-time favorites. In that movie my idol wore aqua blue-green school boy sunglasses. I just had to have them and I hunted them with the fervor that only a smitten teenage fan can bring to such a task. I had purchased replicas of the Richard Gere shades while on our high school senior class trip to Kansas City and added them to my off-to-college ensemble.

My mother asked me if I was sure I wanted to travel with *all* that luggage. She was referring to the set of seven matching pieces of Gucci luggage that I had purchased from my modeling gigs. I answered her with a resounding "Yes!" She was right in questioning my judgment, but naturally, I knew more than my parent. I was eighteen and staging a Grand Entrance. What did Mama know about aesthetics?

When the bus driver called out "Langston!" and set my prized bags onto that dirt, I lost my mind. I will never forget the looks on the poor bystanders' faces when I exited the Greyhound in my bizarre get-up and walked over to my impressive set of Gucci bags. I was ready for the experiences of a lifetime. Parties, new friendships, and the wide vistas of higher learning were on my agenda. What I discovered were red dirt, hard work, and fear. I thought, for the first of many times, *Where have I landed?*

I was definitely from another world to those kids, who stood there baffled. When I asked where the men's dormitory was, one of them, clad in stained grey sweat pants, raised his hand without speaking and pointed out the direction. The mere sight of him to me, and me to him, had rendered us all speechless. I thanked him, Nebraska style – always polite – and started off haughtily towards Breaux Hall, leaving my luggage, my precious Gucci Bags, sitting there in the dirt. Reaching the dorm, I asked the young man sitting at the front desk if they had a service which could help me get my luggage from the bus stop to the dorm.

The man laughed. Having a wonderful time at my expense, he asked, "How much luggage are we talking about – *Mr.?*..."

"Brewer," I answered, and added, "Seven pieces."

He laughed again. In just that moment, an older student entered the dorm.

"Hey, he has a car," the young man said to me. "Ask him…"

"Excuse me sir," I said. "Could I pay you to help me get my luggage to the dormitory?" I asked.

That student nodded and suggested, willingly, that I walk back to my bags and wait there. He'd drive around with his car shortly. Ten to fifteen minutes later he finally showed up. Popping the trunk, he got out – I thought to help me. Boy, was I wrong.

The trunk was filthy. Looking around for a clean surface, any clean surface, I was hyper-aware of my own obsessive compulsive tendencies. I placed the smaller bags gingerly in the trunk – as if "gingerly" would help – and got his permission to place the larger bags onto the back seat. All the while, he stared down at my luggage, eyes as big as dollar coin pieces, and a look of shock frozen on his face. Mama had been right. I'd made my entrance all right, a feat that cost me a cool twenty dollars to drive my bags less than 200 feet to the dormitory, and several weeks of pure hell. I had instantly acquired an indelible reputation: 100% Nebraska corn field.

In coming days, the registration procedure only cemented my outsider image. At the appointed time, a portly black woman looked over her spectacles and shouted at me "Major!" I had no idea what she was talking about. Frozen like a deer in headlights, I asked her what she meant. "Your *Major*," she repeated, "*your major*. What will be your major course of study?" Ah. The light came on. "Music," I managed to say, whereupon she stamped my papers, scribbled something into the corner, and told me to have it approved by the head of the music department. "You know, music is a five-year program," she said, looking for signs of defection. Seeing none, the stern woman indicated that when I returned with the music department's approval stamped on that paper, I would be allowed to register, pay, and begin my new life at Langston University.

Some of the students at Langston resented me, and my luxury luggage. On more than one occasion, ultimately identified persons broke into my room and packed my things into my precious Gucci bags and carried them away, taking even my socks and underwear. (The luggage would be found in a campus creek or behind the bleachers.) I was being brought down to earth, and quickly.

In spite of my stylish arrival and the hazing that followed, I adjusted to Langston quickly. I remember the good days, which were many. I also remember the bad ones, during which my dorm-mates – the luck of the draw had placed me in the midst of some serious campus jocks – attempted to rid the building of my presence.

One night, a classmate of mine, who today is a friend and minister of the Gospel, organized a "pee on David bucket." Interested participants were instructed to stop by his room to deposit their gifts. Dead asleep, I was awakened by thunderous banging on my door. I leapt up and slipped in the urine that had been strategically poured under the door. Falling, I hit my head, and blood began to run down my face. When that failed to intimidate me, they set that same door afire, causing me to emerge, choking and red-faced with the smoke and heat. On several occasions I found myself trapped in the men's bathroom, where the lights would suddenly go out and light bulbs would be lobbed into the shower, keeping me glued in my spot, for hours. When I thought that the water spray had flushed the last pieces of the broken glass down the drain, I would begin the complicated and time-consuming process of carefully picking my way, inch by inch, out of the shower and toward the light switch.

I'd been warned, but no matter what the students threw my way, I would not be broken. I was going to emerge unscathed if it killed me.

Within the first couple months at Langston, I sought out the university's drama department. I met the only acting coach I ever needed, Janet Hollier, who became a force in my life. (Today Ms. Hollier-Davis is a professor at Georgia Perimeter College in Atlanta.) Ms. Hollier cast me as the male lead in a stage adaptation of Charles Dickens's brilliant novella "A Christmas Carol." Rehearsals began in late October 1981, shortly after I arrived for my first year at Langston.

On December 4, opening night, Mama called me moments before the play was to begin. It was important, the switchboard operator said to the Dust Bowl theater manager. (The Dust Bowl theater had been founded by the famed poet and former Wiley College professor, Melvin B. Tolson. His life has been portrayed in a successful film, "The Great Debaters," that starred Denzel Washington. The movie ends as Tolson walks off into the sunset, on his way to Langston. It's a fascinating story.) At any rate, against the theater's protocol, I was called to the telephone at that crucial time before the raising of the curtain.

"Hello, David Lee Brewer," I said.

"One moment David," the operator said. She was putting the call through.

With ten minutes to curtain, I listened with intense disbelief as my mother told me that Grandfather had died. He'd died three days earlier, Mama added. "Your grandmother and I felt it was best for you –, "

I interrupted Mama. "I have to go," I said.

"David, are you OK?" Mama asked.

"No, I'm not OK, but I go on stage in ten minutes. I have to go. I'll call you tomorrow," and I hung up.

I had no time to wallow. Stage management was calling places. I took my place center stage, thinking of my first lines. Then I heard Mr. Eisenhardt's and Grandmother's words stream into my consciousness: "Mistakes are not forgiven in the theater." I had to pull myself together and focus. Seconds later, lights were up, and I was nailing it. My first lines, and indeed the entire first act as Scrooge went well.

When the last line of *A Christmas Carol* had been spoken, I removed the make-up from my face and retreated to my dorm room to mourn. I loved Grandfather and owed him so much. The whole night and well into the following week, I thought of every great seed of wisdom and loving gesture passed on to me by the only man who truly loved me unconditionally.

Long before I'd gotten *the call,* we had lost Grandfather to dementia. I had visited him every Sunday after church with Grandmother. And I remember that I hated seeing him like that, unclear and afraid. He didn't know who I was and I am not sure he even knew Grandmother, except that she was the lady who came to visit every Sunday. Still, the news of his death froze my mind and my heart.

Although Grandmother and Mama had robbed me of the chance to say goodbye, I learned about heartbreak and performance, about personal pain and professional obligation. On a practical level I understood their decision and in the process of forgiving them I absorbed two specific lessons that guide me to this day: (1) The show really must go on, and (2) Never answer the phone the day of a premiere.

The next semester I met Monty Prock, another great professor of dramatic arts at Langston University, who in my junior year would ask me to direct the spring semester play. He told me that it had all been approved by the head of the humanities department, Dr. Joy Flash. Dr. Flash was one of my many supporters while at Langston. I came to believe firmly that my steps had been ordered by unseen providential forces. Grandmother assured me that they'd continue to be, and she was right.

"Of course I am," she would scoff.

At any rate, I auditioned, cast, and directed Claire Booth Luce's *The Women*. That experience taught me about lighting and staging, and at the end of it, we were being nominated for best play at the Oklahoma Theater Festival. One year prior, I had been nominated for the Irene Ryan Award for Excellence in Acting as a solo artist, for my portrayal of Thurio in Guare/MacDermot's musical adaptation of Shakespeare's *Two Gentlemen of Verona* (Irene Ryan was the actress who played Granny on the hit American Television Series *The Beverly Hillbillies*), and now *The Women* was being nominated for the Irene Ryan Award for Excellence in Acting, Theatrical play division. The cast's three wonderfully talented actresses, all new to Langston University that year, were ecstatic, as was I. Not only had the actresses gotten spontaneous standing ovations, but we ranked fifth in the competition. Dr. Flash and Monty Prock were proud. I was humbled, again, by yet another enriching experience at Langston University.

In addition, my then voice teacher at Langston University, Alexis Rainbow, required that all voice majors teach one student as part of their study. "You all are going to help lighten my load – and you will learn a lot in the process," Mrs. Rainbow said. We all thought it was a brilliant idea, especially me. Thus began my quest for knowledge to understand singing on a deeper level, and I read every book I could find on the subject.

As my first official student, I chose Orlando Fowlkes, a rather jovial baritone who sang in choir with me and who took secondary voice lessons with Mrs. Rainbow. A very nice guy, his enthusiasm was greater than his technical understanding of breath. He squeezed his throat like crazy. Had

Orlando possessed good technique and musicianship, I would have learned little. As it was, he challenged me to put into practice all my book learning. And I discovered my true calling as a voice teacher.

By the time I reached graduation day, Langston had afforded me the opportunity to experiment, not only as a student, but also as a fledgling professional singer, dancer, teacher, and artist manager. I had an open playground, so to speak. There was nothing that I wasn't allowed to try out. I'd built a modern dance company and led a modeling troupe, of which several of the club's members went on to become professionals. Between my 19th and 22nd years, in addition to the "garden variety" voice, dance, and acting student I had the privilege of helping to develop, I choreographed, directed, and designed every fraternity and sorority gala held on the campus. Then, the biggest honor of all had been entrusted to me. Together with Robert Harris, Langston's campus activities director, I worked on every facet of the Miss Langston Pageant, coordinating everything from start to finish. It was my baby, all five glorious years. Four of my winners advanced to the finals in the Miss Black Oklahoma Pageant, and two of them, after winning, placed in Miss Black America. I felt grateful, to Langston, God, and my insistent mother. Mama had been right, again.

Six years from the day the Greyhound bus driver had set my Gucci bags in that red dirt, my time at Langston came to an end. On graduation day, May 9, 1987, the ceremony began with my singing the school's anthem, "Dear Langston," and ended traditionally with everyone throwing their caps into the air. Along with my good friends, class mates, and fellow musicians Cassandra Bennett and George Ward, I had begun to realize that *perfection* was something that could never be reached. We nevertheless had spent many an hour trying to attain it. In the process, and under the guidance of a supportive faculty, we had prepared ourselves for this moment.

I was on track, a young aspiring opera singer, with my first professional contract in hand. I boarded my flight in Oklahoma City, at Will Rogers Airport. My journey would continue in Cleveland.

Fate was calling.

3. Ashley Támar

As a young person, I formed the decidedly odd notion that I would grow up to be an opera singer. Because my grandparents had been successful vaudeville performers, my family half-way understood my attraction to singing, acting, and dancing. But opera?! As the child of an educated mother determined that I earn a master's degree, I pleased her by continuing my education beyond a bachelor's degree. At the traditionally black college Langston University, in Oklahoma, I'd learned to teach, and I was now following that path into a master's degree program in music.

I had scholarship offers to continue my studies toward that goal from the New England Conservatory, Temple University, University of Nebraska, Peabody Conservatory, and the Cleveland Institute of Music at Case Western Reserve University (CIM). Cleveland and CIM, also Mrs. Rainbow's *alma mater*, interested me most. I had flown there to audition, and to my surprise the director of the Lyric Opera Cleveland sat in on auditions that day. At the end of my singing "Salut! demeure chaste et pure" from Charles Gounod's opera *Faust*, I was offered my first professional contract to sing the role of Romeo in Gounod's *Romeo et Juliette*. I would also sing an excerpts concert of *Carmen*, singing Don José.

So, at twenty-three, I boarded the plane in Oklahoma City on May 10, 1987, one day after graduation from Langston. I was on schedule not only toward my academic goal, but also toward my career in opera.

* * * * *

Settled in Cleveland, I began *Romeo* rehearsals, quickly establishing a healthy routine. After my morning meditation, I would shower, and then take up my *Romeo* score, going through each act of the opera, phrase by phrase. I had reviewed and remembered everything and would repeat the process at least twice before heading to the theater, just as Grandmother had taught me to do. A strong believer in over-preparation, I was ready.

As opening night neared, Grandmother called.

"Remember your phrasing," she said.

"I know, Grandmother, I have gone over my music many times already and the important phrases – including the subtext – just as you taught me."

Laughing, she told me that she didn't want to seem a nuisance, but she cared. I loved her for all that she had taught me and felt blessed that I had been born into such a tuned-in family.

"There can be no mistakes," Grandmother reminded.

Grandmother then told me that she loved me and reminded me again, "Remember your phrasing."

This time I was the one who laughed and we ended our conversation. I was going to be late if I didn't hurry. Call was at 6:00 pm.

I wolfed down my traditional performance meal, pasta with olive oil and garlic (ala Luciano Pavarotti) and headed to the theater.

The performance was a triumph.

By mid-August, classes at the Cleveland Institute of Music at Case Western Reserve University (CIM) had begun. In addition to the rich musical culture my new home offered, my CIM professors were incredible. Not only my voice teachers, George Vassos and Beverly Rinaldi, but also my opera coach, Linda Jones. My opera professor, Andrew Foldi, was Hungarian born and a Metropolitan Opera legend, renowned as one of the most notable character basses in the company's history. An awesome and difficult person, he had that no-nonsense approach to teaching – like my high school drama teacher, Mr. Eisenhardt, who had also been instrumental in preparing a starry-eyed young David Lee Brewer for the realities of a stage career. Neither Mr. Eisenhardt nor Dr. Clyde Montgomery (my music theory professor and department head at Langston) nor Brenda Seward Jones-Johnson (my first voice teacher at Langston) had ever let anything go by, absolutely nothing. Their discipline had prepared me to appreciate Mr. Foldi's demands and insights. Pointing out my every weakness, he helped me close the gaps between my concepts and their successful implementation. The world of professional opera and music was being revealed to me on a whole new level.

Marshall Griffith, my amazing theory teacher, concentrated on the genius of J.S. Bach in part-writing classes. Carl Topilow, with whom I studied orchestral conducting, took Grandmother's teachings on phrasing to an incredible next step. "Let the music consume you," he taught. "Learn to really listen. Let the music guide your next impulse." Within no time my intent was becoming clear. I had learned to make music part of my fabric. "Serving music is a way of life," Mr. Topilow preached.

Musically a very interesting city, Cleveland boasted one of the top five symphony orchestras in the world, The Cleveland Orchestra, at that time under the direction of Christoph von Dohnányi. Dohnányi was one of the world's best conductors, and as a student of the Cleveland Institute of Music I was allowed access to every rehearsal. Most of the first chair and second chair soloists from the orchestra were professors at CIM and so it was a happening place. I learned so much within its studios and classrooms, and I hung on every word and gesture that I heard in Maestro Dohnányi's rehearsals at Severance Hall. He talked of "seeing it" before you played it, something totally new to me, and then he talked about using "the silence." Grandfather had told me that same thing.

At the age of twenty-three, I heard the incomparable soprano Leontyne Price in Severance Hall. She was the *Prima Donna Assoluta* (The Supreme One), and I will never forget that concert or thinking about how God had touched her throat. She gave all the glory to God and her teacher. No classical musician can have a career without a teacher and Leontyne Price loved hers. She said often that Florence Kimball-Page was her Godsend. After that Leontyne Price concert I was transported to another world by the genius of cellist Yo-Yo Ma, and a few weeks later I would be mesmerized by the violinist Itzakh Perlman. That winter I was being thrilled by the pianist Emanuel Ax, and by spring/summer I was transfixed in my seat after hearing the singers Arleen Auger, Kathleen Battle, and Jessye Norman. I was also introduced to Ms. Battle's and Ms. Norman's remarkable coach Sylvia Olden Lee at Severance Hall.

Sylvia Olden Lee took me under her wing in 1987, becoming my most important interpretation coach ever. A preeminent authority of English-language art song, French *mélodie*, German Lieder, and operatic literature in all the languages, Ms. Lee had been the first African-American coach at the Metropolitan Opera. Now she traveled the world coaching and performing in recitals with the *crème de la crème* of the vocal art. She took me with her often. Study with Ms. Lee required my flying to Philadelphia from Cleveland, and Mama financed those many lessons and trips without one word of complaint. I was indeed a lucky young man.

When I re-discovered Grace Bumbry's recordings in the CIM music library, I listened to her recorded performances, every day without fail. I didn't care what she sang, as long as I could hear *that* voice. I continued to dream of meeting her.

In addition, Sunday talks with Grandmother led me to get serious about my search for a church home. I hadn't yet found a Methodist Church in Cleveland, but then fate intervened in the form of a job offer. Alfred Carter, the director of music at the Mount Zion Congregational Church UCC, had been looking for a tenor – a paid soloist – and someone had told him that I was the singer he was looking for. It wasn't a United Methodist Church, but that it was a Christian church was good enough for Grandmother.

Mount Zion Congregational Church UCC, on Magnolia Boulevard, became my home away from home. There I received God's word and was cared for by a very nurturing and compassionate church family. I enjoyed services there, and Mr. Carter was a knowledgeable musician, a great organist, and always kind. The great black composer Hale Smith was a member of Mount Zion Congregational church, and we talked for hours about music. Also a graduate of the Cleveland Institute of Music, Maestro Smith was very helpful to me as a student. Any need I had was met generously. I loved my life in Cleveland and Reverend Dr. F. Allison Phillips' sermons. He was anointed, and one of the gentlest spirits I have ever known. I got so much out of his teachings.

Prayer for me was a daily ritual, and I often had conversations with God, sometimes just walking down the street. Occasionally a *still small voice* would speak to me, which I ascribed to my spiritual intuition. I knew this voice well. Grandmother had taught me about its whisperings, so we were old acquaintances. Although it came only on rare occasions, I recognized this voice as my guide for life, helping me with important decisions. The reason was not always clear, but I always listened.

In August 1988, my second year at the Cleveland Institute of Music, the still small voice spoke to me. It said, "Move to Houston, Texas."

Without hesitation, I booked a Houston flight that would leave on the following Monday. Having just paid my fall tuition at CIM, I astonished the registrar by asking permission for a leave of absence from the conservatory. The bemused officials granted my unorthodox request and generously extended a full tuition refund.

I said goodbye to my students Alberta Edwards (age sixteen) and Ronald Ixaac Hubbard (age eleven), who studied with me via the CIM preparatory department. Alberta, who would receive a scholarship to Shorter College, in Rome, Georgia, wanted to become an opera singer, like me, she said. Ronald would become an important minister of the clergy. A God fanatic even at eleven years of age, Ronald grew up to found his own church (4 real Church, Cleveland) and is a frequent guest on the Trinity Broadcasting Network [TBN]. Although I adored all my students and appreciated their enthusiasm about music, I grieved particularly at leaving the students at the Sutphen School of Music.

At Sutphen, a community music school dedicated to nurturing inner city children, the kids learned all sorts of cultural things in addition to music. I had been asked to work in the voice department by LaVert Stuart. I loved working there, especially with André, a deaf man whose heartbroken response to my announcement that I was leaving especially tore at my own heart strings. André had waited a lifetime to learn to sing, and now I was leaving him. I could barely speak. I was so sad and ashamed, but I felt compelled to follow what God wanted me to do. It was the only way. I took some solace in the fact that I had indeed helped André to realize his dream. After his singing on the yearly concert, there hadn't been a dry eye in the room.

Naturally, all my friends thought I had taken leave of my senses and wondered how I could just walk away from my perfect life in Cleveland.

Things were going so well, and I had fewer than thirteen credits left in order to finish my master's degree. Was it crazy to leave? I couldn't think about that. I absolutely could not get in the way of destiny. I wasn't haphazardly making this shift in my life and besides, I could always return to Cleveland and the Cleveland Institute of Music: they said so. My professors encouraged me and told me they would miss seeing and hearing me in the classrooms and hallways. When I would announce to my mother that I was going to follow what I described as a "still, small voice" that had urged me to move to Houston, Texas, even Fern began to think of my career path as "odd."

As if things weren't complicated enough – severing my ties with the conservatory and with Mt. Zion – I had a third major obligation in Cleveland. Along with my studies at CIM I had been taken as a principal dancer into the professional dance company that Louis Naylor founded after his return from Europe. The Louis Naylor Modern Dance Company was in residence at the Karamu House, within its modern dance department. I delighted in learning the magnificent history of the theater, where Langston Hughes had premiered his first three plays.

Making the move away from Cleveland brought me face to face with a decision I had been postponing for some years: the choice between singing and dancing. Having trained to the level of "young professional" in both performance arts, I had come to the point where one of them had to predominate. Louis was furious with me. "But you are a born dancer," he cried. Although I understood his sentiment, I was being forced to choose. For two decades I had been happy performing both art forms. At first, when my singing teachers pointed out to me that I'd have to abandon dance if I were going to study singing seriously, I resisted their advice. Wasn't there a way to do both? Surely there was. But no one – neither my dance teachers, nor my singing teachers – agreed with my youthful opinion.

To smooth things over with Louis, I invited him to come to church on my final Sunday. I would be singing a solo and thought perhaps his hearing me sing might help convince him. I was delighted when he agreed. "I think you'll like Mt. Zion," I said.

Sunday morning, Louis showed up on time at my house and we walked together to Mt. Zion under a beautiful August sky, talking all the way there. As we came upon the church I could see George, Carol, Millicent, and other members of the Chancel Choir. Other Mt. Zion members were parking, shaking hands, accepting and giving hugs and kisses on the cheeks, and of course, making a beeline for the door. Getting a good seat is a must in the black church. You have to feel the preacher and for that you need to be as close as possible.

After getting Louis settled, I asked him to save me a seat.

"I'll join you after the Anthem," I said.

I then sped off to the basement for morning choir rehearsal.

It was the six-month anniversary of the installation of Mt. Zion's fabulous pipe organ, completed the previous winter. Dr. F. Allison Phillips, Mt. Zion's pastor, spearheaded the success of its installation, when others before him had let the ball drop. He had done a tremendous job as pastor of Mt. Zion and I was proud to be a parishioner there. I felt that Dr. Phillips represented the kind of man I thought men should be. He treated women well, empowering them as fully vested members of society, not to mention the church community. He was all inclusive and honorable to his own wife. "God loves everyone," he used to say. Because he was so politically active, Mt. Zion was taken seriously in the city.

At the end of choir rehearsal, and just before Alfred headed upstairs to play the organ prelude, Dr. Phillips approached us to pray. Coming directly to me, he took my hand, placing his other on my forehead. The choir surrounded me and I began to tear up. I would truly miss them all. They and Mt. Zion had become my family and were such a blessing on my life. After the prayer, Dr. Phillips told me to listen intensely today. He had been given a word for me, he said. I could hear Alfred playing Pachelbel's Prelude in D minor as I turned toward the stairs. It was grand. After getting into place in the vestibule of the church and at the prelude's closing, Dr. Phillips said "Please stand for the processional and our wonderful choir."

After beginning the service with his traditional Amen, Dr. Phillips complimented the choir. "We have the best choir in Cleveland... Amen," he said. The people clapped on cue. We all smiled, knowing full well that we weren't the best, but it surely felt good to be appreciated for our dedicated service through music.

I suddenly got a chill, as the congregation took their seats. As Dr. Phillips had instructed, I prepared myself to listen intensely to every word. The sermon was taken from I Kings in the Old Testament. Dr. Phillips asked that we bow our heads, and continued. "And God said – ask what I shall give thee. And Solomon said unto God, I am but a little child. I know not how to go out or come in. Give therefore to me, thy servant, an understanding heart to judge thy people, that I may discern between Good and Bad" (I Kings Chapter 3:9). He continued, "On a hillside outside of Jerusalem, which Hebrew religion calls Gibeon, young King Solomon dutifully offered his sacrifice to God, never thinking that it would be the most defining moment of his life."

I got another chill. Like Solomon on that hillside in Gibeon, I was about to serve God in a major way. As yet I had no idea how, but it was his word that was uprooting me. I would really need to remember Dr. Phillips's poignant words on that Sunday in August, he'd reminded. Was it possible that he'd seen my future? At any rate, I had learned such great lessons about faith, hope, and love, and I had Grandmother, Mama, and the church to thank for that. I was in for the ride of my life.

By the time Louis and I parted after Sunday service at Mt. Zion, I felt at peace. It was as though we were parting with God's blessing. I knew that I could have a longer career as a singer than as a dancer, but I wanted to reassure him of my gratitude for his fostering of my dance talents. He had been an incredible teacher, choreographer, mentor, and friend. I could not leave without his knowing how much he meant to me.

On Monday morning, Alfred drove me to Cleveland Hopkins International Airport – an emotional experience. When I arrived at the Cleveland airport, all of my friends surprised me by showing up to wish me well, which made my departure even more difficult. I was leaving it all behind, but I wasn't afraid. I had my orders, God's orders.

* * * * *

I arrived safely in Houston, twenty-four years young, and sweaty. It was hot as heck in the city.

Before leaving Cleveland I had called my friend Heidi Jones, a fabulous mezzo-soprano, whom I had met at the Metropolitan Opera District Council Competition in Tulsa, which also was her home town. Both of us were opera fanatics, and we quickly became friends.

When I told Heidi that I would be moving to Houston, she said that she would arrange an audition with her voice teacher, the famed Greek mezzo soprano Elena Nikolaidi. Madame Nikolaidi had been on the roster at the Metropolitan Opera, and I was both nervous and eager to sing for her. My teacher in Cleveland, George Vassos, also of Greek origin, knew Ms. Nikolaidi and I was grateful that he had provided insight on just how to approach her. I knew that Greek women can have strong personalities but I knew, too, that she couldn't be more demanding than Grandmother.

On the second day after my arrival in Houston, I went to the University promptly at 11:00 for Heidi's scheduled voice lesson. She introduced me to Madame Nikolaidi, a most charismatic and dramatic lady. For my audition I sang the aria from Gaetano Donizetti's *Lucia di Lammermoor* "Fra poco me ricovero," and "Di rigori armato in seno" from *Der Rosenkavalier* by Richard Strauss. These arias were my two war horses, so to speak, and the audition went very well. "I love your top voice," Madame Nikolaidi said (or Ms. Nikki, as we all called her). She accepted me immediately, just like that. Her taking me into her studio at the University of Houston meant I was able to continue my studies towards my Masters of Music degree without missing a beat.

Ms. Nikki was 79 years old in 1988. Towards the end of that semester, a stroke forced her to cut back her teaching load. She held on to me as a student for as long as she could, but ultimately the sad day arrived when she had to let me go too. I found myself uncertain and insecure. Where would my still inner voice lead me now?

I heard Grandmother's teachings. "Trust in the LORD with all thine heart; and lean not unto thine own understanding." (Proverbs 3:5).

66

* * * * *

Although I could have returned to Cleveland, fate was leading me elsewhere. The answer to my dilemma in finding a new voice teacher came via a scholarship offer from the Saint Louis Conservatory of Music, where I would study voice with Stephen W. Smith. Although my time there would be short – unbeknownst to me, the Saint Louis Conservatory had been suffering severe financial and accreditation issues – it proved to be a fruitful detour.

Despite my being on board when the Saint Louis Conservatory ship sank under the weight of its fiscal problems, I found that St. Louis itself offered me several advantages. Moving there in summer 1988. I quickly made friends among the conservatory students and even met the parents and family of my idol, Grace Bumbry, who had grown up in St. Louis. I became friendly with her mother when I attended their church.

During my voice lesson one week, Stephen Smith told me that my idol, Grace Bumbry herself, was coming to hear one of his students, Christine Brewer. Because we possessed identical family names, Christine and I always joked that we were related – an unlikely connection, which any one with eyes could plainly discern. Christine, now one of the world's leading dramatic sopranos, was then in the early stages of her career, nurtured by the Opera Theatre of Saint Louis, which was supporting her audition with Ms. Bumbry. Stephen's disclosure sent me into freak out mode and I began plotting how I would meet the woman who had so captured my operatic imagination.

My music history classroom was positioned with the main door opening onto the foyer, the very foyer that Grace Bumbry would have to traverse when she entered the conservatory's front door. Being very studious, I always sat in the classroom's front row; but on the day *La Bumbry* was to appear I sat in the last seat, in the back row, near the door. I didn't hear a thing my professor said that entire class. My idol would be walking in at any minute, and every atom of my body was tuned to the foyer door.

And then it happened. The Diva arrived, stunning in a black cashmere sweater dress, big hair to beat the band, and pumps with deadly-weapon heels. I quickly stood up, grabbed my Aaron Copland Songs score (Copland had transcribed five of the songs for Ms. Bumbry to sing with orchestra), and slipped out of the classroom. I hoped to get an autograph. Her pianist, Jonathan Morris, smiled as I approached.

Grace Bumbry turned and looked dead at me. She was beautiful. I remember thinking that her head was huge. In fact, in comparison to mine, it *was* large. Singers with big dramatic voices almost always have larger-than-average heads. Her big eyes, exquisitely made up, with false eyelashes, were warm and inviting. A single strand of pearls framed her high-necked collar and her ears were adorned with matching pearl tear-drop earrings. I never thought that I could be star struck, but there I was, my usual aplomb wilted and my gift of gab dried up. After years of dreaming about this moment, I stood there speechless.

"Hello. And you are?" she said to me.

I managed to give her my name, and nothing more. I felt like an idiot. Why couldn't I snap out of it?

"Hello, David. Are you a singer?" she asked. I told her that I was a tenor and added, clumsily, "I am a huge fan." She smiled. I extended my Aaron Copland score and she signed it. She smiled again, wished me good luck, and then moved off to Christine's audition. I stood there, a star-struck groupie, watching her walk away. I couldn't believe it. She and her pianist entered the concert hall, while I looked around to see if my professor had noticed me leaving the room. She had not.

Hurriedly, I took off for the concert hall, where I stood outside with my ear pressed to the door. I listened to every word that Grace Bumbry said to Christine. Meeting Grace Bumbry in real life was more than a thrill for me. It felt like destiny. In the coming years we would remain in contact through her parents and letters.

Shortly after that, the Saint Louis Conservatory went under, but I had returned to Houston long before the conservatory's end, moving in with my Houston friends David Price, Tony Carter, and Charles Dodson. All three were voice majors at the University of Houston. I slept on an air mattress in the living room of their large, three-bedroom apartment on Westheimer Street. They welcomed me warmly, and I have never forgotten their kindness. It seemed as though I was right back where life had intended for me to be.

Again I wondered, "Why am I here?"

I heard the "still small voice" again. This time I was being led to scripture from 2 Timothy 1:4-6: "As I remember your tears, I long to see you, that I may be filled with joy. I am reminded of your sincere faith, a faith that dwelt first in your grandmother and your mother and now, I am sure, dwells in you as well..."

In God's own time, my purpose was about to show itself.

* * * * *

While I awaited further clues from my small inner voice, I began – almost imperceptibly – my career as a fully professional voice teacher. Word circulated that a new vocal coach had just moved to Houston, someone who offered private lessons not merely in singing, but also in the complete performer's art. I had been secretly dreaming of building the complete performer, today called the 360-degree artist.

My very first Houston student, Kijana Wiseman, had a "cross-over" voice. The bird-like character in her singing of high notes reminded me of Grandmother. Kijana not only became the catalyst for my teaching popular-style singing, she also introduced me to an important link to the technical side of the pop music world, her friend Roy Brown.

Roy, who lived in Los Angeles, was one of the world's leading sound engineers. He worked with everyone from Whitney Houston to rock legend Queen and he had amazing stories to tell. Impressed with Kijana's progress under my tutelage, Roy quickly called his cousin Patrice Isley (a.k.a Karen Patrice Roberts), who had been looking for a vocal coach. Then, three months after I gave Karen/Patrice her first lesson, Shevon

Jacobs became my third student in Houston. I also had a slew of students I taught at the University of Houston as a graduate student in voice and opera performance.

In August 1989, at the beginning of the month, Patrice brought along to her lesson a man named Bruce Strickland, an executive with the Pro Line Hair and Cosmetics firm, whom Patrice was considering taking on as her manager. She had been telling him about her studies with me. Wanting to see for himself how things were progressing, Bruce flew over from Dallas to Houston for Patrice's lesson at the University of Houston. After the lesson he told me how nice it was to meet me and that he was thoroughly impressed. He mentioned a Houston woman by the name of Andretta Tillman, with whom he was co-managing a few projects. Bruce asked if he might pass my name on to her. He told me that "Ann," the name he called her, was starting a girl group.

"I'm going over to their rehearsal tonight," Bruce said. Always scouting for talent, he thought that perhaps I'd like to come along, but I had opera rehearsal. I sent Patrice in my stead; she would know what to look for. She, like all my students, even those who study with me today, understood that I didn't accept just anyone into my studio. Talent is never enough, holding close Grandmother's teaching on the book of Matthew (Matthew 13: 45-46): "Again, the kingdom of heaven is like a merchant looking for pearls. When he found one of great value, he went away and sold everything he had and bought it." I was in search of my pearl. As promised, Patrice called after leaving the rehearsal. She told me that she thought the girls overall were worth investigating. Two in particular impressed her.

Two days later my telephone rang. It was Bruce Strickland. "You're going to be getting some calls," he said. "Ann Tillman has been looking for a vocal coach," adding that she "was elated to get your name and number when I told her about your teaching." He also informed me that he had spoken with many of the parents at the rehearsal and that a Carolyn Davis would be calling me to inquire about voice lessons for her daughter. He explained that Carolyn was the mother of a young girl named Ashley, who was one of the singers Ann wanted in her group. "Expect that call within the week," he said. Carolyn called me the next day, even before Ann and I had a chance to speak.

* * * * *

Carolyn and Ashley Davis arrived for Ashley's first lesson on a Tuesday.

Ashley "Támar" was a tallish nine-year-old girl in culottes. Her perfectly coiffed pony tail was dressed with a beautiful blue ribbon, which framed her symmetrically perfect face. Round, with full high cheek bones, Ashley's bone structure suggested that she possessed fabulous high notes and I would delight in helping her find them. Her eyes, although big and round, were deeply set and eager. Behind her eyeglasses, I saw her story, a passion that shone through with love and humility.

I liked her and Carolyn right away. Clearly an educated woman, Carolyn was impeccably dressed. Every hair was in place, and her shoes? – high and Italian.

After a few minutes of conversation, and my customary offering of something to drink, which always helps to break the ice, Ashley was ready to sing. This girl was anything but nervous. Like a race horse in the tight surroundings at the start gate, she was antsy for the start of the audition. She couldn't wait to show me what she could do. "I like you already," I said. No matter what this girl had sounded like I believe I would have taken her. Voice is not the only thing important to a career as a singer. Ashley already had everything else.

I had developed a set of audition criteria that guided me in choosing a singer. One, I had to hear that the voice was inherently beautiful. Two, each singer had to have aura. Aura, that "je ne sais quoi" that makes people want to look at them, was a must. And three, the singer's soul had to shine through. This was the most important of all the criteria and one that shone through with Ashley.

I asked her what she would like to sing.

71

"Amazing Grace," she said.

"Ah – great hymn."

I went over to my keyboard, gave her a C-major chord, and she hummed the chord back to me completely (including the root, third, fifth, and seventh of the chord). OK, she's been exposed to music, I thought to myself. And then she began, even before I could get back to take my seat. Realizing that I might have embarrassed her if I sat down, I turned on my heels and became involved in what she was doing. I could sense, with my back turned, that her face was alive with emotion.

This little girl could throw her head back and holla (a pointed colloquialism in the black community describing a singer's extraordinary vocal gifts). Her tone was stunning. It bristled with energy. It was clear that she had been born for a life on the stage. She was a truly gifted, impressive talent. Her every movement complimented a matching facial expression and she showed intense commitment to the text. With her first tone I heard quality. The timbre of her voice reminded me of candied apples, shiny and delicious sounding. Because it became somewhat hard in certain places, I noted that we would need to work on nuance. I definitely wanted to work with this amazingly talented child.

"She is wonderful. A real star charisma," I said to her mother. "My first order of business will be to help her to sing with more subtlety."

"Subtlety?" Carolyn said.

"Yes subtlety, a suppleness – nuance in the voice. Although wonderful, her singing at the moment can be a bit edgy."

Returning my attention to Ashley I said, "It will require awakening your imagination, but if you would allow, I'd like to help you transform your voice into something ethereal." I wanted to help her to understand that if she wanted to garner attention – to make people really listen – she had to learn to sing softly as well as full out.

It was my opinion that competitiveness in the black Baptist church choir had already inscribed its mark on Ashley Támar's singing. I understood all too well what singing under that kind of pressure could do to a vocal talent. I have a deep respect for Gospel music, but I also know the dangers of some of the stylistic requirements for an authentic performance. Far too often the singer with the biggest voice (chesty sound) is the most celebrated in the black church, so children are encouraged, even expected, to push their voices beyond healthy limits, thus destroying any hope of producing a clear vowel or a free tone for the future. I was glad that my young hopeful was nowhere near that point and I aimed to make sure that her voice remained free and healthy. She was a pearl, pearl number one. The presence of a blessed spirit, Ashley was a breath of fresh air – and only nine years of age.

"OK, let's get started," I said. Ashley prepared herself for what was coming next, and Carolyn looked on eagerly.

"Ashley, you have a harshness in your sound that we are going to rid you of in this lesson," I said.

I explained that the jaw was her problem. Typical of the Gospel style of music, which she had been hearing her entire life, Ashley had been influenced into making an open, full-throated sound that inevitably causes the jaw to stiffen. It is the only way to make that belted sound, so beloved in the black church. "Bad Broadway singers sing with wide open tones, Ashley, but you are not Ethel Merman, my dear. You are a far greater treasure than that," I said. Carolyn laughed, knowingly. Ashley smiled. She hadn't a clue who Ethel Merman was, but I had Ashley's full attention.

"To get to the *free movement* of the lower jaw, I need to help you to understand that its proper action in singing is that it drops downwards and then backward, without any sharp and sudden movement." Asking her to watch me, I yawned. "Did you see what I just did?" I asked.

"Yes, you yawned," Ashley answered.

"Correct. Now you do it."

As soon as she began, I stopped her. "Remember, I said earlier that it would require you to awaken your imagination?"

"Yes," she said.

"Accessing your imagination also means not being afraid to look silly. Now yawn as though you are acting in a school play and make it big enough that your friends, who are partly blind, can see it in the back of the room."

Ashley laughed. "My friends are not blind," she said.

"I know. It's pretend!"

She prepared herself and then she let out the grandest yawn that I had yet seen from a young singer. This girl was a natural-born actress. I can use that, I thought.

"Great. Now did you feel the soft movement of the jaw – back here?" I placed my hand on the masseter muscles at both sides of her face. "Here," I pointed. "The muscle that pokes out when you bite down," I said.

"Oh, wow. I feel it." Ashley yawned again and said, "I feel like a lion."

"Exactly," I answered.

Her little brother Sean, all of three years old, was enthralled. Ashley began to roar like a queen of the jungle and Sean giggled uncontrollably, doubling over and then rolling around on the floor, like a kid at Christmas.

"Yes," I said. "Now we are going to yawn and sing the Ah vowel, and I want you to think chew."

She did it. Instantly her sound changed from bright to warm. She noticed it and stopped. She did it again and burst into laughter. She said it sounded funny, but then said that she felt that she opened up space in the back of her throat.

"Exactly," I said. "Next we are going to sing 'Happy Birthday,' yawning and chewing on an Ah. Do not sing the words," I said.

Ashley did what I asked her. She burst into laughter again. This time I didn't laugh along with her.

"I am serious. I am always serious when it comes to singing," I said. I didn't have to say another word. Ashley's entire countenance changed. She buckled down.

Moving on, I told her that we were going to add the tongue. I demonstrated. "Ashley, watch my tongue," I said.

"Ok."

I began. "Yah, yah, yah, yah," chewing and yawning. I asked her what she saw. She said that she saw that my tongue rested in my mouth and then raised when I sang the vowel, then fell back down.

"Yes. Do you see where the tip is and do you see the curve, when does the curve happen in the exercise?" I did it again. "Yah, yah, yah, yah – ."

74

She answered, "OK, I see the tip of your tongue by your teeth and the curve happens after the tongue goes up and then falls back down."

I stood her in front of the mirror. "Now do it and watch your tongue. Remember what everything is supposed to do."

Ashley did as I asked her to do. She did it perfectly. "Now do you feel the ease of your jaw?" I asked.

"Yes."

"Now sing 'Amazing Grace' again, using this method and thought process." Tears came to her eyes. She stopped. "Now that is your voice, round and beautiful," I said. I asked her to sing the song again completely and without over-exaggerating the technical aspects of what I had just taught her. "We don't want the audience to see you yawning, now do we?"

Ashley laughed again, this time checking to see if laughing was OK.

It was. I laughed back and heartily. "You shouldn't look like a donkey," I said, after which we both fell about laughing.

Carolyn had stopped writing whatever it was that she had been working on. Ashley's little brother Sean had pulled up a chair, and her younger brother Jay, several years older than the three-year-old Sean, was also quiet and paying attention.

Ashley sang the song again and when she got to the high notes, she stopped. She was emotional. Her sound was not only beautiful, but it touched her.

I hugged her and told her that she was extremely gifted. "I look forward to your next lesson and to working on awakening the extraordinary in you and your singing."

Ashley's enthusiasm gleamed. Her spirit and her eyes were full of wonder. I could see the wheels of her brain turning. Her eyes were saying, *what just happened here.* I wanted to scream, *music is what just happened here* and *it begins with you.*

Ashley possessed an inner grace. I was sure she'd make a great singing actress someday.

I turned to Carolyn, who was by now standing next to me, appointment book in hand. "When is Ashley's next lesson?"

"Does every Tuesday work for you?"

"It's perfect." Carolyn scribbled Ashley's next lesson into her appointment book, mumbling to herself under her breath, "Ashley at 4:00 for lesson." Carolyn closed the book, thanked me, and then gathered her things and her children.

I shook Jay's hand, rubbed the top of little Sean's head, and hugged my new nine-year-old protégé good bye. "See y'all next week," I said.

"You can count on it," Carolyn answered.

* * * * *

Most people think of diamonds as being most valuable, but I believe that a rare pearl is something exquisite. Ashley was simply stunning, a gifted and talented child. Patrice had a good eye – and ear – I thought.

If the other girl Bruce had mentioned was as good as Ashley, I was going to enjoy myself immensely building "Ann's girl group."

Ann still hadn't called.

4. Beyoncé Giselle Knowles

"Hello, my name is Celestine Knowles. I got your telephone number from Carolyn Davis. Our daughters are in the same dance group. I am contacting you about voice lessons. You come highly recommended and I was just wondering if you would allow my daughter to audition for you."

Somewhat startled by her choice of words, I greeted Mrs. Knowles warmly and asked her how old her daughter was.

"Eight years old," she said.

I remember thinking that Bruce Strickland said that his friend Ann wanted to build a girl group, but I hadn't suspected he meant "little girls." Intrigued, I asked "How long has your daughter been singing?"

"Since as far back as I can remember," Mrs. Knowles said. "Beyoncé sings around the house all the time. Last year her dance teacher asked if she could put her in a talent show and she won. She blew me away. I didn't know that she could sing like that. That's the reason I'm calling you. I just think that if she is going to do this she should have lessons – *with someone of your education*" Mrs. Knowles said. "I understand that you sing opera," she added.

"Yes, that is right," I answered. "Changing the subject a bit – may I ask you a very direct question, Mrs. Knowles?"

"No, I don't mind at all, what is it?"

"Earlier you said 'if she is going to do this'… what did you mean?"

"Oh, Beyoncé wants to be in the music business," Mrs. Knowles answered.

"Oh, I see. And how does little Beyoncé feel about taking voice lessons?… I asked Carolyn Davis, the same question," I continued. "I am asking if your daughter understands what voice study is all about. Is Beyoncé the one who wants the lessons? I mean, she's very young. Why not let her talents develop naturally and when she's a little older think about voice lessons? The study of singing is no child's play."

"Oh, yes, she is fine with the idea," Mrs. Knowles answered.

When Mrs. Knowles and her daughter arrived for the audition, it was clear that this child was the family's little princess. She was adorable. Little Beyoncé Giselle Knowles was a tiny eight-year-old with a round face, fat cheeks, and a pudgy tummy, typical of a girl her age. Her hair had been perfectly braided in pig tails and beautifully bowed. She wore black patent leather shoes and white socks chosen to perfectly compliment her Sunday dress, which was black and white with puffy shoulders and ruffles at the hem. If she had walked into any Southern Black Church I guarantee all eyes would have been on her. I remember all this vividly, because she looked so picture perfect.

Beyoncé was a little nervous at first so I asked her what she wanted to be when she grew up. She told me emphatically, "A singer." I asked her what she enjoyed most about singing and, again, she answered without hesitation, "The way it makes me feel." I complimented her on her appearance then asked her mother if I could offer her something to drink. Mrs. Knowles asked for a glass of water, and then I sent young Beyoncé into the kitchen.

"My house is your house Beyoncé. Please feel comfortable here; there is no need to be afraid. I love singing as much as you do." I told her. That seemed to relax her.

Beyoncé sheepishly smiled at me.

From my apartment's living/dining room, which doubled as my voice studio, I could see Beyoncé through the opening over the kitchen's breakfast counter. As she looked around for a glass, I followed her movements with great interest. Once she located the glasses, and only then, did I go into the kitchen to help her get one down out of the cupboard. I was checking her manners, and they were indeed impeccable.

When Beyoncé had finished pouring the water, she returned from the kitchen, handing it to her mother, whose smile concerned me. Her look said "stage mother." Beyoncé was her very own world wonder. Nevertheless, I asked my young hopeful what she'd like to sing.

"'Home,' from *The Wiz*," she answered.

"Great, I know that piece," I told her.

"Really?" Beyoncé said.

"Yes, I've sung the Scarecrow onstage," I answered.

Beyoncé smiled broadly. As she readied herself, I was taken off guard. Remarkably, she lowered her eyes, as if to transition into character. I wondered if she'd been coached to present herself in this way. Experience had taught me that pop singers often mimic recordings of famous artists. Very few ever come to me understanding presentation, or even their own sound, style, and musical taste. These are attributes that a singing teacher normally has to develop. However, this little girl was different.

As I understood it from Beyoncé's mother, she'd taken a few lessons with other teachers, but never went back. Perhaps one of them taught her about getting into character, I thought. Anyway, Beyoncé's instinct caught my eye. Suddenly she breathed in, and then opened her mouth to sing.

What she let loose was one of the most believable interpretations I'd ever heard from a child. Her mouth was way too open and the tone, although not harsh, was over energized. Still, something about it grabbed me and wouldn't let me go. She had a distinguished timbre, a voice reminiscent of singers past, similar to Sarah Vaughan's genius. Beyoncé's sound, and her potential, reminded me of molten gold. In addition, I also sensed a type of ferociousness that reminded me of Tina Turner. Nevertheless, it was her phrasing that gave me shivers. She was individual, something that music industry professionals value. Again, I thought it was not every day that I experienced a presence that was uniquely "its own," a sound already so immediately identifiable. Furthermore, she possessed a seemingly innate, physical connection to the text. Could God have sent me a prodigy?

As she continued to sing I closed my eyes. It wasn't just the voice, it was the spirit; it was Beyoncé herself who captured and enraptured me.

"When I think of home I think of a place

Where there's love overflowing.

I wish I was home, I wish I was back there/

With the things I've been knowing."

For a moment I wondered, is this why I am here? Is this girl, this gifted spirit, the reason I had abandoned a perfect life and withdrew from graduate school in Cleveland, moved to Houston, then left Houston only to return? Then I heard it, my still small voice, "She will be the biggest star. Teach her everything."

Completely absorbed by the power of her own singing, Beyoncé had taken flight, right before my eyes, like an elegant swan on the wing.

"Living here in this brand new world might be a fantasy.

But it taught me to love and it's real, it's real, so real to me

And I've learned I must look inside my heart to find

A world full of love, like yours, like mine, like home."

That was it. My eyes were filling with tears. As she reached the climax of the song I was barely able to subdue my emotions.

I'd been transported back to high school and my friend Kathy Tyree's singing of this moving song. In that moment I recalled the love of my family and I knew that little Beyoncé Knowles was able to sing with such tremendous honesty because for her singing was "Home."

Although she had a slight, slow vibrato in the middle register, signaling that she was potentially headed for trouble, I knew I could fix this and that I could guide and teach Beyoncé everything she would need to know about the music business and about using her God-given gift, just as my grandparents had done with me. We were two souls bound by music, and I hoped that she'd listen to me regarding her obvious love for pushing her voice, driving it with "over-emotional" singing (a type of singing I have come to refer to as "wild"). My work would lie in helping her understand that abrasive singing would put a hole in her middle voice, which was the reason for the beginnings of that slower vibrato I heard.

When she finished, I turned to her mother and said, "I'll take her." Beyoncé began to jump up and down and she let out a little joyous squeal. Her reaction startled me. Having only just become acquainted, we didn't know one another at all. But Beyoncé would tell me in later years that she knew I was the teacher for her – she just sensed it.

I stood up, putting both of my hands on her shoulders and leaned down and in toward her so that we were at eye level.

"Are you ready to work very hard?" I asked Beyoncé.

"Yes, I am ready sir," she said.

"Beyoncé, what I mean by hard work is absolute sacrifice for your gift. Will you absolutely devote yourself to your gift?" I had to know this.

"Yes, I am ready. I love singing and I want to sing for the people," she said.

I had one thing left to check out in that audition to make sure that my assessment had been correct: her musical intelligence. I got my portable keyboard and checked her pitch memory and accuracy. I then played various chords and asked her about the emotions they evoked in her. I further checked her memory and listening skills by whispering a simple sentence in her ear and asking her to repeat it back to me. Lastly I showed her pictures, some happy, some disturbing, some showing confusion and some showing surprise. I was checking the reaction of her facial muscles to the pictures, checking micro expressions. She was more than intelligent – she was a natural. Beyoncé Giselle Knowles was prodigious. I told her that if she followed my instructions to the letter she would be a star. She giggled, and with that, I began our first lesson.

"Beyoncé, I have to connect your breath to your tone," I said. "Your voice has a slight, slow vibrato, but I can show you how to solve this issue in ten minutes."

"What is vibrato?" she asked.

"Vibrato is the pulsation one hears between the singing of two tones," I said. Seeing that she hadn't understood me, I sang a phrase to demonstrate, once with a "straight" tone and once again, with vibrato. My newest protégé understood immediately.

I asked her to put her teeth together and explained that it was important not to bite down. "Simply allow your teeth to touch, closed mouth position," I said. Once she did this I asked her to – lightly and without tension – sing a single tone on the Ee vowel, making the ZZZ sound, creating a buzz. She did as I asked and within seconds she felt her diaphragm connect to the breath and tone. We followed this principle up and down the scale, chromatically, and once I arrived at her break (the bridge to her top voice), I took her back down. At the end of the exercise not only was the slow vibrato gone, but she exclaimed, "My voice feels easy."

I told her to begin the song again. What came out this time made even Beyoncé emotional. I was ecstatic. This eight-year-old's sensitivity touched me deeply and gave me joyous affirmation regarding my move to Houston. God had chosen me to teach this young "wunderkind." But would she really do the work? A prodigy without proper guidance will remain merely a talent. Great talent requires unparalleled dedication, on the part of the singer and the teacher, in order to achieve the higher levels of polish and professionalism. I was indeed humbled.

Mrs. Knowles called me after returning home. She said that Beyoncé, who I could hear in the background saying hello, had asked her to call me right away. They wanted to set up the next lesson.

"I'm delighted," I answered.

"Beyoncé is so excited about y'all's work together. All the way home in the car she couldn't stop talking about it, and you."

"How nice," I answered.

Mrs. Knowles also told me that Beyoncé had confessed that for the first time she could imagine that voice study could be fun. After all, Beyoncé was a child, and a smart, musical one at that. She would tell me that she wanted to know how to sing, not just do mindless scales and exercises, as had evidently been the case with those previous teachers. She had no clue how important those mindless scales were to learning how to sing, but she'd find out – enjoying every minute of it, too. I'd already worked the plan in my head.

Anyone could have arrived in an adorable Sunday outfit. But Beyoncé had sunshine in her voice. I knew that this girl had "It."

She would become, so help me God, a star.

* * * * *

Within days of my beginning to teach Ashley Davis and Beyoncé, Andretta "Ann" Tillman called me.

"I apologize for not being able to contact you sooner but I have not been feeling well," Ann said.

"Oh, I hope it's nothing serious," I said.

"Nothing God can't fix," she answered.

Mrs. Tillman's response sounded serious to me, but I abstained from prying any further. It would have been rude. Instead, I asked her when we might possibly meet. I was anxious to hear all about her girl group.

"That's exactly the reason for my call, Mr. Brewer," Ann said.

"Oh, please call me David."

"OK, David. And you should call me Ann," she answered. "So how about coming over to my house this Sunday at around 2:00 in the afternoon for lunch?"

"Perfect," I answered. "Should I bring anything?"

"Just your appetite," Ann said.

Suddenly shifting the conversation, Ann asked if I was a Christian and I told her that I was. "I've never been shy about confessing my love for God," I added. Apparently pleased, Ann then asked my denomination.

"I am Episcopalian." I said. Then I asked Ann if she knew St. James Episcopal Church on Southmore Street?

"Yes, I know that church," Ann said. "Ashley goes to school there."

I hadn't known this.

A highly respected private school in the black community in Houston, The St. James School had been founded in 1971 by the then Rector (Pastor) James Tucker. He and his wife Marjorie Tucker, the St. James School's principal, were wonderful people. Ashley and her brother Jay had been students at the St. James School for a few years already by the time we met.

"Have you met Solange or Mathew?" Ann asked.

"Who are Solange, and Mathew?"

"Solange is Beyoncé's little sister," Ann said. "Mathew is her father."

That Beyoncé had a father was clear – we all have fathers – but I hadn't met him nor had I heard his wife mentioned his name. Neither had little sister Solange come up in Celestine Knowles's conversations. It was time to broach the subject of family in Beyoncé's next lesson. I found it strange behavior – not so much regarding Beyoncé's lack of sharing but rather her mother's. It wasn't usual. Siblings and fathers (husbands) always come up in voice lessons unless there was a reason (trouble) that prevented the student from feeling comfortable enough to talk about their unmentioned parent. Nolan Davis, Ashley's father, and I hadn't met yet, but I'd spoken to him on the telephone on several occasions. Who was this Mathew Knowles, and why was he a secret?

Suddenly, Ann shifted the conversation back to the lunch. "Don't forget to bring a healthy appetite. I'm going to be serving an assortment of egg dishes (scrambled, poached, over easy) and two Quiche Lorraines (one with ham and one without)." Ann continued. "Do you like beef brisket?" she asked.

"Is the Pope Catholic?"

Laughing, Ann told me that she'd planned on preparing the most scrumptious brisket I'd ever tasted. There would also be a choice between fried potato with onions and potato gratin, a pea salad (which I told her was one of my favorites), and homemade pastries. I couldn't wait. It sounded delicious. Before hanging up, Ann asked about wines. "What kind of dessert wines do you prefer?" she asked.

"I loved Portuguese port wines."

"I know just the right one," Ann said. "See you on Sunday!"

After hanging up with Ann, I began running through every possible scenario in my head. I watched the news the entire week and read the most current news magazines for interesting and appropriate table chatter topics and I studied my list of questions about the girl group. (What did Ann plan to do with them, as their manager and financier, and when would I meet the rest of them?)

When Sunday arrived I drove out to Ann's modest, split-level brick home in North Houston, on Strawgrass Street. Anxiously pulling into the driveway, I could see that someone had been anticipating my arrival. A small face, most likely one of Ann's children, had been peering through the sheer curtains. As I put the car in park and gathered my note pad and pencils, I surveyed what looked like a very private and welcoming neighborhood. After greeting one of her neighbors, I rang the doorbell. Seconds later, there she was. Andretta "Ann" Tillman, a tall and gracious woman with very big and welcoming eyes.

"Hi David," Ann said. She gave me a hug and, hands stretched out in the air, Ann beckoned me into the house. Then moving quickly ahead of me down the entrance hallway, she shouted, "This way. I'm still putting the finishing touches on."

"Thank you for the invitation," I shouted back, noticing immediately to my left, the beautifully furnished formal living room, mostly in white, with a baby grand piano serving as the room's focal point. Just beyond that room, before heading down the hallway, I caught a glimpse of a formal dining room. The family room was filled with a massive record collection, a rather large television, a state of the art stereo system, and two blue leather sofas.

"Make yourself comfortable," Ann said, peering through the saloon-style swinging kitchen doors.

"May I peruse your album collection?" I asked.

"Sure, help yourself."

Ann had a huge record collection. This was definitely a music lover's house. Many of the titles were ones my own mother had listened to, back in Omaha. I came across one album that Mama had worn out: Aretha Franklin's "Amazing Grace" was not only a staple in most black households, but seeing it in Ann's collection filled me with nostalgia. Grandmother and I had made an exercise in listening to it. We studied the phrasing, every twist and turn. She was a huge Aretha fan!

Suddenly Ann's children appeared. "Boys!" she called out.

"Yes." Her two young sons appeared in the doorway.

"Introduce yourselves to Mr. Brewer," Ann prompted.

"It's nice to meet you, Sir," they both said – almost in unison.

I extended my hand to little Armon (nine years old), and then to Chris (seven) – both obviously shy. Ann apologized for their "reserved" disposition. I told her about my precociousness as a child and that I had been her children's polar opposite. "I'm sure my mother would have been happy to trade places with you."

Ann laughed, then announced that we could go to the table. "Armon. Chris. Show Mr. Brewer to the table."

Following Ann's boys, I was led into that room that I'd only stolen a glimpse of when I had arrived. It was indeed Ann's formal dining room, and an elegant one at that – wonderfully decorated, complete with what I remember was a cherry wood buffet and sideboard. Armon showed me to my seat.

Carrying the first dishes into the dining room, Ann asked, "Boys, did you remember to wash your hands?"

Thoroughly embarrassed, I had forgotten to wash mine. Excusing myself, I rushed down that hallway again, to the guest toilet. When I returned to the table Ann had already begun serving her children. I noticed that she'd cut into the quiches, giving Armon the one with ham, and Chris the one made of only egg. After finally settling in to my seat, she began passing around one delicious dish after the other. I couldn't have been more delighted. Our first meeting was going well, and Ann was feeding me. The way to my heart is definitely through my stomach. She was delightful and, most important, real. I felt very comfortable in her home.

Well into the meal I began to learn about the group. Ann also told me what I had already heard from Carolyn, that she'd only recently become the official manager of the group. "In fact, two other women preceded me as the group's managers," Ann said. "Denise and Deborah are wonderful women."

* * * * *

Although Denise Seals and Deborah LaDay have been named, in the intervening years, by one author I know about, their important roles in the beginnings of what would become the group Destiny's Child had been ignored, or even obscured, by the Knowles family. On this occasion Ann filled me in on the important details. "Building a group was Denise and Deborah's idea," Ann said. "Denise was enthusiastic, but broke, and she called me for support. I wasn't so sure that I wanted to get involved with girls, but then I met them."

"Why?" I asked.

"Why what?"

"Why were you skeptical of getting involved with little girls?"

"Boys, you may leave the table," Ann said. Once they had left the room, Ann continued. "My husband and daughter were killed in a car crash."

I dropped my Danish, shocked by her candor and devastating words. Before I could pick my face up off the floor, Ann went on to tell me of the circumstances surrounding her loved ones' deaths.

86

* * * * *

On Thursday, the 23rd of October, 1986, Dwight Ray Tillman and his wife, Andretta, were having a disagreement. Dwight was reluctant to drive from their Houston home to Tyler, Texas, to visit Ann's family – not after the long work week he'd had. He suggested that he and Ann remain at home, where they were happily raising their three children, Armon (age six), Christopher (four), and their adorable little two-year-old daughter, Shawna Marie. However, Ann was persistent.

Having been heavily indoctrinated in "the importance of family," Ann always missed hers, especially her seven sisters. Dwight resisted, pointing out that it had been only three months since the last family visit to Tyler – not to mention that Christmas was just around the corner. Still, Dwight knew how this would end, and after work on the next day, he packed his family into the car, and they headed to Tyler for the weekend.

"I convinced him to make the trip. My selfishness is the cause of my pain." Ann blamed herself. "Mama and Daddy were big on family from the word go. They had twelve children (eight girls and four boys), so words like 'dedication' and 'unity' were all we heard growing up."

Ann's mother, Effie Brown, was a firecracker who possessed an iron fist and a silver tongue. Her way was often stern – yet, somehow gentle. She didn't believe in holding back on her sentiments. "I guess she needed to be firm with all dem chilluns," Ann said. Ann's father, Jimmy Brown, was Effie's polar opposite. A reserved man, he was a pillar of self-control and inner strength. Both Effie and Jimmy were faithful members of New Canaan Baptist Church and had served all their adult life, he, as deacon and she, as usher. In significant ways, Ann's parents were mirror images of herself and Dwight.

Over the years I have pieced together the story that Ann began to reveal to me at that first meeting. In 2013 her sister Glenda Stewart recalled, *"It was 9:30 p.m. when the car pulled up to Mama's house. They had had car trouble on the way to Tyler and for this reason they were late getting in. Regardless, Ann drove to my house after getting Dwight, the boys, and*

Shawna settled at Mama's. We could never wait to see one another – not even for a day. I truly loved Ann, as I do all my sisters, but we were favorite sisters. Ann brought with her to Tyler, and to the family, an indescribable harmony whenever she was around. She had an amazing sense of humor and loved to laugh. We could laugh for hours."

Sunday morning church service was festive. Anybody who understands the black Baptist church experience knows that services last all day. New Canaan Baptist Church in Whitehouse, Texas, had just finished its second service, and Ann found herself in the church parking lot chatting up old childhood friends. But time was getting away from her, and she needed to get to her mother's home to pick up her husband, her children, and her nephew Albert. Glenda's husband, Raymond, had prepared the Sunday meal this visit, and the family was to meet at Glenda's for dinner at 5 p.m.

Glenda told me, *"Ann just couldn't resist a good chin wag after church. It didn't matter where she was, she delighted in seeing old classmates and family friends. Most times it was difficult to pull her away from those conversations. All that reminiscing was not my thing, but Ann loved it. She loved people so much. Their stories really interested her. So I expected her to arrive for dinner later than the allotted time. She always did."*

According to Ann, "Our car was still at the mechanic's. The shade tree mechanic, a family friend, had left a message that the alternator needed to be replaced. He told Dwight that he'd be finished that evening around 10:00. Dwight wasn't happy about the pickup time, or the price, but what could we do? We were doing all right financially, both of us having good jobs and all, but three children cut into our budget, and often. I guess that was my fault. I loved buying for the children, especially for my little Shawna. Dwight wouldn't argue with me if I went over budget buying for Shawna."

Despite the car problems, Dwight, Ann, and the children all looked forward to the family get-togethers. Albert, her sister Mae Jo's fourteen-year-old son, came along for the festivities at Glenda's (Albert was Armon and Christopher's favorite cousin). Ann told me that when they walked in the door she could smell the love that had simmered on the stove. The collard greens, candied yams, macaroni and cheese, potato salad, baked beans, green salad, and sweet water cornbread had all been positioned on the table. "We just needed to wash our hands and sit down," Ann said. "Glenda had set a gorgeous table. Dwight exited the house for the back-yard, where Raymond was busy taking the ribs off the grill. They, too, were perfect. The meat fell off the bone.

"Family meals in Tyler were an event, you know," Ann said. "My brothers and brothers-in-law were always competing to one-up the other. My brother Charlie was the favorite cook in the family. He owned a catering company and was the Brisket King of Tyler, but Raymond gave him a run for his money. His ribs were out of this world."

After the meal Ann and Glenda retreated to the back of the house, where they talked about their children and their husbands. "If I remember correctly, football was on the television, and Dwight and Raymond became engrossed in it. The boys and Albert were playing with Glenda's children, and Shawna was with me."

Once again, time had got away from Ann. It always did when she got together with one of her sisters. Dwight suggested they head out.

"Thirty minutes later I finally got in the car. We had to get Albert home and get the car from the mechanic's."

Ann held Shawna on her lap. Dwight had loaded the boys into the back seat. Armon and Christopher were sound asleep. It was October 26, 1986 at 10:30 p.m.

According to Glenda, in later years, *I can remember some details, but not all of them. When Dwight and Ann got ready to go that night, I walked them to the car and then I moved my car into the garage. As I was getting out of my car I heard a big bang and I walked to the edge of my driveway. I could see there had been an accident at the end of my street.*

I started to walk toward the accident and I realized that it was Ann and Dwight. The car was resting part of the way up on the curb and the back end was in the street. My daughter came out of the house and wanted to walk up to the accident with me, but I told her to go back and get her dad.

He was in the shower and he came up to the accident as soon as he got dressed.

In the meantime, there were several other cars that had stopped to help. I proceeded to check on the injured in the car. They were all unconscious – all except little Shawna. I don't remember if I opened the front door where Ann and the baby were sitting, but I went to her first. Armon, Chris, and Albert were in the back seat of the car, and we got them out. Albert was seated behind Dwight and upon impact the seat went back on his legs, crushing his knees. That accident put an end to his football career – a career he had dreamed of since a little child.

Dwight was deceased. He was slumped over the wheel. When I took Shawna from Ann's lap, she made a faint sound and I assumed she was OK – but she wasn't. Before the firemen arrived an unidentified man came over to me and said, 'Let's pray.' I don't remember what he looked like or where he went when we finished praying. When the fireman arrived they started to assess the injuries. When they came over to check on Shawna, they realized that she was severely injured. She was put into the ambulance and rushed to Medical Center Hospital. I think my husband is who called my sister Mae Jo and then proceeded to call other family members...."

"My baby Shawna was asleep in my arms," Ann remembered.

"'Call me when you get home, girl!' Glenda called out to me."

That night, as Glenda pulled her car into the garage, Dwight backed out of the driveway and headed for the intersection where Texas Hwy Loop 323 meets Elm Street (at the corner – two houses away from Glenda's). Suddenly, a horrible bang. Neighbors scream. A speeding drunk driver, traveling south on Loop 323, struck Ann and Dwight's family auto as they sit awaiting a free moment to make the left turn. Dwight is killed instantly, the steering mechanism penetrating his chest. The car is knocked head first up onto the side walk and two-year-old Shawna is ejected from the safety of her mother's arms into the windshield, leaving a hole in it where her head has made contact. Ann, who couldn't free herself from her safety belt, watches her baby girl roll off the dash board and back into her arms. Convulsing, and pinned into her seat, Ann tries to get the situation under control. That is when she notices that Dwight is slumped over the steering wheel. "That damn safety belt – I couldn't get it loose," she told me.

Before my eyes Ann is transported back to that scene. She raises her left arm, stretching it out to the left of her. Every muscle in her body is on alert, her face tense. „Dwight is dead," she says. Beginning to hyperventilate, her body is re-enacting those seconds of horror. She looks down, tugging at her waist. The seat belt. She's pulling at it ferociously. Suddenly, she balls her hand into a fist, screaming out, „This damned belt!" It's jammed. Then falling back into the chair she begins to cry.

The pain of that night erupted from the depths of her soul. Even now, as I think back to that moment, I can feel her agony. Her screams must have been blood-curdling. Ann told me that her sister, Glenda, had said that her daughter had heard them from inside the house.

Then Ann told me, in a voice quivering with emotion, that she couldn't remember anything else. She had blacked out. Her son, Armon, barely conscious in the back seat, saw a man--his uncle, perhaps?–pulling at the back door. The police arrived. Body bags are what he remembers next. His father, his little sister, his mother, all laid out, still, on the side of the road. Are they dead?

Days later Ann awoke from the sedative given to her at the hospital, and the nightmare continued. It's true. Dwight, the love of her life, and Shawna, her baby, are gone. She must pull herself together for her two boys, Armon and Christopher; they need their mother more than ever.

"It is an indescribable pain to lose a child," Ann told me. She has to take a moment before she can speak again. "My whole insides shook. There was a sharp pain, which felt like my blood was on fire."

As if the tragedy of losing her husband and daughter were not enough, Ann discovered that the drunk driver who had taken her husband's and daughter's lives had been released from custody. "No charges were filed," she said. Apparently, the Tyler police let the drunken driver sleep it off and then released him. They hadn't booked him or charged him for murder. Ann called their action racist, "Texas Justice," she said. "In Tyler, Texas, the good ole boy rule still stands prominently." Mad as hell, Ann filed legal claims against the city of Tyler and was awarded a substantial settlement. In addition, Dwight had taken out a life insurance policy with longtime family friend, Al Wilson. That policy had a double indemnity clause.

Now a very wealthy woman, Ann focused her attention on her sons. "Everything I do is for them," she said.

* * * * *

Ann explained that some days it was difficult to get out of bed. However, she knew she had to think of her boys. They gave her purpose. The way she talked about Armon and Chris, I could feel the love. She wanted them to go to college, to get jobs, "stop eating her out of house and home," (this she said laughingly), maybe get married, and definitely give her lots of grandbabies – her exact words. Ann loved children and imagined being surrounded by loads of them.

"Dwight and I wanted more children," she said. "I always wanted another girl, someone who Shawna could share things with, like my sisters and I do." She stopped for a moment to compose herself.

Once she recovered, I asked Ann about re-marriage. No way, she said. She loved Dwight way too much to ever think about bringing someone else into her boys' life. She wanted them to remember their father.

"Armon wants to be a professional basketball player," Ann said. She'd involved him in basketball camps all over Houston. She intended to afford him and Chris every opportunity to succeed. She talked about her best friend, Patricia "Pat" Felton, who was a school teacher and who also had a son who loved basketball. Ann and Pat's boys had met in one of those basketball camps and they had become great friends. Although Chris hadn't identified any real loves yet, Ann told me that he was her sensitive child. "He watches me like a hawk," Ann said. The accident had taken a toll on them all, but Chris was still having nightmares. I thought of the nightmares I'd had after Roy's departure. And although the causes of each of our pains were different, trauma is trauma.

"I want my babies to dream, dream, and dream and not to worry about me." Ann told me, before letting the tears go that she'd been holding back.

Something was terribly off, but again, I didn't pry. In an effort to find her way back to the land of the living, a necessary step for the sake of her boys, Ann delighted in her involvement with *her* new girls group. Grateful to God, she said "They have helped save my life."

Ann's personal story touched me deeply. I naturally assumed that being around young girls would have been much too painful for her, but quite the opposite was true. I understood now that Ashley and Beyoncé – and the other girls in the group, whom I was yet to meet – meant a great deal to my new friend. I got it. Ann saw her daughter, Shawna, in each of their faces. Denise and Deborah had done her a huge service by asking her to become involved, and she planned to take care of them, she intimated. She told me that she never felt right with how things ended for Denise and Deborah, the original managers.

At Ashley's next lesson, I asked Carolyn what she knew about Denise and Deborah's story. Reading Carolyn's signal that the subject of Denise and Deborah was one we should have in private, I changed the subject. However, at the end of Ashley's lesson, when Carolyn and I exchanged our customary hug, she whispered, "I'll call you tonight." That evening, at around 9:00, my phone rang. Carolyn had gotten the kids fed and their homework done, and now that they were in bed she could talk. She had my full attention.

"For two years Denise and Deborah bore expenses, found sources for financial support, and saw to the grooming of their talented young group." Denise and Deborah's problems arose with some of the parents' objections to what Carolyn called Denise's "sharp tongue." Carolyn described Denise as a "to-the-point kinda girl. She called a spade a spade," and sometimes, as I gathered through the conversation with Carolyn, Denise's spade sometimes dug into the wrong ground. "Tina didn't like her," Carolyn concluded.

93

Carolyn told me about a parent meeting held at the Knowles house, where Charles Mitchell, LaTavia Roberson's step-father, spoke bluntly. "I am not sure I want my daughter around such foul language," he said of Denise. Carolyn told me that he had been adamant: "I think the girls need someone with a more *moral* character guiding them." It didn't take Denise and Deborah long to figure out that their days were numbered.

Charles's comments opened the door for the other parents to voice their concerns, and specifically Mathew, Beyoncé's father. "Before you know it," said Carolyn, "that meeting – which started out pretty digni-fied – turned ugly. Mathew Knowles added his two cents, and the meeting got even uglier." His method of pushing Denise and Deborah out for good was to tell them that he had decided to exercise his "Custodial Parent Au-thority." He simply refused to allow Beyoncé to perform until everyone went along with what he wanted.

Carolyn found Mathew's tactics unscrupulous. Still, nothing could pro-tect Denise and Deborah from Mathew's bullying. They lost their nerve. Relentless, he wore them down, so that all he had to do was to wait for their management contract to expire. With them no longer in the picture, it was Mathew who proposed Ann as Denise and Deborah's replacement. He was not opposed to her money. The vote was unanimous. Ann Tillman was voted onto the island as the official manager of Girls Tyme, the name of *her* girl group.

Carolyn painted a daunting description of Beyoncé's father. Was he re-ally like what she described? I couldn't help imagining what he might look like. "His antics keep everyone busy," Carolyn said. Ann mentioned that Mathew was unemployed, having worked in medical sales for Xerox. He had suggested to Ann that he had been searching for a new job, but she couldn't know for sure whether he'd stay in sales.

At Beyoncé's next lesson, I gingerly broached the subject of her little sister and father. Beyoncé apologized for the oversight, while Celestine said that she hadn't thought it important (plain English for "it's none of your damned business," I suspected). It was obvious to me that my ques-tion had irritated Celestine, but maybe I had struck a nerve with her because, like an open faucet, her mouth released a flow of information. Mathew Knowles was hard working and brilliant, she boasted. He sounded like a saint. Now I was even more confused, and intrigued.

Mathew Knowles had gone to Fisk University (the Harvard of black universities). According to Celestine, he had been Xerox's top salesmen in Texas for three consecutive years and that he had earned a "six-figure salary" and that his job ended "this year." The company had actually closed their medical sales division in 1989, but Ann had already intimated that Mathew had been "let go" long before Xerox disbanded the division. It didn't really matter, in the scheme of things. However, I wondered why Celestine made such a point of emphasizing the words *"this year."* And why she added to her already overzealous description, "Mathew is taking a little break." Again, I wondered what she meant.

"He is going to help me with my salon," she said. Her hair salon, Headliners Hair Salon, had only barely opened its doors, in May 1989.

"Wow! Starting a new business is exciting. I know how much work it takes," I said.

Celestine looked at me inquisitively.

"My first business was a traveling hair salon," I said. "Necessity was definitely the mother of that invention. 'David's,' the name of my business, was lucrative and helped save my butt with college tuition back in Oklahoma."

"Very interesting," Celestine answered and then she asked if I was licensed.

"No, I never earned a diploma or certificate, *per se*. I did, however, study with my Aunt Hattie back home. She was a master cosmetologist and a licensed instructor. She taught me everything about the beauty business. I even trained in nail and pedicure services with my first music teacher's daughter, Phyllis Wilson, who owned her own nail salon."

Suddenly, Celestine changed the subject. "Do you know the Montrose area? My salon is in Montrose," she said.

"Yes, I know the area," I answered. Montrose was the upscale home to Houston's gay community.

"Are you seeing anyone?" Celestine asked abruptly. Apologizing for her question's forwardness, she asked, "You're gay aren't you?"

Shocked, I answered, "A little, and no, I'm not seeing anybody." I had just learned my first lesson with Celestine. Asking personal questions would be fair game.

"I just love gay people," Celestine said.

"How nice," was my response.

Shifting my focus to Beyoncé and away from her mother's strange comment about just loving gay people, I asked about her little sister. Instantly it became obvious that I had opened a Pandora's box. Beyoncé lowered her head. Her eyebrows pulled in and up, her head tilted slightly forward and she pressed her lips together, biting at them. I was sure that the nerve I was witnessing was shame. Unbeknownst to her, her face reddened and she tugged at her stomach, ever so gently, which signified deep shame. Before I could verbalize my concern, trying desperately to back respectfully out of the quick sand I'd wandered into, Celestine blurted out that Solange, who was five years Beyoncé's junior, also loved singing and dancing, but "she's not serious." She referred to her younger daughter as lazy – "not like Beyoncé," she said.

Looking directly at Beyoncé, Celestine said "Beyoncé has always wanted to be a singer. Isn't that right, Beyoncé?"

"Yes, Mama," Beyoncé said, while forcing out a half smile.

The child was uncomfortable and embarrassed, which made me uncomfortable. My innocent question about family had turned our wonderful lesson sour. Without hesitation, I ended it. We'd gone over time anyway. Celestine gathered her purse and headed for the door, Beyoncé trailing closely behind. Then, without warning, little Beyoncé did something that she had not done before. She gave me the biggest hug, with all her might.

Celestine said, "Ah – she loves you, David."

Bending down to look Beyoncé in the eye, I said "I think you're pretty special, too." I was sure that she'd become a big name in entertainment.

Beyoncé gave me the biggest smile; this time definitely unstrained. "Thank you for my lesson."

"You're welcome," I answered.

I opened the door and let Celestine and Beyoncé out. Again, Beyoncé hugged me. Just before reaching the stairwell of my apartment complex, Celestine turned back. I heard her voice, but not what she said. I'd been so focused on Beyoncé and why she reacted the way she had when I asked her about her sister.

"I'm sorry. What did you say?" I said to Celestine.

"Would you like to come over for dinner? It will give you a chance to meet Beyoncé's little sister and father, Mathew."

"I'd like that," I said.

Seconds later, mother and daughter were out of sight. Interestingly, Celestine's invitation to break bread never materialized.

The next day, Ann called. "David, would you help me finalize the group?" she asked. Her question to me signified that she wasn't happy with the current setup.

"I'm very interested, Ann" I said. "But I think I'd better meet all the girls first, hear and see them, and then we can talk about it."

"Of course," she answered. "I'll call you Wednesday to set something up for the weekend."

5. Kelly

There was a lot going on in the world in 1989-90. America had a new president (George H. W. Bush, the father), Colin Powell was named the Chairman of the Joint Chiefs of Staff – the first black person to hold that position – the Iran Contra affair became front page news, the Dalai Lama won the Nobel Peace Prize, many prominent people from all walks of life died (movie star Bette Davis, television legend Lucille Ball, author Samuel Beckett, and fighter Sugar Ray Robinson, to name a few), a catastrophic, 7.1 magnitude earthquake in San Francisco claimed the lives of 67, injured more than 3000, and destroyed or damaged more than 100,000 buildings, and the Berlin Wall fell after 28 years.

In Houston, Texas, I was re-focusing Girls Tyme.

* * * * *

Ann and I had agreed to meet on a Saturday at a dance studio on West Orem, where the girls practiced.

"I want to build a little Motown," Ann said.

Knowing the history of the legendary music label, I agreed – with one strong reservation. "I hope that you're not interested in employing Mr. Gordy's methodology. Abuse is not OK," I said.

"Oh God, no," Ann replied. "I want these girls nurtured in love."

I was glad to hear Ann's sentiment. Berry Gordy was rumored to be a hellion. And in my opinion, ruling through intimidation and fear might make for loyal soldiers, but such methods are deadly behavior when raising genius.

Naturally, I was concerned that Ann, being the chief financial officer, and now the group's official manager, would never give me full deciding power, but it was the only way I could agree to taking on artistic development of the group. I was the one who would develop the sound, look and feel of the group, train them in stage deportment and performance, teach dance, acting and modeling, and most importantly, build their voices. However, I was pleasantly surprised by Ann's answer. She started by agreeing to all of my wishes, and then asked if we could keep Beyoncé and Ashley. "They're perfect I think," she added.

"Oh, certainly. In my opinion, Ashley and Beyoncé set the standard," I answered. "Of course, their musical and artistic development would have to be my responsibility."

"Agreed. I trust your judgement, David – totally," Ann said.

I already had the unique sound in my head. Combining the polyphonic genius of Johann Sebastian Bach with the singing brilliance and harmonic fabric of legendary groups, the likes of "The Clark Sisters," the radio and television stars "The Andrews Sisters," and "The Emotions" – in my book, the ever-reigning queens of pop – I was going to build singing phenoms. I wanted to bring quality to the pop music business, and my girls would galvanize it. For this I'd need at least three musically brilliant singers. Four would be even better.

I met Ann over at Darlette's dance studio, as we agreed. Beyoncé had talked about the group and their dance teacher constantly. "Ms. Darlette is so nice," she always said.

Meeting her outside, privately, without her students, I discovered that Darlette Johnson was not only nice, but she was also very sensitive, and unusually kind. She believed that every child should have an opportunity to shine. I agreed with her completely on that valid point. However, when I walked into the rehearsal to which I had been invited, I had serious second thoughts. I saw a group of girls whose work resembled more an aerobics class than an ensemble of cohesive performing artists. There must have been fifty girls, singing, dancing, and fumbling all over each other. I gave them an E for Effort.

Intrigued, I noticed an exceedingly shy little girl whose face lit up the room. "Who is that little girl with the bangs?" I asked Ann.

"Oh, that's Kelly. She's new to the group."

I didn't know if little Kelly could sing, but judging by what I saw, this girl had the star appeal I was looking for. Oddly enough, little Kelly was not Ms. Darlette's reported favorite. Rather, I'd been directed to pay special attention to another girl, KeKe Wyatt. I decided to reserve my final decision until hearing her sing in a private audition, separated from all the "like me – look at me" energy the girls were giving off.

Driving home, I couldn't help thinking about little Kelly and her brilliant smile. Ann said that she hadn't heard her yet, but that Darlette had told her that Kelly missed a lot of rehearsals. It seemed hopeless to Ann, who said – as it turned out, with understated accuracy, "I'm not sure her mother can commit."

I was determined to give little Kelly a chance. Her soul called out to me. There was something about her. Ann said she would see what she could do. I begged her to do more than her best. A couple days later, Ann still hadn't heard back from Kelly's mother.

In our talks about the make-up of our group, I suggested to Ann that we reduce the numbers of girls – significantly. "Denise and Deborah's idea of combining singers and dancers would work. Why not have three singers and three dancers?" I said to Ann.

"I love it," she said.

Although LaTavia Roberson had never sung a day in her life, I had not forgotten that Beyoncé had begged me to find a way to include her good friend in the group. Discovering that LaTavia had a love for rap, I suggested to Ann that LaTavia could become our group's rapper. She had two cousins (Nikki and Nina Taylor) who were sensational natural dancers, and by using cousins, I thought that I'd be able to develop the family atmosphere that I was determined the group needed in order to succeed. It just made sense to take LaTavia and her two cousins. I was getting a three-for-the-price-of-one commitment.

Following the trend of the day, the hip hop duos DJ Jazzy Jeff & the Fresh Prince and the group Kid 'n Play were changing the landscape of music. Not to mention, Beyoncé was Will Smith's biggest fan. Starting out as a rapper under the name "The Fresh Prince," and then as a successful actor on the hit TV show *The Fresh Prince of Bel Air*, he had captivated her. Like most other black kids in the '90s, she never missed an episode of the comedy. LaTavia loved Kid 'n Play. In addition, fashion played a huge part in hip hop culture. Cross Colours Clothing was extremely popular, and the girls loved the brand.

Significantly, LaTavia was already a celebrity, which made my decision even easier. At the age of eight, she had been named a spokesperson for the Pro Line Hair products conglomerate, the major hair care and cosmetics company of which Bruce Strickland was an executive. My relationship to him also played a part in my choosing her. Pro Line's reputation in the black community was comparable to L'Oreal's or Revlon's in the white community. LaTavia's was the face for Pro Line's "Just for Me" campaign. It was a kiddie's permanent hair relaxer advertising blitz that targeted black girls between the ages of six and fourteen. LaTavia had done all the nationwide commercial spots, through television and print media.

Ann and I immediately began holding auditions at her home to choose the third singer. I was disappointed that from the dance group girls Ann had invited, I heard every type of singing imaginable – except excellent singing. It was just dreadful. At the completion of the auditions I had found no one.

Little Keke was indeed very good, but not a fit for the group look or sound, and the little girl that I'd hoped to hear – little Kelly – had not shown up. Kelly's absence from the audition was a real shame. Even Ray Charles would have seen this little girl's charisma and aura. Ann told me that Kelly had moved to Houston from Atlanta and that her mother, although pleasant, was sort of undependable.

Then, almost two weeks later, Ann called me on the telephone. Through LaTavia, she had heard about an eight-year-old girl who, Ann assured me, had "a pretty voice." But Ann had no idea that, for me, the word "pretty" when describing a voice, was jarring. "Pretty" to me usually means a display of an airy, unsupported tone combined with a weak personality. That would not do as far as I was concerned; who wanted to listen to that? But when I arrived at Ann's home, I was surprised and delighted. There she was, little Kelly, eagerly awaiting my arrival. In my mind, Kelly was my third pearl and I hadn't heard one note. She radiated the kind of constant, unquenchable, effervescent light I was looking for.

I promptly introduced myself and asked her right away what she was going to sing. I wasted no time, and even though I didn't know the song she chose, I didn't care. With bated breath I sent up a prayer. I sat back, closed my eyes, and thought, "God, please let this little girl be able to sing."

* * * * *

Kelendria Trené "Kelly" Rowland's was a gifted talent. Not only could she sing, but her nine-year-old *pretty voice* was going to be undeniably beautiful. Her audition went better than well, but I could tell she wasn't convinced. A gorgeous girl, she was exactly what the group needed. She was the third pearl I was looking for. There was something both engaging and sad about her voice and its pathos. Even though it barely projected beyond her lips, I could hear its multiple and fascinating layers.

A bit on the thin side, Kelly wore a white Sunday dress to her audition, with white anklets and black patent leather shoes. Her hair had been curled for church, and at the sides her mother had placed white barrettes. Kelly's little face, although slight, was accented by the cutest pug nose, button eyes, bangs, and a slender cheek and jaw line. Her left eyebrow tended to rise slightly above the right one and although she was a petite nine-year-old, her ambitious nature packed a mean punch. I was elated. Only one thing bothered me. With every fabulous note that she sang she seemed to fight with herself inwardly.

Improving Kelly's ability meant correcting her self-image. Moshe Feldenkrais, in his book titled *Awareness through Movement*, teaches that correcting self-image – which governs our every act – depends upon three factors: heritage, education, and self-education. "The part that is inherited is the most immutable," he wrote. "The biological endowment of the individual – the form and capacity of his nervous system, his bone structure, muscles, tissue, glands, skin, senses – are all determined by his physical heritage long before he has any established identity. His self-image develops from his actions and reactions in the normal course of experience."

As Kelly neared the end of her song, I wondered what her story was. I wondered why fear had such an effect on her. It was obviously one of the reasons for her reluctant sound, but definitely not the only one. Kelly's uncertainty felt more like the result of circumstance than anything else. But I knew something that she did not. Circumstance does not cripple you. Thought does.

"Kelly, you have great high notes in you," I said.

She laughed.

"No, seriously, your cheekbones and slender face tell me that I'm right." It's all about physiology, I added.

"OK," she said.

"You think I'm strange don't you?" I asked. She hadn't a clue what I was talking about, but because I had expressed genuine admiration for her audition, she opted to overlook my quirky excitement about her voice.

"Kelly, have you ever heard the term 'God-given talent'?" I asked.

She said that she had, "…in church."

"Do you know what it means to be a singer with a God-given talent?"

She shook her head, No.

"It suggests that the singer's talent is not only natural, but more importantly, it is a talent so special that it is believed to have been touched by the very hand of God. You have such a talent," I said.

She smiled. It was funny, but I could have sworn her eyes said, "Maybe this guy isn't crazy after all." Kelly Rowland loved compliments.

I went on to explain that many singers have "God-given talent," which in my terms is essentially a perfectly placed instrument. "God-given" did not mean that the singer knew how to sing. And it certainly did not mean that their naturally placed voices would remain intact without the assistance of a capable teacher. In most cases they do not. Study enhances their native abilities and helps to turn a naturally placed voice into a healthy and reliable instrument.

Suddenly Kelly raised her hand, as though she was in school. She had to go to the toilet. Ah – this girl was completely charming.

"What can you tell me about this girl's mother?" I quietly asked Ann, in Kelly's absence.

"Doris is an avid church goer," Ann said.

"OK, but does she understand that *her God* has given her daughter an extraordinary gift? My God is screaming it in my ear."

"I'm not sure," Ann said.

"Well, where was her mother today?"

"Doris had to work, I think" Ann said.

I really wanted to give Kelly's mother, Doris Lovett, the benefit of the doubt. My mother worked two jobs, most all her life. Nevertheless, Fern Brewer showed interest. Doris's lackadaisical attitude gave me pause. "Can we get Doris on the phone? I'd like to talk to her," I said to Ann. "I'd like Doris involved in Kelly's development, if at all possible."

"I'll do it right now," Ann said, leaving the room for the brief moment that it took to make the call.

In the meantime, Kelly returned from the toilet. "Where's Miss Ann?" she asked.

"Calling your mother," I said.

"Oh, she's at church," Kelly told me.

Ann returned to Kelly and me. "There was no answer," she said.

"I know. Kelly just told me that her mother is in church. But would you please keep trying?" I asked. "It is really important that I talk with Doris."

Ann promised that she would.

I turned to Kelly. "OK, young lady. Let's get started," I said. "Our first lesson will be one that I will repeat, in various ways with you, over and over again. It is the most important thing that I will ever teach you, so pay attention. Your musical life depends upon it," I said. Suddenly, I had her undivided attention, and with reason. I had to make it clear that efficiency in singing – for her especially – would mean quieting that mental fuss going on in her head.

Kelly was terribly confused.

"Kelly, how often do you beat yourself up for not understanding quicker?"

Ashamed, she dropped her head. "A lot," she answered.

"We are going to change that outcome, beginning today." Actually, I had already picked up in her audition that little Kelly was brutal on herself. I feared that she was a true pessimistic personality, which in and of itself can be a good thing, but for a singer pessimism can become the noose that hangs you. Singing requires optimism. Kelly approached everything in her life with her own special brand of willpower, simply called overcompensation. She was tiny. Her voice was tiny. Nevertheless, I was determined that she would be seen and heard, no matter what.

I turned to Ann. "Ann, I would love a cup of tea."

"Really?" Ann asked.

"Yes, please."

It was a very warm Houston day, and my wink to Ann suggested that there was a method to my madness. She stood up and went into the kitchen. I knew two things: One, I knew that Ann had an old-fashioned tea kettle that whistled, and two, I knew that she'd play along. After heading off to the kitchen, Kelly and I were able to talk about her dreams.

"Kelly, what do you want to be when you grow up?" I asked.

104

"I want to be a singer. More than anything," she said.

"I'm glad to hear that," I answered.

Ann peeked out of the kitchen. "David, what kind of tea do you want?"

"Oh, hot water and honey would be perfect."

"OK, one hot water and honey coming up," Ann answered, disappearing again into the kitchen.

I could hear that the pot of water was just beginning to hiss. I had just a few seconds before the tea kettle would begin to whistle. I turned to Kelly.

"Kelly, please close your eyes." Taking her by the hand I asked her to keep her eyes closed and to allow her ears to guide her to Ann's kitchen and toward the whistling tea kettle, which had just begun to sound off. "Remember; do not open your eyes. There's no need for fear. I have your hand and won't let it go. I promise."

Nervously, Kelly closed her eyes. Her body tensed up slightly. Her reaction was perfect. I wanted to induce the feeling of confusion and fear, in an effort to create the conflict that had played out in her head. Inch by inch, step by step, we moved toward the kitchen. I led her in the direction of Ann's coffee table, which she bumped into, giving her a shock. Suddenly, she stretched her arms out in front of her.

"Stop," I said.

She froze.

"You are not allowed to use your arms or your hands to help you. Only your feet will take you where you want to go." In order to move forward she'd have to calm down, which she began to do. Her breath, which had sped up after bumping into the table, was settling itself again. Suddenly, the pressure in her hand and arm changed. She was completely focused. The fear had subsided. The correct form of willpower had kicked in. In the words of Moshe Feldenkrais, "To learn we need time, attention and discrimination; to discriminate we must sense. It's the only way to calm the noise."

Seconds later she sensed that she was in front of the door opening. She could hear the tea kettle, which now whistled like crazy. It was very close now. Feeling for the door opening with her left foot, Kelly carefully entered the kitchen. I signaled for Ann to move, and when she did, Kelly turned her head sharply in the direction of the sound. The exercise was working. When I'd removed her sight, her other senses were heightened. She was completely concentrated on the whistle of the tea kettle.

"Open your eyes."

Kelly began to jump up and down. "I found it. I found it," she said.

"Yes, you did. You most certainly did, Kelly."

Kelly's voice, although small and full of air, bristled with vitality. As with Beyoncé and Ashley, I heard an un-buffed pearl, definitely in the rough. She was perfect otherwise and just what I was looking for. Also like Ashley and Beyoncé, she had the natural tear in the voice, which every star talent should have.

In addition to screening Kelly for vocal talent, as I had done with Ashley and Beyoncé, I evaluated her carefully for important qualities necessary for excellence in music. Hand-eye coordination (needed for dance), intellect (needed for rudiments of music), natural phrasing ideas (musical tastes), and a strong support system (family) were all important criteria in forming my idea of an extraordinary group. The last of these criteria, dealing with family, was where things got interesting for me.

I would need to deal with Kelly's absentee mother. Raising genius without family support is next to impossible. This one was going to be challenging, but little Kelly was well worth the difficulties that faced me. In order to teach Kelly successfully I would have to sharpen her senses and teach her that correct use of "mental will power" would become her best friend.

"Never force your will on a thing. You will achieve exactly the opposite."

Kelly nodded her head. She was happy, really happy.

"Welcome to the group," I said. Moments later, I left Ann's house, very excited, and Ann made Kelly some lunch.

I rejoiced in how each girl was very different from the other. I was already working on a plan to teach them how to deliver songs with certainty and skill, no matter the genre, whether rock, pop, soul, R&B, alternative, or crossover. It would develop their ability to move their audience by singing a simple line, without all the frills usually associated with the black voice – key in achieving international success.

Then, just days after auditioning Kelly, I learned that she would not be able to take private voice lessons. Her mother, Doris Lovett, whom I had not yet met, was a housekeeper and nanny by profession and she simply could not afford the lessons. Kelly's position was in jeopardy.

I called Ann at work. It was obvious that we were both concerned that even before Kelly could get started, our vision seemed to be falling apart.

"Ann, we can't lose this girl," I said.

* * * * *

Ashley was always accompanied by her mother, Carolyn, who told me she found the lessons extremely interesting. "Ashley makes progress each week. It is truly amazing to watch your work."

It was true; Ashley had begun to understand what I meant about nuance and brilliance in singing. Her singing was becoming crystalline and precise – exquisite – and her timbre (color) took on fascinating shadings and hues. With each lesson she was quickly becoming a more flexible singer. I couldn't have been more pleased.

In the beginning Beyoncé was also brought to her lessons by her mother. However, Celestine called to tell me that because she needed to keep longer hours at the salon, Mathew would get her to and from her voice lessons. I'd finally meet Beyoncé's father, I thought. Celestine's voice had stress written all over it though. I inquired if all was OK, offering to help if I could. Celestine thanked me and told me that the problem wasn't unmanageable and that she had everything under control. "OK," I said, and offered my help once again and we ended the call.

The first time Mathew was to get Beyoncé to her lesson, she was terribly late. In fact, she was late for every lesson for which her father was responsible. He was often late picking her up, as well, and he frequently didn't show up at all. A confused Beyoncé would sit in my living room listening to me on the phone with her mother, working out arrangements to get her home. Naturally Celestine couldn't leave clients to pick her daughter up from my studio, way out in the suburbs. The embarrassment that filled Beyoncé's face was plain to see. I decided to drive her home myself, which gave me the opportunity to see where she lived. Luckily for me, I knew the neighborhood. My church was only two blocks away.

Once, when Mathew *had* come to get Beyoncé from one of her voice lessons, she and I had not heard his usual signal – honking the horn out front. There he stood, at the front door, tall and thin, with a firm hand-shake. His greeting felt more like a business meeting coming to an end, rather than a comfortable exchange between parent and teacher. With that firm grip, it felt like he was trying to break my fingers. His voice had a self-important ring, and he was uptight, or so it seemed to me.

Mathew's haphazard habits in picking up Beyoncé made me happy that I had decided to schedule her lessons at the end of the day on Wednesdays, just in case. This afforded us a lot of time to get to know one another, and we were soon building a special relationship. She was a remarkable child. Although she had no problem with the display of emotion while singing, able to implement even the simplest directive I gave her in that area, she was painfully shy in company, and she admitted to being afraid of the kids at school. Too often they berated her for being "light skin and pretty."

I wasn't in the least bit shocked at Beyoncé's choice of words. Although I had not grown up thinking of color, I certainly was not ignorant of the age-old problem of color in my world. The black community as a whole has, for many generations, considered the shade of our skins as a determining status symbol. We are to know our place in the pecking order depending on how light or dark our skins are. Residual crap from Slavery, in my community, the cruel saying bites just as woundingly now as it ever did: "If you are black, get back; if you are brown, stick around; if you are light, you are just right." Get the picture? In addition, skin color mattered very much to Beyoncé's parents.

"The girls hate me at school," Beyoncé said.

"Why do the girls at school hate you?"

Beyoncé would say that they told her she thought she was better than they were. They also told her that she thought she was cute. More and more she opened up to me.

"Beyoncé, I was a precocious child," I said.

"What's precocious?" she asked.

"It means several things. One of which is 'advanced for one's age' or it could mean 'spoiled brat.' You can tell me which I was after the story," I said.

My mother had done her student teaching with Ms. Jean Baptiste, who happened also to be my fifth grade teacher. Ms. Baptiste introduced us to the American Revolution, going into some detail about the Boston Massacre. She talked at length about the conflict and about the soldiers who died, but I noticed that she left out an important element.

David's hand in the air. "Ms. Baptiste, did you know that Crispus Attucks fought in the American Revolution and he was the first man killed in the Boston Massacre and that he was black?"

"Yes, I did, but how do you know that?"

"I read it."

"Where?"

"In my mother's books"

That was the day the other children in my "integrated" classroom began to despise me. I spouted off fact after fact that had been left out of the school book. Furthermore, I was too naïve to understand racism; Ms. Baptiste was black, so it could not have occurred to me that there was injustice in the American system of education.

Well, my mother got a call that night and I, in turn, was called downstairs.

"Bring all of my books downstairs right this minute."

Mama placed all the books under lock and key, and with that move I was forced into childhood. I would not be allowed to read books beyond my grade level until I was in eighth grade, in middle school. You might think,

"How awful!" of my mother and Ms. Baptiste. But I had already made a lot of enemies at school by showing off my intelligence. Ms. Baptiste warned Mama that the other children would attack me if she didn't get me under control; in fact, I did find myself running home alone after school every day. It was then that I learned the larger responsibilities of a good teacher. Ms. Jean Baptiste's influence did not feel positive at the time, but today I understand her concerns. She thought she was helping, and my mother agreed. Mama wanted to protect me; she wanted me to have a childhood. But that was the furthest thing from my mind. I hated childhood.

Because I understood that on many levels the way I behaved in school had brought about the attacks that I suffered, I asked Beyoncé if she felt she was doing anything to arouse her classmates' jealousy.

"No, I don't think so. I try to be invisible," she said. "I just go to class and try to be their friend. But they don't like me."

"Kids can be cruel, and the same conflicts you are experiencing are the same ones countless other kids like us live with. Nastiness has no respect of person and will not change over the coming years." What Beyoncé was experiencing came with being a child. "Believe it or not, it will get better," I told her.

"I hope so," she answered.

I feared that little Beyoncé might spend the rest of her life trying to make people like her. She, like Ashley and little Kelly, who still hadn't returned to voice lessons, would always have problems as beautiful flowers amongst the thorns.

"Beyoncé, do you know what a parable is?" I asked.

She said she didn't.

I told her that a parable was sort of like a fable. "Do you know what a fable is?"

"A story," she said.

"Correct, but more importantly, it is a story that Jesus himself tells in the Bible. They are simple stories, using common things like salt, bread, and even sheep, to explain morality.

"Sheep," Beyoncé said, laughing.

"Yes, sheep." Continuing, "I use fables when I teach you," I said. Reaching for my Bible, which lay on the end table next to my couch, I opened it up to the book of Matthew and began to read: "A farmer went out to sow his seed. As he was scattering the seed, some fell along the path, and the birds came and ate it up. Some fell on rocky places, where it did not have much soil. It sprang up quickly, because the soil was shallow. But when the sun came up, the plants were scorched, and they withered because they had no root. Other seed fell among thorns, which grew up and choked the plants. Still other seed fell on good soil, where it produced a crop – a hundred, sixty or thirty times what was sown."

My pupil began to understand. Suddenly, we heard Mathew's car horn. Extremely late, he had arrived to pick Beyoncé up. Gathering her things, Beyoncé thanked me for her lesson and for the talk. She felt much better, she said.

"It was my pleasure, Beyoncé." After she disappeared from sight, I closed the door, both ecstatic and baffled. I definitely heard the words that left her lips as she recounted her classmates' "hatred" for her, but her facial muscles told a different story.

That was the tale I was interested in.

* * * * *

Grandmother and I talked every Sunday. When we spoke on April 15, 1990, she said she wasn't feeling well. Before I could inquire, Grandmother said, "I'm going to Dr. Conner's office tomorrow morning." She knew me so well. "Don't worry. I am in God's hands," she added.

Gingerly changing the subject, Grandmother asked about me. "How are the preparations for your recital going?" she asked.

"Great," I said. "But I'm a bit worried about one of my students."

"Explain."

"I don't know Grandmother, but there's something really special about this little girl. I can see God's grace upon her life. I'm convinced that she can have a great future in music, but her mother is a problem."

"What's her name?" Grandmother asked.

"Kelly Rowland."

I knew what was coming next, so I just bowed my head. Grandmother began to pray fervently for Kelly, as though she'd known her all her life. By the prayer's end, Grandmother had asked God to grant me wisdom. In that moment, I was reminded of Dr. Phillips's sermon on King Solomon back in Cleveland in 1988. He too had talked about wisdom. Grandmother then reminded me that "all things worked together for good, for those who are called according to his purpose." (Romans 8:28) Her words resonated in the deepest part of my soul.

I thanked Grandmother for her prayer and we talked a few minutes more before hanging up. "OK, my heart!" Then she told me not to worry about Kelly, or the group. "And the Lord said unto Joshua 'Fear them not: for I have delivered them into thine hand; there shall not a man of them stand before thee.' (Joshua 10:8) Kelly will be all right."

My grandmother was a powerful woman, a conduit for God's word and purpose in my life. "Thanks again, Grandmother," I said, reminding her to call me after her appointment.

"I promise," she answered.

As I started to hang up the phone, I could hear her voice calling back to me through the receiver. "Hello, Grandmother, did you say something?" I asked.

"Yes, I did. I have been given one last scripture." She told me to read the first book of Peter, I Peter 5:8.

After hanging up, I called Mama right away. I was very concerned. Grandmother hadn't sounded like her usual self.

"Happy Sunday," Mama said.

Without beating around the bush I asked if she'd spoken with Grandmother.

"Why?"

"I just talked to her and she was complaining of stomach pains again," I said. "Maybe it's a good idea to go over and check on her."

Mama said, "As far as I know, she is fine."

"I'm not so sure, Mama."

Grandmother had been in the hospital just months earlier with diverticulitis, an inflammatory disease of the colon.

"I'll call her right away and call you back," Mama said.

An hour later, Mama called me from St. Joseph's Hospital. Grandmother had been admitted. The doctors feared sepsis.

"Doctors have started Mama on a strong battery of antibiotics," Mama said.

It was indeed diverticulitis, and this time it was very serious. Mama could tell that I was anxious, and she promised to keep me posted.

In the meantime, I returned to work on the music for my recital. I also spent some time on two tracks that Preston Middleton, an important Houston-born producer who had made a name for himself out in California, had sent over for Beyoncé. He would become one of her most significant producers in her childhood. We made a studio date, for the day after my recital.

* * * * *

My recital rehearsal had gone splendidly. It couldn't have gone better. I was stronger than ever, and my top voice gleamed. The only glitch: I had inadvertently left the music to Henry Purcell's "If music be the food of love" at a friend's house. Calvin Fuller, my pianist for that recital, said he knew it and that I shouldn't worry about it. We had more than enough time to "go through it on Sunday," he said. I wish that I had listened. Wired from the adrenaline rush of the rehearsal, I called my good friend David Price and told him that I would like to stop by his apartment and pick up the forgotten music. "I'll come over as soon as I drop my things off at my apartment," I said.

David lived just ten minutes' walk from me. As I approached the empty parking lot that I always crossed going to his apartment, my *still small voice* spoke to me, telling me to choose another route. In a euphoric, post-rehearsal state, I did not listen to my senses, a lesson that I had so desperately tried to get across to Kelly. I had also ignored my mother's teachings about being hyper-vigilant as a black boy in America. A million things were going on in my head that evening. Seconds later, I was attacked by seven young men chanting racial slurs. As I fought them off, one of them hit me in my throat.

In mid-fight, and still struggling against my attackers, I automatically checked the state of my voice by uttering a few ums and hums. I am sure this action puzzles anyone who is not a singer. Why would someone under attack stop to check his voice? Being hit in the throat threw me into fight-or-flight mode. I had to regain control of my senses. Instinctively, my body began to slow itself down. The most important thing to me, my voice, was in jeopardy. Together with the instant rush of adrenaline, I fought to focus. I was able to calm myself, fighting them and ultimately getting away from my attackers.

I ran toward the well-lit edge of the parking lot just as a police cruiser happened to be passing. My crazed scream for help stopped the car. God's grace descended, and I was able to escape to safety as my attackers fled into the darkness. However, the same guttural scream that caught the police attention delivered the *coup de grâce* to my voice. This time my ums and hums produced only croaking and pain. To add insult to my injury, the police said they didn't believe my story. How could they have *not* seen my attackers, who had been so perfectly framed under the silhouette of the whiteness of the street lights? Surely they had been visible. The police "investigated" by driving to the corner and turning around.

"Sir, we don't see anyone," they said.

The next morning I went to my otolaryngologist, Dr. Richard Stasney, of the Texas Voice Center, who told me that I was lucky to be alive. I hadn't thought about it, but Dr. Stasney was right. That blow to the larynx could have caused it to collapse, and nothing would have saved me then.

Over the following weeks, Dr. Stasney would monitor my laryngeal healing, and Dr. Pattye Johnstone became my rock. Having left U of H, I had begun private studies with Dr. Johnstone shortly before the accident. A great teacher, she was steadfast and encouraging and would call me

every night to ensure that I was using my voice properly in speaking. Our ten-minute talk would become a ritual with us for one solid year.

Dr. Sands, the sponsor of my recital, wouldn't allow me to cancel it. "Invitations have been sent out and the church will be full," she said. She was absolutely right. I was a professional. I did what any professional agent would do; I called my friends, seeking a replacement. Soprano Heidi Jones and the late mezzo soprano Annette Daniels, both members of the Houston Grand Opera's (HGO)Young Artist Program, showed up in a major way. Together with a fellow Young Artist, the coach-accompanist Mark Trawka, Heidi and Annette sang a beautiful concert in my stead, thereby saving my reputation. Four days later, things finally changed regarding Grandmother's condition.

* * * * *

Nine days after Grandmother had been admitted to St. Joseph's Hospital, I got the call.

She had died. My world imploded.

Through a flood of tears, I listened intently as Mama told me what happened.

"Mama died happy," Mama said.

I didn't understand Mama's off-putting comment.

"She is with your Grandfather," Mama continued. Then she explained herself, "Your Grandmother and Grandfather had a conversation last evening," Mama added.

Apparently, on the eve of Grandmother's intended surgery, Grandfather's spirit visited Grandmother in her room. She had been given a sedative and was unconscious. Mama had listened as Grandmother mumbled her love for my Grandfather.

"It was so beautiful," Mama said

After hanging up, I couldn't get Grandmother's face out of my mind, nor could I shake her last words.

"Read I Peter 5:8," she said.

I had not done as she asked me. Feelings of guilt overwhelmed me. I reached for my bible. Chapter Five, Verse Eight said, "Be sober, be vigilant; because your adversary the devil, as a roaring lion, walks about, seeking whom he may devour."

I got a chill.

Later that evening, I called my sister. I'd be arriving the next morning, getting into Eppley Airport in Omaha at around 10 a.m.

6. Parkwood Street, USA

Grandmother's funeral was the hardest thing that I would ever have to face. How could I just stand up next to her coffin and sing? Even had my voice been healthy, my spirit was a mess. Mama told me I didn't have to sing, but Evelyn Sims's funeral without David singing? Might as well leave out the Lord's Prayer. Still, in spite of those heavy expectations, I remained prayerful. I didn't think that I could do it.

Myers funeral home was packed for Grandmother's service. When the limousine with the family pulled up, we were told to wait and a member of the staff would take us into the chapel. Everything seemed to be going according to plan until they opened the chapel door and Mama saw that the casket was open. The scream she let loose was piercing. Aunt Lee Lee demanded to know who had mistakenly left the casket open; she had given explicit instructions to have it closed. Within seconds, the staff closed the door and took care of the problem. When Mama finally gathered herself we re-entered, this time uneventfully.

As we were being ushered down the aisle to our seat, an incredible pressure came over me. Everyone was staring at me. Suddenly, I felt warm. As if seeing Grandmother, cold and lifeless, had not been enough, people sitting on the edge of the rows began taking my hand. "Be strong, my son," one man said. Another, a woman from Grandmother's high-rise building, touched me and said, "Sing to the glory of God." Did these people really expect me to sing? Of course they did. Everyone in that room had heard the stories about Evelyn's grandson, the opera singer. I began to sweat, managing somehow to sit.

The service began and at every place where the words "musical selection" appeared on the program page, the stares only increased. I looked over at Mama. She wasn't doing well. In fact, she looked a bit flush. I thought she'd faint at any minute. An usher brought her a glass of water, which did not seem to help.

Then it happened. The service came to an end and the pallbearers began to roll the casket out of the funeral home. Suddenly my mouth opened and out came the old Negro spiritual "I'm going to tell God all my troubles when I get home." Mama fainted. Aunt Lee Lee comforted me as I continued to sing through the flood of tears rolling down my face. At first my voice felt like a faint echo of its usual self, then it gradually built in intensity, and I sang Grandmother's beloved spiritual to a heroic conclusion. I was singing for *Ma Grand-mère* (Grandmother had loved to hear me speak French). I couldn't have her buried without hearing my voice one last time. She had discovered it, it was she who formed it, and it was she who taught me to love it.

When I returned to Houston I never said one word about my recent loss to my students, the Knowleses, the other girls' families, to Ann, or to any of my friends. It is what I did. I stifled my feelings, which I am finally learning is not a good thing to do. But back then I felt it was for the best. I didn't know how to deal with death. If Mama and Grandmother hadn't robbed me of the right to bury Grandfather and thus give me the proper opportunity to say goodbye, I might have known what to expect.

In the absence of that I had to prepare for my HGO audition, and Beyoncé's mother made me an offer that I shouldn't refuse.

* * * * *

Headliners Hair Salon, registered with the county court house in May of 1989, was an upscale salon catering to black clientele, but not exclusively. I have already mentioned that Celestine's salon occupied space in a new strip mall in Montrose, a happening Houston area that was frequented by members of the gay community. Many of that community's inhabitants were Celestine's employees, as well as her clients.

Celestine knew that the gay community would help her substantially to reach her long-term goals. As they say, Nobody helps a woman feel self-worth better than the gays. Just think of those "divas" in history whose fame was ignited and celebrated by the adulation of gay men: Josephine Baker, Judy Garland, Liza Minelli, Cher, Bette Davis, Grace Jones, Madonna, and – let us not forget – the opera great Maria Callas. Yes, including the Montrose gay community in Celestine's business increased her cachet. Until she opened that very important door, Headliners would be just another hair shop. Suddenly, it was a colorful salon, and from what I saw, her clientele loved the assortment.

On one of those occasions I visited Headliners to get my own haircut, Celestine and I discussed Kelly. I couldn't understand why Kelly's mother, Doris, was so reluctant to acknowledge her daughter's talent. In my opinion, Doris stood in the way, not only of Kelly's present opportunities, but also of Kelly's future, a future I saw as promising. Acknowledging my frustration, Celestine intimated that she knew no more than I did about Kelly's mother. Still, she offered, "I don't think Doris can afford the lessons. They're poor..." I was a bit startled by Celestine's comment, but asked her to give it some further thought, and I left, still puzzled about what to do about Doris.

Later on that evening, after 11:00, Celestine called me. I thought we were going to finish our discussion about Kelly and Doris. Celestine, however, wanted to know what I really thought of Beyoncé. "In a word," I said to her, "Prodigious." Once again, I reassured Celestine that Beyoncé had superlative native gifts for music, singing, and performance. I ex-

118

plained to her that like other potentially successful artists, Beyoncé would need years of concentrated work. Natural "genius" was a rare gift, and in the world of performance it leads nowhere without years of study and labor to realize that potential.

Once again I mentioned to Celestine my frustration with Kelly's lack of maternal support. The girl group was on the verge of singular accomplishments, if only we could get Kelly securely situated in the fold. Again, Celestine sympathized, but had nothing to add regarding Kelly. She couldn't think of anything that would help reach Doris. In my disappointment I quoted the book of Matthew 5:14-15: "...A city on a hill cannot be hidden..." I was certain that Kelly had a special light, and that God would help me to help her to find a way to let it shine. The Biblical parable about the lamp on the stand told me exactly how I would get to its glow. Celestine took notice that I was a Christian. She really liked that, she said.

A few days later, Celestine called again. She said that she felt bad about not honoring her promise to invite me over for dinner. Wanting to make it up to me, she invited me to lunch.

"I have something I want to talk to you about," she said.

I drove over to Headliners, where Celestine was just finishing up with a client. There was a strange energy in the salon that day. Everyone seemed to be pensive, walking on eggshells. While Celestine dealt with a walk-in, I hung out talking to my barber, whose chair was free. "Hey, what's going on?" I asked. "The energy feels off today."

"Mathew and I got into it," My barber said.

"What happened?"

A lesbian, my barber told me that Mathew had accused her of coming on to a female client. "He's been fucking with me for weeks," she said. "I am tired of his shit."

"Well, how many female clients use your services?" I asked.

"Ex-fuckin-actly...."

It all sounded very strange to me. Then my barber told me that she dared Mathew to fire her, she begged him to actually. "Either produce the 'client' or get out of my face...." She was furious. Apparently, Celestine tried to diffuse the situation, to no avail. "These bitches around here are afraid of Mathew. I ain't afraid of his ass.... *fuckin punk....*" she concluded.

When Celestine's potential new client finally left the salon, Celestine suggested going to the deli in the strip mall where her salon rented space.

"Fine," I said. "Lead the way."

After ordering our sandwiches, Celestine and I began talking about Mathew. Then, after getting seated with our lunch, the conversation shifted to me. "Tell me about your family," Celestine said. "Do you have family in Houston?"

I explained that my family lived elsewhere. "I come from Nebraska," I said. "I see them only on holidays."

Celestine assumed that I must have been lonely not having family around. "On the contrary," I told her, "Mama and I talk every Sunday, and my brother and sister and I talk as often as possible. They are busy with their families."

"Still, there is nothing like having family close," Celestine said.

"Perhaps," I answered.

We had been in the deli for about half an hour when I started to wonder why Celestine hadn't mentioned Beyoncé. In exactly that moment the subject came up.

"I want to thank you," she said.

I didn't understand.

"Just thank you – for everything – for making Beyoncé happy. And for giving her the rides home after her lessons," Celestine said.

"It is no imposition at all, Celestine," I said. Mathew's delinquency in picking her up from lessons had given Beyoncé and me the perfect opportunity to get to know one another better. "Besides," I said to Celestine, "I can give her more time, since I always schedule her as the last student of my day." I continued, "Please don't worry about it."

Looking at her watch, Celestine announced that she needed to get back. "My next client has probably already arrived."

"Oh, OK – I hope that I haven't kept you," I said.

"No, not at all." She hugged me and said that getting to know me had been enlightening. "I enjoyed our talk," she said.

"Thank you for lunch," I said.

Later that evening my telephone rang, again after 11:00 p.m.

"Hi, David. It's Celestine. I hope that I am not disturbing you."

"No, not at all Celestine. What can I do for you?"

"I've been thinking," she said. "Getting Beyoncé to and from her lessons with you, way out in the suburbs, is going to get more difficult. She loves her lessons with you so much. Business is picking up, which means longer hours for me. It's impossible for me to leave work to get her there. You know I can't depend on her father," Celestine said.

"Go on."

"It would be so much easier on everybody, if you – well – would you consider moving into my garage apartment? I just know that you'll love it," Celestine said. "Please give it some thought," she said.

"Ah – OK," I said. I promised that I would.

"All right, thank you, and good-night. I hope that it works out. It would mean the world to Beyoncé to have you closer. She loves you so much."

"I love her too. She is a great student, attentive and respectful – always respectful."

"Thank you," Celestine said, taking full credit for the compliment I had just given to her daughter.

"OK, then." I concluded. "I wish you a good-night."

"Yes, Good night," Celestine said.

We ended the conversation and as I hung up the phone, I considered what had just occurred. I remember thinking that Celestine's invitation – smooth and solicitous – disguised hidden surprises that might prove problematic. However, true to my promise to her, I did give it some thought.

The one-bedroom Westheimer Street apartment where I lived and taught was modern and comfortable. My neighbors were kind and enjoyed the singing that came from my studio during daylight hours. Walking to my car I often heard comments like, "Who was that singing today?" or "'So-and-so' sounded great today." In the Westheimer apartment complex it was the neighborhood kids who had the most fun. You could say that they were my students' first fan base, as they often stood outside the door listening, imitating the opera students or cheering when a singer finally got the high note. Some of them even peered through the windows trying to get a glimpse of what was going on inside. They came to recognize every voice, and if I took on a new student they noticed immediately. I thought my singing students would be a bit distracted by all the attention, but on the contrary – they seemed delighted by their listeners and their blatant curiosity. Beyoncé even laughed at the children's antics. It was a comfortable atmosphere in which to teach.

I hadn't given any thought to moving. Still, the cost of my own private voice lessons, including travel to Dallas, meant that I needed to watch my spending. In addition, I definitely needed to keep my eye on my exorbitant Audi payments and insurance. Judging from the area of Houston where the Knowleses lived, I knew the rent wouldn't be peanuts. And what about air conditioning? I wondered. The $325.00 monthly rent, which included utilities, was a great incentive for me to stay put on Westheimer in 1990. The importance of air conditioning in the heat of a Texas summer cannot be overestimated. The high temperatures and humidity often make life unbearable, and without air-conditioning neither I nor my students would have been able to function. I put it out of my mind and went to sleep.

Celestine, however, had no intention of giving up her idea. Indeed, the apartment Celestine talked about sounded attractive. I resisted making a decision, but she wasn't giving in. Soon she was dangling an enticement I found difficult to ignore.

"If you decide to move into our apartment – which is fabulous, by the way – you'd be making it easier for *all [she stressed the word "all"]* the girls to get to their voice lessons." After the briefest pause: "Including Kelly." Again the briefest pause. Then: "Doris might find it easier, and it would save her on gasoline. She doesn't have much money, you know."

Celestine was right. Since all the families were more centrally located, I had to admit that my moving would make life easier for them. Celestine assured me that I would live independently, that I could continue to have my vocal studio in my home, and that I would be able to come and go as I pleased. In other words, I'd have freedom.

"The apartment has been empty for two years. It would be great to have someone living in it. Who better than you?" she said.

Continuing to counter my resistance, she surprised me by announcing that the rent would be only $50 more per month than I was currently paying. I couldn't believe it. She was asking just $375.00 per month for rent, with all utilities included.

I continued to ponder Celestine's offer. It wouldn't cost me anything to have a look. Still, I wasn't sure that I wanted to live with a student.

Then it hit me – *Farinelli*.

I had learned about the artistry of Carlo Maria Michelangelo Nicola Broschi – stage name Farinelli – at CIM in my Eighteenth Century Performance class. Carlo Broschi was the most famous castrato in all of Italy, and indeed the world. (A "castrato" was a male classical singer who through castration was able to maintain his boyhood vocal purity and quality. In that era, successful castrati – plural of the word "castrato" – achieved great wealth and fame, like the most celebrated rock stars today. In 1994 the very fine, and moving, film *Farinelli*, then in general release, brought this whole subject alive to general movie audiences.)

Young Carlo's father, Salvatore Broschi, a highly ambitious man, was a composer and a choir director at the Cathedral in the city of Naples, Italy. Related to minor members of the Italian aristocracy, Salvatore sought more out of life.

Then tragedy struck. Salvatore, Carlo's scheming father, died unexpectedly, leaving the family in economic turmoil. Carlo fell into a depression and became sick. He mourned his father, feeling lost. Everything had been done for him all his life and now he had no one. He began his quest for a replacement father.

Nicolas Porpora, the most celebrated voice teacher in all of Europe, became Carlo's Godsend, his primary benefactor, and mentor, and he moved the child into his home. As Carlo's every need was seen to, he was required only to study and to take seriously the lessons and wisdom passed onto him by his master-teacher. Carlo had the special quality that Porpora had been looking for in a pupil all his life. Seven years of rigorous training ensued. Under Porpora's guidance, Carlo's singing progressed at lightning speed. At the age of fifteen he made his debut in his master's newly written opera entitled *Angelica e Medoro*. It was a huge success, catapulting young Carlo – now using the stage name "Farinelli" – to fame. Not too long after, all of Europe was crying out the name "Farinelli."

I called Celestine. I had thought about it. I agreed to look at the apartment. We made an appointment and ended the call. I certainly understood Porpora's desire.

Could Beyoncé be my Carlo?

* * * * *

When I entered the Knowleses' garage apartment I fell in love with it immediately. It had a quaint, old-world charm, with lots of windows and double balcony doors that opened into the apartment. Streams of sunlight contributed to the bright and airy feel of the apartment. The balcony looked onto the backyard, where the family had erected a deck for summer barbecues and family get-togethers. An alcove connected the apartment to the family home for easy access. The bedroom was in a loft, and there was a kitchen, dinette space and full bathroom, complete with an antique bathtub. I thought it was a steal, and a definite upgrade, for the rent Celestine was asking. I loved it.

Moving from Westheimer to Parkwood Street in the fall 1990, I felt at home right away. The South MacGregor Way residential area of Houston was filled with tree-lined streets, large homes, manicured lawns, and ambitious professionals. It was often compared to River Oaks, the historic and gated community where the city's wealthiest citizens lived. Like River Oaks, my new neighborhood comprised both upper and upper middle class families. South MacGregor Way was predominately black though. Most of the people living in my new surroundings were families with

124

interesting and impressive stories. I had heard that the parents of the dancer Debbie Allen (from the TV series *Fame*) and her sister, the actress Phylicia Rashad (Clair Huxtable on *The Cosby Show*), lived just around the corner.

The location was perfect because my church, St. James Episcopal, was now only a two-minute drive away. I had become very active at St. James and I ultimately converted to the Episcopal faith from the United Methodist faith in which I had been baptized. St. James was not a large congregation, but it was one that comprised the city's educated black elite: judges, doctors, lawyers, executives for major corporations, newspaper owners, and major journalists, including the city's first black television news anchor, Diana Page. The music program was first-rate, but more important to me was the way I was treated at St. James: like a favored son.

The church community also contained a wonderful school, The St. James School, which Ashley attended and in which Beyoncé and her little sister, Solange, would soon enroll.

Meanwhile, I kept myself busy with my many private voice students, in particular the young charges that I had begun to think of as "My Girls." I adored Ashley and Beyoncé. It may seem silly now, but I had convinced myself that I would always be in their lives, even though I knew that I would not remain their teacher forever. That's not how it works.

A responsible teacher knows that one day the student must go out and conquer on their own. It is necessary to equip them and not cripple them. I would breathe with my girls, and I would cry with them. Tears are inevitable when young singers' protective shields begin to crumble, but eventually they would have to move on. And I would rejoice with them as they triumphed, having learned to set their emotions free and conquer their fears. I was determined to help them to identify their feelings and I promised to guide them in understanding how to display human emotions in singing. Above all, I promised to give my girls the tools they need for life, both in their professional and their private lives so that finding success was an assurance and not luck. I wanted to make them "Fierce," (a word created by the gay community and one I used often when teaching Beyoncé).

In teaching self-introspection, my goal with every student is to help them to self-knowledge. Lost integrity can be regained but only through honesty and if they aren't successful at this task maximum success will be minimal. It becomes necessary to aid them in finding a place for the victim of their past. A singer must live in the present to have a future. Emotional requirements of the profession will demand it. As Ashley, Beyoncé's, and (I fervently hoped) Kelly's teacher, mentor, and musical advisor, I would have to know them much better than they knew themselves. That was and remains my job. Subtle – and not-so-subtle – approaches are needed to nudge the student of singing towards emotional and vocal freedom. Ultimately, I want my singing students and my protégés to be better than I am, and I planned on holding nothing back.

When I had auditioned Kelly the summer of 1989, her voice had been tiny but exquisitely beautiful. In the beginning it was full of air and so small that I had to nearly stand in her mouth to hear her, but it possessed a natural tearfulness and pathos. My goal was to teach her to respect and love her voice – really love it. I wanted her to be able to say to herself that her voice was the most beautiful sound she ever heard. This is crucial in building a real singer. If a singer does not have love and passion for singing and the sound, my work is futile.

The second thing I did with Kelly was teach her to speak. Speak you say? Yes, speak. She read out loud to me and I asked her to elongate all the vowel sounds in the words. Overdo it, I said. Her problem was not technical so much as it was a matter of confidence. Kelly had a God-given, naturally placed voice; I would have to awaken it and her. The reading helped her to become comfortable with hearing the sound of her voice, the way it should be. But just as she began to make noticeable progress, Kelly stopped coming to lessons altogether.

I had become chronically concerned about Kelly's inconsistent attendance. Although the same age, ten, as Beyoncé, she lagged behind them by miles in her vocal progress. Once again I expressed my concerns to Ann Tillman (the super competent business manager of Girls Tyme, and my trusted confidante), who had indeed spoken to Kelly's mother and was close to solving the problem. Without my realizing it, Ann had spoken with Celestine. Finally, having listened to my concerns, and now having heard Ann's insistent urgings, Celestine came to me, pleading Doris's case. Although the inherent beauty with which Kelly sang moved me, I told Celestine that without payment I would not be able to help her. Celestine then agreed to pay for Kelly's lessons.

"Wow, are you sure?" I asked. She assured me; she wanted to help, since Doris could not afford the lessons.

"That's very noble," I said.

"Well, somebody has got to make things right," Celestine answered.

But when Kelly didn't show up for her first pre-paid lesson, Celestine withdrew her offer without hesitation. There was no changing her mind, ever. I completely understood.

I, equally persistent, and now very serious, insisted that if Kelly didn't begin showing up for lessons, she would have to be dropped. Shortly thereafter, Mathew came back to my apartment and asked if he could speak to me. This was in itself confusing. I barely knew the man. Why was he making Kelly's problem his concern?

Mathew pleaded with me to reconsider, "...for the good of the group. They need Kelly and she needs you," were his exact words.

This confused me even further, because Mathew was not the group's manager – Ann was. I found it presumptuous on his part to assume he had any influence on what I decided to do in my studio. He was just another parent, like everyone else (I thought).

In the end I gave way to Ann's pleas to teach Kelly *gratis* – whereupon Ann finally confessed the truth to me. Doris was "not doing so well" – in other words, she had fallen off the wagon.

"Doris is drinking again," Ann told me. "She and Kelly have been living in their car."

Ann decided to take both Doris and Kelly into her home. Deeply touched by little Kelly's plight, I decided to ignore my own guideline – that Freebies inevitably bring about contempt – and I took her on as my only scholarship student. I would teach her for eight years, free of charge, during the entire building phase of the group that would become Destiny's Child, through the signing of their second record deal. There was only one stipulation: Kelly could never miss another lesson. She never did, even if, in her younger years, Ann had to arrange to get her there. Every Saturday for years, Kelly stood before me, eager and ready to learn.

Kelly Rowland, who was a honeyed brown coloring, was a gorgeous little girl, and being semi-homeless was not her only burden. She obsessed compulsively about her very short hair, which was a deeply rooted source of pain for her. I understood this issue, and the need to handle it with sensitivity.

I was aware even at a young age that the men in our culture bear a large share of responsibility for the kind of pain that Kelly felt. As a little boy I saw, learned, and was guilty of offering the ingrained male response toward women with long hair. I heard loud and clear the message sent by my step-father, grandfather, uncles, and male cousins: Texture did not matter – length, however, did. Simply put, long hair seemed an aphrodisiac in the male/female relationship.

In addition, I knew that women and children are no different from adult men in their responses to this sensitive issue. Mothers and aunties everywhere validate a girl child's beauty by the length of her hair, thus undermining the self-esteem of their unfortunate, short-haired sisters. The strong fascination with texture of hair may be a black issue, but length of hair is a female issue. And the long-hair dilemma spans across generations of females in ethnic cultures all over the world.

I told Kelly that hair did not make you beautiful. But it was a losing battle. I was being defeated in every way because of the misguided standards of the culture at large.

Beyond her self-consciousness about hair, Kelly remained afraid of her own shadow and had serious trust issues. I noticed that she behaved differently around male figures than she did with females. I perceived it not as a sexual issue, but more to do with not having positive male role models in her life. She desired the attention and love of a father. (I had known this feeling in my own childhood, but I had not been as dramatically af-

128

fected as Kelly obviously was.) I often saw the look of admiration in her eyes when she was around Beyoncé and her parents. Doris would eventually inform me that Kelly's father was a dead beat, a drunkard and a wife beater and that he would not be showing up any time soon. She had no idea that I knew that she suffered the same vices.

Over the next weeks I became increasingly concerned about Kelly. Something else seemed to be bothering her, but I couldn't put my finger on it. Why didn't she like herself and why was she so negative about her absolutely gorgeous voice? On the day in 1990 when her regular lessons recommenced, her mother, whom I had finally met, asked if she could speak to me in the back yard, behind the Knowles home. I had been living there only a month.

"David, I want your honest opinion," Doris said. "Does Kelly have any talent? Do you think she has a talent for singing?" I replied with a big fat "Yes" and assured her that if she brought Kelly to me regularly, I would prove it to her. I told her that I thought Kelly had a beautiful voice, although it was still extremely small and full of air. "Kelly is a star," I said.

At that moment Kelly rushed outside to ask her mother a question. When her mother told her to wait a minute while she finished talking with me, Kelly anxiously insisted on asking her question. Her mother slapped her hard across the face – so hard that Kelly stumbled backwards, almost losing balance. I was frozen and in shock, unable to move or speak. I felt as though someone had knocked the wind out of me. Suddenly I understood why this young girl was so withdrawn and insecure. She straightened her back, held back the tears, and returned to the house without saying a word.

Doris continued with our conversation as if nothing had happened. She had just slapped her child and it scared the hell out of me, and it was all too familiar. I had not seen anyone hit another human being like that since my childhood, when I would hear the screams of my then young mother when my stepfather beat her. I tried, unsuccessfully, to ignore it and to tell myself that maybe I was reading too much into Doris's behavior. I was consumed with fear for this young girl, the same way I had been as a little boy for my mother and childhood friends whom I had witnessed in abusive situations. Doris seemed extremely nice and loving, but was that only her public persona?

I observed Kelly and saw that she was concerned about who might have seen what happened. Her concern for *who saw*, as opposed to *what happened*, was classic behavior of an abuse sufferer. Most significant to me was Kelly's apparent helplessness. She didn't know what to do. She had no skill for dealing with what had just happened to her and it was obvious, painfully obvious, that what I was seeing was a little girl in survivor mode. She was hiding her pain and had resigned herself – just as my mother had done, many women do, and Kelly would do for years to come – simply to survive the day.

Later that night I found myself deep in thought about what I witnessed. Was this abuse or discipline? The look in Doris's eyes when she struck Kelly was both frightening and familiar to me. It was an unbridled anger that I saw, something dangerous. I'd been here before. I would learn that Doris's normal and automatic form of discipline, which I witnessed repeatedly, was to hit Kelly on her mouth. Kelly was learning that she had no voice and that nothing she had to say mattered. I would spend the next decade trying to convince her otherwise. I would bear witness to the many times she was slapped, cursed, screamed at, called stupid and "dumb ass." Why, I thought helplessly, why hadn't God put me in her house? Doris brutally pushed the boundary of what was humane and legal. It didn't take me long but eventually I figured out that Doris had a serious disorder. I understood her irrational behavior as classic symptoms of bipolar syndrome (Manic-depressive, as it was described at that time. Later, in 2015, Kelly's extraordinary portrayal of Lucious Lyons mother on the Fox Broadcasting Company's hit series Empire recalled for me the complex mother-daughter dynamics that I had witnessed between Doris and the child Kelly.) Thinking of Doris's behavior in a more clinical term, I found ways to deal with the consequences. Kelly will be OK, Grandmother's spirit reminded.

I poured myself into Kelly, giving her the attention of a surrogate father. Because she was almost two years behind Ashley and Beyoncé, convincing her of her abilities would take patience and skill. She had such a beautiful voice – and yet, she suppressed it.

By the end of the summer, Doris had managed to get a job and apartment. I began to devise a plan to "save" Kelly. It was presumptuous of me in hindsight, but then it was all I could think about. I reasoned that if she could get out of her abusive environment, she might be saved. I naively thought that if I spent more time with Kelly, I could protect her, run interference, keep her safe. I would have to be very clever though. I didn't want to upset Doris. She was always under tremendous stress with her work, having to be there for other people's children day and night. But in all honesty, as I weighed Doris and her daughter on my private judicial scale, Kelly was my *only* real concern.

* * * * *

With the new information that I now possessed about Kelly, I implemented several strategies in working with her. Without questioning her directly about her mother's abuse – I wanted to do everything possible to reassure her that she was safe in my studio – I developed a special way of teaching Kelly that would counter the psychological trauma I believed she suffered. I established a calm atmosphere in which she could learn to lay aside her sense of shame and self-hatred, because I knew that she was a special talent. She had the most beautiful voice of all the girls.

I began by offering Kelly the opposite of her mother's behaviors. I gave her heartfelt praise and genuine admiration for her gifts. I told Kelly what her mother wouldn't: that she was beautiful and talented. I promised her that I would help her reach her dreams if she would try to believe in them.

"Do you believe that you can have your dreams come true, Kelly?"

"I don't know," she would reply. I told her to close her eyes and I asked her to tell me stories about beautiful people, places, and things. With each attempt she got better and better. Slowly she began to imagine a world of her own design, where she was safe, and where no one judged her harshly, abused her goodness, or behaved inappropriately toward her. Little did I know that I would spend the next decade fighting to protect her against those very things, which brings me to the point of self-regulation (the art of forgiving one's self for the mistakes he or she makes in performance).

In order for Kelly to sing to the level of her ability, she would have to learn to focus more clearly. Guiding her in principles of metacognition (thinking about one's thoughts), I worked to help her to change her patterns of self-defeating behavior. I believe that the only way to change your world is to change your thought. Kelly's inability to forgive herself was bound up with her belief systems. Every atom, cell, bone, and muscle in her body was hyper-vigilant. My job was to ensure that she learned to believe in her own success, that she could perform well the various tasks I gave her, and that she could trust the positive feedback of my approving words – words that I meant with every fiber of my being. Then I saw her dance, and my heart sank. Not to worry, I told myself. I'd fix that too...

To provide a vocal role model, I introduced Kelly to the work of a major artist, Céline Dion. Her album *Unison* had just appeared on the scene, and I purchased it for Kelly, who was hearing Céline Dion for the first time. I believed that Celine's voice would be a healing force in Kelly's life. I worried that Kelly's insatiable need to be accepted and to fit in would cause her to make the mistake of trying to be an R&B diva. She was not R&B or soul. She had the potential to be one of the greatest pop divas on the planet, I thought. In my opinion, Kelly Rowland is Whitney's successor.

Céline Dion excited Kelly. She began to understand that her sound, her art, and her manner could find a home. The beauty of Céline Dion's texts helped as well. The songs contained messages that I wanted to give to Kelly. They showed strength and love – the right kind of love: self-love. To top it off, the focus on a beautiful and healthy technique in Celine's singing reached my young student. Kelly ate her songs for breakfast, lunch, and dinner.

In the meantime, I worked strategically with Doris. For some reason, I didn't want to accept that the same woman whose laugh and smile could light up a room could be so off balance and cruel. Occasionally I would talk to her about a concern that I had regarding Kelly – in private. By doing so, I hoped that she would go away and give my questions about who Kelly was some thought. I knew that if I could help Doris see Kelly's gift and not be threatened by it, she'd be able to make the necessary shift in her mind that would support the work I needed to do with Kelly in order to switch on that healthy competitive attitude that lay just under her skin. It worked. Doris began to get into Kelly's lessons. She even started bringing her on Saturdays, taking the time from work. She was interested and Kelly was tickled pink. I could now begin to form Kelly the artist. It is amazing what a little encouragement from family will do for a child. But then Doris would slip back into destructive behaviors.

When I work with students who have been exposed to contempt in their childhoods, I remind myself to recognize the irritation that it makes me feel. This is the sign to me that it is contempt that I am facing, and not merely a difficult pupil. If the student has suppressed anger to avoid rejection from his or her parents' manipulations and coercions it will show up in our studio work as confused and unexplainable bouts of rage. Students won't be able to identify the source of their anger and will feel embarrassed. It is imperative that I don't fall into the "reactionary trap." By expressing my displeasure at their behavior I could undermine my authority and destroy confidence. So then the question becomes how to deal with anger and other unwanted feelings toward the pupil, right? Wrong. The student's resisting me, whether intentional or not, is my chance to hear what the problem is. That angry student will tell me exactly what is going on with him or her (their story) while trying to hide the truth from me.

Although Kelly evoked irritation and fear in me, I knew that if I was going to help her, I could not miss the opportunity to learn from her important history. For the student who continually hides, I simply allow those feelings in myself to be called up – we all have them or have experienced them. It is imperative not to ward them off. They hold the key, the breakthrough that is so desperately needed to get to honesty, which is a must in music.

The same holds true, maybe even more so, with the addicted or sexually abused student. Every human being has experienced things – things that are not all good. Those things shape who we are; they form our character and it is that character, and our integrity, that determine if we will belong to the world's finest citizens. Part of a child's healthy development demands that they have their feelings validated.

Author and renowned Swiss psychologist Alice Miller tells us in her book *The Drama of the Gifted Child* that "Until we become sensitive to the child and their 'small child sufferings' the wielding power of the big adults will continue as normal aspect – of the human condition, for hardly anyone pays attention to it or takes it seriously. The victims are 'only children,' their distress is trivialized. But in twenty years' time these children will be adults who will feel compelled to pay it all back to their own children. This is perhaps one reason why adults less often look back nostalgically to the time of their puberty than to that of their childhood. The mixture of longing, expectation, and fear of disappointment, which for most people accompany the remembrance of festivities from childhood can perhaps, be explained by their search for the intensity of feeling they lost back then."

What came forth was the empathy Kelly felt for her parents' sad life stories. It was paramount that she understood that her parents' plight was not necessarily predictive of her own path in life. At the very least, she'd have the chance to concentrate on her destiny – which I hoped would heal her. The images of poor mother and poor daddy were blocking her advancement.

The first step to honesty (openness) is scary. Kelly became increasingly anxious and at the same time displayed a need to throw off constraints. Far too often she reverted backwards to that time when as a child she'd been hurt, becoming the "little girl" all over again in her lessons with me. It was a tight rope walking process, and I knew that if she was going to find success she would have to brave it. I was there to help, I told her. She was not alone, and as long as I could help it, she'd never be.

I would have to teach Kelly with complete openness. That meant looking at my own feelings. To conceptualize her problem was only the first step for me. I had to find a way to help her to rebuke negative history and encourage her to think for herself – something stolen from her in childhood. I promised her that she could reclaim *her* property, so to speak.

If you find this psycho-analysis too esoteric or beside the point for a voice teacher to consider, think again. All you have to do is imagine the adopted child's world. The truth is that they spend much of their lives battling abandonment issues, and their fears are often insurmountable. It takes years to help them get over their *despair* and the *shame*, enough to see their loving adoptive families for what they are. I take it a step further. The student of singing must communicate the feelings of the text and music – someone else's feelings. How? They must be guided through their despair so that they can hear, see, and feel the writer's truth, which ultimately is universal and hits them right over the head, forcing their own truth. Changing the feelings of helplessness to dependency on the teacher is not the answer. Rather, I had to carefully build Kelly's trust in herself and her own powers.

All my girls were such *extraordinary talents*.

7. Group Complete

Beyoncé, Ashley, and Kelly were gifted children. Raw talents, but gifted. When we began our work together in 1989, they hadn't known anything about singing or what it took to have success as a group in one of the most grueling businesses ever. Knowledge is what it would take, and I told them so. Having it would separate them from the rest.

"So you wanna be famous?" I asked them.

I told them the truth. "More often than not, the music business is a very lonely profession; it has been known to break even the best of them." I told them two things about it. One, I told them that it was one of the most thrilling rides they would ever have the opportunity to experience. And two, although thrilling, it could be an unforgiving and cruel business. The artist has to shift between the wants of music executives, family, and fans, and all without losing themselves in the process.

And still they wanted in.

My intent was two-fold from the very beginning. One goal was to help develop in them a sense of group and how each of them fit into it. Secondly, I wanted to equip them to become independent and extraordinary solo artists.

* * * * *

Every human being possesses a unique voice with potential, and its development beyond ordinary depends on numerous factors. The voice itself is so self-evident to us that only its absence, due to hoarseness or a cold for example, makes us aware of it. The apparently simple process of speech is in reality a highly complex act that involves the lungs, vocal cords, oral and nasal cavities, and the lips, as well as the jaw, teeth, ears, and eyes – and, of course, the brain. One has to become a master of this exact complexity to find the kind of success my girls dreamed about.

Beyoncé, Ashley and Kelly wanted Grammy Awards, scores of them.

"Today we are going to learn to sing a simple line, without all the frills and fanfare usually associated with the black voice," I said.

Ethnicity kills a career and environment is everything. You couldn't have the kind of commercial worldwide success I envisioned sounding ethnic. Few can – even Clive Davis knew this when building Whitney Houston, who was quickly becoming "the voice" to watch.

I knew it too.

"Girls, the way to building sensational tight harmonies, which you all will become known for, lies in your understanding of how to produce pure vowels. Every vowel you will sing as a group must be synchronized (meaning the same) and be produced in exactly the same manner," I said.

"But we don't sing vowels, we sing words," Ashley said.

"That is only partly true, Ashley," I answered. "Words are made up of vowels and consonants, so, we most definitely sing vowels. There are very few words that don't have vowels, no matter the language."

"What's a word that has no vowels?" Kelly asked.

"OK Miss Devil's Advocate, technically, words without vowels don't exist, but what I mean is, there are words that don't sound the vowel. Words like "nurse," and "word," for instance, have vowels in them but when you say them you hear no clear a, e, i, o or u vowel sound. There are plenty of words in the English language that fall into this category, and indeed all languages. But you're getting ahead of me."

Although Kelly had jumped the gun, I didn't mind. I welcomed her new attitude with open arms, plus her question was valid. I told my girls that words with no pure vowel sound were normally words that have an r sound and almost always there would be a vowel before the r in the word. I asked Beyoncé, who never spoke when I taught, to give me the vowel found in the word "gypsy." Again, Kelly interjected. "Ah, so there is a word without a vowel." "Is there?" I asked.

"Beyoncé, please sound out the word "gypsy." I turned to Kelly. "So what's the vowel?"

"Well, I hear an EE vowel, but I don't see it in the word," she answered.

"Exactly," I said. "Just because people don't see a thing doesn't mean that it is not there... Hint, hint."

Ashley mentioned that her music teacher at school had told her that y was a vowel, which again was partly correct.

"That's true," I answered. It was exactly for that reason that I'd introduced the word "gypsy" into our discussion. For instance, in the word "Buy," the vowel sound would be a combined AH with EE. In the word "Busy," the vowel sound becomes EE. They got it.

Beyoncé, Kelly, and Ashley had become accustomed to their overly inspired teacher. There was always more coming. I almost never spoke, taught, in terms of single subject matter. Teaching the art and science of singing was like a drug for me. That my girls loved singing just as much as I did, delighted me to no end.

"Any questions?" I asked.

They had none. Satisfied, my girls were perched and ready for phase two.

* * * * *

I asked my girls to say "AH," which is closest to the back of the throat. The first thing they noticed was that the back of their mouth opened, and the soft palate lifted slightly (the soft palate is the soft part of the roof of the mouth, just in front of the uvula). Then I asked them to place their hand (the inner side, where the thumb is) long-ways against their face, just in front of the ear.

"Keep your palm open, the white part facing outward, Beyoncé. Like this," I demonstrated. Then, looking at Kelly and Ashley, I concluded with "Keep your fingers pointing upwards and let your thumbs stretch cross-ways under your chin – like so."

"Leaving your hand in place, speak the EH, EE, OH and OU vowels," I said. "Did you sense them moving in your head?"

They hadn't.

"Try it again. This time whisper the vowels, starting with AH,"

They did it.

"Now speak the EH vowel," I said. "Did you feel it move forward?"

Beyoncé did the exercise again. "Yes," she answered. The other girls then followed suit, answering yes.

"Ok, now start with AH, move to EH, then EE, and OH and end with speaking OU."

They did it.

"Now did you sense the other vowels moving?"

They did.

"Great. Let's do it together," I said.

AH – my hand was facing out, long-ways near my ear, palm open. EH – the girls noticed that my hand moved slightly forward, just forward of the ear and stopping at the side of my face, at the cheek. I continued with EE – again my hand moved forward, this time stopping at the front of the cheek. OH – moved to the smile muscles, and OU – rested on the flower/front of the lips.

"I feel it, I feel it," Ashley said. Kelly chimed in. Beyoncé, however, remained quiet, busy repeating the exercise, over and over again.

"The EH vowel should never be sung in EE's space, and *vice versa*. Every vowel has its own position in your head and are not interchangeable."

They understood.

In addition, I covered what I called "The strange vowel sounds." The "UH" sound in "Love" and the "UHRR" in "Early" were to be resonated in the EH space. I also talked about double syllable vowels (diphthongs), they get special attention. For example, the word "I" has two syllables (two sounds) and therefore must shift to two positions. "I" spoken or sung begins first in AH (back of the mouth) and then moves quickly forward to the EE space (said at the front of the cheek).

My girls were having fun like Christmas, but there was more.*****

Beyoncé came to me breathing incorrectly. "Think about it," I told her. "Breathing happens in the lungs, and the lungs are housed within the rib cage. They do not extend further downward past the last rib," I said. Placing my hand flat against her lower abdominal wall I added, "There should be no outward movement here, in your lower stomach area, Beyoncé. Please do not let your support collapse!" I directed her.

Describing clearly the difference between "intercostal" and "thoracic" breathing, my teacher, Dr. Robert Henry, likened the human voice to a violin's sound, both of which depend upon a body. The violinist's sound depends upon the wood of the instrument, the lacquer and finish, the maker of the violin, and the player's intelligence and skill. The human voice depends upon the thoracic cavity, the vocal folds, nasal passage, head resonators, tongue, the teeth, and understanding the breath and brain of the singer.

Let me explain.

Most people breathe reflexively from the chest, taking air into the lungs in shallow and unsupported spurts, which goes only as far as the front thoracic region. Breathing in this manner produces low blood-oxygen levels. However, when a singer learns to expand the chest, back, and pelvic areas (i.e., to the top of the *gluteus maximus*), allowing the breath to activate all these regions – so-called "intercostal" breathing – without disturbing the stomach's natural position (i.e. belly breathing), they find freedom. Yes, the diaphragm drops, acting as a flexible floor, but the stomach should remain flat, not poke out.

The mastery of isometric contraction of the abdominal muscles, for use in both singing and dancing, meant my girl's understanding that the abdominal muscles should contract, but not shorten or lengthen. "Your abdominal muscles need to remain constant, the same length. In dance you'll gain strength and control. In singing you gain control and vocal power. In both you gain extension – leg and arm extension in dance and range and power in singing." This very intricate and delicate balance of breath, spirit, and mind, required their constant attention and my permanent supervision. Now, in 1990-91, I talked about "Singing on the breath," and my girls listened.

To sing on one's breath, a perfect balance between breath and tone, which I referred to as the velvet zone, must be accomplished. When this is mastered even the youngest of talents will produce a tone of warmth and maturity with absolute clarity. (The "velvet zone" is a term that my colleague, the baritone Roland Burks, who is a fine teacher of singing himself, shared with me. A principle of his then teacher, John Large, the velvet zone, as described in his book "Contributions of Voice Research to Singing," is the warm and cushiony feeling experienced by a singer during vocal freedom).

During our group lessons my girls began to feel a tingly sensation all over their bodies. This kinetic energy happens in every extremity of a well-balanced body. They really felt, individually and as a group, as if their entire body was alive while singing. Correct breathing is absolutely essential to insure proper projection and the surround sound effect, which aids resonance. Pushing past this important sound wave pattern, or opening the mouth too wide at the wrong time, is what took Ashley's voice out of focus and gave it that edgy sound I'd solved. Learning to stay connected to their diaphragm (where getting to surround sound lives) helped them all maintain flexibility and power. And again, with the abdominal wall remaining constant.

Presence in performance, or sensitivity, has everything to do with perception and that special "something" seen behind the eyes. It can never be achieved before the student mastery of breath and vowel placement. Many people say that you either have "it" or you don't, but I do not agree. "It," that special *je ne sais quoi*, is an attitude achieved through inner quiet and self-introspection. It can be taught, and is ultimately won through honesty, which is the only street that will get you to confidence. Confidence begins with learning to have conscious, silent thoughts – thoughts that activated the right facial muscles (learning to activate the true emotion hidden in the text and music). Simply put, I asked Beyoncé, Ashley, and Kelly to mean what they sang: "Think it, put it on your face, and then sing it." That sounds like a simple, even simplistic, notion, but believe me it is not. It describes a complex process that Ashley, Beyoncé, and Kelly would master only after many years of study and practice.

This much detail may seem esoteric to the average reader, but I wasn't building average talents. Just because Beyoncé, Ashley and Kelly were children, didn't mean that I should patronize their intelligence; no responsible teacher should. My girls were genius. All children have in them the potential to awaken their gifts. It takes solid teaching, and an unwavering commitment. My girls had told me their truth. They wanted major success in the music business.

"If you're going to be stars, you will need to know everything about your craft," I told them. I insisted on it.

I got no argument, from any of them.

In my vocal studio I frequently use analogies and metaphors (sometimes even parables) to illustrate the concepts that I'm teaching. One of the useful images I discussed was "Cars." Since the voice is such an intangible instrument, I found that describing it in terms of an automobile helped Beyoncé, Kelly, and Ashley to visualize the ephemeral (the short-lived or transitory meaning). I asked them to describe the color, timbre (tone quality), and brilliance of their voices and to imagine what kind of car would also fit that description.

In my opinion Kelly was driving a Porsche vocally. Her voice was sleek and alluring. To hear her tell it, you would have thought she was driving a Pinto. I argued my case with her and slowly but surely I made progress. Within weeks of my renewed efforts with her, Kelly began to notice that when she spoke, the voice worked fantastically. She just did it, with no extra thought as to how to produce the tone. The sound had body to it and was sonorous. I then told her that singing was an extension of speech and that she would have a warm sound. Now ten years old, I wanted her to sing the words – the same words she had been reading, I told her. But don't forget to give special attention to the length of the vowels, I said. After a period of two months Kelly began producing real tone, a viable tone that shimmered. Just like a well-regulated Porsche.

Beyoncé had a big voice, which she produced effortlessly, but she liked singing wide open tones. This way of singing, left uncorrected, would lead to vocal problems. She sang with an unbridled passion, which I had to contain without squelching. "Beyoncé, you must learn to sing on your interest and not your capital," I told her, in the words of the great soprano Leontyne Price. Beyoncé had to learn to keep something in reserve. Her singing could very quickly become a scream. I had to re-connect her to her diaphragm often, which is how we prevent ourselves from pushing the voice. She had to learn that forcing would actually hinder the desired control she sought. So, I began by paring the sound down to a whisper. I stood her in front of the mirror and stood directly behind her.

"Look at what my tongue is doing."

The tongue is the chief. If the tongue doesn't work, singing doesn't work, I told her. Great articulation can be achieved only through the tongue, and if it is pressured or used otherwise incorrectly, even prayer will not help you. Forcing the sound will make the tongue retract (pull back from the bottom teeth) from the pressure, causing missed notes and harsh sounds.

I began with opening my mouth to its most comfortable hanging position (the natural opening), enough to see the tongue. I asked Beyoncé to notice how my tongue was lying quietly on the floor of my mouth. The tip of the tongue is placed behind the bottom teeth and left there, I told her.

"Now sing an 'AH-EE' on one pitch and allow only the tongue to move. Do not allow the jaw to move, but don't stiffen it."

What Beyoncé saw was that the tongue moved up and down in the center: on "AH" it moved down with a slight curve in the middle of the tongue and on "EE" it rose upwards in the middle, rounding itself off. I then switched to the EH-EE vowel combination. Here she noticed that the tongue while singing an EH vowel lifted up in the middle, as before, but with the singing of the EE vowel the tip of the tongue remained behind the lower teeth (as it does in all these cases) and moved slightly forward. The tongue when singing an OH vowel depressed slightly and seemed to move gently back. OU caused a light lift in the tongue at the tip and then with a forward motion she had the impression that it rested upon the ridge of the bottom front teeth.

The continued mastering of the vowels began to fix her breath – permanently – and then her vibrato. With that I could then build her breath control. Beyoncé's voice would eventually gain unbelievable flexibility. Her runs would be second to no one's, and with the attention to style and technique I required, she would have no peer as a singer. Eventually – but not for some years – I would explain to her that I was teaching her *Bel Canto* methods: the 18th Century Italian singing technique, "beautiful singing" – alla Farinelli. All the girls were being guided in Bel Canto technique. During their course of study, in this most intricate of singing schools, we'd make three important factors our basis: the tongue, the breath, and vowels. First for Beyoncé was making sure she understood breath, the basis of her elasticity and singing *in the pocket,* where control lived. Beyoncé's was a Rolls Royce voice, big, plush, and now smooth.

Ashley's voice was also big, but in a different way from Beyoncé's. I would say she was driving a Ferrari vocally – fast and furious with tons of flash. Although she didn't sing wide open tones, her voice used to have an edgy and hard sound. She often times still attacked the notes. I continued the vowel work with her that I had also given to Beyoncé, which Ashley remembered from her first lesson with me. But recently she and I been concentrating on her approach from the top down, to thin the weight out. It was important that Ashley understand that she was a soprano and would be a soprano. She was not an alto, as her church choir director had told her. Beyoncé was the alto.

Many teachers might think I was unwise – or at least premature – to classify a voice at such a young age. This belief is accurate concerning boys, but by studying physiology and vocal resonance, a competent teacher can determine a projected voice type. Even when she was nine, I heard that Ashley's voice would develop into a first-rate soprano, and I worked with her accordingly. I have never believed in holding back information from children, and especially from Ashley. She soaked it up like a sponge. What was good for me as a child was good for them, if they wanted it. My girls were hungry for knowledge, and they hung on my every word.

In order to guide Ashley to success as a singer, I taught her the importance of head voice, and its use, which is called *voix mixte,* the French name for describing the school of mixing head and chest voice registers. Every voice must learn how to do this in Bel Canto. The fact that it had been my ultimate goal from her first lesson, I asked her to sing the EE and O vowels mostly. My aim was, again, to take all the weight out of the voice in order to make it pliable. Those vowels did that. Once she mastered them she felt an immediate spin in the tone that had not been there before. (Later on in life she would use these very principles to go in and out of head and chest voice seamlessly.)

Ashley's natural tendency was to place her voice forward in an attempt to give it direction and resonance, but I wouldn't allow it. I explained to her that resonance did not need her help. At first she thought I was trying to make her voice small, as did Beyoncé, but I explained to them both that when a singer sounds loud in her own head, the audience hears it as small. Properly produced, the opposite should occur. A singer's voice should sound small to herself, but large and resonant to the listener.

Beyoncé asked me about volume. "How come Whitney Houston's voice is so powerful?"

"Resonance," I said. I went on to explain that resonance was essentially acoustic feedback. It has everything to do with vibration and those sound waves I talked about and nothing to do with projection. It does not come from pushing or trying to focus the voice. It is a mental process which happens through the vibration of bone and cartilage, and employ the muscles of the neck, head, and upper chest to create its perfect balance. "The correct way to get to resonance is through learning to intensify thought." I also told Beyoncé that Whitney Houston's voice was "a natural phenomenon, like Kelly's." Without training, problems arise with these kinds of voices. As the body ages, and shifts through hormonal changes, the first thing that goes is the singer's breath control, then the top voice. A natural talent just opens their mouths and sing. They are almost never aware of what makes their mechanism work and they pay for it in the end. "Whitney's lack of appreciation for study will surely bring ruin," I told Beyoncé.

Beyoncé looked at me perplexed. It was clear that my comments about Whitney had affected her adversely. I told her, "Let me say it this way. Just because a person can sing doesn't mean they know how to sing. Then I told her that Whitney Houston, who had been asked who her voice teacher was, replied, saying God.

"God doesn't teach voice," I said. "He made teachers for that."

Beyoncé understood.

"Remember, knowledge is power!"

All of these basics were the foundation upon which my girls would excel. They had to be taught how to form a cohesive singing group sound.

They learned to master more and more intricate principles over years. To experience them working on, and understanding, these very intricate processes, gave me extreme joy. I was having the time of my life. As nine-, ten- and eleven-year-olds, my girls were learning things usually imparted to aspiring adult singers, and they ate it up. So, when people began to express genuine surprise at their fast-paced progress, I smiled inwardly. Together with them, I'd guided their every step. Sponges, they were children with no preconceived notions about anything. Therefore, I was able to paint beautifully upon their spirits and voices, planting the seeds for a marvelous harvest to come.

"You all will own the music business," I told them. And I had every intention of delivering on that promise.

While never losing sight of returning to the solo stage, and feeling something like pride, I was almost content with the balance in my life. Then Mathew showed up. The knock at my door startled me. No one was supposed to be home. He hadn't been there at breakfast, but yet, here he stood.

"I want to talk to you about Beyoncé…," he said.

Mathew asked me what I *really thought* about his daughter's talent. "…Your daughter is a prodigy," I said, repeating what I'd said to his wife, Celestine, just months earlier.

"Real talent lives in your house," I added.

* * * * *

Mathew Knowles had – and has – no talent, or ear for music. His singing voice was atrocious, to say nothing of his inability to match pitch. At least his wife, Celestine, had somewhat of an ear. She too didn't have much voice, very little actually, but she could at least carry a tune. In addition, she recognized Beyoncé's progress, which pleased both Beyoncé and me greatly. "Beyoncé is singing better than ever," Celestine said.

"I'm so proud of Beyoncé. I've never seen a child like her. She's so serious. She wants to know everything there is to know about music." I continued. "She's definitely going places."

"You think so?" Celestine asked.

"Oh, most definitely. All the girls are," I said. "They are going to turn the music industry on their heads when I'm finished."

While Celestine continued to run Headliners, I increased my commitment to Beyoncé and the other girls. Mathew, however, seemed to be busily hatching secret plans. One day, Ashley's mother, Carolyn Davis, told me that she was concerned about the future of Girls Tyme. She said that she did not trust Mathew and wondered what he was up to. When I asked her what she meant, Carolyn informed me that she and Ann Tillman had been having discussions about Ann's needing to secure her position as manager.

"Secure? I thought she was the manager," I said, "by contract."

"She is the manager," Carolyn replied, "but Mathew has been snooping around trying to get involved," Carolyn concluded.

"Do you think that Mathew wouldn't do a good job?"

"No, I am not saying that he wouldn't. I am saying that his becoming part of management would be unethical. None of us parents should have that position. There is the issue of bias, and a parent as manager could only cause problems. We need a neutral party to avoid any conflict of interest," Carolyn said.

Carolyn's remarks got my attention. Although I had not given it any previous thought, I could imagine the difficulty in creating a fair and equal playing field if just one Girls Tyme parent controlled the entire group's future.

"Well what does Ann think about your theory? Does she agree?" I asked.

"I don't know," Carolyn said, "but she did say that her brother Lornando might be available to help her out."

"Really, does her brother have experience in the music business?" I asked.

"Her brother has more experience than Mathew," Carolyn said. "I am not sure if Mathew intends to work his way into Girls Tyme management, but I have a feeling, deep down, that he is up to no good."

Carolyn had her feelings and I respected them and her. I sensed that she wanted my insights and opinions, but I had neither, even though I lived within the Knowles household. All I knew was that something was off with Mr. Mathew Knowles. I just didn't know what it was. A strange energy permeated the environment. But I held my tongue.

Determined not to rely on my judgment alone, and lacking any of his own, Mathew sought the advice of whiter-skinned music professionals, too often a typical behavior exhibited by people of color with deep roots in the South. Winning the white man's respect was more important to Mathew than brushing his teeth. I'd only known the man about five months, up close and personal, but I'd figured that much out.

Mathew turned to a Columbia Records Representative, Regional A&R, Teresa La Barbera-Whites. Beyoncé, Ashley, and Kelly had successfully recorded a few tracks with a producer whom Ann had flown in from California.

Alonzo "Lonnie" Jackson, from the Oakland area, was an aspiring record producer who Ann said she had a history with. After I suggested to Ann that the girls had advanced vocally enough to resume the recording process, she called Lonnie, paid for his flight, gave him a per diem and ultimately a salary. In the beginning he also lived at Ann's house and then he hooked up with LaTavia's Aunt Yvonne, intimately. (It was a disaster.)

At any rate, Mathew sent the tapes that Lonnie and the girls had been recording with a letter to Mrs. LaBarbera-Whites in Dallas. Some producer who worked at the studio had given him the contact, Mathew said. A couple of days later, Mrs. LaBarbera-Whites called the house. She loved my girls singing, she said. Her enthusiasm was very positive, so much so that she made plans to fly to Houston from Dallas to see them in person.

When Mathew told Beyoncé in front of me, she was ecstatic. She didn't believe it. "You mean it?" she asked.

I smiled.

Beyoncé began to jump up and down with excitement.

Mathew had not mentioned a thing to the other girls, but emphasized to both Beyoncé and me that this coup, and that's exactly what it was, had been all his doing. There was nothing subliminal about it. He just came right out with it.

On Saturday, group rehearsal day, Kelly had her lesson, and then we got to it. I rehearsed the girls within an inch of their lives. After the rehearsal all they could talk about was that someone thought they were good enough to come all the way to Houston.

Laughing, I said. "Of course they do. You haven't been playing hop scotch all these years."

Before 1989, Girls Tyme had been a group of little girls with a dream but no direction. In fact, there had been fifty of them, all cramped into a community dance studio. Now the chosen girls, Beyoncé, Ashley and Kelly delivered another skill set. Their hard work was beginning to pay off. Nothing was certain, they intimated.

"Maybe she won't like us," Kelly said.

"Are you crazy, Kelly?" I asked. I had to catch myself, she was right to be concerned. Kelly Rowland hadn't been working two years on her technique. She was behind the other two girls, but I had confidence in her natural abilities. They would carry her through, for now, I told her.

"You all have worked like ten horses and the fruit of all that labor will be landing tomorrow and each of you will be perfect," I said, looking piercingly through Kelly.

Shrinking, she and the other girls said, "Yes David. We are gonna be good. Don't worry."

In that moment, Mathew knocked on the door.

"David, can you pick Teresa up from Hobby Airport tomorrow?"

"Of course."

He told me that after her flight landed, I was to drive her to the Evelyn Rubenstein Jewish Community Center, "out on South Braeswood," Mathew said. "Do you know it?"

I told Mathew that I knew about where it was but having the address would be better. He turned, without saying a word and walked back to the house. Moments later he returned with the address.

"It is at 5601 S. Braeswood."

I wrote it down and told him not to worry. "I'll get Mrs. LaBarbera-Whites tomorrow and on time," I said.

That evening, Mathew called my house from the kitchen telephone downstairs. "Uh, Ann won't be able to make it tomorrow," he said. "She can't get off work."

"OK," I said, finding his call strange. I was sure that Ann wouldn't miss such an important event.

"Don't forget; after Teresa lands bring her directly to me at the Jewish Community Center," Mathew said.

"Yes, Mathew. I know what to do," I answered. In anticipation, I had already made a sign with her name on it.

I arrived at Hobby, parked my car in the garage, and headed toward the gate. The sign worked.

Teresa LaBarbera-Whites was somewhat tallish, thin, and very person-able. Her hair reminded me of a lion's mane. Big, beautiful, and curly, I could imagine it was a source of great pride. An impressive gray streak ran throughout her locks, which gave her an arresting and engaging look. I couldn't tell her age by looking into her slender face but guessed that she couldn't have been more than thirty-two years old, even with the gray in her hair. She was traveling light and so we headed to my Nissan. Mathew had borrowed my Audi. I still can't believe I trusted him with it.

As we walked to the airport garage, Mrs. LaBarbera-Whites asked me who I was, and my connection to Girls Tyme. I explained, briefly, and on the drive over to the Jewish Community Center she and I got into deep conversations about music.

"Please call me Teresa," she said.

"How long have you been teaching the girls?" she asked.

"I've been teaching them since August, 1989."

150

"Well, they certainly sound great. Are they really as young as Mathew said they are?"

"Yes, they are. Beyoncé's birthday was in September. She is now ten years old. Kelly turned ten several months ago on February 11th and Ashley is eleven."

Our conversation was interesting. It became clear, very quickly, that Teresa cared about the artists she decided to take on. Her voice bristled with excitement as she talked about each artist. When she told me that she had taken on only girls thus far, I started to feel more at ease. She understood their needs and seemed tough enough to protect them.

"I think you're gonna love my girls. They're not only good girls but they work very hard. Everything thing I ask of them, they do, without complaint."

"How often do you see them?"

"I live with Beyoncé, in her parents' garage apartment, so I see her every day. I see Kelly on Saturdays for private lessons and Ashley on Tuesdays. Right now, we have been having group sessions on the weekends, after Kelly's lesson. But that will change soon," I said.

Teresa and I seemed to have lots in common. She told me that her husband was a professional ballet dancer. I had danced professionally. She loved the ballet. I missed it. "I gave it up when I moved to Houston in 1989-90," I said.

"Why?"

"I left it behind to concentrate fully on singing and my own career."

"Oh, you sing, too?" Teresa asked.

"Yes. Opera!"

"Oh Wow! – that explains it," Teresa said.

"Explains what?"

"What I heard in the girls' presentation. I heard a refinement. A developed sound," she said.

The conversation turned to other genres of music and I was pleasantly surprised regarding Teresa's knowledge of Black music. She knew our history and spoke intelligently on matters Black.

"We're here," I said. I parked the car and Teresa and I headed for the front door of the Jewish Community Center.

Mathew was waiting in the lobby. He introduced himself, shaking Teresa's hand gingerly, thank God, and then he led us into the auditorium where the girls were anxiously waiting. Opening the door, I could see my girls already on the stage. They looked stiff. Instinctively, I fell behind Mathew and Teresa, which gave me the opportunity to gesture to them to lighten up. As Teresa and Mathew got closer to them, they all started to move forward to the edge of the stage. So far so good, I thought. I watched with particular attention to their manners. Had they listened during all our conversations about presentation? "If you want to be iconic you must make an iconic impression," I had said.

Suddenly, Beyoncé walked right up to Teresa, who had ascended the stairs to the stage to greet the girls. Extending her hand, she introduced herself. Each girl then responded gracefully and relaxed.

"Nice to meet you all," Teresa said.

I must admit, I was a bit baffled that Ann wasn't there at the audition. I hadn't believed Mathew about her having to work and I hadn't bothered to call and check with her about the validity of what I had been told. It had gotten too late the day before, but I was so sure that she would have found a way to take off work.

All of a sudden I noticed Mathew's changed demeanor. He was on! A peacock couldn't have competed with him on that day. He pranced around like a show horse.

Teresa said that she was ready if the girls were. "David, will you stay with the girls or sit with me?"

"I'll join you," I said.

Mathew's jaws tightened.

Signaling to Teresa, who was about to sit near the front, I suggested we move to the middle of the room. "The sound will be better back here," I said.

Teresa looked at me, a bit unsure at first, but then she followed. Mathew re-ascended the stage and said something to the girls. I started to cough, obtrusively. They were not to let him into their head. They had a job to do. They took their places. They bowed their heads and Mathew gave the signal for the engineer to start the instrumental track. My girls hit every mark. They were singing beautifully and their voices were projecting exceedingly well, even with no microphones. Teresa's body language told me that she liked them, and her facial muscles screamed she loved them. I noticed that her zygomatic and orbicularis muscles, just under the skin, twitched from excitement. She couldn't hide her true feelings from me.

At the end of their song she began to applaud, standing up with the intention of moving in the girls' direction.

"Oh, they have one more song," I said.

Looking at me, now completely assured, Teresa eagerly sat back down. Anticipating the next song, she closed her eyes. It was jaw droppingly beautiful. My girls were singing an *a capella* version I'd set on them of "Amazing Grace." (Beyoncé would eventually revamp it for Destiny's Child.) Teresa was transfixed. Years later, she told me that she had the distinct feeling she had not been listening to children. It was an emotional experience for me. When the girls finished the last chord, Teresa smiled. It was epic.

"They are wonderful," she said, heading towards the stage. I was so proud of my girls. I stayed back in my seat. This was their moment. They were going to change the sound of music. I was sure of it. All those talks about singing on breath, the tongue, the teeth, muscles, the jaw, seeing it, listening to the silence, and playing the movie in your head, just to name a few, had paid off. Great Talents, they were on their way to becoming Genius.

Teresa hugged each girl. "You guys are amazing!" she said.

Beyoncé was elated. Kelly grinned like a Cheshire cat, and Ashley, trying desperately to remain reserved, couldn't help herself and started jumping up and down. Then they all started jumping up and down. Let the giggling and squealing begin, I thought. That Sunday would be one they'd not likely forget. I knew I wouldn't.

A few days later, I learned the truth about Ann's absence at the Jewish Community Center audition. She hadn't had a clue about Teresa's visit, until I innocently recounted the events of the audition in a telephone conversation on Tuesday, after Ashley's lesson. Ann called to talk to me about a song she wanted Ashley to lead. Asking how she was doing, my enthusiasm gleamed. When I broached the subject of how proud I was of her, and indeed all the girls, after their audition for Teresa LaBarbera-Whites, Ann interrupted to ask me to explain what I meant. Oh, no, what had I done?

"Why didn't you tell me about this?" she asked. I swallowed hard and said, "I didn't know that you didn't know. I thought it was you who arranged it. Mathew told me that you couldn't get off work …" Ann was not happy. "He's a damn liar," she said.

Clearly I had made a horrible mistake in mentioning all of this to her, and I will never forget my feelings of embarrassment and dismay. I had been deceived. The next comment slayed me. As it turned out, Teresa had been Ann's contact and Mathew knew it. He had lied about being referred by a producer at the recording studio. "That dirty, low-down bastard," Ann said, from the back of her throat.

I know that Ann called Teresa over the next few days. If she confronted Mathew about his behavior, I never knew it. He didn't say a word or bring it up, and I never did either.

Two Generations of Grandmother Evelyn's Kitchen
Electric range on legs, behind Fern (my mother) sitting with her same-aged nephew, Keith Clayter (Aunt Lee Lee's son, whom I know as "Uncle Keith"). From Grandmother Evelyn's radio on the shelf I got my first musical impressions of the world beyond that kitchen.

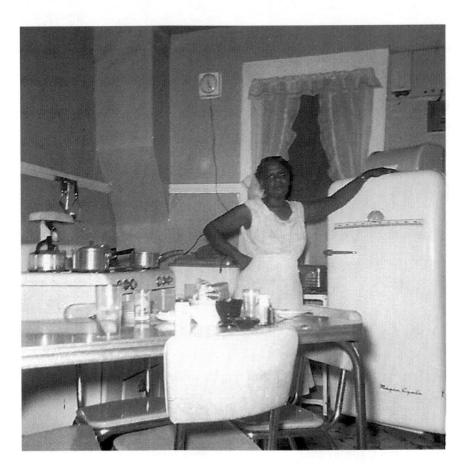

Grandmother Evelyn in my first childhood memories, alongside her fridgidare and her updated electric range (with cooktop lamp and double oven)

Grandmother and Grandfather Sims,
my beloved Grandmother Evelyn (who possessed the beautiful high soprano voice) and Grandfather Charles (the retired vaudeville dancer), who
nurtured and influenced me throughout my childhood

Grandma and Grandpa Dorsey (my father's parents)

Intermission time for Glenn Crytzer's *Savoy Seven Swing Combo* at a fancy dress ball. Gathered in front of the band stand (from left) Aunt Lee Lee, Aunt Sally (first wife of my Uncle Charles), Grandmother Evelyn, and Grandfather

Members of my family gathered at an Omaha banquet table:
(from left) Aunt Beatrice and Uncle William, Great-uncle Earl (Grandmother Evelyn's uncle), Grandmother Evelyn, and Grandfather Sims (others unidentified)

The *Beau Brummel Club*, Omaha 1940s
Top photo: Grandmother Evelyn sits in the middle of the front row (white shoes, ankles crossed) Bottom photo: Grandfather Charles stands on the far left of the front row

Grandmother Evelyn Sims, third from left in the front row, was the vice-president of the XXX, which received a citation from the Salvation Army for her organization's work in establishing North Omaha's first fundraising „Tree of Lights," an annual Salvation Army Christmas fest that continues, decades later, to serve the community's social needs.

Upper photo: Great-grandmother Lula, Aunt Lee Lee, and Great-grandfather Oscar Haskell

Bottom photo: Great-grandfather John Childs

The twelve-year-old Fern Sims (front row, fourth from left), already a member of Omaha's prestigious *Iroquois Drum and Bugle Corps,* was the youngest ever to assume the position of lead majorette.

Daddy (age 17), Mama (age 15, and pregnant with me), Grandmother
Evelyn, and Grandfather Charles. I have often studied their faces in an
attempt to understand this crucial period in their lives.

My twenty-year-old mother surrounded by her three small children: David (age 4), Darryl (3), and Donetta (2)

Ten-year-old David Lee Brewer

Detective Pittman Foxall, center, hand outstretched . . . pleads with Kellogg, surrounded at left.

Shots, Tear Gas Traded

Sister's Pleas, Policemen Quell Man

The pleas of his sister Friday morning finally brought a 20-year-old man out of his apartment after an incident with police.

He was identified as Roy Kellogg, 2960 Patrick Avenue, who was later subdued and taken to police headquarters.

Kellogg, according to his brother Robert, 19, of 2434 Pratt Street, had accidentally wounded James Gill, a friend, with a pistol in Kellogg's apartment about 9:30 a.m. Kellogg's home is in the Pleasant View low-rent public housing project.

A neighbor who heard the shot phoned police, the brother said. Officers in several cruisers answered the call.

Upon arrival, the police called to Kellogg to come outside and he refused, they said.

Kellogg first fired several shots at police, police said.

The police lobbed several tear gas bombs, fired from rifle launchers, into the apartment. Kellogg remained inside.

Police said they did not shoot weapons other than tear gas at Kellogg.

Kellogg's brother Robert, and his sister Carol, 18, also of 2434 Pratt Street, approached the apartment and pleaded with Kellogg to come out.

Carol then entered the apartment to talk to her brother.

Minutes later she stepped out carrying a pistol and Kellogg followed a few steps behind.

As Kellogg emerged, police approached and seized him. A brief scuffle followed.

As officers tried to move Kellogg to a cruiser, Kellogg pushed Detective Pittman Foxall, like Kellogg, a Negro.

Kellogg was then handcuffed, placed in a cruiser and taken to police headquarters.

His sister, Carol, and a friend Lawrence Nero, accompanied Kellogg and the police in the cruiser.

During the shooting, Gill, 24, was taken to County Hospital by the rescue squad. Gill, whose address was not immediately known, was listed in poor condition with a bullet wound in the neck.

Kellogg was being questioned at police headquarters, police said.

Kellogg, his wife and their three children live in the apartment at 2960 Patrick Avenue.

The *Omaha World-Herald* account of Roy Edward Kellogg's shooting of James Gill in our home. With this event, we were nearly rid of Roy's malevolent presence in our lives.

(By permission of *Omaha World-Herald*)

168

In the melee surrounding Roy Edward Kellogg's near-fatal assault on James Gill in our home, the police swarmed our neighborhood. My stepfather Roy, facing the camera in black shirt, was taken in handcuffs to jail.

Lunch with my teachers, 2012. Seated: Mrs. Yolanda Martin and Mrs. Mary Lou Larson. Standing next to me: Mrs. Denise Arnold

Lunch with my teachers, 2014. From left: Prof. Donald Callen Freed (friend of Mark Schulze, seated on far right), David Lee Brewer, Mrs. Yolanda Martin, Mr. James Eisenhardt, Mrs. Denise Arnold, Mr. Mark Schulze

David Brewer (Ebeneezer Scrooge) and John Carter
(Marley's Ghost) gave magnificent performances.

David Lee Brewer, 18, onstage as Ebeneezer Scrooge, Langston University
December 4, 1981, in the Dust Bowl Theater production of *A Christmas Carol.*
(Ten minutes before curtain, my mother had told me that Grandfather
Charles had died.)
*Langston University, "The Lion 1982" (1982). LU Yearbooks, 1980-1989.
Book 4.* http://dclu.langston.edu/archives_yearbooks_19801989/4

In 1990 President George H. W. Bush invited the Langston University Choir to sing a command performance in Washington, D. C. for a major ""Take Pride in America" concert. President Bush had acted on the advice of his Secretary of the Interior, Manuel Lujan, Jr., who had been impressed by the choir's performance at the 1989 Langston University graduation. The Choir received celebrity-status hospitality in our nation's capital city. In the first row, far left: Mrs. Alexis Rainbow (my influential Langston voice teacher) and Mrs. Sarah Phillips; in the top row of the choir, I am third man from the left.

Photo: Alexis Rainbow

Langston University, Langston, Oklahoma (USA): Graduation day, May 9, 1987
From left: Cassandra Bennett (B.A. Music), George Ward (B.A. Music), Denise Wyatt (B.S. Nursing), David Lee Brewer (B.A. Music)
Photo: George Ward

A diverse show, but much too long

By **WILMA SALISBURY**
DANCE/MUSIC CRITIC

Five Cleveland dance companies pooled their talents Saturday night at Shaker Heights High School in "The Family Collective," a production of the Cleveland Project for minority arts.

The Imani African-American Dance Company, Buku-Ire African-American Dance Company, Duffy Liturgical Dance Ensemble, Louis Naylor PDM, Reggie Kelly Dance Theater and guest artist Chuck Davis of Duke University expressed themes of peace, love and respect in a well-intentioned but poorly organized show that went on so interminably that it tried the patience of even the most peace-loving and respectful audience members.

Davis, guiding spirit behind the ambitious collaborative effort, brightened the evening with cameo appearances. A giant elderdancer who moves his huge body with remarkable agility, Davis performed an intense politically oriented solo, "And This Too Shall ...," to the accompaniment of his own singing and poetry recitation and the gentle crooning of "Sometimes I Feel Like a Motherless Child" by a bass from the Duffy Ensemble. A powerful performer, Davis delivered a meaningful message as he kicked at crumpled newspapers and wrapped himself in a red-and-white striped cloth that covered his head. Unfortunately, his solo came at the end of an extremely long first act when many audience members were already heading for the exits.

Davis also appeared as a lazy straw man in "GBoi" (Poro Society), a comic masked dance from Sierra Leone, West Africa. Linda Thomas-Jones sparked Davis's amusing performance with her lively playing of traditional rhythms on a Kelias drum, and the audience was drawn into the cere-

DANCE
THE FAMILY COLLECTIVE

mony as Davis stormed up the aisle in his massive straw costume and dropped his gigantic frame into a woman's lap.

At the end of the three-hour show, Davis pronounced a benediction by asking the audience to join hands and chant his motto, "Peace, love and respect for everybody."

Imani, the aspiring family company directed by Thomas-Jones, made its best impression in "Warrior Children," a dance of strength for young girls accompanied by the Imani drummers. Addressing concepts of peace and love through the eyes of women of color, the company also portrayed a voluptuous earth mother, the struggles of sweet sisters, an affectionate mother-daughter relationship and contemporary women warriors. Adding drama to the music and dance was theatrical narration by Yvetta.

The Imani musicians, one of the most vibrant elements in a program that tended to drag, also assisted Buku-Ire in its colorful presentation of "Peace: the Struggle, the Dream."

The first part of the program featured the Duffy Liturgical Ensemble in theatrical stylizations of sacred rituals. Though more impressive for its singing than its dancing, the ensemble's churchly movement style was energized by the upbeat choreography of Davis and Naylor and the soulful dancing of Naylor and David Brewer.

Naylor's PDM, the newest ensemble on the program, danced "The Family Collective" to poetry by Kahlil Gibran and Jennifer Holiday. Although the illustrative modern dance movements communicated at a kindergarten level of sophistication, the group of seven young dancers showed promise,

and Naylor proved that he is still a compelling stage presence despite waning technique.

The Reggie Kelly Dance Theater, by contrast, projected the showy self-assurance of a slick commercial company. Dancing to taped music, the sexy six-member ensemble brought show-biz flair to their contemporary interpretations of love themes.

Companies as disparate in style and idea as the Reggie Kelly Dance Theater and the Duffy Liturgical Ensemble don't really belong on the same stage. Yet, the evening's wide-ranging repertoire of African folk rituals, Las Vegas-style show dancing, sacred movements from the black church and modern dance set to poetry sprang from common cultural roots.

I was pleased to be singled out for my "soulful dancing" in a review of a 1988 dance concert performed by five Cleveland, Ohio, companies. It was my last public dance appearance before leaving for Houston.
By permission of The Cleveland Plain Dealer

Girls Tyme, circa 1991
Clockwise, beginning with Beyoncé Knowles, kneeling, bottom right:
LaTavia Roberson (facing Beyoncé), Nikki Taylor, Kelly Rowland, Ashley Támar Davis, Nina Taylor
(Photo: The Tillman Estate)

Andretta "Ann" Tillman, with her son Chris, at home on Strawgrass Street, Houston, Texas. The photo was taken after a life-changing automobile accident. While Ann and her two sons survived, her husband and **two-year-old daughter** were killed instantly when a drunk driver broad-sided their car.

(Photo: The Tillman Estate)

Part II

Reluctance

---

8. Basketball Tuesdays

"Beyoncé," I said, "singers must maintain vigilance over their mental state. A voice can be reduced to half its normal size, projection, and quality, if it experiences emotional trauma. Just think of Maria Callas! Once great, she was broken by love. Breath is connected to spirit. Spirit is connected to God, and disturbance of spirit affects the breath." I took a deep breath before adding. "Yes, unhealthy emotions can cripple a performer."

* * * * *

Although the racism I had encountered that fateful night on the streets of Houston had an effect on my psyche, I dared not lose faith or the belief that my voice and the elasticity of the musculature supporting my larynx would fully recover. Still, my emotional eagerness to heal trumped patience, and I pushed myself too quickly. I could still sing, and my physical therapist helped me release the contracted muscles in my neck and back, but the road to full recovery stretched into the distant future.

I attacked working toward my own vocal recovery with a vengeance – in itself a turn of phrase that betrayed my impatience with the process. Still, by speaking words on one pitch to bring the chords together properly, I was able to gently and without force initialize healthy breath flow. I experienced spasms during my ascent to high notes and I felt a pulling sensation in my back, which Dr. Stasney said sounded like occipital nerve trauma. There was definite muscle tension. Still, the work to heal had to be done. No matter the progress, I could expect that I would continue to develop headaches. Dr. Stasney suggested Excedrin, which worked wonderfully in alleviating the discomfort.

I had not developed a wobble, but my breath was still slightly labored, and even though my top voice was still there, it was almost colorless – for a tenor, career-ending. The thought of singing a high C was so painful that even now it brings tears to my eyes just thinking about what I suffered. God, however, smiled on me.

After I achieved proper oscillation of the vocal folds in the middle voice and ultimately even air flow, I began to sing the AH vowel, then EH, EE, OH and OU, on one pitch, with my teeth touching. This helped me to hit my mark of singing the pure vowel, re-anchoring my breath in the body, and keeping the tongue in its proper place. (Making sure that during moments of rest, my tongue rests upward in the roof of the mouth.)

In the third month I spoke the vowels a, e, i, o, u concentrating on projection. One solid month of speaking and then singing the pure vowels, then speaking and singing combinations of the vowels, began to turn things around. The pain, although still present, was beginning to abate. My diaphragm was being worked and I had realigned my breath. I began to trust my voice again. I felt that I would be able to honor my professional recital and concert commitments. Knowing what was ahead of me, I refused to allow myself even a moment of weakness. Private grieving time would have to take a back seat to the daunting task before me: my audition for the Houston Grand Opera chorus.

I arrived on time for my audition, along with the usual assortment of other hopeful singers. I had decided to sing the aria "Dalla sua pace," which was a horrible mistake. Grandmother's death and that text crept up on me with warning. I broke down. The chorus master and a conductor, Richard Bado, gave me a moment to compose myself, which I did. A couple minutes later I returned to the room in control. I began the aria again, this time successfully singing it to the end:

Dalla sua pace la mia dipende
(On her peace of mind depends mine too)/
Quel che a lei piace vita mi rende
(what pleases her gives life to me)/
Quel che le incresce morte mi dà
(what grieves her wounds me to the heart).
S'ella sospira, sospiro anch'io
(If she sighs, I sigh with her)/
È mia quell'ira, quel pianto è mio
(her anger and her sorrow are mine)/
E non ho bene, s'ella non l'ha
(and I cannot know joy unless she shares it).

A week later I got word. HGO offered me a contract for their production of *The Passion of Jonathan Wade,* by the American composer Carlisle Floyd. Maestro Bado had forgiven my mishap – the only time in my career that such generosity had been bestowed upon me.

Winning a position in the HGO chorus was a blessing and a real coup, since Richard Bado had developed the group into a prize-winning ensemble known to be the best opera chorus in the country. I was a soloist, but because of my vocal trauma I had to be smart. By singing in the HGO chorus, not only would I be singing – classical repertoire, at that – but I'd also be perfecting my German, French, and Italian diction. I also would have access to some of the best opera coaches in America. Ultimately, the need to keep my vocal chops up, healing in a safe environment, trumped my ego. I could not let pride rule my brain or my sense for being practical.

Elated that I had won my audition with HGO, Dr. Johnstone continued in 1990-91 putting me through my paces. I sang. I cried. But, I kept at it. With contracts to fulfill at HGO, I began working with Dr. Robert Henry (which Dr. Johnstone allowed, as she said she knew of Dr. Henry's work). After six weeks of working together with Dr. Henry, he offered me the role of Don Jose in *Carmen* for 1993, a couple years off, opposite star mezzo-soprano Debria Brown, who was one of the leads in the upcoming *The Passion of Johnathan Wade* production with HGO.

I worked tirelessly every day in continuing to repair my vocal dilemma. I was not going to cancel that important performance – or any other, for that matter. Dr. Henry had dreamed for a long time of building a training ground for aspiring African-American opera singers. Houston Ebony Opera Guild (HEOG) was the result of his patient work. I had dreamed about singing Don Jose ever since I saw it at the Orpheum Theater in Omaha at sixteen years of age. I had sung the duet in a concert of opera scenes in Cleveland, while at CIM. Dr. Henry was giving me the chance of a lifetime. *Carmen* was now on my calendar for 1993 and I was ecstatic.

* * * * *

Celestine and I talked every evening after she arrived home from work. Sharing her concern regarding her husband, she broke down in front of me.

"I don't know what I am going to do," Celestine said.

"About?"

"Mathew," she said. "I need him to get a job."

It was a very vulnerable moment, and I felt sorry for her.

"Don't worry, Celestine. Women have been doing the damn thing alone for many years. I watched my mother do it and you'll do it, too. You need to stay strong for your girls," I said. "I'm there for you and the girls. We're family now," I said, repeating Celestine's words.

Celestine worked twelve- to fourteen-hour days at the hair salon and Mathew was once again "busy," he reiterated. His response to his children's questions as to his whereabouts? "I'm working on our future." That seemed to pacify Beyoncé, but not Solange. I ignored his big talk, and I kept telling myself, "Don't get involved."

Celestine and I had developed a very close friendship by 1991. She began referring to me in public as her "little brother." We got along great.

There was a mutual respect for one another. She shared with me, on many occasions, her sentiments and expressed her "utmost respect." Most Mondays she and I spent pleasant time together doing things. We went to the movies, went out for lunch, shopped unabatedly for fabric (her favorite pastime), and often visited a woman named Selena, whom she called her sister.

I always had the impression that Celestine thought her family was beneath her. Every word that came out of her mouth, when talking about them, was ever-so-slightly denigrating. "Poor Larry," she'd say about her youngest brother. He never could get it together. Celestine described her sister's *situation* as pitiful.

The first time I met Selena, it was like meeting an old friend. A shade darker than Celestine, she was a strong woman, reliable, and definitely accommodating. Visiting her house for the first time, I learned from family photos that I already knew her son, Johnny. We'd met one another through mutual friends from within Houston's gay community.

"Johnny took care of Beyoncé and Solange for years when they were very little children," Selena told me, while Celestine laid out the various fabrics she'd purchased.

An amazing seamstress, Selena did all of Celestine's sewing, and for years. I swear, if someone had told me that Selena could make people with that sewing machine of hers, I would've believed them, hands down. Her skill was beyond extraordinary. Celestine had only to describe her vision.

"I got it, girl. I'll squeeze it in. When do you need it?" Selena would say. Celestine, always pushing the boundaries, would reply, "Oh –, I need it by Saturday."

Had Celestine forgotten again that Selena had to make the pattern out of newspaper? Of course she hadn't. Still, Celestine pushed. Selena resisted, but she always acquiesced.

The first time I met Celestine's younger brother Larry, I was a bit confused. They couldn't have been more different from one another. I thought that maybe Larry might have been Celestine's brother from another mother, but she swore they had the same parents. At least two shades darker than Celestine, Larry's eyes were a strange color, very light and small. His hair was always cropped short and was bone straight – "white folks straight," Celestine said.

Celestine's niece, Angie Beyincé (who later became Beyoncé's assistant), was Larry's only child, as far as I could tell. I never met a brother or sister, if she had one, and no one other than Angie ever came to the Knowles house. Every summer, without fail, Angie would be dropped off by her father and a woman who Celestine said was her mother.

That woman, ostensibly Larry's wife, was always glued to the passenger seat of Larry's old beat-up truck, never saying a word. She never got out, either. On both occasions, when I'd met her, she nodded her hello with a pleasant smile from the passenger side car window. I don't remember that they ever entered the house. Maybe she was mute, I thought.

"She's never been a talker," Celestine said.

Funnily enough, Aunt Celestine treated Niece Angie, to my way of thinking, with hyper-concern. Aunt Celestine doted on Angie in a cloying manner, and her enthusiasm regarding Angie was almost overbearing.

"How's my Angie doing?" Celestine would ask Larry.

Angie's well-being, even though she presumably had a father and mother, was very important to Celestine. Now, in itself, Celestine's behavior wasn't strange, but Angie seemed to be the only niece or nephew she ever talked about. She almost never talked about Johnny and she couldn't shut up about Angie. Still, when I got too inquisitive, Celestine abruptly changed the subject.

I found it odd.

* * * * *

On a Monday morning I heard screaming in the Knowles house. I rushed over, thinking that it might have been their housekeeper, an undocumented worker from Ecuador named Chunga. At any rate, the closer I got to the door of Beyoncé's room, which was my only internal pathway into the

184

main house from my apartment, I heard Mathew calling someone a Bitch. "You're nothing without me," he said. He was talking to Celestine. I backed out of the house, never wanting them to know that I had heard their boisterous disagreement. My great escape was foiled by Beyoncé's Siamese cat. Just as I was about to head to my apartment, that cat ran in front of me. I stumbled and knocked over some of Beyoncé's trophies. I froze.

"Who's that," Mathew screamed from downstairs.

I could hear him heading upstairs. I high-tailed it out of there, just making it to my apartment before hearing him enter Beyoncé's bedroom. Suddenly I heard Mathew kick Beyoncé's beloved Siamese. "Ugly-ass cat," he yelled.

When he started to descend the three little steps that led from Beyoncé's bedroom into the alcove, I fell to the ground, crawling at an unbelievable rate towards my kitchen. Had I stayed put, Mathew would have known instantly what had actually happened. My door was half-glassed. When he knocked, I moseyed right on up to it, as if nothing had happened. I could see the relief in his face. Once in front of the door, I nonchalantly unlocked it, opening it wide.

"Oh hey, Mathew," I said.

"Can you pick up the kids from school today?" Mathew asked.

I happily agreed and he left. Relieved, I collapsed on the sofa. I had been saved by the cat. Not only was I happy that I had escaped detection, I was also glad that the children hadn't heard their parents' violent exchange.

Checking the clock on my living room wall, I thought, "Oh, I better hurry." It was almost 3:00 p.m. Beyoncé and Solange wouldn't be looking for me. I'd have to park and go inside to pick them up. On the way to the car I couldn't help but wonder: *Who are these people?*

* * * * *

Tuesday was Mathew's basketball evening. Absolutely nothing came between him and Tuesday's basketball appointment. On this basketball Tuesday, I didn't know that Mathew had even left the house. I had no idea that Celestine didn't know that Mathew left the girls home alone, and often. The house was big, and Beyoncé was scared, understandably. She and Solange were too young to be left alone. If Beyoncé heard a creak or a sound, she would come back to my apartment to see if I was home, although she could see lights on. Normally she'd find me there, but unfortunately not on that Tuesday. I had stepped out briefly to run a few errands. Apparently a small problem had arisen, and Beyoncé called her mother at the salon to get some guidance on how to handle it. This time, when Celestine suggested that Beyoncé speak with her father, she discovered that the girls were home alone. She was horrified. A woman had just been arrested, only days before, on live TV, after authorities discovered her young children at home alone.

Celestine cancelled the rest of her appointments and rushed home. When I arrived back home, I could see from my apartment directly into the family room, where the girls were quietly watching television. I also saw Celestine. What was she doing home so early? I rushed down to see if everything was all right, and she began furiously to tell me what Mathew had done.

In the midst of her wrath, Mathew returned from his basketball date. Celestine hit the roof. With no regard for my standing there, she screamed, "What the fuck is your problem?" He replied, "What the fuck are you talking about now?" She screamed that he had left his children home alone. Not a bit remorseful, Mathew ignored her. She called him an irresponsible motherfucker.

Having already witnessed a few of their fights, I wasn't too surprised by Celestine's anger or by Mathew's outraged responses. But I was shocked when Mathew moved toward her with clenched fists and jaw, calling her several unmentionable things. He shouted at Celestine the im-

186

portance of his basketball Tuesdays, and that it was her damned fault if she hadn't arranged a sitter. I had never once seen a gym bag in his hands. I feared that he had been with his "basketball date," a woman who lived south of Houston. Ann, Kenny Moore (Ann's assistant), and I had often discussed Ann's disgust over Mathew's adulterous escapades.

After his comment about the sitter, I understood why Celestine's level of anger was, on a scale of one to ten, a fifteen. No matter how hard she worked, Mathew always found new and ever more disrespectful ways to minimize her efforts. The screaming and berating was reaching pressure cooker stage, and the look in Mathew's eye was like that of a wild animal just before charging.

I looked over and saw that Beyoncé's and Solange's faces were white with fear. Beyoncé had begun to cry. We had never seen her parents' fights reach this level. This was frightening to watch. I had to do something. Solange was shaking like someone on the verge of a nervous breakdown. Doors were slamming, Mathew was spouting off and punching things, Celestine was crying, and I knew I had to get the girls out of there.

Beyoncé and Solange had heard more than enough. I grabbed them, intending to escape to my apartment. Suddenly, Celestine screamed. "Fuck you, Mathew, fuck you! Don't you give a damn about me, or your kids? These are your motherfuckin' kids." To the horror of us all, Mathew viciously replied, "Fuck you and fuck them."

Whenever my stepfather had been on the war path, no matter the time of day or night, I had sprung into action. I had gathered my brother and sister and hid them, under the bed, in the closet, wherever I thought he wouldn't find us. It was dumb, because I wasn't really hiding from anyone, but it was the self-protective action of a frightened child. The screams – well, they would be just unbearable. I hadn't realized to what extent I'd slipped into that old defense mode until I heard Mathew shouting at Celestine, "Fuck you and fuck them." My heart stopped. Did the girls hear that? Of course they did, but I could only pray that they had not understood. We escaped to my apartment, and I closed the door behind us.

Later, I approached Mathew. He was very annoyed by what he called my "butting in" and told me to mind my own fucking business. I told him that their fighting affected my business and I insisted that I had a legitimate interest in the girls' welfare. He got extremely angry and said, "You don't need to worry about a thing. As soon as the fucking money starts rolling in that bitch will calm her ass down and fall in line, believe me." He was talking about Celestine. Did he just call her a bitch, again? Wow!

I ignored his anger and suggested that he tell me when he needed to go out and I would sit with the kids. It was unfathomable that Mathew never thought to tell me he was leaving. Maybe he didn't want me in his business, as he pointed out. And maybe he was right in saying that to me. But I believed he was on the road to destruction. If he didn't pull himself together, his family was going to suffer. In hindsight, I realize that my decision to take on being a "built-in baby sitter" spoke to my devotion and protection of the girls. What voice teacher volunteers to baby-sit? This one did.

* * * * *

While Mathew was figuring out how to market the girls and their career, he couldn't manage to figure out how to pick his children up from school. He forgot them so often that it became a problem with the school, and therefore at home as well. Open fights about the Knowles children erupted. Mind you, he had always been chronically late in getting the children to and from places, but up till now he had never been so completely "forgetful" of his parental responsibilities.

Beyoncé and her little sister, who attended The St. James Episcopal School, were often forced to wait on their father after school, sometimes until way after 6 p.m. Although it was normal for children to be picked up late – sometimes, parents did have to work unexpectedly long hours – Mathew consistently pushed the limits, and with no job for an excuse. The school's posted cut-off time was 5:30 p.m., and if Mathew hadn't shown up by 5 p.m. Beyoncé or Solange would call Celestine at the salon, sending out distress signals. Celestine was working like a slave and resorted to asking everyone, friends and even clients, to pick her children up from school. The Knowles family had only one car – her sporty maroon Chrysler LaBaron – and she had to be at her salon nonstop. Not to mention, Mathew often just took the car without asking her, leaving her stranded.

Mathew's tardiness in picking up his children became unbearable for Solange. The parents at St. James School, who once socialized with the Knowleses, had been discussing Mathew's inappropriate behavior, fodder for their gossip. Naturally, their children repeated what they heard at their dinner tables the next day at school. "Coke-head," they called him, echoing their parents' vile judgments. Little Solange took care of things her way. Kicking and hitting were *forbidden* at St. James but that didn't stop her from attacking her father in the school parking lot, while screaming at her him, "I hate you" and "You make me sick," words that said even under my breath as a child would've gotten me killed. Mathew had no reaction, even when she threw a school book, hitting him squarely in the back, kicking and swinging at him all the way to the car. He ignored her. Anyway, she was nothing to him but a "hellion," he said. However, this display of family affection caused a ruckus with the school's principal.

Mrs. Marjorie Tucker, wife of the St. James Church Pastor James Tucker, and the principal at The St. James School, was fighting mad about Solange's unladylike behavior and about having to wait *again with the Knowles girls*. Whenever Beyoncé and Solange were stranded, Principal Tucker would have to remain with them, because as principal she was ultimately responsible for their safety. To make matters worse, when Mathew did arrive he never showed remorse for being late, which Mrs. Tucker found insulting. She'd just witnessed Solange's response to the situation. Now she was at her wits' end and threatened to remove the Knowles children from the school's roster, effective immediately. Celestine did some fast talking, but Mrs. Tucker held her ground. I didn't know if it would help, but I suggested to Celestine that I might try to speak with Mrs. Tucker. With Celestine's approval and encouragement, I went to the principal, and, speaking as a respected member of the church, I told her why I had come.

"Thank you for seeing me, Mrs. Tucker. I want to talk to you about the Knowles girls."

"I know that you are close to the family and that you teach their girls group, but I am not really supposed to talk to you about Beyoncé and Solange."

"I understand and respect that," I said. "But I don't want to discuss them – *per se*. As a personal favor I am asking you to hear me out. Celestine works like a mad woman, and Mathew's schedule doesn't always allow him to pick the girls up punctually. So if you will reconsider, I promise to take on the responsibility. I promise that you will never have this problem again. I guarantee that I will pick the children up from school every day, and on time." Mrs. Tucker relented and agreed to allow Beyoncé and Solange to stay at St. James. Celestine thanked me and said she owed me one. "Think nothing of it," I said, but I knew that she had yet another hurdle to cross before her position at St. James cleared up.

Mrs. Tucker had hinted to me that neither Mathew's tardiness, nor his daughter's public outburst had been the only factors in her decision to dismiss the girls. I told her I didn't know about anything else, fearing where she was headed and I certainly didn't want to pry. Later, I learned from Beyoncé's teacher Ms. Western that Principal Tucker's concern was also about the Knowleses' late tuition payments. Celestine was severely in arrears. Once again hesitating to become too closely involved, I nevertheless felt it necessary to tell Celestine what I had learned. Celestine was the only one working and was a proud woman; she assured me that she immediately corrected the problem. Beyoncé and Solange were able to stay in school.

Beyoncé and Solange were always ready and waiting for me to pick them up, a responsibility I carried out daily. Having made a promise to Mrs. Tucker and to Celestine, as well as to Beyoncé and Solange, I arrived at St. James on time, without fail and for years. In addition, I found myself caring for the girls in other ways I had never imagined: cooking, driving them to appointments, overseeing their school homework and day-to-day workouts, lessons, and training. I fought within myself over my role in their lives.

* * * * *

On a typical evening, I would make, for instance, Three-Cheese Hamburger Helper, Beyoncé's favorite, for dinner – enough for three. I would ask her if she and her sister had finished their homework, and we would all get ready for dinner up in my apartment. I knew that Beyoncé didn't like the bland microwavable food her mother purchased for them to eat, so when she had any chance to eat my cooking she reveled in it.

Giving Celestine due credit, I know that she insisted on proper vitamins and minerals in her daughters' diet. I had additional motives, however, beyond concern for their general health. In order for Beyoncé to develop as a singer, she needed the right nutrients. In addition to avoiding sugar and too much wheat in our diet, I wanted to provide the vitamins and minerals that would support her developing body and brain.

Celestine, too, had additional motives: she obsessed about Beyoncé's weight. She was the self-appointed Food Police. Beyoncé as a little girl was a bit pudgy, but by no means fat. Still, her mother commented incessantly on what Beyoncé ate and insisted that she do nightly sit ups, reminding her of the sacrifices she would have to make as a *star* singer. That was painful to watch, and I never quite understood the weight attacks. Beyoncé developed bad feelings about herself and became self-conscious about her body, but she loved her mother and therefore was always obedient.

In my opinion Beyoncé had nothing to worry about so long as she took in sufficient protein and minerals. Vitamins B12 and C, as well as the mineral magnesium are all important to a singer and memory. I knew she would be just fine if I could promote those vitamins and minerals in her diet. So I took it upon myself to prepare the right foods for dinner for my-

191

self, because inevitably Beyoncé (and Solange) would end up in my apartment, sitting down to dinner, or snacking from the pots on the stove. I theorized that at Beyoncé's young age, she still carried what is termed "baby fat" and that when she got older her body would naturally re-shape itself, so I was never concerned about her weight.

Celestine and I both knew that if you wanted to make Beyoncé happy, just allow her to sit around in jogging pants and a t-shirt with a plate of cheesecake. She adored cheesecake. However, I would take the higher road to food happiness. In addition to cheesecake, she loved the chopped beef baked potatoes from the Brisket House, fish from Pappadeaux's, and hamburgers at Checker's. Whenever she would have an extraordinary lesson or would feel depressed, I would take her out to one of her favorite places for a vitamin-filled treat and we would talk. I let her talk about everything she was feeling. Her parents' spats (over money, or Mathew's absences) would bother Beyoncé tremendously, and our outings gave her a bit of peace. A deeply sensitive child, Beyoncé would adopt other people's issues as her own. She was way too young to understand that taking on her parents' troubles was unhealthy. It was going to take amazing effort on her part to remain the sweet girl that she was. I began to think about ways in which I could defuse her worries.

* * * * *

Ann paid for everything Girls Tyme needed; in addition, she often bailed the parents out of financial jams. She'd just given Celestine several thousand dollars. In February 1990, a federal tax lien had been placed on the Knowles property. Their house was in jeopardy but Ann's help saved the day. Unfortunately, we were not out of the woods. Celestine used only part of the money toward the debt. She used the rest of the sum to shore up her business by paying off the overdue rent on Headliners space in the mall. She was late on the rent. Ann, the lady that she was, disappointed but non-judgmental, said she understood. Her commitment was tremendous.

Ann even handled the scheduling and logistics of the girls' rehearsal times and places (usually held at the Knowles house – at Celestine's suggestion), leaving me free to supervise the artistic components of their work.

In spite of her strength and sense of pride though, Ann Tillman ultimately had to reveal that she had *Systemic lupus erythematosus.* (She had been diagnosed in 1989, but Ann hadn't talked about her disease with anyone.) Systemic Lupus is a painful, life-threatening autoimmune disease that attacks the skin, joints, blood, kidneys, and other vital organs. When a person has Lupus the body's immune system attacks its own cells and tissues. Ann never wanted anyone to worry about her, nor did she feel comfortable revealing the details of her condition, but she couldn't conceal it any longer. And now I understood more about her tears, earlier, as she had talked about her boys' future.

A few years earlier a college classmate of mine at Langston University had come down with Lupus. At that time, Althea and I had talked about her various options, researching treatments and programs she discovered that the University of Nebraska Medical Center, in Omaha, offered an aggressive therapy with outstanding results. I told Ann about our findings and she said she would look into it. "Maybe the doctors there could help you the same way they helped my classmate," I told Ann, hopefully. Perhaps it had been just plain luck for my classmate, but I was worried for Ann and wanted to offer her some form of encouragement. Not only was she ill with Lupus, but she was still grieving the tragic deaths of her husband and daughter, and was raising her two sons all by herself. The stress alone would prevent remission if she didn't rethink things.

In spite of her decreasing energies, Ann remained active in the girls' lives as their manager and she continued to work for the Houston Light and Power Company. On bad days she would say simply, "Today I have a flare-up." Although she never once complained I could clearly hear the worry in her voice and I prayed for her constantly.

I knew that Ann would have difficult days ahead of her and shared my concerns with Celestine in private. But then I found a new reason to worry. Could my "confidential" discussions with Celestine have had something to do with Carolyn's new-found concerns about Mathew's involvement? It seemed that indeed they had. Soon after Celestine and I discussed Ann's Lupus and its seriousness, Mathew increased his involvement with Girls Tyme – the behavior that had been worrying Carolyn. I vowed that I would not allow myself to be pulled in too deep, but it was inescapable. I was heavily invested by now. I was part of the family and my girls were a part of me.

In the meantime, Mathew Knowles, still unemployed, continued to investigate how he might control the "product," which is how he viewed his daughter and *"her group."* Those words sounded so nasty in his mouth. What did he mean by "product" or "her group"? This was not Beyoncé's group. However, I began to notice that Beyoncé also considered herself first amongst equals. Naturally, I corrected the behavior. She was the prodigy but her extraordinary talent would not ruin the group. I was determined not to let it. "Remember Beyoncé, it is more appropriate to love the art within yourself than yourself in the arts," I preached.

She listened.

* * * * *

My telephone rang incessantly off the hook in 1991-92. My vocal studio had started to develop a certain reputation. Having developed a solid technical approach for the popular singer – so that my students could achieve consistency and what I call "at will" singing – I had quickly acquired a waiting list of students. My girls too were garnering serious attention. Ecstatic that I had not ignored the unknown, I was having the time of my life. One phone call I took brought me my first boy band.

"Hello...I'm calling from Luke Records. I'd like to speak to David Lee Brewer," the male voice on the other end said.

"This is he," I said.

"Ah, Hello – I didn't expect to speak directly to you," the voice on the other line said. "I'd like to talk to you about a boy group we represent called H' Town."

A few weeks later, I met them, all marvelous talents, in my studio. Both their individual and group sound was interesting, but we worked to make it more grounded and more confident. The boys already presented with a masculine and virile sound, so I concentrated on their high notes and their sensitivity. They needed to learn what really fascinated females in the male voice. Their performance needed that certain sweetness. They were in the middle of recording their album and Yes, I delighted immensely in the reputation that I had worked so hard to build.

* * * * *

I was a stickler for great diction. Nothing got past me. My girls' breath could never flow at 100%, creating flawless legato, if the vowel and its placement were not correct. I told them the vowel must be immaculate.

In the meantime, divine influence (my still small voice) suggested I introduce Beyoncé to the opera *Carmen*. Was I hearing correctly? I had no clue why I was being given this directive, but I had learned my lesson with that attack by thugs on Houston's streets. I wasn't going to question or ignore my still small voice ever again. I gave Beyoncé my recording of *Carmen* with Grace Bumbry singing the title role, leaving her to make her own judgements. I felt that since Beyoncé's voice was clearly developing into a true mezzo soprano, she would naturally feel empathy with one of the great mezzo soprano roles in opera, the larger-than-life Carmen.

Beyoncé listened to the entire opera. She loved it, she said, but wanted to know who Grace Bumbry was.

"Grace Bumbry is my idol and mentor," I answered. "She is a trailblazer; a woman of many firsts. She changed a whole country's course on the question of race in culture."

Naturally, what I had just told Beyoncé intrigued her to no end. She wanted to know more and I answered her every question. I always did.

* * * * *

In 1991, I was in the throes of one of my Saturday conversations with Mrs. Melzia Bumbry, Grace Bumbry's mother, about her daughter's taking on the fiery role of Turandot (in Giacomo Puccini's opera of that title), when Beyoncé knocked on my door. She was early, again, for her lesson. Letting her in, I signaled to her that I was on an important call. I continued my pacing back and forth, which I do to this day. It helps me stay concentrated when on the telephone.

"I'll be off in a few minutes," I mouthed to Beyoncé, who disappeared into the kitchen. I knew exactly why. As I continued with Mrs. Bumbry I rounded the corner to the kitchen to see Beyoncé standing over the stove, spoon in hand, taste testing. I smiled. She giggled and replaced the lids on the cooking pots. She tired of the lean cuisine meals and sugarless Jello her mother required she eat. She wasn't allowed to eat like normal people. According to Celestine, Beyoncé was too fat. I remain stunned. It simply was not true. Beyoncé was *never* fat.

Mrs. Bumbry said that her daughter's management didn't want her to sing the icy Princess in Puccini's *Turandot*. Knowing Grace Bumbry by now, and being privy to the story of her career and her choices, I knew that she never left things to chance. Mrs. Bumbry knew this, as well, and assured me that Grace knew what she was doing.

Beyoncé was getting impatient. I gave her *that look* and she took a seat. I'd only be two more minutes, holding my fingers up.

Moments later, I bid Mrs. Bumbry a very fond adieu and we ended the call. Beyoncé was chomping at the bit. "Was that Grace Bumbry?" she asked. Having done her homework, she had read the program notes and knew a little bit more about the superstar singer's path. "No, that was her mother," I said.

"Her mother's still alive?" Beyoncé asked.

I laughed. "Of course she is." (In actuality, Beyoncé's question was only slightly premature. In July 1991, just six months after that telephone call with Mrs. Bumbry, she died. It was a sad day.)

Turning then to our work, Beyoncé and I began to dig into *Carmen*, the libretto and the score. When we got to one of Carmen's big arias, the "Habanera," it was clear to me that Beyoncé had been doing her own soul searching. She had learned to sing the aria not only note-perfect but with fiery feeling.

A few days later, Mathew was screaming into the telephone, shouting, "Girls Tyme needs to be about Beyoncé."

He was talking to Ann.

I wondered why Mathew was ignoring Beyoncé's wishes. She'd made herself clear. "I want to be in the group with my friends," she said.

We all heard it...

* * * * *

Mathew had finally taken a job. He hadn't worked since leaving Xerox and that was back in the late eighties. It was now 1992 and the IRS had become more than a nuisance. They were kicking down the Knowleses' door. Mathew's job was a day late and a dollar short, actually eleven thousand dollars short. Celestine was in over her head and didn't know what to do, she said. She was in arrears with her salon rent payments, her children's private school tuition was going up and she hadn't paid her mortgage in months.

Ann came to Celestine's rescue, loaning her the money to get out of debt. Celestine paid the back rent she owed to keep her salon open and running, and she paid the back mortgage on the house – "only" three months behind at that point. The 1990 IRS bill – some $11,000-plus – would have to wait. It had been a rough year and business, although good, wasn't going great. The rent was exorbitant on Montrose Blvd. I suggested to Celestine that maybe she should begin to look for other possibilities. She said she wanted to try and make it work. "It's such a great location," she said. It was true. Headliners Hair Salon had one of the best addresses in the city, but she couldn't afford it. I wondered why.

"Has Mathew talked to you about his job?" I asked.

"What about his job?"

"He hates it," I answered.

"What do you mean he hates it?"

"He told me just the other day when he came back to my apartment to ask what I thought would be questions about Beyoncé's future."

Mathew was indeed behaving strangely, but I took it as a good sign that he was finally gainfully employed. Nevertheless, when a man hates his job – and Mathew hated his with a passion – trouble is just around the corner. Mad as hell, he said he felt "underappreciated" and complained to me whenever he came back to my apartment. He wanted to "make some real money."

Picker International, the company that had hired Mathew in their medical equipment division, paid the "star salesman" (his words) less than Xerox had – considerably less, he whined.

Mathew Knowles cared about few things. However, he demanded many. Recognition was the cornerstone of his existence. If he didn't get recognition, he was miserable. At any rate, I thought that perhaps Mathew's having not worked for several years might have affected his perception of the insulting "sharp drop in salary." Celestine was just glad that he had a job and, quite frankly, I was too. The family was beyond desperate. How long could they keep the inevitable from their girls? I didn't know.

Mathew's new lease on life, at first a godsend to Celestine, quickly evaporated. She was losing control of her husband. Mathew was once again staying out late at night, and continuing to take Celestine's car from the salon. Embarrassed, Celestine would call me to pick her up. Friends weren't available, she said, which I found strange. She never called upon the people she claimed as her best friends. Perhaps she feared "the neighbors" finding out that she and her husband hated one another. He had started to steal money from the Headliners cash register. She suspected her best friend Vernell and actually accused her of stealing, but ultimately had to confess that it had been Mathew. In a teary scene, Celestine said that

Mathew's drug use had gotten out of hand. I knew all about it. I'd found a very small package of what appeared to be Mathew's wonder drug. It must have fallen out of his jacket pocket, onto the kitchen floor in the Knowles house.

Yes, Celestine had big problems, and so did I.

9. Solange

Solange Piaget Knowles was not only the youngest person in the Knowles house, but she was also the most authentic. There was nothing fake or hidden about her. Either she liked you or she didn't, and vice-versa. You knew where you stood with Solange. Incredibly independent, she was as ambitious as they come. I don't know why her mother was so convinced otherwise.

Mathew referred to his younger daughter, Solange, as "difficult." He maintained that she was defiant, aggressive, and unfocused. Beyoncé, having figured out how to please her parents, could do no wrong. Beyoncé was, from nature, the sweetest child you ever wanted to meet – a trait that endeared her to her father, since she offered no resistance to him, only unquestioning love. Solange was a hellion – again, his interpretation – and Mathew began ignoring her with a vengeance.

Solange wasn't even a thorn in Mathew's or Celestine's side. They patronized her dreams as though they were nothing. She almost didn't exist, and certainly her dreams of singing didn't. It didn't take long before the psychological ramifications of her parents' subliminal messaging began to manifest. Their overt support for, and focus upon, Beyoncé and "her damn group," as Solange called the girls, exacerbated what might have been a normal sibling rivalry. Solange, ever more defiant, set out to get her daddy's attention. Over the years she would force her father to see her by any means.

Outside the door of my over-the-garage apartment was an alcove – really, a walkway that connected my life to that of the Knowles family in the main house. This alcove/hallway was large enough to house a row of sturdy toy chests that contained all of Beyoncé's and Solange's toys. Practical Celestine had had them built, complete with leather-upholstered tops that could serve as seating. Beyoncé used them to lie on when she listened in on my private lessons – all of them, every day – putting her feet up against the wall, ankles crossed. I was used to encountering her there after the students would leave my studio. Or, after a long day of teaching I might say goodbye to my last student at the front door, when there would be a knock at the other door, at the alcove entrance. I would call out "Momento!" in my finest Italian, and there would stand Beyoncé, with her many questions and comments about what she'd been hearing through the walls.

As the months passed, expecting Beyoncé, I would open the door to find Solange. At first surprised, I soon became aware that she had witnessed her older sister's fascination and wanted also to eavesdrop on lessons, especially her sister's. On several occasions I mentioned to Celestine that Solange's talents and eagerness would be well served by having her own voice lessons with me. Celestine insisted that Solange was lazy and less talented and that Beyoncé was the one who needed the special attentions – private lessons with me, in addition to the group's lessons, coachings, and rehearsals.

Solange's effort increased and her longing to be seen had turned its attention in my direction. Trumping her sister, Solange wanted to sit in on Beyoncé's lessons, not in the alcove, but in the studio. Outside the door would no longer do. Beyoncé never said a word, and wouldn't have, even if she had been adamantly against her younger sister's intrusion. Celestine, still not convinced of Solange's serious desire to learn to sing, wasn't budging. Only Beyoncé deserved the lessons. With all Celestine was going through financially, I didn't want to push. Yes, Solange could absolutely sit in on Beyoncé's lessons, but I told her that she'd have to remain manageable – which meant quiet.

"Solange, you may not interrupt Beyoncé's lessons."

* * * * *

The Knowleses' kitchen became infamous during the Girls Tyme-to-Destiny's Child era. It was the place where dreams were made, broken, and stolen. In this kitchen the plotting outweighed the cooking. The Knowleses feasted on "food for thought," and Celestine and Mathew were the chefs. In the best of homes, the kitchen was where friends and family congregated for convivial gatherings over meal preparations and snacks; in this family, conviviality rarely surfaced, and things could turn sour very quickly. It became a personal chopping block, as Mathew and Celestine, in their increasing attempts to control "Beyoncé's" group, hatched their plans. You didn't want to be part of the discussion in the kitchen. If you escaped, you counted yourself fortunate.

It was there, in that kitchen, that Celestine would repeatedly have to face hard facts; it was there that I witnessed her creative attempts to save herself and her family. Conflicts with Mathew and conflicts with the outside world frequently erupted in that space.

A few days after I had allowed Solange to sit in on Beyoncé's lesson, Celestine called me early in the morning from the kitchen phone, nervous and upset. Could I do her a favor? Take the children to school? Rising from my bed, I put on a jogging suit and headed through the alcove toward the Knowles kitchen, wondering about Celestine's call and the reasons for her apparent distress. As I walked through Beyoncé's bedroom (where she never slept, preferring the comfort of sleeping with Solange in her adjoining twin bed) on the way to the main house, I passed Solange coming out of their bathroom. Beyoncé was doing her hair in Solange's room. I spoke briefly to both girls and headed downstairs. I believe it was shortly before 7:00 a.m. When I got to the bottom of the stairs, I made the immediate left turn, passed through the family den, and approached the kitchen table where Celestine sat, nervous and pensive.

"What is it, Celestine?" I whispered. She pointed in the direction of the door that led to the back yard, directing my gaze outside. I couldn't make out the tall man's features, but his Houston Light & Power uniform made it clear who he was. The man was checking the back yard meters. Celestine confessed to me that by tampering with the meters, she had been stealing electricity from the city of Houston. I had never seen her so upset – the kind of upset that said she feared the worst. Understanding her anxiety, I knew to get the children out the door in a hurry, ahead of any confrontation between Celestine and the HL&P man. She feared that he would come to the door, perhaps insist on coming into the house, perhaps…what? Whatever it would be, we knew that her daughters must not experience it. I ran back upstairs.

"Hurry girls," I said. "I'll drive you to school this morning, and we don't want to be late." I decided it would be best to remain upstairs. Having no idea when the HL&P employee might show up at the door, I didn't want either girl to go downstairs and see the "light man." My pacing back and forth irritated Solange.

"Solange, would you please hurry," I said – this time my voice elevated with my urgency.

"Dang, I'm coming," Solange said. "Why are you taking us to school anyway?"

In trying to rush Solange I had failed to notice that Beyoncé had gone downstairs before us. I ran down quickly, calling to Solange to hurry. "David – I am going as fast as I can," she said.

"Shit," I thought, as I once again entered the den. This time I could see Celestine on a telephone call. Her eyes signaled that I needed to hurry. She had taken up the telephone and pretended to be on a business call about the salon. Had Beyoncé bought it? I was not sure, but I do know that she was suspicious. Beyoncé mouthed the question, "Is everything all right?" to her mother. Celestine nodded yes and signaled for the girls to give her a goodbye kiss.

"Have a great day," she said.

Beyoncé, Solange, and I turned to leave the kitchen when suddenly Solange realized she'd forgotten a book she needed for class. "My God, Solange, please hurry. You guys are going to be late!"

202

Had my urgency been too telling? Beyoncé was giving me the eye and I feared that Solange had also sensed that something was off. Beyoncé became very distracted as I ushered them both out of the house and headed to my car. Solange, mumbling under her breath the entire time, reprimanded me for being so harsh. "God-Lee," she said as we finally exited the house.

When I returned from taking the girls to school I went straight into the kitchen. There sat Celestine, now crying uncontrollably. She had been caught red-handed in the crime of stealing electricity. If she had not been so tired the night before, too tired to go to the bank to make the salon's bank deposit, she would not have had the cash to bribe the HL&P employee. It had been the only way to stay out of jail. Celestine's theft, now obvious to the HL&P inspector, made her liable for immediate arrest. Ever creative, and now desperate, she had resorted to the resources at hand. The salon's moneybag lying on the kitchen table, marked for deposit, had been full of cash. Now it was quite flat; all the cash was gone.

Through her tears Celestine told me that it was either give the man all the cash or be taken to jail. She had been stealing electricity for years, not months, and that back bill was enormous. Her ploy had been successful, she was still with us, and her children wouldn't be any the wiser. When I asked how much the bill had been she said that it had been a little more than $1,000. I doubted her story, largely because, the night before in her fatigue, she had forgotten that she had already told me the amount of the night deposit in the envelope, which was much more than $1,000. She'd had one of the best days, and indeed weeks, that she'd had since opening the salon. God had been on her side it seemed, and I told her so.

All that was left in the deposit bag were the checks clients had written her. She prayed they wouldn't bounce. She hoped she had enough money to cover the mortgage – several thousand dollars, which she'd managed to save from Mathew's eager grip (money frequently disappeared from the Headliner's cash register when he was around). But is it enough? I asked. "No," she whimpered, "but I think I have enough to make payroll." She'd have to skip paying herself – again. After that, it was going to take a miracle to solve the mortgage dilemma. The bank had already been threatening foreclosure, she said.

In that moment, I felt such respect and admiration for Celestine. I saw her as an amazing woman. Like my mother, she was making it happen – suffering, but she was making it happen. She said that she would figure something out and thanked me for getting the girls out of the house. Beginning to cry again, she looked devastated and broken. I went upstairs and came back with a rather large envelope filled with cash. It was money I had been saving for a rainy day. I forced her to take $3,000.00, saying that now was not the time for pride. (She took it, and later she paid back every cent.) Mathew was not there that morning. It was 8:35 a.m., and she was late for work.

Celestine needed God's ever-loving grace, now more than ever.

* * * * *

Celestine was now reduced to bended-knee begging. Mathew needed to get another job. She needed help. He said he refused to go back to corporate America. He wanted to make the girls his new career, even though he had no plan how to make that happen. Ann was still manager, and I didn't see her relinquishing her position any time soon. Still, his selfish behavior, coupled with his vices, caused Celestine severe lack of sleep, and her hair, often unkempt in those days, began breaking off in her hand.

After the HL&P incident, whenever she could, Celestine made a special effort to hug and love her girls. She needed to feel special. She not only felt alone – she was. The financial reality of her situation was setting in. She had been late paying for Beyoncé's lessons so many times that I'd lost count. Whatever money she couldn't nail down, Mathew stole. She was losing more than she was taking in. That black hole just kept getting bigger and bigger. She would have to think of something fast, or she would go under.

The Knowles family car was constantly on the blink and she couldn't afford to buy a new one. She had to feed her children. She had to pay her

employees or lose them. And she couldn't take a part time job, because there was no time. Now, Mathew was telling his girls that he spent his nights at "Kinko's," spending thousands of dollars. Celestine backed his story. "Your father is at Kinko's," she would say. No matter how flimsy, her excuse for his behavior seemed to pacify them, and that was all that mattered then. After all, she rationalized, Beyoncé had sung for Teresa, which had to mean that Mathew's trips to Kinko's and his all-night "copying" were for "the family."

Tensions were on the brink of a total collapse. What the hell was he doing, I wondered? The Knowleses had long since stopped having manageable disagreements. Now they just avoided one another, barely speaking. Celestine lost it when she found out that Mathew, after leaving Picker International in 1992, had filed a lawsuit against his former employer, claiming racial bias. The out-of-court settlement provided him the money not only for his extracurricular pleasures at several Houston gentlemen's clubs, but also for massive amounts of cocaine. None of it went to the family. He was using. Celestine kept telling her children, "Daddy is at Kinko's."

Then Mathew went into rehab. Turns out, he had escalated to stronger drugs and even stranger behaviors. Rumor had it that cocaine had long since stopped satisfying his thirst, and had turned to crack cocaine.

By the end of 1992 Beyoncé's parents' strong dislike for one another, then avoidance, had finally turned to disgust. Celestine was losing control of her life and of Mathew, and I began to see below the surface of their hostile relationship. It wasn't pretty. I stayed focused on my girls and Beyoncé.

It could only get better. I just kept telling myself that, over and over again.

* * * * *

Now Celestine informed me that Beyoncé had asked to take more voice lessons, four per week to be exact. Naturally I was hesitant. How would she afford this? She hadn't paid for Beyoncé's lessons in months. The

205

other girls, Ashley and Kelly, were getting only one lesson per week. And what about Beyoncé's little sister, Solange? Were they really not concerned about Solange's feelings of neglect and insecurity? Solange also wanted to be a singer, she said. What about the potential rivalry caused by all the extra attention Beyoncé was getting? Solange already knew that Beyoncé was her parents' priority and she sometimes expressed anger with Beyoncé and "her damn group."

"Do they have to rehearse for so long?" Solange would ask me. "When are they gonna stop? Dang."

The competition between the two became apparent, and Celestine finally asked, "David, can you give Solange a lesson or two? Maybe she would feel better."

I couldn't believe my ears. Hearing Solange's incessant appeals, Celestine could no longer deny her cries.

"Mama, when am I gonna get to sing? I want voice lessons like Beyoncé." She began to ask me regularly, "David, when is my voice lesson?"

Just thinking about Solange tugged at my heartstrings. I found myself more often than not thinking of the Knowles girls before thinking of myself. Although I was there primarily for Beyoncé, I had become sort of a father figure to both Knowles girls. I loved Solange, too. Celestine knew that I adored both of her children and that I would go out of my way for them. Now Solange's talk about singing increased with each passing day and Celestine was being forced to address it.

"David, please. Solange is wearing me out. Can you just give her a little voice lesson – just to make her feel better?"

I let loose a resounding, "What?!"

* * * * *

Celestine told me on several occasions that Solange "changed her mind with the wind." Naturally, since she was Beyoncé and Solange's mother, I

206

wanted to believe Celestine, even though everything I knew about Solange told me that her mother was off base. "Celestine, that child wants to sing and dance," I said. "She has real talent." "Ah – David – Solange is not serious. I don't have money to waste on her," she repeated.

Both of us July babies, Solange and I were kindred spirits in many ways. I understood her ambition and offered her real support where I could. Solange's desire to sing was becoming more and more pressing. One day I heard Beyoncé practicing. Confused as to why she was making mistakes in exercises that she had done perfectly so many times, I opened the door to inquire. At the end of the alcove, pacing in Beyoncé's room, staring in the direction of my apartment, was Solange.

I would have to speak to Celestine, even though I dreaded that conversation. I knew how it would end. Solange had a great head on her shoulders and could focus for hours on things that interested her. Celestine had been so certain that she never took anything seriously that even I began to question Solange's motives. Still, I spoke to Celestine, this time insistent. There was no other way. Solange was going to explode if something didn't happen in her favor – and soon.

When Celestine arrived home, we met as usual at my apartment to discuss the girls' day. If there was anything that she needed to know about, late night was the time to talk about it. I was already giving Kelly lessons for free, and Beyoncé's lessons were being paid sporadically. On this evening I questioned, "How about instead of Beyoncé taking four lessons, Solange gets one of her sessions?"

"No, I think Beyoncé needs her lessons," Celestine said.

So, I taught Beyoncé four private lessons a week (two now gratis) and added Solange to my studio as well, giving her lessons gratis, from my heart. Sympathetic with the child's frustrations, I wished I could have done more for her, but it was clear that her parents' focus was always on Beyoncé. Although I knew why, it didn't feel right that I wouldn't be able to give her lessons consistently. My private voice studio was full and I had started teaching school again – high school English – but when a student cancelled, which was not often, I would give Solange a lesson.

In one of Solange's lessons she snapped at me. Without thinking, I quickly told her that if she didn't want to do what I was asking of her she could "get out." She calmed down and we finished the lesson. There was tension between us that evening when I went downstairs. I gave her a big hug, told her that I loved her and that she could have a lesson the next day. She smiled, and all was well between us again.

I really liked Solange. I had to remind myself that she was just a child when she behaved like a brat. She was always running around the house in a tutu and whenever she had had enough of Beyoncé and her group, she'd call her best friend, Coline Creuzot, over to play. That always meant work. Both little girls had their own ambitions of making it in show business and they would take over the space to develop one of their "modern dances." Everyone had to assemble quietly in the den, myself included, to watch their interpretations. They were actually quite charming, and I felt with proper guidance Solange and Coline could be good. (Coline's mother wanted her to have a childhood and to progress naturally.) But again, within the Knowles family, Solange's talent was regarded as insignificant in comparison to that of her older sister. Not once did Celestine ever voluntarily ask to hear Solange sing, as she often did with Beyoncé.

Having – at least for the time being – secured Celestine's support for my giving formal lessons to Solange, I felt free to turn my attentions to Beyoncé's education. Although still only ten years old, she was advancing rapidly in understanding and skill.

Beyoncé worked harder than anyone I had ever seen and she was driven to be the best. She was an absolutely brilliant pupil, and I would have climbed a mountain to give her vocal lessons. A teacher loves seeing the quest for knowledge in a protégé's eye. Beyoncé really wanted to know the answers and was so easy to teach. She never missed an opportunity to quiz me about a particular singer, their improvements, their mistakes or something that I had said to them. While she should have been doing her homework, she was listening in the alcove, feet up and crossed at the ankles – daily. Inevitably there would be a knock at the door when a singer finished a lesson and Beyoncé would start in with her questions. Sporting the biggest smile, her eyes were wide open. I could read in them that she hungered for more knowledge, especially musical knowledge.

"Was that the nice lady with the big voice? How does she sing so loud? When will I be ready to sing like that?" She referred to my private opera student Carole Dodson, who had a huge sound with a poignantly focused top voice. In addition, she questioned me about Freddie Abney's high notes and runs, then about Cecilia Jackson's robust low tones. Freddie and I had begun working on her first classical recital material, to be performed at Wheeler Avenue Baptist Church the next year. Singing was Beyoncé's life, and for her, every second of every day had to be spent learning something about music. She even asked if she could sit in on Freddie, Carole and Cecilia's lessons. All three ladies agreed. Then Beyoncé began asking if she could sit in on several of my other private students' lessons. I remember a particularly funny situation involving one of those students.

Tony Coles was an impeccable musician who played organ, piano, saxophone, and clarinet, all with a high degree of proficiency. He'd been first chair in the All-City and All-State Orchestras in high school, as well as a promising track star. He was absolutely brilliant – but wayward. He had a difficult time focusing. Nevertheless, his ambition was ever present.

Tony was an all-or-nothing kind a guy. His vocal material was interesting, a la Otis Redding, but his attitude at the age of twenty left me in perpetual, silent screaming mode; if I could only get him to focus.

When I asked if Beyoncé could sit in on his lesson, he emphatically said, "No." The story that follows explains why.

Tony had been hired to play for the recital of my student Freddie Abney. During the entire rehearsal process Tony had been rather understated in his demeanor. Passive almost. After the recital was over, Tony started showing up at my house. He'd heard about what was going on over at my house, he said. When I asked him what he meant he said that students in the music department at Texas Southern University were talking about me.

It soon became clear what they were saying. While Tony visited, listening in on other people's lessons and trying to get me to teach him, he heard Beyoncé singing "Silent Night" in her bedroom. She and I had begun working on the art of improvisation. We studied jazz, both stylistically and historically, with the intent of developing improvisational facility for her pop-recordings-to-be. She listened to the jazz great Sarah Vaughan and a newcomer, Rachelle Ferrell, who for me is the absolute truth in singing.

"Who's that?" Tony asked.

"Oh, that's Beyoncé. She's going to make a million dollars one day."

"Uh – and just how do you know this?" Tony asked.

"Because I am going to make sure of it," I said.

Intrigued with ten-year-old Beyoncé's improvisation skill, Tony listened intensely as she turned the phrase one way and then repeated it, turning it again, this time differently from the time before.

"So that's the little girl everybody says gets all of your time."

I asked Tony to repeat himself.

"Oh, nothing," he said.

I pushed. Had I heard him correctly? And who was everybody?

In Tony's mind, an ever-present feeling began to emerge. Beyoncé was robbing him of me. "She gets all your time," Tony said. "What about us?" he added.

I couldn't help thinking that other students felt the same way as Tony did. Were they, too, feeling cheated? At any rate, it wasn't long before Tony and Beyoncé met. He'd shown up to my house to listen in on lessons, and Beyoncé was in the studio. I didn't think anything of it until we started working on "Precious Lord," and Tony offered his opinion.

"Uh – Beyoncé, your style is off in that phrase," he said.

Beyoncé looked at me. I in turn looked at him. He was out of line, but my stare had absolutely no affect. An expert on liturgical music, Tony felt compelled to help Beyoncé understand how one sings Gospel music.

The man has lost his senses, I thought. He might be right about style, but he was out of line to interrupt a teacher's lesson with another student.

Tony stood up and moved in our direction, towards my keyboard, but the sharp movement of my head screamed that he should sit back down, which he did. He was clearly not thinking straight.

He would later tell a reporter. "David Lee Brewer is one of the most patient people I have ever met…" But, "…as long as you don't get in the way or say anything about his teaching. Oh my God! The sting is worse than any scorpion's bite."

He was right. I laughed on the outside, but on the inside I wanted to kill him. And I was glad that he'd noticed. I have always taken my work seriously.

At Tony's next voice lesson, Beyoncé decided to listen in from her perch outside the door. At the end of his time, Tony went into the toilet. He had been in there several minutes, and since Beyoncé hadn't heard any talking, which usually meant the student had gone out my front door, she knocked at the back hallway entrance.

"Who was that?" she asked.

"Oh, that was Tony."

"Oh…" A long silence followed. Then, after plopping down on the couch Beyoncé said, "He's going to need lots of work."

I almost choked.

It took Tony another fifteen minutes to exit the toilet after hearing what Beyoncé had said. He was undone. When he finally emerged, Beyoncé, whose face had turned red from embarrassment, said, "Oh, hey Tony." Tony didn't say a word, and it was an awkward moment for everyone.

Needless to say, Beyoncé was not welcome in Tony's lessons…ever. Nor did he ever again inquire about hers.

No problem. He had other singers he could listen to. Country singer Chris Gardner came often to lessons with his sons, Max and Kyle, who played with Beyoncé and Solange whenever their father and I worked. Cecilia Jackson also allowed Tony in her lessons. He listened in on Monroe Shannon and Carlondria Dixson's lessons, too.

* * * * *

It was scary. Beyoncé's attitude about music and singing reminded me of me when I was her age. I have never had a student who asked as many questions as she did. Inquisitive was her middle name, and she was always at my apartment, listening, learning and probing my brain, which had made it difficult for me to deny Celestine's request for an increased number of formal lessons, at a huge discount (gratis). In the interim, I committed to teaching Solange as often as I could.

"Feel your feet against the floor, Beyoncé."

Beyoncé was getting good at this. We had identified her sit bones (the big knob called the trochanter at the end of your thigh bone), which if you sit in a chair and place your right and left hand under your butt cheeks, you can feel by moving your hips from side to side.

"It's physiology, Beyoncé," I said.

Following the physiological aspect of movement freed her and the other girls' bodies completely. "It starts with understanding the function of the hips."

Since she was going to be outside my door anyway, lying on her back with her feet up crossed at the ankles on the wall, she might as well get some good hip practice in while she listened in on other people's lessons. I turned everything into a lesson, including how she ate, sat, used her hands to talk, smiled, frowned, laughed and now, even lying on her back, which was not as passive an action as she had thought.

"When you lie here, Beyoncé," I said, pointing, to the leather upholstered benches in the alcove, "utilize the time to become more aware of your own body, your hips and your sit bones.

"Lightly press the ball of your right foot into the wall, and release it. Then the left."

She did as I asked.

"Do it again."

She did.

"Turn it into a game." I added, "Reposition your feet." I told her that one time she could place her feet on the wall perpendicular, one time turning them out, and another by placing one foot slightly higher than the other, "but keep them parallel," I reminded. "The pelvis will move accordingly, every time you press your foot into the wall."

"Like this?" Beyoncé asked.

"Yes, that is good," I said.

"What if I put my feet here?" she asked me.

Beyoncé had moved her feet to a position that was too low on the wall.

"Try to move your hips," I said.

It was difficult for her. And with that, she had her answer.

"I wouldn't suggest going so low that your hips lock themselves. That defeats the purpose of the exercise, which is about perfecting your posture. The goal is free breath for healthy singing. It will also help me help you learn to rise up out of your lower back." Beyoncé, like many women, sat too deeply into her pelvis, which not only looks bad (slumping), but also adds extra stress on the body, not to mention, on the breath.

The next day, my private student Freddie Abney had a lesson. After letting her into the apartment, I rushed back to Beyoncé, who was waiting for me to monitor the hip exercises. As Freddie got settled, she couldn't help notice that Beyoncé was outside the door and that we were doing some strange maneuvers. Unable to help herself, she came out into the alcove and inquired.

"What is that?"

I explained that I was working on fluidity in Beyoncé. "I am preparing Beyoncé for later lessons in the God experience."

"The God experience?" Freddie asked.

"Yes," I said. "Remember our talks about breath and spirit." Breath is connected to spirit. Spirit is connected to God, and any disturbance of spirit affects the breath.

Freddie remembered. But now Beyoncé's inquisitiveness had been piqued.

"When will I learn the God experience?" she asked.

Beyoncé woke every day asking me about what she would learn that day. "One thing at a time, my little ambitious one," I would say to her.

In a nutshell, the God experience in the performance of singing, sport, dance, painting or any other form of art that requires breath and movement, is truth at its most powerful. It begins with learning to achieve complete fluidity and balance in the body and ends with synchronizing breath and emotion.

"Since all movement, even turning one's head, begins in the hips, it is crucial to understand the hips first," I told Beyoncé.

While Beyoncé continued to practice, Freddie and I began her lesson. She had learned the same set of exercises but differently, I told her. I had asked her to walk around the room, while swinging her arms freely. I had also asked her to march while doing the same thing, raising the feet no more than six inches off the ground.

Today I have my students sit, rocking back and forth.

* * * * *

"Beyoncé, where are your shoes?" Celestine asked.

It drove Beyoncé's mother crazy that she walked around barefoot.

"Put some shoes on," Celestine prodded. "That is why your nose is always stopped up."

Celestine insisted that Beyoncé had been waking up hoarse.

"Celestine, Beyoncé is not hoarse and she has never been hoarse. There is a difference between waking up with a rasp and waking up hoarse," I said.

Beyoncé suffered from chronic sinusitis. The antibiotics her mother gave her weren't helping. Then Celestine took her to the doctor. When they returned, Celestine came back to my apartment.

"David, the doctor said that Beyoncé has nodules."

"What? Beyoncé does not have vocal nodules," I said. Outraged by the implication, I assured Celestine that her doctor was flat out wrong.

Completely irritated, I told Celestine that nobody gets vocal nodules at the age of ten. Beyoncé had no medical issues that would support such an odd diagnosis. "Beyoncé definitely doesn't have nodules – or polyps. My ears would have alerted me to those conditions. Their effect on the tone and breath is unmistakable."

214

The next day I picked up Beyoncé from school and took her to see Dr. Stasney, who confirmed that she had neither nodules nor polyps. He did, however, feel that young Beyoncé should consider having surgery to clear her sinuses. I suspected that he might say as much, but surgery was out of the question. Her parents had no insurance. Instead, I shared with Dr. Stasney how I had been helping her find relief.

"I have Beyoncé lie down on the sofa in my living room, while I wash my hands thoroughly. When I return I tell her to open her mouth. Standing behind her, facing the top of her head, I place my forefinger directly onto the middle of her soft palate (the soft area in the back of the roof of the mouth) and press lightly."

Dr. Stasney smiled, "...and the mucous runs freely," he said.

"Exactly," I answered.

When I placed my finger directly onto the middle of Beyoncé's soft palate and gently pressed, maintaining the applied pressure and not moving my finger, all the accumulated mucous began to release, just as Dr. Stasney said.

"Beyoncé, keep the mucous from going down your throat until the most opportune time to spit it out," I would say to her.

Within minutes, she would have cleared the blockage (the size of a small city) in her head, and we were then free to warm her up and sing. Suddenly, Beyoncé's voice would be absolutely clear, completely devoid of any and all bi-noise from the mucous. I simply repeated this non-surgical method as needed, and we pressed on.

Noticing that Beyoncé would remain free of the mucous for days, Celestine was delighted that her daughter had found relief.

"Thank God," Celestine said. "I'm glad she doesn't have nodules."

Answering her with an "I told you so" wouldn't have served anyone or anything. I did, however, remind Celestine that as long as Beyoncé followed the rules of good singing, she would remain nodule free.

* * * * *

I was in an awkward position – living in the midst of the Knowles household, deeply committed to the girls' artistic training, privy to confidential conversations with Celestine, trusted by Carolyn and Ann (both of whom I respected), and too trusting and unsure of how to maintain my balance. Carolyn had her feelings and I respected them and her. I sensed that she wanted my insights and opinions about Mathew's trying to take over management, but I had neither, even though I lived with the Knowles. I certainly knew that things were terribly off with the Knowles family. A strange energy permeated the environment.

I could not formulate any explanations that would help me understand the Knowleses' actions. Once again, I decided they were not my concern – and I chose to ignore them. Ann was a smart woman, and I felt her role as manager was secure. Surely she knew how to handle her business.

David's peace was getting away from him, and it scared me.

I held my tongue…

10. 3 Stars

I kept my mind focused on the powerful charge that I had received. "She will be the biggest star in the world, teach her everything," it said, that still small voice I often heard. Those words had become my mantra.

The recollection of this single thought kept me vigilant, helping me to ignore those constant warning signals going off in my head about Celestine and Mathew. Soon the girls and I would be thrown into what was probably the most important performance of their young careers, at least to them anyway – "Star Search." It would prove to be a milestone event, teaching Beyoncé and the other girls the importance of thinking things through.

Although the girls were ecstatic in anticipation, their television debut would end in disappointment, as Girls Tyme lost the competition. That loss would inspire my increased determination to stand by my principles. As for Mathew: Seizing the opportunity to take control, he would bully his way into the management of Girls Tyme. Convinced that his daughter was his one true way to fortune, he walked over anyone who stood in his way. *His gold mine* was worth fighting for and he'd set out, fanatically using Beyoncé, to achieve complete control. Long after returning from a short "vacation" to a rehab facility, where he had battled cocaine addiction, he set his secret plan in motion. The drugs weren't the only thing that made him feel powerful. The very idea of having complete control gave birth to a monster – full of rage, heading towards disaster. Things were getting eerily weird.

* * * * *

My girls and I had been enjoying every minute of our painstaking and demanding work. We weren't pressured for time, which meant having the freedom to sort out every aspect of their artistic footing and development. I was proudest of Kelly in 1993, who despite her chronic sadness had made great gains. She was going to be a phenomenal talent.

Then, my joy in teaching turned to anxiety when the group's manager, Ann Tillman, dropped a bomb on me. Until now, I had been concentrating on maintaining low-key, non-stressful performance experiences for Girls Tyme, knowing full well that it took time for the brain to catch up with ambition. Their local appearances before relatively small audiences constituted little warmups to an eventual career in major spotlights.

Now, without my knowing it, and with good intentions, Ann had worked on arranging the girls' participation in a nationally televised talent competition. With only three weeks' notice, she informed me that the girls had been selected from thousands of applicants to compete on the nationally syndicated show "Star Search."

She announced her coup proudly in a telephone call to me, "This is something that is going to bring the girls to the attention of the world."

"Yikes," I said. "But Ann, we don't have sufficient time."

"I understand your anxiety," she said. "You are the girls' teacher, but if you feel unprepared…"

"Excuse me," I said, cutting her off. My back was beginning to arch itself and my ego had reared its ugly head. Had she just accused me of slacking off? Of not being prepared? Sensing my new-found levels of testosterone, Ann quickly praised my work.

"Please don't misunderstand me. It was the work you've been doing with the girls that got us noticed. The folks at 'Star Search' and the new producer were impressed with the girls' sound. They called it refined."

The ego is a shameless thing. With that single statement Ann had put my back down and began to win me over. But I have to admit, my problem wasn't really about ego. Kelly Rowland needed years of dance instruction to bring her up to speed, and solving that problem in just three weeks was going to take incredible effort, on all our parts.

"How did the girls come to the notice of 'Star Search'?" I asked Ann.

"We sent a video tape," Ann said. "It was Arne's idea to make it out in California when we were out there recording."

"Who is Arne?" I asked.

"Arne Frager is a major music producer in Sausalito, near San Francisco," Ann answered. Then she asked if I'd heard of the legendary recording studio in California called "The Plant."

"Yes," I answered. I'd heard lots about it from Roy Brown. Many powerful performers have made groundbreaking records over the years (the likes of John Lennon, Queen, Aerosmith, Bruce Springsteen, Frank Zappa, and Jimi Hendrix, to name a few) at The Plant.

"Well, Arne is the owner," Ann said. "He got us on 'Star Search.'"

According to Ann, Lonnie (our Alonzo Jackson) had played the girls' demo for Arne. "Lonnie called me right away, going on and on about how excited Arne was about the girls' sound, and how he couldn't believe they were twelve- and thirteen-year-olds."

After hanging up, I began to make sense of various shards of information I'd gathered. I knew that Ashley and Beyoncé had been flying out to California, to lay down tracks with Lonnie, and now I knew why. Immediately, I headed over to the main house. Maybe Mathew was home. I can't begin to tell you why I thought talking to him would give me solace, but I needed to talk to someone. "Star Search" was a mistake.

As I approached the den, I could hear Carolyn, Ashley's mother, fairly shouting her rage at Mathew. She seemed to be accusing him of foul play. Apparently Arne, Ann, or Lonnie – I hadn't figured out who – had taken Ashley off her solos. Beyoncé was scheduled to re-record her vocals. Mathew claimed that it was not his doing. "I am not the producer, Arne is," he said. I slowly made my way down the stairs, just as Carolyn stormed past me and out the front door. Mathew, stood there, orgasmic, with a shit-eating grin on his face, clearly proud of himself for provoking Carolyn, gloating over her discomfort. What the hell was going on, I thought?

"What was that about, Mathew?"

"Oh, Carolyn's just being emotional," he answered.

I was sure I knew the problem. Lonnie, whom Mathew had wound around his finger, was very likely the reason for the injustice that Ashley had experienced. Lonnie had disrupted our peaceful work more than once. I knew also that he and Mathew shared certain weaknesses – among them, a great, uncontrollable sexual appetite. No wonder they were best buddies. I thought it strange that, all of a sudden, Ashley was a problem in the studio. Lonnie had been berating her, complaining that she was "slow" to deliver in the recording process. Ashley was anything but slow, either in her delivery or her willingness to work hard.

I called Ann.

She explained to me that Ashley's attempts at giving Lonnie what he wanted in the recording studio had been failing miserably. Beyoncé, who had been sitting patiently, awaiting her turn to sing her part, had squirmed about. When she was asked if she thought she could do better, she answered yes. Ashley was then taken out of the studio. Ann had decided. "OK, show me what you can do," Ann said. Beyoncé nailed it, on the first take, and she always would. She was gifted that way.

"Oh my God, Ann, you removed Ashley from her solo because you finally saw Beyoncé's prowess in the recording studio?" I asked. "Beyoncé's studio 'gifts,' are normal for her. They are not special. She is prodigious. She will always hear music and see its structure earlier than the other girls."

Beyoncé saw music as a mathematical formula. She saw and analyzed it with *other eyes and ears*, sensibilities that only the prodigious have. I recognized this and knew what it meant. Ann did not. So, at the end of the day, Ann had made an uninformed decision, one that led us into a quagmire.

Ann's decision had been about the bottom line, about saving valuable recording time. I discovered during our conversation that her savings were dwindling. She'd spent a small fortune already, on her family and friends, as well as a significant amount on Girls Tyme (the group and the parents) and loads on the Knowleses. She'd bailed them out more times than I can remember. "I only thought about efficiency. Beyoncé gave me that," Ann said. "Time is money," she concluded.

My response was, "But it's not Ashley's fault if no one could translate what was being asked of her in the studio."

"It was a decision that I didn't make lightly," Ann said. She said she felt bad, having now realized what she'd done, "but that ship has sailed."

"Still, I wished you had talked to me about it. I could have explained to you and Lonnie the *natural phenomenon of Beyoncé in the recording studio* and thus saved Ashley, and myself – all of us! – the heartache. This has gotten way too messy, Ann."

"I know I've said this," I continued, "but I want to re-iterate that I think you're making a huge mistake, Ann. But it is yours to make."

Carolyn had every right to be upset, but Ann chose not to confirm her suspicions, nor did anyone else. That would have served no one, she said. Celestine said, "What's done is done." Mathew gloated, clearly reveling in his triumph. From me he had learned about Beyoncé's talent and extraordinary gift in music; he used that information to tell Ann (and everyone else) that Beyoncé was the best. Now his daughter had just proven his/my point by her outstanding performance in the recording studio. This situation felt hauntingly evil, as though some outside force had us by the throat and none of us knew how to break the curse. Now, I stood in the middle of a conflict, a battle that had everything to do with Ashley and righteousness. Would she make it?

With Ann's feelings of guilt and Carolyn's anger, the Knowleses were content. They savored the moment when Beyoncé could now take her "rightful" place in front.

Beyoncé, however could not share in her parents' happiness. She hated the strife her skill had caused, taking it very personally. She apologized to Ashley profusely, which proved to be the road to our escape from this swamp. Ashley accepted Beyoncé's apology, and we were able to move on, concentrating on the task at hand. The simplicity of children…what a beautiful thing.

Even with my misgivings about the "Star Search" project, and everything else I'd learned from Ann, I opted to bite the bullet and do everything I could to salvage what little integrity this mess might contain. I thought, if Ashley and Beyoncé could make peace with one another, I too could let go my attitude and concentrate on helping my girls. After all, that is why I was there.

Still, several key factors outside my control threatened to break my resolve: namely, too many chefs in my well-organized kitchen. Egos were on full blast. My girls knew nothing about television. They were both excited and nervous as hell. Nervous energy threatens performance. For them "Star Search" was a huge opportunity. For me it was a nightmare, but I knew what I had to do.

"Girls, I want to tell you a story," I said. "Do y'all know who Albert Einstein is?"

"Duh," LaTavia said.

"OK, Miss Smarty Pants," I answered. "Well, did you know that Einstein was a virtuoso on the violin?"

They looked at one another, wondering where their crazy teacher was headed.

"A little known fact, Albert Einstein was a terrible student. His teachers called him stupid, suggesting his parents think about removing him from school and that he be put into a program where he'd be trained for an easy manual labor job. Insulted, his mother bought him a violin instead."

Beyoncé perked up. "What happened?" she asked.

"I'm glad you asked, Beyoncé. Brain power is what happened next. Einstein used music, and his violin, to relax his mind. He was able to access his subconscious."

I paused for effect. "And that is what we are going to do, right now."

From that moment on, we would begin every group session listening to music, calming music written at 60 beats per minute. My goal was to focus on Kelly's memory and her relaxation, very necessary to the success of our new challenge. Negative energy permeated the Knowles house, and seeped into my studio. Just because Ashley and Beyoncé had moved past the recent issue, Kelly was still scared shitless. Fear is yet another energy, a very debilitating one. I returned to the basics: mind, body, and soul. I would work with their subconscious mind, the "alpha state," and thereby regain a much-needed focus.

I recalled a lecture my eurhythmics professor had given about the power of music to promote super learning, using harmonious, expressive bodily movements in response to improvised music. Certain types of music ease the brainwave pattern taking it into what is called the "alpha state." Adagio movements in classical music, which are around 40 to 60 beats per minute, are perfect thematic material to evoke peace and activate emotion. It is that music, and its slow rhythm, that calms the body and mind functions enough to allow the alpha state of mind to take over. It was going to be the most effective way to increase Kelly's ability to retain the dance steps, calm Ashley's beating heart, and soften Beyoncé's shame.

I walked over to my record collection and found Bach's Cello Suite No. 1 in G major, BMV 1007. I knew that the 60 beats per minute module would work, especially for Kelly, whom I particularly wanted to reach with this method. It would help me to redress her insatiable need for using will power in the wrong way. "Remember, Kelly, we don't force a thing.

We get out of the way and allow it to happen." She knew exactly what I meant. So did the other girls.

"Close your eyes," I said.

They did.

The music started and just like that, there was calm. You could actually feel the tension leave the room. The music had drawn them into relaxation, immediately relieving their stress. Their brains were moving toward a repetitive state receptive to contemplation, which promoted the relaxation and focus I sought. After they listened, I spoke. Softly, so as not to disturb their openness, I explained that I wanted them to listen again.

"This time allow the music to awaken an emotional response in you." I didn't care if it was irritation, as long as they felt something and could articulate it. Getting to great performance begins with imagination, then come questions, conflict, answers, and finally sensitivity. That is where greatness lives.

"OK girls, now we are going to activate kinetic energy." I asked them to stand flat footed, letting their arms hang to their sides. "When the music begins, I want you focused on its calming nature. Let the emotion you feel take control of your mind, body and soul. With your eyes closed, simply let your arms begin to take the weight of your relaxed body. They will begin to feel heavy." When that happened they would be entering a subconscious state. Afterwards I asked them, simply and effortlessly, "to give your mind the command to begin raising your arms, staying focused only on the thought." It took a few tries, but eventually their arms begin to levitate upwards, on their own.

To avoid the risk that the exercise might become boring for Beyoncé and Ashley, who didn't share Kelly's rhythmic problem, I changed the focus every twenty minutes, increasing the difficulty of our work beat by beat. Within a week, camaraderie had returned to our group lessons. The girls would be just fine. Bit by bit, Kelly began to catch on; she was dancing, and in much better rhythm. For the first time her body could anticipate movement. It was beautiful to watch her come into her own. Beyoncé and Ashley – indeed all the girls – were unashamedly supportive.

These lessons began my asking the girls for a six-day week. By the weekend, Ann called. A new decision had been made. Beyoncé was now singing the lead on "All about My Baby," the song they would ultimately perform on "Star Search." That decision put us right back into the mess I'd hoped to have escaped. That song had been set on Ashley! and now this. Emotions again spiraled to a new high. That made me crazy.

"What the hell happened to 'Sunshine?'" I asked.

"Switching to 'All about My Baby' feels better, more today," Ann said. "'Sunshine' is too ballad driven."

"Yes, but "Sunshine," is a song for *singers*. It's what got them noticed," I said. "Not to mention, Beyoncé and Ashley share the lead in 'Sunshine.'"

"True, but 'All about My Baby' can include Nikki, Nina, and LaTavia into the performance for 'Star Search.'"

Ann had a point, but I sensed there was more to this story. I called Lonnie, out in California.

"Lonnie what are you doing?" I asked.

"What do you mean…"

"You know what I mean. You are a musician. You know that 'All about My Baby' is not right for Beyoncé's voice. The key is too low, and Ashley has the stronger chest voice at the moment," I answered.

"I changed the key to fit Beyoncé's voice," Lonnie said. "I think she will do the song the best justice."

I walked around Lonnie's explanation, looking for another window to enter. Perhaps he'd understand, "Look, Lonnie, the tessitura is all wrong in 'All About My Baby.'" (In singing, "tessitura" refers to a song's most musically acceptable and comfortable range for any given singer.) "It sounds as if you wrote it for a male voice," I said. "And why do you insist on Beyoncé singing it choppy? She told me that you were against her singing it the way I prefer, on her body and supported. She doesn't have a small voice, and right now the sound isn't moving past her lips."

"I think the song is perfect the way it is. I want it choppy. Beyoncé shouldn't sing it with a big booming voice. It's pop meets hip-hop," Lonnie said.

224

"Believe me, no one will hear her. You've asked her to technically cut her sound in half. She needs to sing full bodied right now," I answered.

"I've raised the key," Lonnie answered. "What more do you want?"

"A great song would be nice," I answered, hanging up. Lonnie knew that I didn't like the song, everyone did. I apologized for hanging up in his ear, but I'd not likely forget the implications of this conversation. Not for a long time. In addition to berating Ashley, Lonnie had begun referring to Kelly as a little "nappy-headed nigga" in the recording studio. Needless to say, Lonnie and I were at odds from this moment onward.

Mathew supported *Ann's choice* for "All about My Baby," he said. I got it. I really did. I couldn't put this mess on him. He was nothing more than the receiver of an incredible opportunity to push his ideas through. It was true, "All about My Baby" was the high-energy number, up tempo and cool, but still, it was a man's song, pure and simple, period.

Beyoncé returned to feeling uncomfortable with the situation and, being so sensitive, she did not like the bad energy that had reemerged in the group. "You can't always control things," Mathew (of all people!) said. "At the end of the day you just have to do your job and leave the important decisions to people who know what they are doing."

It was the most asinine thing I'd heard from Mathew to date. What was he talking about? "...the people who know what they are doing?" He had no insight musically and absolutely no experience in stage deportment. He didn't know television, lighting, or sound. Already as an undergraduate at Langston University I'd learned about all these factors through Janet Hollier-Davis and Monty Prock, in the drama department. Since then I'd had significant professional experiences, which fed my work with the girls. Mathew had never even sung in a horrible church choir.

Lacking musical acumen, and short on music business smarts, Mathew still had everything he would ever need: a sense for manipulation and a disregard for other people, including his own daughters. Beyoncé, their golden child, was easily manipulated. Mathew's ally in deceit, Mama Celestine, preached family loyalty more frequently than she changed her clothes. Beyoncé, an easy prey, always acquiesced.

A blind man could see how this was going to go. And it really pissed me off that Lonnie was using my girls to advance his own agenda. It seemed that everyone was banking on the girls, including their apparently desperate parents. Mathew had convinced nearly everyone that "Star Search" would make Girls Tyme (i.e., Beyoncé) a star. I, however, smelled disaster. The negativity surrounding this event was overwhelming, even for children who easily bounced back from just about anything.

After my conversation with Lonnie, Celestine came to see me. "Why do you think that Beyoncé shouldn't sing the lead in Orlando?" she asked.

"First of all, I hate that song. But to answer your question, it has to do with physiology. Can't you hear that the song was written for the male voice?" I asked. "Unfortunately, Beyoncé's chest voice is weaker than Ashley's right now, and she and I are in the middle of developing her lift tones, which have to be lightened up so she can move toward singing stunning high notes. I am not allowing her to push on her chest voice. This would undermine our ultimate goal."

It was obvious that Celestine thought differently. Beyoncé could sing anything, according to her. This type of thinking wasn't uncommon. All parents like to believe that their precious offspring is a genius in diapers. They imagine that all it will take is a little guidance, some tactful encouragement, perhaps a Baby Einstein© DVD next to the crib, and by the time the kid is three, the whole world will recognize the parents' genius. And pay them money to get next to it.

"No one can do everything, even if they know how. Beyoncé has learned to respect her physical boundaries in her technical lessons with me," I said. "Do you understand what I'm trying to say, Celestine?" I asked.

Celestine took a moment, looking at me as though I'd stolen her bag of Halloween candy. "I think so," she finally answered, and then she said, "But I have faith in you. Make sure Beyoncé wins!"

I stood there flabbergasted, watching Celestine as she walked away, down the alcove, up the three steps leading into Beyoncé's bedroom and then out of sight. Suddenly, my telephone began to ring. I closed the door and picked up the receiver.

It was Carolyn. Oh shit! I thought…

I decided very quickly that I could not influence any decision about who would sing the lead vocal – Ashley (as we had rehearsed) or Beyoncé (as her parents insisted). That conflict was beyond me right now. I had other fish to fry. I determined the only reasonable thing that I could do within the short time frame I had left was continue to prepare the girls to concentrate more effectively, work on their technique, and deal with the arrangement and interpretation through cleaning up their dance moves.

My girls had long since discontinued their dance lessons with Ms. Darlette and had begun to create their own otherwise effective choreography. I must say, they had good ideas, and the steps were age appropriate, but a bit too energetic, in my opinion.

"Everything has to be understated, not that over-the-top flailing about you all like to do," I told them. They called it "dance," but in television terms, I called it a hot mess. "The moves are too street," I concluded.

I explained to them that a more classic approach would make a better impression, but their twelve-and-thirteen-year-old self-consciousness rejected the idea that applying their beginning ballet training with me would win over a popular public. After all, at close to turning 28, I was old, and furthermore, I was an opera singer. What did I know about performing in the pop world? I knew plenty.

They believed what I was demanding from them was neither hip nor cool. "We don't want to be embarrassed on TV," they all chimed. I smiled, and then insisted. They'd do their dance, but with proper spacing, a perfect instinct for timing, and lines. "I want lines," I said. "Don't forget, if you can't see the audience, the audience can't see you." Mathew, who had asked to sit in on our rehearsal, took note.

"We want to get it right," Beyoncé said.

"Of course you do," I answered. "I hope you *all* do," sending hopeful energy in Kelly's direction, who had made tremendous strides.

"Yes, David," Ashley, and then, Kelly, murmured.

Chiming in, Mathew stood up, saying, "You girls look and sound great." Then he did something that he never did, he shook my hand collegially.

Strange, I thought. Mathew and I had never really gotten along, and I do mean never. What is he up to? I wondered

Just in that moment, LaTavia, Nikki and Nina arrived. We continued with our rehearsal, and I could see that Girls Tyme had come together as a polished group ready for a nationally televised appearance. I'd done all I could do, in the three-week time frame that I'd been given. The girls and I joined hands, giving thanks. They prayed to win. I prayed for their souls, and my spirit.

I was exhausted.

Our environment had hardly been conducive. Mathew's all-nighters had begun to run into mornings. Celestine, ever hard-pressed to come up with an explanation, opted not to tell the truth, but to stick with her Kinko's story. Solange's face screamed that she wasn't buying it. Mama Celestine strongly *suggested* that both girls hide the truth, from the other girls, their friends, and indeed the world.

Innately street smart, Solange continued defiantly to question everything that seemed wrong to her. Mathew hated her questions, and her mother, well, she ignored the ones she didn't want to answer. Beyoncé, the "good" daughter, did what her mother asked, concealing now even her deepest thoughts.

Her parents' marital problems had taken more than its toll on Beyoncé. She began slowly shutting down in 1993. Detesting conflict, she began turning her already introverted self even more inward. Beyoncé's focus had been compromised, with domestic tensions eating into her delight in singing.

In the interim, I increased my commitment to both her and to her mother, Celestine. I actually agreed to help Celestine lie to her children about their father. It felt wrong, and I said so, but Celestine's "I'm their mother" logic trumped my doubts every time. Technically, and in many day-to-day transactions, I might have been raising her children, but of course it was Celestine who controlled them. I understood that.

"Children are not weak and stupid little creatures," I told Celestine.

"I know best," she answered.

It's true. I was not Beyoncé and Solange's parent. However, in my opinion, keeping the truth from them about who their father was would only give birth to their disrespecting him in the long run, rather than feeling empathy for him. I didn't understand Celestine's logic. Yes, Mathew Knowles had major problems.

While Beyoncé withdrew inward, Solange began to show contempt for her father, even at her young age. She'd be seven soon, and had already developed a strong personality. She kicked and punched Mathew whenever an opportunity presented itself, which amounted to several times a month, and she never missed. It didn't take much for her to "go off." Beyoncé pitied Mathew. She loved him, but just couldn't understand him; none of us could. She desperately wanted to know why he behaved the way he did. "Why does Daddy always make Mama cry?" she would ask me. Naturally, I had answers, but Celestine forbade truth.

In the meantime, Ann's health had stabilized, she said. I never once heard her complain, and not surprisingly, she was incredibly upbeat, a common response for someone dealing with chronic illness. My heart went out to her. She'd never admit the excruciating pain and fatigue she suffered, but I knew. Prayers would help, so I got busy sending up scriptures on her behalf, and we increased our talks. I was very concerned about her, and determined to be helpful in any way that I could.

Still a bit upset with Celestine, I couldn't get past the fact that she'd spoken about Ann's health issues in public. Ann had not yet announced the nature, nor the seriousness, of her illness to the entire Girls Tyme family, and not understanding Celestine's motives, at all, I listened intently to her "reasoning." I wasn't buying her attempt to back-pedal, and the look on my face showed it.

"A friend of mine told me that Lupus was fatal," she said. Celestine wanted to know my opinion, "as a member of the family."

In my most unequivocal voice I answered, "Lupus is not always fatal." I continued. "True, every case is individual, but if Ann can control her environment and her stress level she'd most likely be just fine," I added. "I wish you hadn't talked about something so private publicly."

"What's done is done," Celestine answered.

In the end, Celestine sort of apologized, not for what she'd done, but rather that I was so upset about it. Then, as if we'd never discussed it, she and Mathew forged ahead. Right in front of me, in the kitchen, she and Mathew continued discussing Ann's illness. I could not see that theirs were altruistic motives. I heard Celestine say to Mathew that he needed to do something to secure his position. "We are talking about *Beyoncé's* future here," she told him, with pointed emphasis on "Beyoncé." Then Mathew headed off to have another one of his "private meetings" with Ann. It was just sad.

Ann called to tell me about her conversation with Mathew, but I already knew about his offer. When she asked me what I thought about the idea of Mathew's "helping out" with the management of Girls Tyme, I froze. With Carolyn's voice still fresh in my head, and Celestine's defiance choking me, I said, "Is Mathew on the same page with us? Can he be objective?"

"Oh, I think so," Ann said. "He has a vested interest in our success." She believed that Mathew only wanted to help. "He is so thoughtful," Ann concluded.

I changed the subject.

It would be safe to say that Ann never made a clear-cut decision; Mathew simply began arranging meetings and inserting himself into Girls Tyme business. As Ann's condition begin to deteriorate again, Mathew's sudden, authoritative appearance made a *de facto* decision for her. I so wanted to believe Mathew when he assured us that he had Ann's best interest at heart. "I will take care of everything," he told me he'd said to her, in her den. All the while he and Celestine continued their kitchen plotting.

Ann didn't know it, but Carolyn felt it, and I was slowly accepting it. The Knowleses were out for blood.

Then, Ann made an announcement that shocked us all. Mathew would be going in her stead to "Star Search." Not only was that one more strike against the girls, but I was frightened on Ann's behalf; she was having several fingers amputated on May 4, 1993, for what doctors termed "arterial insufficiency" of her right fifth finger. She was found to have black and overtly gangrenous distal joints. She'd been a member of a trial study where adjunctive hyperbaric therapy (a treatment that used oxygen to treat ulcerous extremities in diabetics) was the optimal treatment. According to her medical records, which her mother would give me in 2012, that adjunctive hyperbaric oxygen therapy was supposed to help "release the tendon contracture with acute arterial insufficiency of the finger." It hadn't.

In addition, neither Ann nor Kenny Moore (Ann's former assistant and proposed business partner, whom she'd promised a portion of management) could keep a very important meeting scheduled out in California with Richard Gilbert "Dick" Griffey, the founder of Solar Records. Mr. Griffey was a major player in 1993 and had many of R&B music's leading artists on his roster: The Deele, Dynasty, Klymaxx, Lakeside, Midnight Star and The Whispers, to name a few. As a promoter, Griffey booked tours for artists who included James Brown, Aretha Franklin, and Michael Jackson, acquiring the nickname "Kingpin of Soul Promoters."

Ann tried to reschedule, but Mr. Griffey had only the window of opportunity he'd proposed. Enter Mathew. Due to her condition, Ann's doctor forbade her to fly. Accepting Mathew's offer to help out, she sent him to California in her stead. That would turn out to be an unfortunate decision. When Mathew came back from California his demeanor said everything. Swift and painful changes were inevitable.

* * * * *

Celestine appointed herself as the "wardrobe designer" for the "Star Search" event, and the girls' mothers had agreed that they would shop together for costume fabrics. However, Celestine went out alone to choose materials for the show, purchased satin strips for the costume borders, and asked the other mothers to reimburse her.

In spite of their misgivings the mothers agreed to meet at the Knowleses' house to review what Celestine had purchased. Arriving for the meeting before Celestine got home from the salon, Carolyn and Cheryl (LaTavia's mother) began choosing the colors that they preferred for their daughters. One problem immediately surfaced: there weren't enough colored satin strips to go around, and Carolyn feared (correctly, as it turned out) that Ashley would once again be unfavorably treated. When Celestine arrived home, she blew up. I had never seen this side of her. She completely lost her temper, railing at the other mothers that she was in charge. Carolyn left the house without a satin strip for Ashley's costume, exclaiming, "And do what you want!" Cheryl, too, left without her daughter's fabric.

I was surprised that Celestine was so territorial. Other people had warned me, but I loved her and I didn't want to believe this about Celestine. My barber, for instance, had said that if anyone crossed her in the salon, she would sweetly and surely delete them from her memory bank. She had always been so kind to me, never overtly vicious, and appeared to be considerate and focused. Surely she knew that one person's decision was not the "be all to beat all." The incident with the satin strips was my first close-up evidence that if you interfered with Celestine's control, you'd pay.

In the meantime, I got the message that Ashley had been reduced to rapper on the song for "Star Search" – which already had a rapper in the arrangement. I had spent years building the girls up to be a singing group. I did not like the psychological implication of what was going on, nor could I ignore that this might have an effect on how Teresa, and indeed a signing record label, might view the girls' potential earning power.

"It was the only way to pacify Carolyn," Lonnie said.

"Really?" I answered.

Lonnie's explanation sounded like bullshit to me. I tried one last time to explain myself, believing that my very valid point wouldn't be ignored. "Guys, if two girls rap on the song, the rap itself will draw the most attention. The girls will be called hip-hoppers and hip hop is still seen as mas-

232

culine dominated territory. I'm afraid the judges will get the wrong impression. They are singers." Everyone, including Ann, regarded me attentively and continued stubbornly in their own misguided directions.

Mathew and Celestine's takeover talk had become an everyday thing, and they decided to act two days before Orlando. They devised their approach to Ann. "Don't appear too eager," Celestine said to Mathew, in another one of their *kitchen* conversations. Important to keep in mind: The girls had been looking forward to "Star Search" for some weeks. Ann could not bear to disappoint these twelve- and thirteen-year-olds who had worked so hard.

Mathew showed up to Ann's home, unannounced, only 48 hours before Girls Tyme was to fly to Orlando. "Either I get 50% of management or Beyoncé won't be singing on 'Star Search,' or at any other Girls Tyme function in the future," he said to Ann (as she later reported the conversation to me).

This is the very man whose ass had been saved when Ann had paid Mathew and Celestine's back home mortgage and their hair salon rent, both seriously in arrears. At the time they had a federal tax lien on their house from 1990, and aggressive collection tactics by the government had ensued. So much for thinking he "only wanted to help."

Mathew once again asserted his "Custodial Parental Authority," manipulating Ann as he had done with Deborah and Denise, refusing to allow Beyoncé to perform unless his demands were met. Ann was livid. Mathew had returned from California in more than enough time for Ann to cancel the "Star Search" appearance, the hotels, and the flights; but Mathew and Celestine's calculated punch at the last minute forced Ann's hand.

The Knowleses were winning.

* * * * *

In addition to the more than $150,000 Ann had invested in Girls Tyme's development already (and in extending financial assistance to their parents), she had just spent an additional $7,000.00 on studio costs out in Sausalito. The song the girls were to sing on "Star Search" had been produced in these sessions. Several thousand more dollars went to securing hotel accommodations for five adults and six children in Orlando, as well as flights on Continental Airlines. Cassandra Moore, Kenny Moore's wife, and a Continental Airlines employee, had taken care of all the bookings.

The day quickly arrived for Girls Tyme and their entourage to fly to Orlando for "Star Search." Mathew, Celestine, Carolyn, and Cheryl assembled at the Knowleses' home. My girls were racing up and down the stairs, their energy all abuzz and bouncing off the walls. (Doris, Kelly's mother, was not able to go due to work commitments, and Charlotte, mother of our dancers, also stayed behind.) Alonzo Jackson would meet the families in Orlando.

I was exhausted and confused, feeling contrary, so I examined my attitude. Was I perhaps over-reacting? I was worried about, and for, Kelly. Also I was concerned that there was no children's category in this talent search. Would my girls end up competing against adults? If so, the judges would think, "Oh, how cute," and send them packing. What would that do to their confidence? I kept my fingers crossed and sent up a good one to God asking for his protection and grace for my girls.

Once they arrived in Orlando I spoke to the girls on the telephone every day to remind them of their technique. It was all about repetition. When they got to the point of saying, "We know David, we know," I felt confident that I was reaching them, especially Kelly. As best I could from such a long distance, I encouraged Kelly, trying to calm her obvious nerves. If they got the best of her she'd sing flat. I knew that the girls would hear my voice in their head before going on stage, just as I had heard Grandmother's. Having done everything in my control, I let it go. I had to. Time was up.

As soon as the girls' stage appearance was over I received a call from Celestine, who had promised to call me. The girls were in tears. They had performed well, and they were cute and well-rehearsed, but those factors alone could not possibly sell the judges on Girls Tyme. Just as I had predicted, the misguidance they had received cost them the title. Had I not said that the song "All about My Baby" was all wrong? With both LaTavia and Ashley rapping, singing lost out in the performance.

They had lost the "Star Search" in the manner I had feared – to adults. "Skeleton Crew," the group of rockers that beat my girls, were all much older than they were. Beyoncé, Kelly, and Ashley had been tricked into a false performance. No one had listened to me. Fuck.

I was riled up, to say the least.

* * * * *

The girls arrived back in Houston a few days after the loss with downcast hearts and gloomy faces. At the first opportunity, I explained to my girls the realities of show business and told them they could be proud of their effort. Still furious about the ludicrous repertoire and decisions that other people had made, I continued to obsess about my dire premonitions. Angry, I made a vow never again to allow anyone to come between the girls' artistic development and me.

When the show finally aired, seeing the performance for myself, I felt as if the color had been drained from my body. The very first thing I heard was Ed MacMahon announcing the "Hip-Hop Rapping – Girls Tyme." Shit. All I could see was red. Exactly what I had predicted had come true. The show saw my girls as rappers. Not one mention of the word "singer." Beyoncé, Ashley, and Kelly had been made to look like silly dilettantes – amateurs. It was the messiest crap I ever had to endure.

To top it all off each girl had alternating colors trimming their shorts – that is, everyone except Ashley: Ashley, who along with Beyoncé was a lead singer in Girls Tyme. Ashley's costume had the same color satin piping as the shorts themselves. That choice made her look like an outsider. How did this happen? I asked myself. That incident with the fabric had created a visual discord that represented every flaw in the entire musical performance. Now there was no doubt that complete disruption of the group dynamic would surely follow.

I turned my television off, disgusted.

Worse. "Beyoncé, why are you singing choppy, unsupported and completely opposite of what we'd – you and I – agreed upon?" I asked.

She lowered her head.

"I'm talking to you Beyoncé."

Looking up from the floor, she began to speak. "Daddy told me that I had to do what Lonnie wanted."

* * * * *

A couple days later, I called Ann from the telephone in the Knowles kitchen. It was time to restructure, beginning with a change in ideology. Mathew, whom I asked to be present, balked at my comments, but I didn't care.

"Mathew, the ideology is all wrong here. The thinking has been in too general terms," I said. "In my opinion, we are going to have to think like an equestrian if we are going to find success for the girls."

Judging by the dumb look on his face, I knew I had lost Mathew. Ann, however, chimed in on the other end of the line, attentively and with interest, "Go on, I'd like to hear more."

"An equestrian is not just a horseback rider, and the music business is not just any ol' horse," I said. "We need to develop a formula – combine common sense thinking with tradition. There's only one way to win at anything and that is through quality. By keeping quality at the forefront, we honor tradition. No more haphazard anything."

"But I don't think we've been haphazard," Ann said.

"Of course we have. 'Star Search' was haphazard thinking. Would you go into a boxing ring without a strategy?" I asked. "I didn't want to."

Mathew, in an effort to put me in my place said, "Let's just cut to the chase. It begins with passion and our girls have passion. Passion is all we need."

I had a choice to make. Either I could ignore Mathew's pointless remark, letting him live, or I could take him down with his half-baked idea about passion. I chose the latter.

"Mathew, passion is nothing more than unfocused and unharnessed abandonment, absent of all reason, hence the phrase 'crime of passion.' People kill with passion; they don't win recording contracts with it."

There was a bit of silence. Mathew's stare had turned cold, as I had expected, but again, I didn't give a damn about his bruised ego. I knew plenty of people in the music business who were not trained musically, but were brilliant in the profession. I feared that Mathew would never be among their number.

In any case, I was done keeping my mouth shut.

11. Too tall, too dark and too ugly

Thinking about my life with the Knowles family calls to my mind the New Testament book of Mark, Chapter 4, verses 26-29. "This is what the kingdom of God is like. A man scatters seed on the ground. Night and day, whether he sleeps or gets up, the seed sprouts and grows, though he does not know how. All by itself the soil produces grain – first the stalk, then the head, then the full kernel in the head. As soon as the grain is ripe, he puts the sickle to it, because the harvest has come." As a young man, I was shocked by my realization that Mathew and Celestine were ruining our soil with their own seeds, ones of a self-serving kind.

Mathew and Celestine also had a dream, no doubt about it. For them, "Beyoncé's group" was how they intended to get noticed. What they wanted was admiration. Their overriding goal was to achieve fame and fortune for themselves, and they had begun to use any means necessary, ethical or not, on their quest.

* * * * *

Mathew felt superior after his coup over Ann Tillman. He now owned 50% of management. I will never forget the haughtiness with which he announced his new position. "Things bout to change roun' here," he said. "Der's a new sheriff in town," articulating every word. What followed was one of the most sinister laughs I've ever heard.

Celestine, on the other hand, saw no reason to celebrate. There was better crude buried in Ann's proverbial ground, and Celestine aimed to drill for it. It was she who determined that they would announce Mathew's sharing of the managerial reins after they returned from Orlando. Celestine declared that his anxiousness to cry victory all over town was premature. "*After* 'Star Search,'" she said.

However, Mathew's coercion of Ann had become a footnote to Ann's own critical concerns. While working hard to maintain good face, she was not recovering from that serious surgery. Her doctors weren't sure where the surgery would lead – infection being their main concern – and they warned of the possibility that she might lose more fingers. Both scenarios, as it turned out, would become reality. She developed a terrible infection and most likely would lose another finger because of it. Mathew and Celestine's actions felt so wrong to me. This good woman was fighting for her life, and they were plotting.

While in Orlando, Mathew had called a meeting in which he announced to Celestine, Carolyn, and Cheryl his plans to take over as the Girls Tyme manager. No matter how much Celestine warned against moving too fast, Mathew's need for his little victory speech gnawed at him. He was the manager in charge. Ann's illness had prevented her from going. Being on the set of "Star Search," with all dem white folks calling him sir was like a dream come true. What Carolyn didn't know was that Cheryl, Celestine, and Doris had already secretly signed on with Mathew, back in Houston. He had instructed Cheryl and Celestine that when he made his announcement in Orlando, in front of Carolyn, they were to act as if Mathew's interest in managing the girls was a complete surprise.

238

Mathew planned to show Carolyn, Celestine, and Cheryl a letter, alleg-edly written by a Los Angeles-based music executive named Ruth Carson. While in Orlando, Mathew explained that Ms. Carson was a rising star on the music scene and that she and he had been consulting on behalf of the girls. Although Mathew had refused to give a copy of the letter to the girls' mothers, his special re-reading of Ms. Carson's words (as it was reported to me) left me cold. They were seemingly harsh, trashing Ashley and praising Beyoncé. I hadn't ever heard Mathew or Ann mention a Ruth Carson, but I did know that Mathew himself had been writing a letter in the kitchen before going to Orlando. That letter, which was left sprawled out on the kitchen table, sounded a lot like the one Mathew had just now read aloud, supposedly written by Ruth Carson.

Celestine used her influence to help Mathew in his deception. The oth-er mothers (Carolyn being the skeptical exception) looked up to the wom-an who could seemingly do it all – run a business, hold her marriage to-gether, and raise two beautiful and wonderful girls. Celestine's confidence in her man put them at ease. The women didn't have the facts, but Cheryl, who had loyalty to the patriarch of the family in her DNA, was easily convinced. And it took even less to fool Doris. Without much effort at all, Celestine was able to charm the signatures right out of those two.

That Mathew had secured contact with someone like a Ruth Carson impressed Cheryl and Doris immediately. "Ruth was so wonderful to us," Celestine said, adding that Ruth was, "so excited about the girls' future."

Hearing that, I responded, baffled. I asked Celestine when she had met Ruth.

"Mathew and I met Ruth when were out in California," Celestine said.

Her stare spoke volumes. For a split second, I could have sworn that I saw contempt in her face.

Continuing, Celestine stressed every word: "You remember when we went out to Los Angeles a while back to secure Ken's commitment as group lawyer."

"Oh –, " I said. I had to admit that Celestine's answer was a fact I couldn't refute. I had been responsible for taking full care of Beyoncé and

Solange for five days while she and Mathew had flown out to L.A. to secure legal representation. Attorney Ken Hertz came highly recommended, Celestine had told me.

"This ain't no time for taking no chances," Celestine added. Perplexed, I nodded. She told me that it was, "necessary that I go along." Nevertheless, during my lifespan with the Knowles, which was longer than a decade, I never met a Ruth Carson.

Carolyn Davis, alone, never wavered in her objection to Mathew's becoming manager. Mathew simply ignored Carolyn's feelings. He had begun to look pretty good in Doris and Cheryl's eyes. The truth is, Mathew needed only a quorum of parents on his side to implement his takeover ideas, and with Doris, Celestine, and Cheryl on board he had that.

Carolyn had been calling Ann repeatedly, still hoping to persuade her to name her brother Lorando as co-manager, but Ann assured Carolyn that the girls were "going to be very successful" under Mathew's and her joint management. Carolyn would point out that money is not everything. "What about integrity?" she would repeat. Although I could imagine no one with greater integrity than Ann, I do not know (or, I do not remember) her reply to Carolyn. I know only that Mathew was successful in gaining control of the group.

Mathew's recurring threat to remove Beyoncé from the group if he did not get his way was clearly at the center of Ann's decision. She said, "Mathew is unemployed and he sees the girls as his chance to get into the music business." That statement was eye-opening, because up to that point I had resisted the notion that Mathew's sole interest had been insuring his own fame rather than supporting his daughter's well-being. Ann confessed that Mathew was convinced that Beyoncé's talent would catapult him to the success he envisioned. "He is determined to find success," she said. She never mentioned her own desire to recoup her investment, although I felt sure that she wanted to see a return, if only for the good of her sons' futures.

Mathew's attempts to keep up the appearance of professional courtesy and personal sympathy worked with most of the girls' parents. He couldn't cut Ann out totally, because he still needed her money. Mathew bet that Ann's health would cause a shift in her ability to keep up with her managerial duties with unflagging intensity.

At Celestine's constant urging, Mathew had gone to Ann's house for a showdown. Ann had agreed on Mathew's suggested 50/50 split. His nightly calls to Ann questioning her about strategy and offering up his own half-baked ideas had stressed her immensely. Mathew's obsession was the worst thing for Ann in her condition, since severe stress was detrimental to Ann's health and now her recovery.

Mathew alleged that the doctors would have to amputate her leg. Checking in with Ann, I discovered that Mathew was totally off base. I wondered where he'd gotten his information. It felt to me like *schadenfreude*, a chilling thought. I just couldn't bring myself to believe that he was hoping for Ann's demise, not after all she had done for him and his family. In the meantime, she had started to complain of pain and cold in her hands. Her right distal fifth finger had become discolored. Her doctor had prescribed five sessions of hyperbaric oxygen treatments, to be carried out consecutively, but that treatment, failed to help, too.

"Ann, you must reduce your stress level," her doctor wrote. Her blood pressure was through the roof. She was having dizzy spells.

And just like that, Mathew's new career was official.

* * * * *

In Carolyn's mind Mathew was "unscrupulous and scandalous" and was interested only in helping himself. When she and I talked about the girls' performance in Orlando, I expressed to her my concern about Ashley's unfair treatment. I was afraid that although she seemed to be coping well, the outcome for Ashley was becoming unclear.

"Of course Ashley is upset," Carolyn said. "I raised her to be kind. She is fourteen years old and a sensitive girl. But Nolan and I try to rear our kids by example, showing them resolve when your back is against the wall."

I knew, however, that it was unrealistic to think that negative outcomes – in this case – did not hold an important place in her thinking.

I said, "Ashley was so professional during the whole experience. I was very proud of her. She didn't allow their rude treatment to upset her performance. But is she really all right? Psychologically, I mean."

"We are deeply rooted in our faith in God. Ashley knows two things: that God is with her and that Nolan and I will never let anyone harm her. No amount of money is worth losing your soul," Carolyn said.

"Beyoncé was uneasy about singing over Ashley's vocals," I said.

"Beyoncé is a wonderful girl," Carolyn replied. "She is very sweet and genuinely a good person. She is not to blame for her father's greed. God don't like ugly!"

During our conversation Carolyn disclosed another observation from backstage at "Star Search." Already suspicious of Mathew, she had watched him "like a hawk" the entire time in Orlando. She emphatically asserted that both she and Cheryl saw that Mathew had a long conversation with the show's producer, and that neither of them ever saw him speaking with Ed MacMahon. Carolyn told me that the original question posed by Mathew to that producer had to do with finding out why the girls had received only three out of the possible four talent-rating stars.

That producer had replied, "The lead singer was weak."

Beyoncé had been the lead singer. The producer went on to say that, "the rappers came across stronger."

Several days later Mathew called a meeting. Everyone was assembled in the Knowles dining room, our usual meeting place. In attendance were Kelly and her mother Doris, Beyoncé and her mother Celestine, LaTavia and her mother Cheryl, Nina and Niki and their mother Charlotte, and Ashley and her mother Carolyn. I was also in attendance. Mathew called the meeting to order and announced his newly established position as manager. He distributed contracts that each parent should sign, which he copied from Ann's book on music management, in acknowledgement of the new arrangement. He had just begun to explain the deal he and Ann had agreed upon, when Carolyn interrupted his speech.

"I don't trust you, Mathew," she said calmly, "and to be quite honest, I think it is unethical for a parent to be manager of this group." There was absolute quiet in the room. No one was willing to support Carolyn's assertion that Mathew would stack the cards unevenly in Beyoncé's favor. Only I knew that Beyoncé's "favor" had never entered his mind.

"You didn't even discuss it with the rest of us before harassing Ann," Carolyn went on. "Now, if you and Ann want to strike a deal together, that is your business. But my daughter will not be a part of your narcissism. You pay homage to Beyoncé. I agree that she is a great talent. But Ashley is equally as talented, and I fight for her. I will not allow you to destroy her confidence."

The meeting became heated, with arguments ensuing and tensions escalating. Carolyn repeated her concern, always calmly and matter-of-factly: "I am not going to allow Ashley to be minimized." She called Mathew unethical and his actions suspect. "How can any of us be sure you will treat our girls with dignity and respect in the group?" she asked. One word led to another, and when Mathew had had enough he called out "Doris!" and she signed the prepared contract. He then called out "Cheryl!" and she signed, too. Finally, he called his wife's name, "Tina!" who looked at Carolyn, who wasn't having any of it, and then she signed too. Carolyn stood up and headed for the door, taking Ashley with her. My heart dropped into my socks. You couldn't do the things that the Knowleses did and expect everyone to lie down and take it. Most did, but not Carolyn Davis.

Everyone acted as if what just happened had not happened. I think Celestine believed that she could win Carolyn over, but she had not reckoned with the depth of Carolyn's justified convictions. Mathew, however, did not miss a beat. He did not like being challenged and with a "business is business" shrug, he again called the meeting to order. He pointed out that he had not asked Carolyn to leave. "She left of her own accord," Mathew said. "And good riddance."

I was visibly stunned. It was as if Carolyn had never existed. Not one parent came to Carolyn or Ashley's defense, so I did. I raised valid concerns, which were greeted with silence, then nonchalance, and finally a chilly un-comfortableness that permeated the room. Clearing my throat, I appealed to the group's honor. "We are creating harmful Karma here," I said. I then quoted a scriptural passage, from Galatians (6:7), "Do not be deceived: God cannot be mocked. A man reaps what he sows." Celestine rolled her eyes. This time there was no mistaking contempt. Everyone saw it.

Suddenly Beyoncé burst into tears, shaking and crying uncontrollably. Her friend and co-singer Ashley had just left the group. Don't misunder-stand me when I say that I was glad to see her crying. I hated knowing she was in pain, but I was relieved to see that I had not been the only one af-fected, and her tears gave me some solace.

Celestine gathered up Beyoncé's limp body and took her out of the room, so that Mathew could continue the meeting. Beyoncé, overcome with grief, couldn't walk upright. Completely ignoring his daughter's outburst, as if it had not happened, Mathew continued to outline his vision for restructuring. Oh – there's a word I've heard before, I thought. I made a slight objection and put my two cents in, saying, "Isn't anyone con-cerned about Beyoncé?" No one answered. Mathew hit the table. Had he thought hitting the table would scare me? I stared him down. "Don't you think that Beyoncé should hear the rest of what you have to say if she is going to be the sole leader? It is obvious that you want all the weight to fall upon her now." My words finally evoked a small response from Cher-yl and Doris, whose faces finally signaled concern.

Mathew gave me a nasty look, which I interpreted as, "Stay in your goddam place." "No," he said. It would be the first, but not the last time that I would feel the direct sting of Mathew Knowles. "I'd like to say that I believe you are categorically wrong," I answered, and then Mathew stood up to leave the room, in a real *state*.

Exactly in that moment Beyoncé and Celestine re-appeared. Beyoncé was still very upset. Our eyes met, and I gave her a reassuring look. Mathew ignored her and started to speak again. No one could get a word in edgewise. He wouldn't allow it. It was like watching a child throw a temper tantrum. Celestine apologized to everyone for his behavior, which, compared to what would come later, was only slightly irrational and aggressive. "Tina, I don't need you to apologize for me. That's what's wrong here. We don't have time for weakness," he said. I wasn't sure whether Celestine's apology was sincere, but it didn't matter. It worked. No one liked conflict, least of all Doris and Cheryl.

Mathew continued talking, and Celestine stared at me, now with tears in her eyes. Did she think that I might also walk away? She could see my obvious anger. But I guess I will never really have the answer to that question, because by this time, I adored my girls. I not only lived in the Knowleses' house, I was family. Beyoncé and the other girls had become my surrogate children, the daughters I would never have. I wasn't going anywhere. I was blindly loyal. I wholeheartedly believed I had been called into their lives for a higher purpose.

Still, right was right. The whole matter upset me, and I asked God that evening for wisdom. I had allowed Mathew to rattle me to the point of becoming defensive. Then I remembered Carolyn's comment about narcissism. This would explain everything. Indeed, if Mathew was a true narcissist, I knew exactly how to handle him. I'd have to stroke his ego. Uneasy on the inside, I fell off to sleep. It had been a long, long day and after the end of that life-changing meeting, I didn't know what would be awaiting me in the morning.

All of a sudden I heard screaming. Wanting to ignore whatever was happening in the house, I put the pillow over my head, but I heard Beyoncé crying. In pajamas, I ran into the house via the alcove and through Beyoncé's room – just in time to see Celestine getting up off the floor outside Solange's room. I suspected she had been defending Beyoncé, who was being screamed at by her angry father.

"Don't you ever embarrass me like that again," Mathew said.

While Solange attacked Mathew, Celestine warned against her hitting her father, and I sheltered Beyoncé, moving her toward the safety of my apartment. Suddenly, Mathew stepped threateningly in my direction. Again, I gave him a strong look. That look said, "I dare you."

The war had begun.

*****

No matter what was going on, Beyoncé could sense when something was not right. She was the most sensitive child. She felt absolutely everything and she blamed herself for Ashley's demise. Singing over Ashley's vocals had destroyed the group. She never wanted that – she wanted her own solos, yes – but never to hurt Ashley.

Celestine came back to my apartment that night after Mathew left the house, apologizing profusely to me about his behavior. She had told Beyoncé to go to bed and then she settled in for a long talk. I didn't say a word. Sitting on my couch, she went on and on about how she was going to have to "shield Beyoncé from important decisions." Neither she nor Mathew could assume that Beyoncé would simply follow along, Celestine intimated.

While Celestine continued her speculations, I formulated in my own mind what I would be relaying to my prized pupil. She should remember what happened, and the way it made her feel. "Remember that you are a kind person," I would say. I would go one step further: "Beyoncé, you must remember that you don't think hurting others feels good." She was going to need those words in dealing with her father.

Who was I exactly? I was the person who was developing Mathew's "product" and Celestine's "project." It was I who picked their girls up from school every day, year after year. I was the one getting their dinner on the table and helping them with their homework. Mathew was either committing adultery or getting high on cocaine, and Celestine was working like a slave to make ends meet and trying to keep up with her husband's shenanigans. Celestine regurgitated to her girls that Mathew was spending all of his time at Kinko's. The truth of the matter was: He was an addict who fancied prostitutes. I remember feeling that he would drag the family down and that Beyoncé would suffer most of all. She did not deserve to be implicated by the continuing actions of her shameless father. He would destroy her before it was all over, and I remember asking God to protect her. I prayed for us all.

246

I was beginning to see the error of my ways. Silence had helped to turn the entire situation volatile. Beyoncé was being manipulated for her parents' gain, not hers. They often told Beyoncé that they made their decisions with her best interests at heart. She wanted – no, needed – to believe her parents. What else was she to do?

On the morning after the meeting where everything had fallen apart, I awakened feeling nervous. I had not slept a wink. It was not part of my normal routine to eat breakfast (something my mother always got after me about), but on that day I was hungry. It was as though my body had eaten away at itself in my sleep. I felt empty, agitated, worried, angry and confused. I looked out of the window into the Knowles house from my apartment and saw stillness. It was after 9 a.m., so I reasoned that Celestine would have already dropped Beyoncé and Solange off at school and then gone on to the salon. If Mathew was at home on that morning I didn't see him. Usually he was still asleep at 9 a.m., especially if he had been out all night. Somehow the events of the day before felt like a black cloud hanging overhead. The day felt eerie. I sympathized with Ashley's parents' concern for her safety as Mathew implemented his takeover.

As I was standing there in contemplation, experiencing all kinds of emotions, the telephone rang. Carolyn was on the line, calling to arrange Ashley's next voice lesson. We had a very pleasant chat, which included a brief discussion about the meeting the day before and what had happened there. She was still adamant, but she was very dignified about it all. I was hopeful that the situation would resolve itself and I speculated that maybe, just maybe, Ashley could be re-instated.

Both Carolyn and Nolan Davis were well educated – she with a master's degree, and Nolan with a bachelor's. (Today she is Dr. Carolyn Davis.) These hard-working, loving people were parents of three children, Ashley, Jay and Sean, who were their parents' pride and joy. Carolyn and Nolan were both logical and rational adults and Carolyn reminded me of my grandmother. She provided each of her children with the tools they needed to become healthy, productive citizens. She wanted the best for her children and that included getting an education. She always advised having a backup plan.

Although Nolan (whom I had gotten to know pretty well) was a very present dad, Carolyn was the stronger personality in their household. She was not the typical "meek and mild" Southern woman. She believed in honor, honesty, and God, just as Grandmother did. Nolan supported his wife in every way, admirably so.

Ashley, now in a difficult position, was watching her dream – and her friendship with Beyoncé and Kelly – slip away from her, but she would, of course, respect her parents' decision. She was a wonderful girl who, like the other Girls Tyme singers, dreamed of achieving a starring role in the music business, which she imagined to be an exciting world. I can still hear her and the other girls deep in conversation about finding success. They dreamed big, imagining their first awards acceptance speech and of multiple Grammy Awards and even possibly an Oscar. They talked about making videos and the latest dances. Nothing was more important than rehearsing. My girls wanted to sing and dance all day. For them it was fun, and it gave them a chance to be together – laughing, being girls, and dreaming. This was their way. This was their reality, and "perception is reality." I had taught them that.

Ashley was an excellent student. She was always pleasant and by nature a very happy, well balanced child. Now fourteen years old, she had been with me, under my tutelage, for nearly five years. She was a valued member of my voice studio. I saw her weekly, like clockwork. Every Tuesday at around 4:00 o'clock Ashley stood before me ready for her lesson, never late and always prepared. Even though Beyoncé received four times as many lessons, my work with Ashley meant a great deal to me, and I was proud of her achievements.

The next few lessons after the breakup meeting were extremely hard on us all, especially Ashley. Coming to the house where she had spent so much time and given so much of herself required bravery and fortitude for a fourteen-year-old child. I distinctly remember feeling as though my heart had been ripped out every time she came to a lesson. Inevitably Beyoncé would rush over to my apartment to see Ashley. They'd hug, and it was clear that they loved each other deeply. Beyoncé had returned to the breakup meeting seemingly calm, but in actuality she was not. Celestine called it "moping around" and declared that Beyoncé would get over it. I, however, thought differently. Beyoncé's singing had become subdued in lessons, and she told me that she wanted Ashley restored to her rightful place in the group. "It's my fault," she said, feeling completely responsible for Ashley's banishment. Guilt – very different from shame – was eating her alive.

I asked Carolyn if Mathew had called her to reconcile, and she said that he had. She told me that first Ann called her and then Mathew called, making unreasonable demands. (Ann Tillman and I had talked. I wondered if she had heard about the disagreement and of course she had – at least, she had heard Mathew's version of it. He had informed Ann that Carolyn had left the meeting. Ann asked me to recount my impressions, and with that I had relived the event all over again. I did not tell Ann of the exchange that had taken place outside Solange's room.) Carolyn was convinced that she had chosen correctly in leaving the meeting and saw no possible resolution with Mathew. He wasn't interested in bargaining. Then Carolyn's husband, Nolan, became involved. He and Mathew argued, a lot. Two men protecting their daughters made for some heated telephone conversations.

Within a month of the break-up meeting, Celestine came to me one day after Ashley's lesson. I was surprised that she was at home. She told me that I had to "make a choice."

"Excuse me?" I said.

"Ashley or Beyoncé," she said. "You have to choose between them. If you continue to teach Ashley you will lose Beyoncé, forever."

I was stunned. I couldn't believe she was saying this to me and I asked her if she seriously thought that I could make such a choice. I told her, "I am a voice teacher and my job is to teach voice to whoever needs it." Celestine said, "No. Your job is to teach voice to the person you deem fit."

She was angry and it was clear that she was really serious. I wondered what was really going on between the two sets of parents. My heart was ripped open and it hurt like hell. How could I make such a choice? I loved these girls as if they were my own. I was reminded of the well-known story of King Solomon and two mothers, as told in the Old Testament book of Kings (I, iii, 16-28). Two women fought over a child, arguing their case before him. They both claimed to be the child's rightful mother and Solomon settled the argument by telling his guards to split the child in two, but the real mother spoke up, giving away the child in order to save his life. Beyoncé and Ashley, as an entity, were my child. Even though I was the rightful parent to neither, I loved them both deeply and respected their friendship as inviolate. Celestine was asking me to split them in two. It felt horrible.

Carolyn called me the following day to set up Ashley's new voice lesson for the week coming up. I asked how Ashley was doing. "Just fine," she replied. But when Ashley arrived for her voice lesson I could see that she was not fine. The tensions between the two families were resurfacing in my studio every week on Tuesdays at 4:00 o'clock. Mathew was ignoring Ashley's father, and Carolyn had drawn her determined line in the sand. Mathew would never be ready to discuss an alternate manager, and Celestine promised to make good on her threat. Ashley's pain was real to me, and so was my shame.

The next time Carolyn called I did something that ate at my soul for years. I dropped Ashley from my studio. I told myself I did it to protect Ashley. I even tried reasoning with the Knowleses, but in truth, I feared disobeying God. I felt that I understood why I had been put in Beyoncé's house. I intended to follow orders, the clear message I had received through the aid of my "still small voice." We were doing an incredible work. Perhaps it was better just to move on, I rationalized, to fill the hole that Ashley's departure had created. Ultimately, it was my ego that forced my shameful decision. Too much had been invested, I thought. In hindsight I realize that I could have walked away, and taken Ashley, Kelly, LaTavia, and her two cousins with me, but I didn't. I had been sucked in, totally.

Days later Celestine could see that I was still upset about everything, and that it was diverting my attention. Mathew had passed on the "good news" that I had dropped Ashley. Coming back to my apartment to tell me that I had made the right decision, she told me that it was just as well. "Ashley is talented but she is so big, she towers over the other girls and she is too dark and ugly." There it was, the ugly, age-old problem of blacks in the South: Color. Celestine's "reassurance" served merely to cement the guilt that I felt. My entire insides shook. What in the hell had I done?

There are not many things that I have done in my life that I am utterly ashamed of but dropping Ashley Davis was one of them. I dropped her to keep the peace; my own selfish peace. I felt physically ill and threw up for days. I had hurt a child, down to her very soul. It was in that moment that I really grasped what hell must feel like. I had sold my soul to a creole devil and I didn't like me for a long time. The man staring back at me in the mirror was a complete stranger.

Ashley, please forgive me.

* * * * *

It would take Beyoncé's parents years to cement their older daughter's compliance to their dictates, but they persisted. They became Svengalis, masters of camouflage and deception. They upped the ante. Beyoncé was to be kept out of every major decision. From that moment on, Mathew did not discuss business with the girls. Anything that anyone needed to know was delivered, calculatingly, and at the last minute. "No kid is going to tell me shit," Mathew said. His wife and children were his business. No matter what he did to their souls, it was his business. He was the *master of his castle*, he said.

Beyoncé's parents' behavior would cost Beyoncé in the end, but what was I to do in the meanwhile? I was just the voice teacher, and even though they told me repeatedly that I was "like family," I hadn't felt comfortable butting in. They did say "like" family. My getting in the middle of that family drama, just days earlier, had not been my place. I had reacted, and truth be told, I would have done it again. Celestine felt that if Beyoncé knew the truth she might turn against them. It was clear, at least to them, that in order to get where they wanted to be, they needed to "protect" her from the truth. The Knowles family lies and deceptions began to take root on that day.

A few weeks later, Ann had undergone another surgery; this time to straighten out her fifth finger. Soon after a skin graft had been done on her right palm, she suffered post- contracture release. The finger retracted and wouldn't straighten. She told me that her hand throbbed so much that the pain drove her to removing the splint the doctor put on.

"Ann, is that wise?" I asked.

"The pain was really unbearable. I couldn't take it anymore."

Neither of us believed that removing the splint was a sound idea, but three days postoperatively, her plastic surgeon, Dr. Richard Perlman, noticed she had much bigger problems. The finger showed bruising and some vascularity. She'd have to go back to the hospital immediately for surgery.

Needless to say, I was extremely nervous for her. I didn't know how long she'd be able to keep up her unyielding, positive attitude.

"I'll be fine," she said, showing typical Ann resolve.

* * * * *

However shocking Carolyn's sudden leaving was, just as shocking to me was Celestine's claim that she and Mathew had not intended to get rid of Ashley. In conversations that took place after that disastrous meeting, Celestine insisted that she and her husband had really believed they could persuade Carolyn to come over to their way of thinking. They had not, according to Celestine, ever talked specifically about Carolyn and Ashley in their plans to take over the management of Girls Tyme. No, Carolyn's reaction was a complete surprise, they said.

Not only had the Knowleses' myopia cost me a beloved student, but I had just lost four-and-a-half years of hard work with this precious group, which had just been ripped apart by Mathew Knowles's insatiable need

252

for control. We would have to find a replacement for Ashley: start over from scratch. Well, I didn't want to think about it. Something had to be done, but what? I had to pull myself together.

Beyoncé was devastated. Kelly also had feelings about what transpired with Ashley, but she too had not been free enough to speak up. She always felt powerless. Because she had the softest voice, she believed that she had the least talent (residue of her mother's abuse). Even on good days she found it hard to believe in my truth: that she was a wonderfully gifted singer. What had the events of that meeting brought up in her? The most fragile member of Girls Tyme, Kelly had been adversely affected by the "Star Search" loss. If a good singer with a strong voice like Ashley was expendable, what did all this mean for her? I saw real fear in her eyes.

At Kelly's Saturday lesson, long after kicking Ashley out of my studio, I told her that I would never give up on her. I had been tricked once, never again. Kelly was a precious child in an impossible situation. They all were. Protecting Kelly had become paramount. I still hadn't figured out how to get her into a safer environment, nor was I sure that it was the right thing to do. One of my temporary solutions had been to have group lessons on Saturdays and Sundays. Those weekend lessons often meant the girls would sleep over at the Knowles house so they could be close to me. Celestine approved, because it strengthened "Beyoncé's group." It also was healthy for Beyoncé, but her mother never gave that a second thought. Although I had proposed those weekend sessions specifically to help Kelly, I was also aware of Beyoncé's need for healthy socializing. Kelly needed more than weekend freedom, this was for sure, but for the time being, both girls benefitted from the arrangement.

Privately, I was in profound turmoil. I couldn't face the answer to the question that permeated my thoughts. What kind of man was I? Carrying the weight of Carolyn and Ashley's hatred – as I perceived it – was an unbearable personal burden. That awful day when I said that I thought it best that Ashley find another teacher, Carolyn had said, "Are you seriously telling me that you don't want to teach my daughter?" I just wanted to get off the phone. Carolyn said she was disappointed in me. "I thought you had more integrity," she said. She added, "Shame on you, doing this to a child." Her words all but killed me, but I held my emotions back, something that I knew how to do, and we ended our call. She wished me well, as I did her. I hung up the phone, tears rolling down my face.

So now I had to face a cold hard fact. We were without a third singer. Two singers, a rapper and two dancers would not a group make. It had been weeks since Ashley's departure, and I was certain that dropping Ashley as a private student had spoiled any hope of a reconciliation, so I began looking seriously for someone else.

Having spoken with Ann about my concerns, I went looking for Mathew, who had finally made it clear that Ashley would not be returning due to irreconcilable differences, and nothing anyone said was going to change his mind. He insisted upon everyone's loyalty to him and he resented a problematic person. He would not be undermined. He had become tyrannical. I discovered him sitting, dozing alone in our usual meeting place, the kitchen.

"Mathew," I said.

Startled, he jumped. "Oh – it's you David," he answered.

"We have to consider finding another singer. We can't go on like this," I said.

Mathew surprised me by saying that he was sure he'd already found Ashley's replacement, and that they – all thirteen of them – would show up to audition for me on Saturday. Although encouraged that he was thinking about the group, I worried about Mathew's "sure." He had a terrible eye for talent and he was certifiably tone deaf. I broached the subject of reconciliation with Ashley's parents one last time, but Mathew was not interested. I was not above eating the crow it would require to win Carolyn and Ashley back, but Mathew said, "I insist on getting the respect that is due me."

And so, Saturday arrived and thirteen, virtually talentless girl-next-door types traipsed through the Knowles' home. Not one of them fit, impressive neither in look nor sound. As the last of them left the house, we were startled to hear Beyoncé's voice.

"I know somebody," she said. Having heard each audition from the adjoining room, Beyoncé told her father and me about a little girl who was in her class at The Saint James School. "You saw her, David," Beyoncé said. She reminded me that she had been talking to a girl when I had picked up her and Solange from school the previous day. "You remember?" she asked. "She's pretty, and I think she would fit in perfectly."

"Actually I do," I said to Beyoncé.

"What's her name?" Mathew asked.

"Her name is LeToya."

"LeToya what?" Mathew asked.

"LeToya Luckett."

"Do you think she would be interested?" I asked Beyoncé. "Can she sing?"

"Yes, I think so." Continuing, Beyoncé said "I don't have her number but I can ask her at school."

"OK, cool." I said. Monday was just two days away. Surely our dilemma could wait 48 hours. In a political move, I said, "If she is interested, tell her to have her mother call your father for an appointment on next Saturday."

Beyoncé nodded her head. Mathew grinned from ear to ear. I'd made his day. I played to his grandiosity and self-importance. It was just the first step to gaining control of the situation and him, but it was important. Also, it was the right thing to do. After all, he was management and he was cooperating.

That Saturday, Mathew was sober and actually sociable. Oh how I wished we could see more of the clear Mathew.

I almost liked a clear-headed Mathew.

Girls Tyme, backstage at „Star Search" 1993
Front row, from left: Nina Taylor, Beyoncé Knowles, LaTavia Roberson,
Nikki Taylor.
Center row: Kelly Rowland and Ashley Támar Davis
Top row: Far left Alonzo (Lonnie) Jackson and second from right, Arne
Frager
The others are unidentified.
Photo: The Tillman Estate

The St. James School 1992-93 Class Photo
LeToya Luckett (center row, second from left) and Beyoncé Knowles
(center row, fourth from left) were students in Ms. Western's class
Photo: The St. James School

Autographs (circa 1994) from the boy group *H-Town*, which I had coached

Part III

Passing the threshold

12. LeToya Luckett

During the next week, I heard thirteen singers. Five were OK, two were quite good, and six were impossible. Not one of the thirteen had that special something that would qualify them to fit into our girl group.

Beyoncé then told her father that there was a girl at The St. James School who could sing and that she was pretty and would fit nicely, she thought. He asked her name and set out to inquire about her coming for an audition.

* * * * *

It was a beautiful autumn Saturday in 1993 when LeToya Luckett arrived at the Knowles residence on Parkwood promptly at 3:00 p.m., the time we had agreed upon.

Unbeknownst to me, Celestine had returned home from the salon. Perhaps she wanted to get a look at the girl who Beyoncé was so sure would fit into the group. At any rate, as I came down from my apartment into the main house, I could hear Celeste and Mathew arguing. It was unbelievable. They had taken to harpooning one another in front of company. Beyoncé sat on the family room couch looking lost. I mouthed, "Smile," as I walked by her and then signaled for her to follow me. I felt that although her parents' behavior was disgusting, I knew I could not interfere. My only priority was to protect their daughter.

I was already fifteen minutes late. Halfway down the stairs, I stood stock still. I couldn't grasp what I was witnessing. From that vantage point I could see directly into the dining room, where Mathew and Celestine

259

were sitting. They appeared to be carrying on an intense battle. It was like a puppet theater – I felt that the battle was staged. But why? I turned left into the family room. There I found Beyoncé perched on the couch, pale with shame. LeToya and her mother, Pam, seemed relieved to be distracted by my entrance. After I had already exchanged a few words with Pam, Mathew came into the room and introduced me.

"Pam, this is David. The girls' voice teacher and the artistic director of the group."

"Thank you, Mathew. We've already introduced ourselves," I said. Celestine left the house.

I led the girls and Pam into the next room, and Mathew went to the kitchen to do some telephoning.

I have to say, I was proud of him. Our last big discussion, and we had many, was about his getting my responsibilities clear. I was not just a vocal coach, a term that limits my scope, but rather a voice teacher and an artistic developer. Beyond that, and supporting my work as a teacher of classical singing practices, I incorporated the methods of a psychological vocal therapist. Such a therapist focuses on environmental and/or psychological factors that may contribute to a person's poor vocal habits and skills. Stress in the workplace or in the home, for instance, can seriously limit our vocal powers. My understanding of the whole singer led my desire to develop the complete performing artist. Thus, I was glad that Mathew appeared this time to have acknowledged my importance to the group.

Pam and I greeted one another warmly, shaking one another's hand. I turned my attention to her daughter.

"LeToya is it?" I asked.

"Yes sir!" she said with enthusiasm.

Beyoncé, who had moved into the den from the family room, stood beside me with abounding energy. Beside herself with excitement, she told me, in front of the new girl, "You will like LeToya," to which I replied, "OK. We will see." Beyoncé wanted everything to go off without a hitch. The pride she showed in herself and in LeToya was well placed. This girl certainly had the right look and aura.

LeToya was a gorgeous little girl, a natural beauty, exactly as Beyoncé had described her. Behind her glasses she had the face of an angel, with skin of a golden bronze color. Her long, well cared-for hair surrounded a symmetrically perfect face. LeToya's thin body was impeccably dressed in black and silver lamé. She had one of the smallest thoracic cavities (rib cage area) I had ever seen on a young singer. During our very brief chat together, I heard that LeToya had a bronchial problem, but I decided to broach that subject only after hearing her sing. First things first, I thought.

"What would you like to sing for me, LeToya?" I asked.

She replied, "Lift Every Voice," which is a powerful song written by two brothers, James Weldon and John Rosamond Johnson. It is known as the black national anthem.

"Great," I said.

I gave the signal for her to begin whenever she was ready. Taking a minute to collect herself, she then opened her mouth to sing. From the first tone she had me. Her voice was gorgeous, even though it was all head tone. She had absolutely no bottom in her voice, which didn't disturb me at all. Teaching her to access that part of her voice would be easy, even if it would take years. I was certain that I could teach her to sing just as beautifully there, too. Unable to hold back my excitement I said, "LeToya, do you know you have high notes in you?"

Nervously giggling, LeToya answered, "No. I can't sing high."

"Oh yes, you can. You have high notes galore." My excitement had to do with knowing that a singer with very little bottom voice usually would have a lot of top voice.

I could see Pam in my peripheral vision. She was gleaming. LeToya was the high top girl that I had hoped I would find. Her presence was tremendous. I noticed that Mathew liked our new girl too, but he tried not to show it. With every move she made, you were forced to watch her. She had that something special, what the French call "*je ne sais quoi.*" Like little Beyoncé back at her audition in 1989, LeToya behaved like a singer, one who wanted to be a star. She would round out the top brilliantly in the Girls Tyme sound and chordal structure. I began to think that maybe, just maybe, God wasn't angry with me. He had sent me a viable replacement to fill Ashley's shoes – well, not completely, but at least I wouldn't have to worry any longer.

"Does LeToya have asthma?" I asked Pam.

She answered, "Yes," and then asked if having asthma presented a problem, and she wanted to assure me that LeToya had medication, and her doctor says...I stopped her.

"Don't worry. It is no problem. It affects only the breathing process, but it is totally manageable."

Pam still looked worried. Living with their child's asthma makes most parents hypersensitive.

"Asthma causes the lungs to constrict. I noticed it as soon as I walked into the room. LeToya breathes very shallowly, trying to compensate. Every asthmatic does it," I said. I continued. "Learning to breathe properly will not only enhance her quality of life but both you and she will discover that she will be a lot calmer. She won't fear that she has to gasp for air. It will flow deeply and evenly, which will contribute to her creating a better balance in the exchange of oxygen and carbon dioxide in her blood. However, I will have to break open her rib cage."

At that, both Pam and LeToya looked alarmed.

Laughing, I calmed them. "No, no. Sorry! I don't mean break her rib cage physically – it will be a question of teaching her a special way of increasing her breath intake, so that her lungs, with the help of the intercostal muscles, will better help her. To her it might feel as though something is cracking itself open, here, at her sternum," I said. "And here, at the middle of her back. This process must happen in order to get to the pearl that lies within her – her voice. She will be just fine." They smiled, cautiously.

I looked at LeToya. "OK young lady, let's get to work." And with that, LeToya Nicole Luckett and I began her very first lesson.

"Beyoncé, would you go upstairs and bring me a face towel," I said. "And one of your hair clips or a rubber band."

"OK," she said, jetting up the stairs. Before long, she was back, handing me the items that I had asked for. With the face towel in my left hand and the hair clamp in my right, I pulled LeToya's open hair back and clipped it with Beyoncé's hair clamp.

"LeToya, follow me please," I said.

Beyoncé and Pam followed too. Standing to my left, I could see Mathew out of the corner of my eye as he took a seat in his favorite chair, the place he mostly ever sat in the Knowles house – the kitchen table/breakfast nook. Pam stood at the kitchen's center island counter top, nervously watching.

"LeToya, please stand here," I said.

Placing her directly in front of the sink, I stood to her right. Beyoncé instinctively moved to LeToya's left. I was now in teaching mode. My attention was focused on LeToya entirely. Beyoncé knew what that meant and adjusted accordingly. I turned the cold water on and gave LeToya the face towel while I held my right hand under the water, waiting for it to get cold. It took a few seconds, and when it did, I asked LeToya to cup her hands under the water and then splash it on her face, adding quickly, "And make sure you hold your breath."

A bit apprehensive, LeToya did as I asked.

"One," I counted. "Now wait. And again," I said. We continued like this for about 20 or 30 seconds.

"What does this do?" Pam asked.

"I'm glad you asked. Splashing cold water into the face sends a signal to the brain that LeToya is about to dive into water. The brain sends that information to the body and automatically, without LeToya's help, her body begins to adjust itself so that she can take in more air and hold it longer," I said. "It's neuroscience. In addition, cool water slows the heart rate, calms the mind, and relaxes the body's muscles. With asthmatics the goal is to get as much oxygen into the blood stream as possible. If I had used icy cold water, she'd hyperventilate. Using ice water is dangerous."

Beyoncé was about to burst from the obvious question.

Looking to her I said, "LeToya's chest area and its supporting muscles would tense up and she'd feel panicky. A person with asthma knows and understands hyperventilation."

"Lord, yes," Pam said.

After LeToya had dried her face, she and I returned to the Knowles den. Beyoncé, following closely behind, was careful to hang back so that she didn't interrupt the space I'd created for LeToya.

"LeToya, stretch your arms out in front of you, like this, above your head. Pretend that you want to hug the sun," I said.

She did it, even as she doubted. Her eyebrows gave her away.

"I'm sorry. I forgot to say that you should be happy to hug the sun. Don't doubt the exercise. It causes a frown, causing your eyebrows to pull together and downward, which activates fear in your mind. We want to be happy," I added.

She prepared to do it again.

"Wait. This time really think love. You *really* want to hug the sun and it should put a smile on your face," I said.

"Wow, I can take a deeper breath," she said.

"Did you feel your ribs move up and out? And your back expand?" I asked. "Do it again."

"Yes," she said.

"Do it again. But this time close your mouth. I want you to breathe through the nose only."

She did what I asked her.

"Hold it. Don't move," I said. "Listen to my voice and don't let the air out." I told LeToya that I wanted her to take in more air, without opening her mouth or lowering her arms. "Simply take in more air. Again. Hold it – hold it – hold it."

LeToya's body started to shake.

"Do you feel a pressure, here – at the ribs?"

LeToya nodded her head.

"Those are your intercostal muscles, whose function is to hold the ribs out and up after breathing. OK, let the air out," I said.

Falling about, LeToya let out a little sigh. I laughed. All that oxygen was making her a bit punchy. She had no idea what I was doing, but it was fun like Christmas to her. Turning to Pam, I said, "Well, she certainly follows orders."

We all had another laugh, which I provoked intentionally. It is important to create an atmosphere of calm and joy, especially for the asthmatic singer. Tension and stress are crippling for them.

"This time LeToya, hold your arms outward, as though you are happy to hug your grandmother," I said.

LeToya's face lit up.

"Ah! I see you love your grandmother. I loved mine too."

LeToya prepared herself, raised her arms, which had been resting at her sides and said,

"I feel the pressure here this time," pointing to her chest.

"OK! Great," I said. "Now we are going to alternate. One – arms up; rising up on your tippy toes – then let the air out. And two, arms out – on your tippy toes – let the air out." After repeating this for a few minutes, I grabbed a chair. "Sit down," I said. "Now, while breathing through your nose you are going to hum a note of your choosing, pulsating it while moving your torso from side to side," I said. Demonstrating, I explained that it was a dance move that I was asking her to do, called contraction. "Please allow your shoulders to follow your movements, stretching slightly upwards while popping, that is, contracting your torso."

She did it. She heard a crack. We all did.

"Great. First crack down, two more to go," I said. The top of her vertebrae had cracked, at the base of the neck. Next, I needed it to crack the vertebrae at the shoulder blades and middle back. Seconds later that happened, too.

"OK, now bite down and sing Ee, Ou, Ee, Ou, Ee, Ou, until you run out of breath." I demonstrated. Her body started to shake again. Beyoncé was all eyes and ears.

"Now, keeping your hips still, squaring them in the chair, you are going to isolate your rib cage, moving it forward and upwards to the sky and then contracting backwards, sinking your mid-section and curving the back."

It happened. The last crack, and LeToya, smiling from ear to ear, had become even more loopy. She had never taken in so much air before. "Oxygen is a natural high," I said to Pam, laughing heartily.

I asked LeToya to sing "Lift Every Voice" again. This time the sound was fuller. She had power and everyone in the room heard what I had. Twelve-year-old LeToya Luckett was going places.

I headed toward Mathew, who signaled for me to hold on. He was still sitting in the kitchen, looking ever so busy, having a telephone conversation. After he hung up, he and I talked about LeToya's audition, while she and Beyoncé laughed it up in the den.

"This is the girl I want," I told Mathew. I'd also have to speak to Ann, but I was sure she would back me. Indeed, she said, later, "You have to train her. It's your choice." Peace and happiness had returned to the big house on Parkwood and to the group.

(I, however, would never forget my Ashley. It would be many years before I could put her in the same sentence with my peace and happiness.)

"Pam, we have a rehearsal at 5:00 p.m. today. I'd like to integrate LeToya into the group, sooner rather than later. Can you get her back by 5:00 p.m.?" I asked.

Looking at her watch, Pam said that she could.

"Great."

LeToya had just one hour to get home, change into rehearsal clothes, and return, ready to work. She was being thrown into a fire without water and would have to dodge the flames, finding her way quickly. We had no time to waste. Girls Tyme had an engagement coming up.

I excused myself, shaking Pam's hand again and then turning to LeToya, "Welcome to the group," I said.

LeToya was all smiles. Beyoncé too!

With that, it was time for Kelly's lesson, so I took my leave.

266

Ann had begun to seek out legitimate ways in which she could garner the serious attention she thought the girls deserved. Then Mathew inserted his "thoughts," set on arranging for the girls to sing at what I called, "every cat and dog fight," without very much success. Neither of them got much resistance from me. Local opportunities would only strengthen the girls' performance capabilities. However, having just recently added LeToya to the group, I was hesitant to accept any more public performances until she had had a chance to learn the repertoire and feel more comfortable in the group.

My suggestion that we re-schedule near-future dates did not go over well. Mathew didn't believe in cancellation. I didn't either, of course, but this was no ordinary situation. How could we expect LeToya to perform in only weeks what the other girls had worked on for months, even years? She was still learning the group sound, objective, and vision. Although she was eager to learn, I was still a strange man asking her to do complicated musical and artistic things she had never done before. Mathew was intractable. LeToya would have to learn to trust me. Without the luxury or the comfort of a slow integration, LeToya figured out pretty quickly, she'd have to step up her game.

LeToya worked hard at the difficult task of learning all the steps, getting her voice in order, and smiling at the same time. I knew that she was overwhelmed. I also knew the dangers of stress on her breathing, but we had no time to make allowances for her inexperience. I cancelled a few private students in order to give LeToya the extra time she needed over the next two weeks. I would have to call on every cognitive approach known to man in those lessons, even though LeToya was sharp as a tack. Her mental capacity for high-pressure situations was extraordinary. Still, I kept her asthmatic condition in mind. Again, it and she required a positive and calming atmosphere. LeToya understood instinctively that I expected her to prove that my confidence was well placed. She could not let me down, and she didn't, ever. She worked like ten horses, tension- and asthma-free.

I disliked putting her under extreme pressure and watched carefully for signs of any negative consequences.

The other girls seemed to take to LeToya, and Kelly seemed especially pleased that she had someone whose voice was closer to hers in the group. In the beginning, LeToya felt like an outsider. Kelly understood this feeling and therefore took extra care, showing her the ropes. The two developed a special friendship. LeToya even helped Kelly learn the choreography, because Kelly frequently still fumbled. (I promised myself that this year would be the year I would solve her issues. I was going to get this girl to see her beauty and talent if it killed me.) Beyoncé also enjoyed having LeToya in the group and both she and Kelly constantly talked about how pretty LeToya's hair was – especially Kelly, of course. LeToya had long, silky, thick black hair that hung way past shoulder length.

Beyoncé told me that she had heard LeToya singing one day at school and liked her voice very much. Knowing that Girls Tyme needed a third member, Beyoncé had conquered her customary shyness and mustered up the courage to talk to LeToya.

"Hi, you wanna be in my group?" Beyoncé had said.

Beyoncé had LeToya's complete attention. "What group?" she asked. Beyoncé explained. LeToya told me years later that she was so excited about the possibility of joining Girls Tyme that she couldn't sleep for the anticipation of her audition.

Mathew made it clear to me that Beyoncé was to be the group's sole lead singer and that I should prepare Kelly and LeToya to sing strong background vocals. That was neither my vision nor Beyoncé's. I wanted a group where they all sang solo, and Beyoncé had already spoken adamantly about it. I broached the subject, right in front of her father. I wasn't going to be bullied by a dilettante.

"Daddy, that's old. Nobody will accept us if I sing all the solos," Beyoncé said.

I knew she was right. Beyoncé had an uncanny sense of what was right and what the public wanted and I rarely second-guessed this. Decidedly, I wasn't going to allow Mathew to do it either, not without a serious fight. It was important that Beyoncé learn to think for herself. Some man would always be telling her he knew best, in the music business. We had already begun talking about the importance of developing an individual personality as an artist. I resigned myself to fighting with Beyoncé's parents. Her artistry depended upon the freedom those fights would afford her.

Celestine noticed Beyoncé's natural instincts as well, but she was in full support of Mathew, who insisted he knew best. They needed to control Beyoncé. They could not allow her to start making demands. Celestine began using the word "diva" synonymously with "spoiled brat," as in, "I'm not raising any divas," and, "Don't get any diva ideas that you know how to run this show." Celestine would be caught in public on one occasion, slapping Beyoncé in a music store for, "acting like a diva." Beyoncé believed that the incident had been necessary. Sadly, it wasn't. Her mother's calculated slap had been about maintaining her own position and power, and not about "teaching" her daughter *some humility*. But I digress.

With little effort, Celestine was able to keep Beyoncé under her control. The child began to develop an aversion to the very word "diva" and made it a life-long goal to avoid giving people the impression that she is (what her mother called) a diva, which infuriated me beyond measure.

I, on the other hand, wanted Beyoncé to be a diva – in the original sense of the honorable Italian word. Rather than Celestine's pejorative use, I was actively encouraging Beyoncé to strive for the excellent qualities and accomplishments that earned a celebrated singer the title of "Diva." I wanted Beyoncé's vocal and performance talents to be polished and brilliant enough to justify an honorific that signified "the best." I expected that Beyoncé would be the best, and I made sure that Celestine knew it. I wasn't doing all this work to build the *girl next door*. "She's got to become fierce, step away from that shyness," I said.

However, that did not mean that I wanted Kelly and LeToya to be relegated to a lesser role in Girls Tyme. I wanted them also to be divas, extraordinary in their crafts. All their voices were still under construction, and that meant choosing suitable vocal arrangements, always refining the songs as the girls matured. I explained to Mathew that I didn't want to build a new version of the Supremes, with one Diana Ross in the spotlight and, in the background, the Others. I was interested in a new version of a more polished Emotions or a better-developed EnVogue. My vision was in conflict with Mathew's and there was no talking him out of his opinion or me out of mine.

Suddenly, without warning, Mathew made a major announcement in front of me and the girls, who had heard our exchange. He had changed the group's name.

"Girls, your new name will be '*Somethin' Fresh,*'" he said. Then he placed a flyer of the girls' next performance onto the kitchen counter top. *Somethin' Fresh* stood blazing in the flyer's headline and my girls' picture was next to the announcement of that performance. They were going to be singing at Texas Southern University – in two weeks.

"Thanks for the advanced warning, Mathew," I said.

"You're welcome," Mathew said.

Turning on my heels, I mumbled under my breath, "Asshole."

"What did you say?"

"Are you deaf, too?" I asked. I had come to the end of my patience. I am not a proponent of drug use, but Mathew needed a fix bad. It was bad enough when he was high but if he needed a fix, he was unbearable. The kind of unbearable that could push people to think awful thoughts, and I did.

* * * * *

I was searching desperately for a way to deal with my ever-increasing frustrations with the Knowleses. I tried talking to friends. That didn't work. I tried praying. That didn't work either. Then I got an idea. Remembering Dr. Dunlop, the child psychologist back in Omaha who had counseled my siblings and me after Mama's divorce from my abusive stepfather, I recalled a method he used to help us heal from life with Roy Edward Kellogg. In therapy, we were asked to "talk to the puppet." At first it was slow going – a bit strange, as a matter of fact. But after a few sessions I got the hang of it. Easily forgetting that Dr. Dunlop was in the room, I would say things to that doll, it embarrasses me to recall. They weren't nice, but they were very necessary. What I said and did now to my Mathew and Celestine dolls were far worse.

My beloved landlords on Parkwood Street hadn't a clue that I had a stuffed Donkey, which I called Mathew, and a porcelain Witch doll, whom I called Celestine. Rather than responding verbally to Mama and Papa Knowleses' irritating behavior, I simply returned to my apartment and took it out on my willing substitutes. I stomped on Witch Celestine, several times. I even put her in the oven once at 350 degrees. I yearned to see her melt, but my very own wicked witch of the west was fire proof. Once Beyoncé knocked on the door while I was having a go at Witch Celestine and I threw her behind the couch, cracking her lovely porcelain face. I kicked the hell out of that Donkey. I tried strangling him and I even tried drowning him once, but the damn thing kept floating to the top. Donkey Mathew wouldn't die. Shit! One day the real Mathew had made me so mad, I stuffed Donkey Mathew's head, face first, in a canister of flour, hoping he'd overdose. He didn't. The subsequent shaking he suffered sent flour flying all over the kitchen, while he stared up at me with that shit-eating grin plastered on his furry little face. You know the one. All jack-asses have it.

The things I said to Donkey Mathew and Witch Celestine are unmentionable, believe me. I often substituted the word witch for a similar one when scolding Witch Celestine. I have never used the word "Mother Fucker" in conversation as much as I did with Donkey Mathew. In an effort to make light of my provoked attacks, I often found myself channeling the 70s comedian Flip Wilson. Geraldine Jones, a marvelous and witty character he created for his wildly successful "The Flip Wilson Show" on TV gave life to the phrase, "The devil made me do it." I couldn't help myself. I didn't want to stop. Slapping Witch Celestine and choking the ever-lasting life out of Donkey Mathew felt deliciously good.

By 1993, I had come to resent Beyoncé's parents for who they were and what they insisted upon doing to others. Everyone, especially Beyoncé and the other girls, and yes, even their defiant daughter, Solange, would eventually suffer from their malignant and covert abuse. Taking Solange down a peg or two seemed to give her parents perverse satisfaction. When my conversations with Celestine about Solange's desire to sing merited no real response, I tried talking to her father. But he only wanted to talk about Beyoncé.

"But Mathew, Solange is crying out for attention. Please talk to Celestine. I'm concerned about Solange's psyche. We are paying too much attention to Beyoncé at Solange's expense."

"Fuck Solange," Mathew said, quickly returning to incoherent ramblings about Beyoncé, *his star*.

I felt so ashamed, knowing what I knew. Ignoring a child is a dreadful form of abuse. Each time Mama Celestine threw one of her rocks and then hid her hand, giving special attention to the details that only a mother could give to such a task, I inevitably found myself back in my apartment having another conversation with Witch Celestine. Those moments were especially dark for me, and I didn't understand why. I both loved and detested Celestine, and her husband's sense of entitlement made my ass hurt. I despised them even more for claiming that they were *"doing it all for Beyoncé."* I had been witness to Mama and Papa Knowles throwing Beyoncé under the proverbial bus, and on more than one occasion.

So even though I was ashamed and embarrassed to be abusing a stuffed animal and a porcelain doll, I was grateful for my therapeutic outlet. Prison wasn't for me. Wearing orange was out of the question. The truth is, I needed the surrogates, Donkey Mathew and Witch Celestine, with every passing month more than ever. That jackass and porcelain doll saved lives, including my own.

I had many restless nights, trying to figure out the way to combat Beyoncé's parents' ugliness. They were guilty of so much. I often believed myself to be dreaming, and sometimes I was. For instance, like the time I stabbed Donkey Mathew. That was a real nightmare.

But the real Mathew had taken to waking me out of my sleep, in the middle of the night, expecting me to listen to his absurd plans for the girls. He'd do it to Ann, too, incessantly. So if that dream had been a real nightmare, my irritation was real. The power struggles and underhanded betrayals threatened to break Beyoncé's resolve, not to mention the other girls' confidence. They had already shared their hopes and dreams with me. Now they were sharing their nightmares, ones that became my own.

Call me crazy, but it felt like we were all being controlled by a spirit. I have never felt so crippled in my life. The Knowleses' sugary sweet lie of an idyllic life was debilitating. Even sadder was their believing it. It was as if we had all been put in a trance. Still, I refused to abandon Beyoncé and the other girls. Mathew and Celestine Knowles would not win. So, I came to terms with abusing inanimate objects. It pained me to think that I had no other choice. We were all committed to Beyoncé, especially me. She was an angel who maintained real humility in the eye of her parents' egomaniacal storm. She was a good person. I had to remember that. I just kept telling myself that fact, over and over again.

I know you know that this wasn't a healthy version of Play therapy. But, thank you Dr. Dunlop, wherever you are!

* * * * *

We rehearsed and rehearsed, and LeToya began to catch on. She made it well through her first performance – nervous and sweating all the way, but she made it. She was a natural at not showing her apprehensions to the audience. I never had to teach her that. LeToya and I soon felt secure in working together, and her private voice lessons started going better than well – she was fast and sensitive, and she had an incredible sixth sense about music and performing. All of that was a blessing as we approached our Texas Southern University engagement.

Then Mathew put even more pressure on me by announcing that he had invited Teresa LaBarbera Whites to come back to Houston to hear the reconstituted, newly named Somethin' Fresh. Without telling a soul, Mathew had reconnected with Teresa, keeping her informed of all the new and interesting details of his takeover of management, diminishing Ann's role, and lying like a cheap rug, inflating the significance of *his* re-shaping of the group. This time I did not pick Teresa up from the airport, nor would I hear the girls' performance for her. I didn't even know the girls would be singing for her. Mathew kept all of these pleasures for himself.

According to Beyoncé's account, later, they had barely begun to sing when Mathew suddenly interrupted them. "Stop!" he called out. "I don't care if Teresa is sitting here. You all are not focused." Turning to Beyoncé, he said, "Did you go swimming?" No one said a word. The girls all knew Mathew's feelings on the subject of swimming – one of the rare subjects upon which he and I agreed. He had no idea why swimming affected singers, but he did know that it caused Beyoncé's nose to fill with snot. No one dared reveal the truth, that Beyoncé had, indeed, gone swimming the day before. Mathew made them start over and, fortunately, they were able to "focus" enough to satisfy his need to show himself in control.

After that audition, Teresa came over to the house. It was only then that I learned what had just transpired without me. She told me that she liked the new girl. She asked me how I envisioned weaving her into the sound of the group. "LeToya is the icing," I said, "the icing on a well baked cake. She will give me the top notes and quality of sound that I was developing in Ashley."

"She has something special in her eyes," Teresa said. "Yes," I rejoiced, "and she can sing into the stratosphere. She has a high C in her now, but doesn't have a clue as to how to approach it. But not to worry. She and I will make it a permanent and easy part of her range."

Over the following days my girls and I continued preparing for the Texas Southern University performance. The day before that event, Beyoncé went over to a family friend's house where there were lots of kids. She went swimming – again. She remembered her father's angry reaction, but the other children were having so much fun that Beyoncé, a great lover of the water, couldn't resist. Well, she lost her voice. The next morning

Beyoncé woke up sounding as though ten frogs had taken up residence in her throat. Her head was so stuffed up that it affected her ability to focus on the matter at hand – her singing and her performance.

"You have learned a very valuable lesson," I said. "I don't make these things up, Beyoncé. I tell you these things because I *know* them to be true." I had already warned her against the devastating combination of chlorine and her chronic sinusitis. She apologized profusely.

Mathew had been out all night and when he finally showed up he became furious. I assured him that all would be OK.

"How?! She has no fuckin' voice!" he yelled. Alonzo (Lonnie) was in town for that performance and he, too, was worried, extremely worried. My reassurance seemed to fall on deaf ears. They said, standing there in my living room, that they couldn't imagine how this situation could be saved.

"I can show you better than I can tell you," I said.

By this time Beyoncé was feeling really bad about the difficulties that she had caused. But she had only gone swimming – she didn't have the Plague. I told her not to worry. Since she had not progressed to needing antibiotics, I assured her that I could solve the problem. She knew the drill, but Mathew had never witnessed our process. He had no idea that I could easily relieve Beyoncé's stuffy nose and restore her singing voice to its usual, clear state.

She lay down on the sofa in my living room, while I washed my hands thoroughly. When I returned, she opened her mouth and I placed my forefinger directly onto the middle of her soft palate (the soft area in the back of the roof of the mouth) and pressed lightly. Again, by placing my finger there and gently pressing, without movement, the accumulated mucous began to release.

"Beyoncé, keep the mucous from going down your throat until the most opportune time to spit it out," I said.

Within minutes, she had cleared the blockage (the size of a small city) in her head, and we were then free to warm her up. Lonnie was floored.

After Mathew and Lonnie left my apartment that day, I began warming Beyoncé up with lip trills, and then moved on to light humming. I asked that she keep the throat cavity open and not change its form, nor interfere with the freedom in her back, the two points crucial to effortless singing.

"Purse your lips together," I instructed her, "and with your teeth touching, sing ee ou, ee ou, ee ou. Over and over again, until you run out of breath." Her tone fell into her body and settled in the center of her diaphragm.

Beyoncé noticed that when she sang the ee vowel, her lips and face pulled back into an exaggerated smile, controlled by the zygomatic muscles, just under the skin of her face. When she sang ou the lips protruded, activated by orbicularis oris and the levator labii superioris. Then, I asked her to sing the ee and ah vowels, whispering them. After one-and-one-half hours of slow and calculated work, her voice was once again functioning on the breath. She was still very young, and I needed to insure that she could deliver without being distracted by a stuffed up head and blocked sinus cavity.

"OK, now your voice is flowing on the breath again. Please go to your room and be absolutely quiet," I said. I told her that she could behave normally after one hour, but that she was not to make a sound until that evening, when I would warm up the group again. She did exactly as I instructed her to do, as she always did, and that evening she sang brilliantly.

I'll never forget it and I hope she won't either.

* * * * *

Lonnie was not the only one amazed at Beyoncé's transformation at the Texas Southern University performance. For the first time, I felt a semblance of respect from Mathew regarding my work. Of course, he had acknowledged the progress in the girls over the past four years. But I heard him say many times that any improvements were due to the natural processes of their growing up – nothing to do with me. (Mathew would adopt that story again, years later, telling the press that he was responsible for developing Girls Tyme, Somethin' Fresh, Borderline, Cliché, Da Dolls, Destiny, and, finally, Destiny's Child.)

276

Yes, I had many clues along the way about who the Knowleses were, but when you care about people you tend to look past their faults. My rationalizations of their behavior would bite me in the ass many times in years to come. I consoled myself at that time by always being there for Beyoncé – my Carlo/Farinelli.

The various swimming incidents helped all my girls to have respect for deep knowledge of the voice and of technique. Taking the voice for granted, singers can easily put themselves at risk. Trying to sing when they are sick shows them the folly of that attitude.

"Beyoncé, have you learned your lesson?" I asked.

She had, she said.

We never had this issue again, not during the rest of my time and many years with her. In fact, Beyoncé's swimming capers were lessons to everyone.

13. Power

As a teacher and artistic developer of extraordinary talents I see narcissistic and sociopathic personality disorders, existentialism, and faulty cognitive and behavioral skills every day. Not in my students, mind you, but in the adults who seek my support for their dreams of turning their "child prodigy" into a cash cow. Their demands create an environment that I must deal with, and masterfully. It takes a disciplined mind and well balanced spirit to survive their power plays.

* * * * *

Mathew was garnering negative attention all over Houston, and even Celestine's clients were beginning to talk. Every day she faced new rumors, most of them true. Mathew was into all kinds of kinky things. Word on the street was that the glass dick wasn't the only thing he'd wrapped his hands around. The more I saw and heard, the more I sympathized with Celestine's position. They hadn't been husband and wife for years. I never even saw them hold hands. Naturally, they hugged each other in public whenever they considered it expedient – for photo ops, to name one common occurrence. That was as far as their "affection" for one another went.

Obsessed with tarnishing Celestine's image in the eyes of his daughters, Mathew appeared early one morning – after being out several nights late – with flowers in hand. Beyoncé, who loved her mother dearly, knew that there was tension between the two, so when Mathew asked *her* to pass on his surprise to Celestine, she was elated. She ran into the kitchen, where I sat with a frustrated Celestine.

"Mama! Look what Daddy bought you!"

Naturally, Beyoncé expected her father's flowers to have a positive effect on her mother. Surely, they would soften her mother's obvious anger. Celestine surprised everyone by throwing them to the floor. While a devastated Beyoncé struggled to understand her mother's response, I thought to myself, How cruel – of Mathew, that is, using his own child as a shield against his wife's wrath. Mathew had crossed the line. Damaging Celestine's image in Beyoncé's eyes was punishable by death. None of us knew how he'd eventually pay. For now, she just wanted him gone. "Get OUT!" she screamed. Shattered, Beyoncé burst into tears.

Once again Ann came to the rescue. She was always rescuing this family. According to Kenny Moore, Celestine had thrown Mathew out of the house on more than one occasion. Kenny told me that every time Celestine threw Mathew out, he would show up at Ann's. How accurate "every time" was, I'm not sure, but Mathew spent more than a few nights on Ann's couch. I certainly knew that Ann offered him shelter.

Those were turbulent and sketchy times. Beyoncé longed for a peaceful resolution, and I just wanted them either to finish each other off, or divorce already. Unfortunately, Beyoncé would not get her peace and we would not get relief, not for a long time.

Some days after the flower-offering incident, I saw Mathew in the Galleria Mall, walking proudly with a woman who introduced herself to me as "Diamond." Although it was obvious they were an item, Mathew tried to act as though they were business colleagues. The man was delusional. Very much unemployed, he didn't even own the dust in his pocket, so whatever game he was playing, I wasn't biting. I must say, I was not shocked at all. Who knew better than I that he and his wife despised one another? Theirs was not a marriage. It *was* a business arrangement. Neither was willing to relinquish the claim to the success they'd envisioned for themselves. Still, I couldn't help but feel sorry for the entire lot of them and the situation. It was clear. Diamond, the way she walked, talked, and dressed, was no colleague.

I soon discovered that, although unhappily married, Celestine was not suffering all by herself. Going over to the main house to retrieve my keyboard one afternoon, I happened upon Celestine kissing a man. I recognized him immediately: Richard Lawson, a famous actor. The startled Celestine had no choice but to introduce me. Talk about awkward. She was supposed to be at her salon. I extended my hand to Richard, telling him how much I admired his work. He nodded. "It's a pleasure," he said. After letting him out of the house, Celestine turned. "Richard is my cousin," she said. "He's on that stuff."

Talking a mile a minute, Celestine explained that she had been counseling Richard. He's been on cocaine a long time, she said, and is trying to break the bad habit. She was working awfully hard to convince me of her innocence. I kept thinking, The lady definitely doth protest too much. Why? I hadn't a clue. She should have known I'd be the last one to mention the scene to Mathew. But hey, I thought, what's good for Mathew should be good for her, right? Absolutely not. What she was doing was against everything that she swore she believed in. Celestine Beyincé Knowles was a puritan, a self-proclaimed martyr for Jesus. She never admitted to, or had been caught in the act of doing, anything suspect, not until now anyway. It wasn't biblical, what she was doing. Adultery was a sin, no matter how she spun the story.

No doubt in my mind. Celestine was cheating on her cheating husband with her "Cousin" Richard.

Damn…

* * * * *

Mathew was stealing more money than Celestine could make. Once again, the family car was on the blink, breaking down often, but Mathew was flush with cash.

He'd stolen money out of her purse. Celestine cried.

"Has Mathew looked for a new job?" I asked her.

"No," Celestine answered. Then, in almost the next breath, she voiced her confidence in Mathew's managerial talents.

"Excuse me?" Had I heard correctly?

"Mathew will be great as the manager," she said, wiping her eyes.

"This is new," I observed, hopelessly confused.

Almost from day one of my living with the Knowleses, I had noticed how Celestine berated Mathew and how he belligerently returned the favor. Every day it was something. He wasn't providing for his family; she was an ungrateful Bitch. To counter her claim that he didn't seem to care that they were sinking, he accused her of shitting on his dreams. "Mathew needs to get a job," she'd say to me, over and over. She said far worse to him. It would take me a while to understand that Mathew's belligerence and Celestine's berating came from the same source – shame. But I'm getting ahead of myself. Today, Wife Celestine was pro Husband Mathew. Only God knew what the mood would be tomorrow.

I couldn't help thinking that one day, music executives would see through Mathew's dilettantish posturing and unfounded grandiosity. "You can't fake knowledge in the music business," I said to Celestine. There were just too many things that Mathew had no clue about, things like cross-collateralization for instance and co-mingling, even though he claimed to have degrees in economics and business management. That Mathew didn't have "it," in my opinion, would be putting it mildly. I knew it and God knew it, but Mathew Knowles did not. His obsession with becoming a major player in the music biz – about which he knew nothing – seemed extraordinarily misguided to me. He could pretend, publicly, that he was motivated out of love for his wife and children, but it was clear that Mathew Knowles was driven solely by a need to prove himself. To whom, I didn't know – not yet.

My most telling clue thus far appeared one day hidden in Mathew's own words, "One day, they gon' be bowing at my feet." He swore that he'd been born to *rule the music business*. Interesting choice of words, I thought. The afternoon he delivered his "rule the music business" soliloquy, he and I had been having an intense conversation in the kitchen about Beyoncé. He was still trying to convince me that *our* focus needed to be on her, to the exclusion of the other girls. I would never go for that lunacy, and I told him.

"My daughter is the best," Mathew shouted.

"That may be, but *your daughter, she* doesn't need your *gentle push*. Mathew, you are barking up a very dangerous tree," I answered. He laughed.

I'm out of here, I thought, and I fled both the conversation and the room. No way would I waste another second in a pointless conversation about something Mathew would never understand.

"What, you can't take the truth?" Mathew called out through that shit-eating, Donkey Mathew grin I'd grown to despise. Turning back in the doorway, I said, "Of course I can take the truth, Mathew. If there is anyone who has the qualities to push his way through in the music business, it's you." I had just insulted him and he was still smiling like I'd just called his mother beautiful. His narcissism was extraordinary. Still, I told him that he would be remiss in not learning a few particulars. "It's a tough business, Mathew."

"Nobody's gonna fuck me over," he said.

"Ah – OK," I answered. Then I told him that it's "a wise man who will do at once what the fool does finally" (quoting the 14th-century philosopher and political strategist Niccolò Machiavelli). Mathew and Celestine Knowleses' only card in the deck was their daughter Beyoncé, and *her talent*. Beyoncé's "super parents" intended to ride her like *a race horse*.

"Machiavelli also said, "Everyone sees what you appear to be, few experience what you really are…""

Sadly, six hundred years later, Mathew and Celestine were proving him correct. I had joined the ranks of "the few."

* * * * *

Given the girls' ages in early 1993, I knew that time was on our side. However, the Knowles family's financial situation – and the other parents' perception of their daughters' potential earnings – made them all eager for a quicker return on their investment. My desire to protect their daughters' voices and psyches ran smack dab against their hopes for career and cash flow. I got that. So, I made a call to my friend Roy Brown, out in Los Angeles. It was a long shot, but perhaps I was wrong about the girls not being signable at such a young age. It could be that the music industry would change its formula and their rules to accommodate such extraordinary young talents, ignoring every child labor law known to man…

Roy's wife told me that he was on tour with Brothers Johnson, and that she would pass on my message. (Brothers Johnson was an American funk and R&B duo, the brothers George and Louis Johnson. Wildly successful in the 1970s and 80s, they celebrated a string of hits, most notably "I'll Be Good to You," "Strawberry Letter 23" and "Stomp.") I thanked her and hung up.

I had begun to supervise the studio training my girls so desperately needed. After "Star Search," I started going to all of their recording sessions, especially the ones initiated by Mathew. In those early days I did not know most of the producers and I trusted only one, Preston Middleton. (Competence in this business is a rare commodity.) Mostly, I drove my girls to their studio appointments, and I was always the one who got them home at the end of a long night of recording. Mathew was otherwise occupied.

I was sorry and surprised to learn that Lonnie had been remiss in teaching certain basics for working successfully in the recording studio. Perhaps he thought they were too young to understand even fundamental concepts. I wondered, for instance, why my girls still didn't know how to handle the studio microphone in recording. They were unaware of such dangers as bumping the mic, or their suddenly standing too far back or too close, without alerting the engineer so that he could adjust levels to their change in position. The girls frequently made elementary miscalculations regarding plosive consonants, which can cause "pops" in the recorded sound, and their vowel production, as recorded, was weak. It was important that they understood to apply the theories we worked on in voice lessons to the making of and producing high quality vocal recordings. They were more than old enough, and intelligent enough, and once I stepped in, they embraced the information eagerly.

One day, after finishing a lesson with my private student Cecilia Jackson, I raced back into the house to answer my ringing phone. Roy Brown was calling me back.

"Hey Roy! Brother, I need your help," I said.

"What's up?" he asked.

"Can you help me get a demo of my girls to Quincy Jones, or someone connected at the top of the music business out in California?"

"Sure. Send me the tracks. I'll take a listen to them and get back to you," Roy said.

"They're really wonderful. The girls are on the young side but unbelievably disciplined and talented. I am sure you're going to love them."

"How old are they?"

"They are twelve, going on thirteen years old," I answered.

"What?"

"Yep – twelve and fabulous. Believe me!"

"OK, send me the tape. I'm heading out in two weeks on a USO gig. I'd like to take it with me."

"No problem. I'll overnight it to you," I said. And I did. A couple of days later my telephone rang. It was Roy again.

"Man, these girls are the shit." Roy was ecstatic. He was sure that he could garner interest and promised to get back to me. "Man, nobody is going to believe these girls are twelve."

Still excited about Roy's response, I sought Mathew out over in the main house. He wasn't home, so I left a long and enthusiastic note on the kitchen table. Mathew should come over to my apartment when he arrived. It was "important," my note said.

Several hours later – about 2:00 in the afternoon – he knocked on my door.

I insisted on calling Ann in her HL&P office before he and I talked. I had vowed never again to work behind her back. Busy, she promised to call right back. Ten minutes later she was on the telephone. Mathew and I took the call on the kitchen speakerphone.

"Afternoon, Ann," I said. I explained that the reason for the conference call had to do with a contact of mine named Roy Brown.

"Who is he?" Ann asked.

"Roy Brown is one of the most sought after live-music engineers in the business. He has worked with everybody, including Whitney Houston," I said.

"Where he live?" Mathew said.

"In Los Angeles," I answered. Refocusing on my point, and ignoring Mathew's damn grammar, I said, "He's very well connected. He is a product of Quincy Jones's production school. I've asked him to share the girls' demo with Quincy."

"Oh really," Mathew said. "Who asked for your help?"

"Your wife did Mathew, because of your family's financial situation," I said. I certainly knew that my biting answer would ruffle Mathew's feathers, but my contacting Roy had not been about usurping anyone. "I contacted Roy for his help, and *he'd* like it very much, and *so would I*, if I can pass on *your* private numbers to him so that *you guys* can talk." I'd made my point.

Ann agreed, immediately and appreciatively. "Of course you can give him my number! And thank you, David!" Mathew, however, asked for Roy's number instead of giving his. He was skeptical of my motives, and of me, and he intimated his doubt about Roy's credentials.

"This is legitimate, Mathew. Do you think that I would waste your time? You've known me far too long to believe that I would expose the

284

girls to an imposter," I said. Still, he reiterated his intent. He didn't trust the situation or me.

"I want to check him out with Ruth Carson," he said.

"No problem. In fact, Ann, you should take down Roy's number as well," I answered. "Again, Roy is very reliable. If he says he can help, he can. I'm sure he wouldn't mind hearing from you both."

Ann already had paper and pen in hand. "I'm ready," she said.

Mathew just sat there, a large lump, irritably tucked away in the breakfast nook, sweating in his air conditioned house.

"Uh – Mathew, don't you need some paper and a pen, too?" I asked.

Fumbling through some unpaid bills that Celestine left stacked on the kitchen table, he tore off an edge piece of one of them. Then he looked at me in cold silence, staring right through me, which I took to mean that he was ready.

"Roy's number is 213……", I said.

Ann thanked me again for my untiring commitment and engagement in the girls' lives and future. "Any help is help we can use," she said.

After ending the call, I looked at Mathew, sitting there in all his smelly, disheveled glory. "Now we wait," I said, standing to return to my apartment.

"Nope. I'm calling him now…," Mathew murmured.

"Knock yourself out!"

I couldn't get away from Papa Knowles fast enough. He reeked…of drugs, the late night, and sex. His breath was atrocious, smelling of three-day-old fish and something horribly unidentifiable. Or, better said – unmentionable – which lingered in Mathew's moustache.

* * * * *

It had now been several months since Mathew had initiated his takeover as manager (nominally he was still co-manager with Ann Tillman, but no one would have guessed that from his behavior). With his position solidified, he was on a real ego trip. His moods encompassed both civility and rudeness. We never knew which face he was going to wear, and the atmosphere around the house was, therefore, always strained. His staying out at night, until morning now, had become a thing, which meant louder fighting. Celestine was losing her mind, she said. "Mathew, I need help," she cried, turning the tears on like I'd never seen her do. I guessed she was back to nagging Mathew to give up trying to manage the girls and get a *real* job. Hell, she was even driving me crazy, with all the back and forth. Mathew, in turn, responded by continuing to ignore his wife's "hysterics," undeterred while building his *kingdom* (his word, not mine). He was on an ego-driven trip that only he understood or believed in.

Mathew's lack of knowledge in the business of music began to show through to the other parents. After a family meeting where Pamela Luckett asked Mathew some very pointed – but appropriate – questions, which he could not answer, I once again suggested to him, privately, that he should really consider taking a course in the elements of the music business. I'd heard that the Houston Community College (HCC) offered such a class. Because it was being offered at HCC instead of U of H or Rice University, Houston's larger college campuses, I thought that tuition might be affordable. At that time, even Texas Southern University, a historically black university in Houston, had nothing remotely close to what HCC offered at that time. Today Mathew teaches such a course at TSU about "The Record Industry" to eager students dreaming of making it big in the music biz. As I understand it, his method, which he calls "thinking outside the box," is founded on two principles: One, never give up, and two, find "innovative" ways to turn up the heat. By 1993 we were all devastatingly familiar with Mathew's "innovative" ways.

Since Mathew's famous "STOP and do it again!" scene at the girls' second audition, he had not heard again from Teresa LaBarbera-Whites. It was time to turn up the heat under Teresa. He was feeling ignored, he said. "Teresa needs nudging again." When he finally tracked her down this time, she assured him that she loved the girls, but that, unfortunately, Sony/Columbia records was still not convinced. "But don't worry, I'm not giving up, Mathew," she said, over the telephone loud speaker. She also mentioned that she'd talked with Ann, about the same subject, just days prior. This seemed to irritate Mathew.

"I've got to find a way to light a real fire under Teresa," Mathew said. In his opinion, she'd become passive, he barked. It was obvious, pretty quickly, that he considered Teresa's mentioning Ann "disrespectful" to his genius. After all, he'd brought Teresa to the table – never acknowledging that Teresa had been Ann's contact. He chirped on and on, emphasizing his opinions with many choice words. Sony/Columbia didn't know "what he had to offer," he shouted. Again, I fled the room, and the conversation. Mathew kept talking, oblivious to my sudden disappearance. I could hear him as I went up the stairs, rambling on and on, utterly clueless.

While Ann continued working on securing local performance opportunities, Mathew turned up the flame. Having complained that the labels' executives, producers, and A&R departments, within various genres, always wanted to talk only with Ann, he corralled Celestine in a long conversation about what to do, in the kitchen. Stroking his hair, she suggested he force his position, his power. He shouldn't let Ann punk him, she said. "You are more capable than her, Mathew." What the hell was going on, I thought? Who was Celestine and what the hell was all that stroking-Mathew's-hair about?

The next day, a salivating Mathew rushed home. He had booked the girls to sing at the Black Expo. He said that he'd met someone who knew a woman named Sherry Simmons, who, he said, was the wife of the star producer and multiplatinum songwriter Daryl Simmons. According to Mathew, the "someone" he had met had promised to invite Sherry Simmons to attend the girls' performance at Black Expo that very weekend.

Oh, and something else: "Somethin' Fresh" was out, and "Cliché" was in. True to his pattern, without consulting anyone, Mathew announced the group's third name change. Ann hated it, and Beyoncé called it "the worse name ever," while I wondered what the Houston-born Sherry Simmons would think of it.

On the appointed Saturday my girls and I hopped into my four-door Luxury sports sedan Model B3 type 89 Audi and headed toward downtown Houston. We were met at the front doors by a frantically pacing Mathew Knowles. I looked at my watch. We were on time.

While the girls and I escaped to the staging area, Mathew headed for the toilet. When he returned, much calmer, he introduced me to Sherry, who looked fabulous, standing there in Gucci. "Mrs. Simmons," I said. "It's a pleasure to meet you." Sherry was drop dead gorgeous. We stood in the crowd, exchanging stories about the business and waiting for the show to begin, when suddenly they announced my girls.

Sherry loved them and their performance.

Although thrilling for me, her excitement was also distracting. I needed to concentrate on the girls' performance. Had they hit all their points? Did they make any musical mistakes?

"They are wonderful," Sherry said to me.

Now fully concentrated on the girls, I nodded politely to her without saying a word.

Turning to Mathew she whispered, "You've got a real gold mine." Chest all stuck out, Mathew replied, "We've worked hard." I could've killed him.

Days later, Mathew and Daryl were on the phone. Sherry had come through. Apparently Daryl really liked what he heard on his studio speakers.

"Sherry gave me the tape," he said. "Are these girls really twelve?

"Yes," Mathew answered.

Next, Daryl talked about his plans. "The girls will have to do a showcase, here in Atlanta." When he got off the phone, Mathew's response startled me: "What you think about your boy now, Mama?" he snarled into the air.

Mathew's profane aside to his deceased parent had just given me the major clue I had sought in my ongoing efforts to understand the man. Now I knew who it was that Mathew was obsessed with pleasing: Mother Knowles. Mathew's continual need to annihilate the women in his life had an *Ursprung* – a fundamental source from which his life's motivations flowed. Why had I not put this together before? Certainly he had talked to me about his mother, how he loved, feared, respected, and hated her, all apparently in equal measure. Miriam, he called her, and she had dominated his entire miserable childhood.

No wonder he felt it necessary to dominate – even destroy – Denise, Deborah, Ann, Pamela, and Celestine. No wonder Caroline had infuriated and frustrated him by her stability and integrity. And he was well on the way to ruining his beautiful daughters, Beyoncé and Solange, as well as my entire group of girls. Determined to put a stop to his unscrupulous manipulations of these innocent young women, I went into action. I needed more information. Consulting with my mother, whose professional qualifications included an informed understanding of disturbed family dynamics, I learned the concepts of difficult mothers, and abusive mothers – about the lingering, frequently life-long effects that such parenting has on children.

I spoke with Celestine about Mathew's *Mama*. Because she'd touched on the topic in the past, I felt that she would fill in some of the missing pieces of this puzzle.

"Lou Helen was mean – real mean," Celestine now said.

"Lou Helen?" I asked. "I thought her name was Miriam."

Celestine rolled her eyes. Slowly and methodically, she went on. "Helen – is Mathew's – mother…" reiterating it for me at imbecile speed.

According to Mathew's own recounting of his childhood, Mama *Miriam* Knowles was hell on wheels. Apparently, Lou Helen/Miriam chastised him severely for showing any weakness, no matter how large or small. She had also passed on to him her feelings about skin tone. He would mimic her sarcastically – "Don't have no black ass children," he'd say jokingly. It made my stomach turn. His mother's reference to dark skin, and his joking about it, spoke volumes. It also helped me to understand another of his obsessions, his fascination with "Geechee," a word Mathew used very inappropriately.

Having a "Geechee woman," a term he often used to refer to his wife's heritage, somehow made him feel superior. He believed, as many black people did and do, that "Geechee" represented light-skinned folk (high yellows) with good hair. Even I didn't know back then that "Geechee" was a language and not a people. Derived from a mixture of African, English, and Creole, the language originated with the Gullah people, descendants of West Africa. Celestine was Creole, not Gullah. Celestine's antecedents were Louisiana settlers of mixed race, namely of French and Spanish blood mixed with black (some Francophones and French-colonized Caribbean people). I was clear on one point: Even if Mathew had had all those facts straight, he had inherited from his mother some powerful biases about women and skin color and self-worth. He was in their thrall.

I was relieved – and grateful – that I had finally had a major breakthrough in my efforts to understand the behaviors of this pathetic man. Just when I'd get comfortable with one Mathew, he'd flip the script. Now I could comprehend – even if he didn't – who was driving him. Mathew would frequently call upon his deceased mother to witness whenever he had done something he considered worthy of note in the house on Parkwood. These were inevitably expressions of his frustrated and pent-up feelings, a small boy still trying to get his mother's attention: See Mama? I am worthy of your love, really I am.

At our next group rehearsal, a jovial Mathew exited the downstairs toilet, barely getting it closed behind him, announcing that Cliché had just been taken on by one of America's premiere producers.

"Who Daddy, who?" Beyoncé asked.

"Daryl Simmons," Mathew said.

"Who?"

The girls had no idea who Daryl Simmons was, but they jumped up and down for joy anyway. It just seemed like the right thing to do. They were one step closer. I congratulated them, and Mathew.

"Great save, Mathew," I said.

"It was nothing…" Mathew was as proud as a peacock. Fate had done the work, while Papa Mathew took the credit.

Then suddenly, I saw smudges of Mathew's joviality on his face. The glisten of cocaine residue. As unobtrusively as possible, I raised my thumb to my nose in a signal to him. Wipe Mathew, wipe.

* * * * *

Daryl Simmons was a silent partner at LaFace Records, the hottest new Indie-label during that time. He, Kenneth "Babyface" Edmonds, and Antonio "L.A." Reid were a force majeure as the company's producers and owners. They took the R&B genre by storm. The trio wrote hit after hit, produced and performed on the albums of successful artists like Johnny Gill, Paula Abdul, The Whispers, Sheena Easton, Karyn White and Bobby Brown, to name only a few. Bobby Brown made them a small fortune. Later the trio wrote hits for Boyz II Men, winning a Grammy in the "songwriter of the year" category for the song "End of the Road." They continued to write for that super group and churned out unstoppable hits on Boyz II Men's many multi-platinum albums over the years.

By the time the girls would actually meet Daryl, the dream team, as they were called, had found success once again producing the soundtrack to Whitney Houston's movie "The Body Guard," one of the most successful, highest-grossing music films of all times. (My girls, of course, knew that music. Although superficially thrilling, the title track, "I will always love you," was a dangerous model for my young singers. Beyoncé was particularly drawn to Whitney Huston, and I warned her about emulating Whitney's performance. In my opinion, the strident Gospel tricks would endanger her vocal health.)

After "The Body Guard" soundtrack, released by Arista records, Daryl ventured out on his own, becoming a well-respected producer. He was instrumental in the development of a new singer on the market named Toni Braxton and he wrote and produced on her debut album, which sold more than ten million copies. The album had many hits, but the one that got her the most attention was her debut single called "Another Sad Love

Song," which Daryl had written together with Babyface. (He would play it for me in his car with great pride, as we took a drive to the supermarket when the girls and I visited him later, in Atlanta.) He adored Toni and thought she was the second coming. And he must have been right, because Toni's single was being played by every radio station in the country, regardless of the station's genre specialty. She became what every label hoped they would find in an artist, one who had the ability to cross over and gain fans in many genres. Toni Braxton crossed over into mainstream and became a star overnight.

In the great beyond, Mother Knowles must have been over the moon regarding her son's new "friendship" with Daryl. For Mathew it was better than orgasmic. He'd outwitted Ann, one-upped her. The Cliché parents were also impressed. But it wasn't all smooth sailing. They would need to sign a formal contract; and then there was the matter of a "showcase" for record label reps that Daryl reportedly had in the works. I wondered what kind of hardball Daryl would play and whether Mathew had the where-withal to negotiate a good deal. Daryl Simmons was no lightweight.

Many strategizing meetings were held in the Knowles family kitchen. Then Mathew called Teresa again. "Oh God," I thought. Was he going to gloat?

Not exactly...

* * * * *

Teresa LaBarbera-Whites revealed that she was not doing so well. Her father-in-law, as I understood it, had been diagnosed with cancer, and Teresa and her husband were having a difficult time getting him the necessary treatment. They wanted him to be admitted to a special program in Houston at M. D. Anderson Hospital – one of the most prestigious hospitals and centers for cancer research in the world – but there was a lengthy waiting list. Mathew saw his opportunity. He said he knew exactly how he'd energize Teresa. She'd been too passive in her push with Sony/Columbia,

Mathew maintained. At any rate, after Mathew and Teresa hung up, he dialed 411. Talking with directory assistance, Mathew asked, "Can I have the number for M.D. Anderson hospital?" What was the plan?

A few days later, Mathew and I met in the kitchen. "Teresa's father-in-law is in," Mathew said.

"In what?" I asked.

"I got Teresa's father-in-law a place at M.D. Anderson."

Apparently, Mathew had a contact. During his short time at Picker International Mathew had sold MRI scanners and other major medical equipment to hospitals in the U.S., and M. D. Anderson happened to have been a client. After Mathew had left several messages, the doctor whom he had sought out had finally returned his call.

"Teresa must be ecstatic," I said. There it was again, that shit-eating grin. Mathew was proud of himself. Needless to say, I don't know if Teresa felt indebted to Mathew, but one can reasonably assume so. At any rate, her father-in-law was getting the much-needed care she had hoped for, and Mathew said that he'd be getting more activity out of Teresa.

"She owes me now," Mathew added.

At the same time, Daryl was shaking things up in Atlanta. Preparations for that showcase were shaping up, Mathew said. We still had no concrete date, but Mathew felt that one would be coming through "any time now."

Two days later, Mathew and I were once again sitting in the kitchen, when the telephone rang (thank God he had been home on that morning). On the line was a powerful Sony/Columbia executive, calling about the girls. Teresa LaBarbera-Whites had been working, and the fruit of Mathew's favor was on the phone. Mathew held up his finger, giving me the sign to be quiet, while he continued to speak to the record label executive. I don't remember the person's name, but I remember that Mathew said he was a senior vice president of A&R. Entrenched in conversation, Mathew suddenly scowled. Shit! What was the man saying?

They finished their conversation and I looked at Mathew, curiously. He could see that I wanted to know what transpired during the telephone conversation with Sony/Columbia, but he wasn't forthcoming. He carried on where he had left off with our original meeting, the reason I was sitting in the kitchen on that day.

Mathew had told me that he wanted to build a core team so that "we" could meet "our" goal of "fame."

"Fame," I said. "I have no goal of Fame, Mathew." I had no idea where he'd gotten that I was interested in popular music fame. I asked him.

"Everybody wants fame," Mathew said.

* * * * *

According to Mathew, his management split with Ann gave him sole decision rights. This simply wasn't true. He and Ann were equal partners, but Mathew said he was entitled to full control. Once again, he'd use Beyoncé to deliver one of his most devastating blows.

Ann Tillman and Mathew Knowles had shared a 50/50 split, which came about at the behest of Celestine, who Ann always thought looked out for her. But now Mathew was insisting Ann agree to a 75/25 split in management fees (his favor).

I was in the kitchen when he shouted into the phone at her, "I want 75%."

Ann must have resisted.

Mathew said, "Okay. I'll take Beyoncé and go." Then, before hanging up the phone, he matter-of-factly announced to Ann that Sony/Columbia had called.

Subsequently contacting Teresa, Ann confirmed Sony/Columbia's interest: The label was indeed on the hook, news which put Ann in a difficult position.

When she called Mathew back, he let her do all the talking. He wasn't budging. Then Mathew assured Ann that he had no intention of accepting any "offer." He would hold out for a solo deal for Beyoncé, he boasted.

Ann was between a rock and a hard place. "We can't start out showing dissension in our ranks." Ann explained to him. "Dissension is sudden death in the music industry."

Ann was right. (I can't begin tell you how many acts have lost deals because of problematic parents, attitudes, uncontrolled behaviors…) I will never forget the dismay in her voice. She was so disillusioned with Mathew, but he had her over a barrel. Carolyn had tried to warn her, as she had tried to warn us all.

Later I spoke to Ann privately. "What are you going to do?" I asked her.

"The only thing I can."

When Beyoncé got home from school the next day, she came back to my apartment, sadder than a fish out of water.

"Daddy told me Sony offered me a solo deal," she said.

"What?" I asked. "When?" I wondered. Had Mathew had another conversation with that executive from Sony/Columbia that I didn't know about?

"I don't want to go solo…" Beyoncé said, with tears in her eyes. "I want to sing with my friends…"

"Don't worry, Beyoncé," I said. "Let me talk to your father." I hated to see Beyoncé, or indeed any of my girls, in pain.

A few days later, I found my opportunity to speak to Mathew on Beyoncé's behalf. He just sat there, staring through me, distant – blank – empty. Suddenly the telephone rang. It was Sony/Columbia again. This time Mathew put the call on speaker phone. Apparently, that exec had invited the girls to come to New York for an audition. Could *that* be what he'd said to Mathew in the previous call I'd witnessed? Anyhow, now that same executive was announcing new plans. "It is easier," he said to Mathew. "I can arrive by the end of the week, Friday afternoon," he added.

Mathew looked at me…

I signaled that it was no problem, we'd be ready.

Without missing a beat, Mathew replied. "I'll have everything ready," he said.

"Great! See you Friday."

I smiled from ear to ear: Sony was coming. Mathew mistook my jubilation for praise of him. It had not been. I was rejoicing in God's showing up, right on time. Everything had worked out. Beyoncé wouldn't have to ponder a solo deal. I couldn't wait to tell her; she was going to be so happy, I thought. Mathew headed for the Headliners cash register. He needed money in order to "have everything ready." Celestine agreed.

As usual, Mathew had kept to himself some pertinent information. A serious problem had arisen with Sony/Columbia's interest. They stipulated an exclusive right to hearing the girls, which meant: No Atlanta showcase. Mathew also neglected to inform us that he had signed the agreement with Daryl. As the manager with majority control, he said he didn't need Ann's OK. What would we do?

Mathew's ultimate decision was to play both ends against the middle. Was he out of his damned mind? He was about to be in breach of his agreement with Daryl Simmons, while pissing off Sony/Columbia, one of the most powerful labels in the world. "I'm betting that it will all work out," Mathew said to Celestine and me during a late-night meeting.

"What fucking bet, Mathew?" Celestine exploded. She wanted to know how her husband could have been so stupid. "Did you read that contract, Mathew?" she asked.

Daryl Simmons had full signing rights, repertoire rights, designing rights, songwriting rights, production rights – "and the list goes fuckin' on," Celestine scolded.

I backed out of the kitchen, returning quickly to my apartment. I didn't want to hear any more plotting. My girls would have an important audition in two days. Even though Mathew's decision to gamble was potentially dangerous, I trusted that God knew what he was doing. Then I heard Grandmother's voice in my head – "Satan blesses too, baby." That was indeed a scary thought.

The next day, I picked up Beyoncé and Solange from school. Mathew spent all of Thursday away from home. Celestine wore my ear out, still reeling from the news that Mathew had signed "that contract." While she ranted, I dissociated. I suited up with the full armor of God. "Father, thy will be done."

It's all I had.

After the Sony/Columbia executives had come and gone, my girls and I celebrated at The Brisket House. "Baked potatoes for everyone," I said. They had sung and danced their little hearts out. However, that executive had been adamant. "We want a singing group," he said.

I didn't have the heart to tell the girls about Sony Columbia's stipulation, not after such a wonderful performance. Mathew had not given much thought to the makeup of the group, but now, having majority control as manager, he decided that Sony/Columbia was correct. LaTavia and her two cousins, Nikki and Nina Taylor, were going to be dropped from Cliché.

"Mathew, these are children," I said. "You can't just – kick them out? Just like that – without any consideration?"

"It's business," he answered.

* * * * *

Regardless of my vehement dislike for Mathew, I had to think of a tactful way to handle him and his intention to eliminate LaTavia and her cousins, Nikki and Nina. They – and their parents – had given their lives to the group, and he shouldn't callously dismiss their years of dedication. Mathew was not budging, but there had to be a way. So, I went back to him with a proposal. I suggested to Mathew that maybe LaTavia, Nikki, and Nina could be hired as outside contractors.

"That's a stupid idea," Mathew snarled.

I would have to kowtow to him if I hoped to win. "Please go back to Sony/Columbia," I begged, "and ask them to give me six months to analyze the singing potential of LaTavia, Nikki, and Nina. I'd like to save at least one of them."

"Those girls have zero talent," Mathew said.

"Don't say that, Mathew," I pleaded. "First off, it's not true. And second, these girls love one another. At least give them the chance to prove themselves." I continued. "I'll take on the responsibility of wielding the axe, and protect your reputation as manager, of course." It worked.

Mathew came to me a few days later. Sony/Columbia had agreed to the six months, "But," he added, "I'm giving you one."

"Well then, I'd better get started," I answered.

* * * * *

According to Mathew, Ann was, "not going to make it." He told us that the doctors had all but forecast doom. Again, I was confused. Ann and I discussed her illness frequently, and she never once mentioned that her doctors predicted doom. Quite the contrary, she said, "The doctors are hopeful that with proper treatment and a positive outlook I can beat this thing."

"We have to prepare for the worst," Mathew said.

I remembered Carolyn's suspicions. This situation was potentially ex-plosive, definitely messy.

Ann had kept a small percentage (5%) to secure her boys' futures and because she, "deserved it," she said to me. Had she asked me, I could have told her that Mathew had snowed her. Mathew claimed that it had been his "generosity" that allowed Ann to maintain her 5% percentage.

"Ann is not working half as much as I am to bring viable leads to the table," he boasted – groundlessly.

"Really?" I asked, sarcastically. I knew full well the answer to my own question.

When Celestine found out about Mathew's intended enrollment at HCC, she said nothing. She even ignored the fact that the money to pay the tuition had once again come from her purse. However, Celestine could not abide his jumping the gun with Daryl. His signing "that damn con-tract" was met with her impressive wrath. He had stolen away one of the mightiest weapons in her arsenal – the means to manipulate. And he had done so without any real legal advice. Oh, Mathew said he'd spoken to his HCC professor about the situation, though he admitted that he hadn't shown the man the actual contract.

"Arrogance is going to be your death, Mathew," she said.

Ignoring such rhetoric, I just thought, How typical. In Celestine's mind, everyone was arrogant, including me.

14. I stopped breathing

Mama's response was typical Mama, to the point. During our usual Sunday night chat, we talked about Mathew and his latest rant. "Trust me," Mathew had shouted.

I said to Mama, "He's always complaining that people don't trust him, and by people, I'm sure he means me. He never can understand why *we* fail to see his *rightness*. I think the man is finally losing it, Mama."

"No he's not," said Mama. "He's only regurgitating the messages of his childhood."

How could she say that? Mama had never met Mathew. What did she mean?

"Just consider his repeating patterns of ridicule, disapproval, and rejection. His threatening you all with removing Beyoncé from the group if he doesn't get his way. Holding his own daughter as hostage?!"

"Okay," I answered. I realized I'd told my mother a lot – which she had remembered. "But we can't always use our childhood traumas as reasons for bad behavior."

"Really," Mama said, with just a touch of sarcasm. "The FBI thinks differently, and so do I and my colleagues in mental health. Where do you think patterns form, if not in our childhoods?"

"Well, yes," I said. Good point, Mama.

"Truth can be excruciating for most of us, but ignoring it ends up being even worse. If only we had the courage to face it."

"That's true too!" I said.

"Imagine," Mama said. "Roy Kellogg had a difficult mother. He beat *me*, because his father beat his mother, which was a continuation of what

299

his father saw growing up. The beatings also became Roy's warped answer to his anger with his mother – and by extension, his hatred of all women. He didn't come out of his mother's womb violent. His abusive behavior was learned, and it became an unavoidable habit."

"That's deep, Mama." I repeated her words to myself a few times, even saying "an unavoidable habit" out loud. Then I asked her a tough question – tough for me to voice: When was the first time Roy hit her?

"It was on his mother's birthday. She'd invited us to dinner. I'd brought her flowers, and Roy showed up empty handed. After she scolded him, calling him lazy and thoughtless, he called me outside – for a talk, he said. After helping his mother to finish up in the kitchen, I found Roy outside, smoking. He slapped me – hard – so hard I lost my balance. When I came to myself, I saw that his father had witnessed the whole thing. He was standing on the porch, staring through the screen door. He looked so proud. Roy told me that I'd embarrassed him in front of his father, and that I was never to do it again. Then he walked back into the house. His father gave him a pat on the back, stared at me cold and then smiled..."

I was sorry I'd asked.

"So, it's really quite simple, isn't it? Research shows that boy children who grow up with *abusive* mothers become difficult fathers," Mama declared, pulling me out of my momentary slump. Then Mama told me that children raised by difficult fathers typically exhibit two characteristic behaviors: One, they have the ability to bounce back from trauma or conflict. They must do so, or disappoint Daddy. And two, although bruised, they often times find success. They will most likely turn into overachievers.

"On the other hand," Mama went on, "The *difficult* mother stunts her child's ability to grow emotionally, and to engage socially. Her sons become fuck-ups. Our need for Mama's attention begins already in her womb. We need *her* appreciation, seek *her* understanding. Mathew was and is no different."

"It sounds to me," Mama continued, "that Mathew did not have the option to care. The fear of abandonment and the panic that his childhood

experiences must have caused were threatening, even overwhelming."
Mama added, "I can promise you, those feelings will last him a lifetime."

"What to do then?" I asked.

"I told you," Mama answered. "Get the hell out of there. But since you
won't listen to reason, all you can do is watch, listen closely, and make
yourself aware." Mama told me that I should remember that abusive parents, whether male or female, fix their conditions. They hand out love,
approval, and appreciation judiciously. Issues of perfection and trust will
lie at the heart of their childhood memories. For the rest of their lives –
almost inevitably – they will act out their own fears on other people who
become their victims.

"I can handle myself, Mama, plus…"

"I know! You have to be there for *the girls*," Mama said, jokingly.
"Hell, 'you better hit Mister in the head and think about heaven later,'"
she added, quoting her favorite line from the 1985 Steven Spielberg film
"The Color Purple." Then Mama asked me, "Have you ever wondered
why Solange, from what you've told me, irritates her parents?"

"Because she refuses to play their games," I answered, proud of myself.

"No," Mama answered, sharply. "It's because Solange's knowledge of
what truth tastes like forces Mama and Daddy to choke on their deceptions."

I swallowed hard.

* * * * *

The next day, I called the sisters Cholotte and Cheryl – the mothers of
Nikki, Nina, and LaTavia. I asked if they could come to my apartment for
a brief meeting. They agreed.

I will never forget my shock when Cholotte and Cheryl arrived – both
of them with their daughters. It had not occurred to me to tell them to
come alone. Because I was so nervous about the ugly assignment I'd tak-

en on, it had completely slipped my mind that meetings in the Knowles camp meant everyone's showing up. With no other choice, I invited the five of them in, and began with small talk. I gulped when Cholotte forced me to come to the point. "You seem so official," she said. "What's going on?"

I took a long breath before sharing with them the feedback the Sony/Columbia label senior A&R executive had given regarding the girls' audition. I told them Mathew's decision. The girls burst into tears. Hiding my own dismay, I explained that they'd all have the chance to take voice lessons with me, and at the end of two weeks I would have to choose one of them for the group. Although they felt dejected, they said my proposal sounded fair to them, because they all had, at least, an equal opportunity.

Having survived that first wave of their disappointment, I would gladly have ended the conversation right there. However, I had even more difficult terrain ahead of me. Not wanting to lose momentum, and with their permission, I began immediately to assess their voices and singing talents.

First, the two dancers. Nikki could sing a bit; her sister, Nina, could not sing at all. Since she could not even match pitches, it was clear that she would be out. One month would not have given us enough time to fix the problem. Devastated, she started to cry all over again, which made the other two tear up once again. This was even harder than I thought it would be.

Cholotte was both sympathetic and angry. I was breaking these little girls' hearts. But, if I was going to find a successful end, I couldn't allow myself to get emotional. Nevertheless, it was difficult. I was, after all, human, and I was fond of all three girls. In that moment I despised Mathew and the dreadful position I had put myself into "for the good of the group."

With Nina eliminated, the cousins LaTavia and Nikki were left to work with me for two weeks. Both girls wanted the spot in the group and tried their hardest in our lessons. By the end of that period, LaTavia would emerge the winner. My decision went to her, because she showed me the most natural ability for musical phrasing and interpretation, and because she had the deeper voice, which would provide balance in the group. I

302

needed her low notes to round out the group's chordal structure. Nikki was a soprano, along the lines of Kelly, and she did not meet the overall criteria that this fourth position required.

With that decision, the four-member group was born. Now, in 1993, my original concept, from 1989, might finally be realized.

* * * * *

On the afternoon of LaTavia's first official voice lesson, I picked up Beyoncé and Solange, as usual, at the end of their school day. Beyoncé was beyond ecstatic. Sitting in the front passenger seat, her normal place in my car, she asked, "Can I listen to LaTavia's voice lesson?" I told her that I didn't know if that was such a good idea, not only because private voice lessons are exactly that – private – but also because first lessons are usually bumpy.

"Please David, I promise not to make a noise. I will just sit there like a quiet little mouse. I promise. Pretty please!"

It was always difficult for me to say no to my girls, especially Beyoncé. (As a matter of fact it was hard, and still is sometimes, for me to say "no," period.) I relented, telling Beyoncé that if LaTavia didn't mind, I would allow it. She sat back, cool, calm, and collected, humming. She was confident that LaTavia would be all right with it. Why wouldn't she be? They were best friends and inseparable.

When we arrived home I asked Beyoncé and Solange if they were hungry. Solange asked for a juice, even though what she really wanted was candy. "Solange, you know the rules," I said. Both Knowles girls did. Celestine was clear. "No sweets before dinner." However, it was okay for her to have a juice box, I said.

Focused on Solange, and those darned sweets, I hadn't noticed that Beyoncé had stepped outside into the backyard. Standing on the Knowles deck, she peered through the spaces between the planks of wood in the nine-foot fence her parents had built to separate the backyard from the alleyway. Suddenly, I heard Beyoncé scream, "She's here – she's here." LaTavia's stepfather's car had driven by, she said. Overjoyed, she darted up the stairs, yelling "C'mon David." She flew past Solange's bedroom, then to the left and into her own bedroom, then raced down the three steps and into the alcove that led to my apartment. Quickly disappearing from sight, she'd already let LaTavia into the house by the time I got into the apartment. There they both stood, giggly and all girly, yapping excitedly.

"LaTavia said I can listen to her lesson," Beyoncé said.

Looking to LaTavia, I saw not only her nod of agreement but also a trace of anxiety in her face. We hugged. "Are you all right?" I asked.

She nodded.

"How was school?"

"Good," she answered. Then, out of nowhere, she began anxiously voicing her fears that she would not measure up, that she would make mistakes, that…

"LaTavia, calm down," I said. After all, she'd had private voice lessons with me for a couple of weeks before her acceptance into the group. "Are you sure you don't mind Beyoncé's listening to your voice lesson today?" She wasn't her normal feisty self.

"No, I don't mind," she said.

Ready to begin, I asked Beyoncé to take a seat. She plopped down on the sofa as if she was about to see an exciting movie. That elicited a small chuckle from me, and I asked her, "Who is more nervous here: LaTavia or you, Beyoncé?" At which they both giggled. "All this squealing and gig-gling is giving me a slight earache," I smiled. "OK. Let's settle down. It's time for business."

"Can I take my shoes off?" LaTavia asked, swallowing hard.

"Sure," I answered.

Then, standing directly in front of us, LaTavia readied herself to sing, lowering her head. I could clearly see her larynx ("Adam's apple"). She was continuing to swallow, repeatedly. Why was it taking so long for her to start? I wondered. Then, she opened her mouth and let out a yelp that startled both me and Beyoncé.

During the "deciding phase," two weeks earlier, LaTavia's voice hadn't come across so boldly. Perhaps it was the competition with her cousin Nikki that had softened her dynamic personality? Now the "chosen one," she wasn't holding anything back. But on this day, there was something different, something abnormal. Her sound was harsh, throaty even. As she neared the chorus, I really began to worry. She seemed to be losing control. Her eyes, even wider now, bulged. Her forehead's outer and inner brows had raised, and the brow between the eyebrows had pulled in and downward. Her lips had begun to stretch out across her face, and her jaw was locked. Oh dear, I thought. LaTavia was terrified.

"Stop," I said.

Beyoncé, whose eyes were as big as half-dollars, said, "Wow your voice is – *so* – *big*…"

LaTavia gulped.

"Are you all right?" I asked.

She wasn't. Her breathing had suddenly become shallow, and she clung to her chest. "I don't feel good," she said.

Calmly, I said, "Beyoncé, go into the bathroom, wet a face cloth with hot water, as hot as your hands can stand, and bring it back to me." Was LaTavia having a panic attack?

Beyoncé darted into the bathroom.

As she left, I took LaTavia's hand, placing it on my chest. "Concentrate on my heart beat," I told her. "Talk to me. Tell me exactly: what you are feeling?" I asked.

"I can't breathe," she responded.

"Yes, you can," I answered. "I think you're having a panic attack, LaTavia, but you are not in any danger. It will subside. Just breathe," I said. She needed to know that even though she felt like she was dying, she wouldn't.

In no time, Beyoncé had returned with the soaked and dripping wash cloth, holding it at the corners. It was too hot for her hands. I took it from her. After quickly wringing out the excess water onto the carpet, I placed it over LaTavia's face. "Breathe, my little Diva," I said. She should breathe in the warmth coming off the face cloth, through her nose, I said. "Hold it," I added. "Now let it go, through the mouth, and now again – breathe in – hold it, and now let it go."

She did what I asked, although she remained confused, anxious, and glassy eyed.

Beyoncé, now really worried, asked "What's wrong?"

I gave her the face cloth again, "Re-wet this," I said.

"You're doing great, LaTavia." I needed her to talk to me. "Dare your breath to win," I said.

Her stare said that she thought I was crazy.

"Keep your eyes on me, LaTavia." I told her to curse her breath. "Call it a mother fucker!" I said. "Dare your *damn* breath to *kick your ass!*"

Now shocked, LaTavia's mind had turned to something else besides her panic, which had been my aim.

"LaTavia, I'm not crazy. Talk to your breath, out loud. Let me hear your voice."

She said nothing.

"C'mon breath, kick her ass," I urged, over and over again. "Say it!"

LaTavia started to get angry, which pleased me. Beyoncé couldn't believe what she was seeing and hearing. The look on her face said it all. What's happening? She took LaTavia's hand.

"That's right, get angry," I shouted. "Fight – C'mon, fight!" I said again, continuing to encourage her to talk to me, out loud.

"I'm going to pass out," she said.

"No you're not, believe me," I answered. "Just breathe! Focus on changing your thoughts! Fight, LaTavia. Go inward, and fight your thoughts!" Then I stood next to her, side by side, holding her shoulders, and swaying gently and rhythmically back and forth. "It will subside soon."

And it did subside.

The ten minutes it took for LaTavia's breathing to normalize must've been the longest ten minutes of her life. It is for most panic sufferers. But at the end of the attack she'd learned two things. One: she was OK, and two, she hadn't died. Her problem was in her mind, which according to what I knew about panic attacks, is caused by negative thoughts, probably triggered by some inner conflict, a very deep and personal trauma. That's what I was interested in finding out about. Why had she become so panicky?

Again, Beyoncé spoke out. "What happened, David?"

"LaTavia, had a panic attack," I said. "That's all."

"But why?"

I didn't think I should share my thoughts with Beyoncé. One, my answer would ultimately be upsetting to her and two, handling LaTavia and her fear with extreme sensitivity was more important than satisfying Beyoncé's present curiosity. LaTavia might have known the origin of that fear, but the very fact that she was panicking told me she wasn't ready to deal consciously with whatever it was. I couldn't push. In time I might learn why her body and mind had just behaved so uncontrollably, but now was not that time.

To divert Beyoncé and to reassure LaTavia, I told them about my friend in college, Nikole, a pre-med major from Chicago, who suffered terrible panic attacks. Had done so, apparently, since her childhood.

"What happened?" LaTavia asked.

"Nikole would rather study than eat, but one day I insisted. 'Nikole, you have to get out.' When I went to her dorm and knocked on the door of her room, I discovered that she was in full panic mode. She grabbed me, dragged me to the girl's bathroom, and into the showers. Seconds later I found myself completely soaked, holding Nikole, and telling her to breathe. It was really scary, but I got a quick lesson in panic attacks that day. I learned from Nikole that warm showers help, especially in extreme cases."

"Wow," Beyoncé said. We paused for a few moments while LaTavia continued to calm down.

"Okay, enough of that, girls," I said. "How are you feeling now, LaTavia?"

"Better," LaTavia answered. Then she began to apologize, profusely. She said that she was embarrassed. "I don't want to disappoint you," she said – over and over again.

"It's OK," I answered. "You could never disappoint me. You did an amazing job, didn't she Beyoncé?"

Still a bit stunned, Beyoncé nodded her head, feebly.

"I've never had a panic attack before," LaTavia said.

"Please don't give it another thought." I gave her a reassuring hug.

Nevertheless, my mind raced. I couldn't ignore what I'd just experienced. I had been able to shut off automatic response by asking her to mentally fight with her breath, daring it to win. And the slow swaying, from side to side, triggered a return to voluntary muscle control. You just have to wait out panic attacks. Although mentally draining, they always subside.

Somewhere deep within LaTavia was a pain that she'd either suppressed or was currently dealing with. I didn't know which one, but something was going on. In fact, LaTavia's mother, Cheryl, had called me, days earlier. LaTavia had been having problems at school. Chalking it up to adolescence, Cheryl seemed sure it would pass. She just wanted to warn me, she said. I'd had no idea that I would be required to put into practice some of my theoretical knowledge of how anxiety and panic might manifest.

In Moshe Feldenkrais's 1990 work *Awareness Through Movement* he wrote that slowing one's movements can help calm the person suffering from a panic attack. Furthermore, "Pain that undermines confidence in the body and self is the main cause of deviations from the ideal posture. Pain of this kind reduces the individual's value in his own eyes. Nervous tension rises, which in turn reduces sensitivity once more; so we do not sense continued small deviations from the ideal position and the muscles tense without the individual's even being aware of the effort he is making. Control may become so much distorted that while we think we are doing nothing, we are in fact straining muscles needlessly."

Needing a moment's break, and sensing that Beyoncé and LaTavia could also use a few moments to themselves, I excused myself to the toilet. Feeling a bit overwhelmed, I asked for God's protection over my girls, and me. I felt that I couldn't handle one more problem, and I concentrated on one of my favorite biblical promises: "…God is faithful, and he will not let you be tempted beyond your ability…" 1 Corinthians 10:13. Moments later, I was able to return to the living room, and to my patient students. I clapped my hands reassuringly.

"LaTavia, we are going to begin your session today talking about the principles of 'Light and Easy,'" I said.

"What's that?"

"Light and Easy" is based on the Feldenkrais approach to finding balance in the human body. I explained to LaTavia that it is basically the process of learning "how to turn strenuous movements into good ones – that is, into movements that are first of all effective, and also smooth and easy."

"First up," I said, "is the jaw. Close your mouth," I instructed LaTavia. Taking her hand in mine, I placed her index finger directly on the center of the muscle at the jaw's hinge. "Do you feel the muscle poke out – here, when you bite down, at the back of your jaw, near your ear?"

She said she could.

"This is the first muscle we'll concentrate on. It is called the masseter," I said. The masseter muscle is *a major muscle* of the jaw, responsible for the protraction (forward movement), retraction (backward movement), and side to side movement. "We're going to work there today."

"Now, I want you to drop your jaw, ever so slightly," I said. "Let your hand lie on that muscle, flat – like so," I added. I told LaTavia that she should cup her face, allowing her jaw and chin to rest in the cradle (palm) of her hand. She could even tilt her head to the side. Then I asked her to chew, without saying a word or making sound. "Just let your mouth open and close, softly, and notice the marshmallow feeling happening within the masseter muscle." A voluntary muscle, the *masseter* is paired with the *temporalis muscle* – "Here," I said to LaTavia, touching the side of her head. "The two muscles work together to control every movement the jaw makes, and are very important in singing." Until the muscles move freely in the jaw, the voice will not anchor itself in the diaphragm, the hips, or the facial muscles, nor will they find support.

Connecting LaTavia's breath to tone was going to be extremely challenging, but I had no choice. If I didn't deliver, Mathew would kick LaTavia out of the group. One month was a ridiculous expectation. Her voice was huge. I would have to begin with muscle isolation and then coordination, crucial to all voices, but especially those voices that sing flat and are too raucous to control.

I determined the only solution to this dilemma was to see LaTavia as often as possible. I promised her mother, Cheryl, that she'd have to come three times per week for only one month, and that the rest of her daughter's study would not need to be as intensive, nor as expensive. Her mother agreed, paying the fee gladly.

As expected, LaTavia's sound and jaw became supple with each passing day. So did her confidence. Her tongue lay beautifully in her mouth after our month's work together, and her pitch problem had been all but solved. It would take several more months before she could support the weight of her huge sound fully, but LaTavia had done a tremendous work. I was proud of her, and so were Beyoncé and Cheryl. Singing lessons had produced a more focused and happier LaTavia. We all liked that girl.

Unfortunately, her worrisome behavior in school remained. A very sweet girl, LaTavia could quickly become difficult. She often had a bit of an attitude problem, but I adored her. During our intense history together, she'd criticize herself mercilessly when she made mistakes, even small ones. Sometimes she even got angry with me, but a student's displeasure with my methods never distract me from demanding quality work, so I ignored that. I had to work patiently to keep LaTavia from self-destructing. Through it all, she and I became very close.

When it was time for her to sing for Mathew, she blew him away. Mathew, Ann, the girls, and I all gathered in the Knowles den, listening to her calm *a capella* version of Whitney Houston's "Didn't We Almost Have It All." She nailed it. A sour Mathew stood up and left the room, while the girls clapped their enthusiasm vigorously. Ann winked at me. I'd done it. LaTavia mouthed the words, "Thank you…"

310

It was official. Management agreed that LaTavia had become a viable, fully accepted member of Cliché. I'd never seen her as happy as she was on that day. By the time she and the other girls sang for Teresa LaBarbera Whites again, LaTavia had gotten her huge instrument under control – a credit to her diligence – and she was able to match the other girls' volume levels – loud or soft, as required. Teresa called the new group sound secure. She was very complimentary and noted that "LaTavia's voice is much deeper than Beyoncé's."

I smiled, unable to conceal my joy. "Yes, it is," I said. I thanked Teresa for giving me the six-months grace period I needed to work my little Diva into the fold. "I'm so appreciative," I added.

"I'm sorry," Teresa answered. "Six months? What six-month grace period?"

The look on my face must have been one for the records. Surely, what involuntarily came out of my mouth in that unguarded moment was imprinted indelibly onto my girls' minds. Before I could control it, my tongue rolled out the words "That damn Bastard!" Screaming inwardly, I could have killed Mathew for his deception. Three days later, when I saw him, I gave that asshole what for. Needless to say, his surrogate caught hell, for weeks on end. I tell you, Donkey Mathew saved lives.

* * * * *

A couple weeks after I added LaTavia to the group, Mathew made an important announcement.

"You guys are going to Atlanta," he said. "I have secured you the deal of a lifetime," Mathew boasted.

No one moved. The girls stared at him, wondering what he was talking about. I realized that Mathew had kept the girls in the dark.

"Has Daryl confirmed?" I asked.

"Yes," Mathew answered.

"Confirmed what, Daddy?" Beyoncé asked. The other girls stared at him, holding their breath.

"Daryl called and offered y'all a showcase for major labels," Mathew said. He boasted that Daryl counted on the presence of seven to nine label presidents and CEOs.

There they are, I thought – the girls I know and love. All four of them started screaming and running around the kitchen, dancing the cabbage patch.

"Do you know when?" I asked. "When will the showcase be?"

"Why?" Mathew asked, snidely. "Do you have something more important to do?"

My quick response stopped the girls in their tracks. "Yes, as a matter of fact I do, Mathew." Right in front of them, I said, "I intend to make sure we don't have another 'Star Search' mess. This one will be under my entire control."

"We'll see about that," Mathew said.

"Yes, we most certainly will."

You could have cut the tension with a knife. To break the electric atmosphere, I looked to my girls. Throwing my arms out, I called out "Congratulations!" They ran to me, hugging me tightly, and with that, the dancing started all over again.

Mathew, sitting in the breakfast nook of the Knowles kitchen, looked on with that sour face that had become his trademark of late. Naturally, my comment had ruffled his ever so important tail, but I didn't give a damn. Yes. the Atlanta showcase was a great opportunity. Yes, he had been responsible for our contact with Daryl. But I was the captain of this artistic ship.

Not to mention, Mathew had caused enough trouble, barely escaping Celestine's wrath, just days earlier. Never fully confident in Daryl Simmons, Celestine was nevertheless appalled that Mathew was playing Russian roulette with both Daryl and Sony/Columbia, to whom he had made simultaneous agreements. She feared, correctly, that his duplicity was endangering the girls' chances.

I had repeatedly asked Mathew about his plans. He always responded with his characteristic grunt and the words "That's my business." Naturally, he saw my questions as intrusive. In 1993, anyone who dared to inquire about Master Mathew's decisions got the silent treatment – or worse. But I didn't like surprises, nor does anyone else in the music business, and Mathew was the king of surprise.

I could see that by cheating Daryl, Mathew was cheating everyone on the team, especially the girls, and including Ann, with whom he argued regarding his little ruse. She had been dead set against it, but Mathew had put her in a difficult position. He'd thrown a dangerous ball and Ann felt forced to play Mathew's game.

"Hedging his bets puts us all at risk," I said to her.

"I know," she said, "but questioning Mathew's motives at this stage of the game would be detrimental." All she kept thinking about was the "dissension" that she was determined to keep hidden from the label industry people. "Maybe the situation with Daryl won't pan out before Sony/Columbia sends a real contractual offer."

"Sorry," I answered. "Eventually Mathew is going to get caught, and you are going to be implicated right along with him," I said.

Ann could say nothing to that. Unlike Mathew, she understood the music business.

The fact that many other people would have tried the same unethical means as Mathew gave me no consolation. His stringing along a giant like Sony/Columbia, in violation of the signed contract he had with one of America's premiere producers, was suicidal, and flat out unethical. And the music world is small.

Of course, Mathew didn't want to lose the Sony prospect, and at the same time, he did not want to lose Daryl – not because of any scruples about keeping his word and abiding by the contract he'd signed, but, just in case things didn't work out with Sony. Mathew had no understanding of the obvious ethics, and he ignored the obvious dangers. Deciding that the best thing would be to keep his options open, he was resolved to playing both ends against the middle.

As soon as the now nine confirmed labels wrote that they'd be attending the Atlanta showcase, executives at Sony found out. The grapevine in the music industry is strong and effective. When Sony/Columbia discovered that Mathew had already signed a production deal with Daryl that obligated him to go ahead with the Atlanta showcase, the people at the label were fit to be tied. Hadn't Mathew realized that word would get out? I certainly did. I had tried telling him, but of course, he had merely grunted and said, "Mind your own business."

Mathew's bad decision had turned personal for Sony/Columbia. He'd pissed off the wrong people. Trust, Mathew's favorite word and something he demanded, came up to haunt him for his inability to inspire it. Sony/Columbia reacted predictably. They rescinded their offer. Teresa's hands were tied, and the senior A&R exec who had heard my girls was more than disappointed. He'd returned to Houston and loved the new sound, calling it mature and grounded.

The day Mathew's bubble burst, the apocalypse became reality in the Knowles house. "Stupid motherfucker," Celestine screamed. Beyoncé retired to her bed, depressed.

Left now with no choice but to honor their contract with Daryl, Mathew and Ann wagered everything on Daryl's success. Would the showcase result in a record deal? Daryl had begun to prepare for such an outcome, organizing every detail of the showcase toward that goal. He had even changed the group's name – again – hoping to create a marketable aura around my girls. Da Dolls. Yes, you heard me right. Da Dolls were heading for Atlanta, and their performance there had to be stellar.

I set out to develop a plan to beat all plans, and whenever Mathew tried inserting his cockamamie ideas, I shut him down. I wasn't having it. So yeah, I made my intention clear. I told him, and I told Celestine, point blank, that I'd be in control of this showcase, no questions asked, or they could do it without me. Period.

"Fuck Mathew," I said to Celestine as we conversed that evening, around midnight, when she stopped by my apartment after work.

"Don't worry," she said. "I'll keep Mathew out of your way. The girls need you more than ever. We all do." Celestine hugged me tightly, a bit happy and a lot sad. Her nightmare would continue, at least for now. It looked as though she'd not likely be getting out of debt anytime soon.

"Goodnight," she said.

"Sleep well, or at least try to," I answered.

Her defeated smile broke my heart.

I didn't sleep a wink. I was up all night thinking. What would I do? One thing was for sure. Da Dolls would be prepared for their future iconic status. My chance had finally come to realize my notion of extraordinary singing, and my girls were going to galvanize music.

I would not sleep on the job.

That was for damn sure.

* * * * *

All my girls were talented and each of them held a special place in my being. Beyoncé was my heart; Kelly, my heart's passion; LeToya the joy in my heart, and LaTavia had become my heart's pulse. However, because of her profound insecurities, and because of my profound belief in her talent, I had poured extra thought and teacher-skill into Kelly. I was ecstatic that she was reaping the benefits of her hard work, that she was being noticed by people who mattered.

Daryl adored Kelly's voice, he said. In his opinion, Kelly's voice had a special something in it, a something he had been looking for. We agreed. I'd said that Kelly possessed something special from day one. Then Daryl called her voice "highly commercial sounding," and said that it "gave him goose bumps." I, of course, completely understood his enthusiasm: "When I tell you that Kelendria "Kelly" Trene Rowland has the potential to achieve Whitney Houston success, I mean what I am saying."

Whenever Daryl called the house on group rehearsal day, Kelly would light up like a Christmas tree. She had great respect for him and said so in no uncertain terms. She longed for a male father figure, and she basked in

Daryl's kindness and generosity. At her age, she didn't realize that her respect and admiration for her *producer* intimidated her *manager*. Although Kelly was the child, Mathew responded with childish petulance to Daryl's admiration of the girl's voice. In that behavior, Mathew was following the promptings of his own insecurities, and also those of his wife. "Watch Kelly, Mathew," I overheard Celestine say. Kelly could not be put forward – no way, no how.

What all this meant for me, if I was going to be successful, was that I needed the full armor of God. I just kept reading 1 Peter 5:8, over and over again. Grandmother's words haunted my sleep, and I'd have to remain diligent, vigilant in my vision. Nothing was going to stand between my girls and an exceptional performance.

I got an idea. I called Mama.

* * * * *

It had become my habit to call Omaha every Sunday, checking in on family and friends. This particular Sunday would be more significant than all the others, because I needed guidance in solving the potential problem awaiting my girls. Despite Daryl's attentions and encouragement of Kelly, I still had reason to worry about her. I knew two things for sure: that something had to be done about Kelly's self-hatred and her bouts with depression, and that Mama would have the wisdom I sought. She was planning a trip to Houston, and I'd called to find out when she'd arrive.

Calling Mama on Sunday evening, the 30th of May, from Houston, I was about to hang up when she answered the telephone, panting and short of breath. I asked her why she sounded so agitated.

"I had to go out."

"Let me guess, another client had a crisis."

"How did you know?" she asked.

"It's Sunday evening. Nobody works on Sunday night," I said. "Except you."

Apparently Mama had received a telephone call from the Sarpy County Police Department in Bellevue, Nebraska, where she lived. The police informed her that one of her clients, a methamphetamine user, was holed up in a motel with his young daughter as hostage. He would speak only to Mama, the policeman said. That cop said they were ready to end the standoff by shooting the man, but Mama didn't want that. The client had been doing so well, she said. "What set him off?" she wondered. Mama told the policeman that she was *en route*. When she arrived, the police had been there for two hours; she asked them to give her five minutes.

"I ask one thing," she said. "Do not charge on him. He will only fight you, and this will come to an unfortunate ending. I would like to take him to Immanuel Hospital and check him into the adult psychiatric wing."

The police agreed, but only if the man came out peacefully and cooperatively.

Mama knocked on the door.

I had seen her in action. It is not to be believed. She has such a way with people.

"Bring your ass to the door," Mama said. "You have disrupted my Sunday dinner with your foolishness." The man opened the door, fell into her arms and wept, she said. She entered the motel room and instructed him that the police were ready to kill him and that he needed to let his young daughter go. He did so immediately. She promised him that she would not let the police harm him but he must do as she said. With one hand on her shoulder and the other up in the air, the man followed Mama out of the motel, walking ever so slowly, and got into her car. Flanked by three police cars, Mama drove her client through the streets of Omaha and up to the entrance to Immanuel Hospital, where the medical staff waited to check him in without further incident. She had just walked back into the house when I called.

"Are you OK? Is something the matter?" she asked.

"Everything is fine. I just wanted to ask you when you will arrive here in Houston. I want to plan for your visit."

317

"I will arrive on the 1st of August. I'll call you from the office tomorrow with my detailed flight information," Mama said. "I'm looking forward to seeing your play," Mama added. "I did get it right, didn't I? The play is on the 3rd, right?"

"No, Mama," I answered. "*Opera* – it's not a play. And yes, *the opera* – is on the 3rd, at Miller Outdoor Park."

Ignoring my grumpiness and sensing something was wrong, as mothers seem able to do, Mama asked, "Are you sure everything is all right?"

"Everything is perfect," I said, and we ended the call.

I had decided I wouldn't discuss the real reason for my call. I wanted her to observe the girls without any preconceptions. Sure that she'd agree, I knew that she would instinctively analyze the situation and the girls. I refrained from discussing my concerns about Kelly, as it might have influenced her perceptions.

On June 3, 1993, I joined Dr. Henry's HEOG second season, rehearsing Don José, the leading tenor role in George Bizet's *Carmen*. This production was important for three reasons: one, it was my first time singing the entire opera *Carmen,* and first productions always get extra special attention. Two, Beyoncé and I had already been studying *Carmen* intensely (I still hadn't understood why the still small voice had instructed me to teach her *Carmen,* but I followed directions). And lastly, I would be singing opposite star mezzo soprano Debria Brown, who had sung all over the world.

Ms. Brown had sung a leading role in *The Passion of Johnathan Wade,* my first HGO contract back in 1990-91, when the attack had occurred. She not only remembered me from the chorus of *The Passion of Johnathan Wade,* but she complimented me after our first *Carmen* rehearsal together, two factors that fed my confidence and calmed my nerves. The pain in my throat from the attack was gone, but because of my heavy teaching schedule, I hadn't been onstage in a leading capacity since 1991. The two-year absence had me feeling rusty and nervous.

In Debria Brown's most charming New Orleanian accent, she said, "It is indeed a pleasure to sing with such a fierce singing actor," – here, she snapped her fingers twice – "and those top notes, baby – they are on fire!" I had done my homework, but singing my first production of *Carmen* with Brown broadened my knowledge, and I was able to find more depth in the characters. It also gave me more poignant things to say to Beyoncé in our work together over the ensuing years. For my star pupil, watching the performances was both thrilling and intriguing. She admitted to a mixture of bewilderment and awe when she recounted the evening, her visit backstage, and her enjoyment of the production.

The other girls also thoroughly enjoyed the performances of *Carmen* and they told me so. LaTavia, my little Diva, said "It was cool to see you perform." None of my girls had ever witnessed the intensity with which I did my own onstage work. Kelly and LeToya also complimented me, and they were especially interested in the goings on backstage. It was the first time they got to see what it took to make a big production run smoothly – all the stage hands, dressers, wigs and make-up people, costumers, coaches and stage managers, as well as directors and conductors.

In the days following her attendance at "my" *Carmen*, Beyoncé had tons of questions. Of course she did, I thought. The respect that she brought to every genre of music that I taught her – now including opera – thrilled me. She honored everything about music: the phrasing, the rhythms, the nuances, the intent, and the depth of the text, the composer/arranger – and most importantly, music's emotional requirements.

"I really liked the opera last night," Beyoncé said. Naturally, she "enjoyed the singing the most." Then, suddenly very serious, Beyoncé said, "The Carmen was too old."

Laughing, I explained that opera was far too demanding on the voice to cast the role with someone as young as she's described in the book. (*Carmen* by Prosper Mérimée, written in French in 1845.) "A young girl of fourteen or fifteen wouldn't have the vocal maturity and the breadth of sound, nor the singing technique, to bring such a fiery role as Carmen to life."

Beyoncé nodded that she understood. Then she asked, "Well, why did you choose to sing opera and not pop?".

"My French teacher Mrs. Arnold is responsible for me singing opera," I said. "She'd seen me singing the Scarecrow in *The Wiz* –, "

"You sang *The Wiz*?" Beyoncé asked.

"Yes, already in high school. Remember?" I asked, "I told you that I had sung the *The Wiz*, way back in 1989 at your audition."

"Um –, now I remember," Beyoncé said.

"At any rate," I said. "Mrs. Arnold decided after that performance that I had 'the stuff' opera careers are made of: voice, intellect, and an affinity for foreign languages. So she took me to see the opera *Carmen*. I'll never forget the experience, and I'll never be able to thank her enough for her support."

"Wow," Beyoncé said. "So your teacher meant a lot to you, too!"

I smiled, tearing up. "What a nice compliment," I said. "Yes, Beyoncé," I answered. "I had wonderful and inspiring teachers, ones whose teachings I pass on."

Hanging on my every word, Beyoncé then said, "You have been so inspiring to me too!" She hugged me tightly. "Thanks for being part of my life, David." With that, we continued her voice lesson.

Two days later, I picked Mama up from the former St. Mark's Hotel, near Rice Village, and brought her to my house. She'd agreed to hear my girls.

"Mama, perhaps you should meet them face to face first. It might make them feel less apprehensive," I said.

"OK," Mama answered. "Sounds like a good idea."

We drove straight to the Knowles house, where she not only met all four of my girls, but also Mathew Knowles, putting in one of his rare appearances at the house.

"I've heard so much about you all," Mama said.

The girls greeted her warmly, excited to be meeting my mother. Then Mathew started in. "You have a really wonderful son," he said. "He is a great teacher and has been very helpful. Tina and I think the world of him. He is like family. You must be proud," he said.

I was stunned.

"More than proud," Mama replied, then she looked at me, smiling.

"Well girls, it's time for lessons," I said. Mama and I took my car around the corner to my parking space, and the girls headed over to my apartment from within the main house.

I'd decided the night before to give each girl a 30-minute individual lesson, and then we'd begin group lessons. First up was Kelly, followed by the other three, one by one. As the group lessons started, Mama was suddenly startled.

Enter Solange, in a grand fashion, as only Solange could. She had darted in wearing black leotards and a tutu, pointed her toes, done a pirouette, and then leaped back out of the room in a self-taught full extension. She was not going to allow the other girls to have all of Mama's attention. She had popped into the apartment via the alcove, like a gazelle on Quaaludes.

"What the hell was that?" Mama asked.

"Oh, that was Solange."

"Well, where did she come from?" (Mama could see that there was another entrance to my apartment, and realized that the girls must have used it to get into the apartment before us. But where had Solange come from?) "And where did she go? Did she pop out of the closet?"

I laughed. We all did.

Mama had a great sense of humor and could be refined if need be, but her work and her heart kept her earthy and direct. Even though she dealt with addicts, crazies, spouse abusers, child abusers, the mentally disturbed, and the court systems in Omaha, she had still been startled by the dancing gazelle.

I explained that Solange had aspirations of being a singer and dancer.

"Well, she certainly knows how to make an entrance," Mama said, bringing us all to side-bursting laughter.

At the end of all the lessons (a total of four hours), Mama said, "You girls will have promising careers." Mama told them they had beautiful voices and encouraged them to continue working hard and to never lose faith, looking directly into Kelly's eyes. I could hardly wait to hear her thoughts.

"Thank you," they all chimed, and then, one by one, gave her a hug. Beyoncé was first, followed by Kelly, and then LaTavia and LeToya. Thanking them for their good work that day, I closed the door behind them, and turned to Mama.

"You have a problem," she said.

My heart dropped into my shoes. I took a seat, preparing myself for her analysis. What I got flattened me cold.

"Kelly has been traumatized by physical abuse," Mama said, "but LaTavia is the one in real trouble."

I stopped breathing.

15. Mama

Mama and I went out to dinner that evening, but my appetite did not go with me. I had decided to take her to one of my favorite restaurants, a quaint little place named The Hobbit Hole, now on Richmond Ave. After we got seated I confessed to Mama my ulterior motive for having her observe the lessons. I had been eager to know if my assessment of Kelly's situation had validity; I had not expected that her observations would yield such powerful insights about the other girls.

"Mama, I am developing young stars, and these girls are going to be huge," I said. "I've put so much into them, but I'm still concerned about Kelly's fearful behavior. And now you've told me that LaTavia is an even bigger concern."

"David, I think you are way too invested in these girls," Mama said.

"Yeah, OK – but what can I do about it now?"

"I should correct my statement," Mama said. "I don't believe that the girls are the problem, not really. That father is the piece of work I want to talk about. Where is he from?" Mama asked.

"Mathew? He's from Alabama."

"Well, his mama was definitely a firecracker."

Mama and I had already had a discussion about abusive and difficult mothers. "What makes you say that now?" I asked. "You've just met him."

Her response startled me. "His speech pattern." Mama said. "Mathew's speech is not fluid, and he stammers. Does he have moments where he's cocky and then deeply depressed?"

"Yes," I answered.

Mama said that Mathew's ego was typical. "How is Daddy Knowles' relationship with his wife coming along?"

"Not good," I answered. I did not say to Mama that I had begun to feel that Celestine's nagging of Mathew bordered on emasculation. I didn't need to. Mama had already figured out that Mathew's childhood home and his mother's harsh and belittling treatment of him were no doubt being repeated in his relationship with Celestine. I agreed, having felt for some time that Celestine's harassment exceeded the boundaries of everyday domestic badgering.

"How long has he been on cocaine?" Mama asked.

"What?"

"You heard me," she said.

At just that moment the waitress showed up, offering me a momentary break. But not to fear, as soon as she left the table, Mama dived right back in, repeating her question.

"How long has Mathew been snorting cocaine?" she asked, adding, "His nose is discolored at the edges."

"I don't rightly know," I managed to say, "but I suspect since the mid-eighties."

Celestine had confessed to me that she and Mathew had begun to have serious marital problems shortly after Beyoncé's birth. His drug use, violent outbursts, and physical shoving all contributed to the widening rift between them. I had told Celestine some the stories out of my childhood, memories of seeing my mother physical and verbally abused. She, in turn, opened up with stories about Mathew's behaviors that would've shamed the devil.

I was blown away by how keen Mama's perceptions were. It should have come as no surprise to me, having grown up in Fern's house. Mama's skills for reading family dysfunction never failed to wow me, and I remembered that even as a classroom teacher she'd had a sixth sense about which students lived with abuse at home.

Needing a break from these troublesome thoughts, and because I was beginning to feel a few twinges of hunger, I picked up the menu and buried my head in it. Mama did the same.

I signaled for the waitress. "My mother will have the blackened garlic chicken, with rice, and I will have the Cajun chicken with black beans and rice. Oh, and does my mother's dish come with jalapenos?" I asked the waitress.

"No sir, it doesn't. We can add them if you'd like," she answered.

"Please don't," I said. Then looking at Mama, "You definitely don't want the jalapenos here. They are hot as hell." After the waitress left the table with our orders, I recounted a story about my student Patrice eating the jalapenos and weeping like a baby. Mama listened patiently to my amusing distraction, then:

"I think you should pull back a bit."

"Huh?" Weren't we just talking about jalapenos?

"I think you should pull back a bit – with that family, I mean."

"And how do you suggest I do that? I am convinced that I am exactly where destiny wants me."

"That may be true, but you don't need to live with fate to shape it."

"Ah, Mama, you are suspicious of everybody," I said. I laughed nervously. I knew she was right, dead right, but I was in it now for good. I wasn't going anywhere. My girls had become my family. I loved them.

Presently the waitress returned, and not a moment too soon as far as I was concerned. Turning her attention to dinner, Mama then said, "This looks wonderful."

"It is. Believe me!"

* * * * *

The day after *Carmen* closed, Mama took me to lunch. The fact that I had not abandoned my own dreams of a career on the operatic stage was "reason enough to celebrate," she said. That seemed to give her some solace.

"I've been thinking," she said.

Oh God, I thought. Bracing myself, I was prepared to hear what Mama had to say, but then she did something atypical. She changed the subject. Or did she?

"How do you deal with Beyoncé's shyness?" Mama asked.

"It's still an uphill battle, but she's getting better. The weekend group lessons have helped her tremendously. Having the other girls around helps her with trust. But I may have to up my game. Her mother has started with the 'watch out, Beyoncé!' stories."

"What do you mean?" Mama asked.

"Celestine seems convinced that the kids at school are jealous of Beyoncé and her talent. She keeps telling Beyoncé to 'watch out!' and to be wary of other people's motivations."

"What? That's crazy. Children need socialization," Mama said. "Doesn't she have her sister to share things with?"

"Yes, and No. Solange is such a strong personality that often times, Beyoncé acquiesces to Solange."

"I see," Mama said.

"I've begun teaching her about personal space, which has been interesting, because she is so sensitive. She has a co-dependent personality."

"That's a great one!" Mama answered. Then, "How's her empathy. Have you worked on that with her?"

I didn't understand.

"It's apparent to me that she doesn't know how to handle conflict," Mama said. "It was Beyoncé herself who clued me in on what was going on in her house. Mama and Daddy do more than argue."

"You are right," I said.

"How's the 'little gazelle' doing?'" Mama asked.

"Solange is Solange," I said, recalling Mama's first encounter with her. "She is cocky, demanding, and unrelenting in her quest to become a dancer and a singer. She's her own person, and I value that."

"Is Solange taking regular lessons with you? Consistently, I mean?" Mama asked.

"No, she remains in her sister's shadow. Celestine has not changed her mind about allowing her to have one of Beyoncé's lessons. She insists that Beyoncé needs all four lessons per week. So I have to fit Solange in where and when I can. I even tried talking to Mathew about it, thinking he might be able to talk some sense into Celestine."

"Is Celestine paying you?" Mama asked, point blank.

"Paying me?"

"For all those lessons Beyoncé and Solange are getting?" Mama added.

"Yes," I said, hesitantly, and then I told Mama the truth. Celestine did the best she could, given her financial plight. She couldn't always pay.

"What kind of compromise do you all make?" Mama questioned.

"Whenever she can't pay, I'm supposed to deduct what she owes from the rent. That was her suggestion." Then I added, proudly, "But, I pay her the rent anyway, every month and on time, regardless of her objections."

"My poor naïve baby."

I ignored the feeling Mama's "poor naïve baby" gave me and continued our conversation. "I have not forgotten your warning about giving too much," I said. In turn, I reminded Mama that she was guilty of the same thing. However, she shut me up. "Yes, but I do not live with my work."

* * * * *

My mother was the carbon copy of the mother character (played by Tyne Daly) on the hit American television show "Judging Amy"; she was a social worker on a mission. She gave everything to help children in need. Just like the Tyne Daly character, Mama worked tirelessly protecting children and their rights.

Mama had studied early child development and elementary education at Creighton University. Additional studies in the area of special education awakened in Mama an interest in the welfare of the children she taught. Parents, principals, and colleagues called her an astounding and committed teacher. Nothing slid by her, and she was a stickler for discipline. Mama believed that every child possesses something special, and she went the extra mile to help them. She championed the underdog, and there was always some neighborhood kid at our house needing help with something or other. I remember that a great many of them often stayed for dinner.

Increasingly, Mama felt called to become involved at the family level and she eventually tailored her profession to become a family counselor, a chief liaison to the offices of social work. She loved it, and even worked for the well-known "Boystown," before leaving to take a job with the State of Nebraska. "Now that's where the action is," she once told me. Her specialty became the reconstruction of the dysfunctional family, which brought her in direct contact to the courts, especially the juvenile court system in Omaha.

The young clients she serviced suffered because of chronic alcoholism and drug abuse in the family, as well as physical and emotional trauma inflicted by the adults in their lives. Children placed in danger, children abandoned, children suffering because of mental illness, handicapped children, severely impoverished children, undernourished children, and children crippled by incest all became Mama's passion and personal crusade. Children suffering from generational patterns of dysfunction disturbed her the most: those unable to break the cycle due to circumstances they saw as impossible to change. Completely dedicated, Mama thought about each case individually and never treated anyone like a statistic. I loved running down to the court house after school to watch her in action. Judges and social workers alike praised her in-depth, sometimes raw, but always accurate and humanitarian approach.

Growing up, my brother and sister and I often had a front row seat to Mama's world. The lives she touched and how she touched them made an indelible impression on my siblings and me (my sister eventually followed in her professional footsteps). My mother never revealed her clients' names, but sometimes she felt compelled to talk about the cases. As the oldest of the three siblings I was always interested in discussing their psychology. Sometimes they would invade our lives.

I remember one of Mama's female clients, a disillusioned mother of two children, who was addicted to crack cocaine. Everyone believed the woman was lost – everyone, that is, except Mama. She saw the good in her clients when no one else could.

One night the woman's mother called. "Ms. Brewer," she said, "she is missing again. We haven't seen her in three days." Having an idea where "she" might be, Mama got dressed and headed for crack alley. She entered a crack house, stepping over addicts, needles, and broken vials to retrieve that worried mother's daughter. With absolute resolve, she did her job. A client in need was never denied access to her. But this time, we got a shock. Mama brought the woman home with her, which was definitely against the rules.

"I want you to listen and listen good," Mama said to her. "This is your last chance. You have a court date in the morning and you are going to stand before that judge sober and in control." (They didn't do drug testing back then.) She warned her client that if she didn't pull it together she would lose her children forever. Mama had the client bathe, gave her a warm meal, and put her to sleep on the sofa. To insure the client didn't abandon the plan, Mama slept in a living room chair she'd placed in front of the front door that night.

The next afternoon I skipped school, heading down to family court to watch Mama in action. When she saw me, she gave me "the look." For sure, I could expect a good talking to about skipping fifth period Chemistry, but I didn't care. Seeing the way Mama defended that young mother's right to keep her children was worth the punishment I knew was coming.

"I understand why some mothers have to lose their children," Mama told the judge. "However, this particular young mother shouldn't be one of them." Then Mama went into an argument that I'm sure made even

God proud. I sure as hell was. Mama remains a fierce advocate for women, with a strong sense of empathy with all of humanity. Her sympathies often caused her inner pain.

That day, Mama gave me a ride back to Technical High School and seventh period. "I hate that part of my job," she said to me. "It is never easy to remove children from their home environment, the only environment they know. The crying and screaming rips your heart out." I never forgot those words, nor have I ever forgotten my month long punishment.

That client did clean herself up, got her children back, and to this day calls Mama on Thanksgiving to see how she is doing.

I was and am a proud son.

* * * * *

Mama had taken every opportunity to remind me of my own career over the past years, since my move into the Knowles house. Now, at the end of this Houston visit, she upped her game. We continued our conversation during our Sunday evening drive to the airport for her flight back to Nebraska. After complimenting me on my *Carmen* performance again, she said, "David, those people are taking advantage of you."

"Who, Mama?"

"The Knowleses."

I never wanted to hear that, nor could I accept Mama's being right. I kept trying to steer her back to what she had observed when she had sat in on the girls' lessons. She had astute comments, but when I got to LaTavia, Mama suddenly turned evasive.

"Tell me what you've learned about LaTavia's situation," she said.

"Nothing new, but I watch for signs of abuse, like you said."

LaTavia was a very sweet girl. She possessed a smile that could light up even the darkest room. I adored her. Still, she could be a handful. But Mama knew all of this already. She asked me for information about LaTavia's parents. I wasn't sure what to say.

"Cheryl is a really pretty woman," I began, "with a 'slammin' figure. She's hopelessly devoted to her husband, Charles." Cheryl's devotion to LaTavia's stepfather was obvious to us all. Even the girls would say, "She loves her some Charles!" Mama's voice expressed a colorful "uh-HM" – the one that said, "Answer my question!" Her serious face told me that my attempt to keep the conversation light was going nowhere, and fast. Gingerly, I continued, this time with a bit more substance in my explanation.

"Cheryl is not as attentive to her daughter as she could be – in my opinion," I said. "All of the parents work hard to provide and do their 'best,' I guess. I hate to judge them. As for Charles? He's reasonably nice and extremely well groomed. Still, there's something about him that feels slimy to me."

"Slimy?" Mama asked.

"Well, his behavior and clothes remind me of a slick pimp," I said. "He seems to think he's some stud. His pants are always very tight and suggestive, if you know what I mean, and his shirts are always opened to show his hairy chest. His demeanor seems inappropriate," I concluded. "On the other hand, it's his right to wear tight pants, bulging all over the place, and his shirt open, if he wants."

Mama rolled her eyes, then asked, "Where does he work?"

"He's a Houston police officer, Mama," I answered.

"Really?" Mama said. "In which department?"

"The juvenile division," I said.

With another "Mmm-hmmm," Mama switched the conversation to Kelly.

I told Mama that Kelly seemed to be faring much better than she had been in the past, but that she still was not out of the woods. Doris, Kelly's mother, was definitely an overly strict parent. She had lost her most recent job and was unemployed again. Times were difficult, and Doris suffered from the repeatedly depressing situation she found herself in. "But Kelly manages to get to her lessons, and for that I am most grateful."

"Currently Kelly is living with Ann again, for the umpteenth time," I told Mama. "Ann takes her in out of love, but I worry about the effect on her own health. A single mom with *three* children to raise...?" I knew that

Mama understood that concept. Furthermore, I explained to Mama that Doris had become a real fan of her own daughter and would want to keep her in the group. "My daughter can sing," she would proudly state – a complete about-face for Doris. I reminded Mama that this is the same woman who had originally questioned me in disbelief about her daughter's talents.

"Just be careful!" Mama said.

I had everything under control, I told her. My girls and my work with them was a bit of a sensitive subject with me, and Mama knew it. I protected them fiercely and would have taken on anyone who sought to malign them or their character, which at this point was impeccable.

"So about LaTavia. What's your plan for her voice? Mama asked.

Oh God, I thought. We're back to LaTavia. This was turning out to be an airport ride from hell. Focusing on LaTavia's singing, I explained to Mama how I had been working on stabilizing her. "And she is making progress, both technically and mentally, every day. I have her working on Toni Braxton songs."

"What about Anita Baker songs? I would think she would also be good for LaTavia's deep voice," Mama said.

"Not really," I said. Anita Baker's sliding and scooping, and her unclean diction, wasn't the best example for what LaTavia needed. "Clarity of tone and vowel, as you well know, Mama, are essential in good singing." Not that Toni Braxton was so much better, but her approach served my purposes with LaTavia.

Once again attempting to distract Mama, I said, "I'm having Beyoncé learn an Anita Baker song."

"Oh really, which one?" Mama asked.

"Sweet Love."

"That's my jam…" Mama said, humming its melody.

For a moment Mama let herself be carried away. Sweating bullets and trying to conceal my uneasiness from Mama, I was relieved when she seemed to have made the decision to let me live. Good, I thought. I'm off the hook.

And then I wasn't.

"She is too anxious, and her body is far too developed for a girl her age," Mama said suddenly. While I mulled this blunt comment, Mama said, "She is not present in her body. When she hugged me goodbye, her arms and body felt distant and detached of all emotion."

"Are you talking about Beyoncé, Mama?"

"No! LaTavia."

I reminded Mama that she had observed the girls for only four hours.

Ignoring my remark, Mama said, "Maybe something happened to her at home before she came to her lesson, but something has definitely happened. David, LaTavia splits her mind from her body. She is a perfectionist and she refuses to lose control."

I thought back to LaTavia's panic attack. She'd certainly lost control on that day.

"How does she respond to the other girls?"

"Great," I replied.

"She respects you and trusts you. So watch her. If something is going on you must help her."

My mother was pushing me now. I confessed.

"Mama, I am struggling to find a solution, to help LaTavia find her place in all of this. She is increasingly despondent. I talked to Cheryl, her mother, about it, and Cheryl asked LaTavia what was going on with her, but she quickly replied 'nothing,' and so Cheryl dropped the whole thing." I was quiet for a moment.

"Then I decided to talk with Beyoncé, as her best friend. I wanted to know if she had noticed anything different about LaTavia, or if there was anything going on with LaTavia that she thought I should know about."

"'I don't think so,' Beyoncé said to me."

"I was still puzzling about this when LaTavia's step-father, Charles, brought her to her next lesson. I felt uncomfortable talking about LaTavia with him, but I was desperate. Her mother didn't have a clue what was going on with her. Beyoncé didn't know, and neither did the other girls. I was at a loss, Mama, so I spoke candidly with Charles."

"'Charles, do you know what is going on with LaTavia?' I asked him."

"What did he say?" Mama asked.

"He said that LaTavia had been acting out at home and he had disciplined her. He thought he might have been too strict with her and that perhaps she was angry about being disciplined. He then smiled and said, 'Teenagers! You know how that is.'"

"So then, right in front of me, Charles asked LaTavia if there was something going on with her that she wanted to share. He assured her that he was there to take care of her. But, Mama, he had a strange, disapproving look on his face. It was confusing." I paused, hesitating to go ahead with my story. "Charles always appears genuinely concerned and attentive where LaTavia is concerned. That day she quickly ran over to him and hugged him. She apologized profusely and gave us some cockamamie story about being stressed with all the school work her teachers had been giving her."

Mama asked, "Is she a poor student?"

"No, not at all. LaTavia is an A and B student and to my knowledge gets more As than Bs. She is extremely bright, really, the smartest of all the girls, academically."

"Hmm. Sounds like he's grooming her," Mama said.

"Grooming her?" I asked.

Mama ignored my question. She had heard enough, I guessed, and just like that! the discussion about LaTavia was over.

We had arrived at Houston's Hobby airport. I parked the car, took the suitcases out of the car trunk, and Mama and I headed for the terminal. We had reached the airport in more than enough time. While Mama checked in at the TWA counter, I thought about all the unresolved issues I was too afraid to discuss with her.

My whole insides trembled. Kelly was still a big dilemma for me. I knew that she suffered at the hands of her mother, but what about her father? Could I believe Doris's version of her ex-husband? Kelly's memories of her father were different from Doris's, of course. My own battle with cruel fathers had taught me all about the things that go bump in the night, and the desire to forget. Still, I had no solid evidence about Kelly's father. It was enough for me to stay vigilant against Doris's mood swings and their effect on her daughter. And now Mathew had begun beating up on Kelly verbally in his sporadic "rehearsals." In almost every session, she was reduced to tears.

As for LaTavia, I couldn't push the girl, even if what Mama told me was true. If I was going to get to the heart of the problem, it would take patience. I'd have to wait her out, until she was ready, I thought. Mama swore that LaTavia was being molested, and had been for years. A wise judge of character, Mama's theory had definitely gotten under my skin and she knew it. But I had no proof. I had to stay focused. In exactly three months my girls would be standing in front of nine (the actual number kept changing) record label presidents, CEOs, directors of A&R and major producers.

These thoughts whirred through my brain, and when Mama and I headed to a coffee shop, just opposite her gate, I brought up my kindergarten teacher. "Mama, do you remember Ms. Graham?"

"Ms. Who?" Mama asked.

"Ms. Graham, my kindergarten teacher."

"Ah yes! Why do you ask?"

I reminded Mama about Ms. Graham's "Wonderland." Now, with only moments until she would have to board her flight to Omaha, I quickly told Mama my idea of creating my very own "Wonderland" for my girls. I asked Mama what she thought about the idea of having something like a summer camp, a boot-camp for singers. "I could control the girls' environment and get some great work done in our preparation for Atlanta," I said.

"What's happening in Atlanta?"

"Oh, I'm sorry. I thought I told you," I said. "I guess with the *Carmen* performances, and all our other discussion, I didn't get a chance to mention it. We've made contact with an important producer. The girls are going to be showcased in Atlanta. Important reps from at least nine labels are expected. Their performance will have to be perfect."

"In that case, I think that your summer camp is a very good idea, but I'll say it again – I think you're way too invested in those girls. You are going to be crushed when their parents force them to turn on you."

I looked at Mama.

"You don't seriously believe that Mama and Daddy are going to give you any credit for everything you do – do you?"

The look on my face said it all. I had never thought about it. Not once had I pondered credit. I was far too busy doing the work. Grandmother always said, "Opportunity knocks on everyone's door. Be ready to accept the call." That's what I thought about. My girls would be ready, I had promised myself.

This time Mama spared me her "poor naïve baby." Instead, she smiled, kissed me on the cheek, and waved goodbye. Her flight was boarding. I drove home, a little wiser, but still a lot worried.

I had a summer camp to plan.

* * * * *

The next day, back in the Knowles kitchen, I approached Mathew and Celestine with my idea. We discussed it in detail. I shared with them my observations regarding Kelly, my frustrations, and my hopes for her. I also mentioned that it would be great for Beyoncé to have her around. When I proposed the idea of a summer training camp, Mathew's eyes lit up. A few evenings later, Celestine told me that she and Mathew had agreed to my idea, and would host it on their property. I could proceed immediately.

That very evening Mathew called a group meeting with all the parents present. He explained to them that because of the upcoming Atlanta showcase he was asking for all the girls to spend large chunks of time "on site." He said, "as soon as school lets out in a couple days, we're going to have a 'Summer Camp,'" he named it. "I will need all the girls to live here over the summer for intensive training sessions with David."

Not everyone was happy with relinquishing their daughters six days per week. When would they see them? Doris was concerned that Kelly would become a problem. Pam didn't feel at all comfortable having LeToya spend more than a weekend away from home. Eventually all the parents conceded the need for the intensive rehearsing before the Atlanta showcase. They trusted me, and I promised to honor their request for contact with their girls, even as I impressed upon them the importance of having completely uninterrupted training sessions.

The record labels and industry professionals gathered in Atlanta would be looking for authenticity and confidence in my girls. I had been building on this from day one, but now our precise work could not be frivolously interrupted. I made it clear that not even Mathew would have access to the girls outside of his allotted time. Discovering and maintaining the peak in performance, while breathing, eating, and sleeping it, were my goals for Da Dolls that summer.

* * * * *

The two weeks before the summer training camp was scheduled to begin, I took myself in hand. I focused my energy and I prayed and energized my mind and thoughts. I told myself daily (chanting and believing it) that I would be successful in reaching my goal: helping my girls to achieve the ultimate. I wrote out key words and placed them all over my apartment: words like "routine," "expectation," "greatness," "power of thought," "optimism," "visualize," "keep your eye on the prize" "plan," "gain control," "recover from setbacks," and "stay focused." This intrigued Beyoncé, immensely.

Then I relaxed. I had to relax. For the next three months I would remove from my mental sight everything that didn't belong in my thinking or my world. Nothing else could exist. Beyoncé watched me closely during this time. She watched how I became acutely aware of my mental state, which was about creating the best atmosphere to effect quality in

336

practice, training, and performance. Routine was fundamental. I even awakened early and went to bed early in order to prepare my body for the drastic change in schedule.

One does not simply win. Winning without effort is called luck, and I wasn't interested in teaching luck. I would teach my girls the meaning of discipline and how to have staying power in the music business. I would teach them my "Three Rs of Performance": recognize, replace, and rehearse. Like "readin', writin' and 'rithmetic," my Three Rs were fundamental to my girls' artistic success in our world.

The first step to increasing my girls' mental capacity for Atlanta lay in their understanding the power of the mind's eye. The success of a top performer's use of mental skills (pictures in the mind) requires understanding visualization. For LaTavia and Kelly in particular I repeatedly emphasized the message that they were brilliant, beautiful, and bold. We worked hard to create mental images that would replace the shadows that dominated their thinking with healthy and pleasing pictures.

Becoming exceptional at anything physical, and or mental for that matter, depends upon understanding how to "ease the action," I told LaTavia. Cognitively, she had to learn to recognize the mistake (negative thought), replace it with a better choice (the truth) and then rehearse the new thinking into healthy normalcy (ending her terror). Feldenkrais taught that "When an individual repeatedly experiences a certain difficulty, he usually abandons the activity that he has found hard to master, at which he has not succeeded, or that has proved disagreeable in some way…The limits he thus sets for himself will stop his development not only in the fields that he has decided to abandon, but also in other areas; they may even influence his entire personality."

Talent is what we are born with, but skill and its mastery are what make a success. At some point, talent dies if you don't develop the skill to manage it, which is how you get to maintaining it. In my girls' case, I had already taught them the rudiments of singing skills – the fundamental technical aspects of singing – and now they were ready to advance to more sophisticated thinking. I would concentrate on four stages of mental training: attributes (assessing successful performances), awareness (factors that both help and inhibit successful performance), cognitive and behavioral control (the intellect behind the art), and their self-control (reinforced efficient practice and monitoring).

In the final week of the group sessions before the summer program began, I described the mind-body connection and related it to each girl individually. I wanted my girls to understand focus, emotional engagement, and poise. They needed to know that what comes out of our mouths reflects our thoughts, and that negativity breeds destructivity. No one ever does exceptional work by accident, and if I did my job correctly my girls would begin to learn to put their mind-body-spirit onto a high enough plane to convince those nine labels. I certainly knew that complete mastery of these principles would take years, but by the end of the summer they'd have learned to take genuine jubilation in performance (that state of being where one feels possessed by something unexplainable onstage) to a new level.

To help them to learn visualization and to awaken my girls' imaginations, I used a recording of the orchestral music for Igor Stravinsky's ballet *Rite of Spring*. I explained that the piece is about the "wonder and creative power of spring." I likened it to "the Creation," and the girls responded enthusiastically, saying things like, "Oh, that part sounds like God waking up for the day," and, "That part sounds like the devil." From the music they imagined Adam and Eve and the eating of the apple from the forbidden tree. They had fun learning to hear the music, just as every musician hears it. They had to learn to listen, to hear music, and then to understand that musical sounds were directly linked to emotion. Having identified the fear, relief, birth, punishment, and sacrifice in Stravinsky's work, they understood that music communicates emotions and is an extension of speech.

In the end I told them music was like a movie. The music helps paint the picture of what is about to happen. "Your job is to bring those pictures to life with your voice." I would continue to develop imagery exercises throughout my girls' studies, using everything and every situation to aid

338

me. We observed babies crying to see the miracle of breathing; we observed the swaying of the tree branches during a gentle wind to understand flow and a tensionless body. I had already taught them one of my favorite images: wringing out a washcloth.

I told them that when a singer sings a high note two things happen: the singer employs more energy, and the space narrows (the sensation is of the throat getting smaller, but actually the larynx drops and tilts forward, opening the throat to maximum capacity). Singing high notes, I explained, was like jumping on a trampoline. A springing effect propels the voice upward. The shooting feeling, that the voice is being thrown upwards, takes mental imaging.

The girls and I went to the kitchen sink. I gave them each a washcloth and asked them to wet it, good and wet. Once they did this I asked them to sing a phrase from one of the songs I had assigned – one that required them to ascend to the high voice. Reminding them to give themselves enough leeway before actually having to sing the high note, I asked them to prepare the wet washcloth loosely in their hands, ready to wring the life out of it. As they got to the high note, just before going up, I said to them, "Now! Wring the water out of the rag."

What they sensed was that as the lower ribs squeezed together the space in the throat narrowed while expanding at the back of the mouth. They also noticed that the breath seemed to speed up. The lower ribs acted like the mat of the trampoline; at the same time, as they twisted and wrung the wash cloth, they felt that the squeezing of those ribs gave the breath a push upwards, helping it to travel easily through the narrowing space (the stem of a flower). The sound was propelled upwards and outwards (the blossom of the flower).

This simple, tactile exercise clarified for my girls the physiology of singing high notes. "You can't be afraid of your throat if you want to get to the top of your voice!"

Five plus years of steady and evenly spaced voice lessons had produced assured singers and a group sound to be reckoned with. The Atlanta showcase would require mastery on every level. I would not allow the girls to be undervalued because of age. Every child can achieve excellence. "Create the right environment, and you will discover genius," Ms. Graham always said. I raised the goal to Level Red, and they rose to the occasion beautifully.

My girls now had to be at peace. Peace is where greatness lives. Through finding inner peace and quiet, something Kelly and I had been working on for two years now, they could all open themselves to heightened emotion. That is the key to peak performance. They would become aware of their bodies' reactions to their surroundings, outside forces and internal conflicts; in addition, they would learn to understand how fear of failure might infiltrate their thoughts. How would we increase expectation without creating anxiety? Inner peace was a crucial concept.

A desire to succeed would not suffice; I would encourage in them a healthy drive to succeed. Beyoncé had real drive, while the others possessed desire. Would I be able to encourage Beyoncé's kind of drive in all of them? I might concentrate on such details as mental focus, attitude, and self-regulation, but essentially it is the singer/performer who must implement those ideals. As the common saying goes, "You can lead a horse to water, but you can't make him drink." Articulating my principles would take tireless focus and energy from my side, while practice and consistent study – understanding and doing – would be my girls' job. I asked them to open their minds, and then we began our journey.

Now, how do you begin to find peace in your body, mind and spirit so that your personal best can shine through? I believe that ultimate performance excellence results from achieving five positive states: Drive, Attitude, Focus, Self-regulation and Visualization. I decided that the girls and I would begin with Visualization.

"Visualize your success," I told them. "I want you to dream of having success. Smell it, taste it, touch it, believe in it, fight for it, and most importantly, expect it," I said. "Over the next months I am going to teach you how to get into 'the Zone,' all the time."

I lined up four chairs next to one another. I asked the girls to sit in those chairs (LeToya and Kelly on the ends) and then I asked them to look

340

to their left and repeat the words, "You are beautiful!" to their neighbor. "In the case that you do not have a neighbor to your left, you are to say 'I am beautiful.' Now, look to your right and repeat the same process." We began every group class with this simple, but highly effective routine. Seeing their group members as beautiful validated their importance. They became important as individuals and thus important to the group as a whole. Without each person's belief in herself, all would be lost. Immediately they understood that they were in this together.

Then I asked them to close their eyes and I opened the patio doors. They were to listen – simply listen. They heard birds singing, wind rustling, cars driving by, the soft chatter of neighbors, laughter and stillness. They heard the trees, cats and dogs, and eventually they heard even the constant low lull of heat waves and humidity bouncing off the pavement.

With each sound I was able to teach the beginning stages of the "God experience." They were hearing God all around them. My girls learned they were not alone. Singing was the musical extension of speech representing truth. Someone's truth – the songwriter's truth, your truth or the listener's truth, but make no mistake about it, every song corners truth.

The story and text mean something. My girls had to become super sensitive to subtleties. When I sometimes asked them to tame their brash impulses, these adolescents had a real challenge. By the end of this process they had become hypersensitive.

Through visualization, two things happened: One, they could isolate sound (necessary in concentration exercises) in their memories, and Two, they began to understand recall and sensory perception. Which tree had been rustling? From which direction had they heard the cat or dog? Was the cat or dog in distress? Did the rustle of the tree suggest a beautiful day? Or did it suggest the coming of a storm? And most importantly, how did what they heard make them feel? Then I instructed them to remember those feelings. They would need this skill whenever they sang and performed, building choreography or interpreting song. "Become aware of your environment," I told them, "and stay totally focused, but also be ready to adapt to the unexpected."

Next I checked each girl's explanatory style. I placed a glass of water on the kitchen counter, filled only halfway. "Is the glass half empty or half full?" I asked. Beyoncé said, "Half full," and LaTavia followed suit. Kelly and LeToya both said, "Half empty." I smiled and then poured the water down the drain, placing the glass in the dish rack. Beyoncé wanted to know why I had asked. I told them I would explain later.

The half-filled glass of water test usually brings forth from an optimist the response that the glass is "half full," while the pessimistic response will be "half empty." There are varying factors that determine why people see the half-filled glass of water one way or the other. It was important to identify who was positive by nature and who was negative by nature and to alter the latter perception. It was very important that the girls learned to see their world positively. But I could not force it on them.

They had to believe that they could achieve success at the highest level and not just dream about it. It required active thinking and accepting the responsibility for having a gift. Every inch of them had to ooze confidence. Not a single hair on their head or flinch in their demeanor could insinuate non-confidence.

That two of the girls thought positively and two negatively got my attention. It meant that discord could find its way into my girls' world. The bond of friendship and common purpose needed to be cemented in each girl. They needed to be in one accord. Their environment did not always promote that.

I had my work cut out for me.

On the eve of our "summer camp," I asked the girls not to stay up too late, because I would be waking them up so early in the morning. You should have heard the groans and moans coming from my willing participants. "I don't even get up that early for school," LaTavia said. Her band mates chimed in. Then they noticed I wasn't smiling. I could tell that they didn't know if they liked the new David. I bade them a good evening and let them go for what would be their last night of frivolity.

From the window in my apartment I could see them down in the Knowles family room, having a good ol' time, laughing, feasting on treats, and watching television until after midnight. They were going to be dead tomorrow, but I kept my eye on the prize. I would also be tired, but I would not let them see that. They were about to step into the professional musicians' world. The day was scheduled to start at 5:30 a.m. and end at 10:00 p.m. Six days a week we would follow this schedule for the rest of the summer. This was going to be interesting. Grueling, yes, and fun!

My contemplation was suddenly interrupted by a startling knock on my door. It was Mathew. "How can I be helpful?" he asked.

"Let me think about it," I answered and bade him a friendly "Good night!" No way would I invite Mathew's energy in – no way.

16. The Summer Camp

In a 2002 article about working as A&R for Destiny's Child, Teresa LaBarbera-Whites would tell the interviewer Luci Vázquez, for "Hit Quarters" online magazine, that when Destiny's Child broke through in 1997 they had been rehearsing for that day for nearly eight years.

Frankly, it came as a shock to me when I read the article. Unbeknownst to Teresa, and in her defense, I knew that Mathew had given her inaccurate information. Teresa was quoted as having said: "It was Mathew Knowles's brilliant idea to organize a series of 'summer camps' at his house, in which the girls took part in daily activities which ranged from vocal lessons and choreography to team building skills and workshops in which they studied a variety of successful artists, to determine exactly what it was that had made them successful – all of this guided by a live-in vocal coach, David Brewer, who had moved into the apartment over the garage, and a choreographer, who put to good use the stage that Mathew had constructed in the backyard." End of quote.

Although this is the only article, ever to mention my name and my years of faithful work, the summer camp can't be credited to Mathew, as you will see....

"Beginning" in 1989, I alone had guided the girls, polishing and refining their artistic talents that summer, a six-days-a-week residency at the Knowleses' house. Due to the first summer's success, we would hold two further camps in the summers of 1994 and 1995.

"Atlanta is 80 days away, Girls."

* * * * *

My goal with every student is to help them to self-knowledge. As my pupils' teacher, mentor, and musical advisor, I often know them much better than they know themselves. That is my job. Subtle – and not-so-subtle – approaches are needed to nudge the student of singing towards emotional and vocal freedom. Ultimately, I want my singing students and my protégés to be better than I am, and I hold nothing back.

In all cases I have to go deep into the psyche of the singer. Who are they? What makes them tick? What are the idiosyncrasies they employ in singing? Do they exhibit poor body alignment, or tics that bring about the opposite of what they desire? What are their fears, and where do they originate? Ultimately, I have to assess if the singers can indeed get out of their own way so that their breath may flow uninterrupted. My early interest and studies in the psychology of human behavior combined with my knowledge of vocal technique to good advantage during the summer camp. I expanded my girls' intellect, as well as drove their resolve, and told them that a great singer must possess eight specific characteristics: Desire, Voice, Talent, Vision, Imagination, Technique, Tenacity, and Discipline, in that order.

5:00 a.m. Wake-up

The first morning – like every morning that summer – my alarm clock went off at 5:00 a.m., thirty minutes before I woke the girls. I needed to be focused, with my mind centered on the grueling days, weeks, and months ahead. This behavior raised my girls' understanding of expectation, making clear to them one of the most important factors in being a top performer: preparation. They would become aware, after eventually signing a record contract, that 5:00 a.m. wake-up calls were par for the course. Commitment is Lesson One in *tenacity*.

5:30 a.m. Wake-up Girls

I walked over to the main house, waking Beyoncé and the other girls at 5:30 a.m. Finding them all piled into two twin beds in Solange's room, with her in their midst, I quickly became my mother. Now it was I who was turning on lights, clapping my hands, and cheerily calling out "Wake up, sleepy heads."

Getting them up was a tough and scary proposition for a young man. Ignoring my qualms, I remembered my resolve. I announced to them that they had thirty minutes. "My car leaves at 6:00 a.m., with or without you." There wasn't much time for anything other than washing the slobber off their faces, brushing their teeth, and jumping into their jogging shorts, t-shirts, and gym shoes. "And don't forget your hair ladies – pull it back." Within no time they stood before me, single file, taking their prepared fruit bags and water and piling into my Audi. We were on schedule. I'd have it no other way.

When we arrived at Hermann Park, which was barely a five-minute drive away, I shared with them the ground rule. "Compete only with your-self. It's important to learn that what others do in your profession isn't important to your success. Figure out your *individual approach* to giving your personal best, and then cement it. You all are part of a team, and there can be no weak links."

Before beginning, I asked my girls, "What are we here to do?"

"We are here to learn to visualize our success."

"Good answer, Ladies." They had understood the lessons on team building leading up to this day.

After getting their blood pumping with a fifteen-minute regimen of light warm-ups and stretching (similar to Tai Chi-type movements), we closed our eyes and listened to our surroundings. I then explained that I wanted to teach them an important element in controlling nerves and agitation (restless insides) during performance. I said one word: "breathing."

345

Suddenly, and independent of one another, each girl began peeking questioningly through cracked eyelids.

"I'm talking about breathing for calm, and not breathing for singing," I said. After demonstrating, I then asked the girls to close their eyes again, this time placing their forefinger and thumb just on the inside of their nostrils.

"There are small pockets at the opening of the nostrils, just before where the bone begins. Do you feel it?"

"Yes," they answered politely.

"These two points will help control nerves and your heart rate. Inner peace is everything to the successful performer. Take a slow and steady breath, without tensing, aimed at those pockets in your nostrils. I call it the 'sweet-smelling place.' You will feel a cool air at the soft palette and uvula, which is essential in learning control and calm. Your entire body will begin to feel a bit euphoric eventually. It is like smelling a rose or a sweet-smelling flower. Do you sense what feels like an expansion and rush of energy/air in your chest cavity, shoulders, back, facial muscles, top of head and forehead?"

"Yes."

"Now, please close your eyes and look downward behind your closed eye lids. Keep your eyes shut while looking down. Do you all notice how everything goes really dark?"

"Yes."

"I want you to focus on looking into the middle of that darkness. Search for the middle of that darkness, and breathe through your nose the way I described earlier. You will feel energy in your body, top of head and forehead. We're looking for the feeling of love in your thoughts and body, and you should sense that all your muscles are getting oxygen (especially the arms, buttocks, chest, back and neck), causing them to stretch out a bit. Accept this love-feeling and go with it. Enjoy it and allow it. Do you feel what I just described?"

"Yes."

346

Over time, the sensation strengthened. I then instructed them to open their eyes and to remember the feeling of looking into the darkness behind their closed eyelids. They needed to be able to recreate this sensation with open eyes. "Now look for that energy with open eyes and breathe into the pockets of your nostrils at the same time."

This new breathing concept would take all summer to master. However, when I saw that they had learned the fundamental sequence that morning, we set off on the jogging trail.

We began by walking the trail and then jogging, repeating the process in five-minute intervals, increasing the jogging time each day. Soon we added new interest – and learning – to the jog-walk pattern. When we walked, we snapped our fingers on the right hand, activating the left brain, specifically with regard to combining action with tempo and rhythm in music. When we jogged, we sang and snapped our fingers on the left hand, activating the right brain, specific to the combination of action with melody and emotion in music. My girls quickly realized that nothing came automatically. At first they found it nigh impossible to control their thought and their action, and coordination was exceedingly difficult after each added new thing. Nevertheless, this would change. By the end of the month, we'd hit our 3.5 miles per day goal.

By the second month, my girls were showing increased right-brain function at a much higher rate, without their even realizing it. (While it is true that the left brain is responsible for daily programming, a musician's right hemisphere must be able to turn the academic into instinct.) Next, we'd take perception to the next level.

Perception in music, or the realization that sound is a meaningful phenomenon, is crucial. My girls had already begun this process in my living room, but during the summer camp, my goal was to help them learn to block out distracting sounds. On day two I asked them to focus on one sound, of their choice, something that they heard within nature in the park. Everything else around them should be blocked out. By this point, the perception exercise had increased to being about balancing the so called "will" (left brain) with the "automatic" (right side). Learning to focus the inner ear onto one source, while keeping everything else out of the concentration zone, developed razor-sharp focus, the kind of concentration that would help them to maintain equilibrium and awareness during performance.

I liken this skill to that of a fighter pilot who goes in and out of air pressure (g forces). In dealing with g forces, pilots can experience blood flow away from the brain. They can experience a heightened heart rate, blurred vision, and sweaty palms. The eyes are forced to close in an attempt to facilitate what is happening. And because the eyes are designed for focus, an un-concentrated pilot cannot be focused, because he is overwhelmed by force (external and internal). Dizziness and unclear and jumbled thoughts follow.

Now, singers are not fighter pilots, but similar phenomena happen to singers when they experience extreme nerves. A nervous singer experiences shortness of breath, sweaty palms, an unsettled stomach, blurred vision, and distorted hearing. They forget their words, or their place in the music. Their heart rate increases to the point of dizziness or fainting feelings.

On the jogging trail my girls' muscles were getting maximum oxygen, and the process of oxygen and carbon dioxide exchange could function unobstructed. By the end of the first week, Beyoncé would shiver, and then I noticed that Kelly also shivered. Then it was LeToya's turn and then LaTavia's. That goosebumps moment told me that their bodies had begun to learn focus on the rudiments of concentration. With this process complete, they would be able to block out external noises in order to find constant and even pacing – a condition absolutely necessary for dancing and singing at the same time. It would take weeks to develop their skill to functional level, and even longer for them to master. But we had the time: Today was only the first day of training, and we had exactly 78 days left before Atlanta.

Although he had declared himself ready to "help," Mathew contributed to the cause by his absence. He'd said that he looked forward to the early morning jogs but we never saw him. I guessed that he was busy at Kinko's.

348

8:00 a.m. Breakfast

When we returned to the house from our morning exercise and pacing regimens, the girls had time to shower, have a balanced breakfast with toast, scrambled egg, tomatoes, walnuts, fruit, water, and juice (no bacon or other meat). This nutrition prepared their bodies and their brains for the studies to come on that day.

Next on the agenda would be ear training and music theory. I didn't have the time to make world-class musicians, but I could continue our lessons in counting, rhythm, and ear-training – necessary for chord-building and harmonizing.

10:00 a.m. Ear training and Music Theory

During the ear training and music theory sessions the girls learned the basics of feeling rhythm and pulse in music, understanding time signatures in music, and counting and chord identification skills (major, minor, augmented, and diminished chords) in order to insure tight harmonies and musical phrasing. We practiced such matters as recognizing and understanding music dynamics from pianissimo to forte and every gradation in between.

The girls listened to Bach Chorales, and learned how to hear chord structures through exercises requiring them to sing chords, having been given only the first note. The girls would build four-note chords of various types, depending on the harmony desired. LaTavia might be asked to sing the root of the chord (the base or fundamental tone of the chord) and Beyoncé would then be prompted to sing a third higher (i.e., counting up three tones from the fundamental). Kelly would then sing the fifth in the chord (counting up five tones from the fundamental), and LeToya would sing either the octave (counting up eight tones) or the seventh, depending on the chord we wanted to construct. Then I would switch their roles to insure that they really understood how to sing the proper note after hearing only the fundamental tone. They all learned how to build a solid chord without the aid of their band mates. I was determined that these girls' ability to sing tight harmonies would separate them from the run-of-the-mill groups. It would be their signature.

Because ear training and music theory demand great concentration, I insisted having those lessons in the morning, while they were fresh. We limited those studies to one hour daily. This more than sufficed. Beyoncé loved this theory stuff. She wanted to know everything about music that she could find out, and I would teach her advanced harmonic theory later on.

11:00 a.m. Vocal lessons

Each girl had a thirty-minute technical lesson, which the others observed. Not only did this arrangement make efficient use of time, but it added immeasurably to their understanding of singing and performing. By listening to the strengths and weaknesses of each other, the girls were able to hear and understand what I had been asking of each of them. Giving the individual voice lesson before their mates supported my goal to teach them the importance of self-regulation. Watching me give, and the student accept, constructive suggestions, the girls learned to energize themselves, control their reactions, relax under the pressure of close scrutiny and most importantly, they learned the ability to recover after a defeating moment. The bar had been raised significantly during summer camp.

The ability to recover from setbacks is probably the most crucial attribute to have for a performer. Setbacks (mistakes, missed marks, or failed attempts) in performance make the musician, and especially a singer, crazy, as it usually takes over their thoughts. Having your thoughts consumed by a mistake that has already been made is detrimental, masochistic, and pure torture.

Singers must learn to control their thought processes. In order to sharpen their confidence, I focused on how to react to mishaps. We practiced three things: admitting that we have weaknesses, discovering what those weaknesses are, and then working systematically to eradicate them (using my three R's concept: recognize, replace and rehearse).

1:00 p.m. Lunch

In addition to arranging their meals, I explained the importance of nutrition to good singing. Vitamins and minerals are important for singers because they activate and support a higher capacity for learning. Celestine was helpful, buying the foods I asked for. That the other parents wrote weekly checks for extras costs regarding food, water, lights and toiletries, calmed her tremendously.

The girls' brains, as well as the rest of their bodies, needed a singer's nutritional plan, or we'd be wasting our time. "Tomatoes (loaded with lycopine) have four chambers," I said. Then I showed them a picture of the heart – it too, was red with four chambers. I encouraged eating "grapes on the vine," which vitalized the blood. Walnuts were set out in small dishes around both my house and the Knowleses'. Similar to the shape of the brain (left and right hemisphere, upper cerebrums and lower cerebellums), walnuts help with neuro-transmitters for brain function. Kidney beans, looking exactly like the human kidney, promoting better kidney function. For extra bone strength, the girls ate celery, and rhubarb pie – the only sweet food I allowed in the house. (Being kids, they probably "cheated," but they at least learned something about good nutrition.) Morning runs in the Texas heat, although early morning, still depleted their sodium levels. I couldn't have the sodium being pulled from their bones. And I started preparing avocado dips. The avocado, along with eggplant and pears, not only resembles the womb and cervix in the female, but these foods target the production of hormones, particularly important, I reasoned, for these adolescent girls. (Women should eat an avocado every week to balance hormones, shed unwanted birth weight, and prevent cervical cancer. Did you know it takes exactly nine months for an avocado to become ripened fruit?)

The regimen that we followed every morning became the exacting daily routine for the entire summer program, as well as the two summers following that. Depending on the weekday, the following schedule would adhere to an equally rigorous, but varying calendar.

2:00 p.m. Video study / Artist Study (Mondays – Wednesdays – Fridays)

I introduced the girls to the all-important study of other singers and their performances. Viewing commercial videotapes, we talked together about what constituted success (or failure) in such performers as Queen, Tina Turner, Michael Jackson, Janet Jackson, Barbra Streisand, Gladys

Knight, Mariah Carey, Whitney Houston, and many others. I asked the girls detailed questions about what they saw and heard. I asked them to analyze what made the performances stellar or not. Most important was the artists' performance practice – meaning no street dance.

Video/Artist study class took place three days per week and allowed for my necessary rule of a one-hour digestion period after eating and before going on to any activity that required singing. It is important never to eat and sing directly afterwards, as the stomach is over-tasked if it has to digest food and support singing at the same time. Serious complications such as heartburn can easily result. Every day people experience the feeling of being full and uncomfortable directly after eating. Only burping releases the pressure. Can you imagine singing in this state?

2:00 p.m. Extra voice lessons (Tuesdays – Thursdays – Saturdays)

On alternate days of the video study/artist study classes, I gave extra voice lessons. I dedicated the hour to addressing particular technical difficulties not yet mastered, or to answering questions about performance, movement, singing, acting, and dancing. Because this lesson followed immediately after the lunch hour, the emphasis was more on discussion than on singing.

3:00 p.m. Rehearsals of the songs to be sung in Atlanta

I decided through trial and error which songs best suited the girls and showed them at their ultimate best, and I discussed this process with Daryl. During this hour-and-a-half class, Mathew could join us, if he was available to do so.

The point was to explore the possibilities of songs the girls would sing in Atlanta (original songs Daryl sent over). Often I was given the songs in advance, and then it didn't matter if Mathew showed up. I could do my work without fear of losing time. We had more than enough to do with learning the songs, trying them out, assigning leads, and developing harmonies.

It was in this class that we created the a capella song "Ain't No Sunshine." I based our version on an arrangement by the Emotions. Beyoncé had been chosen to sing the song's lead melody, with LaTavia covering the lows and/or the root in the chorus. Kelly and Beyoncé alternated between singing the third or fifth in the chord, whichever covered the melody, and LeToya covered the extreme highs. LeToya had been successful in learning to consistently access that magical top voice I always knew she had. She was to sing a high C in "Ain't No Sunshine," and it was stunning to hear such beauty and control coming from her young throat. It was going to be the highlight of the a capella number, the icing on the well-baked cake I had spoken of.

This wonderful arrangement would cause a conflict between Mathew, Celestine, and me. Mathew did not want LeToya to shine, and Celestine was irritated that she even possessed the note. She could not stand it that Beyoncé did not and would never have access to the exquisite facility in the upper regions that nature had given to LeToya. Mathew tried to convince me that the song wasn't right for the girls and that LeToya's singing of that high note didn't sound good. Neither of Beyoncé's parents, driven though they were to push her to the forefront, was capable of recognizing the exceeding beauty of her mid-range voice. Instead, they lamented that I "didn't allow her" (or push her) to sing in the high soprano range.

Mathew even tried to force his misguided and definitely uninformed opinion on LeToya herself. I knew better than to listen to his rhetoric, and warned her against taking it on. I cautioned her to ignore his ranting and to continue singing in the way that I had taught her, which was based in science and my concern for her vocal health. Remembering my promise to myself and to them, I was not going to let anyone decide the artistic development of my girls.

4:30 p.m. Studio Class (Mondays – Wednesdays – Fridays)

In the studio class I concentrated on working with each girl to sing selected songs that would challenge their skills and artistry. I chose songs that demanded them to stretch their singing proficiency and musical imaginations, since it would not further their abilities to sing easily achievable songs. In this way, the studio class differed from group lessons, since the girls had the challenge of performing more difficult solo materials for each other. After singing, each girl heard the comments of her band mates, who gave their critiques of the performance. We agreed that constructive comments could not only give much-needed moral support, but also could help everyone to learn and to correct mistakes. The girls never said anything hurtful or demeaning to one another.

4:30 p.m. Acting, Memory and Muscle Development (Tuesdays - Thursdays – Saturdays)

Text painting, a matter of crucial importance in the performance of song, received its due during the summer camp. My girls had to know and understand what they were singing about. Believe me, no one can afford to take for granted their singing in their mother language. Knowing what you are singing about depends not only upon the individual word, but also upon the overt and covert meanings of the word.

In this class I asked the girls to use a song text as the basis for a scenario, write a short script/story, and then act it out as a mini theater piece. This exercise solidified their ability to understand and communicate what they were singing about. The girls also refined their skills in recognizing emotions and communicating them immediately. Again, Beyoncé responded to this class with special enthusiasm and talent.

Memory is essential to the professional singer. Without a sharp memory the ability to have a successful career in the music business will become little more than just a dream. It was a goal of the class to build upon muscle memory (automatic learned response of the singing muscles) as well. I gave extra attention to the muscles used during singing and described them in detail. Each girl understood and then learned how to isolate the control of muscles by focusing on and sensing them. "You can't master a thing until you can see it," I said.

Not only were the muscles for singing important to identify in this class. There were also the muscles used in dance to consider. As a dancer you are taught that a tight center is paramount to good balance, strength and extension. Teachers of singing tell you that it is the exact opposite in our profession. I do not agree. My dance background helped me to be able to instruct my girls in how to get the maximum from both areas and not lose proficiency.

The decision to leave Cleveland for Houston – on an irrational whim, it might seem – tells you the power of my "still, small voice." Let me say it plain: I regard that voice as the universal spirit – God – guiding me, showing me my path. Just as Grandmother stayed close to her faith in God in all decisions, I had learned to heed my private voice. I was merely following the directions that it gave me.

Returning to Houston from my St. Louis detour had brought me face-to-face with a decision I had been postponing for some years: the choice between singing and dancing. Having trained to the level of "young professional" in both performance arts, I had come to the point that one of them had to predominate.

Grandfather's tutorials in front of the television in his living room had set me on the dancer's path before I entered school. With his proud support, Mama enrolled me at age seven in the dance studio of Sondra McSwain, who happened to live in our Omaha neighborhood. A great teacher, Sondra prepared me so well over my years with her that I was able in my mid-teens to accept honest-to-goodness dance engagements. I earned real money dancing in community theater productions, gala events and charity projects. With Grandfather keeping an eye on my development, I had all the dance bases covered.

As a college student in Oklahoma, I not only danced in the Langston University Theater productions, I also founded my own dance company, which gave performances throughout the state. Among the highlights of those years were our performances for the Oklahoma Museum of Fine Art "Arts Series," for the Tulsa Opera under its general director, Edward Purrington, and for the art opening exhibited by famed dancer Geoffrey Holder, whose paintings at the Museum of Fine Art brought in thousands of dollars, all donated to charity. I also joined Ballet Oklahoma where I took advanced classes in ballet.

In Cleveland, in addition to my vocal studies at CIM, I studied the techniques of the great choreographer Merce Cunningham and danced with the Louis Naylor Modern Dance Company as principal soloist. Heeding my voice to leave Cleveland, I was not only interrupting my vocal program, I was also forcing my own decision about dancing.

For two decades I had been happy performing both art forms. At first, when my singing teachers pointed out to me that I'd have to abandon dance if I were going to study singing seriously, I resisted their advice. Wasn't there a way to do both? Surely there was. But no one – neither my dance teachers, nor my singing teachers – agreed with my youthful opinion.

Dance was beginning to create an upheaval in my voice lessons, and vice versa. My CIM voice professor, George Vassos, had already tried to explain the conflict, and then Elena Nikolaidi, in Houston, picked up where he had left off. Now Dr. Johnstone had joined their band wagon. They all were telling me that my "center" was too tight.

Of course my center was tight. A tight center was necessary in dance. Without it there could be no balance. Little by little, I began to sort out the similarities and, more importantly, the differences between the body alignments necessary for singing and dancing. As an amateur, even a pre-professional, I had gotten away with doing both. To be a polished professional, I was being forced to master both.

In dance you must have a strong core. Teachers call it "dancing from your center." This means mastering the engagement of one's abdominal muscles. The idea is to contract, to pull in and up, in your mid-section. Immediately your body begins to align itself and to exert the control needed for professional dance.

Interestingly enough, it is this same region that is most important in singing. However, in singing, the "center" must be loose, my teachers said. Ms. Nikki would walk the room squeezing her rib cage inward and upward during voice lessons. I hadn't a clue what she was doing, and she couldn't explain it. She approached it in several ways, some of which seemed strange to me, but lacking the vocabulary to explain her innate understanding, I remained mystified. It took me years to figure out the delicate balance between strong abdominal support and flexible breath system – all of which involves "the center."

356

Mastering isometric contraction of the abdominal muscles for use in both singing and dancing means that the muscles need to contract, but not shorten or lengthen. They need to remain constant, the same length. In dance you gain strength and control. In singing you gain control and vocal power. In both you gain extension – leg and arm extension in dance and range and power in singing.

Singing, of course, won out, and here I was facing a wonderful group of girls, synchronizing choreography into their vocal performance skills. Sharing with them my own background as a dancer, I not only surprised them, but I also provided them with vivid material from which they could enhance their own connections to dance and stage choreography.

6:00 p.m. Dinner

During the dinner hour, parents could visit their daughters. LeToya's mother came without fail. Cheryl, too, visited often. As a live-in nanny and housekeeper, Doris wasn't able to leave her job, but every so often she would appear – mostly on Saturdays, which was what she could manage – to visit with Kelly. Celestine had only Sunday afternoons (dark days for us) and Mondays available, when the salon was closed, to spend time with Beyoncé, as well as with Solange and the other girls, who also received her motherly attention. (In addition to the dinner hour, parents were permitted to observe – without speaking or interrupting – any classes that involved singing or dancing.)

During this time, I had canceled my other private students, because the training camp took priority. Each of my private students knew the girls and had met them when they came to my apartment for lessons, so all of them understood and supported this arrangement. Everyone was behind this project, but if any of my private students needed or required a lesson I would make myself available during the lunch and dinner breaks.

The girls had become amazingly good. Still, I had never seen or met anyone more focused than Beyoncé. LeToya's and Kelly's voices were no longer full of air, and they were singing beautifully. Both had improved their upper extension, and Kelly's larynx (voice box) had dropped first, giving her voice an uncanny warmth and beauty that gave me goose bumps. LaTavia had developed into a fine singer. She continued to work hard to catch up to the others and had become a very reliable anchor.

Everyone was excited about the showcase in Atlanta, and up to this point the parents had followed my rules, keeping their personal dramas at bay. Sometimes we would see a parent or two (never Mathew) in the morning at Hermann Park, where we usually did our running and endurance training. I had made it clear that no parent was to interfere, as the girls needed to maintain their focus and were not allowed run over to their parent to say hello. We had a job to do, and I needed total commitment. The parents watched in admiration from the sidelines, and the girls, amazingly, did not waver in their concentration. My student Tony Coles, who ran almost every morning in Hermann Park, remembers to this day the focused, sometimes grueling pace that I put the girls through, come rain or shine.

8:00 p.m. Modeling, Dance, and Choreography

During this session I concentrated on the girls' total performance. Because it was too hot to practice in the daytime heat of the Houston summer, I would sometimes switch things around to keep the girls on their toes. I would exchange this class with the scheduled memory and muscle development class.

In the modeling sessions, I connected what they already knew about good singing posture with the ideas of presenting themselves visually onstage. Lifting through the sternum (center of the chest), they learned to project their energy forward in the body so the audience always felt their presence. It lengthened the body and taught balance; then they had to learn to be still without movement, and grab the audience using electromagnetic energy waves. Evidence that they learned this lesson well can be seen in videos like "Baby Boy," "Soldier," "Lose My Breath" and "Stand Up for Love," for instance. Beyoncé's and Kelly's model walk in those videos is sharp and exact, free in the hips, and with attitude from the sternum outward, which they'd learned that summer in my dance sessions.

"How do you know all this stuff?" Beyoncé asked.

"Yeah," said Kelly. "Were you a model, too?"

358

"As a matter of fact I was," I answered. I told them about being discovered in Omaha by a woman named Carol Bailey-Seldon. "I became a professional model when I was fifteen years old." In addition, while in college at Langston University, I formed a club and called it Metamorphosis. I started it to help business majors and any other interested student who wanted to learn the art of presentation. I taught modeling, the psychology behind color, textiles, and shapes – with a heavy concentration on etiquette for the business student.

Once again I told my girls about taking early Saturday morning classes with Louis Naylor when I was new to the Cleveland-based company. This time I used the story by way of introducing the girls to a difficult new floor exercise.

When I got to Cleveland as a student at The Cleveland Institute, it had been a while since I'd taken a floor exercise class in modern dance, but my body soon began to respond to the familiar routines. Muscle memory began to take over.

Louis Naylor had developed a great way to get a dancer's stomach muscles firmed up and the hips squared quickly. It required the dancer to lie on his or her back. Legs were to be parallel to one another, stretched out lengthwise. Once the order for "Pietà" was given (Italian word for "pity"), the pain began. With one swoop of the dancer's breath we all lifted our legs first up, then out and apart (six inches from the ground), into an open position, arms in ballet second position, while arching our backs, holding the pose, and remembering to breathe. The stomach contracts like hell, so does the lower back.

Now lying there on the Knowles family room floor in front of the girls, in Louis's famous pietà position, I was taken back to those exercises. As they followed my lead, the girls' bodies started to shake. I reminded them to breathe into the pain, just as Louis had reminded me. I'd learned many things from him about a dancer's strength and use those principles to this day. Although my girls couldn't hold the pietà position for very long, their competitive nature showed up. No one wanted to be outdone by the other. "Hold on, even if it kills you," I said. Never had a truer thought been had.

Pietà was kicking their butts, but they learned not to show it. The rest of the week they complained that their bodies felt as though they had lifted a thousand pounds. Can you say, "triple lactic acid build up"? It didn't take long before they were old pros at it. And I was the happiest that I'd been in years.

I remember that while teaching my girls ballet, they sometimes laughed at their "old" teacher. I can see them rolling on the floor laughing when I first demonstrated the sissonne. "Sissonne" is a ballet term for a movement named after its originator. It involves a jump from both feet onto one foot, landing front, back, and side-to-side. Not an easy dance movement, it caused surprise and amusement among the girls to see me doing this. However, it helped me to teach them left from right, and to teach them to land and hold the position without wobbling. I also used relevé, the ballet term for "raise." I was an advocate of the French school relevé, which meant rising up onto point smoothly and then releasing. This built their leg calves for high heel shoes. I also introduced them to the towel crunch. They took a small towel, bigger than a face towel but not as big as a bath towel, and put it under their feet, trying repeatedly to scrunch it under the toes. This exercise would build the soles of their feet and point so that they didn't feel the high heel shoes. They felt strong on the balls of the feet, helping them to lead in dance from the ball of the foot to the toe, outwards and upwards. We also worked out modern dance movements focusing on hip isolations, the hands and the wrists. In addition, we worked the neck for head snaps and hair throwing – and my favorite, contractions. Non-dancers might not make sense of all this, but it gives an idea of how involved our work was.

At the end of the second month, it was time to raise the stakes. I took my girls to the shoe store and bought all of them their first pair of high heel dance shoes. I taught them how to move, sing and dance in them, often having to demonstrate while wearing them myself. More laughter.

9:15 p.m. Re-cap of the day/ performance for parents and Mathew (when he was there)

During this segment of the day the girls performed for the parents, sometimes including Mathew, sometimes for him alone. It was during this time that they could show what they were learning and feel a sense of accomplishment. Praise was good for their soul and confidence. By the time the second month rolled around, this session became optional. The girls had made so much progress that by 9:15 I could release them early – unless we needed the work.

At about 9:00 p.m. we might go to the recording studio as well, in order to record the songs that Daryl believed to be serious contenders for self-study. Anything we needed, Ann made sure we got. Mathew even paid for a few sessions, in competition with Ann. He wouldn't be totally outdone. We also made video presentations cataloguing our progress to send to Daryl. He was most happy to get the videos and always called the girls promptly to offer them his admiration and praise.

10:00 p.m. Bedtime

If we didn't have a studio session on Saturday evenings, I'd release my girls at 10:00 p.m. from their strenuous, well-organized day. They would inevitably retreat to the family room in the Knowles house to wind down. Instinctively I knew that they were watching my behavior. Children don't necessarily like to do what they are told to do, so I led by example. After a couple of evenings of seeing lights out at my apartment around 10:30, at the very latest, they followed my example. Two positives began to show themselves: They woke up refreshed in the mornings and they were learning a life lesson about how to prepare for performance. I did not have to preach or even broach the subject. Teaching them – and showing them – how to prepare to win was a formula very important to their success today.

After almost three months of rigorous work they were ready for Atlanta.

* * * * *

I continued teaching, right up to the last minute, even after the girls had returned to their individual homes. Since 1990 I had been emphasizing in our singing lessons how to express appropriate emotions with the reaction

361

of each subsequent facial muscle. After three years, my girls were finally understanding.

Recently I have found in a 2005 *Discover* magazine an article written by Mary Duenwald entitled "The Physiology of Facial Expressions: A self-conscious look of fear, anger, or happiness can reveal more than a lie detector," exactly what I had been teaching in my vocal studio for years. The writer says that "Charles Darwin was convinced that facial expressions don't vary from culture to culture, but by the 1950s most social scientists had come to believe the opposite. To see who was right, Ekman (Paul Ekman, Psychology Professor Emeritus at the University of California at San Francisco, who created the system of micro-expressions used today) traveled to the highlands of Papua New Guinea in 1967 and visited the Fore people, who had never been exposed to movies, television, magazines, or many outsiders. When Ekman showed the Fore photographs of faces with various expressions, they interpreted them exactly as Westerners would. A sad face, for instance, made them wonder if the person's child had died."

Ms. Duenwald goes on to say that "similar studies by other scientists have since shown that facial expressions across the globe fall roughly into seven categories."

Reading Ms. Duenwald's categories prompted me to combine the teachings of this science with some thoughts of my own, as I not only have taught this important subject in my studio, we all had experienced significant ramifications of people's facial expressions in our personal relationships.

SADNESS: The eyelids droop and the inner corner of the eyebrow rises a bit, and in extreme sadness, they usually draw close together. The corner of the mouth and lips pull downward and the lower lip may pout upwards. Frequently I observed these characteristics in Kelly's facial expressions.

SURPRISE: The eyelids widen, and both they and the eyebrows rise upwards. With surprise, the jaw will normally drop open involuntarily. Mama's face, upon seeing Solange the Gazelle for the first time.

ANGER: This one is relatively easy to see. The eyelids, both upper and lower tighten and the brows draw together. In intense cases of anger, the eyelids raise as well. The jaw line juts forward and the lips are always pressed firmly together. Mathew's default expression.

CONTEMPT: It was interesting to my girls that contempt shows itself on only one side of the face. One corner of the mouth will tighten and rise upwards. It seemed to me that Celestine's face was in a state of chronic contempt, not only when dealing with Mathew, but also with others whose thinking was opposed to hers.

DISGUST: We've all seen disgust. Its characteristic nose wrinkling is accompanied by a stiff upper lip, while the lower one protrudes. The expression I tried increasingly to hide when dealing with Mathew.

FEAR: I called this the wide-eyed devil. Fear is characterized by an over-widening of the eyes. The upper lip rises, sort of the way it does when surprised, but in combination with tightened and pulled-together eyebrows, you've got classic fear. Fear began to show itself on several of our faces as our years together continued – fear of loss, of rejection, of failure, of abuse.

HAPPINESS: Can you say big happy smile! There is a difference between happiness and joy. One can *imitate* happy by smiling, but happiness can be achieved only by concentrating on the lower part of the face (the eyelids MUST NOT tighten, but the corners of the mouth do pull up and back). Joy, on the other hand must use both parts of the face (the eyelids MUST tighten and the corners of the mouth pull up and back). The frequent expressions of happiness and joy that my girls displayed on their beautiful faces when singing will live in my memory forever.

These seven categories of facial expressions are fundamental to a singer's repertoire. The word "repertoire" usually conjures the image of appropriate musical materials, songs, and arrangements. A singer's repertoire, on the other hand, includes knowledge of everything human and can never be complete, as the successful performance of a song draws upon the deepest and most mysterious of human emotions.

Leading up to the Atlanta showcase, tensions between Celestine and Mathew seemed to settle some, but only a bit. Mathew was still doing his "disappearing act" and Celestine was still working like a slave. Every day something went on in the Knowles house, that is definitely better left unsaid, and definitely unwritten. At least her mind was at ease, because during the summer camp the girls were never left home alone. Everyone's focus was on the showcase and Atlanta. That was important. Nobody was going to change Mathew.

Although Ann made sure that the financial side of travel to Atlanta went smoothly for the families, Mathew told me that I had to pay my own expenses. He said that Daryl Simmons hadn't felt that a voice teacher was a necessary component of the Da Dolls team. I immediately called Ann, who confirmed that Daryl had indeed raised the question. She also said she was alone in trying to change that, and to explain to him how crucial my presence was in maintaining the girls' performance readiness. I couldn't make heads or tails of it, but in true David style I suppressed the vehement anger I felt. In private, my soul ached. In spirit, I turned to God. Surely this slight couldn't be about my not allowing Mathew in on my summer camp. How childish, I thought. The sheer number of hours it took me to prepare the girls amounted to a fulltime job. To make matter worse, I'd done the work on a contingency basis.

Nobody had had the kind of money that would cover my fee, especially as the idea for the summer camp had come up relatively suddenly. So before I began the three-month training camp, Ann, Mathew, Celestine, and I had had a long talk in the Knowleses' dining room about my workload. We agreed that I would bill management later, when the girls found success. I also intimated that my getting a possible percentage in the girls' earnings might be an option. To that, Ann said, "That's worth investigating." Mathew remained silent. Celestine left the room.

"I have to go to the toilet," she said.

17. Atlanta

Before we left for Atlanta, the Knowleses had a fight, one that escalated quickly to pressure cooker stage. It triggered deep reactions in me, and I believed someone would die that evening. Mathew's escapades had finally reached Parkwood Street. Celestine couldn't stand the sight or the smell of him.

The training camp had come to a close, and we were set to travel to Atlanta, where Daryl's Showcase was to take place. Atlanta was to be Mathew's moment.

Unfortunately for him, Ann and Celestine, combining their feminine ingenuity, foiled Mathew's dream of solo glory. They convinced Daryl that my presence in Atlanta was essential. "You have to be there," Celestine argued. At the ages of twelve and thirteen, my girls were about to cause one of the biggest buzzes in the music industry since the Jackson 5. The LaFace record mogul L.A. Reid, the young singer Usher Raymond, and a whole host of powerful players in the music industry were in attendance. Daryl would set off a war by calling public attention to me and my work as the girls' artistic and vocal coach. And I would finally recognize the enormity of Mathew's egotism.

* * * * *

We arrived in Atlanta to find stretch limousines awaiting us. The girls felt like big celebrities. We were promptly delivered to Daryl Simmons's home. He lived in a private gated community where LaFace Records founder and mogul L.A. Reid also lived with his wife. After Daryl asked when we expected Ann to arrive, he asked about my accommodations. "I'll be staying in the hotel with the parents," I said.

What happened next changed the atmosphere in the room. Daryl suggested that I stay at the house with the girls, which aggravated the hell out of Mathew. Somehow, Celestine must already have known that this might happen. Her look suggested that without hesitation I should thank Daryl and agree. "If it is not too much trouble," I said. "No, it's no problem at all. I think that it makes perfect sense."

Daryl's mansion was very beautiful; smaller than L.A. Reid's, but still quite elegant. (Later, I would pay a visit to the Reid home, the mansion of mansions, where I found an extraordinary entryway chandelier. Mr. Reid was just arriving home as I admired it. I greeted him respectfully, engaging him in a conversation about its splendor. "I'm glad you like it," he said to me, shook my hand and went into the den, where he greeted his children warmly. I must have looked like a country bumpkin in that environment – but that chandelier!)

At any rate, Daryl Simmons's parents were visiting Atlanta while we were there, and his mother was a great cook. While the girls and I stayed with Daryl and Sherry in their home, "everyone else except Doris stayed in hotels."

Doris, who had flown down a few weeks earlier to look for work, was living in Atlanta with family. Briefly reflecting on our arrival at Atlanta's airport, I remembered Kelly's excitement to see her brother, whose existence I had not known about until then. Concern for her mother's plight was temporarily suspended when we observed Kelly's obvious happiness to be reunited with her brother and the rest of the Atlanta family. Apparently Kelly's grandmother, a delightful woman, was raising her brother. He looked just like Kelly, so much so, they could have been twins. He was a very likeable young man. The family reunion had been a short one, and limited to the airport only, as we had lots of work to do.

L.A. Reid's then wife, Perri "Pebbles" Reid, was a dancer/pop artist famous for songs like "Girlfriend" and "Mercedes Boy." She was perhaps most well-known for her discovery of the group T.L.C. She was their manager in 1993, and we were told that she would drop by to meet the girls.

Sherry Simmons, Daryl's wife, had prepared everything for our arrival and was busy showing us our rooms and making sure everyone was comfortable, when the doorbell rang. It was Pebbles. Although professional and somewhat kind, she was not forthcoming with the girls. She did not compliment them even once after they sang for her, and her jealousy seemed obvious to me. She called them "cute." I was insulted. This woman had five notes in her voice, and my girls were "cute"? Ms. Pebbles and I had little to talk about.

Other than going outside of the house for fifteen minutes to get fresh air, I was busy rehearsing with the girls the whole time. With Cheryl Lestrap-Mitchell, LaTavia's mother, Celestine drove out from the hotel to the Simmons's home to visit, but Mathew was nowhere to be found. I neither saw nor heard from him until the sound and lighting check at the showcase venue on the day of dress rehearsal. He showed up then looking bewildered and agitated. In a distracted manner he managed to ask me how the rehearsal had fared. It was as if he intentionally sought to be inaccessible. (This behavior was predictive of a years-long modus operandi, as later on in the girls' career, he was definitely and deliberately inaccessible.)

One evening after everyone had gone to bed, Daryl and I visited in his kitchen for more than an hour. I had not been able to talk with him very much since my arrival. He was either in the recording studio, at the office, or finalizing things for the showcase. Now he asked me how long I had known the girls. When I told him "five years," he looked very puzzled. I didn't understand his perplexed look, but decided not to pry. After an awkward pause, he then asked me, "And how long have you been teaching them?" I proudly answered, "The entire time, five years."

After a brief pause he said, "Oh! I see." Our conversation ended as he told me that he had to get some sleep. It would be a long day tomorrow.

The next morning at breakfast, he pulled me aside. He was interested in my listening to a boy group he was developing. I quickly agreed. "A Few Good Men," Daryl's group, was a vocal quartet, which later, in 1995, released an album titled "Take a Dip."

Daryl asked me to give his boy group a vocal lesson, and he stayed to observe. Afterwards, he thanked me and paid me handsomely. He said that now he was even more excited about hearing the girls live. Daryl must have had some real faith, since he had not seen any of the girls' rehearsals. He told me that Sherry had reported that the girls were well prepared and sounded amazing. Until Atlanta, Daryl's exposure to the girls' singing had been via poor electronic recordings: over the phone, through his car speakers, or in those amateur rehearsal videos Mathew made and sent to him.

When Daryl showed up to the rehearsal at the venue, he found me consulting with the sound and lighting technicians. Accessing my theater training at Langston University, I had amassed credible professional experience in the technical aspects of the stage. Also, I'd worked with formidable recording engineers and producers, in Houston and out in Los Angeles. So, I knew what was needed in both disciplines. I noticed Daryl giving me that same perplexed look he'd given me the night before, standing in his kitchen. At that technical rehearsal, he pulled me to the side and asked me why I was talking to the technicians. I told him that I was going over the lighting design and sound scale I had created for the show.

Daryl promptly told me that at the end of the show he wanted me to come up front, take the mic, and introduce myself to the crowd as the girls' vocal coach. He was very specific and instructed me to introduce, as the girls' encore, "that wonderful song you arranged." "People should know who you are," he said.

While I didn't think that Daryl's request was unreasonable, I had to express my apprehension. Now was not the time to rile up Mathew Knowles. Daryl didn't know Mathew the way I did. Daryl assured me that he did. My demeanor prompted him to speak very honestly with me. "I've seen his ugly side," Daryl said. He then revealed to me that Mathew had told him that I had been hired just a few weeks ago to come in and whip the girls into shape. Daryl said, "Based on my own observations, and after seeing you teach 'A Few Good Men,' it's obvious that you have been the girls' teacher for the years that you say."

I was speechless. Mathew and I had our differences, but I never expected that he would tell such a bald-faced lie. I had worked very hard and was supposed to be family. I couldn't understand why it was necessary to minimize my existence and misrepresent my contributions. I remembered

Mama's perceptions and warnings, now validated by Mathew's behaviors, and I felt like such a fool. Then Daryl said, "Since the encore piece is your arrangement, it should be you who introduces it."

Daryl had discovered the truth and seemed unhappy about it. Despite my fury with Mathew, I told Daryl that I would do as he asked, but that keeping my composure was going to be a challenge. I cannot begin to describe the psychological impact Mathew's blatant lying had on me in Atlanta. It would take all of my mental and physical strength to keep from attacking him on sight. I remember thinking, Too bad Donkey Mathew can't answer my telephone back in Houston – shit! Daryl could easily see my turmoil and reassured me, "Believe me, it's the right thing to do." It was almost as if he were trying to convince me to stand up for myself.

He said, "I have my reasons."

Still a bit fearful of the possible repercussions, I decided to speak with Mathew in advance of the performance about Daryl's request. Gathering myself together, I kept my focus on my girls' showcase. I would not let my anger and disgust with Mathew ruin their hard work. When I told him about Daryl's request, and about his claims, Mathew surprised me by saying, "Oh, great," totally ignoring my asking about his supposed lying. "I think that's a great idea," he added.

Mathew's avoidance of the lying issue irked the hell out of me. Mathew's calm, his non-reaction, had been a reaction, and I didn't like it. Why the hell would he lie like that? It was hurtful and I felt used. Mathew did not want me introducing anything – or speaking at all, for that matter. He'd been caught with his hand in the cookie jar, and still, he shrugged off any indication that he'd done something wrong. His reaction was that of the typical narcissist's response after being caught in a lie. With his "Oh, great – I think it's a great idea…" he could save face and keep control, while I was fighting not to lose it.

To tell you the truth, I felt hatred in that moment. Had Mathew been met with sudden misfortune I wouldn't have shed a tear. Still, I had to focus on the job at hand. I mustn't lose sight of why God had placed me in the girls' lives. I said a silent prayer and extended my hand. Mathew returned the gesture and then I walked away, before I'd say something I'd regret.

I told myself that when the time came, I would walk proudly to that microphone and introduce myself with confidence. No matter how hard I tried, I couldn't get it out of my head that Mathew had reduced me to "a few weeks," after all the years I'd spent developing his "commodity." Then it hit me. The Knowleses wanted to show that the girls' talent was natural and not developed, an age-old crock of shit adopted by many ass-holes in popular music. No one gets anywhere alone, but it should appear, and be part of their story, that the girls, and particularly Beyoncé, simply woke up one morning with fantastic, trained voices and extraordinary performance abilities. I decided right then and there to use the anger that I felt. I became focused in no time flat.

* * * * *

The night of the big showcase finally arrived. Ann had driven safely into Atlanta with Sha Daniels, her nephew Belfrey's girlfriend. Everyone was, understandably, very excited. Daryl Simmons seemed to be the most ex-cited. During these few days he had been convinced by Kelly's voice. Kelly was beginning to shine; the training camp experience had finally reached her. Although Daryl had gained respect for Beyoncé and the entire group, he remained particularly taken by Kelly. He simply loved her sound.

This really seemed to bother Celestine. She knew enough not to show openly that she wasn't excited for Kelly, but at the end of the day it was supposed to be about Beyoncé. Celestine began with her warning whis-pers, ordering Mathew to handle the threat.

When the girls and I arrived at the venue I could feel the intensity of expectation. We were on time, but where was the sound man? I told my-self, David! Stay calm. David! Don't let the girls see you nervous. David! Stay focused! Keep breathing!

This was the first time since my beginning to work with Beyoncé and the others that I was nervous. I was very nervous. Sound check started almost a full 30 minutes late. I hated it that performance details were outside of my control, but I had to deal with it. For instance, there was nothing I could do about Daryl's keeping the costumes a secret. Ever since the "Star Search" costume fiasco, I'd been particularly sensitive on that issue. Now Daryl had control of the costumes for this showcase. The girls hadn't said a word, and believe me, I tried every trick in the book to get it out of them. I even went to Daryl. "I need to know what the costumes look like," I said. My argument was "just in case I need to make adjustments in the choreography to accommodate what you've come up with." Daryl responded, "All I can tell you is, they're wearing pants." I had to relax, I told myself. If there had been a problem with the costume, surely Beyoncé and the others would've spoken up. However, I wasn't sure – shit.

Celestine arrived, clearly on edge. I had no time for her little mini-drama. Our sound check had been late, delaying our last rehearsal. Whatever she wanted to tell me would just have to wait. Perhaps Celestine's worry had something to do with the fact that Mathew had disappeared.

"Where the hell is he?" she asked.

"Try the men's room stall..." I answered. He most likely was snorting something or other, I thought to myself. Walking away, I just kept reminding myself to stay focused. Singing for the invited audience of seven major record labels, a host of producers, and popular music artists in the Atlanta area, all of which Daryl had confirmed the day before with me at breakfast in his kitchen, was serious business.

While getting lost in that inner conversation with myself, I was suddenly interrupted. Daryl wanted to introduce me to L.A. Reid's new artist, who he'd brought with him to the showcase. I excused my girls to go to costumes and make-up, treating the evening as a professional theatrical event, and turned to shake Mr. Reid's hand.

"It's nice to see you again," Mr. Reid said.

"Likewise, sir," I answered. "Who is this extraordinary young man?"

L.A. Reid introduced him as Usher Raymond. This young singer just fourteen years old, had an incredibly strong presence. It was clear to me

371

that he was going places. He shook my hand, and I told him that it was a pleasure to meet him. I would have liked to speak with him a bit longer, but there was no time. There was a problem backstage.

"I'm sorry gentlemen," I said. "Duty calls."

"No problem," Mr. Reid said.

"Go do your thang," Daryl prompted.

I took off for backstage.

A half hour later, my girls and I bowed our heads. It was time to gather for our customary prayer together, which happed before every performance, no matter how big or small. Then they were ready. It was now or never. I hugged each of them, wishing them good luck. "Remember," I said.

"Get out of here David," LaTavia answered. "We got this!" I was so proud of my little Diva. She'd overcome her fears and had turned into a stable and confident anchor.

Walking through the crowd I saw a couple of people who looked familiar. Two of my students from Houston, Scott Sherman and Shevon Jacobs, had driven up to Atlanta with friends, Marilyn Osborne and Kim Hebert-Gregory. They had spent twelve plus hours in the car simply to support the girls and me, which really warmed my heart. Shevon had become a cherished friend and sough-after studio recording artist who could sing her tush off. Scott Sherman, from South Carolina, had won Showtime at the Apollo many times. I had encouraged this wonderful singer, very much in the style of a Luther Vandross, to take his great soul on the road. My friends were all here to share this moment.

I gave them a quick hello, and they cheered me with heartfelt well wishes for a successful evening.

"Excuse me guys," I said. It was time.

"Good luck," they all said, in unison.

"Thanks!"

Taking my place, I signaled to the light man, who began lowering the house lights. On cue, the music started. My girls hit the stage like a whirlwind. They were breathtaking. They hit every mark with military precision. Their modeling, the choreography, and their vocals were on point. The people were in awe. "They're twelve?" I heard some guy ask, who stood just in front of the mixing board. I looked around the room. No one was talking. Each song was followed by thunderous appreciation from the audience. Daryl Simmons shot a video documentation of this unforgettable evening, and in the years since then, clips from this performance have been included in myriad media presentations on the girls.

Da Dolls received standing ovations, and as the appreciative applause continued, Daryl made his way forward, taking the microphone. "Will David Brewer please come up here," he said. I walked up, and he handed me the microphone. "Do your thang man," he whispered. I thanked him as he walked away, smiling. I then turned to the audience. "Hello, my name is David Lee Brewer and I am the vocal coach who trained the girls." With that, the applause started again, complete with whistles and cheers.

Once the applause quieted a bit, I announced that I'd arranged an encore, "Ain't No Sunshine," a song originated by Bill Withers. I explained that our group's arrangement had been patterned after The Emotions. This crowd was familiar with the vocal prowess of The Emotions and appreciated the difficulty of their vocal arrangements. When I announced that twelve-year-old girls were going to attempt The Emotions, I heard someone in the audience yell, "Awwww shit!" I regret that I didn't think to get a copy of the video for my personal records.

Even now I can still remember the evening as though it was yesterday. I'm sure that all the girls can as well. I think the person who may have been the most thrilled was LaTavia. She did it! She was able to hold her own and had learned to balance her huge voice.

I had split the catchy chorus of "Ain't No Sunshine" into three-part harmony, until the end, when LeToya Luckett took over singing a sustained high C above the other girls' percussive rhythm. The audience went wild, once again with standing ovations. She had been nervous about hitting the note, but seeing the audience's reaction she'd put angst to bed. Little Miss LeToya Luckett threw her head back and hollered. She sang the bejesus out of that note, exactly as we'd planned.

I had instructed LeToya to hold it for eight beats, complete with a crescendo, and then repeat it for eight more beats. Mathew's teeth grew long, having asked me earlier on if she had to hold it so long. "Absolutely," I had quickly replied. He didn't like the song and he certainly didn't like that the new girl was getting to shine. Not surprising to me, my high top girl had come through. When the girls released the final note together in perfect harmony, the audience erupted. It was a "goose-bump" moment, a definite memory to hold on to, and their presentation had not contained even a hint of street. We'd managed to erase the memory of that awful "hip hop rapping" performance on "Star Search," just months after it had happened. While the audience continued their cheering, my girls stood there, absolutely stark still. "Hold – hold," I thought to myself. "That's right – take it all in." They didn't move and there was no change in their body or face positions. They had the poise of beautiful little statues, and I stood there a proud papa. I resumed my place downstage and opened my arms wide. "Ladies and Gentlemen," I said, signaling. "Da Dolls." Then they all gracefully bowed together, just as we'd rehearsed so often. The audience went into a frenzy.

After their magical performance that evening, I was bombarded by music company executives. I received so many business cards that my pockets began to bulge. Everybody wanted to talk to me about the girls. Producers, both local and nationally famous, shook my hand. Some even asked about my availability. "I have a girl who needs a you...," one producer said. "Man, that was the fuckin shit. How in the hell did you get twelve-year-olds to blow like that?" another one asked. I answered the questions that pertained to artistic development and signaled for Mathew to come over. I was not equipped to answer those questions pertaining to the future of the group.

It was obvious that there was a problem. Mathew was ignoring me. He looked through and past me, and resolutely avoided looking at me. At first, I thought that he hadn't seen me or hadn't understood that I wanted him to come over. This was not the case at all. After he ignored me the second time, standing alone in the corner like a wounded and spoiled child, I realized that he was actually angry. Mathew was unhappy that the record labels were speaking with me. This was an awkward feeling and moment, but what could I do? I certainly wasn't going to be aloof and stand-offish, or refuse to answer their questions.

I tried to stay focused on the task at hand, but was somewhat distracted by the thoughts of Mathew's unfair and selfish behavior. We were a team. Mathew himself had said so on many occasions. What was going on with him now? Fuck him, I thought. Ann was there, she could answer the questions, and she did – happily. Later, the label representatives were approaching him as well. But by this time however, the damage had been done. Mathew Knowles turned nasty. He had no idea what those music executives, and producers, had been saying to me. The fact that they were speaking with me at all brought out even more of his contempt for me. The tension between us began to feel like frozen butter, and I had no idea how to cut it. I did not want this stress and disharmony, but I was being forced to deal with it.

Despite Mathew's and my "situation," everyone was on a high, especially Ann. She gave me a huge hug. She was so proud, she said. It seemed Daryl was the happiest of all. "Man, that was off the chain," he said, hugging me as well. In his words, he had a "gold mine." Then I noticed my girls. They were chatting up that young singer, Usher Raymond, who stood against the wall, now wearing dark sunglasses.

Beyoncé however, seemed to be searching for something, or someone. Her attention had not been focused on Usher. Our eyes met. Oh my, it was me she sought. When she mouthed the words "Thank you," I excused myself from the chatter, emotional. I loved those girls. My admiration had grown even stronger over the years. They were proud of themselves, as they should have been. They'd done the work, and it was paying off.

When I returned to the room, a round of photo taking had begun. That evening both professional and amateur photographers were busy capturing the girls and the other personalities in attendance. Everyone was wishing them well. The families took promotional photos, and then the girls were shot for photos alone. Mathew and Ann, as managers, posed for pictures with the girls. Next, Daryl Simmons joined in for a few pictures. Then, Mathew abruptly thanked the photographer and sent the girls directly to the limo. It was time to go.

I had been standing there patiently waiting to be called up. I never was, and there was no picture of the girls with me.

This was a defining moment for me in my history with Beyoncé and the girls. It would be the moment where Mathew realized how deep my love and respect for the girls really went and how he could manipulate me. Ray Charles could have seen the disappointment and hurt I was feeling. We were a team, and Mathew intentionally left me out of the team photos. Celestine, who I thought would have intervened, stood by her man.

Although I felt Mathew's harsh treatment to the quick, I held my composure. In hind sight, that may not have been the best move on my part. Perhaps I should have stopped the photographer and asked that my picture be taken with "my girls." At that time though, I was not going to give Mathew the satisfaction of seeing me make an issue out of it. That, however, was beside the point. Asking to be included in some of the pictures would have been the right thing for me to do, and I deserved it. I instead took the high road, something Christianity had taught me and Grandmother insisted upon. Today, I am absolutely clear. The ghetto approach was what was needed, because that is the only thing that Mathew understood. Unfortunately, I was ill equipped to oblige him. I was far from ghetto both in my thinking and in my demeanor.

In all the mayhem, I'd forgotten about my Houston friends. Shevon, who had been watching the discord between Mathew and me from a distance, hugged me. "I'm so sorry," she whispered. "Keep your head up. The girls were amazing. You have done great work," she added. I was close to tears, but I would not cry. "Suck it up, David," I told myself. I thanked Shevon for her kind words, and I reassured her that I was clear on the most important thing: "I serve God, not Mathew." I moved on to thanking Scott, Marilyn, and Kim, silently thinking to myself. "Dearly beloved, avenge not yourselves, but *rather* give place unto wrath: for it is written, Vengeance *is* mine; I will repay, saith the Lord." (Romans 12:19)

"When do you guys drive back?" I asked.

"After the weekend," Scott said.

They invited me out to lunch. I accepted, leaving them for the brief moment it took to get Daryl's permission. I needed to give my friends his address and he'd have to give their names to security, which manned the gated entrance.

"Sure," Daryl said. "It's no problem."

I returned to my friends, gave them Daryl's address, and we parted ways. It had been a long week. I was exhausted, and my girls were in the limo, waiting.

It was a long and an enjoyable ride back to Daryl's house. I was glad that it was just the girls and me. Because they were so happy, I was able to put the negative issues in perspective. The interior of the car was electric with joy and laughter, as they excitedly reminisced, exchanging high-fives, smiles and hugs.

Suddenly, Beyoncé turned to me and said, "Girls..." Then in unison, they all thanked me for all the hard work that I had put in over the years. I could hold back my emotion no longer. A tear fell from my eye. Wiping it away, LaTavia asked, "David, are you crying?" She wanted to know if they "messed up."

"God, no," I answered. "You girls have made me so very proud." And then I hugged them all, one by one, just to make sure that my emotion didn't spoil the mood of celebration. What an awesome evening. I'd never seen my girls as happy as they were at that moment, laughing and giggling and recounting their every move. That is what it had all been about. I wanted and always want to achieve this with my students. A Brewer student knows the difference between okay and very good and what it takes to achieve greatness. On the evening of the Atlanta showcase, I was satisfied, on top of the world.

I felt truly blessed, deeply honored to be my girls' teacher.

We arrived back in Houston to the same hot and humid weather that we had experienced in Atlanta. The girls and I took two days off from their demanding preparations for becoming star performers, and then the disciplined lessons started right up again.

For months to come I remained devastated by Mathew's deception, but did my best to hide it. I couldn't help thinking of Mama's warning. After giving Donkey Mathew a piece of my mind, over several days, I was finally finding my way back to dealing with Manager Mathew. I have always tried to see the best in people and I understand that we all have faults. After all, I understood jealousy and the venom it released. I refused to hate Mathew, but rather put on the "good face" and gathered myself. Typical personality type 9 behavior on the enneagram: Avoiding Conflict.

In his book *The 48 Laws of Power* Robert Greene says: "Never outshine the master. Always make those above you feel comfortably superior. In your desire to please or impress them, do not go too far in displaying your talents or you might accomplish the opposite – inspire fear and insecurity. Make your masters appear more brilliant than they are and you will attain the heights of power." Greene goes on to elaborate on this central theme. He explains that everyone has insecurities. When you show yourself in the world and display your talents, you naturally stir up all kinds of resentment, envy, and other manifestations of insecurity. This is to be expected. You cannot spend your life worrying about the petty feelings of others." According to Greene, "When it comes to power, outshining the master is perhaps the worst mistake of all."

Mathew thought of himself as the master, while I saw him as an unequal. I knew how to manage, and I certainly could have sold Da Dolls to a record label. Hell, Forrest Gump could have! However, I was not the manager for the group – he and Ann were. I never tried to intrude in the business of management. I was the artistic developer. Once I had a conversation with him, and he expressed his suspicions.

"David, I know that you have the desire to manage," he told me. "But you're not the manager, I am. I run this."

When I tried to assure him that I had no such desires, he said I was a liar. Actually, I had never imagined myself as a manager back then. My interest in management would come many years later, long after we had parted company.

Mathew underestimated the incredible amount of time and knowledge it takes to develop an artist, let alone a star artist. Artists – and their managers – who don't value the time that mentors share with them, are those artists who end up believing in their own hype, clouding their reality.

Stevie Wonder once said, "Time is the most precious gift that one can give. The giving of it is often times not appreciated in the moment it is being given."

Understanding what you are doing in music only gives your creativity and talent shine. It does not and will not destroy your ability to touch people, if you were touching people before. The degree of financial success and fame that an artist can achieve in popular music is great, this is clear. But what is success for a singer? Record sales?

Performers must be taught that the public is unforgiving. The old truism, "You are only as good as your last performance," is a sad fact of the singer's life. The public idolizes its stars and expects them to be almost non-human. What makes someone a star? Have you ever asked that question? I will tell you. A star is someone who delivers their art and energy at an extraordinary level, a level that the masses can never obtain. They make you dream about them and want to be them. Simply put, they are not the boy – or the girls – next door.

For the next three years I continued a rigorous weekly routine of private voice lessons with each girl, as well as group classes and studio classes. Group sessions continually dealt with the development of musicianship. Such things as the rudiments of singing in tune, chord-building practices, vowel placement, and rhythmic accuracy were ever-present topics best approached outside the girls' private voice lessons.

The new studio class was different from the class that I had created in preparation for Atlanta. The purpose of the new studio class was to teach advanced performance practices, such as discernment, camaraderie, musical kinetic energy, acoustics, and the sublime. In addition to strictly musical knowledge, the girls needed to dig deeper into the fine points of song performance. Taking the materials that we covered in private technical lessons and group sessions, we moved to a more sophisticated level of understanding how to present a song effectively.

For instance, I assigned weekly songs for each girl to learn, usually a song that dealt with issues where I could work on refinement. Reminding them to put into practice all that they knew from the training camp, their private voice lessons and group sessions, I asked them in these studio classes to concentrate on two things: one, specialized technique in singing (runs, crescendo, decrescendo, vocal turns, and so on) and two, immersion in finding the God in music. Each week, the girls would sing their solos for each other, and we continued to analyze the performances to discover how to make them even better. I had begun teaching the process of thinking like a soloist. All of them had carried their weight in the group admirably in Atlanta. I wanted to continue developing solo characteristics in all of them as well.

Meanwhile, Mathew began having fluctuating group meetings with the girls' parents, ostensibly once every week; he was not always available when he promised. The meetings he did have with the parents became increasingly chaotic, as Mathew arranged things and made important commitments without ever giving anyone a hint of advance notice, not even to Ann. It was as if he was in competition with her. No one understood his behavior. He would regularly put proposals and contracts onto the table for immediate agreement and signing. His methods guaranteed that the parents would experience repeated shocks, and Ann would be left to do the menial work of explaining the contracts' contents.

* * * * *

After settling his new terms with Ann regarding their manager split, Mathew had to secure newly signed management contracts with all the girls – including LeToya Luckett's mother, Pam. The girls themselves were under age, and in the United States the legal age to sign a contract was and still is eighteen. As far as I know this is a universal practice in law. The girls were thirteen by this time. At one of the parent meetings, Mathew produced a contract laying out the terms of his work as the manager of Da Dolls. He sat back and waited for each of the parents to sign.

Pam Luckett, upon receiving her copy, put the contract in her purse and clasped her arms waiting for the next topic. Mathew said, "Uh, Pam, I will need that signed tonight." Pam said in a very calm voice, "Oh, I wasn't aware that we had to sign tonight. I would like to read it and get my legal representative to look it over." Mathew was not having it.

Pam was soft spoken but consequent. She was an educated, sharp woman who worked as a consultant and accountant. Mathew said emphatically, "I need it signed tonight." Pam said, "No, but I will get it back to you as soon as possible." Mathew told her if she didn't sign that LeToya would be out of the group. Silence. We had not long ago had a major success in Atlanta. Now this. It was the Ashley and Carolyn Davis situation all over again.

Pam remained calm, but stood her ground. Mathew remained determined and stood his ground. There was a coldness permeating the room, for what seemed like an eternity. Then Mathew called out, "Doris," just as he had done before, never taking his eyes off of Pam. That was all he had to do. He had only to call out her name, and Doris signed, and then Cheryl, and then Celestine. Pam felt boxed into a corner. "I appreciate everything you have done, but it is my practice never to sign anything until I have read it," she said.

Mathew shouted, "She's out." Pam looked stunned, and Celestine then said, "Pam, don't you have any trust? Mathew has bent over backwards to help the girls, and look at what he has been able to do. We must stick together."

I guess Mathew was right about his wife. The money hadn't begun to roll in, but it was definitely on the horizon. His success in landing Daryl Simmons, which produced a fantastic showcase, had calmed Celestine a bit. Pam repeated her position, and Mathew stood up and left the room. He had three contracts in hand, and one unsigned; we had one ex-singer, LeToya.

The next couple of days went by without incident, and then Mathew called another meeting, this time including Beyoncé. He had drawn up a termination letter. In it, Beyoncé, Kelly, and LaTavia agreed to kick LeToya out of the group for insubordination.

"I'm not having another Carolyn up in here," Mathew said. He was incensed. He said that Pam needed to be taught a lesson and he intended to use Beyoncé to do it. The girls' management contract forbade management or any other entity, outside of group members, to fire a member. Mathew needed Beyoncé to push his plan through. Only one problem: Beyoncé was not in agreement.

"But Daddy, LeToya didn't do anything," Beyoncé said.

Beyoncé was beside herself. She didn't know exactly what to do and when she turned to her mother for help it was quite clear where Celestine's allegiance lay. Still, Beyoncé said that she didn't agree and that it was wrong to kick out LeToya. "This is an adult problem. Why can't you all handle this together and leave us alone?" she said – quite reasonably. Celestine quickly reminded Beyoncé that she was talking to her father. "You are being disrespectful. God doesn't like disobedient children," Mama Celestine said. Beyoncé began to tear up. A few seconds later, with tears running from her eyes, she looked at her father, begging his forgiveness. He didn't say a word.

"You may go to your room," Celestine said.

Beyoncé got up from the table and headed upstairs. I had never seen her so sad. It was clear what her father expected her to do. She would have to sign the letter. It was the only way to force the other girls to sign.

The next day, Mathew called another meeting. Celestine and Beyoncé, Cheryl and LaTavia, and Doris and Kelly were all gathered in the

Knowleses' formal dining room. Mathew had invited me – as a witness, I guessed. Mathew explained that in the contract there was a stipulation for removal of a group member and that the girls had to vote on it unanimously in order for a member to be ousted. He expounded upon his reasons for having to remove LeToya, and then he demanded that the girls sign the documents he had drawn up. Mathew then passed each letter to Celestine, who then passed it on to the other parents. As their daughters read the letter there was a hush that came over that room that I have never, ever felt again. They were all horrified. Celestine handed Beyoncé the ink pen. She signed. Then the other girls signed. It was official. LeToya Luckett had been kicked out of Da Dolls. Suddenly, Beyoncé burst into tears and bolted from the table. Kelly silently dropped her head. LaTavia excused herself from the table to go after Beyoncé, her best friend.

Celestine tried to get Mathew to reconsider. I couldn't believe my eyes and ears. She had tears in her eyes. "Mathew, Beyoncé is devastated. Are you sure?" she asked. What kind of farce was this, I wondered. Mathew stood up, the signed letters in hand, and again, left the room. I just couldn't play along anymore. Following behind him, I asked him if I could speak to him in the kitchen. He walked away from me. I followed, into the bedroom. He turned and screamed at me. I screamed back. It was getting nasty between us. I was ruining his plan. You better believe I was. He asked me to leave his bedroom, but I refused. He moved towards me, and then backed off. Instead, he reached for Celestine's car keys and left the house. Doris and Cheryl didn't know what to think. Once again, Celestine turned on her charm, apologizing profusely for Mathew's bad behavior. She promised to speak to him "…when he calms down. Pam's attitude really hurt him, y'all," she said.

I refused to give in. Two days later, when everything had died down a bit, I set out to talk to Mathew in the kitchen, but this time on bended knee. Almost prostrate before him, I explained that losing LeToya would cost the group valuable time – not to mention (but I did) that they looked and sounded great together. Speaking for myself as well, I told him that I had spent years building the group, then re-building it (after Ashley left), and I was not up to a third time. LeToya's voice type and character were needed in the group. I begged him to find it within himself to forgive Pam for being cautious, to call on her, and to try and work things out.

"Mathew, you are the best business man I have ever known," I said, "You are right to want to corral the situation, but any brilliant business man, such as yourself, would surely look things over before signing." I was laying it on thick, appealing to his ego. Incredibly self-absorbed, he gave no indication that he was even bothered by what I saw as obvious manipulation on my part. I think he felt empowered.

At any rate, I continued. "I am sure Pam didn't mean to offend your person or integrity," I said. Then I used his line: "Do it for the good of the group." He snarled. I saw that I might have pushed the right buttons. When he said he would take my comments under advisement, I left. We had all just entered the gates of hell.

Although none of us recognized it at the time, this was a pivotal moment in the girls' and Beyoncé's history. Perhaps things could have been different if I hadn't allowed them to force me to drop Ashley. That had been *the* pivotal moment. It had led to this one, when I finally gathered up my nerve to stand up to Mathew completely.

Perhaps I could have saved the girls some heartache had I stood up earlier to his senseless abuse, but Mathew had bullied us all into total submission and he didn't appear to be finished. I didn't want a repeat of Atlanta, so I said my piece and left. I had to remind myself: I was there because God had put me there to do a job and I needed to see it through for my own Christian sanity. In addition, Beyoncé was watching me.

How I handled myself in front of my girls was crucial.

One of the great blessings of my life was my association with the brilliant opera coach and teacher Sylvia Olden Lee (1917-2004), who called me "family." Revered by generations of opera singers for her wise guidance, she first joined the coaching staff of the Metropolitan Opera in 1954. In this 1992 photo, she is helping me to shape the role of Don José in Bizet's Carmen.

Every minute spent with Sylvia Olden Lee was of immeasurable value. From the time you entered her presence you were captivated. Music was her life. Teaching definitely was her gift. Her wisdom never stopped flowing, even here--during the supposed break from our Carmen coaching. I miss her terribly. The public knew her as the first African American vocal coach at the Metropolitan Opera. I knew her as a truly great musical mind, a wealth of uncompromising support

Eloquent song

8/93

Jerry Powers photo

Participants in the Houston Ebony Opera Guild recently performed *Highlights of Carmen* at Miller Outdoor Theater in Hermann Park. Debria Brown, a mezzo soprano sings with tenor David Brewer. The opera group is conducted by its founder and director, Robert A. Henry.

I cherish the indelible memories of my first professional appearance as Don José, the tragic principle tenor role in Georges Bizet's opera Carmen. In the 1993 Houston Ebony Grand Opera production, I had the good fortune of the wonderful mezzo-soprano Debria Brown singing the role of the temptress Carmen to my hapless Don José. An amazing colleague, Debria Brown provided me with real lessons in truth and thinking while acting.

Photo: Jerry Powers

Part IV

The Test

18. Gumbo

Beyoncé had moped around the house for days, hoping to get her parents' attention, or shall I say, their empathy. Beyoncé slept horribly the night her father had blown up at LeToya's mother in that meeting. Her friend's dismissal from the group was having a grievous effect on her. Neither of her parents seemed to be concerned, or perhaps they were oblivious to the obvious. I remembered Celestine's words on a similar occasion, "Oh, she'll get over it."

Overly sensitive, Beyoncé turned to her non-empathetic father. He hadn't changed his mind about LeToya, he said, rather sternly. I'd been waiting patiently to bring the subject up, in the kitchen. Tight-lipped, he did say, "I demand to be respected, Goddamn it," which earned a slight, silent chuckle on my part. "Ah Mathew, have a heart," I said. He wasn't having any of it, impervious to my pleading.

The next day, Daryl called me. He started the call by expressing his personal appreciation for my work in Atlanta. He said that he thought I was an amazing teacher and that the girls were lucky to have me. "Hell, I'm lucky to have you," he added. When, after several minutes of light conversation, Daryl hadn't mentioned LeToya, I figured that Mathew hadn't said a word about the blow-up. I rationalized – hoped – that meant that a solution was just around the corner. I hung up, optimistic.

Mathew and Daryl had been engaging in ongoing weekly telephone conversations, which as of late, were making Mathew feel uncomfortable. Something was "going on" with Daryl, but he couldn't put his finger on it, he said.

"Well, the showcase was great," I said. "Didn't he say that the labels were all clamoring for the girls?"

"That's just it," Mathew answered. "Ain't shit happening."

It was true. Daryl had given no indication about a solid offer. He seemed to be in no rush, which was all right by me. In my opinion, and I said this to both Mathew and Celestine, the girls would not and should not think about signing a deal until at least their sixteenth birthdays. "The music business is a beast." Children don't have it easy.

That Daryl was in no rush was cause enough for Mama and Papa Knowles to turn against him. Now, in addition, Daryl and Ann were chatting it up, at least three times per day, sometimes even four. It was intolerable for the Knowleses. Ann's better relationship with Daryl irked Celestine, and it infuriated Mathew. The truth is, while Mathew also conversed with Daryl, his frequent unavailability made a de facto decision for Daryl. Ann was always reachable, always available, and more importantly, competent. Unfortunately, Mathew would never admit that the women in his life were smarter than he was, certainly possessing better social skills.

In my opinion, Daryl was right to move cautiously. An unexpected adversary lurked about. For her own reasons, Celestine had become disillusioned with our producer. That Beyoncé's mother dreamed of being a famous designer was common knowledge around the Knowles camp. However, I knew that she felt defeated by her family background, admitting that her lack of education in fashion would, more likely than not, ruin her chances of acceptance in the world of fashion elite. Celestine knew lots about fabric, but nothing about color, art, or even the history of design – nothing. She dreamed big – of Versace-sized fame. *Her* clothes would never hang in Target, she sniffed.

Despite Celestine's feelings of insecurity, her brash overconfidence led her to suggest that she be made the official stylist for Da Dolls. She got Mathew to propose her idea to Daryl. Apparently, Daryl's answer had been "No."

"Of course, it was," I said to her, late one evening in my apartment. "It's all good, Celestine, but we are talking about you vs. the resources of LaFace records. I'm sure they have a slew of people working for them in that area. That's going to be a hard nut to crack. You have to put things into perspective…"

Her withering look silenced me, ending our little chat.

The very next morning Celestine urged Mathew to "keep an eye and ear out for Daryl." Twenty-four hours after his denial of her request to become the girls' stylist, Mama Celestine became suspicious of everything Daryl Simmons, telling Mathew that she didn't trust him. She reinforced her net of suspicions by wrapping it around Kelly, whose life would never be the same.

"Haven't you noticed?" Celestine asked Mathew.

"Noticed what?" he asked.

"How close Kelly and Daryl are becoming?"

Completely consumed with himself, he hadn't.

Beyoncé's mother had stirred up a hornets' nest. In one of his phone conversations with Kelly, Daryl had mentioned his intention to create a special role for her voice. Now he intended to make good on his promise and do a song with the girls that would cast Kelly in a lead capacity. Naturally, Kelly was elated. Innocently, she could hardly wait to recount to Mathew Daryl's latest and most wonderful news.

"Great," Mathew said. But as a happy Kelly merrily skipped away, thinking she had her manager's support, Mathew's disturbing facial expression told a different story.

Contempt is unmistakable.

Mathew called Beyoncé's mother right away. When she got home, Celestine articulated her sentiments with an arched neck and back, reminding me of a deadly cobra snake. "He has to go," she said. I swear, the next few minutes felt like something straight out of Shakespeare. Mathew reminded his Lady Macbeth that although he was in total agreement with her, they had a signed contract with Daryl. "Which is your goddamn fault," she snapped back. With a lowered head, Mathew tried to shake off Celestine's insult. There it was, that wounded little boy my mother had warned me about.

"Don't let him punk you, Mathew. I don't give a damn what you have to do. Get us out of that goddamn contract."

Celestine had had the last word.

From that point forward, the girls became less available for Daryl's calls, "Homework..." Mathew fibbed. They would never again talk to Daryl directly or individually. Mathew initiated making videos, where all the girls spoke collectively, and he insisted on conference calling. It made sense, he said. Daryl seemed to accept Mathew's excuses, even as Mathew's real motives remained below the surface.

At the same time, Celestine concentrated on a direct undermining of the vulnerable Kelly. She shouldn't become *too familiar* with Daryl, Celestine said ominously to the girl. Kelly should *be careful*, pull back even. Mathew, too, questioned Daryl's motives by suggesting Kelly "never be alone with Daryl in a room." What the hell was that about? I wondered. Then, in the most concerned voice he could muster, Mathew asked Kelly to *trust him*. Trust hell, I thought.

The confused, thirteen-year-old Kelly didn't really understand what was going on, but she sensed danger. Ashley's earlier demise and LeToya's frequent dismissals were powerful reinforcements to the Knowleses' whisper campaign.

During that same period, Pam called. If I remember correctly, that call was on or around the 9th of October. I definitely remember that we discussed Mathew's October 6th answer to her lawyer's letter. Pam had confessed that she was "vehemently against signing Mathew's contract," which I understood. "There are no checks and balances – no way to keep Mathew from doing whatever he wants," Pam added. Having thumbed through the document myself, I noticed that neither he nor Ann could be fired, for any reason. That was a huge red flag to me. I'd never seen a contract without an "out clause," I said to Pam. She hadn't either, she answered. Next, and according to Pam, Mr. Fitzgerald (the Lucketts' attorney) had pointed out that Mathew's action to dismiss LeToya was in direct conflict with his own contract. Just as I had suggested, Mr. Fitzgerald alleged that the "undersigned" had the right to legal counsel.

Mathew's response was deafening. According to him, when laying out the whole matter to me and Celestine, in the kitchen, the clause could not be applied to Pamela Luckett and her daughter. In this, he was correct:

Mathew had no contract from Pam, so how could she be the "under-signed"? Her way was clear. Pam would first have to sign in order to reap the benefits of the contract's stipulations. Until then, she'd have no leg to stand on. A couple days later she signed, LeToya returned to the group, and Mathew Knowles rejoiced in the whipping he'd just given to Pamela Luckett.

Without missing a beat, Beyoncé's daddy called a group meeting. The first order of business was to welcome LeToya back into the fold. Then, with the precision and speed of an attacking rattlesnake, Mathew struck LeToya in a particularly sensitive, personal area. It seems that Daryl and his wife, Sherry, had invited LeToya to become God-sister to their two infant children. Of course neither Daryl nor his wife could have predicted the shit storm that would be caused by their affection for LeToya.

With one hand holding the Lucketts' signed contract, which still need-ed his countersignature, Mathew pushed the telephone across the table in Pam's direction. In front of us all – LeToya, the other girls, and me – Mathew demanded that LeToya's mother call Sherry to decline the invita-tion. If Pam refused, there would be no reconciliation. From that day for-ward, my high top girl was a hyper-vigilant mess around Mathew. She was literally afraid to breathe too loudly.

Thinking about my girls' future, I left at the end of the meeting and made a beeline for my apartment and my Bible. I needed to read some uplifting words. These I found in the book of Psalms, 140:1-4, which was the basis for my prayer: "Rescue *LeToya and Kelly*, Lord, from evildoers; protect *them* from those who devise evil plans in their hearts and stir up war every day. They sharpen their tongues as a serpent. Poison of vipers is on their lips. Keep *me* safe, Lord, from their hands and protect me from their intention to trip up my feet."

My girls were all happy their sister was back in the group. Beyoncé and the other girls chose to ignore Mathew's debilitating power play, which may, in any case, have been a little over their adolescent heads. It could be that Beyoncé had begun to learn that ignoring her father's behav-ior was a safer option.

I, however, saw it all and knew that I would have to remain pragmatic. Mathew's calculated move had just made things a lot harder. I found myself asking, "Who sabotages their own group?" I knew that I'd survive, but I wasn't so sure about my girls.

* * * * *

Ann was very, very ill. That much we all knew. But she was a proud woman and she had kept her most recent health scares secret. She hadn't been forthcoming even with her children, not wanting them to worry. In addition to suffering from Sjödgren's Syndrome, which affected her saliva and tear duct glands, she was now dealing with extreme bouts of edema (water retention), which caused her to gain a great deal of weight.

During a telephone call with Ann, I heard from her that Mathew had been accusing her of not doing her job. Avoiding him and his threats, however, proved difficult. He continually showed up at her house, always in the middle of the night, unannounced and screaming his own special brand of crazy. His startling behavior had reached "a new level," she added. "I think Mathew did drugs in my guest toilet last night," she told me. "I know that the Lord has me in his hands, but I am afraid for my babies. I pray to God every day that he spares me – at least until they both graduate high school."

I was on the verge of losing it. "Ann, you have to protect yourself. You can't allow Mathew to harass you. Please promise me that you will think about you." Her body and health simply couldn't take the mental beating she got every time Mathew was around.

Kenny Moore, Ann's assistant, told me that in response to his appeal for help, his brother-in-law (brother of Kenny's wife, Cassandra), Chauncey, had agreed to move in semi-permanently with Ann. Kenny wanted an older male in the house to protect Ann. She was worn out and now she worried for her children's safety. Mathew's unpredictable outbursts affected Chris, her younger son, in particular. Teary, Ann confessed to me how she hated that her health prevented her from standing up to Mathew. Then she recounted how it grieved her that her fourteen-year-old son "has to bathe me," she said. Armon, who on that day was away at a basketball game, was extremely uncomfortable seeing his mother naked as he washed her body in the bath and took her to the toilet.

During our subsequent telephone conversations, things certainly sounded bad. However, nothing could prepare me for what I saw when I showed up at her house for a surprise visit on her birthday, on March 31, 1994. I hardly recognized her. It was hard to disguise my shock at the fact that the edema had added 40-plus pounds of water weight to her body. Damn! I thought. Despite everything, Ann never wanted pity. Seeing her harsh reality up close gave me a chill that I have never forgotten. I felt horrible.

"Pull yourself together," she whispered.

In just that moment Armon and Chris came downstairs. Ann sat straight up, disguising her pain.

Armon was heading to a basketball practice, he said. And this time, Chris was going to tag along. "Give Mama a kiss," Ann said. A bit embarrassed, both boys did as their mother asked and then left the house. As soon as the door closed behind them, Ann collapsed from the pain. It had taken everything to hold her "everything is all right" demeanor.

Everything was definitely not all right.

When I returned from the downstairs toilet, I asked her if she had taken care of herself contractually with Mathew.

"Yes," she said.

Coughing vigorously, Ann asked Kenny to go into her room and "get my papers." He promptly returned with a grey briefcase. In it were all her contracts, the bills she had paid over the years in support of the girls' future (no small mountain), and her medical records. She flipped through the pages of what was a contract and pointed out a passage I should read. She watched patiently as I perused it, picking it apart. The document that I was looking at – a contract addendum – constituted an amendment to the new 1994 contract, a revision that Ann and Mathew had made when

LaTavia joined the group. In it, Ann had taken that opportunity to add specific language regarding her heirs, in case she didn't outlive the document. (The contract was secure through the year 2000.) I read that her children were to be the recipients of "any and all commissions to be paid to management by the artist," again, in the case of her death. And I saw that both Ann and Mathew had signed it.

Nothing that I read changed the last agreed-upon fiduciary partnership between Ann (5%) and Mathew (15%) in any way. The 1% royalty point, which Ann had insisted upon in the previous version of the contract, had also been carried over. Given her history of unwavering financial support, I was angered that she had to insist upon it. However, as unfair as the 5%-15% split seemed to me, I would sleep better that night knowing that Armon and Christopher's financial welfare and education had been secured. Their mother was earning it with her life, literally.

Just in that moment the doorbell rang. Ann's mother, Effie Brown, had driven up from Tyler, along with Ann's brother, Lorando (Toto), the brother Carolyn had referred to a year earlier. Ms. Brown had not been able to be there in support of Ann's last two hospital stays. Not all together healthy herself, now she and Ann greeted one another warmly. I asked Toto how he and his bandmates were doing.

"We're all good," Toto answered.

"Great."

A year earlier I had coached Ann's boy band Tayste, whose lead singer was her brother Toto. I had helped prepare them for an audition with the label Rap-A-Lot Records. Willie D, a star rapper who was also one of the label's decision-makers, was very high on Tayste. He was also crazy about my girls, really crazy.

One of the reasons for Willie D's enthusiasm was created by a girl who had entered the music business in 1992 – became after one year the most successful newcomer in the U.S. – and by 1994 had most of the critics in raptures. Every one of her albums sold in the millions, and several reached platinum. The girl was none other than Mary J. Blige. Together with Puff Daddy, who was her producer, Mary J. Blige had created a permanent change in direction of the music genre New Jack Swing, a combination of R&B and Hip-Hop. In the wake of her success, many rap labels began looking especially for female singers. Mary J. opened a door that no one had realized was closed. Women began to earn big money – deservedly so. Ann Tillman recognized that – but not Mathew Knowles.

Ann declared herself absolutely against signing my girls with Rap-A-Lot Records – even if the star rapper Willie D was raving about both Tayste and my girls. Ann wisely assessed the situation and remained honest about her priorities for the girls. The Knowleses, however, were flat broke and wanted to get out of their financial hole by any means possible.

"I understand," said Ann to Mathew. "But this deal is not the right thing for our girls. Something really big is waiting for them."

Mathew tried to talk her out of it. Celestine bowed her head in utter disappointment. But I was thrilled with Ann's conviction. Even if she too had less money now than earlier, she never wavered. She was absolutely convinced of her opinion.

To Toto Ann said, "I'll take care of the girls first, to be sure they get the right contract. Then I'll take care of you and your group. Please trust me in this, Toto." And so he did.

In a phone conversation with me, Ann said, "I've been thinking of a really striking name for the girls. I believe that 'Da Dolls' will soon die a graceful death."

A week later, I got an urgent call from Ann. She was beside herself with fear. Belfrey, Ann's nephew, would be driving up the next day with his girlfriend, Sha Daniels, to be with Ann during her upcoming court date, she said.

"What court date?" I asked.

Ann was filing bankruptcy and felt uncertain. She had told no one, not even the Knowleses. I wouldn't either.

On the day of her hearing in bankruptcy court, Ann could barely breathe. Her edema, on that day, was especially severe. She could hardly walk from the exhaustion. In addition to her problem with her foot, which her doctors had diagnosed as "club foot" (usually a defect of one or both feet at birth, Ann's left foot had only recently turned inwards at the ankle, restricting her movements), she had so much fluid in her body that it took her twenty minutes to move only a few yards. Her best friend, Patricia Felton, accompanied her to court on that day.

Many years after that dramatic court appearance, Patricia Felton and I had a frank conversation in Houston to clear up for me what had actually happened in the court house that day. I wanted to know the real story. She obliged. Ann had been forthcoming with me about many points, but not with all of them, so I appreciated Pat's information.

"On the day of Ann's court date," Pat told me, "Ann was not able to make it to the actual court room where the judge was waiting." Ann's lawyer, having been unable to find a wheelchair in the building, asked the judge, as well as the opposition team of lawyers, if it were possible to move the proceedings down the hall, a most unusual request.

Patricia's story continued:

"My client can't make it any further," the lawyer said.

"Any further?" the judge asked.

"Yes, your honor. My client suffers from Lupus and is experiencing shortness of breath and difficulty walking. She is just down the hall, seated in the first free room I could find. Would it please the court, I'd like to beg your indulgence."

After gathering up the files, the stenographer got herself resettled in the room where Ann awaited word. When Ann's lawyer opened the door, allowing the judge and opposition team to pass into the room, their audible gasp was startling.

"Ann began to cry," Pat said. "She was embarrassed. Her entire body was swollen with fluid."

That much I knew. Ann had told me that her edema was life threatening on that day. She also told me that her arms and legs were three times their normal size.

Taking a minute, Pat continued. "The judge and opposition took their seats. In severe pain, Ann nodded her head in answer to the bailiff's question regarding telling the truth, the whole truth, and nothing but the truth. The judge told her that the court needed to hear her answer. She had to speak up."

Pat said that Ann had hesitated. "The fluid buildup caused her speech to be impaired. In order to speak, Ann had to physically push back the fluid in her face by dragging her hands over her cheeks and mouth in order to talk. In tears, she said 'I do,' and the proceeding could begin. By the third recorded point, the opposition stopped the proceedings."

Ann had told me in 1994 that the opposition's lawyer, who represented the bank and her lending company, had stopped the process. Pat now added that he apparently "couldn't take it any longer." She said, "The chief legal counsel for the bank addressed the judge and admitted his shock at Ann's poor health and obvious discomfort. He suggested a compromise, which allowed Ann to stay in her house."

* * * * *

Desperately fearful, Celestine awoke having made a decision. Ann was not in a position to help, she had said. So, Beyoncé's mother, forced to become pro-active about her financial plight, came up with an idea. She would develop a hair magazine and call it "Hair International." All she needed now was to find some investors, which seemed within reach. After all, people believed that she was the owner of "the most successful black hair salon in Houston," as she maintained.

"I'm going to throw a party," she bragged.

Her gamble paid off big – at first.

Celestine expected twenty to thirty people at her shindig. The "Creole culture" of Louisiana was her party theme.

"I'll make a big pot of gumbo," she said (the only time I witnessed her making the dish during my eleven-year tenure).

"Sounds scrumptious, but can everybody eat seafood?" I asked.

"Ah, yes. Good point," Celestine said. After thinking a moment, she continued, "I'll make a smaller pot with chicken."

"Good idea," I said.

Cheryl Cruezot, Celestine's best friend, showed up on the afternoon of the party with members of her restaurant staff from Frenchy's Chicken. They began preparing the hors d'oeuvres trays and the Bunsen burner catering pans, where the gumbo, chicken, red beans and rice and other menu items would be kept warm.

While Cheryl and her staff worked, the girls and I disappeared, heading back to my apartment to rehearse "Ain't No Sunshine." Celestine had requested it, saying that so many people wanted to hear them. They were excited about the event, and after warming them up and rehearsing them thoroughly, I sent them to the main house so that they could get dressed for the party. "We'll be going to the movies later, so think about what you want to change into after you guys perform." By the time I had dressed and returned to the house, Cheryl had transformed the Knowles house from a family home to a festive mini-New Orleans. Celestine had even, as I remember it, ordered a king cake (a New Orleans specialty) for her guests.

Shortly before the arrival of the guests, Celestine descended the staircase looking stunning. Dressed in the orange raw silk suit that her sister, Selena, had tailored, she was perfectly put together. Wearing every diamond ring she owned, she looked every inch the successful entrepreneur. The suit had an embroidered gold pattern imbedded in the orange fabric, and she wore complementary gold shoes. The jacket, fitted at the waist, topped elegant, pencil-legged pants. Selena had cut a tiny groove, a nice touch to the ensemble, at the ankles and the wrists, and Celestine had styled her own hair, setting it off with understated teardrop pearl earrings.

As the potential sponsors arrived, Celestine greeted each of them personally with the charm of an aristocrat of the Deep South. Taking each guest by the hand while exchanging hugs and kisses on the cheek, Celestine played the hostess with the mostest. Many of the women openly admired her large diamonds – which she often pawned so that she could pay her bills. On the day of her swanky affair, she had retrieved them, and just in the nick of time, too. As the compliments flooded in, Celestine Knowles, as humble as I had ever seen her, responded with, "Oh, these old things…" She had turned on the syrup faucet, and her admirers seemed to be lapping it up.

Miraculously, Celestine had managed to corral Mathew for the event. Not only was he present, but he was sober, and most importantly, civil. He handled the male guests, husbands who worked in medicine, law, and real estate, chatting them up with the fervor of a Baptist preacher.

Wearing a dark double-breasted suit, starched white shirt, and polished shoes, Mathew looked dapper. I must admit, it was interesting to see how he and Celestine worked people. No one would have ever believed that they actually hated one another. Celestine spoke in a soft and demure manner, which made Mathew look like a giant, and the perfect husband. She wanted him to come off as the man of his castle, very powerful. For the first time I could actually see why she had married him. They worked together well – to achieve their goal. Not even Beyoncé got the kind of treatment I observed them giving their guests. But of course! These people were important to the Knowles' plan. Celestine's new venture, "Hair International," needed their money.

After mingling for a bit with the guests, soaking in the atmosphere, the girls and I congregated in the hallway. They were ready to sing. Mathew was ready, too. He called for the guests to gather round, stuck out his chest, and exclaimed, "You guys are in for a real treat. My daughter is going to blow your mind." The other girls looked at me, I looked at Mathew, and he carried on, oblivious to the slight of the other girls that he had just delivered. However, with single-minded purpose the girls focused their attention on their performance. They knocked it out of the ballpark. They were fantastic, absolutely brilliant. As had become their custom of late, every note was perfection. The guests cheered them with enthusiastic applause and whistles. I was like a proud papa. After responding to the rush of compliments, the girls and I disappeared. It was time to head off to the movies, one of their favorite pastimes. I hadn't told the girls which film I had planned for them. They only knew that our leaving left Beyoncé's parents to their party.

Several months earlier I had taken the girls to the set of a movie, *Jason's Lyric*, that was being shot in Houston. The tragic love story, staring Allen Payne, Jada Pinkett Smith, and Bokeem Woodbine, promised to be fantastic. At least that is what the critics claimed. Now, in the car, I told the girls which film we were going to see, and they erupted into excited chatter. Part of their excitement arose simply from going out to the movies, away from their parents. The other reason had to do with the "R" rating of this film. For thirteen-year-olds, seeing an R-rated movie had the allure of something forbidden. Naturally, I had checked out both the movie and the story before taking them to see it. There was no overt sexuality depicted on the screen. *Jason's Lyric* was about love, loss, and decision. I felt that they would all profit from seeing it together and discussing it afterwards.

Beyoncé loved the movie. It touched all the girls, but Beyoncé was especially moved. It prompted serious thought, something she'd been pondering and had mentioned to me just days earlier. Not only did the film deal with love, its underlying theme touched on the subjects of choice, and of the consequences of not living one's life for one's self. Beyoncé loved her family and was loyal to them, but her future would ultimately depend upon her own talents and skills, upon her successes. "Life is all about choice, Beyoncé," I would say. "Make the right one and things go well. Make the wrong one and ..." She would just smile, without saying a word.

The look in Beyoncé's eyes on the ride home, after dropping off the other girls at their homes, told me how deeply she'd been affected. As a rule, Beyoncé did not show overtly what she was thinking, not unless she was perplexed beyond all comprehension. On that evening she was clear. She knew full well that she was facing some unpopular choices in her own life, and she dreaded that.

I approached that dread openly. "Beyoncé, you have two choices: Either you can get caught up in adult mess or you can choose to follow your own conscience. Doing what is right is never easy, and it is most always unpopular with the masses – sometimes even with the people you love." Then I said something that startled even me. I couldn't believe the words were coming out of my mouth. "Beyoncé, the ten commandments tell us to honor our mother and father, it does not say we have to like them. There is a difference, you know." Beyoncé's eyes, as big as fifty cent pieces, said everything.

When we arrived home, Celestine came out of her bedroom. She hugged Beyoncé, asked her if she had enjoyed the movie, and then sent her to bed. Minutes later she stood at my door, not to hear about our movie experience, but anxious and excited to tell me about her evening. "Everything was perfect," she said. "We got the money to finance the magazine." With the money now secure through pledges, Celestine could begin to plan seriously. Some of the patrons/sponsors had even given their contributions that very evening. She was justifiably proud of herself. I was so proud of her – a strong black woman who put family first – or so I believed. There was nothing more important to her than how she appeared in her daughters' eyes. They saw what taking care of them looked like, just as I had as a young person, watching my own mother move mountains for her children.

"Can you help me tomorrow?" Celestine asked. She had already begun formulating her first ideas. Tomorrow's talk would be about direction and how she envisioned seeing the magazine layouts, she said.

"Sure," I answered. "I'll get home from church at around 11:30." I looked forward to hearing all about Celestine's vision for the cover.

Mathew was nowhere in sight. She told me that after the party guests had left, he'd gone out for the evening. She then thanked me again and again for always being there for her.

My smile was my answer. "It's my pleasure," I said, wishing her a good night's sleep. A hair magazine was and is an ambitious undertaking.

"Goodnight," Celestine said, hugging me tightly. Then she headed off to bed, going through the alcove, up the three stairs leading into Beyoncé's bedroom, and through the door. I closed my door behind me and turned out the light, happy for Celestine.

Over the next couple months, she and I worked on the magazine at her every free moment. She had finalized the cover design, and we traipsed all over Houston, looking for accessories. In addition, to help her choose the models, I helped her organize the hundreds of photos and stat sheets, a painstaking, tedious process. The Look was crucial, and she was glad for my expertise in reading faces and assessing talent.

The next steps involved deciding on the photographer and arranging the location. Celestine had strategy meetings with her staff regarding the timing of the prep work, and things like hair coloring, chemically relaxing hair, and who got what weave. On the day of the shoot, the atmosphere was crazy cool. The result was amazing. Even Cousin Richard had shown up, all too happy to help. Celestine, who on that day looked better than I had ever seen her, had coerced him into being one of the models. She was a giddy school girl delighted to have been saved by her prince. After the final model walked the space, we celebrated. She'd done it.

Three issues later the magazine folded, and I was left very, very confused.

Celestine's investors were just as shocked, and I dare to say, hot under the collar. They wanted answers. Mathew said he wasn't worried. He had an ironclad contract, he boasted. How secure his contract was or wasn't had nothing to do with me, but their threats felt imminent. Three of the financial backers showed up to the Knowles house, beating on their door. Mathew had promised "great returns on your investments," as one man screamed in the foyer. It got ugly. The complaint was clear. They claimed deception and wanted their "Goddamned money," the woman said.

"You knew the risk," Mathew answered.

"I suspect foul play," another man said.

The first man accused the Knowleses of outright stealing.

Celestine talked to the group with the most apologetic look on her face and in her body that I have ever seen from anyone. Not even the "fatal attraction" actress, Glenn Close, could have played Celestine's part better. She was convincingly distraught. She even cried out loud, claiming, "I poured my life into this project." She was "so sorry that I failed." Bursting into tears, she fled the room, leaving the frustrated and angry investors to Mathew.

In response to Celestine's sudden outburst of emotion, Mathew said. "You'll have to excuse my wife. She's been under strain. This isn't easy for her. I wanted to help my wife realize her dream, but the market says differently. We couldn't have known this outcome," Mathew swore. "We are devastated."

"So are we," the woman said.

Celestine never returned to the meeting. She'd tucked herself away in the safety of her bedroom, behind the locked door. I slipped away to the sanctity of my apartment, away from the heated discussion. I remember thinking, Thank God Beyoncé and Solange aren't at home.

Celestine's theatrics had swayed no one. That trio of investors was out for blood and they returned a couple days later threatening to hire lawyers. They might have known the risk, and maybe it was true that the contract was ironclad, but still the law protects against, "knowingly deceiving people." It's called "Fraud," the women said, and the Knowleses were being accused of it. I understood fraud to be dishonesty calculated for advantage, and the U.S. legal system is specific about its consequences.

The Monday following the investors' meeting, Celestine and I went to Captain Benny's on South Main Street.

"What are you going to do, Celestine?"

"What am I going to do about what?" she said calmly.

"About the sponsors," I said

"Absolutely nothing," she said, thumbing through the menu. "They knew what they were getting into."

"Yes, but Celestine, you could be sued, perhaps even imprisoned."

"No, I can't. My name is not on the contracts," Celestine said. "Mathew's is."

"OK – but – those people's money. They want it back!"

"At the end of the day, it's business," said Celestine.

Her attitude was unnerving me. Had she forgotten that I lived in her house? I heard her and Mathew's conversations. They had them right in front of me, openly and disgustingly so. I didn't want to believe that she and Mathew had committed what clearly felt like fraud to everyone but them. I'd watched Celestine over the years fight like a mad woman in every instance of her life, but with the magazine she just quit. She had never given up, on anything, so why had she just left it, and after only three issues? I asked her. "Reputation is everything in the music business, Celestine," I said. "This kind of thing could follow the girls."

Celestine snapped, saying, "It's none of your damned business, now is it?"

"Excuse me?" I said.

"Mind your damned business. Nobody's angry with you, so why do you care?"

I was mortified. It was clear that Celestine found my moral take on things misplaced. Legally it might not matter if her name wasn't on the contract, but as Mathew's wife and the proprietor of the magazine, she could face serious consequences. Celestine didn't want to hear what I had to say. Only one problem, I wasn't going to allow her to talk to me just any old way. I was family, and I cared about this outcome. Family means togetherness, through thick and thin, and this was definitely one of those thin moments in Celestine's life.

"Celestine, do you think that you are the only one with assets?" I asked. "And of course it's my business, too. I live in your house and those investors saw me there. People know that I live in the garage apartment. I helped you lay the groundwork for the magazine. I don't want to be implicated in any way. If this goes to trial, even in civil court, all persons connected to it could face charges. I don't want to be called before a court, deposed or even thought of as an accomplice, because I am not. I don't understand your attitude about it, Celestine. I can't believe you are not fighting to save the magazine."

Rolling her eyes, Celestine didn't say one word. She stared starkly at me. As I wondered what she was thinking, she began to speak. Through clenched teeth, Celestine said, "Have you decided what you want to eat?" She signaled for the waitress and said, "I'll take the special." Then she looked at me commandingly. "The catfish is great here."

"All right then," I said nervously, and to the waitress, "I'll have the cat-fish with fries. Oh, and would you bring me extra tartar sauce – and extra lemon on the side?"

Noticing that I was still very much in my head about the sponsors' threats, Celestine said, "Oh, David, stop being so damned dramatic." Roll-ing her eyes again, she said, "Gay people."

I lost it. Before I could catch myself I blurted, "And where in the fuck would you be without gay people?"

Celestine's eyes widened, tensing up around the brow, and her mouth dropped open from surprise. Before she could respond I stood up and left the table. She looked as though she could've stabbed me. When I returned she tried to speak. I put up my hand. "Your comment was completely in-appropriate. What does being gay have to do with not wanting to be sued, implicated in, or associated with your shit?"

Back-pedaling, Celestine tried to soften what she'd said, to no avail. I was furious. I chose not to say a word but I wasn't going to let her off the hook so easily for her little slip of the tongue. After that day I became suspicious of everything Celestine.

The meal and the ride home together were tense, to say the least. You could have heard a mouse peeing on cotton. Pulling up to the front of the house, I let Celestine out of the car and then sped off. I had steam to work off before Beyoncé's lesson. I unlocked the burglar bars to my apartment and went inside, heading straight for Witch Celestine. She caught hell that day, as she had on every other occasion Mama Celestine misbehaved.

* * * * *

The house on Parkwood was slipping into a dark place. I remember re-reading my copy of the German philosopher Friedrich Nietzsche's book *Beyond Good and Evil* during this time. Nietzsche said: "Not necessity, not desire – no, the love of power is the demon of men. Let them have everything – health, food, a place to live, entertainment – they are and

407

remain unhappy and low-spirited: for the demon waits and waits and will be satisfied."

Nietzsche also wrote, "Whoever fights monsters should see to it that in the process he does not become a monster. And if you gaze long into an abyss, the abyss will gaze back into you." I took those very poignant words to heart, but it was this statement, "That which does not kill us makes us stronger," that anchored me. Written in 1886, Nietzsche's words are just as relevant today as they were when he wrote them.

Typical behavior of people in a love hate relationship, Mama and Papa Knowles continued on their quest and eventually sought separate-but-equal ways of dissecting their daughters, expecting the girls to choose sides. Beyoncé loved her mother, but she believed that her father was helping her with her career. I was of the opinion that it was an impossible situation for her, and most unfair.

In her frustration, a deeply confused Beyoncé turned to food. Lots of it. "Beyoncé, you must watch what you eat. You have to take better care of yourself. What about your career?" her mother would chide. She ordered a strict diet of "lean-cuisine," "sugar free jello," and water. She put her daughter on a nightly regimen of sit-ups, which Beyoncé did religiously to make her mother happy, sometimes even lying on the floor at her mother's feet. She agonized through the exercises, never saying a word, while Celestine sat comfortably on the family room sofa, with her feet tucked under her, counting each and every grunt. "It's for your own good," Celestine would say.

The saddest day of my life with her was hearing Beyoncé say she wanted to give up singing. Her parents' constant fighting, and now her secret battle with food, brought up feelings of guilt, which conflicted with her desire to become a singer. After all, she told me, it seemed that her parents' fights were about her group. She reasoned that if she didn't have talent, the group wouldn't have existed, and her parents wouldn't have needed to fight.

"Beyoncé, adult problems are exactly that – adult problems. Your parents' problems have nothing to do with you, or your talent."

Mathew and Celestine's problems had everything to do with themselves, his drugs and her desperation and hidden agendas. They were selfish and childish adults haphazardly raising two precious daughters, and they wore on my nerves. I wouldn't tell Beyoncé that her father was a cocaine addict; he'd admit to that himself, some years later. Nor would I say that her mother's habits of control and yearnings for the spotlight were more important to her than life itself.

"Beyoncé, I want you to listen to me and hear me good. Your parents have done and are going to do some not so nice things. Your star is meant to shine bright. Remember that you don't like hurting people. It's not your style at all. And above all, keep your hands clean."

Perhaps I shouldn't have given her that harsh opinion – but I did. I believed in what I said, from the bottom of my heart. I got a jolting reality check the day I found Beyoncé, with her head buried in the refrigerator, stuffing her face full of whatever she could find. That particular time it was chocolate cake. Hugging her, I felt her humiliation, and I promised relief. It was going to be all right. I didn't know how yet, but it would be.

From that day on I was all about Beyoncé. I, as her teacher, could do little to ameliorate the personal hell that trapped her. Narcissistic Family Hell is the worst kind. Today I understand, all too well, that the only way to escape the narcissistic personality is through detachment. In 1994, Beyoncé didn't have that skill. Neither did I. None of us did. But I had an idea.

Desperate, I drove over to Blockbuster video rental, taking Celestine's card. As I had always done, I presented it with my chosen video at the check-out counter. This time there was a problem. The account had been closed due to non-payment of the sum total of eleven or so dollars. I opened my own account, rented the film, and quickly returned to our Parkwood palace.

"Beyoncé, follow me," I said.

She did as I asked.

"Have a seat!" I then walked over to my video machine, and placed the VHS tape into the player.

"What's this?"

"Something special, just for you," I said.

Beyoncé's eyes lit up like a Christmas tree. "What?"

"Beyoncé, no questions please," I answered. "Just watch. And afterwards we can talk about the film," I added. I pressed PLAY on the remote and *What's Love Got to Do with It*, a biopic about Tina Turner, came onto the screen.

I don't think Celestine ever knew about our viewing that film. Nevertheless, at the end of it, Beyoncé's eating binges, her obsession with food, and her self-condemnation disappeared. They vanished. GONE.

Anna Mae Bullock, a.k.a. Tina Turner, had unwittingly saved Beyoncé's life. From that day forward, Beyoncé was obsessed with everything Tina. It was Tina Turner's will to survive, making that decision to love and focus on self, which had made the difference. Beyoncé's sparkle was back, and I will be forever grateful to Tina Turner – Anna Mae Bullock – and *truth*.

Seeing is really believing.

Perhaps I also shouldn't have shared Tina Turner's story with Beyoncé, but I did. My childhood had not been without turmoil. I knew a bit about what she was feeling and told her how I, too, had lived dramatic events as a little boy that were like those that Tina Turner suffered on the screen. I had never seen Beyoncé's father hit her mother, but I'd heard the stories. Tyrannical abuse happened early on in their marriage, I'd been told (something Celestine admitted to later on in life), so omitting the lurid details of my own mother's experiences, I focused on the fact that my stepfather had left scars in me. "The way he beat my mother? And yelled at her and berated her? I have learned from that history," I told Beyoncé. Lead by example, I told myself. I pointed out to her that she had the same opportunity to overcome. Again, her parents' truth did not have to be hers. "Become self-sufficient," I said.

19. Daddy Charles

"Hello!" a female voice said. "May I please speak to David Lee Brewer..."

"Speaking!"

"Hi David, this is Ann Owens, with Houston Grand Opera." Her words startled me. With all the mayhem going on in the Knowles house, I'd forgotten about *Porgy and Bess*, auditioning, or even that they'd said we'd hear back in May.

When Houston Grand Opera had announced auditions for their 1995-96 season production of *Porgy*, I had jumped at the chance. I began preparing immediately. I hadn't auditioned in years. I couldn't afford any mishaps. I got up every morning to do my usual jogging, as well as listening to the sound of silence in Hermann Park. And I visualized success. I read the book *Porgy*, by DuBose Heyward, which was the source for the opera libretto. The book brought back memories of family, struggle, unconditional love, a mother's love, bad seeds in the community, drug and alcohol use, and a father's commitment to family.

All of this flashed through my mind as Ann Owens continued with the reason for her call this morning: to offer me the role of Crabman in the new HGO production of Gershwin's *Porgy and Bess*. Furthermore, they had chosen me to be "first cover" for the great character role of Sportin' Life, the drug dealer.

"Congratulations!" Ann said.

"Wow! Great!" I answered. "This is indeed *good news*." Then I asked, "How long do I have before I need to confirm my participation?"

"We will begin sending contracts out in about a month or so." Congratulating me again, Ann added, "We'd be so glad to have you join our fabulous cast. Rehearsals will begin in December in New York."

Thanking her again, I hung up with a big smile on my face.

411

* * * * *

My only doubts were about leaving the girls too soon. They were *musically* prepared, but they were surrounded by so much negativity. I worried about who would protect them, at their tender age, from their nemeses. I certainly trusted Ann's moral and ethical values, but her health and the Kowleses' conniving had kept me on the alert for some time. Concern for the girls dampened my enthusiasm for signing the HGO contract, but I knew that I had to give the offer serious thought.

We still hadn't heard back from Daryl about a record deal, and time was a-winding down for me. If I was ever going to go after my career, I'd have to be mindful of the "32-year" rule. In opera, tenors who are not singing professionally, at least on the regional operatic circuit, by their 32nd birthday could forget about getting the chance. I was turning 31 in two months.

The telephone rang.

"Mama? Is everything all right? It's not Sunday."

"Everything's fine."

"Guess what Mama! HGO just called me. I got offered good roles in their new production of *Porgy and Bess*!"

"That's wonderful baby. You sound excited."

"Of course I am," I said. "Now I just have to figure out if I'm going to take it and then how to break the news to the girls."

"Are you crazy, David?" Mama shouted.

"No, Mama," I answered. "But my work here isn't quite finished."

After a pregnant silence, Mama managed to regain a neutral tone.

"When do rehearsals start for the play?"

"Opera Mama – opera, and rehearsals start in December. In New York!"

"Oh!" Mama said. "I'll just be arriving and you'll be leaving."

"What do you mean?"

"I got a new job with the Mental Health and Mental Retardation Association of Harris County! I'm moving to Houston in October." Mama said

412

that she'd had several telephone interviews and that her final interview had gone extremely well. She'd been interviewed by the director himself, who had offered her the job on the spot, without need for a face-to-face meeting. Working for the State of Texas, she would have duties almost identical to those she'd had in Nebraska, except this time her clients would be the handicapped and severely abused in the family. Mama also said she'd be working closely with the courts, which was a given.

"Cool beans," I answered.

Of course I was happy for my mother. I love her with all my heart, but, uh, well…had she decided to come live with me? Anticipating my unspoken question, Mama quickly reassured me. "And no, David, I'm not coming to live with you." "Mama, you know you are always welcome," I replied, laughing that she'd read my mind.

Mama knew me well.

After our phone call, I thought about Mama's question as to my sanity, realizing the severity of my decision. Would I sign the HGO contract, accept the two singing assignments, and prepare to spend the 1995-96 season on stage in *Porgy and Bess*?

* * * * *

Who was I kidding?

My power was limited. Yes, as their artistic director I was in charge of the girls' everything. Their complete artistic development was within my sphere. But I was not their parent. That May 1994 I kept telling myself that I was over-reacting, while at the same time I felt an indescribable restlessness within myself. I had become consumed with shielding Beyoncé, Kelly, LeToya, and LaTavia, determined to help them learn to regulate and solve their own problems. I'd made an inroad on Beyoncé's capacity to understand her own fears and to curtail her overeating habits. It helped that I lived in her house. But the other girls? Celestine's covert antipathy toward Kelly, and what I believed were her increasing manipulations of LaTavia to keep LeToya in line were giving me many a sleepless night.

Pretending to be pro-Kelly, Celestine began having little private chats with her. She would stand Kelly in front of the mirror. "Kelly, look at your dark chocolate skin, you're beautiful," Celestine said. The hair on the back of my neck stood up.

Then there was the time she'd "caught Kelly in a lie," she said. On a Sunday evening she called Kelly into private council while I waited to begin her voice lesson. "I understand how you feel Kelly," Celestine said. "I grew up poor, too." What the hell did that mean? I thought. I called Kelly out of that room, and away from what felt like unhealthy advice. "Kelly, I'm ready, whenever you are," I said. I'll never forget the look in Kelly's eyes. "Oh, I'm sorry, Celestine," I said. "Were you finished? I need to get Kelly's extra lesson done before she's picked up."

When I asked Celestine about her attentions toward Kelly, she smoothly declared that they were "faith based." She assured me that helping Kelly was in line with *God's plan*. In 1994 I felt just awful thinking of Celestine so suspiciously. For a long time I fought against my intuition that Celestine actually meant harm to Kelly, while every bone in my body was screaming that I was dead on.

With my longtime interest in human behavior, and even at the risk of indulging in armchair psychology, I delved deeper into persons who suffer from acute personality disorders and mental illnesses. On a fundamental level I was convinced that Doris loved her daughter, but she continued occasionally to snap, abusing Kelly unjustifiably. I wanted to understand Doris better, I really did. My heart went out to her. She could be most charming and very likable, but her extremes of behavior seemed to have a continuing negative effect on her own daughter's fragile self-confidence. Kelly sang well, and then she didn't. It was like climbing Mount Everest again, every time she'd fall off the proverbial singing cloud nine.

Kelly's modus operandi for survival drove her to hiding behind a debilitating self-doubt. She felt herself characterized by chaos and defeatism. "Beyoncé has it all. Their house is so beautiful. It has so many pretty things in it," Kelly said.

414

"Yes, the things are very pretty – beautiful even," I said. I did not share my observation of the other truths. Truths that said that the human beings could be a nightmare. That the human beings were a nightmare. What Kelly didn't know was that the Knowleses' concept of family was largely an illusion. Grandmother used to say, "All that glitters is not gold." Never was there a truer statement.

On one occasion, I learned that Kelly's school principal was often calling her into the school office. I got nervous about this. With all the attention that I had given to her over the years in trying to bring her out of her shell, I feared that I'd turned her into a trouble maker. Oh God, what had I done?

But, no, it wasn't that at all. The school principal had been asking Kelly to serenade the students over the school intercom, to sing a little something, setting the mood for the day. Her voice was and is absolutely beautiful, and this form of praise added significantly to the development of the now fourteen-year-old Kelly. After that her self-confidence emerged slowly and surely. Nothing beats what a little appreciation and the right attention and support will do for a young person. As Grandmother always said, that kind of approval brings out the best in anyone. Her new position at school helped erase her fears of inadequacy, and Kelly glowed. I was so pleased to see her new confidence in lessons and at rehearsals.

Celestine, on the other hand, was not amused. You must understand that Celestine Knowles was not the kind of woman who did things blatantly – for the most part. She used quiet cunning and patience with the passing of time to annihilate the objects of her disapproval. She loved Kelly like a daughter – so she claimed. The fact was, Kelly was not her daughter and never would be. I was so young and naive then. I prided myself on being intelligent, but then I remembered that Mama always said that "book smarts do not a wise man make." As educated as I was, Celestine's street intelligence outsmarted me every time. I'd have to work to keep up, and so would a trusting young Kelly.

In their subtler ways, Beyoncé's parents, like Kelly's mother, were shaping their daughter under the steam press of their self-preoccupation.

Mathew and Celestine habitually lied to their elder daughter in order to preserve her innocent trust in their goodness. Beyoncé knew that some people considered her parents not "nice," but they were her parents. I'd told her to beware of the quagmire they would try to drag her into. She still had a soul and it was clean. So much transpired under the surface in her Parkwood castle, and Beyoncé was happy to remain willfully oblivious to it.

It was in this context that she found company in an idyllic world. Like the Grimm Brothers' Rapunzel, she sat in her window waiting for a rescuing Prince Charming. One Sunday, Beyoncé accompanied Kelly to her church at Abundant Life Cathedral. After the service, one of Kelly's friends drew her aside. "Kelly, who is that?" he asked. "Introduce us."

Within a few weeks, Lyndall Locke, who didn't even own a bicycle, let alone a white horse, began arriving at the castle. Beyoncé was smitten.

My pupil was growing up!

* * * * *

Exposure is central to building a successful artist, and going to concerts was not just about meeting the star. Together, the girls and I studied those performances. What worked? What didn't, and why? It wasn't enough to have watched videos of stars, as we had done during the training camp; now they had to see live performers in action. How star performers interacted with their audiences, and their technical support teams – lighting and sound people, for example – was the goal.

In those years, many top popular acts made their way to Houston for performances, and through my contacts I was able to gain access to the various concerts and to get backstage passes. I took my girls with me everywhere and to every concert, introducing them to everyone. They met many star performers, and of course they were always excited to experience the concerts. Nevertheless, it was their relationship with the hip R&B group SWV (Sisters with Voices) that meant the most to them.

On one particular Saturday in June, shortly before the end of studio class, Solange burst through the alcove door to my apartment. Real dramatic-like, she fell into the room and collapsed onto the floor, while pretending to be out of breath. As soon as she realized all eyes were on her she gasped, "Whoa! Coko is on the phone, y'all." Then scurrying to get up and out of the way, Solange barely missed being trampled, as the girls bolted from their chairs, all at once. They raced over to the main house and the kitchen phone as though life depended upon it. For them, I think it did.

SWV's Cheryl Gamble, also known as "Coko," and the other girls, Tamara "Taj" Johnson and Leanne "Lelee" Lyons, had become real mentors to my girls, and I loved them for it. Not only did they request I bring my girls to their hotel and concert, every time they were in Houston, but after a while their friendship grew so strong that SWV often called the girls from the road, as well, to check in on them. This was one of those moments, and they were ecstatic.

I had hung out with SWV in the late fall of 1992, around the time their debut album, *It's About Time*, was released in October. We'd met through a mutual friend, when they were in town at The Westin Galleria Hotel in Houston. They'd just come back from having lunch and by the end of that conversation we'd become fast friends. They were Christian girls, and I liked them a lot. They had beautiful spirits, which seemed like a perfect match to my girls, whom I'd been teaching for years about the music business. Now it was time for them to see and hear things up close. Naturally, in 1992 SWV had never heard of Da Dolls, but by the time I'd finished talking about my group, they couldn't wait to meet them. That happened a few months later, in 1993, and just as I'd imagined they would, they instantly liked my girls. And vice versa.

I can never forget that first meeting. I picked up Beyoncé and Solange from school, drove Solange to the salon (she was too young to tag along), and returned to the Knowleses. By the time Beyoncé and I pulled up, LeToya and LaTavia were arriving. Kelly was being brought over by Cholotte, Nikki and Nina's mom, who'd gotten past her anger at Mathew for breaking her girls' hearts. Once Kelly arrived, I gave them the news that they would be meeting Sisters With Voices. They immediately pelted me with questions. On the way to the hotel they laughed and babbled about everything and nothing, all at the same time. I thought they'd burst wide open from the anticipation. Arriving a bit early, I parked the car, getting out, and locking everything up reallll sloooww. "C'mon David. Hurry up!" They said.

"Hold on," I said, laughing. "We have plenty of time."

Of course SWV, at that time one of the leading girl bands, thought my girls were really cute. Then they heard them sing. "These girls are going to kick our asses in the future," Coco said. "Wow! They are just twelve years old."

"Yep," I answered, like a proud papa.

Now in the summer of 1994, Coko, Taj, and Lelee were on the phone, sharing stories of being on the road in Atlanta and hearing all about the girls' stellar showcase. Apparently, they'd made a real impression, and word had started to circulate within the business that a hot new girl group, young girls of thirteen and fourteen, were on the horizon. The SWV women excitedly shared this information with us.

My girls started in with their signature squealing, and dancing about. When Beyoncé called her mother to share the news, Celestine called me.

"Is it true?" she asked.

"Yes," I answered.

Later that evening, waiting for Mathew to come home, she talked with me in the den. The girls were long since asleep when Mathew finally walked in from what I remember as an unexplained three-day absence away from home. It was long after midnight.

"Get your *motherfuckin ass* on the phone and find out what the hell is going on!" Celestine said, through clenched teeth, so as not to wake the girls.

"Will you let me fucking get in the house first?" Mathew snarled. After coming out of the bathroom, much more relaxed than when he went in, Mathew gave Celestine his What-the-hell-are-you-bitching-about-now? look.

She explained, and Mathew made a beeline for the kitchen telephone, nearly falling over himself in his rush. I guess it was no problem to call Daryl at 1:45 a.m., I thought. Hell, why should he get off scot free? I wondered to myself. What was good for me and Ann ought to be good for Daryl.

Celestine held up her finger, signaling Mathew to put the phone on speaker phone, which he refused to do. It was true, we hadn't heard a word from Daryl with any proper, or solid feedback. If what SWV said was indeed fact, that the industry was all a-buzz, Celestine wanted to know why they were the last to hear about it. "I want to know what the hell Daryl's game is," she said to me.

Daryl confirmed SWV's report. He told Mathew that he had been talking to a label, two in fact. He also said that he was working out a few details before saying anything, but that he *believed* he had real offers. However, he wasn't ready to reveal any names yet, according to Mathew.

A couple days later, my student Darrell Jones called me to say that Tony Terry, in Houston to perform, was interested in meeting the girls. A year earlier I'd met Tony, through Darrell, and we'd become friendly. A sensational R&B singer, Tony was always on the lookout for new talent. He owned his own production company. I knew that we were under a production deal with Daryl Simmons, but perhaps Daryl would include him as a producer on the record. I couldn't be sure, but I'd asked for his help anyway. Connections are everything.

When the girls and I arrived at The Westin Galleria, Tony was doing his thing, mesmerizing his female audience. He was a regular Don Juan. I hadn't heard a voice like his in pop music since Peabo Bryson, my favorite R&B male singer. Unusually for popular musicians, both singers possess voices of great beauty and uncanny precision.

"He can sing," Beyoncé said.

"Yes, he can!"

Kelly, LeToya, and LaTavia were all eyes, intrigued by the behavior of the seemingly "older women in the room," who my girls thought were embarrassing themselves. Noticing this, I said: "Ladies, the word 'fan' comes from the word 'fanatics.' You too will have them!" Nervous giggle.

"Don't laugh," I added, with a smile. I was amused at their startled reactions to my prophetic words.

At the end of Tony's performance, he escaped, taking us to a nearby Westin Hotel ballroom, where he gave my girls his full attention. His fans would have to wait. Darrell had told him, "These little chicks can blow." Tony Terry leaned back, closed his eyes and prepared himself to be entertained. After hearing the first notes of my girls singing "Ain't No Sunshine," he opened his eyes. They had him. At the end of their performance, he nearly lost his mind. He became so excited that he'd forgotten that "all those women" were clamoring for his attention and autograph. I had too, actually. A woman, most likely the presenter, came in to remind him that his fans were waiting. She apologized, "I really have to steal him away now," looking over at my girls with a huge grin on her face. Winking, she'd signaled that she had heard them through the door. Tony asked us to wait. "Don't go anywhere," he said. "Man, these girls are incredible," he said to me. I promised we'd be there when he returned.

I thought it would be interesting for the girls to see what a real autograph session looked like, up close, and asked that nice presenter lady if we could stand in the background and watch Tony work the hotel lobby. She agreed.

"Now watch and learn, girls," I said. "Even when signing autographs you're at work."

I felt incredibly proud of them. My girls had made impressions on SWV, who shared their story and talent with their management and label, and now Tony Terry was over the moon about them and offered to help.

Roy Brown called the next morning.

"I have a deal," he said to me.

Roy had already shared with Ann and Mathew that Barry Rosenthal had secured the attention of Elektra Records. When he gave me the news, my mental wheels went into overdrive. Elektra's director, CEO Sylvia Rhone, had been at the Atlanta Showcase. She was Daryl's good friend. Could this mean that the business between Roy, Ann, and Mathew, was in direct conflict with Daryl? Although he hadn't given Mathew the name of the label he believed was interested, either of the two, I suspected correctly that Elektra was the one Daryl was bringing to the table. Roy talked about a $600,000 payday.

"Thank God," Celestine sighed. I could tell that she'd begun mentally to spend the advance money. She said she liked the sound of Roy's figure. "Mathew," she added, "We now have a ball park figure of what it's worth." I wondered who, or what, "it" was, and why she'd chosen those words if she referred to the girls. Not likely to get an answer, I let it go, worried. Elektra records had EnVogue on their roster. Would my girls get the attention they deserved? In any case, we had a problem. Could it be that two people were courting the same label?

What budget would Daryl propose? I wondered.

* * * * *

Though Mama had come to tolerate my enthusiasm for the girls, there came a Sunday in July when she interrupted my monologue to express her concern about my overall goals. Mama now quizzed me seriously about my singing plans.

"Are you going to take the HGO contract or not?"

"I'm still not sure. There's so much going on here. But I have time to decide. I haven't received the contract yet."

Satisfied that I was still taking the HGO opportunity seriously, Mama returned to the girls, pushing me for details about Kelly, then Beyoncé, and ultimately, the dreaded topic of LaTavia. I knew what Mama wanted to hear, but I simply had nothing definitive to say to her. I could only tell her that although LaTavia's panic attacks had all but disappeared, her attitude in school "was getting worse," according to her mother, Cheryl. "I don't know what to do," I said to Mama. Her suspicions, even as she repeated them, still had a powerful effect on me.

Mama reiterated, "Essentially, it's all-or-nothing with LaTavia." Then Mama asked me to think back to our lessons. "Go way back in your work with her," she said. "What was LaTavia like, say, a year ago – two years ago?"

My response was, "Full of life."

"And how is she now…?"

"Mama, you know the answer to that question. We've talked about it."

"Humor me," Mama said. "Tell me again."

"Well, she's unhappy, a lot," I answered. "She's irritable most of the time and suffers from terrible mood swings."

"Mood swings?" Mama asked. "With you?"

"No, with her mother."

"How is she with Charles?" Mama asked.

"Responsive, and in my opinion, a bit overzealous."

"I would imagine that LaTavia switches back and forth between difficulty with appraisal of self and the chaotic and unstable relationship she has with her mother – hence *splitting*. In my opinion, LaTavia has problems seeing that her parents have both positive and negative qualities combined. I think she sees one as all good, the other as all bad. I'm going to take a stab at this and say that Charles is a very bad man," Mama concluded.

It wasn't even a month later…

* * * * *

As Charles Mitchell drove out of the alleyway, a strange feeling came over me. My heart began to race when LaTavia and I moved into the living room of my apartment to begin the lesson. She was like a zombie, mumbling a greeting, and moving on cue, but she wasn't in her body. What I saw didn't look or feel like panic, but still, I was concerned for her, terrified actually. She was on automatic pilot. Where was her sass?

"You seem a little tight today, LaTavia," I said.

She moaned, her eyes glassed over.

I started the lesson as I always did, placing my hands at the nape of her neck, just at the hair line. Dealing first with the tension in her posture, I

422

said, "OK, let your head fall into your body." I reminded her to drop her shoulders. She was like a soldier, stiff as a board. "LaTavia, let your head go. We've done this a hundred times." My disapproving tone was upsetting her. "Hey, take it easy," I said. She began to shake. When I placed my hands on her shoulders the shaking stopped. But when I lay my forearm across the top of her chest area, near the collar bone (a typical voice-teacher gesture that helps to settle singers downwards into their bodies), she began to cry.

"OK," I said. "Let's sit down."

She walked over to the couch, wiping her eyes and sniffling. I told her to have a seat and went into the kitchen to get her a glass of water. Standing at the sink I said a silent prayer for her and myself. My God, I thought. Could Mama have been right? I felt sick.

When I returned to the living room, glass in hand, and holding a box of Kleenex, LaTavia stared me straight in my eye. "Charles has been touching me," she said. I dropped the water, and LaTavia burst into tears, crying uncontrollably. My eyes were filling up. I went to her. Just as I prepared to sit, there was a knock at the door, then banging. It was Beyoncé. As usual, she'd come to eavesdrop on LaTavia's lesson, from the hallway adjacent to her bedroom. She'd seen Charles's car leaving the alleyway and had taken her place on the toy chest outside my door.

I opened the door a crack to speak with her. Concerned, Beyoncé asked if she could come in, to which I said, "No." Now was not the time. I had to devote my full attention to LaTavia. "I'll talk to you later, Beyoncé."

"Is LaTavia all right? I just wanna know if she is OK," Beyoncé said.

"She's fine," I said. "We will talk later, Beyoncé." I closed the door quietly and turned back to the sofa, where LaTavia sat, still weeping. "How long has this been going on?" I asked her.

"I was eight," she answered.

Devastated, I barely maintained composure. I began to rewind, replaying every scene, every hug between Charles and his step-daughter. My body tensed as I remembered every articulated syllable of Charles Mitchell's false praise, now clearly identifiable as an attempt to control her, or as my mother had so plainly put it, "groom her" to insure secrecy. Everything about him suddenly repulsed me. What had this man done to my "little diva?" I asked myself.

While pacing the floor in thought, I happened by my window. From there I could look down into the Knowles family room. I saw that Beyoncé, who had returned to the main house, was staring up helplessly at my apartment. Bonded in a very special way, Beyoncé and LaTavia were almost like twins. What one felt the other experienced. They loved each other, and Beyoncé was beside herself with worry. She was most likely wondering why I had lied to her for the first time. I turned to LaTavia and then moved toward the phone. I would call the police.

Wait! I thought. Charles *is* the police – Houston Police – and an officer of many years, in the juvenile division, of all places. What would he do to LaTavia? What would he do to me? How would this affect my girls, the group, and their future? I hung up the phone. One thing was clear. Had I called the police, LaTavia might have been immediately removed from her home and mother. And what about the coveted Elektra deal? I had to think this through, talk to Cheryl first. It was as if time had stopped. I didn't feel myself breathing. My heart thumped, as if at any minute it would jump out of my chest.

Somehow, I managed to call Charles.

"Hello Charles, it's David. I'd like to bring LaTavia home a bit later. I want to give her extra time. There are a few technical things I want to review with her," I said. He agreed, and we both hung up.

I'd just bought myself a bit of time. I had to figure out what to do, before LaTavia had to face Charles again. Going back there would surely be frightening for her, especially after having revealed his crimes, but she would eventually have to go home. I shuddered with the dread of that moment.

My next move was to call Cheryl, but LaTavia stopped me, telling me that her mother knew nothing of this abuse. She was scared to tell her, LaTavia said. Her words brought to mind Mama's telling me how often she had witnessed the denial of the mothers in these cases. I prayed for a different outcome, for LaTavia's sake. I knew that Cheryl was dependent upon Charles. She adored him. For the time being, in this moment, I had to provide LaTavia with support and love. She had trusted me enough to tell me the awful truth; I was hard pressed to honor that.

As reason kicked in, I decided to give LaTavia some key points, things I had learned in teaching seminars, to help her in the situation. I would explain what she should do, until we could talk to her mother. "Listen carefully, LaTavia," I said. "Memorize these things!"

"Number one, the next time Charles tries anything with you, in the loudest voice possible, YELL: 'STOP IT!'"

"Two, if he tries to force you or hit you or intimidate you in any way, attack him. Bite, kick, and scream. Leave bruises that he would have to explain to your mother."

"Three, tell your mother what has been going on."

"Four, do not be surprised if your mother doubts your story. Because she loves Charles, she might become angry with you at first, and try to defend Charles."

LaTavia's frightened look killed me.

"I'm afraid it's true, LaTavia. Accusing someone of molestation is serious. It's shocking, even, and if your mother truly is not aware of this abuse, she will have a hard time accepting this news. Please remember: I believe you. I'm on your side. I know that you are telling the truth. This is not your fault." I just kept repeating that, over and over again.

Lastly, I explained to her that she had to tell both her parents that I knew. "Besides telling Charles to stop, of course," I said to LaTavia, "this is the most important thing. They need to know that someone outside the family knows Charles's secret."

LaTavia promised me she would do these things, and then started to tear up again. "Don't cry LaTavia. It's going to be all right," I said. Seconds later I reached her mother's voice mailbox and left a message for her to call me back. When she did, I asked her to come to my house. "It's about LaTavia," I said.

"What's she done now?" Cheryl asked.

"Nothing, but we have to talk about why she's been so despondent. It's important, Cheryl," I said. "Can you come tonight?"

"I can't tonight. Charles and I have plans. But I could come tomorrow."

"OK, tomorrow would be fine," I said. "Oh, Cheryl," I added. "What time are you and Charles going out tonight? I have kept LaTavia overtime in the studio. I wanted to give her a longer lesson and need to know when I should have her home."

"We will be leaving around 7:00 p.m. But LaTavia has a key," she said.

"OK, great. Then I'll see you tomorrow. And please bring LaTavia with you!"

"OK, see you tomorrow," Cheryl said, and hung up.

I let LaTavia sit there for a while, absolutely quiet if she wanted. I asked her if she would like to have a bite to eat with me, as I hadn't had dinner. We drove to Frenchy's Chicken on Scott Street, not far from the house. I assured her that she was safe now. She'd have to go home, for sure, but she had to understand how important it was to act normally. "Your mother thinks you have been acting out in lessons, that you are troubled somehow, and defiant. Make sure you don't change her perception, LaTavia, before tomorrow, when I have a chance to speak with her."

LaTavia said she understood, and then she thanked me for listening. We ate, and she talked. I listened. It was important for us both that I listen, for as long as she needed me to. While LaTavia talked or not talked, my mind continuously spun, flooding itself with one nightmare after another. After a couple of hours, and two helpings of peach cobbler later, it was 7:00 p.m., safe for her to go home. Before she got out of my car I reminded her of what she should do if Charles tried anything. I reminded her again, "None of this is your fault. It will all be OK," I added. "Call me if you need me."

"I promise," she said and went into the house.

On the way back home I remembered Beyoncé. She had been waiting to talk to me and must have been out of her mind by now. As I expected, Beyoncé was waiting with bated breath. When I told her what had taken place – choosing my words carefully, giving her honesty without too much detail – she broke down into tears. She was devastated, as was I. That her best friend and our precious group member, the funny and brave LaTavia, had to live with such a nightmare overwhelmed us both.

That evening, when Celestine came in from the salon, I sat down with her and Mathew, who was, unusually, at home. I told them what had transpired. Celestine ran into the bathroom and vomited. Mathew looked as if he'd been pulled back into a horrible memory. His body went instantly numb. Cold and glassy-eyed, he stood up without saying a word and left the house.

I didn't sleep so well that night, nor would I, not for a long time. I'm just finding a bit of peace with the writing of this book.

* * * * *

The next day Cheryl showed up at my house, on time, and with LaTavia. I asked if she wanted something to drink and she asked for a glass of water. I took two glasses down. My throat was as dry as a powder keg. I called to LaTavia to help me in the kitchen.

"Did anything happen last evening?" I asked.

"No, Mama was still home when you dropped me off."

"Are you ready?" I asked. She was, she said, and then she hugged me tightly.

When we re-entered the living room, Cheryl began apologizing for LaTavia's bad attitude. I stopped her.

"LaTavia's attitude is not really the reason for this meeting," I said. Cheryl looked confused.

I explained to her that LaTavia had told me that Charles had molested her and that it had been going on since she was eight years old. I gave LaTavia a reassuring look and then focused my attention on her mother.

After a moment's silence, Cheryl spoke.

"Is this true, LaTavia?" she asked.

LaTavia nodded, then mumbled "Yes." Cheryl hit the roof. I had suspected that she would find it difficult to accept her daughter's reality, but I had not expected her response to be so brutal.

"You're a damn liar," Cheryl said. "I don't believe you." She accused LaTavia of having a jealous nature. I couldn't believe it.

"She has always been jealous of my relationship with Charles," Cheryl said. "She has never liked him and was angry with me when I married him. We have caught her in several lies recently." She paused. "I don't know what to think."

"Cheryl, you must believe her first and then question her motives later – if you really think that it's warranted."

LaTavia tried to say something. Cheryl interrupted her.

"Cheryl, let her speak. Perhaps the reason she didn't like your husband is connected with what she told me. It seems that his abuse of LaTavia began almost immediately after your marriage."

Cheryl began to cry and shake. LaTavia got up to go hug her mother, but she pulled away. Suddenly, Cheryl turned to me and said, "I don't believe her." She accused LaTavia once again of never liking Charles and then said that she needed proof.

"Can you prove that Charles touched you?" Cheryl asked her daughter.

LaTavia broke into tears.

"Cheryl, please show a bit more empathy. You haven't been abused," I said. Or had she been? Had Mathew, I wondered?

"But I have no proof," Cheryl said. "What can I do without proof? Without proof, nobody has been abused." Cheryl then said that Charles's friends on the police force "will support him."

"Cheryl, it took real courage for LaTavia to come forward. We can't be dismissive. I too thought about 'proof,' but a child doesn't need – or even have – proof. And this is not just any child. This is LaTavia. Your daughter. The accusation is enough to initiate an investigation. We can't deal with this haphazardly. This is a serious allegation. We must discuss the next step. Obviously she cannot go back to your place with Charles in that house."

Again, Cheryl said, "Without proof, I can't do anything."

Bewildered, I was fighting to maintain my patience. I didn't understand what kind of proof Cheryl thought that a thirteen-year-old could offer.

"LaTavia's word isn't enough for you?" I asked Cheryl.

"No, it's not. Charles is a police officer. He's loved at work, is a great husband and has been a good provider," Cheryl said.

"That may be, but he is a horrible step-father." It was important that we stay focused on the problem at hand. I wanted to talk about the next steps. Charles needed to be reported, and yes, it would be ugly and probably even scary, but it was necessary. "Charles cannot be allowed to stay in the house," I said.

"Nobody is calling the police," Cheryl said. "If you call the police, I will deny everything."

I was floored. LaTavia's tears suddenly stopped. She looked to me for help. I picked up the phone and began to dial.

"David, please. Let me handle this. This is my problem now. I am her mother. Give me the opportunity to get to the bottom of this. I promise that I will handle it."

LaTavia dropped her head.

"Nope, there is no way that LaTavia is going back home," I said. Setting the telephone receiver back into its cradle, I suggested that she be allowed to stay the rest of the week and through the weekend at Beyoncé's house, which Cheryl agreed was a good idea. It would give Cheryl time, space I knew she needed. Talking to Charles about this should have been the logical next step, but it was obvious to me that there was no logic at work here. Not for Cheryl there wasn't. It was not my concern what she told her husband. My responsibility was my student's safety.

Cheryl and Celestine talked via telephone. Celestine gave her approval without reservation. Then Cheryl drove home and returned with clothing for LaTavia's weekend stay with the Knowleses.

Three days later Charles called my house. He'd be coming with Cheryl to pick up LaTavia on Sunday. "You've been warned," he said.

"What the hell is that supposed to mean?" I asked.

"Nothing – nothing at all," Charles answered.

When Mr. and Mrs. Mitchell arrived on Sunday to pick up LaTavia from Beyoncé's house, Charles walked in with a smug swagger. Cheryl was dolled up to the nines, smelling of sweet perfume. Nothing had changed between them it seemed – Cheryl was still the doting wife and Charles the loving husband.

For me everything had changed. LaTavia was the unwilling participant in his deviant behavior – only now, I realized just how powerless I was. Calling the truth would land LaTavia in foster care where things could be worse. Mama had told me horror stories about kids in foster care. Charles would win. His wife supported him.

While LaTavia went upstairs to gather her things, Charles asked to speak to me in private. I obliged. Naturally he denied any wrongdoing. He explained to me how "these things worked." He took false reports every day, he said. "These cases are so difficult to prove, you know." When LaTavia returned downstairs, Charles turned to walk away from me. I called out to him, "Charles, touch her again and you'll have hell to pay." He smiled, nodded his head once, and said, "LaTavia, are you ready to go?"

Celestine and Mathew had no comments, either for Cheryl, or for Charles. They felt that it wasn't their place to get involved. (Ann also told me, later, that she felt it was LaTavia's mother's responsibility to solve the problem.) I rationalized that as long as the abuse was stopped, I had done the best I could by LaTavia.

"I don't want to get kicked out of the group," she told me at her next lesson.

"You won't, LaTavia," I answered.

"I know our relationship is bad, but I love my mother. I don't want to lose her. Charles hasn't done it again."

Two years later he would, while I was singing in Cleveland. After learning from Beyoncé what happened, I called the police. I didn't care what Cheryl said. The police woman with whom I spoke told me that unless the victim "herself," came forward to "press charges," there would be nothing

430

that the police could do. Did they really expect a child to file a complaint? "Yes, we most certainly do," the police woman said. Before hanging up, she added "Or her mother can file for the victim." She didn't know me "from Adam," the police woman said. My accusation was being made against one of their own, and I was not the victim. I hung up the phone in angry frustration, and called Cheryl. She promised that she would "take care of it."

I felt like I was trapped in Hell. No doubt, LaTavia felt the same.

As I understand it, Texas still has no statute of limitations on what Charles Mitchell did. Yet he roams Houston, a free man.

20. Beyoncé's depression

Mathew remained cautious, rudely so. Both Berry and Roy pushed to talk percentage, but Mathew wasn't a fan of playing with others. Instead, he pushed Daryl harder to spring into action. Daryl still wasn't ready, to reveal the labels or to be pushed. Neither made Celestine happy. "I'm gon have to light a fire under Daryl's ass too," Mathew said. What was Beyoncé's father thinking, I wondered? Daryl alone had full and final deciding rights.

Through all my years with Mathew Knowles, I had countless opportunities to observe that he demanded from everyone a particularly unpleasant brand of worship: either you were with him or you were a threat, with no subtleties or nuances between those extremes. In addition to making Ann's life a living hell, accusing her of not keeping her word on just about everything, he'd even started banning his daughter Solange from the area of the house where group meetings took place. He claimed that Ann was not keeping up with her fiduciary duties and that Solange, well, her defiance disturbed him. I could see that Beyoncé wanted to speak out, but in each case she ultimately remained silent, retreating even deeper within herself.

* * * * *

"Ambivalence" is a psychological term that I discovered had its origins with Sigmund Freud, who taught that "Ambivalence was the foundation to understanding the simultaneous and debilitating presence of love and hate." Beyoncé's parents had become masters of the game. They despised one another, yet they came together in matters concerning the future, specifically, the future of their own desires. Two things became clear. Beyoncé would give the devil her very soul to save her parents' marriage, and two, they couldn't give a damn. Winning was so much more important than love. So, on Mondays, Celestine liked Mathew. On basketball Tuesdays, he was once again, "a piece of shit...," amongst other things.

Beyoncé heard every single horrible word her parents screamed at one another. Like many kids Beyoncé's age, she was naturally frightened by the thought that her parents might divorce and she assumed that she could prevent it by a perfect performance of her role: the good daughter. Girls love their fathers. Still, although she loved both her parents dearly, her mother's welfare ultimately became her overriding focus. Celestine was able to take advantage of Beyoncé, confusing her even further by whispered accusations and innuendos about Mathew.

Beyoncé continued to probe my thoughts. "Do you think that Mama and Daddy love each other?" she would ask. I would not break my cardinal rule about discussing Beyoncé's parents in an unflattering light.

"I can't answer that...," I answered.

A week later, after a long day of teaching I was saying goodbye to my last student at the front door when I suddenly heard a knock at the other door, the entrance to the alcove that connected my apartment with the family home. Had Beyoncé been eaves-dropping on that last lesson? Heading toward the alcove door, I called to her in Italian, "*Momento!* I'm coming, Beyoncé. Hold your horses," I called, rounding the corner. When I reached the door I saw that it was Mathew, not Beyoncé. What could he want? I opened the door and invited him in.

432

"Hey, David. How's it going?" Mathew asked, as he entered my apartment and took a seat.

"Oh, I'm making it all right. What can I do for you?" I closed the door.

"I have a proposition for you," Mathew said. I regarded him warily.

"I know that you want to get into the music business in a big way and that you have dreams of becoming a manager..." I didn't know where he was getting his information, but his opening gambit made me immediately suspicious. I had no delusions of show biz grandeur and I certainly did not imagine myself managing in the pop world. My goal, to be a successful opera singer, had nothing to do with that world. When I wasn't teaching and coaching other singers, I spent every waking moment working on my own craft and dreaming of opera, only opera. But, I heard Mathew out. I was interested in what he had to say. He had never been so solicitous with me before, and I was curious to know what he was up to this time.

My girls and their singing had begun to attract serious attention in the press and among admirers throughout Houston and the surrounding areas. Everyone who heard them celebrated "their sound." Now, at fourteen years of age, they were being produced by the Grammy Award-winning Daryl Simmons, of Boyz II Men and Toni Braxton fame. I took quiet consolation from their achievements thus far, even though I knew that Mathew had tried to deny my role in their successes. But what did that have to do with his "proposition"?

This boost in the girls' reputation had given Mathew a new cockiness – and unwarranted pride in himself. He had not discovered anyone and he certainly had never developed the girls artistically. Even though his "successes" were questionable, I can't begin to count the number of times I heard people say, "Those girls are going to make them all rich." He was already riding someone's coattails for his own profit.

Nevertheless, on the basis of Da Dolls' increasing fame, every man, woman, and child with a dream had begun to knock on his door seeking management. In the eyes of all those admiring hopefuls, Mathew felt like the king of show business. "You know I have begun taking on other groups and solo artists," he said. "Yes," I replied, noticing that Mathew was in one of his invincible moods today. I didn't know if it was the cocaine or the countless words of praise for Da Dolls that puffed his chest. Hopefuls were clamoring to be part of the Mathew Knowles winning team, flattering his ego beyond reason. Among these hopefuls was a group of boys (Adagio) who Mathew thought were the Second Coming. He took them on and began to rehearse them, but, in my opinion, to no avail. I had seen and heard them. The rehearsals were futile. I found the boys' attempts at singing almost embarrassing, and Mathew's attempts at developing their talent laughable. As I recall, only two of them had any voice at all.

My thoughts swam gratefully away from whatever Mathew was saying about his boys. Having taken on another spectacular duo boy group named "Second Verse," youngsters who had truer talent, I had no interest in hearing about Mathew's scraggly crew.

I preferred thinking about the girls, of whom I was so proud. Impressed by their fortitude, I respected them as young artists, and I had gained their respect for my years of teaching. We often knew what the other was thinking before words had even been spoken. Bonds like that fuel the teacher/student relationship. A great teacher has something to say and has many worthy and valuable experiences to share. It takes an equally talented student to master those intricate and time-consuming principles. Over the past months, particularly since discovering LaTavia's personal struggles, I had begun to understand the worth of my teaching. In supporting LaTavia, the girls and I had all grown....

These drifting thoughts came to an abrupt end when I tuned in once again to Mathew. He was continuing his "proposition" to me.

"I was wondering if you would have a listen to my boy group?" Mathew was saying. "They are really talented. I believe they could be the next Boyz II Men." Was Mathew dreaming? Stifling a laugh, I thought he must have taken leave of his senses. Then I remembered all the other people whom he had paraded in front of me. He thought they all had talent.

"OK, but what can I do for you?" I repeated.

"I want you to take my boys on and clean their sound up. Prepare them to be really great. You know how much I respect your work. Quite frankly, well, you are the best at what you do. Just the other day Teresa [Teresa LaBarbera-Whites] and I were discussing you. She thinks that you are great as well."

What's all this ego-stroking about? I wondered.

"Why, when Daryl Simmons said that the girls were sounding 'too classical,' I defended your position," Mathew said. He was losing me.

"I told him that I trusted you totally and that you were the best. If David said the girls' sound was not classical, then it wasn't. I sided with you. You know what you are talking about." Mathew paused and smiled, waiting for me to nibble at his bait.

"I am happy to share my empire with you," Mathew said proudly, while sliding his body forward in the chair, *in a state*. "I can offer you a 10% share of management of the boys. That's half of the 20% I normally get for management."

Still waiting in vain for a real reaction from me, Mathew continued, "The only thing is that I would have full deciding power."

Biting my tongue, I took a deep breath.

"Mathew, I appreciate your offer and am *truly* honored that you would consider sharing your empire with me. However, I'm afraid I don't agree with you about the boys. You know that as a voice teacher I try to support even the least-talented individual. So I can give your boys a few lessons. But in my opinion they don't have what it takes to become star performers."

Mathew's face changed. He did not like my response. "OK, you have a point, but that is why I am coming to you. If anyone can help them it is you," he said.

I could tell that Mathew was not going to give up trying to convince me. "OK, they have a bit of talent," they did. "Again, I appreciate your confidence, but I can't promise you they will be stars. I just can't." He lowered his eyes, clearly disappointed.

Then I said, "However, if you feel so strongly about these boys I will consider helping you if you give me a 2% share in Da Dolls. You can keep your 10% of the boys. I don't care about them. But I do care about my girls. I know they are star talents. I have invested my own blood, sweat, and tears in developing them, and they will change music. I'm sure of it."

As if coming out of a trance, Mathew raised his eyes slowly and refocused. I thought I was watching a slow-motion film. He stared at me.

"Never," Mathew said, through clenched teeth. "In a Million. Fucking. Years."

Had I heard correctly? I asked him to repeat himself and he did so, enunciating each word as if we had tuned into a program for the hard of hearing. Then he stood up and walked out of my apartment.

I was mortified. Just five minutes ago I was the greatest thing since the invention of peanut butter and bread and now I was not worth 2%. Well, wasn't that a kick in the ass?

The next day Celestine came to me to smooth things over. She was aware of Mathew's little ploy. She said that it had been her idea that he come to me. Celestine and I talked extensively, but I hadn't changed my mind. When I tried explaining myself to her, she said – disingenuously – that she understood my rationale.

I knew in that moment that my conversation with Mathew had changed everything for me. I could no longer ignore one hard cold fact: The Knowleses were trying to take advantage of me. I told Celestine exactly that. "On the contrary," she exclaimed. Celestine continued talking, attempting to pump my ego with the fervor of an evangelist. I tuned her out, no longer interested in dancing to her brand of faith.

Eventually the three of us got around to "letting bygones be bygones," even though I would never feel the same way again about my surrogate family. Mathew never apologized for the callous way he had spoken with me and although I agreed to forgive, I could not forget. No matter how hard I tried, I couldn't forget the awfulness of it all. Although it took me some time to realize it, Mathew's declamation "Never in a million fucking years" had cracked my resolve to ignore my own welfare in favor of that of the girls. He had pierced my strong exterior and gained the capacity to annihilate me.

For a long while, Mathew and I stayed clear of one another. At Celestine's behest, and to attempt a truce, I took his precious boys into my voice studio (with my 2% offer still on the table). For approximately two months I gave them some lessons. It didn't take them long to become unhappy with Mathew's management style, which they found crude and spiteful. Hoping for a sympathetic ear, they decided to talk to me. I was emphatic. "You must find a way to talk to him and express your concerns directly," I said, "or you will have to walk away from him and his management offer."

Soon Mathew was at my apartment again, banging on the door ferociously. Apparently the boys had taken my advice and had tried to talk things over with him. With predictable anger, he had rebuffed their attempts at an open discussion. Now he turned his venom on me, claiming that I was trying to break the relationship that he was building with the boys so that I could steal the group from him. "You are trying to turn my boys against me. Do it again and you will never teach Beyoncé again."

I took slow, deep breaths and turned my mind toward calming thoughts. Or at least I tried to. Incensed, I asked him to leave my apartment immediately. I reminded him that I had already explained to him that his boys were untalented. Since his demeaning attitude regarding the 2%, I had promised myself that I would never again ignore my feelings about him. "I would never try to ruin a working relationship between you and your clients. It is not my way, nor is it my business.

"And for the record, Beyoncé is not doing me any damn favor. Beyoncé ain't teaching me shit. Got that!?" He had never seen me react to him in this way. My strong defiance seemed to get a moment of grudging respect from him. But I wasn't looking for respect. I was looking for the damn doorknob, because if he didn't get out of my apartment I would not be able to control what I said or did next. And I hate to lose control. I slammed the door on his backside, almost breaking the glass.

Naturally, Celestine reached out. "How's my little brother doing?" she asked. Once again she'd called to clean up her husband's mess, apologizing.

"To tell you the truth, Celestine, it is my fault," I said.

"What do you mean?"

"Nothing changes, unless it changes," I said. It was simple. Mathew would never apologize and I would no longer forgive his rudeness. "It is I who will change, not Mathew. I can no longer accept your apologizing for a grown man."

With a nervousness in her voice and clinging to her role – one of her roles – as her husband's defender, Celestine replied, "You know Mathew, David."

And to that, I said, "Exactly. I most certainly do."

She abruptly changed the subject. "The air conditioner in the car went out yesterday," Celestine said, ever so gingerly. "Can I borrow your car? Or do you have time to take me to the fabric store tomorrow? We can go to lunch afterwards, on me."

"If I don't have to substitute teach tomorrow, sure," I answered. (I had recently put myself on the "sub list" for local public high school classes.) "We can get an early start on the day," I concluded, ending the call. Then I had a row with Mathew's donkey surrogate.

* * * * *

I slept brilliantly after my Sunday night tussle with Donkey Mathew over the real Mathew's biting "Never in a million fucking years." Celestine's attempts to calm me, even after she admitted that it had been her idea that Mathew talk to me, had failed miserably. I didn't care who said what to whom; Mathew's bad behavior was inexcusable.

Indeed, I wasn't called the next morning, so with a freed-up Monday, I called Celestine. I could see from my window that she'd begun her morning meditation, reading the Bible in the family room. She'd been reading the Good Book like an evangelist as of late. Something was bothering her, I thought.

438

"Good morning Celestine," I said. "I don't have to teach today, so we can leave at about 9:30 a.m., if that's good for you.

"Yes, wonderful," she answered.

"Are you OK?" I asked.

"Yes, why do you ask?"

"You don't sound like yourself, that's all." I told her that I'd be over after I had some breakfast.

"Great." Celestine said. "I'll be waiting…"

After putting the breakfast dishes in the sink, I headed over to the main house, through Beyoncé's bedroom. I heard her singing. Why wasn't she in school, I wondered? "Oh my God," I thought. "Not that damn tape again."

I made my way down the semi-spiraled staircase, dreading the scene that was about to take place. Celestine intended to remind me of her position. My skin began to crawl. Whenever Mama Celestine felt that I was getting too big for my britches, she pulled out tapes of the seven-year-old Beyoncé shouting out "Home," from *The Wiz*, you know the one. It was her first audition piece for me. With each viewing, Celestine's *point* was to remind me how blessed I was to have met Beyoncé, and not the other way around.

Trying to keep things light, I said, "You're in a reminiscing mood today."

"Oh, David. It's you," she said, as though I'd startled her. Then drawing my attention to the video, she said "Isn't she just awesome?"

"Even more so now, after learning *how* to sing."

Ignoring my sarcasm, Celestine asked if I was ready to go. "Where would you like to go for lunch today?"

"Wendy's."

"Did you say Wendy's?" she asked.

"Yep, Wendy's," I answered. "Got a taste for a Frosty©."

The conversation to and from the fabric store was pleasant enough. Celestine was in one of her "everything's wonderful" moods. You know the one, so happy it hurts – phony as hell, and riding my last nerve. Well, at least she's consistent, I thought. She's paving the road toward a bumpy detour.

I'd awakened consecrated. I didn't want to fight, argue, or even disagree. I hated the back-biting, the unnecessary wielding of her "I'm Beyoncé's mother" power. It was so unnecessary. Beyond my annoyance, I was a little embarrassed on Celestine's behalf. No one would ever pay attention to Beyoncé because of her mother; she would always capture an audience with the radiance of her voice. We'd been down this road, but Celestine never gave up trying. I'd never change my mind. I knew my worth and I refused to give up the peace I felt on that Monday morning, not even for my "big sister" Celestine. I meant every syllable of the "Fuck Mathew" I'd yelled at her the night before.

Several hours later, we pulled into Wendy's on Cullen Street. While standing in line, and from out of nowhere, Celestine said, "Don't be so modest!"

"What's that, Celestine?"

"Don't be so modest," she repeated.

"What do you mean?" I knew exactly where she was headed, and I wasn't up for it. "Ah, Celestine, let's just enjoy our lunch. We've had such a nice morning." But Celestine was on a mission. It was in her eyes.

"If you want me to apologize for throwing Mathew out of my apartment, you'll be waiting forever," I said. Even their threats to remove Beyoncé from my life had stopped affecting me.

Going from the counter to the table, and sitting together with our food, Celestine barely paused for breath, delivering a long and monotonous soliloquy about Beyoncé's talent.

Finally, I held up my finger. Pointing to my already nearly empty Wendy's Frosty cup, I begged her indulgence, mouthing "I'll be right back." And then said, "Please hold that thought."

When I returned to the table, and before my butt could hit the seat, Celestine came out with it. "If anybody knows how blessed Beyoncé is, it's you."

"True," I said, easing myself into the chair. "What's your point?" Damn, I thought, Let's just get to it. I wanted to hear her say "it" out loud.

"David, you're being arrogant again," she said.

Chuckling, I answered, "And again: No, I'm not." I hated it when Celestine called me names. Every time I didn't act or think the way she wanted, she would haul out the same tired *go-to* words, calculated to deflate me. When she wasn't branding me "arrogant," I was "bourgeois." Her tiresome name-calling had finally pierced my armor.

By now, the end of 1994, I was determined to speak truth – not *my* truth but *the* truth. Honesty was hard for the Knowleses to take, especially my new brand of in-your-face honesty.

"Celestine, we are family. Why must we beat around the bush?" I said. "What's going on with you?"

Staring me down like a police chief, Celestine said, "Beyoncé is very gifted." Pause for effect. "She has *always* been gifted."

"I'm sure that you believe that, Celestine." She looked at me expectantly as I continued, "Most gifted children will remain gifted, but very few will become genius. Beyoncé will."

Celestine's face darkened, her gaze narrowing to a steely stare. The conversation wasn't going according to her plan.

The handling, however, was going perfectly for me. It had revealed her true purpose. It was turning out that she intended our little pow-wow to corral me about what I'd said to Mathew, just a day earlier: "And for the record, Beyoncé is not doing me any damn favor. Beyoncé is not teaching me a damn thing..." Celestine's invitation to lunch was about putting things into the *proper* perspective, and by clever cajoling, she intended to correct me and my *arrogance* – again.

Taking a different tack, I said, "You are absolutely right, Celestine. Any teacher would be honored to teach the likes of Beyoncé. She is so respectful, never rude. And she and I have always been on the same page." I took a last sip of my Frosty, while Celestine glowered. "So why the brow-beating?

"You see, Celestine, there are many children, even in that People's workshop video, who are undoubtedly just as talented..."

Interrupting me, Celestine blurted, "Yes, but they weren't special."

In the most cynical voice I could muster, I said, "Ah! Right!! – Thanks for clearing that up." Looking for an end to this unpleasant conversation, I said, "Celestine, I have always wanted to ask you something."

"What's that, David?"

"Why didn't you and Mathew notice Beyoncé's gift – I mean before Ms. Darlette's observation of it?" I asked.

"We did. I noticed that Beyoncé was special at birth."

"Yes, you've intimated that, but I'm not talking about your average 'my baby is the best' belief. I'm talking about real action. Why had it taken a talent show to realize Beyoncé's talent, to say nothing of her prodigious qualities?"

Celestine started to respond.

Interrupting, I continued. "I think it's because you and Mathew, like other parents do, saw Beyoncé's 'singing around the house' as child's play – cute, as a matter of fact. No offense intended, Celestine."

I'd hit a nerve, or so her behavior felt to me. Celestine stood up, excusing herself to the ladies room. Her eyes screamed that she could no longer suffer my defiance. When she returned, I picked up where I'd left off, unabashed and definitely unapologetic. "Celestine, can we stop with the manipulation. You know I adore Beyoncé. Yes, she's gifted, but so are a lot of people. Why, the black church is full of gifted children – who, by the way, will never become genius in their craft."

"What's your *point*?"

"My *point* is: Please show a little respect. Beyoncé has been blessed with a rare and extraordinary opportunity, one that is to my knowledge, not commonplace."

"Oh, really. And what's that?" Celestine asked, rolling her eyes.

"God's placing a competent teacher in her house," I said to her. Celestine stared at me, stiff-lipped.

"I know you'd like to think that my moving into your house was your doing, but none of this is you," I said. "And it's not me, either." Continuing the tone of the conversation on a more spiritual plane, I asked Celestine to imagine what her own life might have been had God granted her the luxury of having, say, a young Gianni Versace as her mentor. "Can you imagine, Celestine, if he had lived in your house when you were eight years old, and you had had access to him 24/7?"

"What, so now you're comparing yourself to Versace?" she said with the most patronizing tone.

"No, the world will do that, just as soon as Beyoncé opens up her mouth and unleashes what I've taught her. I am just getting started. And believe me, my work will be heard on radios all over the world." Silence. "Now, that – *was arrogance*," I said.

Celestine wanted my head on a silver platter. I could feel it. She neither acknowledged my reference to her thwarted ambitions to become a fashion designer, nor did she offer a witty comeback. She simply continued to pierce the air between us with a cold, black, emotionless stare. Then, suddenly, just when I thought she'd given up, she let loose a penetrating insult.

"Beyoncé is great," she began. "I know you want to be an opera singer, David, but do you really think you have the talent for it? I mean, *you're such a great teacher.*"

Ignoring her obtuse remarks, I went on. "Singing is subjective, Celestine. Uninformed fans are always ready with an opinion. Beyoncé certainly is smart enough to guard against this by concentrating solely on her singing, which is becoming nothing short of spectacular with every inhalation of air. And that fact, my dear Celestine, keeps me in your house." The fact that the woman hadn't paid me a dime in two years could have substantiated my commitment to teaching Beyoncé – and the other girls. But wanting to avoid further controversy, I left that topic alone.

"Oh, my – have I upset you?" Celestine asked.

"No, not at all. We're family. We're just talking, brother to sister and vice versa, right?"

"Right," she answered.

And with that, Celestine's little drama died a quick death, along with her sugar-sweet nice nastiness. She'd had her say, and I had made my point. Now she knew. I wasn't going to be handled by anyone – anymore. Still, I could expect retaliation. You always could with Beyoncé's mama.

I finished off the last bites of my burger, and then Celestine and I headed for the car. We still had to take fabric to Selena's.

"It's such a beautiful day isn't it," Celestine said.

"Yes, it is."

In typical Celestine fashion, she'd come, thrown her rocks, and was now ready to move on, as if the last hour hadn't happened.

* * * * *

Confessing the escalating internal conflict between Mathew and me, Celestine sought allies in the other mothers. Cheryl and Pam needed to fall into formation, Celestine suggested. Doris gave her support over the phone. "We need to protect our assets," Celestine said, betraying her *true concern*: the girls' – her – financial success. "As women, we have to stick together," Celestine told her manipulated followers. Both Cheryl and Pam agreed.

I asked Pam what she thought Celestine's motive was.

"You! I think she was talking about you."

"Interesting," I answered.

Pam suggested that Celestine had gone a bit further in her explanation. I remember her saying to me that Celestine warned that even though Mathew and David weren't getting along, "We need David."

"Strange indeed," I said, recalling our Wendy's conversation.

Everybody, especially Celestine, knew that Pam and I had developed a friendship.

"You and Pam sure are getting close," Celestine said.

"Yes, we are. She's nice," I answered.

444

"Yes, she is," Celestine said, with just a hint of sarcasm.

Pam and I had spent serious amounts of time strategizing in order to lessen her daughter's suffering. Our primary concern was LeToya's health, regardless of whether or not Mathew would make good on his threat to dismiss her from the group. That common goal brought us together.

As Celestine had guessed, my attitude had more than changed. Hearing words like "Never in a million fucking years" does something to a person. That affected me deeply, and not in a good way. I was an *asset* – apparently, a valuable one, but I already knew this. However, in Mathew's mind I should remain a liability, and with good reason.

From a layman's point of view, asset and liability are easy to understand. I, however, had to be absolutely sure of my suspicions. Wondering how people in business understood the concept, I took out my Webster's dictionary, looking up the words for a more concise definition. I read that an asset provides a future economic benefit, while liabilities present future obligation.

I got it. Mathew didn't plan on including me in the profits. He owed me nothing, he said, and more importantly, I owed him nothing. Not even my hand in friendship. However, Daryl's attentions, ironically, made my job more difficult. Mathew and Celestine both resented Kelly's improving self-image, and even more, they continued to resent Daryl's admiration for her talents.

As I worked to vitalize her ego, Beyoncé suddenly developed a problem with how Kelly was singing. Never harsh in the beginning, she was calculating. I will never forget Beyoncé asking her father right out why he always picked on Kelly, right in front of the other girls.

"She's weak," Mathew answered.

I was stunned, but not totally surprised. Mathew had yelled the same harsh accusation at Beyoncé, in jest. Weak! Mathew hated weak. But Beyoncé remained disconnected, a mental state compounded by her mother's chiding Kelly about her getting too close to Daryl. I told Beyoncé the truth. "Your mother sees Kelly as a threat to your rising star," I said.

Shocked, Beyoncé said, "But we are all different."

What else could she say? She hadn't expected that I would side with Kelly. I couldn't have said it better.

"Exactly," I answered. "And each of you is sublimely talented too..."

My intent was clear.

* * * * *

By September each new day on Parkwood Street gave a real and ever changing face to fear, self-worth, pride, and vulnerability. Although I found it difficult to ignore the parental power struggles, Beyoncé, the group, and my sanity depended upon it. Psychological factors can break or make the prodigy. I was opting for the latter, keeping in mind that my relationships with my "actual students" were most important. The child prodigy will remain a mere talent without consistent and competent guidance, this is a fact. Beyoncé and I had a wonderful relationship, but it was always clear: her parents were raising her, her parents were forming her character. I was familiar with the fight for power between a positive teaching influence and the parent, but Mathew Knowles's pathology – and now Celestine's – had intensified.

When Ann Owens had called again, it was to leave a message of inquiry. Why hadn't I mailed my signed contract? Calling her back, I told her that I intended to participate in the production. "I just need to figure out how to honor my previous commitments." She agreed to give me another few days.

"We really want you for the production," Ann concluded.

"Thank you, Ann, for your patience." I promised to get back to her with the contract before the end of the month.

The next evening, Mathew scheduled a Dolls group meeting and requested my presence. The parents, the girls, and I assembled in the Knowles house. He didn't beat around the bush. "Ann and me *[sic]* have discussed the breakdown...," he said.

Pam interrupted. "Breakdown?"

446

"I'm coming to that," Mathew said.

He went on to explain that after consulting with *industry professionals*, namely his lawyer Kenneth Hertz and the mysterious Ruth Carson, "I have made a decision regarding the group's future financial distributions." Mathew said that he had worked out a fair breakdown of *his* fiduciary duty to the girls, as follows: Beyoncé Giselle Knowles (45%), Kelendria Trené Rowland (25%), LeToya Nicole Luckett (15%), and LaTavia Marie Roberson (15%).

I let loose an audible gasp. No one else so much as moved.

Staring me down, Mathew boasted that those "industry professionals" agreed with him, that since Beyoncé was the leader of the group and because she was the one who did the most work (at this, I had to suppress my urge to scream), she should get the most return. Who knows if anyone, including Kenneth Hertz (hired as the girls' attorney), ever made such a ridiculous statement? It was and is common-place in the industry that bands agree to an even split. There are exceptions to that norm, but nonetheless, it is the norm. Although no one was privy to the supposed conversation between Mathew and these "industry professionals," I did remember Mathew's pattern of hiding his own nefarious ideas under the cover of the reputations and titles of real (or imaginary) professionals.

Still no one said a word. Not even a sense of right and fairness made an appearance in answer to this ridiculous percentage/split. I didn't know if Pam and Cheryl were in shock, or if they had not heard Mathew correctly. I searched their faces to find any traces of surprise, anger, or even frustration, but discerned nothing. There was not one wrinkle in their expressions. Wow, I thought. Did they understand what Mathew's audacious proposal meant? I certainly did. It meant that LeToya, LaTavia, and Kelly were Beyoncé's background singers. They would never be treated fairly and they would never be equal. Life was about to become impossible in this group. At that moment, I easily predicted doom. The meeting broke up without further discussion. The next day, I turned to Celestine for answers, but then found out that fiduciary duties toward the group were the least of their worries. She had bigger fish to fry.

For months now, Celestine had been somewhat off., and for the past two weeks she'd been acting even stranger than Mathew. Re-intensifying her demands that Mathew get a job reaped no immediate response. I'd never seen her so desperate, not even while squirming her way out of the stealing electricity from HL&P fiasco.

Mathew had, in fact, gone out and gotten a job, this time with a company called Phillips Medical Systems. It lasted, as I recall, a very short time, maybe a month or two, at an even more considerable decrease in salary. His new sales position took him somewhere just outside the city of Houston, Mathew said. The highlight of his employment with Phillips Medical was the company car he got (a copper-colored Ford Tempo), which delighted him. He had grown weary of sharing the only car in the family (a Chrysler that was constantly breaking down, and not the Jaguar that Beyoncé re-members her father driving). It appeared that Mathew was making an effort, and I actually gained a bit of respect for him because of it. His family need-ed him and he'd stepped up to the plate with this new behavior.

I was, however, just as surprised that in the end, Celestine wasn't near-ly as hopeful as I was about Mathew's "right on time" new job. "It's too late," she said to me. They'd had to file bankruptcy for the second or third time – I'd lost track – and there was still the yet-to-be-resolved 1990 fed-eral tax lien. Already, the second such threat had been delivered in the mail, with an even bigger tax payment that threatened to choke the life out of Celestine's family.

My bit of respect for Mathew lasted but an eye-blink moment. No sooner had we heard that he'd been hired, we heard that he'd been fired. He said he'd left the job, quitting because it was *beneath him*. Neverthe-less, this unfortunate turn of events, which I expected to raise Celestine's blood pressure, instead caused her to walk around the house and through her days, perpetually numb.

Celestine called Ann, their faithful rescuer in time of need. Having barely survived her own bankruptcy, Ann maintained that she could no longer help the Knowleses out of their major debt. Increasing medical care costs, severe vascular problems, and other concerns that resulted from her

448

newly diagnosed club foot and old edema concerns left her no wriggle room, spiritually or financially. She explained to Celestine that she must now protect her own scant funds with a fierce focus. Ann finally had to admit that although she had deep compassion for Celestine's plight, she hadn't caused the Knowleses' problems, and she was in no position to rescue them. As Ann was explaining these things, Celestine's face drooped. Whatever were they talking about, I wondered? At the end of that early morning kitchen conversation, Celestine said wanly, "I understand," while in her face I read raw anger.

A few days later – it was after Mathew's quitting, or firing – I entered the main house to find myself in the midst of another, familiar domestic drama. Celestine was standing in the middle of the kitchen crying uncontrollably and calling him every kind of mother-fucker, while Mathew, unmoved by Celestine's passion, sheltered himself in the breakfast nook, high and lordly – definitely high. As it turned out, Celestine's tirade wasn't misplaced this time. Not only did she accuse Mathew of taking money from the family business, this time to buy that Ford Tempo from the company when he'd left, but she also held in her hand a devastating letter.

Because she had not paid the agreed upon monthly IRS payments, in over a year, she told me, the government agency was moving to seize their home. Eviction. In 48 hours.

Shit.

Having fought the good fight, Celestine was now being forced to accept her fate. She was losing the love of her life, her house, and with it all the appearance of prestige and wealth its walls had afforded her. In a quick glance I took in her fear and suddenly understood every cut of Celestine's eye, every slant of her mouth I'd witnessed over the past months. Now all that was left to do was to pack up the house, their memories and their possessions, and work out a good story. Her children's lives and futures were at stake, she said.

Suddenly, standing before me, she turned off the tears and turned on the smiles – just like that – she was *happy*, so happy it hurts. She was desperate as hell, but sticking to it. As the world continued to turn, I knew that I'd have no problem adjusting. I wasn't so sure about Celestine's psyche. Hers looked like a nervous breakdown waiting to happen.

That evening, Celestine came back to my apartment and explained the situation fully. She did not want her girls to know just how bad things were and she swore me to secrecy again. She was always swearing me to some sort of secrecy. This time the lie felt particularly wrong – not to mention I was beginning to feel irritation that she'd gambled with all our lives and existence. Although her protesting had become sort of a broken record, I promised her that I would keep her secret. I felt as though I'd been hit over the head with a baseball bat.

Just before going to bed, I turned to Romans 14:23. I read: "But whoever has doubts is condemned if he eats, because the eating is not from faith; and everything that does not come from faith is sin." Plainly put, if I believed that something I was doing wasn't right and I did it anyway, I was sinning. Mathew Knowles was not of faith. His wife's tongue was that of a serpent. The next day, after service at St. James Episcopal Church, I asked Father Tucker with help interpreting the confusing scripture. He assured me that my battles with the Knowleses, and in particular Mathew, were not synonymous with the Romans 14:23 interpretation of sin. "Rather, your problem sounds like pride to me," Father Tucker concluded. Suddenly, the light bulb went on. He was right. In that instance it became clear, flooding in like a tsunami over me. Mathew's "Never in a million fucking years" had bruised my pride and ego. Both were repairable.

I let my anger go. Eviction was a bumpy enough ride.

* * * * *

I felt compelled to care about Celestine's family and financial problems. I hadn't created them, not a one. Yet I was almost religiously devoted to that family. It felt like worship, like I was boxed into a corner. Celestine had stolen electricity, cable, souls, and even my joy, she had clung to anything that might help her escape feelings of shame, and I remained helplessly devoted to her. I felt anger and I chastised myself for feeling it. Why hadn't she reached out to me, I asked myself? I certainly could have helped – paid even more rent – loaned her more money. My bank account was full and I had no dependents.

The next morning, I awakened with a heavy heart. Once again, I returned to the kitchen with an envelope. When I walked back in, with my contribution in hand, Celestine was on the phone with Ann. She'd also reconsidered, and like me, she was offering help, even though she could not afford it. Neither of us was *prepared* to pay the overwhelming debt that Celestine and Mathew had racked up. It was all proving to be too much for her: troubles with her salon's landlord, David Gibbs, regarding back rents; the shame of getting caught at poaching electricity and barely escaping jail; Mathew's stealing money from the family business; inability to pay herself a full salary; and now the threat of indeed a second tax lien. Still, the most we were willing to do was help with moving costs, put some money in Celestine's pocket, and help shore up back salon rents, which again had become steep. In addition, Ann promised her the money for the first and last month's rent on a new place to live.

I found myself deep in thought, about everything. When, and what, would Celestine tell her children, I wondered? They would surely ask a million questions. It seemed the cost of Celestine's love for silence had finally caught up to her. Although they *still* didn't know of their father's serious drug addiction, Beyoncé and Solange now had to live with the consequences of their father's dilatory behavior. How would Celestine explain all that?

Later that evening, I expressed my concerns to Celestine. By way of reply, she told me of her plan. She would sell the house in time to beat the IRS deadlines. (The final threat had finally arrived in the post.)

"Celestine, do you really think that you can sell this house in 48 hours? It is next to impossible. The closing process alone can take weeks."

"I have to trust that God will make a way," she said. She also said that when she sold the house – "and I will" – she would "secure your place in the deal. It is not fair that you would have to move due to our problems," she

451

said. I assured her that such thinking couldn't have been further my mind. Emotionally invested, I was concerned only about her and the children.

For the next two days Celestine did not sleep, nor did she go to the salon. She focused on selling that house. Which she accomplished. By the eleventh hour, she had not only found a buyer, but she had closed the deal.

With only minutes to spare, Celestine and the buyer had signed the contracts. The house now belonged to a man named Steven Williams (I believe I remember the name correctly). He was a youngish and upwardly mobile black developer who had been buying up many of the properties in and around the neighborhood. He would acquire the houses, restore them or partially re-construct them, and then re-sell them, and always at a significant profit.

I asked Celestine how she had managed to pull it off. "I gave him the house," she said. She explained that she had taken a huge loss, to the tune of thousands of dollars, in order to close the deal under the deadline and salvage what was left of her credit history. It was a noble thought, but improbable, I thought.

"I have two girls to think about. If music doesn't work out for Beyoncé, I need to make sure she can go to college," Celestine told me. Beyoncé was now fourteen and a half, and would be ready for college in four to five years. I was sympathetic, but Celestine's thinking was unrealistic. None of us is above having to file bankruptcy, but the black mark on the family credit would last at least seven years and possibly longer, that is, if the creditor chose to re-issue the debt, starting the seven-year process all over again.

"I'm sure that all will turn out to plan," I said. "Beyoncé has a bright future. No worries there. Just concentrate on the right now."

Celestine started to cry. She continued to lose in selling that house, not even earning enough from the equity to rid herself of the IRS threat, she said. She hadn't paid enough into it to get anything out. A dark cloud loomed overhead, and I fought within myself to find some sense in it all. It was obvious that Celestine was stuck in that self-protecting space called denial.

452

A friend was what she needed. She sat, broke and angry, while Mathew continued to party. She was desperate for support. She talked. I listened. She cried some more. I understood.

Celestine's sense of defeat was palpable. When Doris called to offer her sympathy, Celestine could barely muster up enough humility to thank her. "I appreciate your call," Celestine said, through clenched teeth, and then slammed the phone down. It's hard to fathom, even today, just how quickly Celestine's smile and sweet disposition could turn to absolute and unbridled anger. When she had collected herself after Doris's perceived "insult," she turned to me. She said, with pride, "I have secured your place. The new owner promised that you do not have to move."

I couldn't bear to burst her bubble, not after the exchange I'd just witnessed between her and Doris. Celestine hadn't saved me from anything. She didn't know that the new owner had already stopped by the apartment. I'd be able to stay in my place above the garage, he'd said, but only as long as it took him to do the renovations to the main house, an estimated period of six months. After that, he said, they would begin work on the garage apartment, and then I would have to vacate the premises.

Celestine got back home late, around 11 p.m., and we talked in the Knowles family room. I remember having put her girls to bed around 8:45 p.m. By 12:45 a.m., Mathew walked through the front door. He entered the family room, walking right past us with neither a glance nor a word. After retrieving what he'd come home to get, he turned to leave. Before he could disappear from the room Celestine said to him, "Mathew, I sold the house today." Without turning, Mathew said, "Have you found another one?" Celestine burst into tears, and Mathew took his exit.

I'd never seen the likes of their dysfunction.

Exhausted, Celestine and I called it a night. She disappeared into her bedroom and I headed to my apartment. On the way, I passed Solange's room and noticed a very awake Beyoncé, whose expression broke my heart. She'd heard every word. The next three days, she didn't eat, drink, nor go to school. She stayed right there in that bed.

Beyoncé was depressed.

21. Goodbye Parkwood

Hard times had forced Celestine to sacrifice her pride, and even her integrity. She was in a bad way. I had urged her to accept my offer of financial help, my chief concern being Beyoncé and Solange's school tuitions. Again, I could afford it, and we were *family*. However, I did not have the kind of money that she needed to salvage the mortgage on their home.

As their eviction became reality, Celestine and I drove over to a few properties she was thinking of renting. One she'd found, a mid-sized but spacious home, had a small pool in the backyard.

"Beyoncé would be so happy here," Celestine said.

"Yes, she would," I agreed. "We know how she loves swimming."

In the end, Celestine sensibly chose the least expensive of the three houses we looked at. Beyoncé and Solange dealt with their new reality in different ways: Beyoncé remained selflessly devoted to her mother, always the good daughter, and Solange was mad as hell. Beyoncé, as expected, blamed herself, and I observed that Solange was in total agreement with her. The family's financial predicament was indeed Beyoncé's fault. Everything was her sister's fault. Hers, and her "damn group."

Mathew remained vehement in his effort to set LeToya and her mother straight. Having commandeered the group for occasional rehearsals, he had become increasingly Joe-Jackson-like – without Joe Jackson's musical acumen. Now he decided to teach the Lucketts a lesson they'd not forget – ostensibly because LeToya had come late to *his* rehearsal. Personally, I was amazed that he had managed to show up at all and, for a change, on time. I was on hand as he began his "rehearsal" with the three other girls.

"I'm sorry we're late," Pam said as she and her daughter rushed in. "LeToya had an asthma attack and I had to take her to the doctor."

"Oh my," I said, genuinely alarmed.

Mathew said nothing. Annoyed, he continued shouting orders at the girls.

In the kitchen two days later, Mathew, Celestine, and I talked about the incident. It was late, the children were asleep, and he ranted on, calling

Pam "a bitch," comparing her to "that bitch Carolyn Davis." I remember thinking that someday, somebody was going to whip Mathew's ass for that kind of talk. He stormed out of the house, slamming the door behind him.

"Celestine, neither Pam nor Carolyn is a bitch," I said. Celestine had no response, tacitly acceding to her husband's crude assessment.

Mathew and Pam could have spoken the same language, the same business jargon, but they didn't. Pam's degree in accounting, as well as her knowledge of economics and standard business practices, were the real beam pole in Mathew's eye. It was obvious to me that Mathew had missed many a class session in his business education. How embarrassing for him, her intellect must have been. She never said a word to Mathew's surprising and unorthodox business tactics. Pam had learned to expect his unethical ways, but she couldn't hide her baffled look. None of us could. Her steady gaze said *idiot*. Mathew recognized that look, and in response his blood pressure would skyrocket. I remember his eyes. They'd go dark.

Over the next weeks, apparently in response to Celestine's intervention, I got a call from Pam. Always articulate and clear-headed, Pam said to me now – gently, but matter-of-factly, "I don't trust Mathew around my daughter. Now he wants to adopt LeToya."

"Excuse me?" I said.

"You didn't know?"

"I didn't," I answered.

Pam went on to tell me that Mathew had called her with some nonsense about becoming the legal guardian – of all the girls.

"It's true. Mathew believes his lunacy. He says that things would be much easier if he was in control, without having to answer to us, to the parents."

"He said that?"

"Yes, those exact words."

"That's crazy," I said.

"It's ludicrous," Pam replied.

Of course Pam fought Mathew on the "legal guardian" issue. He actually had had papers drawn up. *Was* he crazy?

I called Celestine. "No worries," she said. "None of the girls' parents have agreed to the idea." Thank God, I thought. Someone has some sense. Then I heard from Celestine that Doris had actually considered it.

Pam, of course, was dead set against it and said so. "I just can't agree to that. I won't agree to that. For the life of me, I can't see what the problem is for me to bring LeToya to rehearsal and pick her up afterwards. She needs to be at home. Mathew can call me over-protective all he wants, but I will not turn my daughter over to someone else. She is my responsibility."

Mathew chose not to respond to Pam's unequivocal "No!" – not just yet, anyway. I was sure he would be plotting another round. Pam's argument, for me, was built firmly on the unshakable logic of a mature, sane mother. Mathew called Pam's "motherly logic" disrespectful. Celestine called it arrogance. The next time I spoke with Donkey Mathew and Witch Celestine, I called them both damn fools.

* * * * *

It had become increasingly difficult to quell the rumors surrounding Mathew's extracurricular activities. The latest word was that he'd started to do *anything* for a fix. Was he escalating? The implications were too much for Celestine to bear and, although shamed beyond all understanding, she defended her husband's honor (I use the term loosely). She clung to her fictions within the household, and remained overtly happy – so happy it hurt, and at the same time careful as hell. Beyoncé believed her mother's every explanation, whereas Solange would hang her head, listen carefully, pull her mouth back into a smile, and say, "Sure, Mama. Whatever you say." I loved that child.

Robert Greene, in his book *The 48 Laws of Power*, has pointed out that throughout history, a court has always formed itself around the person in power – king, queen, emperor, leader. "Violent and overt power moves were frowned upon," Greene adds. "Instead of using coercion or outright

456

treachery, the perfect courtier got his way through seduction, charm, deception, and subtle strategy, always planning several moves ahead." I saw that life in the Knowles court was, in Greene's words, "a never-ending game, requiring constant vigilance and tactical thinking."

* * * * *

Seduction, charm, and deception had heretofore worked for Celestine, but by now she had become perpetually angry. She'd not likely get over losing her house any time soon, which intensified her focus on Beyoncé's career, and the threat to her own future fame. The successes of the *group* meant relatively little to her. I settled in and just rode her unpredictable waves.

One day Mathew announced to me and Beyoncé that Doris had moved away from Houston. "She took that job in Atlanta," he said.

"Where's Kelly?" I asked.

"At Ann's."

Thank God, I thought. Ann had convinced Doris to leave Kelly in her care. Ann's boys, Armon and Chris, treated Kelly like a blood sister. Nevertheless, Celestine chose to butt in. "Go and bring Kelly to me," she said to Mathew. Every fiber of my body lit up. I said, "Now is not the right time, Celestine. Kelly needs time to process, and you guys just got settled into the new house on Braes Meadow Drive." Sure that Kelly was wrestling with feelings of abandonment, I added, "I think Ann's house is the best place for her right now."

Celestine insisted.

I was completely dismayed by Celestine's attitude toward Kelly over the years. She'd had her chance to help Kelly. All those times I had asked her to consider taking Kelly in, she had refused. "I don't want to get in the middle of it," she would say. Now, she proclaimed that she was only thinking about Kelly's "welfare." Both her rhetoric and her reasoning felt disingenuous. Kelly's welfare? I didn't believe a word of it.

When Ann learned of Mama Celestine's intention, she put up one hell of a fight. I rejoiced, but ultimately Celestine was able to convince Doris that it was not wise for Kelly to be around "all them boys," and the decision came down: Kelly would live with the Knowleses. Yes, Ann still had power, but no one *feared her*.

In spite of Kelly's long-held, envious feelings about Beyoncé's wonderful environment, now that she was going to be living in it, she began to have misgivings. It was one thing to be over at the Knowleses' house all the time for rehearsals, but now Kelly would have to depend on them solely for her every need. Being beholden is a form of extreme psychological anxiety. She was afraid to take a glass of water in the Knowles house unless someone else was having one. She ate only when the family ate and she didn't dare go into the refrigerator without asking. Mathew's unpleasantness in rehearsals escalated tenfold, which felt to me as though he wanted specifically to break Kelly's spirit. He said that he was "just toughening her up," since, in his flawed opinion, she was the weakest member of the group – another of Beyoncé's father's spectacular delusions.

I realized that fighting with the Knowleses had become the central dilemma of my life. Mathew's overtly abusive language and Celestine's covert manipulations were wearing me down. If I would attempt to shield the girls, or deflect Mathew's criticism of them, he would respond with "I know what's best," or "Stay out of my damn business." I would respond, "You mean OUR business?" which might silence Mathew for the time being. He'd back off the girls for a bit, and then it would start all over again. Those verbal wrestling matches were draining, since every time Mathew went after one of the girls verbally, I had to reinforce my protective safety net.

Beyoncé knew that her parents lied to her continually, and that they regularly perpetrated "small" deceptions by excluding her from the knowledge of their actions. People called Mathew and Celestine "unkind" right to her face. And even though Beyoncé hadn't crossed over to blind loyalty, she coped with the pressures of her parents' fighting, and their negative opinions, by dissociating, which would become a worrisome habit. I knew that she had a clean soul, but having been left in the dark for so long, Beyoncé was developing a type of sensory deprivation. If she could see no evil, then there was no evil. The other girls, however, were *seeing* very clearly.

* * * * *

To the casual observer, the Knowleses' manipulations might have appeared harmless, so masterfully did they disguise them. However, both Celestine and Mathew had upped the ante. Their methods were symptoms of an obsessive greed. Within the family, these machinations were having increasingly detrimental effects on their daughters. I continued to worry about Solange.

Solange began to complain about everything Beyoncé. Not too long after the move from Parkwood Street to Braesmeadow, Solange – out of spite – even got Beyoncé's boyfriend, Lyndall, banned from the house.

On a Sunday evening, I had been teaching and rehearsing the girls in their new home. Lyndall had come over to the house to visit after the rehearsal. He and Beyoncé were in Beyoncé's room watching television. As Celestine and I visited in the kitchen/den area, we were interrupted by what sounded like a loud thump and screaming. The noise was coming from upstairs, so we headed in that direction. Suddenly, Lyndall scurried past us, Mathew hot on his trail.

Beyoncé came running downstairs behind her father, screaming and crying. She didn't understand his behavior. As Celestine comforted her, it came out that Solange had told her father that Beyoncé and her boyfriend had been upstairs kissing. (Beyoncé had done something or other to upset Solange and now Solange was getting her revenge.) Beyoncé swore that she had done nothing wrong. It was clear to me that Solange was seeking attention by any means necessary. Celestine must have thought the same thing, because she insisted that Solange confess the truth, which she did. Solange had indeed lied, but the damage had been done.

It was at this point that Beyoncé realized that a boyfriend would be out of the question. Mathew forbade boyfriends from that day on. "You can't find success and have a boyfriend too," he declared. Celestine, however, said otherwise. She won that argument.

Inevitably, the waters again muddied.

Not so long after the great Lyndall chase, Pam had arrived to fetch LeToya from what had been a brilliant rehearsal. I heard Kelly call out, "LeToya, your savior is here," as she walked away from the front door of the Knowles home. She left Pam standing in the doorway. I hadn't seen that coming, not at all.

Apparently, no one, especially Beyoncé and LaTavia had seen the developing rift between Kelly and LeToya. I suspected that Kelly's being let down again by her own mother had everything to do with her snippiness. I watched, listened, and corrected. "That behavior will never do, Kelly," I said. Miss Kelly was misdirecting all her resentments, which Mathew and Celestine had been fueling for months, at the group sister LeToya, who made an easy target for Kelly's anger. LeToya, with her long, silky, black hair, LeToya, with her doting mother, had aroused every jealousy Mathew and Celestine could encourage in Kelly. LeToya's mother, Pam, was their target, and their gentle whisperings in Kelly's ear promoted a harmful return to her old self-image problems. Crippled against lashing out at Mathew and Celestine, Kelly made LeToya her personal punching bag.

In addition to the Knowleses' subliminal messaging, Kelly's sadness regarding her mother's abandonment – no matter how temporary – developed quickly into an overt fear of her surrogate father, Mathew. I had been able to protect her against attack while on the Knowles property, but I didn't live with them anymore. Damn, I thought. Celestine had played her hand well. One thing was very clear: Kelly had become the Knowleses very own Cinderella. She would never attend the ball, nor put her foot in a glass slipper.

I could barely contain my anger.

Once again, Celestine put pressure on me to have Beyoncé sing high notes. "Sooner rather than later," she said. My patience with this tiresome conversation had worn thin, and I resented Celestine's disrespect. She knew absolutely nothing about singing, nothing. For the umpteenth time, I attempted to explain.

Beyoncé is a mezzo-soprano, I told Celestine. She was not a soprano like Kelly, definitely not like LeToya, and she would never be one, I said. I was determined to set these young voices on the right track, so that they would remain secure and able to expand with age. I told Beyoncé's mother that forcing Beyoncé to push the top of her voice at the neglect of the bottom would shorten her range and that her middle voice would develop problems. For years we had done painstaking work to insure Beyoncé's vocal health, and I would not risk that precious voice just to please a mother who did not understand a thing about singing. I didn't care if she had been a Veltone (the high school singing group Celestine swore she'd been a member of). Her singing was amateurish and her knowledge of fundamental vocal truths was nil.

That Sunday, after our group rehearsals, the girls sang for Celestine and Solange, as they sometimes did. I clearly remember the feeling of pride Kelly's singing gave me that evening. She'd had an Ah-ha! moment in her lesson earlier that day, and her performance that evening was clear evidence of it. Everyone in the room sat up in surprise as Kelly suddenly gave it her all. Her singing was beyond amazing, beyond glorious. It was obvious that she finally understood what I meant by being centered in all four points – the points necessary for exceptional singing: the soft palate, the larynx, the diaphragm, and the hips.

Celestine telephoned me later that evening. There was something that "concerned" her. She asked if we could meet at my Parkwood Street garage apartment the next day.

When we met I was completely unprepared for Celestine's "concern." What she said sent me over the edge. "David, Kelly is beginning to sound too much like Beyoncé," she said solicitously. "Isn't there something that you can do?"

I exploded. I began to see red and I tried unsuccessfully to calm myself "I am sick of your shit."

She looked at me, wide eyed. I vowed that she had no right to speak with me that way, or to challenge my professional expertise.

"Celestine, the only way to ensure that *Kelly* not be as good as Beyoncé would be to under-teach her. And that is not going to fucking happen." I was enraged.

"I'm sorry you feel that way," Celestine said, back-pedaling. "That is not what I meant at all. I just think that Kelly should develop her own way of singing."

"Bullshit," I said. "Do you really think that I don't know what is going on? I have known ever since Daryl admitted to loving Kelly's sound."

"Again, I'm sorry you feel that way," she said even more disingenuously than the first time.

I felt an explosion coming on. "Your intentions are in no way noble and pure. What the hell does 'I'm sorry you feel that way' even mean? Are you threatening me – again? And another thing. Who calls a special meeting for crap like this? I consider yours the ultimate manipulation and insultingly dishonest." I told Celestine again that I thought Beyoncé was a star talent and that none of her contemporaries would overshadow her. "She will be simply the best and she is earning the right to be. She works like no one else I know to be good at her craft. She does not need your Goddamned meddling."

Trying to get hold of my emotions, I focused on breathing. My insides shook. Memories raced back to Ashley, and to all the other times that Celestine Knowles had attempted to manipulate me with threats of taking Beyoncé away from me. I could've slapped the shit out of Celestine. Instead I continued, using harsh words that I later would ask God's forgiveness for, and even hers.

"Celestine, you know that I love all the girls. You also know I hold Beyoncé in high esteem. Beyoncé for me is a special student. She is every teacher's dream: a host of discipline, determination, and sheer talent. She shows respect for other people and their talents."

Celestine was momentarily speechless.

462

"I have taught her to be considerate and to be kind toward and with all her musical colleagues. Why can't you and your husband take a clue from your daughter? I cannot and will not sign off on your insanity any longer. I just can't do it. I will not serve you. I belong to God, and he sent me to Beyoncé."

Celestine said she was shocked by my behavior. "There's no need for all the cursing," she said.

"What? Well aren't you the pot calling the kettle black!" Celestine had a habit of calling her enemies some very un-Christian names. On those occasions, her *gutter behavior* shocked even me. "Please leave my home, Celestine. Now!!"

After she left, head high and pleased at the way she'd handled me *and* my Kelly, I reached behind the couch. Witch Celestine was in for it.

* * * * *

After what Celestine had just pulled, my life with Beyoncé's family was clearly coming to an end. I was embarrassed by how emotional I'd gotten. I felt used, having believed their lies. I just couldn't anymore. I would not harm Kelly, under-teach her, or entertain thoughts of under-teaching her, even if it meant losing Celestine and Mathew's precious Beyoncé.

The next day I felt worse than awful. Celestine called me. She wanted to talk about the disagreement, and I did too.

During our phone conversation, Celestine mentioned how proud she was to have helped me. Then she intimated that it had been an honor for me to live in her house, from both our points of view, she added. She'd upgraded me, she suggested.

Ignoring her patronizing tone, I told her what a joy it had been to teach her daughter as well as picking her up from school, helping her with her homework, making sure she ate, putting her to bed at night. I continued, beginning to ramble. I mentioned things like all-night recording studio sessions that I hadn't charged for, the thousands of dollars I'd loaned her, those extra lessons for Solange. I mentioned, too, Ann's help and support of the Knowles family, and that Ann and I had always both acted out of love and compassion. No, I had been the contributor. Celestine hadn't paid me in years for lessons, I said, and I never badgered her for one red cent. As Celestine began to realize that I was presenting her with a laundry list of services for which she owed me both gratitude and money, she assembled her weapons for a rebuttal.

Celestine spoke. "Nobody asked you to do anything for free. It's your own damn fault if you don't know your own worth."

My fury returned within an instant. "I'm going to be hanging up now, Celestine." I'd just been bitten, and Celestine's cobra bite had taken full effect. True to her nature, she had slithered in, delivering one final blow.

"I didn't mean that the way it sounds, David."

"Ah – of course you did, Celestine, but it's OK. You're right. It's all been a question of self-worth. You have a nice day now, you hear."

I hung up, completely done.

So now Celestine was angry, I thought. It was clear that she resented my brand of in-your-face honesty, and for forcing her to look at her own shame. I had done all those things, those good deeds, to help her. I wanted to ease the daily pressures she was facing, recalling my own mother's dedication in the process. But now, by dredging up those good deeds in anger, I had unwittingly broken a major common-sense rule. In Robert Greene's book *The 48 Laws of Power*, the author puts it this way in Rule Number 13. "Appeal to people's interest, never to their mercy or gratitude. If you need to turn to an ally for help, do not bother to remind him or her of your past assistance and good deeds. They will find a way to ignore you." I learned about these powerful words too late in life. Too bad I hadn't had Greene's book handy in the spring of 1994.

I signed the HGO *Porgy and Bess* contract, put it in the return envelope, and drove it to the post office. It was time to go, even though the still small voice that usually guided me had not yet spoken to my conscious mind.

I simply couldn't take it anymore.

464

The next day, on a Monday, Celestine invited me to the movies. She was paying, she said. We drove over to Meyerland Mall in Bellaire (an affluent subdivision of Houston) to see the film *Philadelphia*. It was, and is, a powerful movie. AIDS was still a very serious topic in the world. Medicines had gotten more effective, but people were still dying. I remember that neither Celestine nor I had been able to hold back the tears during the scene where Tom Hanks, the protagonist, translates the operatic aria "La mamma morta," sung by Maria Callas in the background. He analyses the music, inexorably pulling his co-star, Denzel Washington, along with the entire audience, into the drama.

Celestine looked at me, her tears flowing. She didn't know anything about opera, she said, but "that scene touched me deeply." She expressed great interest in Maria Callas.

"I have plenty of her recordings at home where she sings that aria. You're welcome to borrow them."

"Thank you so much, David. I would like that."

"It's my pleasure," I said. Although my sentiment was genuine, I was no fool. I wouldn't be swayed, not by a movie, not anymore.

* * * * *

"I told Celestine that I'm leaving."

"Oh?" Mama said. "What was her response?"

"She reacted the way I had expected," I said. "She *said* she doesn't want me to go. She said that the girls would be devastated to lose me and then she asked me to consider staying on. I had to explain to her the unwritten 32-years rule."

"Have you told the girls?" Mama asked.

"Yes," I said. "Beyoncé and the other girls were shocked, and sad. They quizzed me as to my reasoning. I told them about my chance to sing on tour with Houston Grand Opera. I couldn't bring myself to tell them the truth, Mama, that Celestine and Mathew had pushed me one too many times."

465

"So what's the solution going to be?" she asked.

"I agreed to continue my work with the girls. I promised to fly to Houston in between cities on the tour when time allowed."

"David. Please don't tell me you volunteered to pay for your own flights." (Shit! I thought to myself. My mother knew me well. Of course I had volunteered to absorb exactly that expense.) My silence was Mama's answer. "You are a grown man. It's your business." I knew that this was a vote of no-confidence in my judgment, and a sign of her disapproval. A comment from Mama like that really meant "You'll learn…"

I told Mama that the girls knew *Porgy and Bess* from Whitney Houston's version of the duet "I loves you, Porgy." "I explained to the girls that HGO is staging the entire opera for a big tour. I told them that the tour actually begins in Houston at HGO, and that I'll invite them to go to the premiere as my special guests." Then I told Mama that Kelly had asked if they would ever really see me again.

"What did you say?"

"I said, 'Don't worry; you are not getting rid of me that easily.' That made them laugh. Then I said seriously, I'll be back in Houston after Christmas. Then I answered Kelly's question directly. 'I will never leave you – unless you all don't want me in your lives anymore!'"

"David!" Mama said. "That's emotional blackmail. That's not fair. You shouldn't put those girls in a position you know they will never be able to honor."

Mama was right.

"I believe the girls appreciate you. That is not the problem," Mama pointed out. Chastened, I nodded in agreement.

* * * * *

It was a cold December 1994 in New York, and the city was buzzing with holiday excitement. The rehearsals for the Houston Grand Opera *Porgy and Bess* U.S. tour were beginning, and after Christmas the cast would be flown back to Houston. The tour would take us to eleven cities, and I had planned time for the girls' voice lessons between performances in Dallas and San Diego (6 days), Seattle and Cleveland (6 days), Cleveland and Minneapolis (13 days), Minneapolis and Miami (6 days), Miami and San Francisco (6 days), and Costa Mesa and Portland, Oregon (20 days).

I knew that I would miss Beyoncé and the others, but I hadn't counted on the level of separation anxiety I felt. With each telephone call – and there were many – my longing only increased. Beyoncé said repeatedly that she missed me. "I need a voice lesson, bad," she would say. Apparently Daryl Simmons had been talking seriously to a record label. As it turned out, he had settled on Elektra Records. My thoughts returned to Roy, and to Barry Rosenthal, their offer to help, and Mathew's ultimate disrespect. Memories of those ugly scenes with Mathew killed my homesick feelings.

Porgy rehearsals came to a close two days before Christmas. On Christmas Day, I called the Knowles residence from my New York apartment, a third floor walk-up at 127th Street and Madison Ave, in Harlem. Celestine answered the telephone. She was overjoyed to hear from me she said, happy, so happy it hurt.

"We heard from Daryl," she said.

"That's great news!"

"The showcase is planned for the end of February, or the beginning of March. But as you know, that could change."

"Congrats," I said. "I know you're delighted."

She ignored my statement. "So, when do you come back again? The girls can hardly wait. That's all they've been talking about."

"Tomorrow," I answered. "I fly into Intercontinental on American Airlines, flight 1683 at 12:45."

"Well, your room will be ready," Celestine said.

"Oh, that's nice of you, but my mother lives in Houston now. Did you forget?" I answered.

"Ah, yes. I did. Sorry. But you know you are welcome."

"Yes, I do. Thank you."

"How's Gregory?" Celestine asked.

"Oh, Gregory is fine. He is already in Miami, with family."

"Well, tell him I said hello," Celestine said. I could hear Beyoncé and Kelly in the background. "Hold on David, these girls are chomping at the bit to talk to you. Have a Merry Christmas."

"Merry Christmas, Celestine," I said.

After speaking with Beyoncé and Kelly, I called LaTavia, and then LeToya and Pam. Then I called Gregory.

Gregory and I had started dating the previous year, immediately after my *Porgy* audition. We'd met through my best buddy, Roland Burks, a baritone and a colleague from my days at the University of Houston and HGO. Celestine had immediately liked Gregory – also a baritone. She thought he was "just an all-around great guy." He had helped her move into the new rental property on Braes Meadow Drive. Even Mathew liked him, a lot. I'd never seen Papa Mathew show kindness to anyone, in all the years I'd known him, but he and Gregory got along unusually well. The girls thought he was "cute," and even "*fine…*" they all said, embarrassed and hiding behind their fourteen-year-old nervous laughter.

Genetically advantaged, Gregory was what you called – plainly put – gorgeous. His hair was jet black and both wavy and curly. He sported a well-manicured mustache and goatee, and his eyes sparkled. Deeply set, they highlighted his perfectly squared jaw line. He had strong cheekbones, and perfect lips, but it was his kindness that had won me over – that and his cooking. Oh my God, could Gregory cook. Slightly taller than me, standing at 5′ 11″, he'd discovered the way to my heart. Still, I couldn't help wondering if Gregory was the "handsome bad boy" who would be the bearer of unwanted tension in my life. Walking down the streets of New York with him could be an unnerving experience, what with all the undisguised attentions streaming in his direction.

On the flight to Houston I revisited Celestine's comments that Kelly was sounding "too much like Beyoncé." An essential part of honing your singing skills is about emulating the good you hear. I don't know any singers who didn't or don't copy someone. It's one way you learn to find your own sound and style. So what was really bothering Celestine about

468

Kelly's sounding "like" Beyoncé? It was clear to me that Kelly's beauty of voice bothered Celestine. I wondered: Did she also realize that Kelly had the most beautiful voice of all the girls? I did.

Once again I found myself comparing Beyoncé and the opera superstar Maria Callas. In fact, I occasionally had told Beyoncé that for me, she was "the Callas of R&B/Soul." The two of them were similar in many admirable ways. They also had in common a dark side: their mothers.

Callas was said to have been a model student. Her first teacher, Maria Trivella, said in interviews, "She was fanatical, uncompromising and dedicated to her studies." I would say the same of Beyoncé. Callas had been overweight, and her mother, like Celestine with Beyoncé (who was *not* overweight), had chided her because of it. Callas had only one other sibling, a younger and thinner sister, with whom she found herself in constant conflict. Think of Beyoncé and Solange. Yes, these two devoted students of singing had major things in common: extraordinary talents, unstinting work habits, and their mothers.

I was getting tense, all over again. Finally, we were landing. A tropical climate! I welcomed the sunshine.

* * * * *

Silvia Rhone, then Elektra's CEO, was undoubtedly the most powerful woman in the music industry. She was black, regal, no-nonsense – and great friends with Daryl Simmons. She and I had met, independently of my girls, in Los Angeles in early 1994. Through my pupils Patrice Roberts-Isley and Scott Sherman, who were both living in L.A., I was introduced to L Simone, daughter of the legendary singer Nina Simone. Lisa – or L, as she demanded I call her – became my pupil. She had given a showcase that Silvia Rhone attended. Recognizing who Ms. Rhone was, I took the opportunity to re-introduce myself. She remembered me.

"Didn't we meet in Atlanta?" she asked. I reminded her it had been at the showcase for "Da Dolls."

"Ah, yes," she replied. Her simple question about how the girls were doing prompted me to a long, rhapsodic account of all their successes. I did not even try to hide my pride in their accomplishments. Then we discussed L's performance.

Ms. Rhone liked L Simone and told me that she'd wished she hadn't sung so many cover songs in her show. Later, I passed on to Mathew my special insight about what Ms. Rhone expected from an artist. Once he got over the shock that I'd gotten my information straight from the "horse's mouth," he confessed to me, again, his worries. Mathew's incessant nagging about "Beyoncé's preparation" for the second Atlanta showcase that Daryl was planning wore on my patience. I had prepared Beyoncé, and indeed all the girls, down to their last atom over the almost seven and a half years that I had been their mentor. My answer to his concerns about "Beyoncé's preparation" was short and to the point. "What have I been doing all these years? Of course she's ready. They *all* are...."

"Elektra is an outstanding label," I said to Ann in a phone call. They housed world-famous artists such as Metallica, AC/DC, Motley Crue, Tracy Chapman, The Doors, Missy Elliott, Queen, The Beach Boys, and En Vogue, to name a few. Despite the label's prestige, I had real concerns, which I had always kept to myself but now shared with Ann. "I am doubtful that my girls will get the attention they deserved at Elektra. Elektra still has En Vogue on its roster."

"I know," Ann said. "But, one step at a time. We haven't gotten the deal yet. Let's cross that bridge when we come to it."

"Fair enough," I answered.

Ann told me, and Celestine confirmed, that Mathew had already starting boasting all over town. His new king-of-the-mountain attitude didn't set well either with his wife, or with Ann. Like everyone, she too had an ego – always understated, but it was there. Ann and Mathew struggled for dominance as managers, but Ann had a hand up on him – money. The Knowleses needed her money, so they played nice.

That Ann wasn't "as flush as she had been" had no bearing on anything. She wasn't yet totally penniless, and she had an ace in the hole. Her nephew Belfrey, one of the region's most active drug dealers, was rumored to have had strong ties to Colombian cartels. Once Belfrey came onto the scene, flush with cash, Mathew went but so far. It was rumored that Mathew had gotten his cocaine through Belfrey. That truth would certainly have prevented him from rocking the boat, I thought. Mathew, on the brink of financial ruin, and needing Belfrey's support, so to say, could not afford to offend his alleged source.

A spiritual woman, Ann anguished over asking Belfrey for money altogether, but felt she had no other choice. He'd given Ann $25,000, which she used to pay for flights, hotels, and per diems, as well as some of her own bills. As I understood it, Belfrey had been helping out his Aunt Ann for quite some time. She didn't have a recoupment agreement with Mathew in place should he make good on his threat to remove Beyoncé. This deal had to work the way Mathew had stipulated. She had to "play ball," she said. It was either honor her fiduciary responsibility or lose Beyoncé. Mathew had been clear, and Ann had invested way too much to gamble with other constellations, she said.

Because I'd have some distance from the Houston day-to-day, while on tour with *Porgy*, I would have the luxury of envisioning other possibilities. I remember quizzing Ann, asking her if things would be so bad if Mathew took Beyoncé and left.

"Beyoncé is great," she said.

"Yes, she is. Her success is certain. But the other girls also have success in their futures," I answered. "Why not let her have Mathew's solo career?" I asked. It was a rhetorical question, as I still supported Beyoncé's desire to keep the group together. Still, I was concerned for Ann.

My main reason for even broaching the difficult subject was Ann's health. Her doctors warned against stress, and the combination of financial problems and the music business spelled STRESS in all caps. Mathew was an insurmountable hardship on her. She didn't look well, she continued to work at HL&P out of necessity, and she was retaining water again, which usually meant that her kidneys were being affected by her illness. She assured me that she didn't have kidney disease. She took more medicine, the water retention subsided, and all would be "well" again, until the next flare up. In my opinion, Mathew Knowleses' antics were killing Ann Tillman, literally.

* * * * *

On January 27, 1995, "my" *Porgy and Bess* started its United States tour with performances in the home of this new production, the Houston Grand Opera. That I write "my" *Porgy and Bess* indicates the profound effect of that experience on my life and career. It is engraved indelibly in my memory. In fact, this was David Gockley's and Hope Clarke's *Porgy and Bess*, and I was thrilled and honored to be a member of their company.

David Gockley, the esteemed general manager of the HGO (who, after more than thirty years in Houston would continue his brilliant career as general manager of the San Francisco Opera), was well known for his love of the opera *Porgy and Bess,* and for his monumental productions. Having decided on a black director for his new production of *Porgy and Bess*, Gockley turned to the renowned dancer and choreographer Hope Clarke. A brilliant dancer and television actress, Clarke had been a principal with both the Katherine Dunham and Alvin Ailey companies, and she had recently been nominated for Tony and Drama Desk awards for her choreography of the Broadway show *Jelly's Last Jam,* a George C. Wolfe production. Under her direction, this HGO *Porgy and Bess* would gain a reputation as one of the most outstanding productions in the history of American opera.

Born in Washington, D.C., in 1941, Clarke had lived through a time none of us in the cast knew about first-hand. On the first day of rehearsal in Houston she reminded us all that we came from tradition – a tradition deeply rooted in hard work, pride, and compassion. She talked of a black people who watched out for one another, who helped to raise each other's children. Long before Hillary Rodham Clinton's book *It Takes a Village*, Clarke pointed out to us cast members that in the black community, no

472

child was left to raise himself. Neighbors would chastise a child for infractions, after which the parents would confirm their own expectations for the child's right behavior. Clarke filled our *Porgy and Bess* production with pictures of a characteristic black society and their way of life. She called attention to the necessity for women to shop for clothes via mail order catalogues, because black people would not have been allowed to go into stores.

In the *Porgy and Bess* crowd scenes onstage Clarke created vignettes of hair braiding and Double Dutch jump roping, of children sitting with a school teacher learning to read, of mothers cooking, wringing laundry, and placing hot cakes on window sills. Men returned home from a long day at work to loving families and wives. I even learned to roll dice, a skill that growing up in Omaha hadn't afforded me. Ours was a production that recreated a time and place where black people were rooted in pride and faith in God. We would "share all those intricacies with the audience," Clarke said.

In a later interview with the *Los Angeles Times,* Clarke explained, "I want African Americans who come to see the opera to be proud that an African American is directing ... and to recognize the people on stage. I wanted to draw a community which we could find today: It could be any poor community, but one with pride." And in an *Opera News* interview she said, "In my production, everybody works. Everybody has some type of job. Just because you are poor doesn't mean you have to be slovenly or ignorant."

Her direction was brave and it rang true, especially regarding the factual and cultural aspects of the Gullah people – the people about whom DuBose Heywood had written his novel and the play, *Porgy,* which he subsequently converted to the libretto for Gershwin's opera *Porgy and Bess.* Clarke did indeed portray a true story of the Gullah community, one that humanized their condition.

For my star pupil, Beyoncé, and the girls whom she referred to as "her sisters," watching the performance of *Porgy and Bess* was both thrilling and intriguing. It was not their first experience of a live, full-length opera performance. They had come to that 1993 *Carmen* in Hermann Park. They had also seen the HEOG production of *Il Trovatore*, as well as the 1994 double bill of Bernstein's *Trouble in Tahiti* (in which my partner, Gregory, had the leading role) and Menotti's *The Medium* (in which I took an important acting role, of Toby, the deaf mute). Those experiences had afforded my girls the opportunity to learn more about what the focused intensity and the commitment of a highly trained, professional artist, looked like.

Now they were bouncing off the walls, from a mixture of bewilderment and awe, when they recounted the evening of the premiere, their visit backstage, and their enjoyment of the *Porgy and Bess* production. "Especially the singing," Beyoncé yelped. She called both my performance and the show "inspiring." LaTavia, my little diva, said, "It was cool to see you dance." Celestine reminded me, ever so gingerly, that I was a superior teacher. She just couldn't help herself. I actually felt sorry for her. The woman wanted what she wanted, whatever that was.

HGO's stage was massive. I remember Beyoncé's asking if she could go out onto the stage. With the permission of the stage director I took her center stage and introduced her to my world. Looking out into that grand opera house, I was sure, would be an experience she'd not likely forget. "Sing something," I said. "Anything." When she heard the ease with which her voice bounced back to her in the Wortham Center (HGO's home), she became emotional. "That's right Beyoncé, dream – feel your success." She told me that she could, and suddenly she understood what singing for me must have felt like.

In the days following Beyoncé's attendance of *Porgy and Bess*, as usual, she had endless questions for me. Her curiosity for all things music was indeed extraordinary and spoke to everything that made her a prodigious talent. The respect and genuine interest that she had for every genre of music that I'd introduced her to and taught her – including opera – thrilled me. She honored everything about our art form and singing: the phrasing, rhythms, nuances, intent, and the depth of the text, the composer/arranger – and most importantly, music's emotional requirements.

* * * * *

It wasn't easy to leave Houston after that last performance of *Porgy and Bess*. The four girls saw that final performance, and our subsequent backstage visit warmed my heart tremendously. It was there that we said our real goodbyes. Although they knew that I would continue to be their teacher, sadness filled the air. I had devoted myself to them for almost eight years, spending more time with them than their own parents. Taking good care of my own vocal health, and setting a good example for the girls, I had never allowed myself the luxury of too much extracurricular activity. Still, we had reached a major turning point in our relationship, and my teaching would now take place between my performances in other cities – intervals during which I would not be physically on Houston soil. I was so proud of the work we had done.

Truth be told, I started to feel less angry at Celestine and more thankful that her cruelty had pushed me out of the nest. Had she – and Mathew – not insulted me to the extent they did, I might still have been paying resentful homage to the Knowleses. I also thanked God for Mama's nagging me, and her persistence that I should keep my eye on the prize – my own prize, not the Knowleses'.

Kelly asked me how long the tour would last. I told her that the tour was to last through July of 1995 and would conclude with the performances at Portland Opera. All the girls were intrigued by the travelling I would be doing, and the singing in so many different cities – for different audiences! It was no secret that they dreamed of putting themselves into the same situation. They had been visualizing their success for years, and success was definitely on the horizon. I knew it. The girls and all the adults involved were anxiously awaiting the call from Daryl, which finally came through. The Elektra showcase had been set. They were ready.

"You have worked hard. We always knew this day would come. Keep the faith," I said, as I boarded the bus bound for Dallas with the rest of the *Porgy and Bess* cast. I reminded the girls of the Bible verse in the Book of Matthew, Chapter 21, verse 21: "And Jesus answered them. 'Truly, I say to you, if you have faith and do not doubt, you will not only do what has been done to the fig tree, but even if you say to this mountain, 'Be taken up and thrown into the sea,' it will happen."

I hugged them all tightly and boarded the tour bus.

22. No one escapes

Earlier, during the New York music rehearsals, I had been approached by my colleague Lou Ann Strohman about becoming the male American Guild of Musical Artists union representative for the *Porgy and Bess* tour. ("AGMA" is the union that represents opera singers, ballet and other dancers, opera directors, backstage production personnel, and others.) Although I was honored, I knew that it would be a demanding responsibility, which I did not take lightly. In actuality, I had fought for my girls for so long I wanted a break from that kind of responsibility. I had joined the *Porgy and Bess* tour looking for healthy escape into singing and acting, but it seemed that social responsibility had followed me. Lou Ann finally won me over during the Dallas leg of the tour. One of the perks was having my own suite, in every subsequent city.

Having dealt with Ann's illness and the Knowleses' greed, I stood ready to face the very human problems that would arise during the 1995-96 HGO tour of *Porgy and Bess*. Living with the Knowleses had trained me to adopt an unflappable, no-nonsense demeanor in the face of opposition, an attitude that would be sorely needed in the situations and problems that Lou Ann Strohman and I were about to encounter. Taking on union issues, I became the spokesperson for my colleagues regarding their rights. I am known for being respectfully outspoken, which is exactly what Lou Ann wanted in a partner. One has to be passionate, but rooted in factual details – especially when fighting for justice.

We in the cast quickly became family for one another. Living, working, and traveling together, we were repeatedly challenged to prove the depth

476

of our commitment. The test came in many forms, none more demanding than in our relationship with a young colleague whom we called "Staplefoot." He was dying of AIDS.

Staplefoot's membership and presence in the *Porgy and Bess* touring company challenged us all at every turn. Lou Ann and I had to deal with the legalities of his being a formal member of the cast, which included putting safety assurances in place at each venue. As Staplefoot's union representatives Lou Ann and I became his counselors, his friends, and his advocates with the union – whose leadership had naturally expressed concerns. I received an instant, head-spinning tutorial in human rights and how to handle delicate situations with grace and discretion.

Even though I did not expect at first that Staplefoot faced imminent death, I recognized that the HGO's decision to hire this wonderful, but sick, artist spoke to the extraordinary level of commitment and compassion of David Gockley's organization. My colleagues, both onstage and backstage, constantly amazed me. Everyone looked out for Staplefoot. I observed with great interest the dynamics of each person's relationship to him. We were all connected and working together. The way in which each person dealt with the sensitivity of the situation was a lesson in love and humility.

Curiously, I'd been prepared years earlier for the psychological effects of AIDS through, of all people, Beyoncé. When she was still very young, her uncle Johnny had died from the disease, and it had been a traumatic experience for her. As her voice teacher, I had had intimate knowledge of all of Beyoncé's feelings and fears, especially regarding her uncle's death. Quite frankly, all illness frightened Beyoncé. She didn't understand AIDS, and her mother had insisted she visit her dying uncle in the hospital. I'd never seen fear in Beyoncé's eyes until that moment. She was terrified and became physically ill. I felt that Celestine's insistence was misplaced, but of course I had kept quiet.

Union business, teaching, and performing seven to eight shows per week would keep me busy. I would become resident voice teacher to 65% of the cast – principals and chorus alike. Although I found it all challenging, what did I have to complain about? Nightly, with the raising of each curtain, we all had the unique pleasure of exposing the audience to love and community – the ideas of family. I took that seriously. After living for so long amongst the Knowleses, I needed to remember what a healthy family felt and looked like. The complex community and family environment that we achieved was one of the real beauties of Gershwin's *Porgy and Bess* – as staged by Hope Clarke.

* * * * *

I must say, I looked forward to our last Sunday matinee performance in Dallas. Teresa LaBarbera-Whites promised to come, and she'd bring her husband. There wasn't an empty seat in the 3,400-seat facility on February 26th 1995. "I finally get to see you on the stage," Teresa said, calling me in my hotel to thank me for having arranged the tickets. "Please," I answered. "I'm glad to do it."

After the performance Teresa went on and on about the production, the dancing and the singing. "Your voice is amazing!" I thanked her from the bottom of my heart.

"And your dancing is pretty spectacular too," her husband said. As he was a professional ballet dancer, I took his words to heart. Then my teacher walked in.

"Dr. Johnstone," I said. "You made it."

"I wouldn't have missed it for the world." She'd been ill and I wasn't sure she would be up to making the drive from Denton, Texas, where she lived, to downtown Dallas.

I introduced her to the Whites, who were genuinely happy to meet the teacher's teacher. Teresa had not known about my being attacked on Houston streets some years earlier, nor could she imagine what I'd endured in order to arrive at this day. "I'm even more impressed now," she concluded.

Back at the hotel, I called Beyoncé. She and Kelly were OK, she said, and rehearsal had gone great. After hanging up, my telephone rang. It was

Jim Ireland, calling me from his office, on a Sunday. "I have some great news for you," he said.

In re-negotiating my contract in Dallas, as the new union representative, I had explained my situation to company management. "I am building the next superstar girl group," I had said, "and have to make trips to Houston in order to teach them." I didn't know if honesty would work, but I believed in telling the truth. No sense in lying. Grandmother used to say, "Somebody always sees and hears you, Baby." At any rate, I was told that I would have to speak to Jim Ireland, who was director of productions at HGO. I knew Mr. Ireland well from my earlier days at HGO, and I prayed for the best. Despite his reputation for being difficult, he delighted me with his response. "The special travel considerations you asked for will be met. It's absolutely no problem, David. John *[Maestro John Demain, our conductor]* told me that you are teaching the cast." (I had begun by working with my very good friend Marquita Lister – our first-cast Bess – and word had spread quickly.) "You are saving us money by keeping everyone vocally healthy. HGO thanks you, and I thank you!"

I was floored, and remain eternally grateful (and so should my girls!). HGO's generosity was huge. It meant that I would be afforded the luxury of flying back to Houston whenever I wanted, joining the cast in the next city from there, even though my home base was now New York.

Late one evening, Mathew called me. Deep in the middle of the night, the phone rang in my suite at the Excelsior Hotel on West 81st Street, in New York. Who is calling me at 3:30 in the morning? I wondered. Reaching for the phone, fumbling in the dark, and eventually finding the receiver, I answered.

"Hello."

"David – it's Mathew. I got a song I want you to hear." Music was blaring in the background.

It still hadn't registered who was on the telephone. "Mathew, is that you?"

"Listen to this," he said, holding the phone up into the air. He shouted, "I got it – I got it."

"Got what Mathew?" I asked. "What are you talking about? What do you have?"

"This song right here is going to get us the deal with Elektra," he shouted. "Wide Open!"

Ah, how I hated being the bearer of bad news, but Mathew's discovery sounded like an R&B disaster to me.

"Mathew, you know I try to see things from all angles before reacting, but my gut tells me that this song is not going to do what you think it will. Let's talk about this in the morning."

"What – What did you say?"

"I said, I don't think this song fits our girls. It sounds like it was written with the male voice in mind." Mathew knew very well that I had already rehearsed the girls within an inch of their life on a more appropriate track. Nonetheless, he said that he had made an executive decision.

I sat up in the bed and asked Mathew about Ann's opinion. She had failed to mention the song change in our talk the day before. Of course he had not consulted with Ann.

"Fuck Ann," Mathew said.

"Back it up Mathew," I said crossly. "What are you talking about? I've been training the girls to sing live into the natural acoustic of a room – without microphones. What if Elektra wants to hear them without microphones? Projection is important."

I thought I heard him breathing, so I continued. "This song is too low, for too long! In that range their voices cannot speak at a high enough frequency to be heard, let alone to impress anyone." My increasing annoyance with him spilled over. "Even an idiot can hear that this song won't show the girls off at their maximum capabilities."

"What? What did you say?" Mathew said aggressively.

Had it been 3:30 in the afternoon, I might have used a more tactful word, but I needed to get his attention. And it felt good for me to tell him what I really thought. Mathew Knowles was an idiot.

"Mathew, this is exactly why I asked you to speak with me about this tomorrow morning. It's 3:30 *A.M.* I don't want to get into a fight with you, but I am tired. Repertoire is not your area of expertise. We have already agreed about that."

"Don't worry, they will sing on your fuckin breath," Mathew growled. His spooky laughter sounded possessed.

"*Breath* – won't help them Mathew." I asked myself why I was having this conversation. I hated talking to Mathew in this state. He was on some type of new crazy.

Before he could sputter a reply, I continued, trying once again to be tactful and articulating each word clearly. "Again: It is my professional opinion that a wrong choice of song has been made here. I am extremely concerned that this song could become a deal breaker. If I were Elektra, I wouldn't sign a girl group coming in with that song. Not only does it not show the female voice in a good light, it makes it obvious that whoever is handling A&R doesn't have much experience. You don't want that, Mathew, believe me. The key is all wrong. Plus, I have trained the girls to sing challenging repertoire, the best available songs. To me 'Wide Open' feels like ordinary, girl-next-door material."

There was a long silence. Had Mathew dozed off again? His constant calling at unreasonable times of the night – and predictably high – had long since begun to wear on me. I could always tell when he had been sucking on the glass dick.

"Mathew?"

"I believe people will like it. It's catchy," he said.

Beyond frustrated, I screamed, "So are crabs, but I wouldn't want those either." I hung up the phone, called him a few choice names, and tried to get back to sleep. Mathew Knowles would make even Jesus Christ cuss – and out loud.

I unplugged the phone. "Now," I said to myself, nestling myself into one of the most comfortable pillows I'd ever slept on.

Mathew had already declared, and begun spreading the word amongst the parents, that I had abandoned the girls in their hour of need. Several Houston friends and colleagues had heard about it. In his uniquely eloquent way, he was summing up his feelings: "Fuck David. He abandoned us when we needed his ass most."

The fact that I had done no such thing – just like any other uncomfortable facts in his world – never deterred Mathew in his need to malign me. Mathew's crass comment about my abandoning the girls in their "hour of need" was totally unfounded. I had abandoned no one. I was sure that Celestine, in her own covert way, was supporting this fabrication. She most likely initiated it. Of course I was concerned that their manipulation of facts could change the way the girls felt about me. Even so, I had to trust that Beyoncé, Kelly, LaTavia, and LeToya were smarter than that, hoping they'd not believe Beyoncé's parents lies. I prayed they would not forget my devotion to them all these years. Our work together, and my ongoing attentions would surely only strengthen our bond.

But what if I was wrong…

I returned to Houston on the morning of February 27th. Mama had gotten settled into her house in Bellaire, on Hillcrest Street. She had met a man named George, who seemed nice enough. On the surface he seemed devoted, but I had learned not to be too naïve: Things didn't always seem the way they appeared. I dropped my bags off at Mama's home and then drove immediately to the Knowles house.

After our lessons, Kelly told me that Ann was in Tomball Regional Hospital. When I called her in the hospital she seemed to be getting along okay. I say "seemed," because it would not be accurate to say she was well. She wasn't. Several days after her discharge I visited her at home, flowers in hand. That was March 5th, 1995, the day before I would fly out to the West Coast to join the cast of *Porgy and Bess* for performances with San Diego Opera. Despite having very little body strength, Ann tried to rise from her chair. I insisted she remain seated and leaned down instead to hug her. She flinched. Worried by her reaction, I quickly apologized. I

482

hadn't known that she had been suffering from excruciating ulcerated lesions on her back. Even touching them, not to mention the pressure applied from my overzealous hug, caused her unbearable pain.

As she offered me a seat, the telephone rang. She answered by putting the caller on speaker phone, as it pained her to hold the receiver. It was Mathew. I have never heard such screaming in all my life – well, actually I had – from Mathew himself, and from my stepfather just before he would unleash one of his beatings on my mother.

"I don't give a damn if you did just get out of the hospital. Do you have the money?" Mathew shouted through the phone. I assumed Mathew referred to the money needed to fly the girls out to Atlanta for the Elektra showcase, which Daryl had now reconfirmed was reportedly less than two weeks away.

"Mathew, I am not feeling very well. Can we talk about this later?" Ann was embarrassed by his behavior.

"Ann, do you have the fuckin' money or not?"

"Yes, Mathew I have the money, but can we talk about this later?" she repeated. Without warning, we heard a dial tone. He had hung up the phone. Visibly shaken, Ann confessed to me that Mathew often called using such language.

Chauncey Wooden (Kenny Moore's brother-in-law) answered Ann's telephone when I called her on the next morning, March 6, 1995. I remember the date vividly, because it was the day following Mathew's nasty "Do you have the fuckin' money or not?" telephone call, and before I was to go to the airport. I wanted to check on Ann. Chauncey told me, guardedly, that Ann was "unavailable." When I asked the reason, Chauncey revealed that she had taken a sedative in order to calm herself.

It seems that Mathew, in all his entitled glory, had decided to call on Ann in person to collect that money – in the middle of the night. Ann, as responsible as they come, certainly would not rescind her fiduciary obligations toward the girls, and she refused to give Mathew the money. Ann had invested her life savings and an incredible amount of love and energy in them already. In addition to help from Belfrey, she had even secured outside financial sponsorship in Atlanta, through the assistance of a gen-

483

tleman friend named Jesse. Jesse didn't seem trustworthy, but neither he nor his scruples were my business. If Ann liked him, I liked him. However, I wanted to know why Mathew would press her for money. And in the middle of the night? I smelled drugs – or worse.

It proved to be worse.

* * * * *

Today, I understand the significance of Mama's wisdom, but back then I was honor-bound. Grandmother's telling of the biblical figure that had five talents, from the book of Matthew, remained ever present. God had blessed me with a gift for music and teaching, lending me extraordinary instincts and insight. Surely it would aid my girls in becoming the phenomenal group I envisioned. After all, I could never forget that it had been *God's grace* that had put me in their lives, and that hadn't happened without reason. Thus I gave freely, with my whole heart. As a Christian I had been taught to do so. When it came to the parents of my girls, it became increasingly important to remember the words of Sir Francis Bacon: "In order for the light to shine, the darkness must be present."

I remained steadfast, reminding myself that "God's will be done." I had no interest in conformity, but rather in remaining true to what was good and decent. Beyoncé and my girls were good and true.

Elektra's CEO, Silvia Rhone, had taken charge immediately. Her first mandate was, "That name has to go," she said. She hated Daryl's naming the group "Da Dolls."

She got no argument from us.

A re-focused Celestine said to me, "This record deal is long overdue. They need you now more than ever." All too happy to oblige, I got to work, intensifying my efforts.

My girls would be fantastic. We'd practiced for this day already for more than seven years.

484

* * * * *

In April 1995 on a few days' break from the *Porgy and Bess* tour, I saw clearly that the girls were ready for a completely new level of vocal achievement, learning to connect breath to thought. We'd done all the necessary fundamental training for it, and now they were ready to implement a more sophisticated approach to the singer's art in all its complexity.

"I call it 'the God experience,'" I said.

"The God experience!" Beyoncé said. She'd been waiting for this day.

"Yes, the God experience! This aspect of singing pulls at the very soul – it is the heartbeat to discovering how to tap into emotion all the time. It's about realizing instinct, trusting it." The girls looked doubtful. "This is not an airy-fairy concept," I reassured them.

Great singing, much like success in athletics, has everything to do with understanding "flow." On that day, I compared their lessons in singing to the training of the Olympic track and field athlete Carl Lewis, who was at the end of his phenomenal success and fame in 1995.

"Carl Lewis's coach, Tom Tellez, had revolutionized track and field," I told the girls. "His extensive study of anatomy and physiology had helped set Carl Lewis apart."

Through biomechanics (the study of external and internal forces on the body), Carl's coach was able to maximize his performance based on knowledge of physics of motion, gravity, and structure. Tellez understood that isolating every significant movement, from the sprinter's start in the blocks to the finish, would help him to teach efficiency and lead his athletes to peak performance. Combining kinesiology (the study of movement) with biomechanics made champions out of the talented athletes he trained (a very impressive list of track and field stars).

Similarly, a competent singer needs to engage certain specific physical and mental processes. Mastering the complexity of breath and its sensation (understanding that each emotion has its own audible breath), tending to the diaphragm (anchoring the sound/tone, aiding in support), and connecting the hips, larynx, facial muscles, and diaphragm to the breath and soft palate visually through the cry – these are the details that support effortless singing and visualization (which is what I had been referring to as "text painting"). Now, all these separate and important elements needed to become one simultaneous process. It would be an emotional experience, but my girls were ready.

"You all are my champions," I said to all four of them. "As most exceptional singing talents are, you have been born with natural gifts. My job has been to awaken the extraordinary in you."

Kelly said, "Wow, you really believe in us."

"Yes, I do. I handpicked each of you for your potential and your unique native abilities. But to galvanize music, you must become singing athletes of a special kind. I have worked out every facet of your learning, just the way Carl Lewis's trainer did. That includes the physiological and psychological aspects of performance." In addition, I pointed out that, like Carl Lewis, they had listened, never questioned, and had learned to trust their body, mind, and spirits unconditionally. Tellez called Carl the perfect student athlete, and for me, so too were my girls.

I continued my analogy of singing to athletics. "Remember our talks about maximizing the even exchange of oxygen and carbon dioxide in the blood in performance?" I asked them.

"Yes," they all said in unison. We all had experienced that in a very real way through our jogs in Hermann Park.

"Well, buckle your seat belts. You're headed for the ethereal – the next, ultimate level in great singing.

Each singer, I said, has to figure out the shape of their soul and then remain pliable. "You must be like water," I told them. "Water takes on the shape of whatever it comes into contact with. In order to touch, to move people, we must take on the form of our listener." They looked at me inquisitively.

I told my girls to imagine they were water. Water has form and yet no form. It is soft, yet it is hard, and strong enough to penetrate stone.

"Water, like you, must always be allowed flexibility," I said. "You must always be pliable with your audience. For me, the audience is like a vase. You as the singer begin your journey by pouring your energy (the water) into the listener (the vase). Inserting a flower (intent) provides the audience with the story. Water (your energy) wraps around the stem of the flower (the intent, the message) and produces a powerful effect on the listener. The two of you become one."

I explained to the girls that nothing in the universe is still. Of course, an object can be at rest, but the forces deep within, and surrounding, that still object are in motion. I reminded them that there is motion in all things – even in silence – even in water. "As singers, even when we are silent, our bodies and spirits are in motion, ready to energize and make audible our voices. A complete harmony with the universe is what I am after. Our performances begin in the dressing room. Before you reach the stage you'd better already be *in motion* – or better, *in thought* – about wrapping the audience up in the story."

I took them into the kitchen and poured water onto the counter top. What started as a simple puddle began to expand outward.

"Do you see how the water continues to slowly and evenly spread itself out as if to take over the entire counter?" I asked. "The water never makes a sharp shift in its direction. There are no sudden movements."

I reminded the girls that whenever I had talked about elongating the vowels (singing vowel to vowel so as to not change the intensity or energy given to each note), legato, singing on the breath, flexibility, and consuming the audience (surround sound) – I was describing the physics of singing, a process that simple puddle of water was now showing them.

I then took it a step further. I explained to them the meaning of kinetic and potential energy. Kinetic energy is energy in motion. Potential energy is energy that stands still. Asking my girls to shift their attention, I turned to the kitchen stove and lit one burner. I asked Kelly to hold her hand high above the flame. "Kelly, if kinetic energy is energy in motion, would you call the flame kinetic energy?"

"Yes, because the flames seem to dance, and that is movement, isn't it?" she replied. You are partly right, I told her. "Although the flame is in motion, it remains itself in place, does it not?"

"Yes," she said.

"What do you feel coming off the flame?"

"Heat," she said.

"Exactly. The flame is the source. Let us say that it represents your body – your instrument. The heat you feel, wafting upwards and against your hand, is the real kinetic energy (cognitive kinetics). It is the heat that remains stable, unwavering (no sudden movement) – anchored in its job, if you will. In singing it becomes the thought that must be constant and most important, *continuous* in its motion. That motion, the energy wafting upwards in continuous motion, represents the work that breath and thought have to do. Energized breath and thought become singing."

"LeToya, do you feel how the heat coming off the flame feels constant? It makes no sudden, sharp or jutting movement. The flame might flicker and leap, but the heat is constant." LeToya gave an affirmative nod. Beyoncé, deep in thought and hanging on my every word, remained silent – taking it all in, as was usual for her. LaTavia, happy to tell us that she had just studied the difference between kinetic and potential energy in science class, chimed in, "Does the heat become like the movie in our head you always talk about?" Absolutely, I said. She'd nailed it. "The movie is the story – the meaning behind the text. Your job is to unfold the story, not spring it on us."

A very determined Beyoncé, Kelly, LeToya, and LaTavia had learned all about discipline over the past seven plus years. Carefully implementing the formula that I believed determined success, I had devoted myself – mind, body, and soul – to the process that would lead them to achieving their own goals. I had recognized their talent and ignited their creativity, always making clear the importance of music in the human experience. I talked of gratitude and treated them with loving kindness in order that they learn important lessons on giving. Having designed our work together to create cohesiveness as well as independence, the importance of personal responsibility had been emphasized in teaching them how to think about their eventual brand. They were instructed to reflect on the beauty of their spirit, allowing it to shine through the beauty of their singing.

I continually reminded all of them that the world worked in spiritual ways. "What you do will come back to you. What you think will come out of your mouth, and thus into your life," I would say. I warned Beyoncé against believing the hype. Understanding the superficial nature of PR, and the ambitious parent, I told Beyoncé that "Your fans – the whole world – will tell you that you're great," I scolded, "but remember, it will never be you who will be truly great, but rather your humanity. Be careful of loving the applause. Excessive accolades can play tricks on your mind and lure you into accepting the morals of the majority."

"You must resist this," I would say. "Il pubblico si costruisce solo a strappare giù." (The public builds you up only to tear you down.) Even though Beyoncé didn't understand the Italian, she was drawn to my habit of expressing myself in other languages. Foreign exposure, of any sort, helped all of them to visualize a much larger world than their own, which I believe is a very necessary part of the puzzle in dealing with fame. I didn't want them believing that they deserved special acceptance just because they were American – or excellent. America's freedom's is what makes American artist beloved. A girl in Africa can dream, but without certain freedoms and experiences her world remains small.

"If you want to reach an international audience, you must think with the inter-nationality that is needed."

* * * * *

The girls won their Elektra Audition. A very happy Beyoncé and the other girls were finally in Atlanta, recording. I was shocked to find out that they were not being housed at Daryl's house. His studio was there, and he had plenty of room, but instead the girls were housed in his assistant's basement. According to Beyoncé, the room was not bigger than a thimble in size.

"We have a couch and some cots to sleep on," Beyoncé said.

I couldn't imagine it. Celestine was insulted, out of her mind. She couldn't fathom that her baby was sleeping on a cot and suggested to

Mathew and Ann that the girls return at once to Houston to complete the recording. That was out of the question. Neither Beyoncé nor the other girls wanted to return to Houston. I was glad to know that they wouldn't even consider it. They were finally experiencing some much-needed independence. All they wanted to do was record and shop. They were good girls who were in heaven – seventh heaven, Kelly said. They were even earning a per diem.

"Lennox Mall, here we come," Beyoncé told me during my weekly call with her.

If I remember correctly, they were getting $150.00 per week, and all they did, when they weren't in morning tutoring sessions or the recording booth, was shop. Beyoncé loved to shop. Their favorite stores were Macy's and a shop called Contempo Casual. I was amazed at how they were able to make $150.00 last. Beyoncé and I had a good laugh when I told her that at her age I had a hard time holding on to even $10.

While the girls delighted in their new-found freedom, Mathew complained about Daryl, who, according to Mathew, had not spent sufficient time with the girls. In a phone call to Houston, Mathew swore that he knew why Daryl had dragged his feet in getting the recording deal, and why he was ignoring the girls now. Apparently, Daryl's boy band "A Few Good Men" (those boys I had given lessons to when the girls were twelve and in Atlanta for their first showcase) were struggling in the studio. They were scheduled to release their album on September 26, 1995, and they weren't close to finishing. Daryl's attentions had been diverted to helping them. Mathew screamed, "Those fuckin' boys can't sing. Daryl needs to be concentrating on us."

I disagreed with Mathew's comment about the boys' singing. I did, however, think that they had not developed a special sound yet, and I wished that I could have been more helpful, since unlike Mathew's "star" boy band, all the members of "A Few Good Men" could definitely sing. Celestine contributed her own sour opinion, insisting again, "Don't let Daryl punk you, Mathew." I hung up the phone, having heard enough.

I remember the argument Mathew and I had about song repertoire, the selection of songs, when the girls were to sing for Elektra. An obsessed Mathew hated not having control. He had demanded of Daryl that he be given a say in the repertoire. He was no A&R (Artist and Repertoire) expert, but neither was Daryl. Repertoire is an entirely different horse to mount than, say, producing the record or managing the artist. A&R specializes in both managing the artist and choosing the optimal music for the record. It is the A&R decision that can make or break a project, and most beginning artists will never be allowed a controlling voice in the decision-making process.

* * * * *

My private life was also showing signs of discord. Something was terribly off between Gregory and me, and had been for months. Matthew 7:7 says, "Ask, and it will be given to you; seek, and you will find; knock and it will be opened to you." Despite the fact that I had met his parents, and received their approval, a growing tension told me to ask, seek, and knock on the door.

I prayed. I broached the subject with Gregory. He said nothing. I pressed harder. What he finally confessed shook me to the core.

On June 1st, two weeks after a harmonious dinner with his family in Miami, Gregory admitted to having had a torrid affair. According to him, he and a man named "Gerardo" had been seeing one another since my singing in Cleveland. My hurt turned to rage.

Still furious on June 3, I returned to my suite at the Cathedral Hill Hotel after the evening performance of *Porgy and Bess* at San Francisco Opera, to discover that Gregory had telephoned – again. He had already left 24 messages on the hotel answering service, all of which I had ignored. Number 25 was no different. My focus had to remain on my work, period. San Francisco Opera was an important station in my career. Singing well, especially there, was a must. Not to mention, my girls, in the midst of recording their first professional album demos ever, were calling me constantly.

The following day I left San Francisco with the *Porgy* cast, heading for Los Angeles. Unbeknownst to me, Gregory was headed there, too.

Shortly after check-in at the Intercontinental Hotel on South Olive Street in downtown L.A., I called Ann, desperate to find out what was going on with my girls in Atlanta. Mathew hadn't been available to me for weeks, and Ann now said to me that no one had heard from him in days. Daryl had been frantically trying to reach him, and so had Celestine. While deep in conversation with Ann, I heard a knock at the door.

"Ann, could you hold on. The bellman is at the door with my luggage."

"Who is it?" I asked.

"It's me," the voice said, on the other side of the door – a voice I knew well. "I've come to ask for your forgiveness." Having failed to connect with me by telephone, Gregory had decided to talk with me face to face. I opened the door quickly, letting him in to avoid a scene. I hate scenes.

"What are you doing here?" I asked.

"Aren't I going to get a hug?"

"Don't push your luck," I replied, and turned on my heels. "Please come in."

"What's up with the formality?" Gregory asked.

The look I gave him said everything. What was I going to do now? A big part of my troubles was staring me in the face. I had never been as disillusioned with a human being as I was at that moment with Gregory. He, on the other hand, forged ahead. He had arrived with a purpose. On many levels my uneasiness pleased him. The level of my anger, he said, was "proof that I cared."

"Of course I care," I told him.

"C'mon David, I am sorry," he said, grabbing my arm.

As I wrestled myself free, Gregory said, "I bet if I was your precious Beyoncé, you'd forgive me."

"What did you say? What the hell does Beyoncé have to do with this?"

No answer. Gregory didn't say one audible word, but rather let the look on his face do all the talking. His stare suggested that I'd ignored him, and our relationship, by putting Beyoncé first. Irritated, I turned to walk away from him, only then noticing the telephone receiver lying on the bed where I'd left it.

I had forgotten Ann, who was patiently waiting so that we could finish our conversation. Hurrying to the phone, I asked her forgiveness and promised that I would call her right back. "No problem," she said. "Take your time." She had heard the entire exchange between Gregory and me. She wished me luck in resolving our issues.

"Give Gregory my very best, and take care of you, David," Ann said. She told me that I'd be able to reach her at home after 7:00 p.m. if I needed to talk.

It was customary on tour that our travel day was slated a free day, and in Los Angeles our first official day off happened to be the next day after arrival. This had never happened before. It seemed as though the universe was aiding Gregory. For two solid days Gregory and I discussed – well – he talked and I listened, without interruption. We were two intelligent adults, I thought. Even in my quandary, I reassured myself: You can do this.

"It just happened," Gregory said.

"Really – well it's never 'just' happened to me." Trying to push my buttons, he agreed, calling me "perfect."

Was he calling my character into question here – *Really?* A part of me wanted to forgive him immediately and just move on. Forgiveness was a big one for me. I was still figuring that one out. Maybe this happened for a reason, I thought. Nope, I said to that stupid idea. It's fucked up. That is what it is. It's fucked up. I was determined to remain dignified to the end.

Performances came to an end in Los Angeles, and those in Costa Mesa, California, brought more of the same: Nightly we sang to sell out houses, and nightly we took multiple curtain calls. The Houston *Porgy and Bess* was a huge success, ultimately earning HGO and the host American opera houses an estimated $18 million dollars through ticket sales.

Gregory and I began to sort through our problems. I wasn't so sure we'd make it. If only I had followed my first instinct, I thought, the one that had told me to beware the handsome bad boy. Hopelessly stuck, I remembered the conversation that I'd had with Father Tucker when I'd sought his advice.

* * * * *

Father Tucker had responded to my questions about forgiveness by recounting for me the parable of Jesus and the moneylender. He read to me from the New Testament, Luke 7:41-47:

"Two men owed money to a certain moneylender. One owed him five hundred denarii, and the other fifty. Neither of them had the money to pay him back, so he canceled the debts of both. Now which of them will love him more?"

Simon replied, "I suppose the one who had the bigger debt cancelled."

"You have judged correctly," Jesus said.

Then he turned toward the woman and said to Simon, "Do you see this woman? I came into your house. You did not give me any water for my feet, but she wet my feet with her tears and wiped them with her hair. You did not give me a kiss, but this woman, from the time I entered, has not stopped kissing my feet. You did not put oil on my head, but she has poured perfume on my feet.

Therefore, I tell you, her many sins have been forgiven – for she loved much. But he who has been forgiven little, loves little."

Finishing his reading, Father Tucker told me that forgiveness was synonymous with grace. He gave me a moment to absorb that concept. Then he asked me what I thought Jesus was saying to the Pharisee Simon.

I replied, "Simon the Pharisee might have been a bigger sinner than the woman, but he didn't know it."

"OK, that's interesting," Father Tucker answered. He then asked me what I thought about redemption.

494

"Redemption comes through acknowledgment," I answered.

"Excellent. So what are you willing to acknowledge?" Father Tucker asked.

I couldn't answer. I didn't want to answer, and then I said, "I have some soul searching to do I guess."

"David, you can't know grace until you can admit that you too are a sinner," Father Tucker said. "But don't worry. God has a way of waking us up. You'll be fine. No one escapes."

"Escapes what?" I asked.

"That's for me to know and you to find out."

The next drama wasn't too far off.

23. A cry for help

I was furious – *at Mathew.* He wanted Kelly out of the group.

"He's found a replacement," Ann said.

"Really? Who?"

"Are you sitting down?" Ann paused, then choked out the name. "Keke Wyatt."

I hit the roof. What the hell is going on in my absence? I wondered. I had heard Keke as a child in Houston. I liked her. I had nothing against her. She sang beautifully, but she didn't fit the group then, and I was sure she wouldn't fit now.

As I understood it, Kelly had done nothing to deserve the ill treatment. Apparently, several of the producers hired to work on the girls' demos for Elektra liked Kelly's voice and singing. Of course they did, I thought. So now the Knowleses were intensifying their campaign to shut Kelly down for good. When was this going to end? I wondered. Ann assured me that Kelly had not yet been told, and I begged her not to. I was never sure whether she ever found out about her near-exile.

So much depends on reputation in the music business. Some fabricate it, some embellish to gain it, some lie for it, some omit the truth, some annihilate the competition, some pay for it, some steal it, and some will even kill for it. How far were the Knowleses willing to go to ensure Beyoncé's supremacy over everyone?

Again, Beyoncé's talent didn't need their constant push. No one was going to usurp her, not with her talent and after all the work she'd put in. Kelly too was brilliant, in her own way. She was no threat to Beyoncé's climb and Beyoncé was no threat to Kelly's. It was clear that the producers recognized Beyoncé's vocal genius. For their purposes, whatever they were, they also liked Kelly's singing for its own values. Neither their intentions nor Celestine and Mathew's pushing would change Beyoncé's course, and Kelly, too, like all my girls, deserved a fair shot at fulfilling her promise. I had heard her brilliance in that nine-year-old whisper. By educating her – equipping her with a very real weapon, her own talent – which I hoped she wouldn't betray – I wanted to help Kelly escape her family's generational dysfunction.

Her child would not live in a car....

But then Fate came knocking. None of this, not Kelly, not Beyoncé, mattered in the end. No, once again, Mathew had conjured up confusion.

Ann told me that amongst other hare-brained ideas, Mathew had allegedly talked Daryl into letting him hire no-names to work on the "demos" that would determine the girls' Elektra album direction. Whether that was fully accurate, I can't swear, but when the astute Sylvia Rhone heard the resulting poor-quality demo recordings, she hit the roof. I did too, once I heard them. The production was third-rate – amateurish, at best.

Furthermore, according to Ann, Elektra executives discovered and were understandably angry over the misappropriation of monies they'd given for the hiring of producers. It couldn't be accurately accounted for. It was suspected, and even said, that Mathew had pocketed most of it. I got it, on good authority, that missing money wasn't Mathew's only fault with the label. Without further discussion, Elektra called off the entire deal. Eight months into the contract with Elektra and my girls were dropped.

496

On the day Elektra's dismissal letter arrived they cried like babies. They didn't understand why their dream had ended, and so abruptly. One day they were recording, the next they were on a plane headed for Houston.

"It all happened so quickly," Beyoncé said.

It took everything I had to keep silent.

Celestine, however, did not. She'd had enough. She, her girls, and Kelly left Mathew sitting in the middle of an empty house and moved into a rented two-bedroom condominium. Ann's nephew Belfrey Brown and a couple of his friends helped move Celestine that day to their new palace on Newcastle Street. I have never forgotten it. I doubt if Mathew ever did. Years later I would learn that he'd been sitting right there while Celestine, Belfrey, and his helpers packed up everything. No fight, no argument, just a face reflecting a shameless good-riddance attitude.

I can remember driving over to the Braesmeadow Drive dwelling in 1995 to find Mathew curled up on the floor. Was it a dream? As I entered the back door, he got up, wiped his eyes, and stared starkly into mine. When I inquired as to his family's whereabouts, his response shook me in my soul. That much is vivid. He said, "Fuck them. They'll be back when the fuckin money starts to roll in."

I turned and left the house. 1995 was turning out to be just what fate had meant it to be, a fucked-up year for us all.

Gregory, and now this.

* * * * *

We had beautiful late-July weather in Portland, Oregon, our last performance and stop on the *Porgy and Bess* National Tour. The tour had been outstanding in every way. I'd learned so much, mostly about myself. Boy, was I thankful for those lessons. Now I needed some quiet. Regardless of all the union business, performance stress, and death, and despite the fighting with Gregory, I was finding peace.

While I waited in the lobby of the Imperial Hotel in downtown Portland for my former Langston University professor and voice teacher Mrs. Rainbow to arrive, I let my mind drift. Mrs. Rainbow knew all about my girls, and my long years of work with them. We'd talked about them often via telephone and over dinner, whenever I'd travel back to Oklahoma. She found my experience of "raising future pop stars" to be intriguing. I hadn't spoken to her since the tour dates in San Diego, and now she and I, together with her daughters Ariana and Anastasia, had a lunch date. It was a satisfying day, connecting my past and my present with Mrs. Rainbow.

By this time, I was beginning to hear from Beyoncé that she had developed an aversion to sharing her personal space with Kelly. She told me that she hated having to live in a "small apartment," as she accurately called their new two-bedroom place. When Kelly had moved into Beyoncé's home, naturally the girls needed a period of adjustment. Now, in addition to her "small apartment" experience, she confessed to me during a phone call, "Before Solange came along I got all the attention, then I *had to* learn to share. Now I have to share with two people."

I couldn't believe what I was hearing. "Every sibling feels that way, at some point or other," I answered. Beyoncé's words disturbed me deeply. They oozed from her lips as though she was expressing undoubted and inalienable rights. Every human being eventually must leave childhood behind, and Beyoncé needed to remember that she was better than her worst self. I spoke my mind. I explained to her, "All people suffer setbacks." She too would have things to overcome in life, I said, to which she replied, "I know, but we are broke. We have no money."

"Pride goes before destruction and a haughty spirit before a fall," I said, quoting a famous proverb to her. "Beyoncé, you have been warned. Enough said."

* * * * *

By September, three of my girls had auditioned for Houston's version of the High School for the Performing and Visual Arts (HSPVA). Beyoncé

498

and LeToya got in, Kelly did not. I just didn't want to believe that Kelly, with her beautiful voice, sensitive phrasing and passion, hadn't given her all at the HSPVA audition.

When I finally got her on the phone from New York, it was obvious that something traumatic was going on with her. The negative-self talk had not only returned, but it had intensified. Kelly sounded like she'd resolved herself to being substandard. I assured her, once again, of her talent, but to no avail. I even tried telling her that I knew the head of the voice department at HSPVA, a Mrs. Bonner, and that I promised to look into it.

Her response? "Whatever."

It was most unsettling, to say the least.

At any rate, I called Mrs. Patricia Bonner, whom I had met years ago through my student Shevon Jacobs-Loftin, an HSPVA graduate. A dedicated teacher, Mrs. Bonner lived for music, just as I did. Always on the lookout for voice teachers to help her "babies," as she called them, Mrs. Bonner asked Shevon if she knew someone who could help two students that Mrs. Bonner felt had great potential, and could benefit from patient instruction. Days later (this was 1990-91), Mosha Phillips and Jacqueline Pugh joined my studio, to positive results. An easy person to talk to, Mrs. Bonner now was agreeing to answer my questions about Kelly truthfully.

"Kelly has a beautiful voice, but she lacks the confidence needed for matriculation at HSPVA."

I was floored. "Really?" I asked. After a slight pause, I continued. "Kelly is an amazing singer, extraordinary, as a matter of fact." I knew that Kelly could sing her butt off, but only if she dared to show it.

"Maybe, but on the day of her audition she didn't exhibit that." Mrs. Bonner continued, "It sounded as if she was holding back. When she was prompted to give more, she gave less."

I thanked Mrs. Bonner, and hung up the phone. What was I going to do? As hard as I'd worked to motivate Kelly, her past *was* determining her future. Then I thought, no wait. Kelly had sabotaged her own audition. And she hadn't lived in the Knowles house a full year. Fuck…

On my next flight to Houston, I sat my girls down.

"Girls, I want to tell you a story." I read to them aloud from the Book of Matthew. "There once was a man who sowed good seed in his field. But while everyone was sleeping, his enemy came and sowed weeds among the wheat, and went away. When the wheat sprouted and formed heads, then the weeds also appeared.

"The owner's servants came to him and said, 'Sir, didn't you sow good seed in your field? Where then did the weeds come from?'

"'An enemy did this,' he replied.

"The servants asked him, 'Do you want us to go and pull them up?'

"'No,' he answered, 'because while you are pulling the weeds, you may root up the wheat with them. Let both grow together until the harvest. At that time I will tell the harvesters: First collect the weeds and tie them in bundles to be burned; then gather the wheat and bring it into the barn.'"

"Then God left the crowd and went into the house. His disciples came to him and said. 'Explain to us the parable of the weeds in the field.'

"God answered. 'The one who sowed the good seed is the Son of Man. The field is the world, and the good seed stands for the sons of the kingdom. The weeds are the sons of the evil one, and the enemy who sows them is the devil. The harvest is the end of the age, and the harvesters are angels.

"'As the weeds are pulled up and burned in the fire, so it will be at the end of the age. The Son of Man will send out his angels, and they will weed out of his kingdom everything that causes sin and all who do evil. They will throw them into the fiery furnace, where there will be weeping and gnashing of teeth. Then the righteous will shine like the sun in the kingdom of their Father. He who has ears, let him hear.'"

I completed the reading, waiting for a reaction.

Perplexed, my girls looked at me bashfully. I let the words of the parable sink in. Then, after a brief discussion about what I sensed was going on with them while I was away, we went on with our rehearsal. They'd understand the deeper point soon enough. The music business would show them no mercy. And neither would Celestine and Mathew Knowles, their feared, if not fearless, leaders.

Excited about my Cleveland Opera debut in Verdi's opera *Rigoletto*, I packed my suitcase. David Bamberger had made good on his offer to bring me back to Cleveland, and in addition to my debut with the company, I had been offered another opportunity. A young soprano, Helen Todd, and I had been hired to sing excerpts from *Rigoletto* for inner city school children. "Great," I thought.

I boarded my flight to New York's LaGuardia Airport, fulfilled and grateful. My own coffers were filling up handsomely.

1996 was certainly turning out to be a better year!

* * * * *

As expected, Teresa still championed the girls' talents, but nonetheless, winning over executives at Columbia would be no easy feat. No one there had forgotten Mathew's ploy to play them against Daryl, with whom he had a signed contract. And now Mathew had allegedly stolen money, from Elektra records of all places. Still, Ann hoped that Teresa could help her scale the wall of deceit that Mathew had built. Plus, she hoped that Daryl's removing himself from the project would help Columbia forgive the past.

Celestine continued to speak accusingly about Teresa's past "inability" to secure serious interest from her colleagues at Columbia Records.

"Nonsense," I said.

Celestine's pessimistic and dismissive way of thinking covered her own "generational" attitude. A somewhat warped traditionalist, Celestine believed women to be powerless. Ignored by her own father, she'd come to understand that men were better at a negotiation table. That's what she said, anyway.

I said to her, "Teresa is respected in the business, and is an amazing A&R. I can't imagine that she wouldn't be able to bring her male colleagues to the table – if you think that's so important." I felt confident in Teresa's position.

"We'll see," Celestine answered.

* * * * *

When Teresa asked why the Elektra deal had been lost, Ann opted to tell the truth, which infuriated Mathew. Her honesty embarrassed him. Still, Ann held her ground. Teresa deserved honesty, Ann said. After all, they needed her now – more than ever.

Teresa, acutely aware of who Mathew was, in all his effervescent glory, came up with an idea. The answer could be in finding a well-established producer, one who produced hits, one who could oversee the entire project – and *the money*. Naturally Mathew was insulted, but what could he say? Ann too would be suspect in Sony Columbia's eyes. Mathew would not sit alone in that hot seat. However, Teresa generously gave him the benefit of the doubt. In fact she didn't want to believe that he had pocketed the girls' future, but she would be no fool. Convinced that finding the right producer was the first order of business, Ann suggested to Teresa that she had the perfect person in mind.

Ann contacted her old friend Alonzo "Lonnie" Jackson, who had long since returned to the Oakland, California, area. Lonnie and the girls had a long history, and Ann trusted him. According to Ann, Lonnie was great friends with D'Wayne Wiggins, who was producer extraordinaire in 1995-96, and a member of the wildly successful boy band Tony, Toni, Toné.

"He'd make the perfect producer for us," Ann said.

"I think that is a brilliant idea, Ann," I agreed.

"Yes, Teresa thinks so too."

However, Mathew's ego had once again been bruised. Who cares? I thought to myself. Mathew was not the consummate professional who'd satisfy Teresa and her colleagues at Columbia. D'Wayne Wiggins, however, would. "I'm working on getting him to the table," Ann said.

According to Ann, Teresa believed with every fiber of her body that she'd be successful. "The time is right," Ann added. "Not to mention, D'Wayne understands the group dynamic from the inside out."

Teresa's plan worked like a charm. Beyoncé told me that Sony/Columbia had agreed to hear them *without* a demo. With D'Wayne Wiggins on board,

502

the production deal could be signed and in the can by December. He and his company, "Grassroots," had received word from Columbia, as had Ann and Mathew. The girls were being granted a live audition in New York. If I remember correctly, their audition was to take place in January. I recall planning to re-arrange my ticket to be in Houston earlier, so that I could prepare them.

I was already scheduled to land in Houston on January 12th, as the HGO had called a January 14th brush-up rehearsal for *Porgy*. We were scheduled to take the opera on tour to Japan. I can recall telling Beyoncé that I'd fly in earlier in order to work with the group. And I definitely haven't forgotten that I said, "I will be in Tokyo when you guys audition in New York, but I promise you that you'll be ready."

Then, after I had talked to the other girls, expressing my excitement about their upcoming audition, Beyoncé passed the phone to Mathew, who was chomping at the bit.

"Hey, David," Mathew said. He asked when I planned on arriving, adding, "Man this is it. Sony. The big time."

"I'll re-arrange my flight to land in Houston on January 1st."

"OK," Mathew said. "The girls are excited to go to New York. While we are there we want to go to the studio. Can you block out the time, giving me a date in mid-January?"

"I can't be there, Mathew. Sorry. I have *Porgy* brush-up rehearsals in Houston for the Japan tour," I answered. "I'm not scheduled to even be in Houston until the 12th, but I'll call HGO now and have my ticket changed." I added, "I'm sure it won't be a problem,"

There was an awkward silence. After a few seconds, Mathew then said to me that I needed to make a decision.

"What do you mean, Mathew? Naturally I am going to make arrangements to prepare the girls. You don't need to worry," I said.

He responded, "It is either your career or Beyoncé."

I lost it.

"Go fuck yourself. I am not Beyoncé's servant," I screamed. "I am the goddam gift-giver here, and don't *you* ever fucking forget it." I slammed the telephone down. Mathew's narcissism brought out the absolute worst in me. Seeing only red in that moment, I had forgotten that Mathew had turned on the speaker phone. According to her mother, in a conversation with me later that night, Beyoncé had heard every awful word. Celestine called me to apologize again for Mathew. Beyoncé was in tears, she said.

I hadn't been raised to be non-empathetic. Naturally I understood and do understand the human condition, but in dealing with Mathew I had trouble remembering that scripture says, in Colossians: "Put on then, as God's chosen ones, holy and beloved, compassionate hearts, kindness, humility, meekness, and patience, bearing with one another and, if one has a complaint against another, forgiving each other; as the Lord has forgiven you, so you also must forgive. And above all these put on love, which binds everything together in perfect harmony."

I landed in Houston on January 1, as I'd promised. Mathew stayed far away from me. Whether by choice or luck, I was glad he did. He'd gotten one thing right. The Sony Columbia audition was the big time. Everything had to go off without a hitch; none of us needed his antics. My girls had been preparing now for eight long years. All their dreams were about to become reality. They were more than ready. They were sensational.

* * * * *

The cast of *Porgy and Bess* arrived in Tokyo on January 27th 1996. An electrifying city, Tokyo reminded me of New York, and specifically Times Square, except that in Tokyo most of the city seemed to be lit up all the time. I'd never seen anything like it. Not even New York was so alive. It felt as though a billion people were walking around on the very block where you were. I was both fascinated and exhausted, all at the same time.

On the evening of February 5th, I'd received a message. Awaking the next morning, I opened the envelope that had been slid under my hotel suite door and saw that it was from Ann.

"Call me ASAP," it said.

504

I spent the whole day anxious. I wanted to call Ann immediately but the time difference of some fourteen hours held me back. It was still the middle of the night in Houston. I decided to phone her at my midnight. I knew that she often had problems sleeping, falling off to sleep around 2:00 a.m. or so. Plus, she needed every second of her mornings to get out of the door on time, because of her illness and various handicaps. Any deviation might throw her off schedule, so I waited for 10 a.m. Houston time.

"HL&P, this is Ann."

"Ann, this is David. I received your message this morning. You called?"

"Yes, what time is it over there?"

"It's midnight," I answered.

"Oh, well, are you sitting down? Are you somewhere you can talk?" Ann asked.

"Yes, I am," I answered. "Out with it."

Ann giggled. She knew that I knew the reason for her call.

"Have you heard anything from Columbia Records?" I asked.

"Yes, we heard yesterday."

"Well?"

There was a long silence. The suspense was killing me. Then Ann said, "The girls WON their audition."

I screamed, in that moment not caring that I'd awakened half the hotel. "Oh my God! What did they sing? I want to hear all about it."

"They sang 'Are You Ready' and 'Ain't No Sunshine,'" Ann said.

Had I heard correctly? "Did you say 'Ain't No Sunshine'?" *My* 'Ain't No Sunshine'? The one I arranged?"

"Yes, and it was the deal closer. The girls sang brilliantly."

"I know what you are thinking," Ann said. "Beyoncé chose to sing it at the last minute, in honor of you. And just like in Atlanta, the record executives lost it. The girls gave it everything they had. They were amazing," Ann said.

I was out. Gone. Canned.

Mathew said I'd made my choice. I didn't argue.

Celestine began frantically trying to reach me in Nagoya, Japan. She imagined that she could sweet-talk me into ignoring Mathew's most recent abrasive behavior. "So be it, Celestine," I said to her. "I'm sorry, but teaching Beyoncé and *her group* is not God's only purpose for me. I wasn't born just so I could serve her, or them. That is crazy, and most unfair."

Celestine asked me to give her some time to smooth things over with Mathew. "I'm sure that I can get him to see things my way," she added.

"Take all the time you need," I answered.

That same week, Ann and I had quite a different conversation. Months earlier, they – Ann, the girls, the families – had been in an uproar. The issue: Mathew's overbearing, self-indulgent grandiosity, and his absolute need for artistic and production control had threatened the girls' deal with D'Wayne Wiggins.

D'Wayne had signed the girls to an ambitious production deal, under the auspices of his Grassroots production label. But now, according to Ann, D'Wayne had become disillusioned with Mathew. Apparently Beyoncé's father had insisted she be recognized and made lead singer on *all* the tracks.

"So, he's still on that?" I asked Ann.

"Hold your horses," Ann answered. "That's not the half of it." Ann said that Mathew had furthermore insisted that Beyoncé be included as writer on the tracks.

"What?" I asked, completely dumbfounded.

"It doesn't end there," Ann answered. "Mathew also suggested that Solange be given a chance to write. Mathew apparently said that 'Solange is pretty good.,' and then he said, 'I think she should have a crack at it.'"

"A *crack* at it," I repeated, laughing heartily. The man was crazy, absolutely crazy, I thought to myself.

"Yes, can you believe it? The gall," Ann answered. "And then, after all that, Mathew had the nerve to say, 'It can't be that difficult.'"

I couldn't help myself. My laughter had turned hysterical. "Mathew's got balls," I said, when I could speak. "Donkey balls, but balls none the less."

Ann, too, could barely continue, which I was happy to hear. She hadn't laughed much over the past year.

For me it was clear what would happen next. I hadn't known that all this had been going on even long before I'd flown to Houston to prepare the Sony Columbia audition.

"Why didn't you tell me, Ann?" I asked.

"You know me," she answered. "I'd much rather find a solution than to keep a mess going."

Ann was quite right. Finding the solution should have been all that mattered. And yes, I did know her.

Despite my love for the girls, I was fascinated by this ludicrous turn of events. It was deliciously good. Served Mathew right. D'Wayne threatened to recall his generous offer, and by June 3rd, he had.

The phone calls between New York and Houston heated up. As far as Mathew was concerned, "D'Wayne's black ass" could "stay in fucking Oakland."

Celestine, too, was dead set against the idea of another producer contract. "We don't need another production deal," she said.

"Really Celestine?" I asked. "Perhaps you're right, but you guys are sabotaging Teresa – and the girls' future – with your insistence on having it your way."

"I don't think what we're asking is unreasonable," Celestine answered. She added a resounding, "Case closed."

Celestine could be a beast.

When I talked with Beyoncé a few days later she was beside herself with worry. Nevertheless, she had her orders. Her mother had said she was to remain loyal. "I have everything under control," Celestine had said to her.

"Beyoncé, it's all going to work out."

She didn't answer.

"Remember what I told you," I added. "Once again: You *are* going to make it, and in spite of your parents. Becoming a great singer is part of your destiny – God's glorious plan for your life."

Still, Beyoncé remained despondent. All those years of adverse stimuli were sucking the life out of her.

As a result, years of ups and downs, of twists and turns and of disappointment, Beyoncé had now become lethargic. She had already begun to guard herself in counter-productive ways, especially after her parents separated, but now she seemed less awake, and with every call she was getting worse. Solange even had to pull her from her bed to come to the phone. She admitted that she hadn't eaten in days. Her voice was audibly weak, feeble even. More introverted than usual, she had wrapped herself in an isolation that ate at her like a cankerous sore. Damn them, I said to myself.

Celestine let Beyoncé sulk, which was an indulgence that I was firmly against. I reached out to her at the salon. I talked and talked, even – in my frustration – shouting my concerns, but "whatever Celestine's baby wanted, baby was allowed to do."

"Beyoncé's going to be just fine," she said. "And you know what?"

"What?"

"So will you."

"This is not about me, Celestine. This is about Beyoncé. Her depression is getting worse," I said.

Celestine said nothing.

I wanted so much to believe that Beyoncé's mother was taking her bouts with depression to heart, but her reaction said differently. Celestine and Mathew's primary focus had always been toughening up their precious Beyoncé. In actuality they were destroying her ability to cope. Nevertheless, I just couldn't abandon my student, even if I was *still out*, as Celestine hinted. How does one raise genius and just walk away, uncaring, and detached? You don't. I certainly couldn't.

Ann's efforts to keep D'Wayne and Mathew's discord from Teresa and Sony Columbia had failed miserably. "Not to worry," was Teresa's alleged response. I was glad when Ann told me that Teresa said that she had an idea how to solve the problem. I prayed that it would work.

Celestine swore to me that neither she nor Mathew was against having a star producer on board, which I believed was a fantastic lie. After I called her out about it, she admitted that it was D'Wayne himself, and his ability, that she and Mathew had questioned.

"You thought the same thing about Daryl," I said.

"And I was right," Celestine answered.

There was no point in arguing. Celestine was always right, even if she'd never admit that it had been her hand that had forced Daryl's fate. Nevertheless, I believed that nothing would keep my girls from destiny. They were too good – better than good – exceptional.

I remember thinking that it would be Beyoncé who would pay the high spiritual price for her parents' greed. Still, making Celestine and Mathew my vehement enemy wasn't my goal, so I kept my moral conviction tied up with my tongue – bound in a knot. Still, I could admit to myself that their motives were questionable, challenging all understanding. With my new-found independence, I simply refused to return to covert search and destroy missions with Donkey Mathew and Witch Celestine. I'd put that craziness behind me, for good.

My further attempts to reach out to Mathew went unanswered, and even Celestine remained unusually quiet. I was supposed to head to Houston to continue with the girls' lessons. I had promised the girls, but Celestine felt that they needed a break. "They are so depressed," she said. "Of course," I answered. But after calling each girl at home, I discovered that the only one deeply depressed was Beyoncé. In my opinion, it seemed that she was shutting down more and more, with each passing conversation we had.

Celestine remained strangely nonchalant.

Despite Celestine's attempt at a smoke screen, I knew that Beyoncé's depression was less about the Elektra debacle and more about her parents' state of affairs. Her worst nightmare had come true. Mathew and Celestine were separated, and a traumatized Beyoncé saw divorce on the horizon. It wasn't just because Mathew and Celestine couldn't take one another anymore. Celestine's decision to leave Mathew had everything to do with her need to force a change from him. I asked myself when women would learn that trying to change a man was the worst – and least effective – thing you could do to him. Mathew could give a damn about Celestine's ultimatums. It was all about him. He was great, completely self-absorbed. Yes, it was Beyoncé's parents who depressed her. And in my opinion, they'd tarnish her very soul if she wasn't careful. I was sure of it.

In a bold move, Mama Celestine suddenly decided to sit Beyoncé down for a chat. "It's time," Celestine said. She'd aimed to tell Beyoncé "the truth." I don't know exactly what Celestine told her, and I didn't ask, but it must have been a life- changing exposé of her father, as interpreted by her mother. After that I wouldn't recognize my student. Beyoncé began to use foul language, aimed at her father. The contempt and resentment that I had predicted would come had shown its ugly face and, according to the other girls, it wasn't pretty. I was speechless when I witnessed her wrath for myself, even as I secretly rationalized, in my own mind, that these outbursts signaled "better late than never." Kelly, LeToya, and LaTavia liked their new and improved sister.

I did not.

Ignoring his daughter, Mathew forged ahead, torching everyone and everything in his path. In 1994 he had told Beyoncé that one day she'd understand the necessity to "kill everything in your way," as explanation for his throwing LeToya out of the group. "Sometimes you have to shoot," he concluded. I guess Beyoncé was now a believer in his directive. However, Mathew hadn't expected to be the object of her first killing. In answer to her newly found aggression, he twisted information and spun blatant untruths, selectively omitting anything that didn't favor his purpose. Mathew incessantly maneuvered us into corners by circulating false information. That confused the public perception, and it confused us. "The product" – *his group* – began to doubt their own memory, perception, and sanity.

510

I called Mama.

In our conversation, I described to Mama an old black-and-white film that resembled our situation. She said, "Oh, the movie you're talking about is called 'Gaslight,' I think. I believe it starred Ingrid Bergman." I hunted the film down. This 1944 thriller was a dead-on mirror of what was happening to us, and of Mathew's psychopathy in action. After watching it, I called Ann with my new realization. She was clearly shocked when I said, "Perhaps I shouldn't say this, but our fighting with Mathew isn't working. Let's let the white folks handle him. He'll listen to them, and only them."

Mathew Knowles had underestimated Silvia Rhone, the CEO at Elektra Records and the most powerful black woman in the music business. When she dropped the girls from Elektra, he called her a "black ass dike bitch." Knowing all of that, Mama had commented succinctly, "He's not about to disrespect the good white folks at Columbia Records."

She "knew Mathew's kind," and so did I.

Most black people do.

Happily, by the end of January, the fruit that was Teresa's idea had ripened. Joy had returned to the Knowles house – well, almost. Sony's decision was to keep D'Wayne, offering him a direct deal with the label. He'd remain in charge, the girls' producer, oversee the money, and be the go-to man for the label with management. A livid Mathew had been forced to acquiesce.

Celestine took special delight in informing me that I was *back in*, officially. This was shortly before Ann's call to me in Tokyo.

Now, on February 14th, a relieved Beyoncé, and her equally happy sisters, breathed an elongated sigh of relief.

But, true to the familiar pattern, the next problem was just around the corner.

During a long and expensive call with Beyoncé from my hotel in Osaka, on February 17th, I learned that she and the other girls were now in a battle to hold on to their most recent name: "Destiny." Da Dolls were gone, and Destiny waited in the wings. Except...

511

"There is a girl group in Mississippi who has the name 'Destiny,'" Beyoncé said.

"Well, what about buying the name from them? Have your father and Ann looked into that? Destiny is such a fitting name."

"We like it too," Beyoncé answered. "Columbia told us though that if the girls refused to sell it, we would definitely have to change ours."

"Ah, OK. Well, let's wait and see," I said.

"When are you coming back to Houston?" Beyoncé asked. "I need a voice lesson, real bad."

"We leave Osaka in the morning and I'll be in Houston three days later – after I change out my suitcase," I added.

"Good," she answered.

By the time I returned to the U.S., Mathew and Celestine had reconciled. She'd moved back into the house with Mathew, a different house but on the same Braes Meadow Drive, some three or so months after having left it.

Mathew had called it.

The fucking money was about to roll in.

* * * * *

At our first lesson and rehearsal after their successful Sony Columbia audition, Beyoncé could hardly wait to tell me about the room they auditioned in, at Sony headquarters in New York. She revealed that it was so small, they could have reached out and touched the executives.

"By the way, I heard that you all sang 'Ain't No Sunshine,'" I said.

"Yes, and we were fierce," LaTavia said, snapping her fingers twice in a Z formation. She'd become such a hag.

The girls fell about. They were having fun like Christmas. So was I. I loved seeing them happy, full of laughter. A puzzled Beyoncé asked, "Hey, wait a minute. How do you know we sang that song?"

"Ann told me," I answered. "And thank you for thinking of me. It was very noble of you to suggest it, Beyoncé." That had been my moment – to let Beyoncé know just how much I appreciated her acknowledgment.

With the warmest smile on her face that I'd ever seen from her, Beyoncé said, "It felt right."

Now I smiled. "Well, when Ann told me that you sang that song, I got a little emotional," I said.

"Ah –, " Kelly said.

"I'm so incredibly proud of you all," I concluded.

Hugs were overflowing.

"Hey, are you going to be in town for our signing party?" Kelly asked.

"I don't think so. It's in summer and I'll be singing in Milan, Italy, on the *Porgy* tour. But you know I'll be there in spirit," I answered. "You all must know by now; I am always with you."

"Uh – like – every time we take a breath," LaTavia said.

Once again they fell about.

I was one proud papa! Suddenly, I clapped my hands together. "Okay you girls. Enough with the fun – it's time to work." We had lots to do, continuing our studies in Feldenkrais: "Thinking While Acting" (listen, carry through, and adjust), "Freeing Action from Wasted Energy" (eliminating useless movement), and "Breathing Rhythm" (adjusting the breath to the speed of movement).

* * * * *

Performances at La Scala, Italy's premier opera house and mecca to all opera singers, were going well. It was touch and go at first. Not because of any mishap, but due to the stage itself. La Scala's stage is a beast.

We had arrived in Milan by way of Alitalia Airlines on July 7th. The heat was tremendous, worse than any humid day in Houston or Miami, if you can imagine that. Check-in at The Hotel D'Uomo went without incident. My suite was beautifully situated, complete with a small balcony, which faced Milan's famous Cathedral. Every morning, I took breakfast on that balcony, soaking up Milanese life, and of course the city's love for music. It was everywhere.

Almost immediately after checking in to the hotel, I headed over alone to the opera house. Standing in the foyer of La Scala, I quickly became overwhelmed with nostalgia. I had dreamed of standing where some of the world's greatest opera legends had stood, including my mentor, Grace Bumbry. I'd be seeing what they saw, hearing what she heard, and experiencing the enthusiastic Milanese audience, a special breed of Italians known for booing even the best of them, if they didn't like a singer. I couldn't wait to sing on that stage.

La Scala was just as I'd imagined it, but singing in "heaven" would require us all to make some adjustments. Typical of opera singers everywhere, I yearned to try out my voice on the stage. With just the ghost light to dispel the darkness, I sang a few phrases. Nothing came back. Suddenly I heard a voice from out in the house somewhere, *"Se si vuole essere ascoltati, si deve cantare in questo punto del palcoscenico."* (If you want to be heard you will have to sing on this point on the stage.) Those wise words came from Teatro alla Scala's very own fire chief, who unbeknownst to me had been listening. He was a man so breathtakingly beautiful, that Michelangelo himself would have marveled. Noticing my stare, he told me his name and then said, "I am head fireman." Suddenly, it was warm, very warm. "Breathe, David. Breathe," I told myself.

"Mecca is dead as wood," he said in a thick Italian accent.

I smiled, nervously. "Si, è vero." (Yes, it's true.) And that is exactly what the stage of La Scala was – aged wood.

It was also the reason the theater has its own fire department. The way those glorious planks soaked up sound would put "Bounty," the American paper towel brand, and its slogan to shame. Absolutely nothing sung upstage, anywhere on the stage, could be heard out in the house.

The next morning, our first rehearsal day, Amy Hutchinson, our resident assistant director, announced that we would have only four days to re-block the show.

The cast's murmur became a dull roar.

"I know this is alarming, but we have no other choice. We're going to have to completely re-block it, pulling everything down center stage," Amy added. Then running forward to the spot she'd meant, she said, "Here. Right here is where all solo lines will have to be sung. Stand here and don't move," Amy concluded.

"OK, that's easy," someone answered. "But what about those of us who have business to do on stage? Where do we go?"

"You have to play everything here, in this space," Amy answered. "Start from where your original blocking had put you, and then move your sung business downstage, staying in this marked area."

Now the cast was really grumbling.

"I know," Amy said. "But believe me, you won't be heard otherwise."

"Oh," somebody said. "Girl, that's all you had to say," another one added.

That good-humored remark broke the tension, and we fell about. Then we got down to the grueling work, with very little time to complete the task. If your memory was bad, you were in trouble. A few of my less experienced colleagues quickly became frustrated. I remember wishing that my girls had been there, in Italy. If ever there was a lesson in "Thinking while acting," re-staging *Porgy* at La Scala was it. In the words of Moshe Feldenkrais, "It is much more difficult to change a habit than one might think, as all who have ever tried know."

I had harped repeatedly to Beyoncé, Kelly, LeToya, and LaTavia, about awareness, connection, and movement, while paying close attention to time and space. These were principles that I'd learned as a professional dancer, studying Merce Cunningham's technique. But it was also an important exercise and process in the study of movement, initiated and developed by martial arts guru Moshe Feldenkrais. In his words, thinking while acting was about learning to hear instructions while carrying out an exercise, and how to make the necessary adjustments without stopping the movement itself.

* * * * *

I called Ann to check in on her and see how she was doing.

"I've been better," she answered.

There was something strange in her voice. I didn't know what it was, but when I pushed her for an explanation, she changed the subject.

"How's Milan?" Ann asked.

Taking a few minutes, I resigned myself to the fact that whatever bothered her, she didn't want to discuss and answered, "La Scala is amazing. The house is an acoustical nightmare, but the fans here are amazing," I added. "I'll never forget the long autograph lines we enjoy nightly."

"And speaking of enthusiastic fans," I continued. "I had lunch yesterday with my mentor Grace Bumbry."

"Really," Ann said. "That must have been exciting."

"It was," I answered. "She drove in from Lugano, Switzerland, where she lives. It's only about 45 minutes outside Milan." I added. "Have you ever heard of the famous designer 'Biki'? I asked.

Ann had not.

"Well, she is a direct descendant of Puccini – his granddaughter, as a matter of fact," I said. "At any rate, she's one of Grace's dress designers, so we agreed to meet at Biki's atelier," I added. Then I told Ann that Grace was having two dresses made.

"Two?" Ann asked.

"Yes, one she will wear to the famous Vienna Opera Ball, and the other to an important engagement in Athens."

"Wow," Ann answered.

"She looked stunning, even if the dress was being held together by pins," I added.

We both laughed.

After Grace had finished up with the dress fitting, we headed to lunch. Grace's recommendation was that we eat at Ristorante Galleria because they had air conditioning, which in 1996 was still a precious commodity in Europe, and especially in Italy, where summer temperatures can be unbearable.

516

"Ann, she'd driven the Rolls Royce. We went to lunch in style," I boasted. "Naturally, I was excited. I have never ridden in a Rolls Royce before. Hell, I'd never even stood next to one before," I concluded.

"Don't make me laugh. It hurts," Ann said.

I apologized and then continued. "When we drove up to the restaurant people started to stare. But once we got out of the car, I understood why," I told Ann. "The Italians started screaming 'Bumbry, Bumbry, La grande cantante lirica' *[Bumbry, Bumbry, the great opera singer]*. They erupted into cheers, with some rather rambunctious clapping."

"Within seconds there was a mob. The Maître d' and his staff came out to help us into the restaurant, which was no easy feat. The Milanese people go crazy for opera. I felt like I was with a rock star. Did you know they call Grace the 'Aretha of Opera'?" I added.

"Really?" Ann answered.

"It goes without saying, we got the best table."

"It sounds like quite the lunch date."

"I had a great time," I answered. "Afterwards Grace dropped me at my hotel. You should have seen the faces of the hotel staff," I added. "From that moment on I was treated like royalty at the Hotel D'Uomo."

"You are living the life," Ann said.

"How are our girls?" I asked Ann.

"The girls are great. They are still recording out in California with D'Wayne, and making me proud," Ann answered. "The tracks sound great and their singing is even greater. The harmonies are so tight."

Ann couldn't see it, but her last words were music to my ears. Then Ann said, "Too bad you weren't here for the signing party."

"Yes, I hate I missed it, but did you take pictures?"

"Yep. My sister took a slew of them. I'll send them to you. They should have arrived by the time you return home from Italy."

"Great," I said.

"When do you get back?"

"On my birthday, July 22nd," I answered.

A few days later, I called to check in on Ann again. Her older son, Armon, told me that she was sleeping. I promised to call back. When I got Ann on the phone, I could not believe my ears. Something was really off with her. Ann seemed distant, further away than the other day. Her entire demeanor seemed controlled.

"Ann is everything all right?" I asked. "You seem a bit stressed." Coughing, and beating her chest to loosen the heavy phlegm buildup in her bronchial tubes, Ann took a breath and began to speak but then she stopped.

"Mama, are you all right?" her son Armon asked, who had obviously rushed into the room.

It took a few seconds, but Ann finally was able to answer. "Yes, Baby, Mama is all right. I just swallowed wrong, sweetie. Would you get me some water?"

"Ann, should I call you back?" I asked. "I can call you back." She didn't sound good. This phone call was tiring her, I thought.

"No, give me a minute," she answered. Then she whispered, "I'm glad you called actually. I need to talk to *someone*."

Just in that moment, I heard Armon's voice again. "Here Mama," he said. He'd brought her the glass of water.

Ann reminded Armon that she needed a straw. Then, suddenly I heard the voice of Ann's best friend, Patricia Felton, in the background. She and her husband, Vincent, had arrived to take Armon to his game. Their son played on the same basketball team. Suddenly, I heard Pat calling for Chris.

"We're going to be late, Chris," Pat said.

Seconds later, I heard Ann shout, "Look after your brother, Armon," and then she thanked Pat.

"Mama, are you sure you're going to be OK? I don't have to go to the game tonight," Armon said.

"How are you going to get to the NBA if you start skipping games?" Ann asked. "No, you go to your game, Baby. Mama will be all right," Ann added.

"Are you sure?" Armon asked again.

"Yes. Now get out of here, boy," Ann said.

My mind was racing. I could hear the boys and Pat leave the room. A few seconds later, Ann became emotional. Slowly, and with great effort, she began to speak. "I'm worried about Chris," Ann finally said.

"What about Chris?" I asked.

Apparently, Chris had carved the words "If my mother dies, I am going to die" into Ann's dining room table.

My eyes welled up.

Her son's pain was ripping Ann apart. I felt my heart drop into my shoes. Ann continued. "I'm so afraid for my babies," she said, now openly sobbing. "I don't want to die. I pray every day that God spare me."

It was obvious. Chris's words were a cry for help. I could well imagine his pain and confusion. He was just thirteen years old in 1996, and adored his mother. He still hadn't ever really gotten over his dad and little sister's death, and now his mother might die. It was too much for him. Years later, Armon confessed to me that going out the door, and to that basketball game, had been a very difficult thing to do. He understood how sick his mother was, as did Chris. Essentially, Ann's children had been reliving the five stages of grief, over and over again, since 1986. That fateful night permeated their lives, and their dreams, Armon told me. Chris was in despair that he could not change the situation.

Naturally, it took a few minutes before I could speak again. When I did I asked Ann if she'd considered getting professional help for the boys.

"Yes, I've asked my main doctor for some referrals."

In the meantime, she'd continue to take her troubles to the Lord, she said. "He is still a just God," she added.

What a brave woman, I thought.

Part V

The final ordeal

24. Ann's Death

Only a few days into *Porgy* performances in Milan, I received a severe shock. Dead asleep, I was awakened in my hotel suite by a telephone call at 4 o'clock in the morning.

"Hello," I said, rather annoyed.

"David," the voice on the other end said. "This is Tanginique."

"Who?"

"*Tangie!* I work with your mother. I'm Warren's wife. Warren – George's brother." My sleepy brain slowly began to make sense of what my mother's colleague was saying. In my mind, I could see my mother back in Houston. She had settled into a new life – a new job, a new house, and a new beau, George, the man she'd eventually marry. But what was the reason for this call?

"Ah yes," I said. "What can I do for you Tangie?"

"I'm sorry to wake you," she said, hesitatingly, "but it's about your mother." I waited for her to continue, and after a few second that seemed minutes, she said, "It's about Fern."

Now sitting straight up in the bed, I reached over and turned on the lamp and looked at the clock. "Is my mother all right? Is she alive?" I asked, as calmly as I could manage.

"Oh God, yes," Tangie answered. Apologizing profusely for alarming me, while trying lamely to backtrack from her ambiguity, she tried another tack, which only made matters worse. "Fern is okay. But she's not safe."

"What do you mean?" I told myself to breathe and pushed Tangie to get to the point. "What's this about, Tangie?" I asked.

"It's about George."

"George?'"

"Yes, and drugs," Tangie added.

"Drugs?" I didn't understand. "Are you trying to tell me that my mother is on drugs?"

"No, George is, and because of it your mother is in danger," Tangie said. "Fern has been sleeping in a chair with a butcher knife."

"What?" I got up and began pacing the floor as I listened to Tangie.

According to her, Mama hadn't left her house in days. She said that my mother had had a visitor, a local drug dealer, and that things threatened to "escalate." "I'm frightened for your mother," Tangie added.

"Okay, stop," I said. I had to call my mother. It felt as though the blood was draining from my body. I thanked Tangie for her call, and for her candor. "I have to hang up now," I said.

Mama's phone rang and rang. "C'mon Mama, pick up," I mumbled to myself. Finally, she answered. I listened as my mother told me about George's little problem. She'd only just found out, she said. I found her words hard to take, or to believe. It was her job to see such things. Sensing my blood pressure rising, Mama said, "I need to correct what Tangie told you." Mama swore that she'd received only a strange telephone call. "No one has come to the house."

"Well, Mama, that makes me feel so much better," I said facetiously.

"There's something else," Mama went on. "Both George and your car are missing."

I stopped breathing, again. Had I heard Mama correctly? Of course I had. Swallowing hard, I asked, in utter disbelief and angry as hell, if Mama had called the police.

"Yes, I filed a police report, but I didn't have the license plate number, or the registration, or the insurance papers to give them. And I was too embarrassed to call you."

Silence.

"Are you still there, baby?" Mama asked.

"Yes, Mama, I am still here." I was furious. Before leaving the country, I'd asked her specifically not to let George drive my cars. Now, for rea-

522

sons I didn't care to hear – she'd fallen in love with the man – she'd taken the chance. Not only could she not complete the police report without getting information from me, she also had no way to get to or from work. She revealed that my second car, a Nissan Stanza, which she also had in her possession, was on the mend. She hadn't told me that either.

"Okay, Mama," I said, completely agitated and avoiding the subject of love. I gave a shit about George's drug addiction. Then I heard Father Tucker's voice in my head. I recalled our discussion about Simon the Pharisee and the money lender. I got a chill. My grandmother's voice also came rushing in. She'd taught me that in every problem there was an opportunity. I understood. God was getting my attention. The thing that I hated the most in Mathew Knowles, his drug addiction, had come to my family. Fighting back tears, I said "Mama, I'm going to need the case number on the police report."

"Baby, I didn't want to bother you with this," Mama answered.

"*JUST* – give me the case number, Mama – *please*." It was becoming increasingly difficult to suppress my urgent need to scream, but I had to. Ashamed, I apologetically explained, "I need it to arrange a rental car for you, Mama."

"Oh, I understand," she answered.

A few minutes later she returned to the phone. After jotting down the police report number on the hotel note pad next to the phone, I told my mother that I would get back to her as soon as possible. I called my insurance agent. After about twenty minutes of conversation, we had everything arranged.

I called Mama back. "Someone from State Farm is going to call you," I told her. "A rental car will be delivered to you at home tomorrow by Enterprise rental cars. In the meantime, my insurance agent will follow up with the police."

"I'm sorry that this happened, and that it has upset you so much," she said – again.

"No problem, Mama," I lied. Dissembling as best I could, I added, "What's done is done. I'm just glad to know the truth. I can't help you unless I know the truth," I said. "Don't you remember those words? You used them when I was a child." Mama said she did. We had a moment, and then I was back to her transportation problem. I wanted to forgive, but as I said, that was a big one for me. "Everything is taken care of, Mama. I'm just glad you're okay." That much, at least, was an honest conclusion.

"You're a good son," Mama answered.

Muffling my disappointment, I managed to say, "And you've been an even better mother." Truth be told, all I could see was the blank checkbook I kept in my car's glove compartment. Two days later my bank reported that my account was more than $6,000 short. And on July 21st, after the last *Porgy* performance, I talked to the Houston police. They'd found George, but not my car. What I found out from my mother sent me reeling. George had given my car to the drug dealer for a fix.

Fuck….

* * * * *

I landed in New York on July 22nd, in the late afternoon.

"Have you opened your birthday gift?" Gregory asked. Miles away, he'd called to congratulate me.

"Oh God," I said. I'd completely forgotten the huge box in the bedroom. "The phone's been ringing nonstop ever since I walked in the door," I answered. "Hold on." With the phone on my ear, held up by my left shoulder, I opened the package. Inside the first box was another box, and then another, and yet another. Finally, I opened what appeared to be the last of the boxes. "Gregory, what have you done?" I asked.

"Just open it…"

"Hold your horses. I am…" I looked expectantly at the last one. "Is it jewelry?" I asked.

"David, open the dang box."

"OK. I'm just playing." Inside was the most handsome diamond cross, set in white gold, with brilliant stones. "It's perfect," I said to Gregory. "I love it," and I really did. "It's beautiful," I added.

"I'm glad," Gregory said.

Gregory had worked hard to win back my confidence after his affair. I appreciated the effort and told him so.

We chatted comfortably for fifteen or twenty minutes, and before we hung up the telephone, Gregory suddenly remembered that Mathew had sent a CD to our apartment. "Oh, and Ann sent something too," he added. "Both packages are there in the living room on the fireplace mantle."

"Hold on, Gregory." I hurried to the living room, at the other end of the apartment.

"Well?" Gregory said.

"Momento. I just got the thing opened," I answered. "Ah, pictures – from the girls' signing party in Houston. And Ann wrote a note." I read it aloud:

"The evening was wonderful. D'Wayne flew in from Oakland and Kim Burse came in from New York. You haven't met her yet [*I never did meet her*], she is a junior A&R at Columbia. Enjoy!"

I began flipping through the pictures, giving a play-by-play for Gregory's benefit.

"Here's some of Ann," I said. "She looks so proud," I added. Then I came to the pictures of Preston Middleton, one with the girls and their mothers, which is just one of my treasured mementos from that time, and one of Ann's sons. There were many photos of people I didn't know. Then I happened onto a picture of Charles, LaTavia's abuser, which gave me the willies. "She looks so uncomfortable, all hugged up with his pedophile ass," I said to Gregory.

When I came to the girls' performance pictures I found myself checking out their mouths for correct vowel formations. I hated the costumes, another one of Celestine's disastrous ensembles. The girls wore black shiny pants and ankle boots, white jackets, and strange-looking leopard (or tiger) print shirts. They looked hideous. And Beyoncé appeared to be bursting the seam of her pants. She'd gained weight, which was always a sign that things weren't well in Camelot. Then I happened upon one that disturbed me to the core.

"Houston, we have a problem."

"What is it?" Gregory asked.

"I'm holding a picture of the four girls. Beyoncé seems to be openly scolding Kelly in what looks like the middle of their live performance."

What the hell was going on? I wondered.

* * * * *

The very next day I flew to Houston. I wasted no time confronting Beyoncé and Kelly, together, about the picture.

"What is this?" I asked, passing it to Beyoncé. She lowered her head, and an even more embarrassed Kelly followed her lead.

"I'm talking to you ladies. What's going on?"

Again they said nothing. Fifteen years old, and the cat had their tongue. I decided not to push.

"Whatever it is, it ends here, right now – today. Understood?"

Both girls, heads still bowed, nodded.

I'd made my point.

After our rehearsal, I found out from Mathew that Sony Columbia, D'Wayne, and Ann had finally settled on the final budget of $324,742.00 for the girls' first album. He was furious. Celestine had managed to keep Mathew out of the talks. In this she'd been dead right. King Mathew so believed in his own royalty, he insisted on "making" everyone at the label respect him. His bullish method of engaging with people at Sony Columbia was certainly one way of looking at things. Celestine, however, instinctively insisted, "It's time to surrender." How canny, I thought.

Rule number 22 in Robert Greene's 1998 book *The 48 Laws of Power* teaches how using surrender transforms weakness into power: "When you are weaker, never fight for honor's sake; choose surrender instead. Surrender gives you time to recover, time to torment and irritate your conqueror, time to wait for his power to wane. Do not give him the satisfaction of fighting and defeating you – surrender first. By turning the other cheek, you infuriate and unsettle him. Make surrender a tool for power."

At that time, in November 1996, Celestine's reason for surrender was a tad bit different from the one I would later read in Greene's book. She chose surrender not to regroup and irritate her conqueror, but rather as a device to ingratiate herself with the girls' new professional network. Celestine aimed to acquire something more important to herself – reputation. "A good reputation and respect are worth much more than silver and gold." (Proverbs 22:1-3.) Celestine still dreamed of becoming a fashion designer, obsessing about it, nonstop. Not only would Beyoncé's talents light her own way, they'd also provide the way for Celestine's own dismal star to shine. Mathew needed to "shut the fuck up," she reiterated.

Further trouble had re-appeared on her horizon in the form of a lawsuit against her and Mathew brought by Vance Publishing Company, which had produced Celestine's short-lived hair magazine. Technically, Vance was suing Mathew Knowles, but it was Celestine who hadn't paid the bill. It was her magazine, and she'd failed to remit even one red cent. Had she ever intended to pay? I wondered. I couldn't help thinking about our fight in Captain Benny's. Mama and Papa Knowles had knowingly committed fraud. Now Vance Publishing was out for blood, and I can't say as I blamed them. She certainly had made money from sales, and had surplus from her "sponsors."

During this trip to Houston, I also had a chance to see Ann. Since she always professed, in our phone calls, that she was doing well, I was eager to see for myself just how far she was slipping. I'd heard from Beyoncé that Kelly said things were bad.

During my last call with Ann in July '96 from Milan, she had confessed that she was "just happy to be alive."

"What?" I asked.

"I almost left here," Ann answered.

Almost died, she meant. "What happened?" I asked.

"Acute appendicitis is what happened," Ann answered. "I ignored it, thinking it was just one more pain."

"My God, Ann."

"I'll be fine," Ann answered, diverting the conversation to other topics.

A bit jarred, I wondered how much more my dear friend could take. I recalled her numberless trips to the hospital and the surgeries. As a result of her Lupus, she had suffered severe edema, connective tissue disorder, arterial deficiency, and palmar contractures. She had also dealt with horrific finger amputations, both at the distal joint and complete finger amputations, all due to the Raynaud's Syndrome, which her doctors had diagnosed in 1990. By 1994 she'd add chronic pulmonary fibrosis, lesions, asthma, and then acute bronchitis to her long list of ailments, and now she lay at home recuperating from a bout of acute appendicitis.

Ann described briefly her hospitalization on April 3rd. Doctors had been forced to perform yet another palm scar contracture skin graft surgery. That time they'd taken skin from her forearm. As had happened in the past, the wound wasn't healing properly. By the end of the month, Ann again experienced pain in her hand. "My finger feels cold," she said. We both knew what that meant. Her last finger would have to be amputated, doctors said. That left her thumb, a stump, and more bandages for her boys to change.

Although I was able to witness the situation up close, I understood it fully only many years later, in 2012, when her dying mother revealed to me just how much pain my friend had really been in. That year, during a telephone call with Mrs. Effie Brown, she told me everything. I then read the very detailed notes in Ann's medical records. Mrs. Brown would give me those notes, shortly before her death, along with her fervent request that I "avenge her daughter." "I don't believe in revenge," I said to Mrs. Brown, "but I can tell the truth." Her reply, "good church folk talk," made me smile. "That's good enough for me, baby," she said.

In my opinion, Celestine resented Ann. Ann's generosity took her back to her poor childhood and servitude. Still, she'd turned on her best June Cleaver persona in 1996. Now she was determined do everything possible to ingratiate herself with the Sony Columbia people. They too had refused Celestine's offer to provide her styling brilliance to the girls' stagewear.

In a telephone conversation, Beyoncé confirmed for me that things had been going well in the recording sessions, but that the songs themselves were "old," Beyoncé said.

"They sound like the music my mother likes," she said.

This came as no surprise to me. All young people find the music of yesteryear outdated and not cool, but I was hearing this from Beyoncé, whom I'd taught well. She had learned and become quite good at discerning what was a hit. "We have no hit," she said.

"Beyoncé, if there are no hits on the album, you have to say something. Speak up," I told her.

My shy Beyoncé didn't have the nerve.

"No problem. I am back in Houston in three days. You can play some of them for me and we will develop a strategy."

When I listened to the four songs that the girls had recorded thus far, I heard what Beyoncé had described. The songs were R&B driven, but certainly not sixteen-year-old friendly. "Hey, this one is great," I said to Beyoncé. The track was called "Killing Time." Beyoncé liked it too. "I am feeling how you are singing this. Your use of the vibrato sounds like time ticking away. You can hear the waiting – the anticipation," I said. I could feel her smile beaming through the phone line.

Then there was a song called "Never Had a Love Like Mine," which I thought had potential. Kelly's vocals leapt off the recording. "Mama doesn't like that one," Beyoncé said. I thought to myself, Of course she doesn't. However, I avoided giving an opinion. I wasn't touching that with a ten-foot pole. I didn't need to. Beyoncé's silence said it didn't need discussing. My student was becoming wise to the ways of the world, and to those of her mother.

"David, did you and Beyoncé talk about the album?" Celestine asked me later.

"Yes," I answered. "We discussed it." I wanted to know why she'd asked such a question.

"What do you think?"

"I think Beyoncé is on point," I said, knowing full well that what I had just said meant that Mathew and Ann would get an ear full. My plan worked. Mama Celestine had a way of twisting people's arms. Beyoncé's dilemma would be solved, promptly. And neither she nor I would have to fight the fight.

What I didn't talk about was my disappointment. I hadn't heard the other girls' voices. Why weren't they being included in the recording process? Beyoncé's voice was all over the track. It was clear that Celestine and Mathew delighted in this fact, but had D'Wayne, like everyone else, caved to the Knowleses' pressure? An album with Beyoncé singing all the parts was fraudulent. Destiny was a group of four singers, not just Beyoncé. Did Sony really intend to pass off an album they'd marketed as the next big thing in girl group sounds, as a fraudulent representation by just one member? Of course they didn't.

"They don't have a clue that it's *all Beyoncé*," Mathew said. I was livid. What was our fearless leader up to?

In the meantime, D'Wayne announced that Sony Pictures had chosen "Killing Time" for an upcoming movie called "Men in Black," starring Beyoncé's childhood funny man hero, Will Smith. The complete sound track, "Men in Black: The Album," had a title track that had a planned release date of June 1997. It featured performances by Will Smith and Cheryl "Coko" Gamble, from SWV. Beyoncé had gotten hold of a copy of the song. It was hot – real hot. "Coko sounds amazing," she said. I agreed. Then she played the final mix of "Killing Time" for me. The song, produced by D'Wayne Wiggins and written by him and Tara Stinson, made me emotional. "Brava Diva!" There was nothing more to say. Beyoncé had nailed it. She brought youth to a song influenced and driven heavily by R&B. She'd found "her way" of speaking up. Even today, Beyoncé gives her opinion through her singing.

"Isn't Beyoncé magnificent?" Celestine said, ecstatically. "I told you so," she concluded.

You told *me* so? I thought. Poor Celestine. No, if anyone knew what Beyoncé was truly capable of, it was me.

* * * * *

The girls continued their lessons with me and spent many hours every week in the recording studio. Their progress pleased Ann, but she was suffering, now more than ever.

On January 9, 1997, Ann's chief medical physician, Dr. Louis Berman, forbade her to return to work at HL&P. That's when Ann's best friend, Pat Felton, drove her to the Baylor College of Medicine, where Ann saw her rheumatologist, Dr. Sandra Sessoms. According to Pat, who at Ann's request sat in on the conversation, Dr. Sessoms told Ann that she had the worst form of Lupus she'd ever seen. Her prognosis was dire. "I need to be absolutely transparent here, Mrs. Tillman," Dr. Sessoms said. "I fear we are too late, but I'm going to treat you anyway. You never know." Then she asked Ann, "Are you a praying woman?"

"Yes," Ann answered.

"Start right this minute."

Kelly, who had accompanied Ann and Pat to Dr. Sessoms' office that day, sat in the waiting room, devastated, broken. The woman she'd come to love like a mother, who had saved her and Doris from living in their parked car on the street, and had housed and fed and loved her, was dying.

"Ann, I can see from your test results that you have an abnormally high degree of stress in your life."

"Yes, she does, Dr. Sessoms," Pat said. "She's a music manager. Her group just signed a huge record deal with Sony."

"Uh – hmmm," Dr. Sessoms said. "Well, as of today you have to concentrate on getting better. No more stress," Dr. Sessoms concluded. She wanted to start Ann on a Cytoxan Chemotherapy regimen. "Cyclophosphamide aggressively kills cancer cells," Dr. Sessoms said. Picking up the telephone, she ordered that the new protocol begin immediately.

Ann's first treatment of chemo knocked her flat on her derriere. Ann's medical records show that although her system improved remarkably (her hand began to heal after years), she experienced insomnia, agitation, and anxiety, which presented over a period of several days. Ann also professed

531

to being frightened, confused, and increasingly disillusioned with the medical care delivery system in general. She stated that she had at times felt like she might want to just bring everything to an end, though she vehemently denied meaning suicide. "I've never had suicidal thoughts," she swore. The records show otherwise. She flatly refused psychiatric treatment, again and again. She jokingly told me, "Black folks don't do that." But a blind man could see the truth. Ann was severely depressed, and Mathew's vicious demands weren't helping.

On March 17 Ann presented with pain in her thumb. Distal right thumb. On the evening of April 4th Ann suffered an attack of asthmatic bronchitis. Several days later, just to add to her stress, she lost her insurance with Met Life. Having problems healing from the bronchitis, Ann was admitted to the hospital. Dr. Marque Hunter introduced intravenous antibiotics, high doses of cortisone, and other supportive care. "Reinstatement of her suspended treatment of Cytoxan was long overdue," he wrote. At almost the same time Ann's thumb began to ulcerate. Dr. Berman told her that he could do nothing else other than to use Duragesic (a pain med), oral morphine, and oral hydrocortisone to manage her pain. Her wheezing had subsided, but the cough would remain a few more days. In addition, she suffered a minor dyspnea (shortness of breath). As soon as Ann began "to ambulate," Dr. Hunter gave her the Cytoxan treatment, which she had resisted. She got better.

On the day of her discharge, she was pre-medicated with Phenergan and one gram of Cytoxan. Sedated and mildly nauseated, she made it through to the afternoon, when the nausea subsided a bit. Pat picked her up from the hospital, drove her home, and put her into bed.

On April 24th a frantic Kelly drove Ann to Tomball Regional Hospital, scared to death and racing dangerously through the red lights. Pat Felton, covered in vomit, held onto Ann in the backseat. The Cytoxan, which her test results showed was working, had affected her pulmonary circulation, and she became sicker than she'd ever been in her life. It was ischemia (an insufficient supply of blood to an organ, usually due to a blocked artery). The tissue was deprived of oxygen because her blood wasn't circulating.

The blood vessels were under attack and quickly dying off, due to worsening vasculitis.

"Your cardiopulmonary course is in constant decline," Dr. Sessoms told Ann.

"What does that mean?" family members asked.

In plain words, it meant that Ann's veins were shit, killed off by her disease.

In addition, Ann had to be "bloused" (dosed) with parenteral steroids. She had had a blood clot in her hand, treated by surgery on March 18th. Where in her hand exactly, her medical record does not explain. It does suggest that circulation was being affected to her hand and thumb, which explains her pain. Now, she was presenting with an active connective tissue disorder with vasculitis. Ann was dyspneic, wheezing with shortness of breath, and hypoxic because of the difficulty getting oxygen into the blood stream. The surgery, while alleviating some of the pain in her hand, had done nothing against her emotional distress. She was extraordinarily anxious.

Pat was by Ann's side when she returned to Room 366 from the O.R. Seeing that Ann was cared for, Pat left, returning to Ann's Crescent Moon home to check on Armon and Chris, who should have returned from a basketball game. An hour or so later, Mathew and Celestine walked into Ann's hospital room. Hooked up to several intravenous lines, and sedated, she was resting. The two flanked her bed. When they called to her, she awoke. Their conversation left Ann in tears.

Enter Christopher Williams, a young Nigerian producer, whom Ann had taken under her wing. Christopher had produced Ann's rapper "B-Boy," and the two had developed a close friendship over the years. Ann had written, on July 22nd 1996, almost a year earlier: "To Whom It May Concern: This letter is to certify that Christopher A. Williams has continuously assisted me over the past three years, do *[sic]* to a chronic medical condition in which I have lost three fingers on my right hand. Christopher has been very instrumental in helping maintain and perform day to day task with my adolescent sons. Sincerely, Ann Tillman." Ann's letter and determination helped Christopher obtain a visa that permitted him to remain in the U.S. (Today Christopher lives and works in Los Angeles.)

Christopher had seen the Knowleses as they left the hospital. He and his wife, Melanie, were parking their car as Mathew and Celestine left the building. According to Christopher, they had a dark and agitated look. By the time Christopher and Melanie got upstairs and to Ann's room, she was a mess, crying uncontrollably. When he asked Ann what was wrong, she told him that the Knowleses told her that "if you can't do your damn job then you need to step aside." Ann told me exactly the same thing, over the telephone. She added that the Knowleses had said that they "didn't want Mathew held up contractually, preventing him from acting as sole manager when she died." Yes, those were Ann's words to me. I was horrified. Never in my life had I heard such psychological abuse. I had to acknowledge that Mathew and Celestine's selfishness had reached new heights.

Despite her severely weakened state, Ann refused to give up her managerial rights. That would no doubt have angered Mathew and Celestine, anger that Christopher could clearly read when he observed them leaving the hospital.

A few days after the scene with Mathew and Celestine, Ann was released from the hospital. However, only a couple of weeks later, on May 14th, 1997, Ann called Pat Felton, around 4:00 p.m. "Pat can you come?" she said. "It's time." Her children had just left the house, she told Pat. "I asked Armon to take Chris with him to basketball practice."

Pat rushed over to Ann's, her heart pounding. Frightened, and half out of her mind, she pulled into Ann's driveway, weeping. Pat told me that she had prayed the whole way. Ann's choice of words, "It's time," had arrested her spirit. When she walked into Ann's house, her mother, Effie, who had come up to Houston a few days earlier, was trying to dress Ann. Pat began to help.

"My God, it was so difficult to lift her. Ann's edema was the worst it had ever been. She was dead weight. Ann couldn't help lift herself." Finally, they got her into the wheelchair she'd been given for home use. The next problem. "How are we going to get her up into Ann's truck?" Pat asked herself. Running back into the house, she rummaged through Ann's telephone book. She called a neighbor, the father of one of Armon's friends. A fireman, he was trained for such situations. He happened to be home and he was able to go to Ann's home and hoist her up into the truck. "The screams were awful. Ann was in so much pain." Pat knew that there was something terribly wrong.

"Ann finally got settled," Pat told me. "I started the car, put it in drive, and made my way out of the circular drive. Ann asked me to drive slowly." The tears began to flow from Pat's eyes. Ann was acting strangely, Pat said. "Drive slow, Pat. I want to look at my house, one last time." Pat began to shake, unable to speak, and she did as Ann had asked. "'Stop,'" Ann said. "We sat there, about five minutes. Ann just stared at her house."

"Then, she raised the power window and said, 'OK, we can go now.'"

Pat told me that she had to drive carefully, paying attention to any bumps in the road. Every jerk sent Ann into a frenzy. "She wanted to stop for gas," Pat said.

"Who wanted to stop for gas?" I asked.

"Ann did."

"Why?"

"I think she wanted to feel like the day was going to be just like any other day. I certainly did not need to stop for gas." Then Pat told me that Ann wanted to stop and look at the cows. "I just kept praying, and driving."

Finally, they pulled into the emergency entrance of Park Plaza hospital, in downtown Houston. According to Pat, it was approximately 6:30 p.m., maybe closer to 7:00.

"Mrs. Tillman where have you been? Dr. Berman called us hours ago. We've been expecting you since 4:00 p.m."

It took hospital staff, four nurses, and two doctors, to carefully take Ann down from her truck and try to set her into the wheelchair. By this time, not even the wheelchair could accommodate her swelling body. The doctors called for a gurney.

Ann was wheeled into emergency. Intravenous lines and a heart rhythm machine were hooked up, and they placed oxygen tubes in her nose. They tried unsuccessfully to remove the fluid from her body. She crashed. "Code Blue," the nurse yelled. Asked to step away from Ann, Pat was directed away from the area. Another nurse cut Ann's blouse off her. Seconds later, they had a pulse.

In just that moment, Cholotte walked into the emergency room entrance. She and Ann had been friends since before Girls Tyme. Pat saw her and gratefully fell into her arms. "Ann's heart just stopped," she said tearfully. Cholotte began to tear up. "But they saved her," Pat continued. Although they were relieved, both women realized that things were very different this time. They'd been down a similar road with Ann, but this was much different.

Around 2:30 a.m. doctors told Pat that Ann had been stabilized. They suggested she go home to get some rest. They were going to review the charts, and come up with a game plan.

"Will she be all right, Doctor?" Pat asked.

"We're doing all we can. Your friend is a very sick woman. It doesn't look good." the doctor said.

Worn out, Pat stayed another few minutes. After drinking a coffee, she attempted to drive home. It was 3:00 a.m. Vincent, her husband, had been calling her hour by hour. "He even offered to drive to the hospital to pick me up," Pat said.

The next morning, Ann called Pat at 7:00 a.m. "Pat, when you were here I was in intermediate ICU. Now they've moved me to critical ICU," Ann said.

"What do you mean, Ann?"

"They said that I almost didn't make it."

Pat's tears began to well up.

"Pat, are you still there?"

"Yes," Pat said.

"Can you come now? And can you bring my mother?"

536

Pat called Cholotte, who lived just minutes away. Together, with Cholotte driving, they took Ann's truck, picked up Effie, and headed to the hospital.

"I told the boys their mother was in the hospital," Grandmother Effie told Pat. According to Effie, Chris had asked, "Is Mama all right?" Effie told him that she was stable. "Everything's going to be all right, baby. You know your mama is a fighter," she added. Pat then confessed to Effie that Ann had died, twice already. Effie rejected Pat's words. After a brief exchange of heated comments between the women, the car became silent. Pat, sitting in the back seat, began to cry. She said that she had never been so frightened in her life.

When the three finally got downtown and walked into the ICU of Park Plaza Hospital, Ann was in good spirits, although on morphine for the pain. It was approximately 8:30 a.m., and Ann was sitting up in the bed, laughing with the nurse, who was administering some procedure or other.

"Thank God," Effie said.

"I'm sorry," the nurse said. "Only one person is allowed in the ICU."

Ann asked Pat to stay, and then asked Cholotte if she would take her mother to the cafeteria. "Mama have you had breakfast?" She hadn't. "Where's my purse?" Ann asked. "It's somewhere around here." Cholotte told Ann not to worry. She'd cover the breakfast. They would see her later. As soon as they were out of sight, Ann broke down. An emotional wreck herself, Pat took Ann's hand.

The nurse came in and began to unlock the wheels to Ann's bed around 10:30 a.m. They were taking her to radiology. "What's going on?" Pat asked. "We have to run some tests," the nurse answered. "Can my friend go with me?" Ann asked. "Yes," said the nurse.

Pat and Ann talked about their boys, and mid-sentence, Ann said, "Pat, I'm cold." Pat went to look for a blanket. When she returned Ann's body was still, eyes wide open. Was she sleeping? Pat wondered. She called to Ann. No response. It was happening again.

Pat stopped a nurse, who asked Ann if she could hear her. "Tell me what's wrong, Ann." Ann couldn't speak. Then, without warning, Ann sat up on the gurney, her eyes rolled back in her head, and she flopped back down. Her organs were failing.

The nurse called out. "Code Blue!" She yelled. "Code Blue!" Then she climbed up onto the gurney, pumping away. The doctors came running, shouting, "Get her to ICU. Stat...." With that nurse straddling Ann and pumping her chest as if her own life depended on it, Ann was whisked away down the hall and into the elevator. Once again, she'd been saved.

Pat was totally spent. She'd been suffering alongside Ann since 1989, having been diagnosed with Lupus herself, not long after Ann's diagnosis. Pat didn't know what she was going to do. "You're going to do what I do. Take care of your family and enjoy every minute of it," Ann once told her. All this went through her mind as she stepped into the elevator, heading for the cafeteria, to find Cholotte and Effie. Through tears, she told the two women what had happened. Cholotte began to cry. Effie stood up, shouting. "Stop saying that!" she screamed at Pat, and left the cafeteria. She made a beeline toward ICU, and Ann. It took a few minutes for Pat to calm down, and in the midst of Cholotte's calming Pat, she broke down completely.

By approximately 11:25 a.m., Cholotte and Pat had collected themselves sufficiently to return to ICU. As they emerged from the elevator, Pat saw Keith, Ann's deceased husband's brother, just steps away from Ann. Pat thought it strange, since "Ann hated him," Pat said. Would Ann have called him?

Walking down the hall, they could hear Effie talking, rather boisterously. In fact, she was screaming, Pat told me.

As she got closer to Ann's room, she saw a woman whose back was turned to her. She was taking something away from Ann, who now was on a heavy morphine drip. "It looked like papers," Pat said. The woman turned to face Effie, who had asked angrily, "What are you doing here?" It was Celestine Knowles.

As Celestine put the papers into her purse, Effie called out, "Ann! Can't this wait?" She was livid. Apparently, Ann had just signed some sort of contract. But why?

"This is important, Mama. Tina is my friend," Ann answered. She slurred, 'She is going to take care of some important business for me.'"

"What business was she talking about?" I asked Effie, during our 2012 telephone call.

"I don't know. I wish I did." Effie was adamant that Celestine's behavior "didn't feel friendly to me." Then she told me that "Ann was loopy, talkin out her head. She wasn't herself at all."

Continuing, now with an unbridled anger, Ann's mother said to me that Celestine turned, smiled, and casually left the ICU. On the way to the elevator she nodded her greetings to a bewildered Pat and Cholotte.

A year later, in my 2013 conversation with Pat, she fully corroborated Effie's account. "Did you see Mathew?" I asked Pat.

"No, just Tina. The look on that woman's face…" Pat said. "It still haunts me."

The elevator door closed. Celestine was out of sight. She had left the hospital.

Now weeping openly, Pat remembered that Ann was euphoric, and hallucinating. "Her body was fighting like hell to get oxygen." The doctors adjusted the oxygen levels. Ann began to come back. Two hours elapsed while the doctors worked feverishly. Somewhere between 2:30 and 2:45 p.m. Ann yelped, "I can't breathe." She flat-lined. Pat screamed, "Ann – Ann – *wake up*!"

Ann was dead.

25. Beyoncé in trouble

My girls were forbidden to attend Ann's funeral in Tyler. Mathew's orders. He also tried to keep them from the memorial service in Houston. However, Pamela Luckett, who found Beyoncé's father's decision unacceptable, insisted on attending, with her daughter, LeToya. "Ann was kind to me and my child. This is crazy," Pam said to Mathew. "C'mon LeToya. You and I are going." As she left the room, Mathew yelled, "Then take all of them!" The other three girls bolted for the door, relieved that – no matter how rudely – he had acquiesced.

When Pam and the four girls arrived at the Houston memorial service, embarrassingly late, the church was packed, and they had trouble finding any place to sit. Grieving, and ashamed, they were forced to take seats in the back row. Not only had they been robbed of the opportunity to say goodbye to Ann, they were also denied the chance to sing or even to speak. Mathew had refused the family's request on both counts. No singing in Tyler or in Houston

The Brown family had played a tape at Ann's funeral in Tyler. In Houston, Ann's other artists sang. Among the mourners were many people who had loved and admired her, including young talents whom Ann had given substantial financial assistance and guidance. That only one of my girls' parents showed up to the memorial service was unsettling to those who knew how important the girls and their families had been to Ann. No one was more appalled than I was. It was all so incomprehensible and tragic. Mathew's behavior had a profound psychological impact on Beyoncé, resulting in guilt like I'd never seen.

After the memorial service, Mathew showed up at Ann's home to confront her family with what he considered unfinished business. In a 2013 interview, Kenny Moore recalled for me that Mathew was demanding that they give him "some damn master tapes." Kenny told me that one of Ann's brothers said to Mathew, "Man, we just buried my sister. Let's not do this." Several witnesses confirmed what happened next: "Fuck Ann," Mathew shouted. A fight ensued. Mathew Knowles escaped with his scrawny little life. Even though appalled, I took an uncanny pleasure in hearing that someone had finally fulfilled my prediction that sometime, somehow, someone was going to whip Mathew's ass for his outrageous talk. I am sorry to have missed it.

Fourteen days later, I got a call from Celestine. The girls – now Destiny's Child – were in New York and "desperate to see you," Beyoncé's mother said.

* * * * *

I got home late on May 29th, 1997. Shevon Jacobs-Loftin, her boyfriend Cesar Hernandez, and my good friend Roland Burks, who was in New York from Austria, all took me out to dinner that night to celebrate. I'd just made my Carnegie Hall debut, singing the Mozart Mass in C minor. The next morning my telephone rang.

"David," a female voice said.

I recognized it right away. "Hi Celestine," I answered. "How are you?"

"I'm good. It's nice to hear your voice." She said that she was well. "Listen, we are in New York and the girls asked me to call you. They would love for you to come by the hotel tonight, after they are back from their photo shoot. Do you know the Regency?" *[Today it's the Empire Hotel.]*

"Yes," I said. "It's across the street from the Metropolitan Opera."

"That's it. Can I tell them that you will come? They love you so much!" Celestine was buttering me up, hard. What was she up to this time? Still, I hadn't seen my girls in nearly five months, so I agreed.

"And I them," I answered. "Yes, tell them I'll be there."

That evening I showered and dressed and then headed down to West 63rd Street. It took me about fifteen minutes to get from Harlem to Lincoln Center, following a familiar route: the Number 2 express train to 72nd street, and the Number 1 local to 65th.

At the Regency, I first called Cheryl, who was with the girls as chaperone. "Hi Cheryl, it's David. I'm in the lobby." She gave me her room number and I headed upstairs.

I was a bit nervous. When I knocked on the door, prankster LeToya, jokingly disguising her voice, said, "Who is it," in a very high pitch. "Open the door, girl," I said, much like I imagine Mama would've – real teacher-like.

Suddenly the door flung open. Standing before me were my heart, my heart's passion, the joy in my heart, and my heart's pulse. I couldn't have been happier. We all hugged, delighted to see one another again.

My beautiful girls were becoming beautiful young women. Celestine had taken extreme measures with Kelly's hair, cutting and shaping it into a dramatically short style. Naturally I wanted to know about that, along with other news from the girls' lives.

After our happy catch-up conversation, Celestine came to the point. "*We* are recording a new song at Chung King Studios tomorrow. Do you know it?"

"Yes," I said. "I know it well." I had worked with some pretty impressive producers there – also some wanna-be-famous producers – coaching their artists in recording sessions.

"Can you come?"

"Of course," I answered.

My girls jumped up and down – all the thanks I needed in that moment.

The next morning, May 31st, 1997, I arrived 45 minutes early at the Chung King recording studios, 170 Varick Street, for a scheduled 12:00 noon session.

Immediately I ran into Teresa LaBarbera-Whites as she emerged from the elevator with the girls. "David," she said, hugging me. "How are you doing?"

"I'm good, Teresa. It's great to see you again."

As I hugged the girls, she asked about my singing and I told her that I'd just made my Carnegie Hall debut singing the Mozart Mass in C minor. "Oh my God," Teresa answered. "I wish I had known. It would've been great to hear you again."

Celestine, always in earshot of everybody's conversation, said, "You've heard David sing?" As if a great secret had been kept from her.

"Yes, in Dallas," Teresa answered. "He invited me and my husband to *Porgy and Bess*. It was awesome, and he was amazing."

"Yes, he does have a beautiful voice," Celestine said.

As I let Celestine's near-compliment roll off my back, I noticed that Beyoncé had moved to a quiet corner, studying her music. Good girl, I thought.

Conversation now turned to why I was there. Teresa explained that the girls were going to be recording a song called "No, No, No." It had been created by a production team out of Newark (3 Boyz from Newark) – more specifically, Vincent Herbert, Rob Fusari, Mary Brown, and Calvin Gaines. (Vincent is today listed as A&R for Lady GaGa, who was actually discovered by Fusari. It was Rob Fusari who introduced GaGa to Interscope and Vincent Herbert.)

That Vincent was late irritated Teresa, but she would do nothing about it. "Producers are often late, especially when working with newcomers," she said. She explained that producers are always paid in advance, so since they already have their money, they hold the trump card. You didn't want to piss them off.

"That's good information to keep in mind," I said.

"Yes, so we'll just have to be patient."

"No problem. I've cleared my day."

Along about 3:30 p.m., more than three hours late, Vincent walked off the elevator. Teresa introduced me. His lyricist I already knew. "Hi Mary," I said, hugging her tightly.

"David. What are you doing here?" she asked.

"The group you're recording today, I told you about them. These are the girls I trained in Houston."

"You two know each other?" Teresa asked.

"Yes, David is our voice teacher," Mary said, referring to her group, which Wyclef Jean had shown interest in. Teresa's ears perked up. Turning back to me, Mary added, "Now I know why their voices sound so amazing."

I smiled like it was Christmas.

While Vincent and Mary disappeared into Studio 2, the "Blue Room," to set things up, Teresa and I continued talking. She explained to me the background for today's session. I saw clearly that Celestine was frowning her disapproval, thinking that I couldn't see her.

"The girls were signed to a one-album deal," Teresa said. "My bosses are happy with the girls' work. They are confident in their potential, but as it stands now, the album has no hits. We really need two strong singles."

I looked at Celestine, whose frown turned to a thin smile. "My gut tells me that 'No, No, No' is one of those hits we're looking for," Teresa concluded. Without missing a beat, I said, "OK, so where's the room where I can warm up my little sirens?"

"Right this way," Teresa said.

Clapping my hands, I called out, "Girls, follow me. It's time to work."

"The singing needs to be great," Celestine said.

I controlled my urge for sarcasm and said instead, "No problem. I've got it!"

Beyoncé was supposed to record first in this multi-track session, but her old nemesis, blockage in the sinus cavities, was making things difficult. "Beyoncé, my dear Beyoncé," I said. "You've been walking around with no shoes on again." She lowered her head, mischievously smiling.

Not much had changed, and old habits die hard. In all probability, Beyoncé will always walk around barefoot, getting a stuffed nose because of it. At any rate, I went to the men's room to wash my hands, and she assumed the position. Teresa looked on in wonderment as I began the process of removing the mucous from Beyoncé, who was lying down on a couch with her head tipped back. I placed my forefinger on the usual spot and within minutes she was clear. "Well, I never," Teresa said. Twenty minutes later, my Diva was clear and ready to knock it out of the box!

Little Miss Beyoncé had developed into quite the studio musician. She could lay down a track, in a matter of hours, mistake-free. She had already given the other girls their parts, which made my warming them up and rehearsing them a breeze. We discussed, both individually and collectively, their vocal colors (they should all keep their sound bright), shadings (pop style), the importance of the vowel (clean and resonant), and some alternative phrasing ideas (tell the story and employ the use of the swell tone). I warned against typical R&B heavy and soulful singing, and they listened.

Then I told them that I had an idea for the bridge, but "naturally, I'll have to clear it with Vincent."

"What is it?" Beyoncé asked.

"Bach…"

She smiled. The girls all knew exactly what I had in mind. The bridge should sound like a choir, a sultry one, but a choir.

Upon entering Studio 2, I could tell that Mary had been working. Vincent Herbert didn't know me from Adam, and apparently, no one had mentioned that he'd have a vocal coach in the studio. Having sensed that I was treading on his territory, I proceeded with caution and tact. With his back already down, he welcomed me warmly into his session. And that is exactly whose session it would remain, his. I was already clear about my role as the vocal expert in relationship to his role as the recording producer. I am only ever in a recording studio to translate the producer's wishes to the singer, in a technical language that gets them the best emotional result. Nothing more, nothing less.

Beyoncé began the session and was singing like a goddess. She laid down her lines in the verses and her part of the chorus fairly quickly. Now Kelly was up. She entered the booth confidently, ready to sing, but both her singing and her technique were off. What I heard was not indicative of my work. What happened? I wondered. (After their little break from lessons with me, back when Celestine and Mathew separated and the girls had been dropped by Elektra records, Kelly had regressed. I'd fix the issues and go away again, only to find when I returned that everything Kelly and I had done to correct the problems would have been forgotten. It was most unnerving.) Now, in Chung King Studio 2, Mathew walked in and everything went to hell. Kelly became a bumbling vocal mess. He'd only just arrived, he said. The session stopped briefly, just long enough for everyone to greet him.

When we began again, and Kelly opened her mouth after that short break, she sounded worse than terrible. Mathew's insidious deprecation had had a powerful effect. Kelly could not find her rhythm again, nor her breath. Vincent's frustration was becoming obvious. Mathew suggested "Just let Beyoncé finish the track." I was horrified.

"Let's take a break," Vincent said.

The girls disappeared into the green room. Celestine flitted around the studio, in her element. June Cleaver had made everybody her friend. "Oh, just call me Miss Tina," she told the receptionist, who began sharing a private moment with June/Celestine/Tina.

I went into the green room, where LeToya was already talking on the phone. LaTavia was lying on the sofa, which I found strange. Something was up with her. She wasn't her usual perky self. Naturally, I asked if her sluggish demeanor had anything to do with her mother, or Charles. It didn't, she answered. So, what the hell was going on around here? I thought. Again, Beyoncé studied her music.

Kelly sat in a corner, eyes cast down, kicking herself. I walked over and took her chin in my hand. "Lift your head, Kelly," I said. "I know. No worries. I'm back. It's all going to be different." I was relieved that she gave me a smile.

I went out into the hall to have a little chat with Mathew. There was no time like the present.

"Man, the girls rocked their audition for Sony," Mathew said. "You really should have been there."

I let him talk.

He continued, oblivious to my silence, posturing like crazy. His boasting rose to new heights. When he took a breath, I saw my chance.

"Isn't it sad about Ann?" I said.

He was thrown off. "Uh – yes – it is. She was a great person."

I looked at him. "We all miss her very much," he added, lamely.

"She respected you so much, Mathew," I said. "Why, just before she died, she told me that she could rest easy, and that you had everything under control." His bright smile could have shattered darkness.

"Yes, she told me the same thing."

"Really," I answered. "I'm so glad you got your flowers while she was still alive."

Mathew was so full of bullshit. Didn't he know that I knew that he and his wife had badgered Ann in her final days? "At any rate, sorry for interrupting you, Mathew. What were you saying?"

Mathew picked up right where he left off, even more pompous than before. According to him, in the middle of the girls' first audition song for label executives, the door had opened, and in walked the big boss, Sony's CEO, Tommy Mottola. (Mottola discovered Mariah Carey and then married her.) Mathew went on to say that Tommy Mottola apologized for being late, took his seat in an impressive conference room with a long shiny table, and then signaled for the girls to continue. Naturally, Mr. Mottola had seated himself next to Mathew. They were "surrounded by music executive royalty" (label presidents Michael Mauldin and Don Ienner). After the girls' last note, Mr. Mottola (or, as Mathew said, "Tommy") yelled "Carte Blanche!" "It was huge," Mathew boasted. "No one gets 'Carte Blanche.'"

"That is great, Mathew."

I could have challenged Mathew with what I already knew. One: a recording budget of \$324,742 – down from a proposed budget of \$540,000 – was hardly "Carte Blanche." Two: Beyoncé had already told me that their audition had been in a small room. Those "executives" had sat around on couches, so close, she had said, "that we could put our arms out and touch them." She had made no mention of a shiny table, or of Tommy Mottola. Typical Mathew, I thought. But I did not challenge him. Rather, I continued pumping his ego throughout the evening and night, as the recording session wore on.

After the break, Vincent agreed to try Mathew's idea. Beyoncé was to sing all the parts and harmonies, and the other girls – well, they were left at the side. Vincent told me what he wanted to hear, and I translated it to Beyoncé in technical singer's terms. Vincent and I worked well together. All those years of studying chordal structures, text painting, and Bach had made Beyoncé unstoppable. Had the other girls stopped working on what they'd learned? Of course they hadn't. They had simply been cut off. But instead of fighting Mathew, I chose to surrender – for now.

In the meantime, we'd come to the bridge. God was with me. Vincent and Mary began discussing it. They hadn't quite figured out how or what they wanted to do with it. I spoke up, respectfully of course.

"I have an idea," I said.

"Let's hear it." Vincent said.

I told Vincent that I could show him better than I could tell him. I asked if he would humor me. He agreed.

Beyoncé, I said, was to sing the words "yes" and "no" breathily, with no vibrato and with a slow and deliberate swell effect on the note, releasing it upwards. (Crescendo and decrescendo.) "Creep in and out, evenly," I said to her. "The sound has to be absolutely smooth for this to work." She nailed it. Just as I had told Ann, Beyoncé's prowess in the recording studio was natural. She implemented her technique, for sure, but that she was so fast had everything to do with her prodigious gifts. The end result was stunning, and Vincent was over the moon.

Teresa, sensing a break-through in her dilemma, said, "I believe this song is going to be a hit." She left the recording studio, phone in hand. Talking to Wyclef Jean's people, Teresa said that she was sure that Wyclef was the right producer for realizing a vision she had. They must have agreed to get it to him, because Teresa said, "Great, I'll send the song over just as soon as it's fully mixed."

With the session over, Teresa asked Vincent for the mix, just as soon as he could get it to her. He promised, thanked me, and shook my hand. I kissed Mary on the cheek, and they left.

"Welcome back, David," Teresa said. "I'll never go into the studio again without a vocal coach." (It was a new concept in 1997.)

"Are you back, David?" Celestine asked.

"I've never left," I said to her. Looking at both Celestine and Teresa, I said, "However, I can't abandon my career. I won't abandon my career. From now on, lessons will need to be paid for, including Kelly's, flights, and every second spent in the recording studio, too."

Teresa agreed. "No problem. Mathew just needs to submit the bills," she said. Then she told me that she'd work personally to push the paperwork through.

"Great. Then we have a deal."

After all those exhausting hours, I left Chung King Studios with a piece of paper that the girls had slipped to me. On the way uptown in the train, I read it. Their autograph, and the beautiful words: "Best Voice Teacher. Thanks."

Although everyone was excited that Wyclef Jean had agreed to work on my girls' first album, nobody knew what to expect. After meeting him, however, I did. He had an aura of pure genius. He was quirky, extremely sensitive, and down to earth. He traveled with his "motivation" in a plastic bag, and kept his creativity close. He was a creative beast of a different species.

The remix of "No, No, No" turned out amazingly. Most of what you've heard or read about Beyoncé's recording process is accurate. Of course Mathew added his own fanciful fabrication, that Beyoncé sang so fast because Wyclef had had to catch an airline flight within the hour. The real reasons for the pace actually make a better story, but Mathew never did let the truth guide his pronouncements.

The full truth is that Wyclef was ready to record the chorus of "No, No, No." Jokingly, he said, "And hurry up, girl!" Beyoncé started to sing the chorus real fast, "You mean like this?" she asked, singing and laughing wildly. Wyclef stopped her, asked her to repeat what she'd just done. He had asked the engineer, James Hoover, from Digital Studios in Houston, to press the Record button. It was different, very different. Beyoncé thought Wyclef's idea was crazy, but he said, "Nah girl. When the thugs hear this they gon' go wild." He was right, of course. The single sold millions and made Destiny's Child a household name instantly.

In my opinion, Wyclef Jean is in the same league as Prince and Bob Dylan. He is also hardest man in show business to get on the phone. You would have to meet him on the street or in a recording studio somewhere if you wanted to pin him down for something or speak with him directly, which is not as difficult to do as it may sound. Wyclef Jean is a star who has never hidden himself from the public. He can still be seen walking down the street in New York or sitting in a corner booth at local restaurants. I remember meeting him on 43rd Street in lower Manhattan, a year after we'd first met. He was walking with a female colleague.

Just back in town from France, I was *en route* to the restaurant B Smiths, with a friend, Barron Coleman.

"Wyclef" I exclaimed.

Startled, he said, "Do I owe you some money?"

I laughed. It was typical Wyclef to make a joke. "Not a cent," I said, "but if you want to give me some I am not going to turn it down." He laughed and said, "I am a broke man, my brother." Still laughing, we hugged one another. I introduced Barron, and Wyclef introduced the singer who accompanied him, who was clearly curious to understand how we knew one another.

"This is David," he told her, "Destiny's Child's vocal coach. Hey," he said, turning to me, "didn't you do Mary Brown's group too?"

"Yep," I said. "That's me."

* * * * *

Mathew issued his new contract, with the girls' final name change, on June 9th 1997. The legalization of the name change from Destiny to Destiny's Child would happen nearly three years later, in February 2000. We always thought that it had been legal, because Sony Columbia had also changed their contracts, conforming with Mathew's usage. Furthermore, Sony Columbia could abandon talks with that girls group Destiny, in Mississippi.

The idea for the remix of "No, No, No" was all Teresa LaBarbera-Whites. Her vision was to release two versions of the same song, as a single and as a track on the album. That had never been done before. It created a buzz and much conversation. People argued their points. Who liked which and why became fodder for radio disc jockeys, while the girls' record climbed the charts. Sales were great.

The second such undertaking, of the same idea, happened with a track called "With Me," which was first produced by Jermaine Dupri and remixed by Master P, the hottest rapper in the game in 1997-98. Also recorded in Houston, the song did well, but in my opinion, it couldn't touch the freshness Wyclef brought with his second production on the album.

This time he brought Fugee's member, Pras, along to the studio. The result was a song called "Illusion."

* * * * *

The Wyclef version of "Illusion" was to be a spinoff of the great song from the 80's "Just an Illusion," by Imagination. It would replace a song called "Never had a love like mine," which Celestine hated. It had a lengthy solo that Kelly sang beautifully, and Beyoncé's mother complained to the girls, relentlessly, that the song was "too old" for them. Her nagging worked. After a while, the girls began to hear what a misinformed Celestine heard and complained to Teresa about it. It would be eventually dropped from the album, and replaced with Wyclef magic. With that, Beyoncé was one step further to being accepted officially as the group's unmitigated leader.

Teresa called me at home. She needed me in the studio. "We will be recording another Wyclef song. It should be interesting."

"Wyclef?" No problem. "I'll be there."

Wyclef arrived to the Chung King studios at 7:30 p.m. I will never forget it. We had been there since 12:00 noon waiting for him. After saying hello, greeting Teresa, and hugging the girls, he disappeared into the Blue Room. No one, and I do mean no one, was to interrupt him. And no one did.

Anyone who knows Wyclef knows that he creates on the spot. He started writing "Illusions" from scratch, at about 8:30 p.m. Well, at least enough of the music, he told Teresa, so that the girls could record on the track. "I'll add the other sounds later, but record the rap tonight." In just that moment, Pras, from the Fugees and the Refugee camp, emerged from the elevator. We greeted one another warmly, having met at several rehearsals of Mary Brown's group, which he and Wyclef had decided to take under their wing. Five and one half hours later, the song was finished. It was 2:00 a.m.

Wyclef Jean called for the girls. LeToya and LaTavia had to be awakened. At that signal, Kelly hung up her telephone, and Beyoncé came out of her trance. She'd been studying the text the entire time, organizing the movie in her head. She was in the middle of one of those "scenes" when I called out to her. We all entered the studio, Celestine included (I don't remember if Teresa was there then).

"Are y'all ready?" Wyclef asked.

"Yes," they all chimed in unison.

The engineer started the track. It kicked. It was hot, youthful, funky, totally Wyclef. The other song it replaced didn't compare, I had to admit. We listened, bobbing our heads, and even dancing to the fresh beat. By the second musical phrase it was clear in my head what the vocal production would be. I heard possibilities for modulation, rhythmic syncopation, highs, lows, sultry, sass, and more important, Bach-style chords. Suddenly, we heard the rap. Pras had already laid his contribution on the track. I looked at LaTavia, in the same moment that Wyclef pointed to her. She was to counter Pras. Then he pointed to LeToya. "I want you on the highs," he said, demonstrating in his raspy falsetto. Kelly would fill out the chorus, and do a sort of response to Beyoncé's call. She would sing the lead. I'd never seen the girls so happy. They all had a part. Wyclef intended to use them all.

Pras and I had a moment.

"You killed it, my brother," I said. He thanked me. "I love the line about Princess Diana," who had just died, shortly before the recording of this album, in September 1997.

A wonderful and personable mensch, Pras was way cool. The girls loved him, and I enjoyed working with him. He was always even-keeled, never off balance, sort of like my all-time favorite rapper, Treach, from "Naughty by Nature." There are just some people who bring a smile to your face, they are so kind. Pras and Treach were two of those people. The last time I would see Treach, in person, would be at a New York birthday bash for Sister 2 Sister Magazine, but that is a story that will come later, one absolutely essential to the story of Destiny's Child, the girls, and the deprecating Mathew and Celestine Knowles.

552

In the midst of our little celebration, Beyoncé, who was the most excited, whispered to me that she was "so tired of doing all the work."

"Well, you should have a talk with your parents about that," I said.

She looked at me, as if to say, What do you mean? "You do all the work, because your parents want it that way." Beyoncé lowered her head. "I know," she answered.

Before Wyclef could begin recording the girls, I asked his indulgence. "Beyoncé's nose and sinuses are blocked."

With a look of embarrassment, Beyoncé said, "I'm fine." I knew better, but I humored her. There comes a time when a teacher must realize that the student is no longer a baby. Their individualism begins to emerge. Beyoncé had exhibited her independence on that evening, at that moment, and I wisely stood back. She entered the booth, with her mental movie all worked out and written into the margins of her printed text, and proceeded to sing the opening lines.

"Stop," Wyclef said. "Do you have a cold?" he asked.

I didn't have to say a word. An honest Beyoncé answered, "No sir, I need to clear the mucous out of my head and sinuses."

I smiled.

Wyclef looked at me and said, "Isn't that what a cold is?"

I laughed heartily and replied, "Sure, but Beyoncé's problem is not a cold." It was difficult to explain, and I told him that I could show him what I meant.

Beyoncé walked into Studio 2 from the booth, and the girls, who had been waiting their turn, moved off the black leather sofa. They all knew the drill. I left, headed to the men's room, and washed my hands.

On my way back to the studio, I heard Celestine screaming. Mathew had arrived.

Having been absent the entire day, Mathew had sauntered in, close to 3:00 a.m., smelling like soap. Celestine understood where he'd been, but I knew the exact address. Mathew's New York hangout and church, so to speak, was a strip club called Flash Dancers, on Broadway, billed as the ultimate in adult entertainment. Of all the clubs he frequented – in Chicago, Houston, Los Angeles – Flash Dancers in Manhattan was one of Mathew's clear favorites. I remember saying to Mathew once, "Wait till you get to Europe, Mathew, I hear the clubs over there are on another level." He blushed from embarrassment, and then asked me all about them. I told him what I'd heard, of course. I was making him my friend....

Now, on this most important occasion for the girls, the group, for *Beyoncé,* Mama Celestine yelled a few revelations of her own. "Get your mother fuckin' ass in that Goddamned Studio, Mathew," she yelled. "You need to put a stop to this shit."

I stopped in my tracks. Celestine's yelps always revealed crucial information, and I had the feeling that her present outburst would tell me what I needed to know in order to win the evening.

"What the fuck are you talking about?" Mathew whispered loudly.

"Wyclef wants those little bitches to sing on the song, all of them. Get your ass...."

Mathew fell all over himself getting out of the green room and into the studio. Celestine followed him, not too far behind. Our eyes locked. I smiled. She frowned, mad as hell. I nodded, and entered the studio behind her.

Beyoncé had already assumed the position. Wyclef and the engineer sat there, perplexed but humoring me. "Tilt your head back, Beyoncé," I said. Then I placed my forefinger into her mouth and held it gently on her soft palate, standing over her and approaching the roof of her mouth from behind. A few minutes later she coughed up a huge blob of mucous. Wyclef laughingly shouted, "Oh shit, that was dope."

"Now she's ready."

Beyoncé returned to the booth, clear as a bell, and Wyclef was amazed. So was the engineer. (Listening to the final recording of the album, one can easily hear when Beyoncé was a bit stuffed up, and when I'd cleared the mucous.)

During the whole removing-the-mucous scene, Mathew and his lovely wife stayed out of the room. I was sure they were strategizing. "I think it's great that you want to use all the girls on the track," I said to Wyclef.

"No question," he said. "They're a group."

"Sure they are," I added, smiling broadly. I winked at LeToya and LaTavia, who sat there eagerly awaiting their turn to get into that studio. Kelly looked like a deer in headlights. Mathew was there. I called her over to me. "Sit here, next to me Kelly." She did as I asked, shaking, but she did it.

I must say, I really enjoy working together with Wyclef. His mind works a mile a second. You can't sleep on him or you'll get lost. Beyoncé was unbelievable in the studio, having laid down all her vocals in just under two hours. It was now 5:00 a.m. LeToya was next up. We left the room to warm her up, and ten minutes later re-entered the studio. She went directly into the booth, with her text. I entered the studio. Mathew followed closed behind. I took my seat at the control board, and Wyclef and the engineer began setting microphone levels on LeToya.

"Can you hear me?" Wyclef asked.

She nodded.

He explained what he wanted, exactly. Wyclef's vision for the song was to have LeToya sing the top part of the chorus and the Oo oo oo oo ahs (from a sample of the song "Just an Illusion"). It needed to be airy, very soft, and in tune, he said to me. And then she would sing on a modulated section of the chorus (Can it be that, can it be that, can it be that, can it be that). Wyclef said that he wanted to begin with the modulation chorus. "I'm going to play it back to you. Listen to Beyoncé's ground note. Copy her color and lightness." LeToya said she understood.

While all this was going on, Celestine called Beyoncé out of the studio. She wanted to order a pizza for the girls, she told her, and Beyoncé knew what the other girls liked. I guessed that Celestine wanted to hold Beyoncé hostage. They didn't come back to the session for a while.

As the two of them left, Mathew came back into the studio. He stood directly behind us – Wyclef and me, Kelly who sat next to me, and the engineer. He was facing the booth glass. LaTavia had curled up on the couch, anxious.

Wyclef announced that we'd be starting. I smiled encouragingly at LeToya. The music started and, looking down at her paper, she began to sing. The first notes came out great, but then her voice cracked. I quickly turned to see an intimidating Mathew, arms folded and looking disgusted. I now knew how Mathew had controlled the girls.

"Are you cool?" Wyclef asked LeToya.

She nodded, swallowing.

"OK, let her try it again," Wyclef said, signaling to the engineer.

This time, things went much better, but still, the LeToya that I had trained and knew wasn't in that booth. Wyclef recorded three more takes, then turned to me. "I want her to sound like an echo," he said.

I asked Wyclef's indulgence, once again. I went into the booth under the pretense of doing some exercises to help LeToya's find Wyclef's directive. Fully aware that if they had pushed the communication button, the one that allowed the producer to talk to and hear the singer, all would be lost. Instead, I took LeToya's pencil, faking that I was giving her a technical approach, and wrote: "I know that Mathew is trying to intimidate you. Ignore him and watch me. I am on your side and will guide you."

Then I told LeToya that Wyclef wanted her to sound like an echo. "You know how to do this," I added. I reminded her of our work on releasing a tone, upwards and always without closing the throat to do it. She understood, she said. "I'm counting on it. You are great. Remember that you are the best person for this portion of the song and no one can do it but you. Don't let me or Wyclef down." Hugging her, I whispered into her ear, "Sing the hell out of it, Diva!"

Wyclef started the session again, and she nailed it, every glorious note. Mathew left the studio and we were free to record an absolutely, breathtakingly easy track. The girls hadn't sung so effortlessly on the entire album.

Mathew and Celestine had lost. Kelly sang her part, "It's just an Illusion," LaTavia did the rap "Boy I love you but I gotta let you go" perfectly, and Beyoncé had sung an absolutely perfect guide for all the chords and filler parts. Her ad libs were great.

"Illusion" turned out to be a perfect recording on a strategically well played evening. I noted to myself, with satisfaction, the irony of the title. I'd worry about the repercussions later.

The session ended at 7:30 a.m., twelve full hours after we'd begun. While Wyclef and the engineer started working on the rough mix, the girls and I went into the green room, where Celestine sat in contemplation. Mathew had disappeared.

I thanked Wyclef for the amazing experience. He thanked me. Then I hugged all the girls goodnight and embraced Celestine intensely. "Thanks for keeping Beyoncé with you," I whispered, "while I took care of that little mess."

If it hadn't been clear before that I was on to her, it was now.

I knew that I had the label on my side. I'd played my hand well. Teresa was absolutely convinced as to what I brought to the table.

Executives at Sony Columbia, namely Teresa and Michael Mauldin, loved the sound of the last recordings. Teresa told me she had one more.

"I know. Beyoncé has already called me."

The song was Lionel Richie's "Sail On," and Beyoncé and I had talked about inverting the melodic content. (Melodic inversion means that you start on the same note, and then move your melody in the opposite direction. The benefit is that the second phrase bears a kind of intangible connection to the first one.)

The result was *familial*.

* * * * *

In November 1997 I was excited to appear in the premiere of an opera, *Amistad*, by America's most prolific black composer, Anthony Davis. The Lyric Opera of Chicago – one of the top opera houses in the United States – was producing it under the direction of the exciting, legendary George C. Wolff, producer of New York's Joseph Papp Public Theatre. The eminent American conductor Dennis Russell Davies was the music director.

Already into the run of ten performances of *Amistad*, I was excited to spend some time with my girls, who were on their first record-signing tour of the U.S. It had been less than a year since the release of their single "No, No, No," and they had flown into Chicago to do record store appearances and to record with R. Kelly. I met them at the South Side record store that was hosting their signing, and later they came for voice lessons at my temporary Chicago home, which I'd rented from my good friends Clifford and Herrece Fields.

My friend Nikole, from Langston University, and I had just finished our Chinese take-out, when my girls pulled up in front of the house. We smiled to see the curious neighborhood kids gathering around the white limousine. The girls had their moment, greeting their young fans, and then they rang the doorbell. I invited my girls into the house, and we embraced each other with heartfelt hugs.

"Girls, this is my friend Nikole," I said. LaTavia and Beyoncé looked at one another. "Yes," I said. "That Nikole." Nikole looked at me, questioningly. "I'll explain later," I said to her. They signed an autographed picture for Nikole's adorable three-year-old nephew, Justin, who was already a fan and who could sing all the words to "No, No, No."

After Nikole had left, the girls and I got down to business and worked on the song that they would be recording with R. Kelly that evening. Again, Kelly's technique had become faulty. What the hell was going on with her? I asked myself.

At the end of the lessons I promised that I would try to stop by the recording studio after that evening's *Amistad* performance. However, a post-performance press event ran late, and I called the studio to make my apologies. I took care of myself: Having to sing in two days, I knew that I needed plenty of rest, especially when dealing with the bitter Chicago winter.

"I'll see you guys in Houston next week," I said.

My girls had been booked for the Keenan Ivory Wayans show, their first U.S. television appearance. They were bouncing off the walls with excitement. I don't think I ever heard from Mathew as much as I did during this time. He was wearing on my nerves.

* * * * *

By February 12, 1998, five days from the release of my girls' debut album, my telephone was ringing off the hook. It was 5:00 am. I felt Gregory's gentle nudge against my right shoulder. "It's for you," he said, searching for my hand in the darkness of our bedroom. Taking the receiver, I asked him with a crackly voice, "Who is it?"

"It's Mathew," Gregory murmured.

Of course it was. Only Mathew Knowles would call you at 5:00 a.m. with his bullshit and without apology. He'd been harassing me since Chicago. Now more than slightly irritated, I took a deep breath.

"Hello."

"Beyoncé can't sing," Mathew slurred.

Exasperated, I let out an audible sigh and said, "Mathew, it is 5:00 a.m."

"Beyoncé can't sing," he repeated.

"What do you mean, Beyoncé can't sing?" I was so over his sense of entitlement by now.

Mathew rambled on about some of everything, but from what I could make out, Beyoncé had lost her voice after "the show." I remember thinking What damned show? But I kept my cool. It was clear that he was high. He'd been partying with God knows who, and if I waited long enough I would probably get to the bottom of things. I'd been in this predicament many times with Mathew over the years. I knew what to expect from him when he was coming down off a cocaine high. For my own security, I quickly jotted down the number on the caller ID, hoping that he was calling from a hotel, someplace traceable. I took nothing for granted with Mathew Knowles.

I knew that he and Destiny's Child were on a small promotional tour that Sony Columbia President Michael Mauldin spearheaded. This so-called "Soul of Power Tour" had been designed to introduce newcomer acts Jagged Edge, Destiny's Child, and a very young Kimberly Scott. I didn't know where they were on the tour at the time of Mathew's disturbing call.

"Where are you Mathew?" I asked. He still wasn't making any sense. Over and over again he repeated that Beyoncé couldn't sing. Now I was beginning to worry. I contemplated hanging up and calling back. I could try the various aliases that I knew Beyoncé assumed when traveling, but then, what if this wasn't a hotel. In just that second, I heard the voice of a woman, and it wasn't Celestine's. Just as I thought, Mathew wasn't alone. He hardly ever was on the road. Wait a minute, I could call Cheryl, I thought.

Cheryl LaStrap Mitchell – LaTavia Roberson's mother – was the Destiny's Child chaperone. She didn't travel under an alias, so I knew that I could call her. I knew that calling Celestine was out of the question. That was a road I refused to travel down. She'd find out soon enough, I thought, but not from me. Nope, calling her wouldn't bring about calm – not at all. I decided to try again to get through to the chemically altered Mathew. He was likely to notice that he was talking, and then hang up because he couldn't remember to whom, or why.

I shouted into the phone, but Mathew just kept rambling about absolutely nothing. The voice of his female companion was so clear, it was obvious that she lay right next to him. I hoped that if I shouted loudly enough, she would hear me. I called for her to take the phone. Gregory thought I had lost my damned mind. Shaking his head, he retreated to the kitchen for a glass of water while I tried desperately to make sense out of Mathew's gibberish.

"Mathew, what is going on with Beyoncé? Mathew – Mathew – Beyoncé – what is going on with Beyoncé?" Still not getting any satisfactory response, I asked him if he could remember her room number. No answer. "Are you in a hotel?" I asked. No answer. Damn. Mathew had dozed off mid-sentence. I was so tired of the drug-induced moments. "Mathew, Mathew!!!" I screamed. Suddenly, the fog lifted. We were out of the twilight zone.

I was able to ascertain that Beyoncé had insisted that Mathew call me. Probably, many hours before this. Apparently, she had been singing a club date in a smoke-filled room and her voice had suffered a hit from all the smoke. Mathew was clueless, but Beyoncé knew that she was having an allergic reaction. She couldn't remember what medication I had told her would stop these symptoms.

"Go to the drug store and buy Benadryl," I said to Mathew. "Beyoncé should take one tablet, and drink a glass of milk. Better yet, eat ice cream. The cold ice cream will help reduce the swelling of her vocal cords and more importantly, coat her throat and keep her cords moist."

"Mathew?" I said. "Are you still there?" What – I couldn't believe it.

He'd hung up.

The next day, I found myself anxious and rushing home from the Number 2 express train. Rehearsals had run late. Destiny's Child was going to appear on *The Keenan Ivory Wayans Show* and I wondered how Beyoncé's voice was. Having walked into the apartment, just in time, Gregory yelled for me to hurry. "The girls are about to come on," he said. I dropped my satchel and made a beeline for our bedroom, where I'd heard Gregory calling to me from.

The show host, Keenan Ivory Wayans, had begun to introduce my girls. Suddenly the camera cut away to them. The music started, and the poses that their new choreographer, Frank Gatson, had set to the opening looked gorgeous. I could barely contain myself. Gregory, too, was just as anxious as I was.

The girls looked great. Debra Gineyard, the stylist that Sony Columbia had assigned to the girls, had dressed them in the clothes she'd chosen for them to wear in the *No, No, No* Part I video. Beyoncé's hair had been finger waved, but it didn't look quite like Celestine's work. I wondered if she'd even traveled to Los Angeles. A very talented hair stylist, Celestine was furious when Sony Columbia returned with an unequivocal no to her request to style the girls. She had "great ideas," I remember her boasting. But Debra Gineyard was their girl. Stephanie Gayle, who, if my memory serves me correctly, was on the product management staff at Sony Columbia then, told me that Debra was one of their favorites.

When Beyoncé started to sing her opening line, "Boy I know you want me, I can see it in your eyes," I leaned in further toward the TV screen.

Her breathing was off. I could hear it. Tensing, I started coaching her through my bedroom television. "She can't hear you, David," Gregory said, laughing. Annoyed, I pulled away from him, because something was terribly off. Shit! Shit! Shit! "Mathew! You didn't give her the Benadryl," I shouted.

To the average listener, Beyoncé would have sounded fabulous, but she was having a problem with her breath and she was pushing her voice, something she never did. She was behind the rhythm, and at one point she made an audible blip. Gregory heard what I heard. I began to pray, immediately, and fervently. It was obvious that Mathew hadn't followed my instructions the night before. All of a sudden the phone rang. I motioned to Gregory to get it. I was far too invested in my prayer to move. He handed the receiver to me, shaking me out of my fervent concentration. "It's for you," he said. I continued praying. "David, Sony Columbia Records is on the line." I wrapped up my prayer, asked Jesus's blessing, and took the phone.

"David," said a male voice.

"Yes, speaking."

"This is Michael Mauldin."

"Yes, Mr. Mauldin," I said. The president of Sony Columbia, and father of superstar rapper/producer Jermaine Dupri (JD), was on the phone. He'd gotten my number from Stephanie Gayle. "Are you watching?" Mr. Mauldin asked. I assured him that I was – painfully so.

"What do you think is going on?" Mr. Mauldin asked.

"An allergic reaction, sir."

"Can it be fixed?"

"Oh, yes sir, very easily," I answered.

"What do you have planned for tomorrow?" Mr. Mauldin asked.

"I have a coaching at the Metropolitan Opera for my next role in Madrid," I said.

Mr. Mauldin asked me to please cancel. "I need you in Washington," he said.

He explained that the next Destiny's Child television performance was only a few days off. The show would be Black Entertainment Television's

(BET) *Teen Summit* and it, too, would be before a live audience. "Everything and everyone needs to be on point," Mr. Mauldin said. "Someone will call you in the morning with the details."

"Yes, sir," I said. We ended the call.

Seconds later, Stephanie Gayle was on the line. "I just got off the phone with Mathew. He told me that Beyoncé is tired and just needs a good night's sleep. Did Michael call you?" she asked.

I told her that I had just finished a telephone call with him.

"I *told* Mathew that we needed you on this damn tour," she said. Shocked, I hadn't heard anything about her request. Mathew had kept that bit of information to himself. "You have to go to Washington," she said. I was all too willing.

"That was Mr. Mauldin's sentiment also," I said.

"Good," she said. "Fuck Mathew. I don't care what he thinks. I'll call you in the morning." Stephanie promised to coordinate with Mauldin's office, saying that either she or his office would call me around 9:30 a.m. "Somebody will definitely call you."

"No worries," I said to her. I promised to be home, awaiting the call.

"Please go and fix the problem, David. We have a lot riding on these girls' success and I know you understand that."

"I will fix the problem. It's a rather simple fix, as a matter of fact," I said.

The next morning, at promptly 9:30, my telephone rang. It was Mr. Mauldin's secretary. I would be picked up by limousine at 11:00 a.m. and driven to LaGuardia Airport, where I would take a flight to Washington D.C. I was given the name of the driver who would be awaiting my arrival in the domestic terminal of Dulles Airport. Stephanie called shortly thereafter.

"Did you get the call?"

"Yes, I did," I said. "The car is picking me up at 11:00."

"Great, somebody from the product department at Columbia will show up in Washington."

26. Little Ugly

My flight landed at Dulles International Airport on time. I didn't see the driver anywhere. Heading for the pay phone to call Sony Columbia in New York, I saw Mathew walking down the corridor. I'd recognize that lope anywhere, bad knees, big feet and all. I took a deep breath and walked in his direction.

Mathew offered to carry my overnight bag for me. "No, I have it," I said.

"Boy, I'm glad to see you," Mathew said. I smiled and asked about Beyoncé. "She's in the car. You can ask her yourself," Mathew answered.

Excited to be seeing my girls, I sped up my pace.

Just before getting to the exit door, Mathew said proudly, "Ya know you have real power when you can get your vocal coach flown in at a moment's notice."

Was he taking the credit? Of course he was. I laughed it off. I simply agreed with him and quietly reminded myself to maintain that fake-ass smile I had plastered on my face. "Don't get sucked into his Ahab spirit, David," I thought to myself.

Not knowing that Mr. Mauldin had called me, Mathew truly believed that he had caused my appearance on the scene. That the president of Columbia Records himself had summoned me would have been too much for his ego to bear. How boring, I thought. His daughter was in trouble, and he obsessed about his own importance. All I cared about was what was going on with Beyoncé. She was the reason I had changed my schedule and flew to Washington.

Leaving the terminal through the double-glassed sliding doors, I saw the door to the limousine fly open, and Kelly, LeToya, and LaTavia ran in my direction. Ecstatically happy, they hugged me, all at the same time. Beyoncé had stayed by the car door, and as I got closer to her I could see that she had a huge smile on her face. She hugged me and whispered into my ear, "Thank you for coming." Her voice sounded terrible. It was a raspy mess. Her cords were more swollen than I had anticipated. I took her by the arm and while the other girls got into the car, I assured her that we'd get the problem under control. "Your voice is fine. I promise you. It is fine," I said. Her problem was a simple allergic reaction – to what, I had no idea, but it sure as hell wasn't smoke.

Once in the limousine, I smelled a sweet scent. "Who is wearing perfume?" I asked. It was LeToya. The aroma permeated the car with the insistence of funeral lilies. In that moment, I realized that I'd forgotten to talk about the dangers of wearing perfume around singers, most likely because my girls, still young, had not shown any interest in perfume or make-up until now. I asked LeToya to switch places with LaTavia, who sat next to Beyoncé in the limousine. Within seconds Beyoncé began sneezing violently. Quickly, LeToya moved away and LaTavia reclaimed her spot. I didn't need to say a word. Actions spoke louder than anything I could have said at that moment.

Mathew? He stared out of the window, oblivious to anyone else.

I knocked on the glass that separated us from the driver.

"Excuse me, sir. We need to get to a drug store ASAP," I said. Then, I asked the driver to crack all of the windows.

The driver made a right turn, and sped up. Within minutes we had arrived at a rather large Walgreens pharmacy. Beyoncé and I quickly got out of the car and headed into the store, looking for the cold and allergy medicines. Spotting the Benadryl, I opened the box, took out two tablets, found a bottle of water on a nearby shelf, and urged her to take the medicine right then and there. She swallowed the pills. Then we headed over to the frozen foods aisle.

"Beyoncé, choose your favorite ice cream," I said. Celestine always forbade her those kinds of indulgences, claiming inaccurately that Beyoncé was fat. A smile lit up Beyoncé's face. She knew that I was on her side, completely. As she chose her ice cream, I looked around for some serious spoons – not those feeble white plastic ones, which break at the slightest pressure, but some good, strong clear plastic spoons that will dig right into hard frozen ice cream.

"Go on Beyoncé, open it," I said.

"Right here, in the store?" she asked.

"Yes, right here in the store. We'll have to hurry. Those Benadryl tablets are going to start working in about ten minutes. We don't want to have to carry you into the hotel, unconscious. You're a big star," I said. Beyoncé laughed. "You're crazy, boy. I ain't gon be sleep in ten minutes," she said.

A Walgreens employee had been watching us. Realizing how our behavior must have looked, I turned to him. "Sorry, we intend to pay. We aren't taste testing," I said. Embarrassed, the employee laughed. Then his eyes opened wider as he recognized Beyoncé from the night before on the *Keenan Ivory Wayans* show. When he asked her for an autograph, I suggested he follow us to the register to get it. "We're in a hurry," I explained. Beyoncé didn't think she'd be asleep in ten minutes, but I knew better. I paid for the ice cream, the Benadryl, and the spoons and we left the Walgreens. She had just made her first fan happy, and it felt good, she said. She was all smiles from that moment on – but sleepy, she admitted. We both laughed and got into the car. Although we reported the incident in detail to our companions in the limo, Beyoncé's father registered no interest.

When we arrived at the hotel, I saw my friend Sandra Hyslop waiting for me in the lobby. She'd come to pick me up. We had work to do on our Roland Hayes project and were beginning preparations for professional recitals we had coming up in the United States. We greeted each other warmly, and I told Sandra about the emergency that had arisen. "Beyoncé, this is Sandra Hyslop, my good friend and pianist."

"Nice to meet you, ma'am," Beyoncé said. Sandra shook Beyoncé's hand while the other girls filed out of the car and into the hotel. Sandra met all of them, one by one. Mathew took immediate charge at the front desk. I waited until he was finished assigning everyone their rooms and then introduced him to Sandra. He too said how nice it was to meet her. When I told him that Sandra had been the editor of *SYMPHONY* magazine, as well as my pianist, he started with the how-wonderful-is-David bull crap. I let him talk. He needed the moment. Ignoring his obsequious manner, Sandra was very gracious. I had to get Beyoncé into bed and told

Sandra that I'd be right back. "Take your time," she said. And then a very groggy Beyoncé and I headed for the elevators.

No one was to disturb Beyoncé. I gave strict orders to the hotel front desk staff that she would be allowed to eat a hamburger, NO CHEESE, and French Fries for dinner and yes, she was allowed to have another *big bowl* of ice cream. Beyoncé was thrilled: a hamburger, fries, and ice cream. She thought she had died and gone to heaven. "You should travel with us more often," she joked. In the elevator I told the other girls that I would give them each a thirty-minute lesson that evening, when I returned from my own rehearsal with Sandra.

I got Beyoncé settled into her room. While she went into the toilet, I pulled back the covers and removed the little chocolates that the house-keeper had left on the pillows. Sometimes, depending on the chocolate, a singer can have adverse reactions, such as reflux. That was the last thing we needed. Beyoncé came out of the bathroom. "You were right," she giggled. "I'm really sleepy." I laughed. "I told you so." She took her night clothes in hand, and I took my leave. At the door she gave me a heartfelt hug and thanked me, again, for coming. "I appreciate you so much," Beyoncé said. "Girl, you know I'd walk on water to help you," I said. She laughed at that Biblical reference.

As I left her room, my thoughts turned to her recent interest in the subjects of church and faith. She'd been going to church about a year or so, and she wanted to know my opinions on faith too. That girl asked more questions than a lawyer. She was such a wonderful girl, a good girl, with a good heart. She was going to be huge.

The next morning when Beyoncé awakened, she called me in my room, just as I had asked her to do. I told her that I was just getting out of the shower and would be there shortly. I heard another voice. "Beyoncé, is someone else there with you? You are supposed to be on vocal rest," I said. "Yes, Mama came this morning." A red flag went up in my brain. I hurried to Beyoncé's room.

Knocking on the door, I let myself in with the key that had been given to me by hotel front desk staff the day before. When I called out to Beyoncé, Celestine answered. I walked into the sleeping area, and there she was, stroking Beyoncé's hair, just as I'd seen so many times before. Suddenly, a Biblical reference for her behavior popped into my mind: the story of Jezebel and Ahab. However, I had no time for metaphors and analogies.

Turning my attention to Beyoncé, I asked "Beyoncé, how are you feeling? We need to get to work." Celestine's presence was a problem. I asked her to leave Beyoncé and me alone. Reluctantly, she honored my request. Walking her to the door, I whispered that Beyoncé's successful performance depended upon quiet and calm so that she could concentrate. "I hope you understand?" I added. I knew that Celestine would agree to disappear if it helped Beyoncé to give a stellar performance. I just wanted her gone.

After getting Beyoncé centered and focused, I began warming up her voice with light movement. Soon we found ourselves humming and following an even lighter regimen of yawns and staccato exercises (meant to help her cords come together in a healthy way), and then we spoke-sang. I had purposely chosen Anita Baker's "Sweet Love" for our warm-up song. Beyoncé had learned it with me when she was fourteen years old. Her body would remember the healthy way that she had first sung it and would thus trick itself into realignment. Singing songs that activate positive muscle memory is the most efficient way to correct problems. We had exactly four hours before the limo would take us over to BET.

Next we did lots of slurring exercises, using the vowels Ah, Eh and OO, and I incorporated a Do Re Me Re Do Ti Do scale into the exercises. This took her above and below those crucial shifts in registers that helped her to connect better to her diaphragm and breath. Within 45 minutes her breath had realigned itself and she was now ready to begin light singing. We spoke the first line to Anita Baker's song, aware of the position of the throat and mouth when speaking, and then singing it in the same unaltered position. Thirty minutes later, she was ready to actually sing the song. She was doing brilliantly and began to smile. She knew that everything was going to be OK. Mid-sentence she stopped, hugging me tightly. Then she stepped back quickly and fell into the rhythm of our work again.

Suddenly there was a knock on the door. Debra Ginyard, Destiny's Child stylist, and Quincy Jackson, then the girls' assigned product manager, had arrived. (Today Quincy is Vice President of Marketing for Def Jam Records.) I hadn't expected Quincy, but was glad to see her. "Right on time you guys," I said, giving both Debra and Quincy hugs. Debra began laying out clothes on Beyoncé's bed for her to look at. In that moment, the other girls were knocking on the door, and Celestine was with them. I could tell that getting back into Beyoncé's room delighted her above all else. "Beyoncé, don't say a word," I said.

Beyoncé chose a black leather jacket and an almost cream-colored top and bottom combination. Debra, who never forced the girls' decision, then had the green light to fit the other girls in complimentary colors. She was brilliant at her job. You could tell that she absolutely loved what she did, and to boot, she was the sweetest girl.

I noticed Celestine over in the corner giving Quincy an earful about something. I could almost bet she was complaining. Celestine didn't like Debra and had taken to calling her out in front of the girls. "That girl sure is ugly," she would say. Before long Celestine was referring to Debra simply as "Little Ugly." She knew enough not to do so in front of Sony executives, Quincy, Stephanie, or Debra herself. That would have been a non-Christian thing to do, Celestine said. Then she'd laugh sinisterly. I was horrified.

She called Debra "Little Ugly" so much that the girls began referring to their stylist by the same name. As if they couldn't remember the girl's name. "Little Ugly" this, and "Little Ugly" that. In front of the girls I admonished Celestine, told her that she was wrong. "Oh David, lighten up. I'm just joking. The girls know I'm just joking." Some joke.

Debra announced that all the girls had decided on their outfits and had been fitted. Then she rushed away to make last-minute alterations. Cheryl and Mathew had just joined us when Quincy suggested we begin preparing to head downstairs. "The limo will be here for us in about thirty minutes," she said.

Beyoncé's room looked as though a cyclone had hit it. Her clothing almost never hung on hangers. The floor seemed to do just fine. Even as a young child on Parkwood Street, Beyoncé had been this way. The other girls left Beyoncé's room to go gather their own things, and Quincy headed out the door, asking me to follow. "Sorry, Quincy, my work is not finished here." I briefly talked with Quincy outside the door in the hallway. Celestine stayed behind, making herself invaluable as Beyoncé dressed.

"Well, how is she?" Quincy asked.

"All is well, no worries. Her voice flows like butter again."

Beyoncé's vocal cords were still swollen, no doubt about it, but I had used the cold ice cream to reduce the swelling, the Benadryl to render her unconscious so that she couldn't talk and do further damage, and Anita Baker to release adrenaline and a few other feel-good juices to the thalamus of her brain. "Beyoncé is going to be just fine, Quincy. I promise."

"Thank you, David."

Realizing that I had left Beyoncé to her mother's wiles long enough, I pulled out my key and entered Beyoncé's room, announcing myself again. I had ten minutes to undo whatever Celestine might have whispered. As I entered the room I could hear her telling Beyoncé how important this performance was and that the label was looking at her. "Give your all," I heard her say. "Beyoncé, you will sing on your breath. You are not to push." Celestine knew by this time that she completely wore out my last nerve whenever she'd dispense her "vocal wisdom." No longer under the illusion that I was "family," I spoke my mind freely, unafraid. "Oh, I didn't mean to suggest…" Celestine began, looking at me pointedly. Seeing her to the door, I just smiled and closed it behind her. Beyoncé was my priority. She retreated to the bathroom to get dressed.

The limo had arrived. As Beyoncé and I walked to the elevator, I continued to speak quietly about those things she would have to remember during her performance. "Remember to keep your hips square. Dance using your upper body in block form and for God's sake, ride the breath," I said. When we reached the lobby, the other girls were there, waiting for us. Mathew was at the front desk talking with the hotel front desk staff, about what? I don't know. I believe Quincy was talking to the driver. Debra, still sewing and making alterations, had her head buried in her work.

Then it happened. Celestine emerged from the elevator carrying black boots, high-heeled boots that she had purchased for Beyoncé to wear. In her mother's opinion, Beyoncé looked too short on television. Holding out the boots to Beyoncé, she looked at Debra, who had a puzzled look on her face. "I hope you don't mind," Celestine said. Debra shook her head. "No problem," she said, returning to her work on the alterations.

When we arrived at the BET headquarters, I suggested that Beyoncé should be first up in the make-up chair. I never left her side. While the house make-up artist painted her face, I continued to warm up her voice, now concentrating on both the major and minor zygomatic muscles, which run along the side of the face and cheek toward the corner of the lips, and the masseter muscle, which is the big muscle near the back of the jaw. It pokes out when you bite down. We finished off by connecting her to the gluteus medius, the muscle just under the gluteus maximus muscle (her butt muscles), and which was the final step in anchoring her. Now she could play her instrument without fear of its getting away from her.

Beyoncé suggested to the girls that they change the order in which they would sing the songs. "I think we should begin with 'With Me Part I' and then sing 'No, No, No Part II.'" Yep, I was proud of my pupil. She had learned well. "With Me Part I," the more lyrical song, would give her time to get her nerves under control.

Agreeing, the other girls began getting made up. First up was Kelly. LeToya was next, then LaTavia. I stayed with each of them and warmed them up, as I had done with Beyoncé. Every once in a while, I would look back. Beyoncé was in the corner, going over her choreography, mouthing the words and breathing. While pacing, sometimes with her eyes closed, she was getting into the zone. Celestine was with me in the make-up area, making last-minute suggestions to the hair and make-up team regarding the girls' hair. I don't remember the head make-up artist's name, but he was fabulous. I had never seen my girls so perfectly coifed.

When they were ready, I assembled the girls for harmony warm-ups. We sang major and minor chords. I switched who sang the base and who sang the seventh of the chord often. It made them focus. They never knew who was going to have to sing the root of the chord (which I signaled by pointing to the girl who was supposed to sing it, thumb down) and the seventh of the chord (thumb up). Then I would point to the girls who would sing the third and fifth of the chord. It was a bit like directing a flight into the air terminal parking position. When the stage manager called "Places!" they were ready.

Taking Beyoncé's arm, I had her breathe through the sweet points in the nose, all the while talking to her. "I'm going to stay on my breath," I said. "I'm going to keep flexible on my breath and not push," I added. "I'm going to knock this performance out of the box," I concluded. Entering the backstage area, we could all see the fans. The show had gone to commercial break and the young people in the studio audience were busy chatting away. The stage manager told my girls to take their places. She did a ten-second countdown and the show host announced that *Teen Summit* was back. As she introduced Destiny's Child, I looked out onto the stage at Beyoncé. She was praying silently.

Suddenly the music started and she moved into action. She was brilliant. They all were brilliant. Beyoncé rode her breath. The flexibility in her voice was there and she was singing in the middle of the vowel. She kept her hips square and anchored, moving her entire body as a block from the waist up. I was like a proud papa. My work had been done.

The audience went wild, especially when Kelly sang her part. Audiences loved Kelly. They were in awe of Beyoncé. "With Me Part I" ended perfectly. The audience erupted in applause. The show cut to commercial break. I ran out on stage and handed Beyoncé a bottle of water I'd brought with me from the hotel. She drank some, gave it back to me, and never left the zone. She barely recognized that I was there, just as it should be. Back from commercial break, the host announced "No, No, No Part II." The music started; then the poses; then the choreography. Their lines were perfect and their spacing was good, too. This time Beyoncé nailed the

572

opening line, "Boy I know you want me, I can see it in your eyes." She was in the groove, completely on the beat and singing the song better than she had in a long time. Quincy squeezed my arm, kissing me on the cheek, all the while dancing and mouthing the words "thank you." We were both dancing. Mathew and Celestine stood in the background. *Teen Summit* was a complete success.

After the performance we all gathered back in the green room. The girls and I took a picture together, and they signed my album, autographing it with very heartfelt words. Mathew had not allowed them to thank me individually in the liner notes of their album. He allowed my name to be included in the list of miscellaneous people to be acknowledged. I am glad that I pushed through on this occasion. The only picture of the girls and me that I own is the photo we took at BET that day. That photo and their autographs are treasured possessions.

As the girls signed the album cover, I was in deep conversation with Quincy, who was on the phone with a very happy Columbia Records president. She gave me the thumbs up. Celestine looked at me with contempt. Her stare felt to me like sheer hatred. My days would be numbered. I was sure of it. You didn't cross Celestine and walk away. She was going to pay me back; I just didn't know how. No matter the consequences, I was glad that God had put me in my girls' lives. Even if it meant losing them to an ambitious and determined Mama Celestine.

I gave silent thanks, hugged my girls, and took my leave. The limo was waiting to take me back to the airport. It was time to go home. On my way to Dulles I read the girls' autographs.

From Beyoncé: "Thanks 4 all you've taught me. You have been inspiring to me and I love you. Thanx 4 being a part of my life. Thank you!"

From LeToya: "To my friend and vocal coach, Thankx 4 taking my voice to another voice. God Bless."

From LaTavia: "To David, Thankx 4 sticking By me through my rough times and my Bad attitudes. I Love You Guy!"

From Kelly: "David, words cannot express my thoughts & love to you! Stay in my life always O.K. Love you 4-ever!"

* * * * *

Sony Columbia spent a small fortune on the "Soul Power Tour," which Michael Mauldin himself initiated. Already in December of 1997, Mauldin had orchestrated interviews in music magazines about the tour, which was to help promote his baby acts Destiny's Child, Jagged Edge, and the eleven-year-old singer Kimberly Scott. The *R&R Magazine* reporter Tara O'Quinn wrote a profile of my girls, calling them sensational. "Destiny's Child is a group blessed with *real* talent," she wrote. "The successful blend of genuine vocal ability makes their music 'ear friendly.' No hype, no studio tricks, just God-given talent flowing through the speakers whenever "No, No, No" is played. What Houston has released on the music industry is gripping."

After the publication of Tara O'Quinn's *R&R* profile, a journalist from *The Sun Reporter* in San Francisco published a review of Destiny's Child's debut album. He quoted the girls. "'We're young but we're surely not new to the game,' Beyoncé said *[the reporter helped the readers by explaining that Beyoncé rhymed with fiancé]* – a stunning, honey-complexioned beauty with a big powerful lead voice. 'Yes,' adds pretty Kelly, also an outstanding lead singer, 'we've been singing together for so long and know each other's voices so well, we just naturally bring out the best of each other when we're in the studio or on stage. Personally, we're closer than most real sisters.'"

The tone of the entire article is extremely positive. "It's obvious that Destiny's Child is a well-crafted collaborative effort," *The Sun Reporter* wrote. The journalist called Destiny's Child a "totally committed group at its passionate center." He went on to say that the group was "Already being compared to classic groups like the Supremes and the Emotions." He closes out the article with a prediction. "Beginning with the chart ascension of 'No No No,' the success forecast for Destiny's Child is undeniably 'Yes, Yes, YES!'"

I read that article over and over again while sitting in business class on my trans-Atlantic flight to Paris. I planned a vacation to visit friends before having to head back to America for performances. I loved Paris and

574

stayed at the Hotel Louvre, a swank upscale oasis not far from the famous museum from which it took its name. Naturally, I kept up with Beyoncé and the other girls. Beyoncé's perfume allergy was under control and the other girls were enjoying the tour. I couldn't have been prouder of them. My contacts at Sony swore that they had never seen a group so well prepared. I beamed.

* * * * *

My girls' debut album had made its appearance on February 17th, 1998, and already they had been nominated for three Soul Train awards. While I was still in Paris, my girls would be in Los Angeles, sitting in the audience at Shrine Auditorium, for the Lady of Soul Train Awards. Sony Columbia had released their singles in November 1997 and they had done reasonably well. (By early 1999, they had sold millions and had been certified Platinum.) There was a 50/50 chance they'd win a Soul Train Award, but my girls knew that they were up against some stiff competition. Destiny's Child had been nominated along with SWV, Escape, Total, Mia, Queen Pen, Sparkle, and industry Veteran EnVogue. Although they were new on the scene, I felt confident, and I had told them so before I left for Europe.

"From your mouth to God's ear," Beyoncé said.

I spent the whole day wandering around Paris on February 27th. I walked the Champs-Élysées, Paris's most famous avenue, bought some peppermints at Maxim's, and had lunch with my friends at the Eiffel Tower. I didn't talk to Beyoncé and the other girls on that day. Paris was nine hours ahead of California, and I didn't have their itinerary. Mathew had stopped sharing things like that with me, even before Washington. In addition, calls from Europe, especially from the Hotel Louvre, were not what they are today. Calling Houston from my room was still very expensive. Sure, I was doing well financially, but nowhere near rich, so I opted for sending Destiny's Child my positive energy via prayer and the literal airwaves.

When I awakened on February 28th I found a note that the concierge had slipped under my door. Gregory had called from Nashville, where he was singing *Tosca*. "They won," the note said. I don't know if I was doing a holy dance or the huck-a-buck, but I was dancing. I was beyond happy. Suddenly my telephone rang. Running to it to catch the call, I answered excitedly.

"Gregory," I called out.

"No, it's not Gregory, Mr. Brewer."

"Tony, is that you?"

"Yep," he said. Tony Coles, who has remained a loyal friend since 1991, was doing his own little dance. "I can't believe it. I can't believe it. The girls won all three of their awards."

"What did you say?" I asked.

"Destiny's Child won all three of their nominations," Tony repeated.

Tony reminded me that I had told him on Christmas in 1991, when Beyoncé was ten years old, that this day would come. Beyoncé had been singing "Silent Night," a song we had been working on in her lesson, and at the moment Tony showed up to my studio she had begun to sing her improvisations on the melody. In her room, at the end of the alcove that connected my apartment to the main house, Beyoncé was busy singing her heart out. She made an interesting turn in the opening phrase that captured Tony's attention. "Who is that singing?" he asked.

"Oh, that's Beyoncé." Tony hadn't met her yet. "She's going to make a million dollars one day," I said.

Looking at me like I had just crapped my pants, Tony asked, "Oh really, and just how do you know that?"

"Because I am going to make sure of it," I said. "It's part of God's plan." When I think about it, that was a pretty cocky thing to say, but I *was* sure of it. Although he'd been raised by a mother who was a minister of the Gospel, Tony was skeptical of my prediction. He thought it fantasy and said so. Now, many years later, my jubilation reminded Tony of my expressions of faith. As my shouts and Thank You Jesuses were winding down to a huffy puffy but happy calm, I returned the phone to my ear. Tony was still waiting.

"I'm sorry. Please excuse me," I said. "I just couldn't contain myself."

"No problem. You said that they would be successful and now they are on their way. I can't believe I sat in that house all those years, watching it all unfold," Tony said. Then my mother grabbed the phone from Tony. Turns out he was calling from her house in Houston. She was overjoyed.

"Congratulations, baby. I know you are proud and Mama is proud of you. You worked hard and it paid off."

Mama and I talked for a couple minutes and then she excused herself to remove the laundry from the dryer before having to head out to work. She gave the phone back to Tony, who had stopped by to make the long distance call to Paris.

I was finally able to get the details. Tony told me that the first award was for the Best R&B Soul Single of 1998, for Group, Band or Duo. The girls were up against SWV, Total and Escape and they won. Then he told me that the second award was for Best R&B Soul or Rap by a New Artist. Destiny's Child was up against Mia, Queen Pen and Sparkle. My girls won. Finally, we came to the biggie. Best R&B Soul Album of the Year by Group, Band or Duo. My girls were up against the Duo Changing faces, EnVogue and SWV, and they won that too.

"And guess what?" Tony added.

"What, what? Don't make me beg!" I said. I could barely take the excitement.

"Beyoncé thanked you. She thanked you first and then somebody named Frank. Then she thanked her mama for her styling and then Mathew as manager."

I began to tear up. Then, "Wait – hold up." I asked Tony to repeat what he had just said.

"What do you mean?" Tony asked.

"Go back to the Celestine part."

"Beyoncé thanked you as her vocal coach, somebody named Frank (Destiny's Child choreographer), Tina her stylist, and…"

"Stop," I shouted. "Did you say Celestine was her stylist?"

"Yes. Why is that so shocking?" Tony asked.

"It is so shocking because Celestine is not the stylist, Debra Ginyard is."

"Well, I don't know anything about no Debra, but Beyoncé said her mama was the stylist."

I was thoroughly confused. What had happened to Debra? Then it came back to me. Not only had Beyoncé begun complaining about her work, she had been accusing Debra of intentionally making them look "old." Those had been her exact words to me.

"But Beyoncé, you always liked Debra," I said, puzzled – until I realized whose words she was parroting – "making us look old…"

Celestine. Her calling Debra "Little Ugly" had paid off.

Subsequently, I heard that Sony Columbia Records felt bad about taking Debra off the Destiny's Child job. They'd had no time to find a replacement, Stephanie said. So, Celestine offered to dress the girls for free. Of course she did, I thought. I felt sick and angry, all at the same time. A few months later my girls would perform in Australia. Afterwards, Celestine was named stylist. She'd won. I felt horrible for Debra, wondering what Celestine's poisonous bite had done to that sweet girl's reputation.

A few weeks later, I found out that Mathew had attacked Beyoncé backstage after the Lady of Soul Train Awards and continued his ranting in the hotel. According to LeToya, he was pissed off that Beyoncé had thanked me first. LaTavia added that he demanded of Beyoncé that she was never to say my name again in public, an order that she dutifully fulfilled.

* * * * *

In autumn 1998 I phoned the Knowles home repeatedly from Lisbon, Portugal, and Madrid. In the first week of July, rehearsals had begun in Lisbon for the world premiere of Philip Glass's opera *O Corvo Branco* (The White Raven), which took place on September 26, 1998. By October '98, I had traveled with the rest of the cast to Madrid for performances at the Teatro Real, Madrid's premier opera house.

578

Because I would be out of the U. S. for several weeks in summer 1998, and at the same time, the girls would be on tour, Mathew and Celestine and I agreed that we should set up a lesson schedule for early December, when we were all back in Houston. During that summer and then several times in the fall, I phoned the Knowles home repeatedly from New York, Lisbon, and Madrid. In the first week of July, rehearsals had begun in Lisbon for the world premiere of Philip Glass's opera *O Corvo Branco* (The White Raven), which took place on September 26, 1998. I still hadn't heard from Mathew. In October I traveled with the rest of the cast to Madrid for rehearsals and performances at the Teatro Real, Madrid's premier opera house, and I still hadn't heard from him.

I did hear, however, from Beyoncé, once. She called me at home in New York before I left for Portugal, where I would join the rest of the cast for *O Corvo Branco* rehearsals. She and the other girls were on the Boyz II Men Evolution Tour, as one of the opening acts, together with R&B male groups Dru Hill and K-Ci & Jo-Jo. Beyoncé said that she didn't have a lot of time, but that she wanted to give me a heads up. "I gave Wanyá your number."

"What's up?" I asked.

According to Beyoncé, the Boyz II Men lead singer, Wanyá Morris, was suffering from vocal nodules.

"Oh," I said. "That's not good. I'm sure you guys have had to cancel a few performances."

"Yes, several."

"Well, tell him he can call me at any time." And then I gave Beyoncé my hotel numbers in Lisbon and Madrid, adding "…just in case." I didn't know when he'd call, or if he'd call. "As you know, Beyoncé, vocal nodules isn't something you can get rid of overnight. But it's definitely a solvable problem. It's important for him to react decisively."

"Yeah, that's what I told him," Beyoncé answered. "I hope he calls you. He's such a nice person and a good singer."

I suddenly heard a distant voice on Beyoncé's end of the line. She covered the phone receiver briefly.

"I'm sorry," Beyoncé said. "I'm back." Then she asked when I would be home. "The tour is over on July 25th, but we aren't going to be doing the whole thing," she said.

"I'll be heading home in early December," I told her. "Madrid performances of *The White Raven* are scheduled for November 28 to December 5, and on December 4th there'll be a live television broadcast in Madrid. It's a tight performance schedule. I'm sorry that I can't get away to join you guys on tour."

She offered no reply.

"Beyoncé, are you still there?" I asked.

"Uh-huh."

I asked if her father had mentioned my having called him. "I've left at least ten messages on Mathew's business line in the house. I need to set up your lessons."

"Lessons?" Beyoncé asked in a distracted voice.

"Yes," I answered. "I even called your mother," I added. "She promised that your father would get back to me soon, but I haven't heard from him. Is he so busy?"

"Yes, I think so," Beyoncé answered.

"Beyoncé, is everything all right?"

"Oh, sure."

Trying to break through her sudden reticence, I repeated that her mother had promised to have Mathew call me, and Beyoncé said, "Well, I hope he calls you back soon, because I need a voice lesson really bad."

"That's exactly why I've been trying to reach him. I know that the whole group needs a tune-up," I said. She didn't say anything else, so I finished the conversation with, "It won't be long before I'm standing in front of you all. Take care, and I can't wait to see you."

"Me too," she said.

* * * * *

On approximately December 15, 1998, Gregory and I drove over to the Knowles house. I'd gone to see the girls, to hear their completed tracks, and to present Mathew with my bill for the work I'd done during the Atlanta showcase, Elektra records, and the summer camp months. (The actual bill was more than $15,000.00, but in typical David fashion, I had cut the bill to a little more than $7,500.00. It was close to Christmas, and I was doing well financially, so I felt generous.)

After we had heard the tracks, Gregory and I were finishing our conversation with Celestine and Mathew. Solange was sitting on the couch, and Beyoncé and Kelly were upstairs, in their bedrooms, most likely talking on their teen lines to their boyfriends, Lyndall and some Greek guy Kelly was secretly dating.

That's when I presented my invoice to Mathew. "You can take your time paying it," I said, passing the envelope to him.

"What is this?" he asked.

"It's the bill for my work during the training camp back in 1993, '94, and '95, including the preparation for Elektra records. We agreed I would present it when the girls found success."

"What? Elektra fell through, and I don't remember agreeing to paying you for back work. And what work?"

I was stunned. My demeanor instantly turned to quiet, but obvious, rage.

"Let's go, David," Gregory said, taking my arm, holding it tightly. In retrospect, I can see that my reaction to Mathew's oversight must have been frightening.

Also realizing the magnitude of Mathew's callousness, Celestine quickly asked me, to "remain calm." Turning to her husband, she reminded him, "Mathew, he did do the work."

"He sure did, Daddy," Solange said.

Mathew looked at me and shouted, "I'm tired of niggas trying to cash in on the girls' success."

"What did you say to me?" I yelled, "Really Mathew, you mean like you've been doing for years? *You asshole.*" Not even his insult "Never in a million fucking years" had upset me as much as his "niggas trying to cash in" comment. First off, I wasn't a "nigga" and two, I wasn't a thief. He was.

Beyoncé came downstairs, curious to know what was going on. She passed her father in the hallway as he stormed into his bedroom/office.

"I'll talk to him," Celestine said.

"Let's go, David," Gregory now insisted.

In just that moment Mathew returned with a typed note, full of grammatical and punctuation errors, but clear in its intention. "Destiny's Child will pay David Lee Brewer a total of $4,000.00 for services rendered in 1993, and all subsequent summers..." Signing this document would mean my agreeing that for $4,000 the debt would be rendered "paid in full."

I balled it up and threw it in Mathew's face. "I'm not some punk ass, Mathew. You agreed, and you are going to pay me."

An indescribable anger seized me. Gregory grabbed me again and managed to get me out of the house. Life was at risk – Mathew's life, to be exact. I was out of my mind with rage.

The next day Beyoncé called me at my mother's. "Daddy, didn't mean it," she said. "Please don't be mad."

I listened, quietly.

Then Celestine took the phone. "Please reconsider. Beyoncé doesn't want to lose you as her teacher. Take the money. We're all going to make so much more in the future. Take the $4,000.00 David," she repeated, "or you won't get anything."

"Did you just say I won't get anything? This is me, Celestine. David. After all these years, you dare say that to me? You really don't give a shit about me, do you?"

She said nothing.

I hung up, having a Witch Celestine flashback.

O Corvo Branco (White Raven), a five-act opera by the American composer Philip Glass, had its premiere at Expo '98 in Lisbon, September 1998. The title refers to a myth in which Apollo turns a white crow to black, and the opera uses the crow as a symbol of lost innocence. As a member of that cast, I sang not only in the Lisbon premiere, but also in subsequent Madrid performances. The photo (above) is of a dress rehearsal in Madrid.

Photos: Javier del Real

Following a June 2000 Los Angeles concert, a tribute to the great African-American tenor Roland Hayes, I posed with my pianist, Sandra Hyslop (in polka-dot skirt), and my Langston University acting teacher, Janet Hollier-Davis (now a professor at Perimeter College, Georgia State University, Atlanta).

27. Girl, Bye

That Sunday, the 20th of December, my mother's phone rang. Mama handed me the receiver. It was Celestine. She wanted to "talk," another one of those talks that I had learned to despise. "Can't we find a compromise?" she asked me.

It took a minute, but I choked out a response. "I'm not sure we can, Celestine. I want my money, all $7,500.00 of it."

"I understand," Celestine said. "Just come to the house. Let's talk. We've always been able to talk. Beyoncé is just torn up about what happened."

What Beyoncé felt, in that moment, had nothing to do with our disagreement. This was business.

"I'm not sure this can be fixed, Celestine. So much was said. Let me think about it."

Then I added, "I'll call you in the morning."

"OK," she answered.

The next morning, my gut told me to stay in bed. My mother, however, talked me into hearing Celestine out.

"David, we must face our demons," she said.

* * * * *

By December, things at the Knowles house were bad. Mathew's head had swollen to the size of a small country. His behavior was even more unbelievable than anything you've read thus far about him. Apparently, Mathew was having his umpteenth affair, this time with the sister of his bookkeeper at Music World Management, Linda Ragland. Celestine was furious.

Mathew needed to pay, and dearly.

On December 21st 1998, Mathew realized, possibly for the first time, that Celestine wore the pants. Celestine was determined that Daddy

Mathew would learn the lessons that she was teaching. She alone controlled his future.

After several of Celestine's rants, crying spells, and near fainting, Beyoncé fired her father.

"Daddy, you are fired."

Merry Christmas, I thought.

To save himself, Mathew broke down, confessed his drug addiction to Beyoncé, and promised to re-enter rehab. He then revealed yet another fact. A shocked Beyoncé listened as her father admitted to being "a sex addict." The reason for the admission: his urge to explain that there was an excuse for his behavior – in other words, it wasn't his fault. My God, the man had laid it on thick. A horrified Beyoncé, trying desperately to hold her ground, felt sorry for her father. Her little sister, Solange, did not.

Satisfied with her orchestrated outcome, Beyoncé's mother then said, "Beyoncé, Mathew is your father. In this family we remain loyal."

And with that, a teary Beyoncé Giselle Knowles took it all back. Had Celestine just played her daughter? Of course she had, like a fiddle. Daddy's job was saved, and a vindicated Mathew hugged his daughter – the first time he'd ever done such a thing since my knowing him. It was a Tiny Tim moment, for sure.

Hallmark has nothing on the Knowleses.

To tell the truth, Mathew wasn't ashamed of his drug abuse and sex addiction. No, not a bit. He would recount it all, years later, in an interview he enjoyed giving to The National Enquirer. Saving himself by any means necessary, Mathew even kept his word and went to rehab, the very next day. However, this time he wouldn't actually check himself in. No, he was going to kick drugs as an outpatient. Typical, I thought. I said to Celestine, "I mean, who tries to quit drugs as an outpatient?"

Needless to say, that didn't work so well. In no time, Mathew was right back to his habit and Beyoncé was left to wrestle with the ugly truth. Her father had used his "situation" to bamboozle her.

Mathew's spending had gotten up to almost a thousand dollars a day, Celestine confided. Perhaps that was a lie, but she told it. Nevertheless, his effort didn't feel serious to me. Nor was Solange convinced, who by 1999 would finally get some attention. I continued to remind Beyoncé privately to "just keep your hands clean." I could only pray that she would listen. So far, so good. But her patience was wearing thin. Celestine saw to that, as I witnessed one time at close range.

The girls were in New York for interviews. It must have been about 1:00 a.m. when I prepared to leave their hotel and head to my apartment uptown. LeToya, LaTavia, and Kelly had already gone to their rooms, and Beyoncé and I were saying our final goodbye, when the telephone rang.

"Hold on," she said.

I closed the door and walked back into the room. Beyoncé was talking to her mother.

"Hi, Mama," I heard her say.

From the look on Beyoncé's face, which darkened almost immediately after greeting her mother, Celestine's call was not a pleasant one. Beyoncé sat on the bed, downtrodden. Her breathing seemed labored. Nervously picking at her jeans, she answered her mother's question. "No, Mama. I haven't seen Daddy….," and then, "What's going on?"

After a few minutes' conversation, Celestine and Beyoncé ended the call. Completely distracted, she began to pace in the room like a caged panther.

"What's up, Beyoncé?"

I waited a few moments, and then I asked her again.

"What's going on? Is everything all right?"

"I have to find Daddy," she answered, and started to put her shoes on. She was definitely not okay.

"How do you plan to do that?" I asked. "We don't even know his room number." In all the years my girls traveled professionally, Mathew refused to give anyone his room number, except Cheryl, when she acted as chaperone. And he said that she was allowed to bother him only in case of an emergency.

Completely exasperated, Beyoncé sat down in the chair in the room, her head in her hands. I felt bad for her. This wasn't the first time Celestine had pulled this crap, but something was different about this time.

When Beyoncé finally raised her head, a tear ran down her left cheek. It was always her left cheek. Gingerly, I reminded her that we'd talked about this. "Beyoncé, this is actually between your parents."

The next morning, Beyoncé confronted her father in the limousine on the way to the interview – right in front of all of us – including the driver.

"Where were you, Daddy?" she demanded.

"That's my business," he answered.

With that, she flipped out. I didn't recognize her. She had turned into a beast, cursing and threatening to remove Mathew from his position as the group's manager. I was glad she hadn't had a weapon. Mathew's only response was to say, "Beyoncé, watch how you talk to me in front of people."

In that brief, volatile exchange, I saw clearly that Beyoncé's relationship with her father had changed forever.

* * * * *

Along with Celestine's manipulations of Beyoncé, her conniving against Kelly drove me crazy. She launched her undercover campaign against Kelly's greatest vulnerabilities: her sensitivity about her dark skin color, her despair over her hair style, her lack of confidence in her (beautiful) soprano voice, and her lack of a stable home life. I watched in dismay as Celestine repeatedly found ways to poke at Kelly's spirit.

Celestine constantly told Kelly that she sang like an angel – in itself, a lovely gesture – and then immediately she would remind the girl that she should never sing "too loud." I can't tell you how many times snake-in-the-grass Celestine pointed out to Kelly, ever so tenderly, that her voice became unpleasant when she sang too loudly. I heard, "Don't allow your voice to shine brighter than Beyoncé's." Kelly heard, "You're no good." As a result, Kelly would then hold back, which was the opposite of what I was teaching her, asking of her.

Other times Beyoncé's mother made Kelly's gorgeous skin her target. Celestine loved to stand with Kelly in front of a mirror and, cupping the

588

child's face in her hands, say, "Look at your chocolate skin, Kelly. It's beautiful," knowing full well that Kelly was hyper-sensitive about her darker skin color.

Eventually I found out what had happened to Kelly's hair, and why. According to Beyoncé's manipulative mother and Beyoncé herself, Kelly had become *boastful* (Celestine's opinion, of course), had taken to calling herself the "second lead singer" in *Beyoncé's group*. Kelly was still living under the delusion that Celestine cared about her. In fact, all my girls lived with that delusion for a long time. With no Ann around, and with me frequently gone, on the road, they had lost the two adults in their lives who could help make sense of the conflicting messages they got. I could deflect the hostility when Celestine nagged at me that Kelly was "beginning to sound too much like Beyoncé," but on their own, LeToya, LaTavia, and Kelly didn't stand a chance.

I confronted Celestine on several occasions about the things that I saw as suspicious. When she mowed Kelly's hair right down to stubble, talks got serious. Celestine and I had talked so often about Kelly's self-love, or rather the lack thereof. Kelly's aversion to short hair in general, and her despair about the "uneven" look of her own hair, were well known within our circle. Why then did Celestine fucking chop it off? Immediately after seeing the pictures from Destiny's Child's very first album photo shoot, I asked Celestine how she could do such a thing, "...knowing what you know?"

She claimed absolute innocence.

"Celestine, even us boy children, regardless of where we might come from, can recall screaming on the day our mothers took us to a barber shop for that first hair-chopping experience," I said. "You know how sensitive Kelly is about her hair. Even if you didn't know Kelly, you surely know, from your line of work, how much women count on the look of their hair to define themselves."

Celestine remained staunchly convicted in her fantasy. She'd not done anything to harm Kelly, she repeated. "I would never do such a thing."

I didn't believe her.

589

In later years, when the girls, as Destiny's Child, began to appear before more sophisticated audiences, Celestine shared with me her stylistic vision for the group. Beyoncé's mother reasoned that one girl should be blond, one should be a sassy red head, one should be a brunette, and the other, well, she had to have short hair. It wasn't personal, she reiterated. "I think Kelly is beautiful, but somebody has to have the short hair." Absolutely sure that she'd done right by Kelly, Celestine shifted the topic to "Beyoncé's commercial success." I reminded her, "You mean the group's commercial success?"

"Of course," she answered. "You know what I mean."

I most certainly did, and so did the "other girls," I told her. "Celestine, Destiny's Child is a group. It is *NOT* Beyoncé alone."

"That's true. But Beyoncé does most of the work."

"I'm sure that's what you and your husband would like to believe," I answered. "But your saying that over and over again does not make it so."

Innocent of all these manipulations, Kelly seemed to be oblivious. Celestine would promise me she'd be more sensitive to Kelly's needs, but naturally, she didn't keep her word. It wouldn't take long before she was in manipulative mode again. She had even accused the girl of lying. I'll never forget that teary scene, Celestine whispering her sweet accusations into Kelly's ear. In my opinion, it was this incident that finally broke her delicate spirit. The Kelly I'd come to know and love hated lying. It began to occur to me that she might possibly, out of sheer self-defense, adopt dissembling – even lying – as a coping device.

Now, to most, Celestine's compliments might sound harmless. You might even think that ole David is off his rocker. LaTavia was the darkest in the group, definitely darker than Kelly, you might say. However, LaTavia was no threat to Celestine. LaTavia wasn't the one with the color complex, Kelly was. And although LeToya was the one with the brilliant – and the highest – soprano voice, the one that soared way above Beyoncé's, Celestine focused on Kelly.

I will never forget the day, during the 1993 summer camp, when I found three of the girls outside sunbathing – for the second time. After a strenuous morning of jogging and drilling vocals, they were supposed to be resting. I didn't eat with them that day, but before our next session was to begin, I happened passed my balcony doors and saw a scene that horrified me. There they were, clad in bathing suits, basking in the Houston heat. I flung open the double doors.

"Girls, why are you guys sunbathing?" I already knew the answer to that question, but I needed to confirm my suspicions.

"Miss Tina told us to," Kelly said.

My blood pressure shot up. I thought I had made myself clear the first time Celestine had suggested that the girls get out into the sun.

"And where is Miss Beyoncé?"

"In the house," said LeToya.

Beyond furious, I said, "And that is exactly where you all are going. Are you crazy?" They quickly did as I asked.

Realizing that my reaction might have come across as scolding, I patiently explained to the girls – once again – that my concern was for their physical and vocal health.

"Girls, singers can't afford to lose moisture, either in their throats or their bodies. The sun is incredibly draining. Plus, my to-do list is already overloaded. I don't need to add 'solve unnecessary muscle cramps' to it. Our training will only get more intense."

They understood, nodding their sorry heads.

I went immediately to the telephone to call the salon. Not only had Celestine ignored my professional warnings about the harmful effects of the sun, but she had also interfered that week with my rehearsal schedule in what I saw as a challenge to my teaching. I'd had enough of her damn meddling, and it was time to push reset, to re-establish the boundaries.

Earlier that week, knowing full well of my background as a professional performer and choreographer of dance and modeling, Celestine had nevertheless taken it upon herself to send a modeling "instructor" to one of my rehearsals. On that evening, after our dinner break, I had heard music playing outside. Pleased that my girls were taking initiative, I went to the balcony doors and looked out. What I saw sent me reeling. A strange man had the girls lined up, moving them around our rehearsal stage (The Deck).

I quickly headed downstairs. "Excuse me," I said. "What's going on here?"

"Hi, Tina sent me over to work with the girls on their modeling."

If this guy was a modeling instructor, then I'm Jesus Christ. He was a hot mess, incompetent, unprofessional.

Irritated, I stopped the "modeling" session, hoping he'd take the hint, and suggested that we move on to our own dance rehearsal.

As the girls got into formation, our uninvited guest took a seat.

I shot him a look.

"Oh, may I watch?"

I answered curtly, not bothering to hide my disgust, "If you'd like."

A few minutes into the rehearsal, the girls began to giggle. I turned just in time to see what looked like the worst attempt at a pirouette that I have ever seen. Talk about bad Wonder Woman impressions. This guy was a joke. I hit the roof. Then I walked him to the door. Closing it behind me, I turned to see four snickering girls falling about. I wasn't having it.

"Girls, let's take 10! I'll be right back," I said, and then made a beeline for my apartment and the telephone.

"Hi Celestine, Sorry to call you at the salon. I hope I'm not disturbing you…." With that, unsolicited visitors were history.

Now, two days later, I was calling her again.

"Sorry to bother you at work, Celestine, but I need to clarify something right now. Can you explain why you insist on suggesting that the girls sunbathe?"

"I did what?"

"Sunbathe. The girls say that you suggested – again – that they should sunbathe today."

"What's the problem?" she said, "I thought it would be something fun for them to do together."

"Mm," I said. "And to be clear. What's the reason you suggested that Beyoncé not join them out on the HOT deck?"

I could sense Celestine's blood boiling. After scrambling her brain to come up with a plausible answer, she said, "Beyoncé burns so easily...."

I couldn't help myself. I laughed out loud. "Seriously," I said.

Begging her majesty's indulgence, I said, "I mean this with all the love in my heart, Celestine, and please don't misunderstand me, but I was serious when I talked with you the other day about the harmful effects of the sun on the singer. I won't bother to repeat that information, because I know that you remember it.

Celestine said nothing, but I swear I heard a hiss coming through the line.

I went on. "For the last time, the sun is detrimental to our work."

"How so?" Celestine asked, in a tone that managed to sound both innocent and flippant.

"Dehydration," I answered. "Plus, black folks don't sunbathe."

"I have to get back to my client," Celestine snapped.

"No problem. And again, sorry for bothering you at work."

"See you tonight," she said.

"Sure thing."*

*Celestine stubbornly maintained that practice with the girls, even after they were finding success as Destiny's Child. In an interview in SiSTER 2 Sister magazine in December 2000, the singer Farrah said of Mathew and Celestine: "... They also had me suntanning." Asked whether Beyoncé, too, was tanning, Farrah replied, "No. I think that's why they didn't have her tanning. My assumption was that every time I looked at a picture, she stood out more because she was the bright one. Not because she was the prettiest, but because she was lighter." When asked who told her to tan, Farrah said, "The mother. She's like the stylist and she was like, "You look prettier darker.""

* * * * *

Each time I battled the Knowleses, I did so with a full and open heart, which left me dangerously vulnerable. Even when I wasn't the one taking the direct verbal beating, my soul suffered like hell. It sounds harsh, accusing someone's mother of calculatingly vicious motives, but Beyoncé's mother earned my censure, over and over again. I kept asking myself, How many people did my mother set out to annihilate so that I could get my dream job on the opera stage? The answer? Zero.

During our weekly phone call, Mama reminded me that a woman's resolve is a fierce thing. "Having Beyoncé at the center of Destiny's Child is necessary for Celestine's rise," she said. "Imagine it. She will most likely claim to have selflessly sacrificed herself for Beyoncé, swearing she was forced to downsize her house on Parkwood. She might even drop a tear while blaming her husband for everything. And Beyoncé will believe her. You can set your watch to it."

I was speechless.

"David, most of the claims will be fabricated. You know that, and I know it, but will the public? I have seen it a hundred times, if not a thousand. Dealing with a mother set on proving her value to her children is no easy task."

Mama's words were anything but comforting.

"I'm sorry, Baby. But unfortunately, it's the way of the world. Most people can't be trusted. Jealousy is real. Their lies sound plausible. Just be careful, sweetheart."

I looked at Mama, not knowing how to reply.

"David, do you see how I just whispered unsuspecting poison into your ears?" Mama asked. "We are pros at it. I'm warning you, never underestimate a mother on a mission."

About six months later, Mama's words still echoed in my soul. I had already told her about my argument with Mathew – the one that Gregory dragged me out of his house about – over the $7,500.00 he owed me.

"Mathew transferred $4,000.00 today to my account, and after I refused to accept anything other than full payment. Henry (Henry Holmes, my U.S. accountant) said that fighting him would cost me more than the amount. He said I should seriously consider accepting the payment, and moving on."

"Sounds like sound advice, David."

As much as it gnawed at me, I left it.

* * * * *

Destiny's Child's breakthrough success would come after the release of their sophomore album, *The Writing's on the Wall*, on July 28, 1999. (I believe my girls adopted that title after I had talked to Beyoncé about the Biblical story of Belshazzar's feast.)

As Wyclef would so eloquently put it, my young divas "went from a dream to the young Supremes." Their album *The Writing's on the Wall* immediately registered at number six on the *Billboard* 2000 album chart, and for the remainder of 1999, Destiny's Child continued to top charts and boast impressive sales. By June 2001 they would sell eleven million records worldwide, and receive a whopping $9,000,000.00 (nine million dollars) in royalties. Their first single, "Bills, Bills, Bills" climbed to number one, just weeks after it first aired on the radio, and it remained on *Billboard*'s singles chart for nine consecutive weeks. It was official. Destiny's Child, by all accounts, was a tremendous international success.

No longer shy about speaking up, Beyoncé led the group's assertion of musical independence. "We want this album to be in our voice," she said. At Sony Columbia, Teresa listened.

Sony Columbia brought in big guns with Kevin "She'kspere" Briggs, who served as lead producer on *The Writing's on the Wall*. He had just produced and co-written TLC's hit single "No Scrubs," in December '98, and the previous June (also 1998). During this period, I was continuing to sandwich in the girls' lessons as frequently as we could get our calendars coordinated.

That summer when the girls' first single from the new album was released, I was in Houston, singing Puccini's opera *Madama Butterfly* with Houston Grand Opera. I heard the radio deejay for 97.9, The Box, announce "Bills, Bills, Bills" as I was driving. "This is the new one from

Destiny's Child," said the announcer. Reaching over and turning up the volume, I heard the first line. "At first we started out real cool." The text went right through me. My foot hit the brake, and I pulled over to avoid an accident as I listened to the entire song, emotionally transfixed by what I heard. Mathew never gave free copies of the album, not even to his supposed team members, so I rushed over to Tower Records (today a Kinko's), on Shepard Street at Hwy 59, and bought it. My girls had found their authentic voice, which pleased me to no end. At the same time, the record made me extremely uncomfortable, and it slowly dawned on me that my uneasiness was God talking to me. This album was going to be prophetic in every way – I just didn't know how.

Kelly Rowland and I had been working on Whitney Houston materials off and on for several years already. They were not only right for her voice, they were crucial to her understanding of an essential element in singing, a concept I called "taking flight." To breathe in honesty, and then let it soar, was the goal. On the Saturday in question, Kelly and I had been working on Whitney's "I'm your baby tonight." Kelly sang the hell out of it. It was if the song had been tailor-made for her. Her singing of runs was on point, and the high notes – my God, her high notes. They were simply exquisite – LeToya Luckett quality. Kelly felt herself. She even interpolated a few upper notes that hadn't been written. I rejoiced that she was singing from a very powerful space. Beyoncé, who had been observing the lesson, praised Kelly.

I didn't realize that Mama Celestine had come home. It's important to explain here that by this time, 1999, Kelly had – perhaps unconsciously – adapted two voices: one that soared with me, open and free, and one that she pulled back when singing in front of Celestine, a voice that never projected louder than Beyoncé's. Thus, as I approached Celestine that day, sitting in the family room, she was clearly angry. In retrospect, I realized that she was furious, thinking that Kelly and I had betrayed her. Yes, it sounds crazy, but she who betrayed others so easily could see betrayal in the fact that Kelly was an eager and successful student of singing, and that I was her eager and successful teacher. That professional relationship, of course, had nothing to do with Beyoncé's Celestine. When I asked her if everything was all right, she looked at me cuttingly, then said, "I'm just tired."

A few days later, on the Sunday evening before I would fly off to Germany, Celestine called me at my mother's house. "David, I need to talk to you." Memories of other such requests from Celestine flooded in. Carefully, and with my best manners, I asked her if we could talk over the phone.

"I don't want Beyoncé to hear me," she answered.

Shit, I thought. I really wasn't up for a fight, but I agreed to meet with Celestine on Monday, while the girls were at school.

I prepared for Armageddon.

* * * * *

Our heart-to-heart was the most unpleasant conversation that I have ever had in my life, with anyone. If Celestine and I ever disagreed about anything, ever, in my teaching of her daughter, it was about the top of Beyoncé's voice. I was determined to set it correctly so that it would remain secure and expand with age. Celestine wanted her daughter to sing higher notes, and as soon as possible.

Exasperated, I repeated myself. "Celestine, stretching the top of Beyoncé's voice at the neglect of the bottom will eventually shorten her range. Her middle voice would develop problems." Still, Celestine pushed, this time accusing me of purposely neglecting Beyoncé's top voice. She wanted what she wanted. The truth was, she knew little about singing and absolutely nothing about teaching. She hadn't ever even sat in on a voice lesson, ever. On she pushed, her offensive aggression undiminished by my sensible concern for her daughter's health and long-term career.

This Monday's conversation was no different. The same old, tired Why aren't you teaching her to sing high? Then she upped the ante by challenging me, "What am I paying you for?"

"Excuse me? You haven't paid me in years, Celestine. More important-ly, money has never had any bearing on what I *will* or *will not do* with *my students*," I said. "What are you suggesting? I really want to know."

"Beyoncé should sing the highest in the group!"

No longer willing to beat around the bush with Beyoncé's mother, I said, "Oh, I see. You mean higher than Kelly. Riiiight."

A bit embarrassed that I would call her out, directly, Beyoncé's mother stiffened her back and answered, "Yes, and better than Kelly's high notes. Damn it."

I asked Celestine what her real problem was with Kelly. "You've been riding this girl for years." I already knew the answer, even the one she'd give, but I reminded her that Kelly had done the work, just as Beyoncé had. "She deserves to enjoy her own success, to the fullest."

In a Glenn Close moment, Celestine's mouth flew open. She was abso-lutely flabbergasted. She swore her innocence. She loved Kelly, she said.

"Right," I said sarcastically. "Celestine, we have had this conversation so many times I've lost count. Do we really have to revisit this tired ass topic?" I asked. "Again, Beyoncé is a mezzo-soprano, she is not a sopra-no, nor will she ever be one. She sings fabulous high notes, but in the manner that her voice type should approach them technically. It is far too dangerous to push her to sing another way, just for your ego's sake."

"I brought you in to make Beyoncé the best, not Kelly."

"What?" I asked. "You didn't bring me into anywhere. God gives me my orders. He brought me to Houston, and into your lives."

"No, that was me," Celestine reiterated. "I think you just don't want Beyoncé to sing high notes."

"That is preposterous, Celestine. Again, Beyoncé sings fabulous high notes. I ain't going to ask her to throw her fucking head back and scream. That ain't happening. I've left no stone unturned, with any of my girls."

"And that's another thing. Beyoncé is my daughter. She is not one of your girls."

Where was this heading? I paused in order to quiet my mounting anger. "Listen Celestine," I repeated, calmly. "I simply will not risk Beyoncé's vocal health, and all the exceptional work that we have done thus far, because of her mother's insatiable need to be famous."

Now it was Celestine who was silent.

"That's right. I said it. Do you think I don't know what this is all about?" *Basta!* "I know who you are."

"And who am I, David?" Celestine snapped.

"Some people would call you Jezebel," I answered.

Celestine started to yell. "Beyoncé is the best thing...."

"What? That ever happened to me? She's the only blessed person on the planet? Is that your message? Get a grip, lady." I laughed. "I gave Beyoncé that voice, not you. She is definitely not the best thing that has ever happened to me."

Celestine screamed, "God gave Beyoncé her voice."

"No, God gave her talent, and then he gave her me," I answered. "Again, everyone has a voice. Everyone has talent. You sound silly."

Challenging Celestine on her very misguided belief, I continued. "Celestine, no one is going to care about your designs if Beyoncé can't sing. She's a singer, not a model, and definitely not your damn student."

"You're not the only voice teacher," Celestine blurted.

"You Bitch. Are you serious now?" I said. "That's exactly what I'm talking about." I paused for a quick breath. "Surely you fucking jest."

But, no, this was no joke. I was being fired. That was the purpose of this drama. Did she not know the danger of taking Beyoncé to just any teacher? I did, and I told her so. "Be careful Celestine, get the wrong teacher, and Beyoncé will be ruined. Hell, I could ruin her voice in fifteen minutes."

Celestine's eyes bugged out.

"You couldn't possibly think that I would harm my own student?" Of course she could. Promptly clarifying what I meant, I said, "I know it, God knows it, and your ass knows it. Beyoncé did not wake up fabulous, and with a well-trained voice. None of us does."

Celestine's reaction was typical of someone with her pathology. "You have always been jealous – of me, and of Beyoncé."

"That's just desperate, Celestine. Sad actually," I answered. "You're right though, about one thing at least. I am definitely not the only voice teacher on the planet. However, I do be da one you have choked for more than a decade.

"Now listen up! Today is the last day you get to minimize me, ever."

Celestine started to speak, and I cut her off.

"PLUS. You should know that I know all about Kim Wood Sandusky."

"What..."

"You heard me. What, did you think that I wouldn't find out, Celestine, that you have sneaked both Kelly and Beyoncé to her behind my back? Teresa told me, innocently, but she told me. She doesn't know that you are evil incarnate."

Startled into silence, Celestine looked at me in disbelief.

"And another thing, how long do you and Mathew intend to hold back the wonderful Kim Woods Sandusky from LeToya and LaTavia?"

Celestine finally spit her fury out. Leaning into my face, she screamed that I was "an arrogant bastard."

How original, I thought.

"First of all, leave my father out of it. And secondly, go straight to hell where you fucking belong."

I wished her luck and headed for the door.

She tried once more to speak.

"Girl, bye," I shouted, throwing my hand up.

The next day, prompted by her mother, Beyoncé called me, in tears, and apologetic. I sympathized with her, but not enough to change my mind. Stick a fork in me, I was done. Finished.

"Don't worry, Beyoncé, you're going to be fine. I have left no stone unturned. You've been trained better than most opera singers and definitely better than any of your contemporaries. Only you can break you," I said. I wished her luck. "Please promise me that you'll remember the rules."

Sniffling, she promised, adding, "I love you."

"I love you more."

Then, at my request, Beyoncé passed the phone to Kelly.

"Kelly," I said. "Have you talked to your mother?"

"No, not yet," she answered.

"Kelly, you *must* talk to your mother," I concluded, emphasizing every word: "This. Is. About. Your. Life."

I hated walking away, but lives were at stake. I had finally realized that I had to be sober, had to be vigilant, had to recognize that my adversary, the roaring lioness, paced relentlessly around me.

Naturally, Lion Celestine called me a couple days later, after my talk with Beyoncé and Kelly. She was giving me "one last chance to come on board." She required absolute dedication though, to Beyoncé and to her future, she said.

"Correction," I answered. "You mean your future. I've made sure that Beyoncé's future is secure. She's good. In fact, she'll do great."

Realizing that she was getting little wiggle room, Celestine made one last-ditch effort. "The girls are going to be in New York Friday, signing autographs at Tower Records on Broadway," she said.

"Nice," I answered. "I'm in New York on Friday. I'll stop by."

And I did.

I stood in a line that stretched around three or four city blocks, and for hours. Security told me, "No exceptions." Inching forward, I was finally in sight of the signing table. My girls had already seen me, several fans back. I could tell they were uncomfortable, so I approached them jovially, arms stretched open. They were familiar with that body language. I still loved them. Of course I did. They had done nothing to cause our unfortunate separation. At any rate, I put the CD down on the table. LeToya stood up, hugging me first. LaTavia followed, then Kelly, and finally Beyoncé. Was she dissociating? Probably, I thought. Her hug was a bit distant, but not at all cold. She then whispered, "I'm sorry," with which I'm sure she had just broken her mother's cardinal rule about loyalty.

I knew how the Knowleses operated. When you're out, you are dead to them. I didn't mind. I was not dead to my girls. It was their respect that I enjoyed over the years. Beyoncé signed her name, and then the other girls signed theirs, drawing hearts, and even one or two xoxo kisses under their signature. Then LaTavia handed me my recording back, lovingly.

"I love you all, very much," I said reassuringly.

My girls waved goodbye, and just like that, I was history. This time, for the last time. I was at peace.

The Knowles family was Kim Wood Sandusky's problem now.

* * * * *

In the aftermath of that "higher notes" storm, Celestine and I talked a few times. The girls had been on tour with TLC since October 27th, as their opening act, singing seventeen dates on a 29-day schedule. Along the way, to their already packed concert calendar, Celestine told me that they had added cities in Texas, Massachusetts, Georgia, Indiana, and Canada.

I was busy myself, making a recording in San Diego for KOCH International records of an opera called *Tania*, by Anthony Davis. From San Diego, I found out that LeToya and LaTavia were dating Brandon and Brian Casey, members of the R&B quartet Jagged Edge. "Mathew can't be happy about that," I thought. When I finally was able to catch up with him he was more than irritated with the idea. "I hear the Soul Power Tour was a success….," I said.

He was not amused.

I must say, neither was Beyoncé, but because she was having her own personal boyfriend drama, she kept her feelings to herself, at least in the beginning. Lyndall Locke had cheated on Beyoncé in 1999, for what I believe was his third infraction.

Now, putting the pieces together, I suspected that Lyndall must have been the reason for her distance on the telephone during that call from Madrid, and why she was so not there. The very thing she'd learned to hate in her father's behavior was whipping her through Lyndall. Infidelity is a hard one, even for the best of them, but for Beyoncé it was the pain of all pains. She'd shared her soul with Lyndall. I'd kept her secret, but I wanted her to know that her emotional state was normal, as painful as it all felt. "Beyoncé, I have told you many times. What we fear shows up." I begged her to not get bogged down with what Lyndall did or didn't do. "Your purpose is bigger than who he is to you, sweetie. Think rationally. Lyndall is your first love. He certainly will not be the last one. Young love is the hardest, but this, too, shall pass." (Soon after this conversation, she met Shawn Carter, a.k.a. Jay-Z.)

For all that Mathew despised Lyndall, Beyoncé's little boyfriend wasn't the real threat. Lyndall, Mathew coldly maintained, was a nothing of a boy who'd never amount to anything. No, Manager Mathew needed to turn his focus onto the larger problem, one that threatened to derail his well laid plan. The Casey Twins – or, as Mathew so primitively referred to them, "those niggas" – were trash to him. "I know their mother-fuckin' ass like the back of my hand," Papa Knowles said. They had LeToya and LaTavia's noses wide open. To say that my girls were smitten would be an understatement. Brandon and Brian, several years older than my high top girl and my little Diva, had become their ride to the ball. They played right into the teenage-girl fantasy about "dating older men."

"I knew I shouldn't have agreed to that fuckin' Soul Power Tour," Mathew said. He cursed the day he had let Columbia President Michael Mauldin talk him into allowing the girls to join that "ghetto tour," he said. Mathew went on and on about LeToya and LaTavia, calling them several unmentionable names. "Whores" comes to mind.

Mama Celestine – also concerned about protecting the cash cow – guided her husband in this case, convincing Mathew that LeToya and LaTavia were "ruining the girls' wholesome images." Celestine had always – understandably, as the mother of lovely little girls – been prone to warning her daughters about unseemly behavior. "Remember, Beyoncé..." she would begin, as a prelude to such age-old adages as "A good girl is as a good girl does." I had long since noticed that Celestine's "Remember, Beyoncé...." would inevitably be followed by a piously clothed warning calculated to repress Beyoncé's instincts for expressing her own personality. This time, Celestine believed that her daughter's fame and fortune were threatened by the "unladylike" behavior of LeToya and LaTavia; their infatuations with undesirable boyfriends might undermine the group's pure public image. By the end of 1999, whenever Celestine disparaged LeToya and LaTavia, both Beyoncé and Kelly knew not to defend them.

I remember thinking, "Let the games begin.

* * * * *

All the while Mathew was ranting about the Casey twins, my girls were continuing to perform in the U. S., and they were anticipating an important European tour. Suddenly, a truly serious issue arose: LeToya took ill. A pernicious bronchitis led her doctor to forbid her taking part in performances in Baton Rouge, Louisiana, and subsequent cities. Her mother, Pam, did some fast talking, aware that Mathew could easily deem LeToya a "leaving member," pursuant to the clause/phrase written into the girls' Sony Columbia contract. Pam promised the doctor that she would join the U.S. tour for a week to nurse her daughter back to health. With that, LeToya's doctor gave in to her desperate request.

Immediately Pam called Mathew with the good news – or attempted to call him. He was nowhere to be found. Teresa LaBarbera-Whites said that she hadn't heard from him in days, and Celestine hadn't a clue where he was. Left with no other choice, Pam called Kenneth Hertz, the attorney for Destiny's Child. Frustrated with Mathew's constant disappearing, Hertz told Pam to fax over the doctor's release while his office booked LeToya's flight. Pam purchased her own ticket, as LeToya put their bags into Pam's car. The two hurried, barely making the Baton Rouge flight in time to join Destiny's Child and Jagged Edge.

That evening, after a valiant performance, all the girls, Pam, and the boys of Jagged Edge boarded the tour bus. Craig, the tour's road manager (whose last name I don't recall), received a call from a furious Mathew.

604

He insisted that Craig should throw Pam Luckett off the tour bus immediately. They were in the middle of Nowhere, Louisiana. Mathew "explained" that Pam wasn't covered by the group's insurance. (Whether Mathew's claim was the truth or not remains to be proven.) I remember that it was late at night, dark, and desolate. Pam had no idea where she was. LeToya, Brandon and Brian Casey, and their bandmates, all protested. Outraged that someone would have the gall to kick "someone's mama off the bus," the guys got off the bus with the women. Brian Casey would also say that he and the guys of Jagged Edge "were just so disgusted," adding that "not for one minute did those girls [Beyoncé and Kelly] put themselves into LeToya's shoes."

Hearing all of this from Pam after the fact, I was floored.

Later, Beyoncé and Kelly told me that LaTavia and LeToya were "different" – whatever that meant. They would tell Vibe magazine, a year later, that the two "changed when boys got in their heads." That's certainly true of many teenage girls, and I would remind Beyoncé and Kelly that they, too, had become "different" when they experienced their own first relationships. "Beyoncé, have you forgotten all the crazy thoughts and things you did when you took up with Lyndall?" I asked her. "And you too, Kelly," I added. "You do remember your young Greek boy friend? – the one that you kept hidden from Mathew?" They could not – did not – argue with my reasonable approach to the matter.

Not long after this incident, it was LaTavia's turn to feel Mathew's wrath. She fell "sick" and would need to be hospitalized, Cheryl said. "What bad luck," I thought. That is, until Mathew yelled into the phone that Brandon Casey was at fault. Mathew was disgusted, he added. "It's her own damn fault." Shocked, I can recall that I thought that regardless of who was or was not "at fault," her doctors were refusing to give my little Diva the release to travel. I had no ideas for Mathew. It simply wasn't my problem anymore. However, I wasn't going to be rude. I considered suggesting he call Kim Wood Sandusky. Instead, I listened, interested to get Mathew's version of the crisis, knowing that I could check it against Cheryl's more reliable accounting of the situation.

Concerned about LaTavia, I called her mother for information about her daughter's prognosis. Cheryl confirmed that the doctor had forbidden travel. "Ma'am," he said, "I don't think your daughter will make that flight." Cheryl, having become a more responsible mother, said she could not put her daughter's health in danger. LaTavia, who was still suffering from a very high fever, could barely stand and or walk, not without excruciating pain.

On travel day, LeToya showed up at the Knowles house, on time, to take the limousine to the airport. She found Mathew on the phone, making it clear to someone that if LaTavia didn't show up at the airport she'd be out of the group. LeToya told me that she assumed he was talking to Cheryl, and that he had yelled those words into the phone.

Cheryl found herself caught in a difficult dilemma. Her daughter's career was on the line, and so was her own job. She was, reportedly, earning an annual salary of around $40,000 as the girls' chaperone. By showing up at the airport herself, could she save her daughter's position? Her own? That was the plan. And so, Cheryl did the only thing she could. She did her job, showing up at the airport for the flight, hopeful that her being there with a solid medical explanation would satisfy Mathew. It did not.

When Cheryl told Mathew about the doctor's refusal to release her daughter, Mathew began screaming. His anger was epic, "brutal," LeToya told me. "Cheryl burst into tears," she said, but Mathew remained "a butthole." Cheryl's next move was to call the doctor. Perhaps, Mathew would believer her then. He gave a shit, having heard the doctor say, "I'm sorry, Mrs. Mitchell, but your daughter isn't going anywhere." And that was that.

"Mathew walked over to us," LeToya then told me. Matter-of-factly, he "pointed to Junella *[the group's official choreographer]* and told her that she was going to take LaTavia's place."

Many years later, LeToya would fill in a very important gap in the scene. She recalled for me that she had called her mother, Pam: "Mama, call that lawyer." Pam did as her daughter asked. "That lawyer" was the entertainment attorney Randall Bowman. He told LeToya in no uncertain terms to "make sure you and Cheryl get on that plane."

According to LeToya, Beyoncé and Kelly stood by silently with bowed heads through the whole episode.

The Europe tour went relatively well. Junella Segura did take LaTavia's place, as Mathew had instructed, standing in to complete the look of four. She didn't know the vocal parts, so she lip-synched, safely covered by the girls' use of their TV tracks for those performances. However, Beyoncé confessed later that they'd actually barely escaped ridicule. The press was asking questions. When Kelly once began to explain that "LaTavia is…" Beyoncé cut her off with a look. The way Beyoncé made it sound, she'd cut Kelly pretty rudely, then told the reporter that "Doctors wouldn't allow LaTavia to travel," and continued with how "her health is most important." And that LaTavia would be "joining us for the next set of gigs." Things were fine, Beyoncé swore, and she hadn't lied. They were sisters, forever.

Those very legitimate questions came sort of on the heels of the girls' previous March 28th, 1998, Germany performance on *Top of the Pops* (equivalent to *American Bandstand,* or *The Soul Train*), singing "No, No, No" to a packed TV studio audience. Then, reporters saw a cohesive group, but now, some in the press compared Destiny's Child with the German girl band Tic Tac Toe. Once friends, Tic Tac Toe had had two wildly successful albums and then disintegrated from infighting.

Beyoncé calmly assured her fans that "there are no problems in Destiny's Child."

TO: THE BEST
VOICE Teacher:
DAVID

You know how much me
You taught me and
I thank you so much
I Love you always.
Beyoncé "97"

David,
You were a big
help to me & you
know it. Thank U!
U Love You!!
your little DIVA,
La Tavia

David you
are the best.
I lae you with
all of my heart
LeTaya

David, Words cannot express how much you helped me + me I still need you though. you know I love you! thank u!! God Bless!!

I was touched to receive these expressions of the girls' feelings, which they wrote to me immediately after we wrapped up the recording of Destiny's Child "No, No, No." Recorded with Vincent Herbert at the Chung King Studios in New York City, May 31, 1997, "No, No, No" would become a smash hit and would win two Soul Train Lady of Soul awards in 1998.

608

"Destiny" (circa. 1995)
From left: Kelly (before
Celestine cropped her
hair), Beyoncé, LeToya,
LaTavia

From left.: Kelly,
Beyoncé,
LeToya and
LaTavia

Photos:
The Tillman Estate

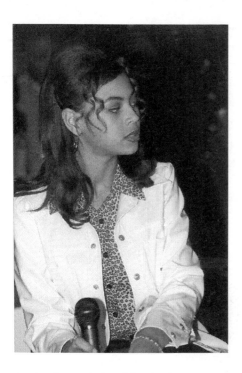

At the Sony Columbia signing party
in 1996 Beyoncé and Kelly

Kelly Rowland

Photos: The Tillman Estate

Destiny's Child: My girls…
"The Performance"
Photo: The Tillman Estate

Solange Knowles (circa age 11) poses with *Destiny* and Chauncey Woodin
Photo: The Tillman Estate

Ann was so proud!!

From left: Mathew Knowles, Kim Burse (A&R at Sony Columbia), D'Wayne Wiggins, Ann Tillman

Photso: The Tillman Estate

613

LaTavia Roberson and her stepfather, Charles Mitchell

Destiny's Child and their mothers: My girls, front row from left: Beyoncé, LeToya, LaTavia, Kelly. The mothers, top row from left: Celestine Knowles, Pamela Luckett, Cheryl LaStrap Mitchell, Doris Lovett

Beyoncé, age sixteen

Photos: The Tillman Estate

Kelly at the Grand Marriott Hotel, New York City, 1998

LeToya Luckett, our jokester, at the Grand Marriott Hotel,
New York City, 1998

LaTavia at the Grand Marriott Hotel, New York City, signing the pre-autographed pictures

Beyoncé at the Grand Marriott Hotel, New York City, 1998.

Part VI

The road back

Intermezzo

New York, early spring 1999

The memory is crystal-clear. At exactly 8:30 a.m. I was awakened by my still small voice. Just as it had done in Cleveland in 1988, it was giving me my next assignment in clear terms. "You're going to Germany," it said. And again – just as I'd done in Cleveland – I unhesitantly reached for the phone. This time I called my New York travel agent, Roswitha Sterbal, to rebook my already-scheduled return flight from Paris to New York. "I want to add a month-long stopover in Berlin," I said. It was no problem, Roswitha reassured me: "You're flying business class." Within the hour everything had been arranged. I would now fly from Paris to New York via a stop-over in Berlin.

In March/April 1999, directly after landing in Germany's capital, I sang auditions for Theater Freiburg, the Komische Opera Berlin, Stuttgart Opera, and The German National Theater, Weimar. The first lucrative contract came from Weimar. After a successful round of auditions, I returned to New York, and the next day flew directly to Houston from LaGuardia Airport. Before leaving Germany, I had been hired to sing the title role in Faust, the masterpiece by French composer Charles Gounod. Richard Bado, my long-time coach at HGO, was expecting me.

My first Faust had to be stellar!

28. The breakup – Part I

Denial

LaTavia Roberson lay on her grandparents' couch recuperating from her hospital stay, terribly disillusioned. Since the group's return from Europe, LaTavia's best friend and band mate, Beyoncé Knowles, had ignored her. According to LaTavia, neither Beyoncé nor Kelly had so much as called her. Ah, I thought. Typical. "The ole Knowles silent treatment." I knew it well. We all did. Whenever Mathew and Celestine suspected anyone of "disloyalty," their term for any number of behaviors, they would give the perpetrator their silent treatment. Even if innocent of the charge of disloyalty, the accused person would usually give in under their abuse – passive/aggressive, I believe is the term for such a tactic. LaTavia was certainly having trouble coping with her best friend's new attitude. "It's not fair," she thought out loud.

In the waning months of 1999, when Celestine started referring to LeToya as a "troublemaker," the other girls fell in line and began to *perceive* her as a trouble maker. Beyoncé's mother enjoyed her quiet campaign against LeToya, who was in reality only the innocent conduit to Celestine's real target: Pam, LeToya's mother.

Seeking to substantiate LeToya's supposed defiance, and her questioning of Mathew's business ethics, Celestine said, "Pam put that shit in her head." LeToya had asked Mathew for a simple accounting of Destiny's Child's finances, a request that was "out of line," Celestine said. "But LeToya has always shown a propensity for business," I observed during one of our phone conversations. Mama Celestine sucked her teeth in the telephone.

Neither Mathew nor Celestine intended to give LeToya any respect for her business savvy, and definitely not for her above average intelligence. Sharp as a tack they did not need. Compliance and Loyalty, that's what they demanded. Celestine harped constantly. LeToya this, LeToya that. The girl had done nothing wrong. She never did.

Now it was LaTavia's turn to be in the Knowleses hot seat. When I learned that Beyoncé and Kelly had not so much as phoned their convalescing friend and sister, I feared the worst. Destiny's Child's next performance – still without LaTavia – took place around December 13th at Houston's Compaq Center (now The Lakewood Church). After the concert LeToya Luckett announced that she was planning to go see LaTavia, Beyoncé and Kelly opted out, silently indicating their disapproval of making contact with their erstwhile friend and bandmate. For LaTavia that snub was the last straw. Her psyche began to fracture under the pressure of not understanding. Why the hell would Beyoncé stab her friend, her sister in the back? LaTavia had supported her through her relationship with Lyndall, unequivocally so.

LaTavia was being gaslighted, that's what was going on. Typical of someone who is subjected to such tactics, LaTavia started to doubt her own recollections. "I thought I was crazy," she told me. The Knowleses referred to her as "promiscuous," and a "fast girl." "Remember, Beyoncé," Celestine said insincerely, "she's been through a lot." There she was, the Celestine I knew, pious devil, with her whispered insinuations. How does dating and sleeping with one person make you *promiscuous*? Celestine aimed to use LaTavia's recent, horrific life experience against her. Her innuendos increased the girl's feelings of paranoia. I'd never been so happy to be on the outs with anyone in my life. My flight back to New York and then on to Germany couldn't come fast enough. I never wanted to hear Celestine's whisperings again.

* * * * *

Upon my arrival in Leipzig I went immediately to my hotel to check in, and then on to the Thomaskirche [St. Thomas Church], where Johann Sebastian Bach, my favorite composer, had served the final 27 years of his life. From 1723 to 1750 he had played the organ, directed the choir, and composed incessantly. In that church, he had written many of the chorales that my girls had sung as I taught them how to hear chords and understand harmony. I could hardly wait to see what he saw, sit where he most likely sat, and above all, hear the magnificent organ in the church where he had played for so many years. Listening to its recorded sounds on CDs or in PBS broadcasts had whetted my longing to hear the instrument live. It was grand.

As I walked through the Thomaskirche's enormous doorways for the first time, I heard an impressive ensemble rehearsing one of my all-time favorites, certainly one of Bach's most recognizable chorales. I became emotional with the sounds of "Jesu bleibet meine Freude" [Jesu, joy of man's desiring], in that church, in the most authentic Bach style and coloration I'd ever heard. I thought of my girls, wishing that they were here to absorb that sound, to experience the intimate connection with musical history. I imagined calling them after my performance to share my Thomaskirche experience with them. "Jesu bleibet meine Freude" had special meaning for me that day.

After leaving the church, I headed back to the Marriott Hotel, where Opera Leipzig was housing me in a beautiful suite. I had planned to have dinner at 4:30 in my suite, counting on the punctuality of room service to help me stay on schedule. I was determined to adhere to the rule about allowing a full hour for the digestion of my food before singing. The discomfort of singing on a full stomach can't be overestimated.

After my meal, at precisely 5:45, room service carried away my tray and I jumped in the shower. By 6:10 p.m., I was headed out the door. Careful to wrap up nicely, but not overly layered, I walked over to the opera house, just five minutes away. The security guard, a pleasant man, gave me directions to the artist's scheduling and services office. When I walked in, the secretary greeted me warmly, took my coat, and told me the director wanted to see me.

I couldn't have imagined why. She opened the door and ushered me in. Sitting in a high-backed black leather chair, staring out of the window, was a tall and slightly greying man. When he turned around to me, I let out a whoop.

"Axel Joliet!"

Before me sat the former artistic director of Houston Grand Opera, a fan of my voice, and now the head of artist services and planning for Opera Leipzig.

All smiles, he asked, "How long has it been?"

"My God, at least seven years," I answered. "I think it was 1992 or '93 when I saw you last."

"Yes, I think you're right," he said, and embraced me heartily. "How are you?"

"Great," I answered.

Axel and I chatted a while, catching up. Of course, I told him a bit about my girls. He'd heard of them, he said. Destiny's Child was just beginning to become well-known in Germany. Suddenly, I noticed the small clock on his desk. Shit, I thought. I was five minutes behind my schedule.

I stood up, apologizing. He understood, standing to shake my hand. I made a beeline for my dressing room, a rather opulent space with a shiny black upright piano, placed strategically against the wall and away from the windows, as it should be. Taking my music out of my satchel, I began my warmups, lightly connecting my breath to my diaphragm.

At 7:25 a young woman who introduced herself as my guide for the next few days fetched me and took me to the conductor for our 7:30 p.m. rehearsal. "It will be in Maestro's studio," she said.

The great Russian conductor Michail Vladimirovich Jurowski was a giant in the classical music world. He had chosen to open the New Year's Eve concert at Leipzig opera with the opening scene from *Faust*.

Maestro Jusowski, a tall man, had a penetrating gaze. I sensed immediately that he was being waited on, hand and foot, by his wife. My face must have given away what I was thinking, because Mrs. Jurowski began to explain that her husband worked too hard. "He's had two mild scares, already," she said. She referred to his heart. Another woman, his mother-in-law, sat quietly in the corner, looking on approvingly at her daughter's careful ministrations. The Maestro had only to look in the direction of something he wanted, and she brought it to him. Her affection was endearing. And so, it appeared that we were going to have an audience for our private rehearsal.

Sitting down to the piano, the Maestro got right to work. His personality, his aura, and his attention to detail got my respect. He began playing the introduction to my aria. On cue, I came in, completely in the music. After about a minute or so, he paused. "Your French is superb," he said, in a strong, Russian-accented English. Then without missing a beat, he carried on, exactly where he'd left off. Adjusting quickly to the abrupt stop in rhythm, I had just enough time to mouth "Thank you," but barely. The first high note was just around the corner of that last phrase.

The next day we had our first and only orchestra rehearsal in the hall. My colleagues were arriving backstage, unpacking their instruments as I entered. Nodding my greetings, I made my own preparation for the rehearsal. As I was setting up my personal recording device, Maestro called my name and began to introduce me, even before I got up next to him at the podium. Maestro told the orchestra that finding me had been "ein Glückstreffer" (a lucky discovery). I quickly made my way to his side, bowing and acknowledging the orchestra's applause.

Maestro raised his baton and our rehearsal began.

Standing in front of the Gewandhaus Orchestra of Leipzig, one of the oldest and best orchestras in the world, was a dream come true. The sound that poured out of them gave me goosebumps.

My mentor, the legendary American soprano Grace Bumbry, had once passed along to me some wise words of the renowned conductor and prodigy Lorin Maazel: "There are only three reasons for a singer to be nervous. One, you don't know your music. Two, you don't know your text. Or three, you're thinking about yourself." No, I had a handle on all three. I was prepared. Nothing was going to come between me and a successful performance.

* * * * *

Backstage at the opera house on New Year's Eve, the Maestro and I exchanged the traditional opera singer's good luck sign – mock-spitting three times over the colleague's shoulder. Greeted with generous applause upon entering from the wings, I made my way ahead of Maestro Jurowski through the orchestra and took my place front and center, next to the conductor's podium. As soon as I sensed absolute stillness in the opera house, I raised my eyes to signal my readiness. Maestro Jurowski raised his baton for the orchestra's introduction. One minute and fifteen seconds later my moment arrived.

I had already entered Faust's world, a dark and despairing place. Aged and desperate, I sang Faust's opening words, "Rien! En vain j'interroge" [Nothing! In vain I ask]. Cursing science and faith, Faust – I – came to the crucial moment: I called for infernal guidance. Enter Mephistopheles (Satan). So achingly did I yearn for the return of my lost youth, I traded my soul for the devil's deceitful promises. Faust's feelings and his desperation matched my own. I understood my character's frustrations.

At the end of that magical evening the audience erupted with Bravos – a perfect ending to an inspired performance. It was a success. My colleagues and I received ten curtain calls that night. I had known my music, I had known my text, and my thoughts were entirely anchored in the character and essence of Faust and his confrontation with Satan. David Lee Brewer – the man – did not exist in that performance.

Before going out with the cast for our post-concert celebration, I stopped by my hotel to drop off my stage make-up case and garment bag. On the way I passed what seemed to be thousands of people celebrating and drinking champagne. Because this was the eve of the new millennium, 2000, Leipzig's fireworks had special meaning.

As I made my way through all the crowds on the street after the concert, my cell phone rang. Pam Luckett was on the line from the United States. I asked Pam to hold on and made my way into the hotel. Quickly I handed over my belongings to the bellman and searched for a quiet corner in order to talk. The raucous band playing in the lounge drove me on to the men's room. Once there, I listened, speechless, as Pam told me the reason for her call.

LeToya and LaTavia had had a blazing blowup with Mathew. Apparently, things had come to a head. What started out as a desire to bring Mathew to the table had quickly turned sour.

A whirlwind was about to hit Destiny's Child.

* * * * *

No one was happier about the breakup of Destiny's Child than Celestine. She was getting what she wanted. When I finally was able to get her on the phone on January 3rd, 2000, a Monday, she said, "Those little ungrateful bitches are done." She explained that she'd "warned Beyoncé" about those "tramps."

I had nothing to say to that.

The day before, after landing in New York from Leipzig, I'd talked to a much kinder and more forthcoming Beyoncé on the Knowles girls' private telephone line. Already suffering emotionally, she managed to tell me that LeToya and LaTavia had "fired Daddy."

"What do you mean?" I asked.

"They wrote a letter disaffirming their contract," Beyoncé answered. Then she added, "They want their own manager."

I would later learn what the letter said: "As of this moment, please do not transact any further business on my behalf, individually or as a member of Destiny's Child. You do not have any authority to do so."

"OK…" I now said to Beyoncé. After a pause, I asked her if she understood what "disaffirmance" meant.

She didn't.

"Well, it means that after you girls turned eighteen, the law expects you to rethink things, renegotiate your contracts. Your management contract with Mathew is invalid now, even your Sony Columbia contract has expired."

Although she said nothing, I knew that Beyoncé was listening with close attention to my every word. I went on, telling Beyoncé that she and Kelly had the legal right to renegotiate their contracts. "It is the law, all over the world," I said.

Still she listened, silently.

Moving on, I asked Beyoncé what she thought the next step was.

After a slight pause, Beyoncé spoke. "Daddy wants me to go solo." She then told me that her father had had a long conversation with the group's attorney, Kenneth Hertz, the controlling partner at Hertz Lichtenstein & Young LLP, in Los Angeles. Beyoncé alleged that Ken Hertz had told her that she would "have to quit the group."

"What do you want to do?" I asked.

"I don't know. I just don't want the group to break up," Beyoncé answered.

"Then it won't," I said.

In exactly that moment we were interrupted. I could hear Mathew yelling for Beyoncé in the background.

"I'm just about to get off the phone, Daddy," she called out. Then, whispering into the receiver, she said to me, "I gotta go."

We ended the call.

* * * * *

Celestine said to me that LeToya and LaTavia thought they could bully them into doing what they wanted. She laughed sinisterly. Beyoncé, following her mother's lead, would be quoted in *Vibe Magazine*: "[I think] we could've talked about [the problem] and figured out some kind of agreement. But they waited until our most vulnerable time and sent this disaffirmation letter, 'cause they felt like we would have to give them whatever they asked for. And the day they sent it we were devastated," said Beyoncé.

Within days, magazine articles, a serious onslaught of television news reports, and rampant rumors all supported completely fictitious accounts of a scandalous breakup of Destiny's Child. Understanding what was really going on – and what had, from the beginning, led up to this point – I kept my own counsel and told no one what I knew.

A gullible public seemed to believe every word Beyoncé and her "family" were saying in the press, most of it lies. Mama had warned me. She had not told me they would use the girls to sell their special brand of bullshit. Kelly overtly praised Mathew, as did Beyoncé, attempting to be subtle. Kelly called him her "hero." "Mathew has sacrificed so much for us," Kelly said in one interview. "He didn't have to take me in. He didn't have to sell his house and his cars for us. He didn't have to give up his life for Destiny's Child." That's not all he didn't have to do, I thought. I could have thrown up.

Still, I understood where Kelly's loyalty came from, and more importantly, why she was scared to go against the Knowles. Their overt, as well as their subliminal, messages to her had been effective. I understood clearly why she believed she owed them a lot.

Yes, Mathew and Celestine could make their false claims without any fear of being refuted. Their professed feelings of great pride in their child, their struggle, their self-sacrifice, their selflessness in the nourishment of their child's talent – these are universally adopted themes that parents of star performers, no matter the idiom, have made for generations.

I recalled author and renowned psychologist Alice Miller's powerful words, "Until we become sensitive to the child and their 'small child sufferings' the wielding power of the big adults will continue as normal aspect – of the human condition, for hardly anyone pays attention to it or takes it seriously." The victims are "only children," and their distress is trivialized. Kelly couldn't dare to recognize her own suffering and speak out against these saviors.

Buried beneath the Knowles crap lay the stinky truth. Beyoncé's parents were thieves. They had been stealing money from Destiny's Child for years – even when what they were stealing was the money that Ann Tillman had quietly and generously advanced to support the group. Over years, Beyoncé had begun to learn the truth of their deceptions. Her mother confessed the sin, and then required her to remain loyal for "family." According to Mama Celestine, Mathew could be in a lot of trouble if outsiders learned the truth. That must not happen. Beyoncé needed to "keep things in perspective." The whispered "think about your career" was enough to renew any wavering loyalty.

Of course Celestine never admitted her complicity in the evil that Mathew had perpetrated. Any degree of transparency would have exposed her as well.

Now Beyoncé's "ungrateful sisters" were attempting to open a new Pandora's box. They needed to be silenced. Beyoncé couldn't protect her friends because it would go against "Family." It was just that simple.

If LeToya and LaTavia's claim of "Misappropriation of Funds" ever saw the light of day, the truth is that both Knowleses could possibly face not only huge fines but also imprisonment. The Texas Statute and Code was clear: The penalty for embezzling money of $20,000 or more, but less than $100,000, carried with it a $10,000 fine, and one (and up to 10) years of imprisonment, or both.

In short, Mathew was guilty as charged: of the unsavory act of double-billing. His deceptions had begun long years before the break-up of Destiny's Child.

"You girls owe me $50,000," he had said in 1995. At an emergency group meeting with the parents of Destiny's Child, manager Mathew passed out a document outlining his financial contribution to the girls' development, a long and ambiguous list of false debits assigned to the girls's earnings from 1992 to October 1995. It was a blatant fabrication of the facts. My suspicions were rooted in history, his-story, which one could trace right back to the Biblical story of Jesus and the money lenders.

Now, Mathew was building a case for his noble self-sacrifice and tireless work on behalf of the group. He presented an invoice for bogus and overly inflated telephone charges of an estimated $7,500 (which sum would increase with every interview he ever gave).

Then there was the $5,000 that Mathew listed under the heading "miscellaneous costs." I couldn't believe my ears. Mathew was masterfully passing off his "unexpected financial commitments" as legitimate. He claimed pompously that they were "things you don't normally get receipts for." So, of course, he did not submit any.

On one occasion, when Mathew raised the issue of "unforeseen costs" during the Summer Camp, I lost it.

"Ludicrous," I blurted out.

Mathew shot me a stern look.

It was, however, too late to take the outburst back. All I could do was shrug my shoulders, and mouth the word "Sorry," for all to see and understand.

Had Mathew forgotten that the girls' parents had dropped off checks with their daughters? every Sunday night, during the summer camps? every year? Both he and Celestine ignored that detail. However, I certainly could recall those checks covering the burden of extra costs for food and utilities. Why, they even included Chunga, the maid, in their claims for remuneration from the parents. As I was sure that my girls' parents had also not forgotten writing those checks, I had expected them to speak up at any minute. Not a word. Nothing came. Not a peep. No outrage. Not even a perplexed look.

I was stunned.

Celestine then asked, "It is standard practice that management would be reimbursed, isn't it?"

Her proud husband answered, "Yes, it is, Tina." And then he added, smiling incongruously at his supportive wife, "I expect every dime, too."

Another flagrant charge of $5,000 on Mathew's list made the hairs on the back of my neck stand at attention. When I read that Mathew was billing my girls $5,000 for voice lessons (!), it was clear that he'd grossly overstated his bill. I cleared my throat, again, this time coughing conspicuously, and definitely aiming to interrupt. But again, not one person in the room spoke up. Neither Mathew nor his wife had paid me for voice lessons since 1993, shortly before preparations for the Atlanta Showcase began. In fact, Mathew never paid me for voice lessons, ever, yet there the charge stood, in gleaming black figures.

Much later, in 2012, I would hold the proof in my hand that the Knowleses had indeed done what I'd known for years. During a telephone call with Ann Tillman's mother, Effie Brown, I learned that Ann's sons, Armon and Chris Tillman, had been denied their rightful inheritance. "Them boys was robbed," Effie Brown told me.

In 2001 the family filed a $38,000,000 legal claim against Destiny's Child, Sony Entertainment, and Mathew Knowles. Depositions were taken on February 19th 2002, in Houston, Texas, at attorney Ben Hall's Yoakum Boulevard offices.

I was horrified to hear that Mathew had not honored his 5% fiduciary duty to Ann's estate. He hadn't even tried to contact her children, claiming under oath that he didn't know how to reach them. Of course, he lied. I know that he had Glenda's telephone number (Ann's sister), and that he had called her. Nevertheless, Armon and Chris got nothing even close to the agreed-upon 5% commission of everything Destiny's Child had made since 1998. It appears that the "management contract," which had been signed by both Mathew and Ann, and that proved their 15%-5% split, had "gone missing."

"How did it disappear, Ma'am?" I asked Mrs. Brown.

"Them Knowleses," she answered. Ann's mother believed that Mathew had "paid Keith to steal it." She was talking about the boys' uncle, their father's brother, Keith Tillman, who had visited Ann unexpectedly in the hospital on the day she died. Keith had also been the only one in Ann's house, outside of Mrs. Brown and Ann's boys, during that time. Mrs. Brown believed that Ann asked him to do her a favor that required his visiting the house. Apparently, that favor would end up costing the boys their inheritance, Mrs. Brown suggested.

My heart fell into my shoes. Ann had never had much good to say about Keith, her brother-in-law. She had confided in me that he wasn't an attentive uncle. She regarded him as an opportunist. (How he got custody of Ann's boys I still do not know.) Now, in 2012, her mother didn't appear to like him very much either.

"After Ann died," Mrs. Brown told me, "Keith bought a new house. His ass had always been broke, and then he even took his wife on a cruise."

What Mrs. Brown said next shook my very spirit. Apparently, Ann's signature on that contract, which Celestine had secured under shady circumstances at Ann's hospital death bed, is what sealed the deal in favor of the Knowleses. By 2002 it, too, had come up "missing." No one could substantiate that the contract even existed. Kenny Moore and I were the only two people who knew of its existence, and Kenny wasn't talking. His wife, Cassandra, was afraid of the Knowleses, because they were rich and famous, Kenny told me. So, he left the boys hanging, agreeing to pass on to their lawyer, Ben Hall, only the papers he had in his possession. He declined even to give an affidavit. I was in Europe, totally out of reach. The boys had no clue where I was, or that I even knew, not until I reached out to them in 2011.

Mrs. Brown's grandsons' inheritance was gone.

"I'm gon' send you these papers, Baby," Mrs. Brown said. "Maybe you can do something with 'em."

We ended the call.

As I waited for the papers to arrive, I thought about the years of Ann's honest devotion and work on behalf of Girls Tyme-Destiny's Child, about her generous financial support of the group, and her special love for Kelly. Also, I couldn't help thinking about Ann's untiring commitment to the Knowles family. So when Mrs. Brown swore that Kelly had denied her daughter, "just like Judas did to Jesus," I sat up, in shock and disbelief. It was inconceivable to me, especially after all Ann had done for Kelly – and Kelly's mother – that she would do such a thing.

Ann's heirs, her two sons, received only one-half of the one percent royalty, which amounted to $1.25 million before lawyer fees and taxes – not even close to Ann's 5% contractual commission. Mathew helped himself to the other half percent, while Celestine suggested the girls sing tributes to Ann. I guess her piety made her feel better about what she'd done on Ann's death bed.

Mathew claimed, "Ann gave up her rights to management." Had she really? Was giving up her rights to management (upon her death) the same as giving up her 5% percentage in everything Destiny's Child? Her money had financed their climb. I can only tell you, the woman I knew, in devotion to her sons, would've cut her left hand off before denying them what she had worked so hard to secure, their rightful inheritance.

Fact is, the lawyer of Destiny's Child, Kenneth Hertz, ended up with Ann's 5%. Whether he knew that it came on the back of a dead woman or not is inconsequential now, isn't it? The money is gone, and Ann's intentions for her sons were denied them. But hey, Mathew's cronies got paid.

I had always wondered why Hertz's helping Mathew felt slimy, unethical to me. He was the girls' lawyer, not Mathew's. He should've gathered his clients to talk things out, even if through a mediator, but that never happened. Pam told me that he had never even called the house. Their only encounter was his buying LeToya that airline ticket to Baton Rouge – which she surely would have been reimbursed for. Pam also said that she was unaware whether Cheryl ever got a call from Hertz. She did know, however, that he was getting a percentage of Destiny's Child. That was the money honestly due to me, and to Ann's heirs.

Henry Hertz, also an attorney, helped Mathew shore up his power and control over his situation. "Trademark the name," he advised Mathew, referring to "Destiny's Child." He drew up the papers himself – a highly unethical act, not to mention illegal per the Sony Columbia contract, which said, "The artist owns the exclusive right to the name…" Both men, feeling entitled, simply steam-rolled the contract. Weeks later it was done. It was official. Mathew Knowles owned the name "Destiny's Child."

As a consequence, Mathew was free to make Destiny's Child look like anything he wanted. Additionally, Kenneth Hertz could now legally confer with Mathew without raising ethics questions. In an interview with *Vibe* Magazine, Mathew asserted that "Destiny's Child is bigger than its members for the same reason that it doesn't matter who runs Coca-Cola…It's a trademark. It allows you to be able to change members. As long as you got a hit song, there will always be a Destiny's Child. The day there's not a hit song it don't matter if Beyoncé's singing. If you ain't got no hit songs, it's gone. It's as simple as that."

The Knowleses were finally in business, and the speed with which they moved to annihilate LeToya and LaTavia after this single event was mind blowing. "One down, two little bitches to go," Celestine joked.

Oddly, the *Vibe* article's author unwittingly revealed Celestine's type and special brand of harshness with a quote from the music historian Patricia Romanowski, co-author of *Supreme Faith* and *Temptations*. "Such pronouncements may sound terribly cold… in order to survive in the dog-eat-dog music industry you've got to play hardball, and no one does it better than family-run organizations." Romanowski continued, "There's a high level of discipline in these entities. You're either with the team or you're not. Nobody takes any crap, because the whole family is at risk," she wrote. "The groups that succeed are less forgiving. They get rid of the problem. It's very Darwinian, survival of the fittest."

I can never make peace with the greed and the injustice in this business.

* * * * *

Every cent that I knew Mama and Papa Knowles had been syphoning was indeed charged back to Destiny's Child. As LeToya and LaTavia so rightly suspected, they had been paying for a variety of personal Knowles expenses: multiple and excessive car repairs, bailing out Celestine's salon when the rent was months in arrears, the Knowles family housekeeper, Chunga – all paid with the girls' money. Mathew had even maintained two open day accounts at the Hilton Hotel, next door to Houston's Caligula Club, and The Embassy Suites Hotel, where Beyoncé's daddy enjoyed his regulars. His extramarital affairs were legion – and expensive to maintain. I'll never forget one particular fight, as I feared that Celestine would kill him. Mathew claimed that he'd kept the hotel accounts in order to house clients, Sony officials visiting Houston, and guest producers, even though most of the girls' recording took place outside of Houston. All those ploys were marginally feasible, but Mathew's claim, that he'd spent many nights in those hotels with his wife, was decidedly not.

Then there was the double billing, co-mingling of accounts (as, for instance, when a person with fiduciary responsibility mixes trust money with that of others), and fraudulent commission sums. When Mathew Knowles, under oath, was asked why attorney Kenneth Hertz, Destiny's Child's legal counsel, earned a 5% commission, his attorney advised him not to answer, and he followed that instruction. Mathew was taking 50% of merchandising monies, with no contract, and he had even borrowed $50,000.00 dollars from the girls' booking agency, signing an agreement that clearly stipulated that it was a "personal loan." How he paid it back, or who paid it back, or whether it was paid back is still not clear. And that's not the half of it.

Mathew's head of payroll, a woman named Linda Ragland, confronted Beyoncé's father over his illegal commingling of accounts. In a straightforward memo, Ms. Ragland insisted that Mathew hire a certified public accountant. She wrote: "Until at such time as when bank accounts are properly set up separating Destiny's Child's funds, Music World funds, Synature funds and all others, I will no longer handle office expense payments, payroll, etc." She concluded, "I am requesting to work from my home office for the week until these issues are addressed."

What happened next was completely predictable. Mathew fired Ragland – at Celestine's behest. I already knew this. Celestine had ulterior motives. Not only was Ragland "dangerous," she told me, but getting rid of her seemed a bit of poetic justice for Celestine, so to speak. Mathew had been having an affair with Ragland's sister, and Celestine learned (whether or not it was true) that he'd confessed to the sister a heinous crime during a night of passion. Suspecting that the woman had confided in friends, Celestine took immediate action. She accosted the woman in the streets of Houston, threatening her about her "damned mouth." It wasn't one of Celestine's finer moments.

Now, years later, in 2002, Ben Hall, a lawyer for the Tillman estate (Armon and Chris Tillman, Effie Brown, and Lorando Brown, Ann's brother) asked Mathew, for the court depositions, whether he "knew that his financial records were not in order when Linda Ragland pointed it out."

Mathew's response could be interpreted as an act of perjury. "No, I didn't," he lied.

Then Ben Hall asked Mathew Knowles to read a document he handed him (called Exhibit 90). Mathew perused it, then Hall said, "Exhibit 90 is your memo back to Linda Ragland terminating her after she brought to your attention that the financial records were not in order; is that right?"

"Yes," Mathew answered.

Scandalous. (Contrary to popular belief, oft times an artist's worst nightmare and greatest enemy will be family, the personal networks, people whom they love and trust. Beware, artists!)

The deposition papers also confirmed that Beyoncé's father had paid for lap dances with the Destiny's Child credit card. I knew about this too. Celestine hit the roof when it happened. "Stupid bastard," she yelled. "How could he have been so dumb to leave a paper trail?" she asked me. She didn't expect an answer. She was merely venting.

Then, shocked, I read about his tax fraud, which I hadn't known about at the time. Mathew had claimed Kelly Rowland as his "third daughter" on his 1997, '98 and '99 tax returns. He'd had the option, and might I say, the more appropriate option, to check the box "dependent." That was Kelly's official and legal status in the Knowles house. Instead, Mathew wrote in the name "Kelendria Knowles." His actions were clearly and indisputably illegal.

In his continuing quest to assassinate Beyoncé's problematic sisters, LeToya and LaTavia, Mathew shamelessly and unabashedly spewed one foul lie after the other. Ken Hertz had told him to check in with the record label to find out where they stood on Beyoncé's going solo. As I understood it from Beyoncé, during our second telephone call, "Daddy called the label..." Twisting the truth, Mathew had portrayed LeToya and LaTavia as discipline problems. He'd been covering for them all the while, he told his Sony Columbia contacts. Nevertheless, the label had not signed off on the group breakup. Not yet anyway. For Sony Columbia, it was about business. And then there was the upcoming shooting of the "Say My Name" video. Dissension within the ranks, especially at this critical juncture, was potentially disastrous for Destiny's Child and the label.

So, in a last-ditch effort, Mathew tried Celestine's suggestion. It was time. "Tell them that the girls didn't sing on the album," she said. I understood her to mean Sony Columbia. In addition, Mathew would say, "Ask the girls' producers." This was a crucial point. Mathew needed professional substantiation for his claim that he'd been covering up LeToya and LaTavia's inabilities in the studio for years.

While Mathew implemented Celestine's plan, she too got busy. Why was she sneaking around and chatting up Brandon and Brian Casey? I wondered if Mathew knew about that. At the same time, neither she nor Mathew was taking or returning phone calls from Pam, Cheryl, or Bowman. How could these Jagged Edge boys help her case? In the end, the Knowleses had only to play up the "leaving member" clause, which Beyoncé's mother understood before we all did. We thought the clause referred only to failure to show up for work. Even Beyoncé believed this, Mathew too. Celestine was getting her ducks in a row, for reasons that I'd finally understand – in the year 2002.

At this time, however, in 2000, we all had a different understanding. "Leaving member" addressed only the members whose contributions were essential to the sound of the group and or act. The Knowles had systematically killed LeToya and LaTavia, legally. Had my going on the *Porgy* tour opened them up to attack? I wondered if this had been Celestine's plan all along. It became clear to me that it was. Still, I shuddered to think that she would really kill Beyoncé's group, destroy her friendships, and turn her against me, all so she could be her daughter's "savior." Such thinking was abhorrent to me – it seemed purely evil – but it would explain why she and Mathew were so contemptuous when I suggested that it was fraudulent to sell a CD of a group called Destiny's Child with only one girl singing on it.

Again, singers beware.

Why hadn't my girls' parents spoken up at the group meeting in 1995? At that time, Mathew announced that "...after consulting with industry professionals" (he meant Destiny's Child lawyer Kenneth Hertz, and the mysterious Ruth Carson), Mathew "made a decision regarding the group's future financial distributions." Mathew said that he had "worked out a fair breakdown of his fiduciary duty to the girls, as follows: Beyoncé Giselle Knowles (45%), Kelendria Trené Rowland (25%), LeToya Nicole Luckett (15%), and LaTavia Marie Roberson (15%)."

I gasped, audibly. Mathew's lunacy was unethical, and definitely not in line with standard practices in the business. Sony came to the girls' rescue. They insisted upon equal splits, 25% of the total when it came to royalties, placing it into the contract. (On their Jon B tour together, Brandon and Brian had actually shown their girlfriends their checks. That had opened the girls' eyes to the realities of equal distribution of a group's earnings.) I hope they've learned what I have after many years of inner turmoil, that "Silence is never Golden." My high-top girl and my Little Diva were choking on their contrition. We all were finding it hard to breathe. Our compliance, the fear of our worst nightmare, management, and the hunger to belong, to feel like family, would be our downfall.

Finally, Celestine delivered the coup de grâce. Mathew was to convey to Don Ienner that Beyoncé had written a personal letter to the label, explaining her position. Only she could make her plea to "go solo," her mother said. The letter should depict how angry she was, "disappointed and just plain fed up."

All of this is substantiated in the court depositions, which confirmed that Beyoncé had signed the letter – but I knew that she had not composed it. I'd helped Beyoncé with her homework for years. I knew her writing style and inflection. This letter was not Beyoncé's. Rather, it read like her mother's breezy, crass chatter. It was clear to me that Celestine had dictated this letter. It was dated January 17th, 2000, a little more than a month after Bowman hand delivered LeToya and LaTavia's "Letter of Disaffirmance." Beyoncé (allegedly) wrote: "I have shared some of the best moments in my life with the two of you by my side. I have also shared some of the worst." Beyoncé continued, citing several transgressions that she claimed were perpetrated against her by her bandmates LeToya and LaTavia. "I never complained when you didn't sing one note on numerous songs on the album. I've never complained that when I was working my butt off in the studio, as I did on the last album, that the two of you were both either sleeping or on your phones approximately 80 percent of the time. I never complained when the two of you were lipsinging *[sic]* to my vocals on some of the videos and onstage. In fact, I only helped make our contributions appear to be equal to the public." In conclusion, "Beyoncé" wrote, "Approximately every three weeks [or less] there is 'drama' caused by one or both of you! It has been this way for at least the past two years and I don't deserve this!" It reeked of Celestine's babble. At the end of the letter, my girls' future, their fate, would be sealed. Its words were scathing.

Dependable Kelly, who didn't matter as much as Beyoncé in the growing political battle, was also forced to lie. Her letter, also printed in *Vibe* Magazine's February 2001 issue, wrote: "I think it's so funny how every time there is something good going on with Destiny's Child, one of you will spring something on us [Beyoncé and me] ... And before, I've tried to forgive and forget and move on, but I refuse to be run over and receive punches from y'all. Y'all have taught me not to take crap from anyone and to always watch your own back..."

I felt sick.

Then, Celestine finished off the "tramps." She claimed, "From the time LeToya got in the group there was always drama, always jealousy, always madness." The truth of the matter is, neither girl had been a problem, nor caused drama, nor been jealous, nor created madness. They were sweet girls, who in their formative years were neither calculating, manipulative, nor deceitful. Gifted children, they never lied to me, never dissembled, never acted from ulterior motives. Their childish fantasies tended toward princess dresses and Prince Charming, not huge bank accounts. Money did not motivate them to perform; they sang and danced from pure joy.

Beyoncé, the prodigy, wasn't the one desperate for celebrity, favor, and reputation. I came to see, rather, that her parents were systematically replacing those innocent childhoods with the cynicism of desperate adults. The fact that Pam and Cheryl hadn't sensed or heeded the dangers that Celestine posed, meant that their children ultimately had to pay. I'd never seen character assassination so well played out. Saint Celestine had tricked all of us.

Reading the *Vibe* article, I tried to ignore the web of lies that Beyoncé's mother was creating. "People don't know all the crap that we've been through with LeToya and LaTavia." The writer suggests that by the time the disaffirmance happened, Beyoncé and Kelly had been miserable. "It was the last insult they could take," Celestine adds. She concludes in her artless manner, "You give people an inch and they take a mile, and that's basically what happened. Beyoncé and Kelly kissed their butts all the time, spoke to them first, and then went into the studio and did all the work."

I'd read enough. Screaming at the page, as if the journalist could hear me, I yelled "She's a lying....witch."

The next time I talked to Beyoncé, I didn't recognize her. Almost catatonic in her depression, she had been in bed for weeks. And again, Mama Celestine had allowed the sulking, just as the biblical figure Jezebel had whenever her weak husband, Ahab, fell into bed, moping about something he'd been denied.

Celestine (a true Jezebel spirit, in my opinion) allowed Beyoncé's sullen, sulking behavior, because it always worked to her benefit. When she'd had enough, just as Jezebel did ["How is it that your spirit is so sullen that you are not eating food?" – 1 Kgs. 21:5], Celestine would ask pretty much the same question, stroking Beyoncé's hair, again, just as Jezebel stroked Ahab's hair in the biblical story. I'd seen Celestine's process. Beyoncé would answer her mother in much the same way Ahab does. She would accept blame. Nevertheless, Beyoncé said, "I don't think it's the right time to go solo." She believed the fans would be angry with her, not forgive her and blame her. The leader always gets blamed, she reasoned. (A fact that I'd tried to impress upon her.)

Celestine promised to find a solution. ["Arise, eat bread, and let your heart be joyful; I will give you the vineyard of Naboth the Jezreelite" – 1

Kgs. 21:7] It was Celestine who did the leg work, discovering through the girl's choreographer, Junella Segura, that a native of Illinois, a girl named Tenitra Michelle Williams, could be a proper replacement for LeToya. Celestine arranged for Williams to fly to Houston, and even paid for the ticket and picked her up from the airport herself. Mathew's testimony confirmed, "Tina and Beyoncé and Kelly brought her to our home." [Jezebel sits down and writes a letter. She is going to pay two false witnesses to testify that they heard Naboth blaspheme God and the king, so that both he and his sons would be stoned to death and the king would be free to lay claim to his land – cf. 2 Kgs. 9:26] Celestine's goal seemed clear to me. Like Jezebel, she was guided by a specific philosophy. "Take what you want and destroy anyone who stands in your way."

Beyoncé and Kelly already knew Tenitra Michelle as an R&B artist, Monica's background singer. She auditioned. With renewed hope, Beyoncé came out of her depression. Her mother had saved the day, just as Jezebel had. And like Ahab, Beyoncé wasn't interested in knowing the details. At the end of that audition, LeToya and LaTavia (Naboth, and his sons, in my opinion) were metaphorically killed, dismissed, stoned to death. "We'll need one more girl," Celestine said. She got busy again.

Enter Farrah Franklin, the second replacement.

The Original Destiny's Child

me because I thought they were trying to make me look or be like LaTavia and I wanted to have my own identity. They also had me suntanning.

niki: Really? Were you the only one in the group that they had tanning?
Farrah: They had me and Michelle tanning.

niki: They didn't have Beyoncé tanning? I mean, she's the lightest one in the group.
Farrah: No. I think that's why they didn't have her tanning. My assumption was that every time I looked at a picture, she stood out more because she was the bright one. Not because she was the prettiest, but because she was lighter. I never realized like, "Okay, I'm tanning." I'm thinking I like to be dark. So I'm like, "Oh, I get to go to the tanning salon for free." I had to tan. I had to change my whole hairstyle.

niki: So who told you that you had to tan?
Farrah: The mother. She's like the stylist and she was like, "You look prettier darker."

niki: When you came into the group was it pretty much stated that Beyoncé's father would be your manager as

well? I know that was a problem with LeToya and LaTavia. So did he become your manager as well?
Farrah: Yes.

niki: How did you feel about the styling of the group? Was there anything about the clothes that you didn't necessarily care about?
Farrah: Well, it was awkward wearing their old clothes.

niki: We did an interview with LaTavia and LeToya and they mentioned that you and Michelle were wearing their clothes that they paid for. Was there ever a time that you and Michelle spoke to LaTavia and LeToya?
Farrah: No.

niki: When did the real problems start with the group?
Farrah: Like I said, her mom was doing the hair. My hair started breaking and my hair is real. Pretty much everyone in the group has some pieces or a weave. I'm the only one in the group that didn't have anything. So when my hair started breaking, of course I'm gonna be like "What's going on?" So there were problems because I would complain about my hair breaking. I'm like, "This is my hair." I didn't like the red anymore. They were like, "There needs to be a redhead in the

Farrah Franklin

From Beyoncé: "Thanks 4 all you've taught me. You have been inspiring to me and I love you. Thanx 4 being a part of my life. Thank you!"

From LeToya: "To my friend and vocal coach, Thankx 4 taking my voice to another voice. God Bless."

From LaTavia: "To David, Thankx 4 sticking By me through my rough times and my Bad attitudes. I Love You Guy!"

From Kelly: "David, words cannot express my thoughts & love to you! Stay in my life always O.K. Love you 4-ever!"

29. The breakup – Part II

Having spent so many years with Destiny's Child – from its founding, and through all the name changes – and with the Knowles family, I had expected to enjoy an ongoing, amicable relationship with them all, even when I no longer worked actively with the girls. But on February 15th 2000, the day Destiny's Child's "Say My Name" video made its debut on MTV and BET, all those expectations evaporated.

Sitting in our apartment in New York, Gregory and I watched in disbelief as the "Say My Name" video, directed by Joseph Kahn, exposed the group in all its new show-biz dishonesty. Their every sung word revealed to me that the musical values and performance integrity that my girls and I had worked for since 1989 were going up in public relations smoke. The four girls, two of whom I'd never seen before, were surrounded by dancers who were apparently meant to camouflage the fact that these girls were only pretending to be a group. Beyoncé and Kelly were joined by a girl named Michelle, and another they would introduce as Farrah, substitutes whom Celestine and Mathew had invited to jerk, gyrate, and pose their way into Destiny's Child history. It was a travesty.

I silently recalled scripture. "Never take your own revenge, beloved, but leave room for the wrath of God, for it is written, "VENGEANCE IS MINE, I WILL REPAY," says the Lord." (Romans 12:19) Tears began to roll down my face.

A month later, the angry LeToya and LaTavia fought back. On March 21, 2000, they filed a petition against Mathew, Beyoncé, Kelly, and Sony Columbia in the district courts of Houston, Texas.

I left for Monte Carlo.

* * * * *

Gregory's fourth affair happened while I was away singing in the South of France. It would ruin our friendship. I didn't want to talk about it, I just wanted out. I got it, I truly did. Gregory's sister had passed and I hadn't been there, so he intimated that his grief made him do it. Malarkey, I thought, even though I still loved him.

Our last goodbye, which took place over the telephone, was a hard one. We suffered and reminisced our way through a short conversation. I liked Gregory's sister, I even loved her, and would always be fond of him, but I loved me more. "No more betrayal," I whispered silently to myself. I just didn't have it in me to make the *effort*.

"Again, I'm sorry about your sister," I said. He thanked me. But, I wondered, would anything ever be enough for him? I recalled to him my promise to fly back and forth from Germany, for the relationship. He remembered.

I asked to be let off the hook. He agreed, saying "I'm sorry." Then he ended things, abruptly and matter-of-factly. I was too tired to care. "Well then," I said. And after what seemed like an unending pregnant silence, I heard him sniffle. My answer was a hardened heart. I wished him well. "Likewise," he said. Then we hung up.

I walked towards the window. Was my car service on time? It was. Depressed and yet shamefully relieved, I questioned my feelings. Had I stopped caring about everyone, becoming cold? What was going on with me? I didn't like the man staring back at me in the mirror and I'd not liked him for a long time. Picking up my luggage, which was filled with pictures of my life with Gregory, I headed downstairs and gave the key to his cousins, our landlords. I hugged Shirley and shook Vincent's hand, who apologized for his cousin's behavior. "Pray for him," he said. I promised that I would, and I did. Seconds later I was heading for JFK International Airport and my new life.

Twenty hours or so later, I put the key into the lock of my new home, a perfect two-bedroom apartment in Weimar, Germany, and *I breathed*.

There had been no kitchen when I signed the lease, a few months earlier, after performances in France with the famed conductor Christoph Eschenbach. Only an ugly sink and a cheap stove stood in the rather large kitchen space. I asked my new landlord, Herr Roland Biskop, if he minded purchasing a full kitchen for me, and a washer/dryer (which finally broke down in 2016, while I was writing this book). I had paid the first and last months' rent, plus a healthy deposit (three months' rent), before leaving for New York. Now back in Germany for good, I walked into the nearly empty apartment at Puschkinstraße 3, grateful for its shelter.

I had chosen my building because it placed me in the heart of cultural history, where I had daily reminders of three of the 18th and 19th centuries' greatest writers. First, Alexander Puschkin, for whom my street was named, was the father of Russian literature, and a black man. My new home was a stone's throw from the house in which the revered poet Johann von Goethe had lived. From my window I could see his home, now a much-visited museum. Just around the corner was Friedrich Schiller's house-turned-museum, which I passed daily on my way to the opera house. These were constant reminders of those famous eighteenth-century giants. I had sung their words many times, in everything from Schubert songs to Beethoven's Ninth Symphony, which uses Schiller's "Ode to Joy" for its last movement.

As promised, Frau Ulrike Biskop, my landlord's wife, had seen to the installation of the washer/dryer as well as a new kitchen. European apartments have fewer built-in features than Americans are used to, and my Puschkinstraße kitchen required significant attention in order to make it useful even to a bachelor tenor. She had thoughtfully purchased silverware for me, and a portable clothing rack, for which I reimbursed her directly after my arrival.

There were only three working light bulbs in my new home: one in the kitchen, one in the bathroom, and one in the hallway. I had no furniture yet, but Frau Biskop had taken care of my telephone installation (she'd even bought the telephone) in advance of my arrival. We had filled out the necessary paperwork together – she in Weimar, and I in New York. After a couple of weeks I had received her email confirmation. Deutsche Telekom had given her my new telephone number, which I promptly passed on to Celestine at the salon, and Pam.

With this good start, I quickly turned to the rest of the apartment. The first thing I did on August 15th was unpack, sort my laundry by color, and walk to the dollar store I'd seen on the corner. I needed laundry detergent, fabric softener, and garbage bags, for those memories I had decided I didn't want to keep. And in that instance, I faced my first real hurdle – *the German language*. Although I had sung in German – poetic German, literary German – I wasn't able to speak one ordinary sentence, not even a little bit.

I entered the store, smiling at the nice woman behind the counter. A bit nervous, I opened my mouth and began.

"Uh, Hello," I said.

"Hallo," she answered.

"Do you have laundry detergent and garbage bags?" I asked.

The store clerk didn't understand.

I walked outside, asking several people if they spoke English. No one did. Shit, I thought, and then quickly re-entered the store, this time looking around for myself. The laundry detergent was easy to spot, but the garbage bags? I return to the front of the store, with a bit more hope. Stay focused, David, I told myself. Forgetting my manners, I leaned over the counter. But then I instantly pulled back, apologizing profusely for my threatening behavior. I was sure the very white German woman behind the counter harbored a fear of black men. America had taught me that most white women did. Nevertheless, I was no longer *in Kansas*, so to speak. Germany appeared to be different, nothing like I'd heard. Not only had I not seen any Nazis, the store clerk hadn't flinched. I hadn't frightened her at all. In fact, she joined me in my search for whatever it was that I was looking for behind her counter. Then I saw it, tucked away, just under the cash register, a miniature garbage can. Pointing, I said "There – *that*." She understood.

"Ahhhhhhhh – Müllsacken," she said.

I repeated her words, and somehow her accent too. "Yes, Müll – sacken," articulating every syllable with painstaking focus.

"Da drüben, letztes Regal, unten links," the woman said, rapidly firing off her words.

I didn't understand.

"Komm mit," she signaled.

I smiled with understanding. "Come with me" was a phrase I'd sung. Her gesturing hand also helped. I did as she asked, conscious not to invade her space. Once at the back of the store, she pointed. There they were, the garbage bags, just as she'd said, at the back of the store, on the last shelf and to the left. Tickled pink, I picked up a roll, using the picture on the wrapper to determine the right size, and she and I returned to the front of the store. While ringing the items up, ever so slowly, the clerk asked, "Where come you....?"

I didn't understand.

"Home your....?"

"Uh – Uh – *Oh*," I said. The light bulb came on. "I am from New York."

"Ohhhhhhhhhhhhhhh, New York," she answered. Then with the most perplexed look I think I have ever seen on a human face, she hesitated. "Ugh," she grunted in frustration. Then, trying again, she asked "Visit?"

"Ah, no," I answered. "I am here for work."

Now it was she who repeated my words. "Wuh – urk....," smiling. She understood. Then she asked, "What do you?"

I'd gotten the hang of things and answered valiantly, "I am an opera singer."

"Oooooooooooouuuuuuuuu," she answered. "Am Theater?"

"Yes, at the theater," I said.

Then, handing me my bags, the woman offered me her hand and said, "Please hold the line!"

I smiled, knowing better than to laugh or even giggle. Instead, I shook her hand, thanked her, and took my laundry detergent and garbage bags and left the store.

"Auf Wiedersehen," she called out.

Turning to her, and with the biggest smile on my face, I answered "Yes, Auf Wiedersehen."

I was going to be just fine.

(I later understood why the woman said "Please hold the line" instead of "It was nice to meet you." It was most likely the only complete English phrase she'd heard. Germany had just started adding the English translation "Please hold the line" – after the German phrase "Bitte, warten" – when you were put on hold on the telephone. I was now in the former East Germany, where the people had lived behind Berlin's Wall, forced to deal with Russian oppression and their despised language. Although picturesque Weimar was a center of culture in 1999, it would take years before English would be a widespread option in the Thüringen region.)

Frau Biskop's clothing rack now came in handy. After hanging my clean white clothes, I put the next load into the washer and headed out into town, looking for a supermarket and Anno 1900, a fabulous little restaurant oasis where I'd eaten in 1999, the night before my audition at the opera house. (It remains one of my favorites in all of Germany.) On the way to the supermarket, I passed an Arko chocolatier (chocolate shop) and decided to go in. The place was full of clients, so I browsed until someone was free to help me. Suddenly, a middle-aged woman came over, extended her hand and welcomed me to Weimar. "You're the guy from New York, the opera singer, aren't you?" she asked. Stunned, I nodded yes, unable to speak. Less than two hours after leaving the dollar store, word had spread. I'd have to be careful.

Weimar was small.

* * * * *

I had just made it. The grocery store was about to close. "Fünfzehn Minuten noch, Junger Mann" [fifteen minutes left, young man), the older woman said. I had time to buy cereal, milk and some breakfast food before heading to the Anno 1900, whose owner, a young man in his early twenties, remembered me from the year before. I ordered Roulade (Rolled and stuffed beef, with gravy), Thüringer Klöße (A delicacy from the region, which is a large ball-shaped potato dumplings), and Rotkohl (Red Cabbage). The restaurant owner, in a perfect Americanized English, suggested a burgundy wine. I told him I didn't drink. "I never drink," I added. He insisted, and I thought, "What the hell...." I told him to bring me his "best." He said that he knew the perfect one to compliment my meal. After dinner, I returned to my apartment and prepared for a long night. I had to sleep on the floor.

The next day, Stephan Bahr, who lived in Weimar and taught accordion at the local music school, picked me up at 10:00. A friend of my friend and travel agent, Roswitha Sterbal, Stephan had agreed to take me furniture shopping, suggesting we go directly to a local furniture store with "good sturdy quality merchandise." Möbelhaus Helmreich, established in 1914, was quaint but fully stocked. Within hours I had furnished my entire apartment: closets, sideboards, linens, blankets, lamps, glassware, dishes, a kitchen table and chairs, living room chairs, floor lamps, and rugs, etc. "Wir liefern die Sachen morgen" [We will deliver the things tomorrow], the owner promised. Stephan had already ordered the couch, which he and I agreed upon over email, from the furniture store Otto, which made shopping by catalogue in Germany easy. It would arrive by the end of the week, they said. All that was left to do was to buy my bed and pillows. Stephan took me to a store called Röller, in Erfurt, the next town over. Things were shaping up.

On August 17th, after lunch at Anno 1900, I happened upon a tall good-looking man, who wore his hair cut close to the scalp. He was riding his bike, on his way home for lunch. Stopped dead in his tracks, and obviously interested in striking up a conversation, he introduced himself as Ralf Hebig. After a few minutes of struggling back and forth, between his fractured English and my even worse German, it became clear that we had "a certain something in common." We agreed to meet later that evening, where he'd promised to introduce me to his life partner. Disappointed, I agreed, maintaining the utmost decorum and respect for what I saw as his *unavailability*. Ralf, his partner, Tino Schreiber (who is today his husband), and I got along fantastically. We have remained friends, and I spend my birthday with them, and Ralf's mother, every year, at their family home in the country.

After Ralf rode away on his bike that day, I headed for the artist entrance of the opera house. There I met Andreas Henning, the assistant conductor (*Kapellmeister*) in the house, who would be on the podium for the *Don Giovanni* that would be my first opera at Weimar.

"Hi, David," he said. His English was even better than that of the owner of Anno 1900.

"Ah, hello. Maestro," I answered, shaking his extended hand.

"How was your trip? Are you getting along OK?" Andreas asked.

"Oh yes, I've even purchased all my furniture." Andreas could not believe that everything would be delivered right away. I explained that I'd bought locally and paid in cash, which apparently made a big difference to the merchants.

"How's your German coming along?"

Perplexed by his question, I answered "I've been here only two days. But don't worry, I'll learn it...."

Andreas looked ill. His brow began to sweat, and the color seemed to be leaving his body. "I don't understand," he said. Then, looking me straight in the eye, he said, "Please don't tell me that you've learned *Don Giovanni* in Italian?"

"Of course, I did." My agent had told me that Weimar's production was an original-language *Wiederaufnahme* [a production revived from a previous season].

"Oh, God," he answered. "No, we are doing it German."

Now it was I who felt sick. I had seven days before the first and only rehearsal with the orchestra, and only three days after that before the opening. My legs went numb, and I felt that any minute my heart would stop from the shock. "I have to go," I said, nervously.

"Wait, where are you going?" Andreas asked.

"Home, I have work to do."

I have never seen such a look of pure horror as appeared on Andreas's face in that moment. His angst was real. "This is a catastrophe," he said.

"No worries," I answered, as I started to run away.

"Momento," Andreas said. "You'll need the right version." Pulling himself together he said, "Go up to the third floor and ask the music librarian for the correct German score. She'll know."

I did as Andreas suggested, and then I made a beeline for my apartment. Realizing that I'd have to cancel my meeting up with Ralf and Tino, I cracked open the *Don Giovanni* score and began pacing.

When my new acquaintances rang the bell, I explained. Ralf and Tino understood, but were intrigued. How did I plan to pull off the impossible? "Du kannst kein Deutsch!" [You can't speak German], they said, emphasizing the obvious. "No problem," I said. "I'm a good musician." And then I added, "I sing German with an excellent accent," explaining that I'd studied the phonetics of the language since the age of eighteen.

Ours was not an easy conversation, as I had to use my dictionary for every word. Ralf and Tino showed incredible patience, but I had no time to lollygag. They left, and I took out my laptop, opened a Microsoft Word document, and began to type out the text. Then I translated the German text into English. This tedious process took a good 24 hours. It helped that I had already translated the Italian into English. My mental movie was complete, and I had worked out every phrase. I "merely" had to get the German into my head, my voice, my tongue, my memory. (I wished my girls had been there to see my process, having told them a million times about the importance of memory. In classical music, no memory means no career.)

Seven days later, I stood in front of the orchestra, and a terrified Andreas. I'd done it. Memorized almost everything. In German. Although I made three small word flubs, I felt pretty good. Andreas was astounded. However, the chief conductor, Professor Dr. Georg Albrecht, was less than happy. Calling me to the side, and showing great concern, he wanted to know why I was having memory problems. I thought I would pass out from fear. Suddenly, Andreas, stepped in, reminding him that I'd learned the German in seven days.

"*Schaffen sie das, Herr Brewer?*" [Will you make it, Mr. Brewer?] Professor Albrecht asked grimly.

"Yes, I promise," I answered in English. Professor Albrecht then switched to English. "OK," he said. "I trust you." He still seemed a bit suspicious of my claiming to have learned the German text in only seven days.

The next day, August 25th, I had a three-hour staging and blocking rehearsal with the assistant stage director, Gisela Bohne. As she told me where and when to move, I kept saying "Ja wohl!" [Yes, sure!] My American colleague, a soprano named Cynthia Jacobs, laughed. "You don't understand anything she's saying, do you?" I smiled at her perception. The assistant director, a legend at the house, was very clear with her gestures. From the old school, she made it easy for me to understand her. Her eyes and body language told the story for her. I thought about my girls again, but only for a brief second. "I'll be fine," I told Cynthia.

Opening night, stage management was calling "Places!" over the loud speaker. I rehearsed my phrasing up to the last second, just as Grandmother had taught me to do. From my dressing room to the stage, I ran the movie of my opening scene through my head. Suddenly, the lights lowered in the house. My colleagues were in place onstage, and I heard applause that sounded like a million pairs of hands. Maestro Henning took his place at the podium and began to conduct the Weimar Staatskapelle in the Overture to *Don Giovanni*. "They all came to see the handsome black man," the stage manager whispered, showing me a local newspaper article. Apparently, people were talking all over town. I was the only black person in Weimar, which sort of explained the full house.

Seconds later, I heard my music and made my first entrance. My Donna Anna, a wonderful soprano named, Romelia Lichtenstein, focused her eyes on me, trying to help guide me into my first position. By the mid-section of the duet it became clear that I knew where I was and what I was doing. I could feel the dark cloud of doubt lifting from the stage. I was consecrated, wrapped up in God's grace. To my right, sitting on the third row, were Ralf and Tino and all their friends. Tino's sister had driven into town for the performance from Magdeburg, a couple hours away. To my left I could see the lady from the dollar store.

Don Giovanni was a success. I can still feel the adrenaline. I'd never been so focused in my life – well, maybe in Atlanta, when my girls sang for those record labels. This moment matched that one, in its own way. When I appeared for my bows, I could not believe the enthusiastic response. The audience went wild, stomping, cheering, and clapping in a steady repetitive rhythm. At the combined curtain call Cynthia Jacobs, who sang Donna Elvira on that evening, whispered, "The rhythmic clapping means they really like it."

While I was removing my make-up, there was a knock at my dressing room door. A woman and her young son greeted me, the small boy hiding behind his mother. "Mein Name ist Silke, Silke Kuhn," she said [My name is Silke, Silke Kuhn], "und das hier ist mein Sohn, Jonas." [And this is my son, Jonas.] Silke's ten-year-old son stood there, wide-eyed. I extended my hand, saying, "It's a pleasure to meet you, Jonas." When Silke told me that he'd just started learning English, I replied that I was just beginning to learn German. She asked if Jonas could be my pen pal, which was his idea, she said. I thought this was brilliant. Children speak in a simpler language pattern, and I hoped that he would not be judgmental of my halting attempts to learn his language. Instead he found it "putzig" [charming]. After that first meeting, Jonas began to write me short notes in German and I answered in English.

It worked out well, for the both of us, and by December I'd meet the entire Kuhn family: Jonas's grandmother, Molly, and his grandpa, Horst, Silke's husband, Jens, and their small daughter, Josefa. I'd meet his aunt and her family and I'd even meet the neighborhood Santa. I became an honorary Kuhn, gratefully accepting Silke's invitation to Christmas Eve dinner. Today, Jonas, whom I adopted as my little German brother, works in television and film.

Weimar had quickly become an enormous blessing, my very own personal place of refuge where I could escape Destiny's Child drama, and Gregory, whom I thought of daily. God had granted me the space to find my footing, and I was grateful. I even found a great church, the evangelical congregation at the *Stadtkirche Sankt Peter und Paul* [the city Church of Saint Peter and Saint Paul]. In addition, my new friends Ralf and Tino did something truly remarkable. Every Friday night for an entire year, provided I didn't have a performance, they invited me to their apartment for dinner. All their friends would show up. We ate great food, we drank wine, we laughed, and we talked, a lot. Exactly the point, Ralf pointed out: they were teaching me German. I remain touched beyond words, and I have never forgotten their gigantic gesture, or their generosity – *ever.* With their help, I became proficient in their language. Within six or seven months, I could even argue in German – with bad grammar, but I could get the job done.

The second Friday in December, I got home late. Dinner at Ralf and Tino's went long, as they and their friends Claudia, Simone, Lazlo, and Sabina explained to me the history of the Berlin Wall, and its many ramifications. Naturally, I was fascinated. The stories were of incredible family sacrifice. Mothers lost contact with their children, brothers and sisters were alienated from one another and from their families. Before we knew it, the evening had flown. Getting home quickly from Ralf and Tino's house, I climbed the four flights of stairs to my apartment. As I put the key in the door, I could hear my telephone ringing. It was 1:45 a.m. Who was calling me at this ungodly hour? Fearing the worst, I rushed in and answered, just in time.

"Hello," I said.

"David," a man's voice on the other end of the telephone said.

"*Mathew?*" I asked.

"Yeah, Man," Beyoncé's father said. "How you been?"

* * * * *

Mathew Knowles had called to ask me if I would testify on his behalf in the upcoming depositions. "Those little bitches are suing us," he said, laughing nervously. After a few seconds of silence, I answered. "Mathew, of course I will testify, but please be advised – I plan to tell the truth." Mathew intimated that he'd have it no other way, speaking in an English so mangled that I wasn't really sure what he was saying. Then we hung up. I never heard from him again. Typical, I thought.

I celebrated 2001 with Ralf and Tino at Claudia's bar. It was a great evening. Weimar Opera performances started up again on the 4th of January, which made me think about Celestine. It was her 47th birthday. I'd turned 37, that past July. Leaving those reminiscences, I checked my emails before going to bed and saw that Alan had written me.

In November of 2000, during the run of *Der Rosenkavalier* in Weimar, I had met Alan Behr. He would not only become my New York lawyer, but also, along with his beautiful and charming wife, Julie, a great confidante and friend. Today, he is a partner at Phillips Nizer in New York.

Alan had been in Germany writing a travel book. His target audience were those who wished to study East German history, maybe even travel throughout the region. A native of New Orleans, Alan was an avid opera lover who frequently attended performances in New York, where he and Julie lived. On the night he came to the opera in Weimar, I was singing the character role of the Italian Tenor, who has one gorgeous aria in the first act of *Der Rosenkavalier*. My costume was a purple satin fat suit, with rhinestone buttons, and the most ostentatious wig. My character's look, patterned after Luciano Pavarotti, in all his round glory, made the thin· *gorgeous me* unrecognizable.

This role always makes a short night for the tenor, as the sole aria ends the first act. With extra time on my hands I decided to watch the rest of the opera, after the intermission. That is where I met Alan, who asked if I was American. Our brief conversation revealed his purpose in being in East Germany, and he asked to interview me for his book "The Long Way Home." We met the next day for lunch at Anno 1900, the beginning of our warm friendship.

Now, on January 4th, 2001, I thought of him and Julie, calling to wish them a Happy New Year. Almost immediately after putting the receiver back on its base, my phone rang.

"Hallo, bei Brewer," I said (Hello, Brewer residence), answering the call in the German tradition. The voice on the other end said, "Uhm. Hello, David is that you?" "Yes, this is David." In that second I recognized the voice of Pam Luckett. "Pam!" I shouted, "I was literally, just in this moment, thinking about you guys. How are you?" She said that they were all healthy and that she couldn't complain.

Because I had not talked to her since summer 2000, I had many questions. Pam explained that LeToya and LaTavia had suffered tremendously the past year. To my inquiry about LaTavia, Pam said that she had made a full recovery and was doing well. The two girls were preparing to participate in depositions for their upcoming lawsuit against Mathew, Beyoncé, Kelly, and Sony Columbia, which I already knew about.

We continued to make small talk for a bit, and then Pam came to the reason for her call. LeToya and LaTavia were in the beginning stages of building a new girl group. Would I be interested in helping? even taking over the development of the group?

Avoiding a direct answer to her inquiry, I asked how they planned to find the other two members, since Pam had not mentioned any other names. "Through auditions," Pam said.

"They want to make the decision themselves, to find singers they click with." Considering what they'd been through, I understood and accepted their terms immediately. The idea was to re-create my original concept of four girls.

Then Pam and I got around to talking about the Knowleses. "Mathew has been up to his old tricks," she said, "But he is no longer important in the scheme of things. Beyoncé is now the problem."

"Beyoncé? how is she the problem?" My mind popped to attention.

Pam replied that Beyoncé had taken to giving interviews trashing LeToya and LaTavia. Both the girls were understandably very upset about Beyoncé's vicious attacks. I guessed she and Kelly were fighting back because of the lawsuit, but at the time of this phone conversation with Pam, I didn't fully understand why. (Just a few weeks later, *Vibe* Magazine quoted Beyoncé, who called LeToya "tone deaf.") Still, Pam's allegations had me in shock. I had to ask her, again and again, to repeat what she'd just said.

Pam feared that LeToya was falling into depression, and she told me that LaTavia had started drinking, that she'd even gotten some DUI citations. These problems were not public knowledge, Pam told me. They certainly had not been reported in the German press. However, my mother would tell me something about a national radio disc jockey's comment that Beyoncé was "kicking people off the Destiny's Child Island." Pam asked me if I would give an interview to counter the claims that Beyoncé had made. I agreed to do so.

A couple weeks later, on the 18th of January, 2001, my telephone rang. I studied the number in the display window and, recognizing that it was a U.S. caller, I answered in the American way. "Hello." A pleasant woman's voice announced herself as Joy Reid, founder and editor of *Truyu* Magazine. I greeted her politely, telling her that I had been expecting her call. Joy and I had a few minutes of small talk and then she repeated what Pam told me, that Beyoncé had claimed that LeToya was tone deaf.

Joy's next comment threw me for a loop. She asked me if I had read the article in which Celestine had talked about me. Apparently Beyoncé's mama had given an interview with a London gab magazine, which quoted her as saying that she had allowed me to live in a back room of the Knowles home, rent free, in exchange for voice lessons. She also said that Celestine never gave my name to the interviewer and so the reporter simply referred to me as the "unnamed voice teacher."

Suddenly, I found myself asking, David why did you agree to this interview? All these lies were upsetting. I swallowed and said to Joy, "There is nobody on this planet who knows their *[Destiny's Child's]* voices better than I do because I built them... None of them are tone deaf. All of them can sing... It's just flat wrong. I don't know why [Beyoncé] said that."

I didn't hold back. The next month, I interviewed with *SiSTER2Sister* (S2) Magazine.

* * * * *

Celestine must have been loving herself, I thought. Michelle Williams, a background singer, and Farrah Franklin, whom Mathew slandered with the sobriquet "video whore," weren't going to cause problems. But

LeToya and LaTavia wanted justice, and I felt that they deserved it. They shouldn't just go away, shrivel up, and die.

When asked to depose, Mathew swore that he'd done nothing wrong. He even pointed to audits he himself commissioned, to the tune of an alleged, whopping $30,000. The "audit" purportedly proved he'd not acted "improperly managing the group's money." Not only was that a complete load of horse shit, just like his "audit" was, but I was sure he'd steal again if given the chance. I even wondered if he'd stolen from Beyoncé, independent of Destiny's Child. At any rate, LeToya and LaTavia weren't buying his special brand of bullshit anymore, and neither did the attorney Randy Bowman, who wrote in a letter: "Until a forensic accountant has looked through these records, we don't know if all the money that was paid to Destiny's Child is reflected in those audits," Bowman said. "We have no way of knowing if he received a million dollars and accounted for $400,000 of it in the context of the records he turned over. So until we know everything that came in and what he did with it, we can't have confidence in any of the records."

Beyoncé swore that "our attorneys talk every day," which was not true. She claimed that "They got letters from us and calls from us." Another lie. Then, ".... and they got a letter from the label....," which was her first true statement. However, that letter only discussed the ousted girls' "ceasing to perform as Destiny's Child."

Just as public gossip and fan suspicions began to die down, Farrah Franklin got fired, after just five months. Her reason: Mathew Knowles. Mathew Knowles's reason: unprofessionalism, and missed promotional dates and performances. Sound familiar? This *fact* explained that radio disc jockey's comments Mama had told me about. Rumors were running rampant, worse than a runaway wild horse. "Something's not right with that group," some people were saying. "It's that father. He's shady," others swore. My personal favorite was people's summation that Destiny's Child equaled nepotism at its best. Bingo! I thought. But no, the ever present and looming threat of prison remained the real problem.

A completely docile Kelly remained loyal to the Knowleses. I suspected as much, I told Pam. Taking into account Kelly's need simply to survive, I did not blame her, but she wasn't innocent. Still, what she and Beyoncé were doing was tantamount to inciting a small revolution. I can't begin to describe how upsetting Mathew's false claims were to me, when I finally read them for myself in those depositions (Luckett, et al vs. Knowles, et al, Vol. 1, 1-29-02). Yes, I certainly knew that lunacy hung out in Mathew's head, but now he and his cronies (Beyoncé, Kelly, and their team of lawyers), were actively advocating the complete take-down of innocent girls. Girls – young women – who were telling the truth.

What the public doesn't know, and maybe not even the girls themselves, is that sources inside Music World Management told me that the courts had insisted upon appointing an *ad litem* to the case. Her assignment was to review the girl's minor contracts, all of them, from 1993 onward, keeping only their best interest in her focus. Susan Bruning was that *ad litem*, and her findings threw a massive monkey wrench into an already foul Knowles operation. Ms. Bruning wrote: "The minors do not yet have financial structures in place to enable them to preserve, for their future personal use and benefit, a reasonable amount of the income they derive from their professional activities. I believe it is important that financial trust be established to ensure that each minor will have the opportunity in the future to use and benefit personally from the income derived by her during her minority. Sony has agreed to accept letters of direction from the minors instructing Sony to pay income due to minors directly into such trusts, when established."

Ms. Bruning's statement did two things: One, it exposed Mathew's illegal intention, and two, it got Sony off the hook. The girls dropped their suit against Sony, satisfied that both old royalty amounts and new figures would be calculated and sent to each girl directly. In addition, as I understood it from LeToya and LaTavia themselves, during talks we had at LaTavia's dining room table in Atlanta, they'd been thinking of dropping their claims against Beyoncé and Kelly, feeling guilty about suing their "sisters," whom they still loved. I know for a fact that they felt that they had had no other choice but to sue, and that their only beef was with Mathew. They wanted to expose him and his unscrupulous practices. Think again.

"They want money, so we'll give them money," Celestine maintained. I'd called her at the salon. She swore the ousted girls were opportunists. So, she'd agreed with Mathew, she said. This meant making a settlement offer. Now, I knew Mathew. Way too wrapped up in his ego, he had abrogated to Celestine the creation of a settlement idea. It was only Celestine's idea, and she was determined that it would work. Lawyers everywhere would much prefer settlement deals over going to court. The odds are unpredictable in court proceedings. A settlement was "free money," without all the hassle.

There was only one problem that I could see: the girls' relationship with their attorney, Randy Bowman. He was smart and tough, and he had the Knowleses over a barrel. He'd never agree to this settlement. Then I found out that Pam had allowed herself to be talked into changing lawyers, recommending that the girls go with Warren Fitzgerald, who lived in Houston and had begged her to let him take over the case. LeToya and LaTavia fired their Dallas-based attorney, which I still consider their biggest mistake.

The Knowleses were now perfectly positioned. Mathew Knowles's crony Louis Bush, oh he of no scruples, had taken over Linda Ragland's position in payroll at Music World Management. He and Warren Fitzgerald were "homeboys," from the same neighborhood in Acres homes.

Louis gained the confidence of Warren. He wouldn't lie to him, Warren thought. Swearing that Destiny's Child "didn't have it like that," Louis added, "not like people think." Warren Fitzgerald then talked *seriously* to his new clients, who naively agreed, falling into the money trap that Celestine had set for them. They believed their lawyer when he told them that settling was the right thing to do. It was the winning move, everyone thought. Warren had bought into Louis's lie, hook, line, and sinker.

A settlement was reached. $850,000 was the sum, and to show good faith, Mathew's lawyers agreed to play ball and not obstruct the deal the girls made with Sony to have back and future monies placed into their trust accounts directly. Randy Bowman's wise counsel, to ask for audits, financial records, and bank statements, was never acted upon. The

Knowleses had escaped prison once again. With that settlement, the suit against Beyoncé and Kelly would be dropped, and Mathew would enjoy the benefits of Celestine's brilliant manipulation. A non-disclosure agreement forever sealed the real evidence of his wrong-doing from the public. With that Celestine was free to become the brand she is today.

Having agreed to help with LeToya and LaTavia's girl group, "Anjel," I flew to Atlanta in late winter 2001 to begin working with them. After checking into my hotel suite, I drove directly to LaTavia's house on Glenwood Avenue. At my destination. I punched in the code at the security gate that protected the property. When I knocked on LaTavia's front door, a man's voice called back to me. "Hold on, I'm coming," he said. Suddenly, and to my complete surprise, I found myself standing face-to-face with Louis Bush. We greeted one another cordially, and then he got in his car drove away.

I entered the house and ascended the long staircase, which led to the first level of LaTavia's two-story town home. I called out to her and she replied from the bathroom, "I'll be right there." I took a seat at the dining room table, just opposite her cozy kitchen and waited. Suddenly she appeared, looking much thinner than I remembered. She'd had a nose job. After our old, familiar bear hug, we chatted a bit. Then I got right to it.

"Why is Louis Bush in your house?" I asked.

"You know Louis?"

"Yes, he works for Mathew," I said. Apparently, Louis had been fired and he had been "helping" LaTavia – buy her house, invest her money, and, and, and.

"LaTavia, be careful," I said. Then I asked, "Are you sure you can trust that man?"

"I think so," she answered.

"I'm not so sure," I concluded.

At any rate, Louis was still living in Houston, from what I could gather. "He's traveling back and forth to Atlanta, to *help me*," LaTavia reiterated.

Destiny's Child's third album, "Survivor," was about to be released, on May 1st 2001, which we all anticipated with bated breath. Even though the settlement had been reached and committed to paper, the $850,00.00 split hadn't reached LeToya and LaTavia's bank account. Their back-royalty checks had been deposited.

* * * * *

Deep into my first sessions with Anjel, I'd gotten LeToya and LaTavia back on track vocally – actually, pretty easily. Their new bandmate, Nativida "Nati" Quinones, reminded me of Jennifer Lopez, flat singing and all.

An absolutely gorgeous girl, Nati had great raw material, but could sometimes sing terribly flat, and go off key so bad, that you didn't recognize the song or its key anymore. She had been living in Hartford, Connecticut, when she was "discovered" by Linda Casey, Brandon and Brian's mother. I quickly gained her trust and we began to address her pitch problems. It should be said, Nati was not tone deaf, not in any way. The problem was a technical one, easily solved. Developing her into a fine singer would be a piece of cake, and I told her so. By August, her pitch problem was solved, and I would return to Germany. Rehearsals for the opera *Die Zauberflöte*, by Wolfgang Amadeus Mozart, began in Weimar on the 25th of August. I would sing the role of Tamino, the romantic male lead in the opera.

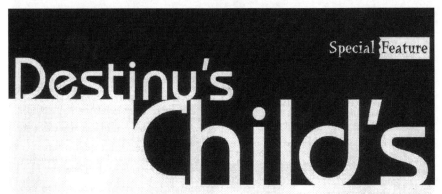

Special Feature

Destiny's Child's

Longtime voice coach David Brewer.
He answers, "Can any of them sing?"

interviewed by niki turner

So much has been said about the vocal ability of Destiny's Child and its former members, LaTavia and LeToya, that I figured, who would know better about their skills than their former vocal coach, David Brewer? We got in touch with David and this is what he said:

"I began working with Beyoncé and Ashley Davis when they were 8 and 9 respectively. [Ashley] was the original member who left the group.

This interview appeared in the May 2001 issue of *Sister2Sister* magazine. Shortly before the magazine's interviewer Niki Turner contacted me, Beyoncé had been quoted in *Vibe* magazine (February 2001) stating that LeToya Luckett was "tone deaf...." I was, of course, exceedingly upset at this unfounded allegation.

The title character in the five-act French opera *Werther*, by Jules Masse-net, became one of my signature roles. It is a demanding role that I have sung frequently in European opera houses, always garnering positive re-views.
Photo: Erika Fernschild

Curtain call, opening night of *Werther* performances in Weimar (February 24, 2001). Based on Johann von Goethe's "The Sorrows of young Werther," the text came to life on that evening. Standing ovations for everyone! What a marvelous cast; and even greater was starring in my favorite role, just steps away where Goethe had lived.

Photo: Erika Fernschild

30. Anjel

Anger

Destiny's Child's third album, "Survivor," released on the 1st of May, 2001, immediately – in its first week – shot to #1 in the pop listings and received unanimously rave reviews. It would sell more than 15,000,000 copies.

I listened to "Survivor" with a heavy heart. We all were being attacked in the song's lyrics (LeToya, LaTavia and myself). What had become of the group that I had so carefully built? When the album track number 13 emerged from my CD player, I was incredulous. "Story of Beauty" detailed LaTavia's molestation to the letter. Utterly shocked that Beyoncé would think it appropriate to expose LaTavia's vulnerability in a pop song, over a catchy beat, I relived the pains of that whole episode: Charles's sinful behavior toward his step-daughter, his smug self-assurance of impunity, and LaTavia's suffering. And now? Beyoncé's "best friend" kicked out of the group, her character trashed, and integrity undermined with lies, and for what? Family loyalty?

Later, in 2002, Beyoncé called her former sisters LaTavia and LeToya "bad seeds." "Now all the bad seeds are out of Destiny's Child," she said. "Go to hell, Beyoncé," I yelled at my television in frustration and anger.

"Bad seeds," I muttered to her image on the screen, "are people who are congenitally disposed to evil deeds, which means, Ms. Beyoncé, that you had better look to your own genes. With a mother and a father who have proven themselves capable of despicable deeds, you might want to be careful about casting aspersions. The shoe you're trying to force on LaTavia's feet might fit your own…"

Shame on the entire lot of them.

Beyoncé's parents by this time had solidified their fabrications about the Knowles Family History. How they had sacrificed everything to be the girl's savior. How Mathew had given up a six-figure job to devote himself to his daughter. How noble they were. Just imagine.

Hats off, Celestine, I thought. What a formidable influence she'd been. What was it that she said? *"Take what you want and destroy anyone who stands in your way."*

Who was the Bad Seed?

In September 2001the magazine *Ebony* published a piece by Lynn Norment, "THE UNTOLD STORY OF HOW Tina & Mathew Knowles Created the Destiny's Child Gold Mine." The article details how Mathew and Celestine Knowles had founded, prepared, and built the girls group Destiny's Child. According to Norment's version, which she had received straight from the horse's mouth, "In 1989, while at Tina's salon, the Knowleses received an inquiry about creating a girl group around Beyoncé." Hogwash.... "Over a year's time, 40 to 50 girls from various ethnicities participated," Celestine said. Norment continued. "Tina focused on styling the girls' hair and creating their costumes."

Good Lord, if their lies weren't so insulting to me – and to Andretta Tillman – I'd have laughed. I asked myself whether the untruths, the linguistic syntax of the words Ms. Norment wrote and published, were direct quotes of the Knowleses. Might she have misinterpreted them? Were they really such miserly people that they could not acknowledge the dedication – musical and financial – that Ann and I had provided along their road to success?

Today, when I read that article, I can vividly recall wishing the Knowleses real harm, death even. Sure, I begged God's forgiveness. It's unChristian to hate, and I had heard and believed, "Don't do things for credit, do them from the heart." But I wanted what every human being wants and what every artist deeply desires: not to be forgotten. I wanted the recognition I deserved for my work and I wanted the applause that I had earned. I am no less a Christian for that. I know this now. Furthermore, I loved those girls, and after eleven years of close work with them, nurturing them, and creating a musical partnership with them, I was devastated to be guillotined from their lives.

Beyoncé's parents were shamelessly taking full credit for the girls' every success. Worse yet, Beyoncé and Kelly were acceding to the lie.

Ebony's egregious account of Beyoncé and Destiny's Child's rise completely denied the truth. I was being erased from the history of what many call "the greatest girl group of all time," certainly in American history, and was damn mad about it. Their fabrication became the accepted version of the Knowles story, not only in *Ebony*, but also throughout the media, whose extensive covering of this phenomenal girl group had reached an international readership.

Their betrayal had more than choked my spirit. Suddenly Grandmother's voice came to me, "Do not let your heart be troubled. Trust in God, and trust also in me."

In the book of Proverbs 6:16-19, King Solomon wrote: "There are six things that the LORD hates, seven that are an abomination to him: haughty eyes, a lying tongue, and hands that shed innocent blood, a heart that devises wicked plans, feet that make haste to run to evil, a false witness who breathes out lies, and one who sows discord among brothers." With Grandmother's voice echoing in my soul, I began a six-year journey of healing.

From the years 2001 to 2007, those lessons in wisdom, understanding, God's commandments, the breaking of God's laws, and comparing God's way to Man's, were my way back to peace. Beyoncé's rejection of God's way will inevitably bite her in the rear end. Only a wise person escapes.

For now, I'll continue with my story. I was beginning to realize a number one truth: the power of Relationship.

* * * * *

Bargaining

In February 2001, I was only days away from my opening in the title role of Jules Massenet's *Werther*, the French opera masterpiece based on the novella by Goethe. Living and singing in Goethe's town, Weimar, only added to my anticipation of singing this great and demanding tenor role.

On February 21 my publicist, Tony Coles, called me from the U.S. to report the results of Destiny's Child Grammy Award nominations for

"Song of the Year" and "Record of the Year," which I had already heard about.

"They won," Tony said.

"In which category?" I asked.

"Best R&B Vocal Performance by a Duo or Group, for 'Say My Name,'" Tony answered. Then he said, "They got booed."

A sharp pain shot up my spine. "Booed!? What was Beyoncé's reaction?"

"Panic," Tony said. "She was definitely affected. She sang off key. And I have never heard Beyoncé sing out of tune."

I hadn't either. I couldn't believe my ears when the video of Destiny's Child's February 21st performance surfaced months later on the internet. Tony had called it right. Beyoncé's unnerved reaction to the audience's booing was audible. Was it poetic justice for the senseless and vicious attacks she and Kelly had launched against LeToya and LaTavia? When I was able to reach Pam, in Atlanta, she told me that LeToya, LaTavia, and Nati had been in Los Angeles, at the Grammy Award ceremonies. They had heard the booing live, and they were doing just fine, Pam said.

The popular celebrity news show "Revealed" then did a story on Destiny's Child and the Grammy Awards. The E Network show featured cameo appearances by Beyoncé, Mathew, and Kelly, with the moderator Jules Asner. Ms. Asner's lead-in was, "The disharmony came to a head in December of 1999, when Mathew Knowles received a letter from lawyers of LaTavia Roberson and LeToya Luckett demanding their own separate managers. But what LaTavia and LeToya didn't realize was, that their days in Destiny's Child were numbered." Ms. Asner then said, "Although the exact reason for the split is unclear, one thing was certain, LaTavia and LeToya were out of Destiny's Child."

Mathew Knowles: "I was disappointed. I felt angry because I did work my butt off for them, so I was also really angry, because attorneys, which are not my favorite people, they can really screw up a lot of stuff."

Next, Beyoncé let loose, crushing her former bandmates with untruths. The lie that I found most significant was, "We tried everything to prevent having to no longer be together. We tried psychologist...," then she stumbled.

"Church," Kelly whispered, then said, "Prayer..."

Beyoncé picked up where she'd left off, "...everything you can possibly think of but really, in reality, some people are just not meant to be together, and God has his will and his will be done."

I was enraged. Now Beyoncé was making God responsible, doubling down, just like the child of narcissistic parents would. In their ignorance, she and Kelly were giving me a new sense of purpose.

I was determined to take Anjel all the way.

The next season, on February 27th, 2002, Tony and I watched the Grammy Award ceremonies on television in Houston at my mother's house, before I flew to Atlanta to work with Anjel. Destiny's Child had been nominated once again. This time their album "Survivor" was nominated for Best R&B Album. However, they won the Grammy for Best R&B Vocal Performance by a Duo or Group, for the *song* "Survivor," not the album. (Beyoncé has yet to win Album of the Year, something she always imagined when she dreamed out loud as a kid.)

* * * * *

Delta Flight 0015 from Frankfurt to Hartsfield-Jackson Atlanta International Airport landed at 3:25 p.m. on April 13, 2002. Anjel had received a formal invitation to perform on April 30 at the *SiSTER2Sister Magazine*'s 13th Anniversary birthday bash in New York. I had accepted the invitation, regardless of Brandon and Brian Casey's very vocal objections. (That they were still influential with Anjel was a constant source of aggravation to me.) I disembarked into the Atlanta spring focused, ready to kick some ass.

The girls opted to sing two originals, "Lonely" and "Lingerie." As Anjel's new manager, I asked my friend the attorney Alan Behr, who was well aware of my work with Destiny's Child and Anjel, to check in with

BMG (Bertelsmann Music Group). "Can you feel out BMG for me to see if they'd be potentially interested in my new girl group?"

A week later, word came back.

"It's all set," Alan told me.

"Great!" I answered. I told no one.

Next, I set out to secure television. Eager to keep the girls' trust and respect, I suggested that their Louis Bush "do something" to prove his worth. I suspected correctly that he would call his friend Sheila Eldridge, a New Jersey publicist, who quickly organized an appearance on Fox television's "Good Day New York" for the girls. She too wanted in on the team, which I wasn't against. "Good Day New York" was the luck we needed. At that time, there was no better platform than live television. Not to mention, this appearance would save us a bundle and alleviate the need to rent space for a showcase. "It will air the morning of April 30th, at 7:45 a.m.," Sheila Eldridge said. I called Alan immediately.

I then called in a favor from Devon Cass, star photographer and make-up artist, who agreed to do the girls' makeup for "Good Day New York" as well as for a photo shoot. My own personal photographer, Devon was definitely the right person to help me. "Make them feel like stars and they'll act like stars," I said. Then, I called Tony Coles, my publicist. "I'll need you in Atlanta the last week, before we fly to New York."

"What's up?"

"Strategy, and I need your instinct, especially when it comes to Brandon and Brian Casey."

"I don't understand," Tony said.

"I think they are sabotaging me and the girls. I have it on good authority that they have been paid off to hold the girls back."

He agreed, and I booked his flight, putting him up at Extended Stay Suites, in the upscale Atlanta neighborhood Buckhead.

* * * * *

Brandon and Brian Casey were classic jerks, and terribly homophobic. I could care less what they thought about me, but no man who treats women the way they did would ever get my respect. I certainly knew they were trying to influence the girls' trust in me, and now I had a good reason why. The Casey brothers and the Knowles parents deserved each other.

Preparing for the New York appearances, I spoke very little with Brandon and Brian. I hadn't flown all the way from Germany to kiss their asses. The brothers reminded me of my asinine sociopathic father. I found them terribly shallow and insecure. I had good reason to suspect them. They had blocked everything thus far. And now they were yelping about New York and the S2S birthday bash. "We're against the girls going to New York," they told me. I asked why, curious to see what they'd come up with. "They're not ready," was their response. Laughing heartily, I answered, "I'll be the judge of that, gentlemen."

Brandon's treatment of LaTavia's "non-singing, non-talented ass," incensed me. "Girl, don't listen to that crap," I said. Brandon berated her talent constantly, and toyed with her emotionally. He picked fights unnecessarily, and in my opinion, kept LaTavia off her A-game. When I jokingly insulted him, saying that he had only five pinched off notes in his throat (he had six), LaTavia said she loved him. She was absolutely dedicated to him and wanted to please him, no matter what. Sound familiar?

Brandon and Brian, together with their bandmates from Jagged Edge, had never won an American Music Award, or a Grammy. "They simply aren't versatile enough," I said to LaTavia. "For me, they are mediocre." LaTavia didn't know quite know what to make of my candor. I sensed she was hurt by what I'd said, so I backed off, praying that her boyfriend's influence didn't ruin her completely. Furthermore, I was worried about her drinking. She wasn't as strong as she'd like to think she was, not in 2002.

Brian's terrorizing of LeToya had also become chronic. I suspected that it had gone on for months, possibly even longer. The way I heard it, his normal modus operandi was to bang on her door at 3 a.m., screaming

674

at the top of this fucking lungs. It got so bad, neighbors had to call the police. Then, he switched to incessant calling on the phone. Ring, ring – LeToya would not pick up. He'd leave a message, saying, "LeToya, I love you. You the best thing that ever happen to me." Then five seconds later she was a "bad made up bitch" who thought she was cute. "You ain't even that fine," he would yell into the phone. Another five seconds would go by and there he'd be again, this time crying, "I love you, LeToya. Pick up the phone." Silence – Silence – *wait for it* – "Fuck you then, you ugly skinny bitch." My God, the things he said to my high top girl made me want to kill him. She begged me to let her handle it. It was crazy, pure craziness. This would go on for hours, or at least the tape Pam played for me went on for that long. After receiving my copy from Pam, I played it for Tony over the phone. His reaction was classic Tony Coles.

"He's certifiable...."

With that insanity as our backdrop, Tony and I worked in the recording studio to prepare the intro track, and he consulted on the mixes of the two tracks the girls had decided to sing. I refused to wait another minute on the Caseys, who had promised more than once to get the girls into the studio. They'd done nothing.

The media were interested in what LeToya and LaTavia had to say, but Brandon and Brian were categorically against press. "No press is bad press," I said. Kelly and Beyoncé were still spreading their lies every chance they got, continuing to demean and blame LeToya and LaTavia. Still, the Casey twins wanted no parts of negative campaigning, they said.

"I don't agree," I said to the girls. "I can easily disprove the lies that they are spreading about you."

I had had enough and I called Sheila. "Please set up radio interviews. Nothing is off limits," I said to her. With less than six days to New York, we were on target.

On the last day of recordings, April 26th, 2002, LeToya nonchalantly sauntered in to the studio, daring anyone to call her on her chronic tardiness.

"Miss Luckett, please go into the booth," I said. She said nothing.

After the headphones and levels check, my high top girl announced that she was ready. I gave the cue for the engineer to start the music. Her lackluster sound startled me. "Are you all right?" I asked.

No reply.

We started again. I stopped her. "Tony, do you hear what I mean?" I asked. He nodded his head, yes. I hit the mute button, "Try it again," I said. "This song is sensual, about somebody touching your spot. C'mon girl, you guys wrote it." She sang the first phrase and then stopped. "Why did you stop?" I asked. LeToya's response was, "I'm waiting to see what ol' boy gotta say," referring to Tony.

I insisted we take a break. LaTavia, threw up her hands. Neither of us understood LeToya's sudden negative attitude. When we tried again, LeToya's performance was even worse. "My God, LeToya what is wrong with you today?" I asked in frustration. "I have never heard you sing like this, not once in all these years. Do whatever you need to do, but you've got to nail this song. Hell, touch yourself if you have to," I said, jokingly.

LeToya removed her headphones and threw them to the ground. Once out of the booth she cursed me out as though I was her enemy. I'd never heard such foul-mouthed language from her, ever. When she finished, she turned and stormed out of the studio. Tony followed, outraged. A few minutes later, he returned, asking why I had let LeToya talk to me like that. "She's a Princess," I answered, opting for the softer explanation for what I was really thinking. It rhymes with itch.

"Well, Princess has left the building," Tony said.

"What are you talking about?"

"She's gone. She got in her drop top Mercedes and sped off."

Before I could say anything, LaTavia had already entered the booth and was ready to go with her section. Always professional, LaTavia finished brilliantly. Her low tones had gotten so sexy. She knocked it out of the box.

Suddenly, the door opened. It was LeToya, still silent. We exchanged glances. Her eyes said, Don't even think of asking me to apologize. In fact, I'm still waiting on her apology. The headphone and e-cue levels were reset to her voice and we started. She was back. The girl I knew, that unbelievably clear and focused singer, had returned. She laid it down, an awesome performance.

"Good," I said. "And curse me like that again, we're going to have a serious problem."

I didn't give a damn what LeToya's problem was. Short of a death in the family, neither I nor the music business would care. She needed to pull it together. New York was just as much her opportunity as it was anyone's. After a bit of research, I found out that one of LeToya's group sisters had slept with Brian. "Typical," I said to Tony. "He's like a sociopath." I then called LeToya and shared with her what I had heard about her boyfriend. "He and Brandon have been paid to keep you back."

"By who?"

"Guess."

The next day Brian called me, thirteen times. I never answered.

* * * * *

Our flight to New York left Hartsfield-Jackson Atlanta International airport on April 28th, 2002. Getting checked in was a hassle. Fans were coming from everywhere. "Do you girls finally see what I mean?" They'd been duped for years, and now they and their mothers were witness to the truth of their own popularity with the Destiny's Child fans.

I suggested that the girls' mothers lock arms with their daughters while walking through the airport. This worked. A red cap at Air Tran Airlines had all the luggage on his cart, so that all our hands and feet were free, just in case we needed to sprint to safety. Sure, some fans pushed their way into the girls' space, but nothing like what could've been had we done things differently. We had no budget for bodyguards or security. Creativity is what we could afford and so I used it to our advantage.

Finally, we had made it through control and were resting quietly at our gate. With more than one hour to spare, Pam, and I, and Tiffany's mother,

Celestine, relaxed into friendly chatter and laughter. Cheryl and LaTavia sat off to one side, by themselves. Strange, I thought, but nothing more.

Landing in New York, we found the limousine and car service drivers waiting just on the other side of baggage claim. Cheryl seemed put out. Was she really upset that the mothers were being asked to ride in chauffeur-driven Mercedes? So it seemed. Strange, I thought, but nothing more.

On our ride to the hotel, B2K called the girls on their cell phones. Friends from way back, the very successful R&B quartet had also flown in for the S2S birthday bash. Looking to me for approval, I nodded. Everything was set. "Of course, you guys can meet B2K," my eyes said. After the call ended, I begged their indulgence. "Just promise me you won't wear yourselves out, and for God's sake, don't stay out too late." They needed to remember why we were here. "We have early radio interviews." Almost in unison, they answered, "We know Daddy," then fell about laughing.

Jason Sky, the girls' stylist, was due to land later that afternoon, his message said. I replied that his car would be waiting outside baggage claim. He should call me if there were any problems. And then my telephone rang. It was Jillian, Jason's boss, and the shop owner who dressed the girls, calling to say that business was keeping her in Atlanta. I promised to call her after the performance, and our scheduled photo shoot with Devon. She wished us good luck and we ended the call.

"Thanks, Pam," I mouthed. She'd taken care of getting the girls checked in at the front desk while I was on the phone. Again, I noticed Cheryl, staring off in the distance. She looked troubled. This time, I went over to her. "Is everything all right?" I asked. "Can I help you in some way?"

"Oh, no. Nothing's wrong," she answered.

"Okay, well let me know if anything changes and I can be helpful." We all headed to our rooms – no suites this time – and I closed the door. A few moments of peace, I thought. Wrong. My telephone rang incessantly. Who are these people? I asked, and How in the hell did they get my number? I finally understood why music managers never answer their phones. I turned it off and lay down on the bed, falling off to sleep. I was exhausted.

The next morning, on April 29th, Pam and I had an early breakfast, and she thanked me for jumping in when the girls needed me.

"LeToya is in a much better place," she said.

"Yes, she is." I had recognized, already in 2001, at our initial lesson, that LeToya was suffering from existential depression. She was questioning life and its meaning, a classic symptom of the condition. Its debilitating effect on artists cannot be overestimated. I decided not to share with Pam that LeToya had cursed me out a couple days earlier. Pam still thought LeToya incapable of such behavior. Instead, I opted to close with, "Music is a powerful medicine." Pam agreed, and I moved on.

After breakfast, we headed out to the first radio interview, which Sheila Eldridge had also set up. It went off without a hitch. After the third one, which had been definitely explosive, we headed back into Manhattan from the New Jersey radio station. On the way, the girls were hungry. Seeing a McDonald's, our driver pulled off the highway and into the golden arches parking lot.

Cheryl opted to wait in the van, and I stayed with her. Something was bothering her. We could use the quiet to talk, I thought. Perhaps she was ready to tell me the truth, instead of always making herself scarce, standoffish. I was glad I did. She bared her soul. For the first time, I felt connected to Cheryl, spiritually. It didn't take long before we were talking about Charles, who she admitted had finally confessed. Tearfully, she shared with me her reaction to Charles's blaming LaTavia. "LaTavia was eight, Charles, eight fucking years old," she said she told him. "Tell me how an eight-year-old child can turn on a grown ass man?"

After a moment of choked silence, Cheryl was able to continue. Realizing that he'd been discovered, Charles tried to recant. When that didn't work, he threatened Cheryl. He and his cop cronies would take care of her, he told her. "Well, I guess I'd better watch out too then," I said. Then looking at Cheryl seriously, I said, "Fuck Charles, ain't nobody scared of his horrible ass."

I could see the girls coming back. "Thanks for the talk, Cheryl, and for your apology. It means the world."

"I owed it to you," she answered.

* * * * *

Devon Cass stood in front of my hotel room door on April 30th at 4:30 a.m. ready to make up the girls. As planned, at exactly 4:45, he began with LaTavia. I could always count on her to be on time. She and Devon hit it off immediately. Next in the chair was Nati, and then Tiffany. He ended the session with LeToya at 6:30 a.m., which gave us exactly thirty minutes before we had to leave. While Devon packed up, my hotel phone rang. It was the concierge. "Sir, the limousine is downstairs," he said. Calling each girl, I asked them to hurry. We'd meet in the lobby. "We can't be late," I reminded them.

To our annoyance, LeToya emerged from the elevator one minute before the limo was scheduled to leave. I gave her a look. "Sorry," she said. I prayed that morning traffic in Manhattan would smile on us. We were cutting it close, but we were on time.

The "Good Day New York" interviewer was very pleasant. While he chatted with the girls about how the show would run, I called Alan. BMG would be watching, he said. The head of A&R had just telephoned him at home. "OK," I said. "Great. I'll call you back. We are about to start soon and I have to turn off my phone."

We were up next, after commercial. At exactly 7:45, the host opened with, "Today you are not only in for a musical treat, but may I be so bold as to say, a visual treat as well." Anjel was fierce and everybody in that room knew it. Towards the end of what turned out to be a great interview, the host concluded with, "You guys must be thrilled, because you really have the stuff. You are poised and ready to launch." Then it was time to sing. Naturally they knocked it out of the park.

I was a proud papa.

As soon as the girls finished singing and "Good Day New York" cut to commercial, I left the room, switching on my phone. "Sheila, I'm out here if you need me." I said. Alan answered on the first ring. "Great news," he said. "BMG wants a sit-down as soon as possible, and are very interested in signing the girls. Congratulations!" he concluded. Elated, I thanked Alan. "I'll call you back once we get to the photography studio."

680

Devon's was our next stop. Jason called. I put him on speaker phone. "You guys were amazing," he said, and then he promised to jump in a taxi and meet us at Devon's eastside studio. I gave him the address once more, and hung up.

* * * * *

When Anjel arrived at the Puck Building, at 295 Lafayette St, the press went crazy. Apparently, they'd all seen my new girls on "Good Day New York." Photographers snapped what felt like hundreds of pictures on the red carpet. And journalists from various magazines and news organizations fired questions at them. "You girls are gorgeous," one reporter said. Another said that Anjel was going "to give Destiny's Child a run for their money." I couldn't have been happier, waiting to escort Anjel into the building. Suddenly the center of attention on that star-studded evening, Anjel was being greeted by guests at the S2S birthday bash. Everyone who was anybody in music, film, and entertainment law and journalism was there.

After getting Anjel settled in their dressing room, Devon, Jason, and a very pregnant girl named Elaine (our rented hair stylist for the day), got to work preparing the girls. Shevon, my student and friend, who had recorded for Rhino records, acted as the girls' chaperone. I was grateful that she'd been able to help, because LeToya and LaTavia knew her well. While Shevon dealt with keeping the girls' parents out of the dressing room, I set off to find our stage (there were three) and the designated soundman.

"What is this crap?" I asked our engineer. The sound board looked like a tinker toy, plastic and cheap. "This is not what we agreed upon."

"I just work here, sir," he said, and signaled the big boss to come over.

"What's the problem?" the man asked.

"Sir, I sent you a technical rider with all my requests. Here is *your email*, confirming receipt of the rider, and that I would have what I asked for. Do you see that?" I asked.

681

The man admitted that he'd written the email and then explained that there must have been a mix up. Apparently, the sounding board positioned at Stage II, where we were to perform, should've been set up for Stage III, and vice versa. "We will switch them right away," the boss said. "Please, give me half an hour."

I returned to my girls. Everything was fine, Shevon said. Thirty minutes later things escalated. The sound system, although bigger and more stable-looking, still sounded like shit.

"I'm sorry," I said. "This is not what I asked for. My girls won't be singing."

Just then, an assistant of the S2S magazine owner, Jaime Brown, passed by. Getting her attention, I asked her to pass on my regrets to Jaime, who was in the main hall celebrating. "The sound system isn't what I expected, ordered, or can accept. We are leaving."

"Wait a minute," the girl said, rushing off.

A minute later, Jaime was hugging me. "What's wrong, David?"

"Hi, Jaime," I said. "This sound system is the problem. I don't have faith that it will give us a powerful enough output to do even a good per-formance, let alone a stellar one. It's just too risky, on a night like tonight. Not to mention, I asked for cordless microphones, and they've given us four cord mics," I concluded.

Jaime asked me what she could do to rectify the problem. "We can get you the cordless mics," she said. The sound company boss corrected her. They didn't have enough. Additional cordless mics weren't part of the package deal S2S had negotiated.

"Not my problem," I quickly remarked.

"Wait, David. There must be a way!"

I called Roy Brown in Los Angeles. Completely ignoring the sound man, I passed my cell to the engineer. "If this man tells me that the sound system that you have presented me with is powerful enough to do the job, we'll sing. If not, no deal." Then, I headed off to my girls, who had been patiently waiting in the dressing room. It was already 11:15 or so. We should've been on stage performing at 11:00. "Girls, we may have to leave without singing," I said, explaining that the sound system wasn't right.

In just that minute, Jaime walked into the dressing room. After handing me my cell phone, she greeted the girls, and I talked to Roy. "Man, I was able to help increase the quality by 65%," he said, "but you're right. The sounding board is on the cheap side. Because I can't assess the noise factor, and the acoustic of the room, I won't be able to guarantee that the girls would come across powerfully."

I hung up, looking at Jaime. The look on my face was clear. We were cancelling. "I'm sorry," I said.

She really wanted the girls to sing. She'd talked them up in the magazine. "Please sing," she added. "For me?"

"Uh, Jaime, can you give us a few minutes?"

I gathered the girls around. "I know Jaime has been good to you guys, and it would be nice to sing, but in my professional opinion, it's too risky." LeToya asked, "Will we be embarrassed if we sing?" My answer was, "Absolutely not. It's just that the sound board can pump out only about 70% of the volume needed for you guys to be heard over the noise in the room. We've pushed it to its maximum. I think it's too big a risk."

After speaking amongst themselves, they decided to honor their commitment to Jaime.

"Okay, give me a minute," I said, reluctantly. "While I go do a sound check, you guys run through both songs. And adjust your choreography. Take out any forward movement. They don't have cordless mics. We can't have the cords getting tangled. And I think it's a good idea to use the TV tracks, complete with background vocals and ad libs. It will help fill in the sound at the chorus and bridge, just in case the audience gets too rowdy."

"No problem," LaTavia said. We'd practiced for this.

* * * * *

Anjel took the stage and the audience erupted, cheering them on. As soon as I sensed a perfect stillness, I cued the engineer.

The girls were sensational, hitting all their points. They were focused and had worked out the necessary changes in the choreography, only coming forward during solo lines. The rest they did in place, delivering convincingly enough to keep the audience's attention. We were OK. So far, so good, I thought. Just as I thought, the TV track at the chorus filled out the sound optimally.

Then, I noticed that LaTavia was drunk, not sloppy drunk, but definitely tipsy. When had she had time to drink? Where, I wondered? Realizing she had slowed down her solo line a bit, she kicked into gear. I spotted Cheryl, who stood under overhead lights, which illuminated a strong negative disposition coming off of her. Suddenly, she ran from the room, crying. Had LaTavia seen her, I wondered? Of course, she had. I only hoped that Cheryl's action wouldn't derail the performance. It didn't, thank God.

At the end of the first song the audience erupted. Devon, Shevon, Jason, and Elaine were clapping feverishly. I was taken back to Atlanta. It was déjà vu, all over again. Whistles and cheers reverberated from the audience. The girls called B2K on stage and signaled for the next song to start. They were on fire, loving every second.

Jaime was elated, blowing kisses. By the second song's end, she looked as though she could jump out of her skin from joy, hugging all the girls tightly. "You girls sang your butts off," she said. The sound system, although not great, had not embarrassed them. Thanks, Roy Brown! I thought. Still, not everyone was happy. Back at the hotel, trouble brewed.

* * * * *

Anger

After the S2S performance, I told the girls that I would meet them at the hotel as soon as I had finished up at the Puck building. Several music executives had approached me, giving me their cards. I hadn't heard one negative thing, which delighted me to no end. Even Brandon and Brian congratulated the girls, LaTavia had said. She'd called them after the performance to give them a report. It was truly a joyous atmosphere in the girls' dressing room. Nati's mother and family were close to tears, they were so proud. Even Frank Gatson, the choreographer for EnVogue and for Beyoncé, was complimentary. "David, you did it again. They sound amazing," he said. Then he insulted the choreographer Robin Dunn, who I wanted to bring on board as Anjel's choreographer, insinuating that she was incompetent. Was he angling for me to consider him? No way. He worked for Destiny's Child.

About 45 minutes after the girls had left, the limousine driver called me on my cell. He was outside. I asked Shevon to stay with me. We'd take her home first and them me, I told the driver. Then I called Pam, who was prepared to meet me in the hotel lobby so she could take care of the limo bill. "Just call me when you're close," she said.

In the lobby I ran into Jason. While Pam paid the driver, he and I talked. He said he'd enjoyed the performance. I asked him if he knew where the girls were, as I had good news for them. He answered, "They're all in LaTavia's room."

When Pam came back into the building, she went on and on about how beautiful the girls sounded. Heading to the elevators, we both thanked Jason for his work. "The girls looked amazing," Pam said.

"I think we're going to be seeing lots more of Jason in the future," I said.

He smiled, but said nothing.

Pam got off on her floor and Jason and I continued on to LaTavia's floor.

"Is everything all right?" I asked.

"I'll let the girls tell you," he said.

I didn't understand, but I didn't say another word. Talking to the stylist about group business wasn't exactly appropriate.

When I knocked on LaTavia's door, Nati answered it. As I rounded the short entryway, which led into the sleeping area of the room, the conversation stopped cold. "What's going on?" I asked.

I opened my mouth to ask another question and Cheryl exploded, cursing me out. She called me a mother fucker, a bastard, and even a son of a bitch. Stunned, I could only stand there with my mouth hanging open.

Then I saw it. An almost empty bottle of what looked to be E&J Brandy was sitting on the night table, near the bed. Apparently, Cheryl was outraged because the girls had embarrassed themselves with that "fucking awful performance." She swore that she hadn't been able to hear the girls.

Pulling myself together, I disagreed with Cheryl. I had just spent the last hours talking with music executives who thought differently. Did that mean nothing to Cheryl?

"Girls, are you going to listen seriously to this crap? You heard the audience's response." No one so much as moved. "Uh, Hello. Is everyone suddenly deaf?"

Then Cheryl got up from the bed and screamed in my face, "Fuck you, David. This mother fucking shit ain't gon go down like this, not this time. You ain't gon be running nothing up in here," she screamed. Her breath was atrocious. "Cheryl, you're drunk," I said, which upset her tipsy daughter. According to LaTavia, I'd cost them their chance for a deal.

"That's not true, girls. You decided to sing. I gave you guys the choice and I thought your reasoning was sound. Everyone I talked to loved your performance."

Cheryl started in again. "Shut the hell up, Cheryl," I yelled. She started to move towards me, but LaTavia grabbed her. Then LeToya said, "It's your job to protect us. Just look after us in the future, that's all I'm asking," she said.

"What are you talking about?" I said, whereupon Miss Luckett finished me off. "Mathew was a butt hole, but he would have never let us sing in that kind of situation," she said.

Had I heard correctly? LeToya?! the girl that Mathew had kicked out of Destiny's Child, was she defending her abuser? I took a deep breath. In fact, I took three.

With tears in my eyes, I said quietly. "Congratulations. BMG has offered you guys a deal."

I turned and headed for the door. Just before it closed, I could hear the girls screaming, and dancing around the room. They were happy, but they'd just lost their manager. Sure, I'd finish the deal, and they would pay me a finder's fee, but I was done. Comparing me to Mathew had been the last insult I could take. It was simply too much for me to bear.

The next morning, the mood was subdued, strained. Pam and I got everybody all checked out, and then we all got into our separate cars. Cheryl didn't look my way, and for everyone's sake I didn't look hers. On the ride to the airport, the air inside the limousine was thick. Tiffany tried to lighten the mood, but it was pointless. How do you come back from last night? I thought. I'm sure the girls were contemplating the same thing.

LaTavia apologized for her mother's behavior. I said nothing. Then she apologized for her own bad behavior. "Get some help," I said, looking her in the eyes. "Promise me." She promised.

I told the girls that after my concert in Berlin, on May 31st, I'd return to the U.S. for talks with BMG. "You girls will have to fly to New York at that time." The deal was safe. "I have an appointment to talk with the head of A&R next week from Germany." We pulled up to the Air Tran curbside service at LaGuardia Airport and checked our bags to Atlanta.

My flight back to Germany left on May 3rd in late afternoon, heading back to Frankfurt. I was anxious to get back home. Pam, who had stayed over with LeToya a couple days, met me at the airport. We sat together, talking and having a light snack. "You did it," Pam said. "No, we did it," I answered. "We are a team, nothing like our last situation." I sensed that Pam wanted to discuss what happened in LaTavia's room. I, however, did not. She didn't push me, and for that I was grateful. She reached inside her purse and pulled out a manila envelope. Inside was the production deal the girls had signed with Brandon and Brian. "Great, I look forward to delving into this on the plane," I said. "It's a long flight," I added. We stood up, giving one another a hug and then parted ways. "I'll call you in a couple days," I said. "And thank you, for all you do." Pam smiled.

On the flight home to Germany I began to read the production deal. It took me exactly fifteen seconds to realize that what I was reading was not a production deal, but rather a recording contract. Shit, what was I going to do? We couldn't sign a deal with BMG if the girls already were under a recording contract. This was a nightmare. I'd trusted my students, which was obviously an error in judgement. I'd had no reason not to believe what they told me.

Suddenly, a few pages of the contract fell out of my hand. I looked down, noticing the signature page, where clearly LeToya, LaTavia, and Nati had signed. Now, as I retrieved the pages from the floor, I saw an even more distressing document: a cover letter from Randy Bowman, who had unequivocally advised the girls against signing what he called an unserviceable contract. He had clearly informed them that they weren't signing a production deal, but rather a record deal.

Fuck, Fuck, Fuck….

The next day, Saturday, May 4th, my flight landed in Germany. When I walked into my apartment in Weimar, my phone's message light blinked. Alan had called. I should call him in the office on Monday about BMG.

I had a whole forty-eight hours to figure out what I was going to say. I'd been blindsided by this mess. Fearing for my reputation, all I could think about was BMG considering us to be unserious. Then I got angry. It was obvious that these girls and their parents, like so many in the music business, expected me to pull a fucking rabbit out of a hat. That's what good managers do, they say. We're supposed to put out fires, fix artist fuck-ups, constantly. This time I was going to be the one suffering the third-degree burns.

I wanted BMG badly, and only Alan and I knew why. BMG was the one label the Knowleses had no influence over. German-owned, the label had massive international reach and was a serious player in the U.S. market. Signing with them was best of both worlds. What was I going to say to Alan? He'd also put his reputation on the line.

I don't think I have ever been as nervous as I was on May 6th, Call Alan Day. I picked up the phone, calling his office at exactly 10:00 a.m. New York time.

"Hi Alan, it's David."

"Hey David, how was your flight?"

"It was great," I answered.

"So, you got my message about BMG?" Alan asked. "They are hot for Anjel. In all the years I've dealt with them, I've never seen them this excited about anyone."

"Yes, about that," I said. "We have a problem."

"Go on."

I told Alan the truth. I had trusted my girls and then I told him that I had screwed up royally. "I should've demanded they give me the contract sooner, but they were so sure they'd signed a production deal." But now here we stood, in quagmire. Alan assured me that our problem wasn't as bad as it seemed. "I understand that Brandon and Brian are the boyfriends of the two ousted members of Destiny's Child?" I answered that Alan was indeed correct. "OK," he said. "No worries. I'll give BMG a call and get back to you." I asked Alan what he was going to tell them. "The truth," he answered. "Don't worry," he added. "I'll get back to you in a day or so."

Immediately afterwards, I called LaTavia at home and asked if she could gather the girls together for a conference call, in about an hour. When I called back, I held on while each girl connected to the other over three-way calling, and then I talked, candidly.

"Girls, can you all explain to me why you guys would sign a recording contract with Brandon and Brian?"

The silence was broken by Tiffany.

"I haven't signed anything," she said.

I told her that I knew that, "Please don't sign anything with those jerks. That you haven't signed might be our silver lining. Brandon and Brian couldn't sell hot butter."

"For the life of me, I can't figure out why in the hell you guys would sign with those losers. They don't even have distribution, and from what I hear they ain't getting it. And without it, they can't move one CD you'd record. And they call themselves a record label – what a fucking joke."

Nobody said a word.

LeToya asked, "So, what do you suggest we do?"

689

I told her to sit tight, do nothing. "Don't talk to anyone." I had Alan on the case. "Alan and I just talked. He's just put in a call to BMG and will get back to me in a day or so. We will figure a way out of this damned mess."

No one spoke. We ended the call.

A couple minutes after hanging up, I called LaTavia back. She hadn't said a word during the conference call, which I took to mean that she didn't agree with what I had to say about her boyfriend. However, I needed her to understand that her "man" had not been looking out for her. He did not have her best interest at heart. I did. My God, how many times I've heard the horror stories of women who trusted their "boyfriends" in this business. You could write a book, full of sob stories.

Suddenly, Brandon picked up the phone. "Hey, David, this is Brandon. Did you say that the girls shouldn't have signed with us and that we were losers?"

Swallowing hard, I quickly denied it, saying, "No, I didn't." Brandon repeated his question. Once again, I denied it, feeling trapped. I couldn't take it back. Wait, yes I could, I thought. I didn't care for Brandon and Brian Casey. Just as I was about to confess my sin, LaTavia stunned me, screaming, "David, you are exactly what my mother said you were – a fucking liar."

"Excuse me?"

"You are a fucking liar and I trusted you. Brandon was on the phone listening to our conversation the whole time."

I lost it. "LaTavia, why would you do such a thing?"

"I wanted to prove everybody wrong and show them that you were honest."

I admitted that I shouldn't have lied, but she'd put me in an impossible situation. Then I asked, "Brandon, are you still there?" He said that he was. "Great," I said. With LaTavia still listening, I asked, "Brandon do you want what's best for LaTavia?" He swore total allegiance to her and said that he would never stand in the way of her dreams. "Well, that's good to know, because I'm close to finding a solution that will suit everyone, and it sure would help LaTavia if you stood by the words you just spoke."

LaTavia slammed down the phone.

I called the other girls immediately, who were shocked by what their bandmate had done. She had seriously jeopardized the group's future. LeToya promised to talk to her, to try and talk some sense into her. Then I reached out to LaTavia again, three times. The third time was a charm. She answered. "LaTavia, I can't believe that…" She stopped me. "Why did you lie?" she asked. "Isn't it obvious?" I answered. LaTavia said that I had hurt her. "Excuse me?" I said. "I hurt you?" I couldn't believe my ears. "I love you and have only ever fought for your well-being." I tried to protect her. "I know," LaTavia answered. "That's what makes this so difficult." And with that she hung up on me again.

Alan called me the next day. "Great news!" He told me that after talking amongst themselves, A&R at BMG New York wanted the girls. They were willing to discuss buying the Casey twins out of their contract, and were open to talking about keeping the boys connected to the project as producers. I shared with Alan that such a move could cost up to a million dollars with these boys. Alan's response was, "Hey, what can I say. They want the girls." It was indeed great news. Unexpected and fantastic fucking news.

I called the girls, unable to reach LaTavia. "BMG is willing to buy the boys out of their contract, and Alan was able to get them to agree to talk about the boys staying on board as your producers on the album." They were ecstatic.

When I called Brandon on his cell, he didn't answer. I then called Brian. I explained that BMG wanted the girls, offering to buy out the Casey contract and keep the boys on as producers.

"Oh, really," Brian said.

"Yep," I answered. "I'm not shitting you."

"We'll just see about that," Brian said, and then he hung up in my ear.

The deal of a lifetime had just fallen apart. Embarrassed beyond belief, I'd eventually come to terms with LaTavia's stupid behaviors, but it would take many years. I would never lay eyes on her again. Nor on LeToya.

Shortly after the deal fell apart, Brandon left LaTavia. "Tragic?" I thought. "Typical."

Some allegiance.

Right:
This publicity shot of Anjel resulted from the photo session with Devon Cass during that ill-fated week when Anjel performed at the *Sister2Sister* magazine birthday celebration in New York City. From the floor up: LeToya Luckett, Tiffany Beaudoin-Walton, LaTavia Roberson, and Nativida "Nati" Quinones-Jones
Photo: Devon Cass Photography NYC

When Anjel arrived for their performance at the *Sister2Sister* magazine birthday celebration, we discovered that the contractually guaranteed sound system had not been provided. I discussed the situation with LeToya (right, in pink) in the presence of my surrogate sister Shevon Jacobs-Loftin (middle, in black), a former Rhino records recording artist
Photo: Devon Cass Photography, NYC

Anjel surrounds me immediately after their performance at the 13th annual birthday celebration for Sister2Sister magazine, April 30, 2002, in New York City. They were sensational.

Anjel performed at the 2002 birthday celebration of *Sister2Sister* magazine. *Photos: Devon Cass Photography NYC*

31. Nothing changes until it changes

The Velodrom
Berlin, June 1, 2002

"No one is allowed to touch Beyoncé!"

I hadn't expected to hear those words. Just whose idea had it been to have Beyoncé's isolation secured by such a peculiar phrase? Strange, I thought. I was being ushered into a room where Beyoncé, Kelly, and Michelle Williams (I was looking forward to meeting her) were greeting a select group of their fans. As I entered the room, they were signing autographs and posing for pictures. While some asked for group photos with Destiny's Child, most wanted to take pictures with Beyoncé. Very few requested individual pictures with Kelly, or with Michelle, who was eyeing me conspicuously from the side. And guess what? No one was touching Beyoncé, who, in my opinion, either was high on marijuana or she had taken some very, very strong medication. Her highness was unmistakably lit.

"Hello, David," Beyoncé said. "What are you doing here?"

"I live here," I answered. "In Germany." I told Beyoncé that I'd had a performance in Berlin the night before and decided to stay over to see their concert.

Genuinely surprised, Beyoncé said she hadn't heard. Her parents certainly knew, I thought. I'd called Celestine at the salon to give her my new Weimar telephone number. Still, Beyoncé's reaction was the confirmation of a suspicion I'd been harboring for some time. She and Kelly had never received even one of the letters or the birthday cards I'd sent.

Suddenly, Michelle interrupted. "Oh, you're David. I have heard so many wonderful things about you."

"Really....?"

"Yes, and please forgive me," she said. "I didn't mean to interrupt." She concluded with, "I'm Michelle," stretching out her hand.

"Nice to meet you, Michelle." Then I added, brazenly, "Why, you are even prettier than your pictures. They don't do you justice."

Slightly embarrassed, Michelle smiled and thanked me. And then Beyoncé called out to Kelly, who hadn't even looked my way. Upon receiving Beyoncé's disapproving look, Miss Kelly acquiesced.

"Hi, David," she said, dry as a powder keg.

Hugging me seemed to be a great imposition. Poor thing, I thought. What the hell was her problem? Quickly, I turned my attention back to the more pleasant Michelle. "How are you liking being in Destiny's Child?"

"I'm loving it. It's a lot of hard work, but I love it."

"Boy, don't I know it," I answered.

Suddenly, the girls' tour manager stepped into the room. "It's time," he said, pointing to his watch. I asked Beyoncé if I could leave my small bag with her crew and pick it up after the concert. I didn't want to schlepp it through the concert venue. To my left, I could see the tour manger shaking his big head. However, Beyoncé agreed, saying yes. Some flunky or other moved in my direction, took my bag, and disappeared from my view almost as fast as I'd asked the question.

"You can pick it up at the artist entrance – after the show," the tour manager said.

"Sure thing."

Making my way into the Velodrom, I observed the Destiny's Child crowd. From my seat, I allowed my thoughts to wander over the years that had led up to this moment – from hearing tiny Beyoncé for the first time, to now, in this large hall, aquiver with the anticipation of thousands of fans. The dimming lights interrupted my reminiscing, and as the music began, the spotlight shone onto a young girl. I recognized that voice, the way it excited and then disappointed. It was Solange. She was opening for her sister – and her "damn group."

Solange and two dancers, Destiny's Child's opening act, worked hard to entertain the crowd, singing to playback. No special lights, no anything. Just the three of them, all alone on that big ole stage. The songs were, I realized, merely OK. Sad, I thought. Although she was undeniably talented, Solange hadn't grown vocally or artistically, not even a little bit. Naturally, I thought of Celestine and her stubborn refusal to allow her younger daughter even a fraction of the training that she considered the birthright of her older daughter.

With the crowd now awaiting the entrance of Destiny's Child, Beyoncé's voice rang through the concert hall. Just as I remembered, she had started singing backstage, unseen. Her fans went wild. She set the tone for the entire concert, an energy-packed entertainment, beautiful to the eye as well as to the ear. I noted, with satisfaction, that it was all worth the price of admission.

Beyoncé had kept every aspect of our work together intact, even the drag queen sparkle I'd worked into the fabric of her performance during the last years. (I had studied the craftsmanship of a local Houston drag artist named Corwin Hawkins, a.k.a., Amazing Grace, and had passed on aspects of his brilliant performances to Beyoncé. She can thank the performer named "Amazing Grace" for the hair-blowing fan that became one of her signatures.)

My sole disappointment with the evening was Kelly. Her voice never emerged from its hiding place, and her performance was lackluster. Was it her new teacher, or had Kelly slipped back into that deep emotional trap from her childhood? Praise the Lord, it was not my problem now.

After the last song I made my way backstage. My access was relatively easy, because I knew the Velodrom management from my having been there so many times with my German star singers. I was certainly no threat. "Of course," security said, letting me through the barrier, and the supervisor who gave his permission remembered my fervent pre-concert conversation with Destiny's Child in the greenroom.

I came to the stage entrance and exit area just as Kelly was coming off with some of the male dancers. Seeing me, she quickly slowed down. Suddenly, she hit one of the dancers over the head and took off running. Naturally, he followed suit, and the two of them ran right past me. Twelve years ago, I had hesitated taking Kelly on for free, but I'd so believed in her sweetness and in her talent. Now, in 2002, her former gratitude had turned to contempt. Ms. Kelly was a Star! One who, but for me, would still be living in a car. Or had her surrogate "father" so poisoned her young mind against me? These confused thoughts flashed through my mind as I watched her disappear round a corner.

My momentary disappointment was replaced by the pleasure of encountering Michelle as she came off the stage. Obviously embarrassed by her bandmate's behavior, she stopped, looked me square in the eye, and shook my hand. "It was very nice to meet you, David," she said. "And you too, Michelle. Congratulations!" What character, I thought. Above and beyond all else, I could see that Tenitra Michelle Williams had been raised well. I was grateful for her impeccable manners.

I could see Beyoncé in the distance, giving orders, verbally handling some poor man in the backstage crew. As she started down the hallway in my direction, accompanied by her massive body guard, her eyes fixed on me. I had read about "Big Shorty" in magazine articles. Standing 6 feet 6 inches tall and weighing at least 400 plus pounds, he cut quite a menacing figure. The distance between Beyoncé and me was closing when Big Shorty said, "Step Back!"

I looked at Beyoncé, perplexed. Was I dreaming? Wasn't she going to tell him that I was no threat to her?

Absolutely not. She just stood there, a smile painted on her face, falsely effervescent. Had she just dissociated? Of course, she had. Having to look around Big Shorty's massive frame even to make eye contact, I congratulated her on a great concert.

"Thank you," she said.

Big Shorty repositioned himself, allowing for a face-to-face conversation.

"I'm glad to hear that you've kept up your technique."

"Thank you," Beyoncé answered.

Stretching out my left hand, which prompted a reaction from Big Shorty, I said, "It was a pleasure to have been chosen to develop that throat of yours."

Again, Beyoncé said, "Thank you."

"My God, what have they done to you?"

"Thank you," she answered.

I was done. "Excuse me, Big Shorty," I said. "Where can I find my suitcase?"

"Down that hallway and to the left." He added, "It's in the production office at the end of the hall. You can't miss it."

"So, you know exactly who I am," I said.

Big Shorty just smiled.

I could see that Beyoncé remained standing there with her father's shit-eating grin plastered on her face. Stunned into silence, I took my leave of her empty shell.

Once I'd gotten out of view, I stopped. "Breathe, David. Calm down!" I said to myself. It took a minutes before I could continue. In my confused state, I suddenly doubted my whereabouts. Had I made a wrong turn? Shaking, I had to stop again. I was so angry, I felt as though I might be having a heart attack. Then, I saw my suitcase. As if through a muffled screen, I could hear a girl's voice. Oblivious to just about everything, I entered the room. Suddenly, I heard a yelp, which helped to pull me back into reality. The young girl I'd heard was jumping into my arms, scream-ing, "David. Oh, my God, David...."

It was Solange.

"It's so good to see you!"

Hugging her warmly, I started to come back to myself.

"How are you, Solange?"

"Good," she answered. Then, in typical Solange Knowles style, she came right out with it. "How was my performance?"

Fighting back tears, I managed to say, "It was good, Solange."

"Are you all right?" she asked.

I couldn't answer her, or maybe I did.

"What happened?" she asked.

"Oh, it's nothing. What have you been up to?" Solange deserved my full attention. She was not Beyoncé.

Oddly, it was in this moment that I realized my first real truth on the road back to me – Relationship. Relationship remembers. It feels like family. It is not judgmental, nor hurtful. And it never ignores, nor deval-ues. Had I not had real relationships with my girls? Solange considered me family. She had expected nothing, appreciated everything, and unlike her sister, she loved me back.

I wished her luck and took my leave.

* * * * *

March 12, 2003

In my Weimar studio, I was working with one of my American voice students, David Young. An operatic bass, David had been selected to sing in the regional rounds of the Metropolitan Opera National Council Awards auditions, in Kansas City, Missouri. He had just finished his lesson when the mobile telephone I loan all my students began to ring. David answered it, and then handed it to me. "It's for you." I thought surely that he hadn't heard correctly. Who could be calling me on this phone? I hadn't used the number for myself in at least two years. I asked him, under my breath, if he knew who was calling and he said "VH1." I took the phone and answered quickly with a resounding Hello!

"Hello! am I speaking with David Lee Brewer?" inquired the young woman on the other end of the phone.

"Yes."

"Hi! my name is Jessica Paul and I am one of the producers for VH1's tribute show 'Driven,' have you heard of it" she asked.

"Yes, I have. How can I help you, Jessica?"

Jessica told me that she was calling because VH1 was doing a show on Beyoncé. It would be called "Beyoncé Driven" and they wanted to know if they could interview me.

"I live in Germany," I answered.

"That's not a problem. We are prepared to send a camera team." Jessica then said that Beyoncé had told her during their conceptual talks, that if they were going to do a serious story about her life, they should really call David Brewer. Jessica's words shook me. "Beyoncé told me that you are probably the most influential in terms of her artistry and singing."

701

"Excuse me?" I said. As if yesterday, I remember my astonishment. I was dumfounded and emotional all at the same time. After that backstage fiasco in Berlin, I had come to believe that Beyoncé had no feelings about our work together, at all. Had she come to her senses? Now I was hearing from this television producer, a complete stranger, that those years had meant something to her. Perhaps, I'd been wrong about her. Had I just become that teacher who after many years hears from a grateful student?

"I'd be delighted to do the interview," I said.

"Great! that is exactly what I like to hear," Jessica answered. "I'll get back to you with a date we can have our camera team there."

"That won't – won't be necessary," I said. "By chance, I'm flying to New York City in the morning for performances at New York City Opera and will land at JFK tomorrow." (I was flying into the U.S. to sing the Philip Glass opera *O Corvo Branco*, which I had premiered in Lisbon at the Expo in 1998. Sung in Portuguese, performances would be at the New York City Opera under the auspices of The Lincoln Center Festival.) "I arrive on Wednesday, March 12th. Perhaps we can meet Thursday or Friday?"

"Friday would be perfect," Jessica answered. We agreed on a 1:30 meeting time.

I slept fitfully that night – if at all. I tossed and turned, tip-toed past the spare bedroom where David Young was sleeping, made several trips to the kitchen (eating all the chocolate I had in the house, even helping myself to David's), read several magazines and articles about opera, and finally used the time to answer fan requests for pictures and autographs. That call from VH1 had completely unnerved me. I kept telling myself, while pacing throughout the apartment, that everything would be great. Regardless of my most valiant efforts, I was completely undone.

The next morning David and I took a train from Weimar to Frankfurt, where our flight was scheduled to depart from the International Airport. On the train to Frankfurt David asked, "Are you going to be all right?"

"I'm sorry?" I said.

"Last evening – you didn't sleep much," he said, laughing. "At one point I thought I heard you take a shower. That was about 4:30 a.m."

I could only laugh.

Our plane touched down on time in New York at John F. Kennedy airport around 15:30. I wished David good luck with the Met auditions, and he went off to his connecting flight for South Carolina.

I gathered my luggage and headed for the exit. A driver awaited to drive me to the apartment that the Lincoln Center Festival had rented for me. On the way, I called Jessica.

"I'm in New York," I said.

"Great, I look forward to meeting you on Friday."

Then I called Shevon to confirm our dinner reservation for Thursday evening at Dallas BBQ on West 42nd.

I remember that the chilly weather on the day of the interview called for my brown turtleneck sweater and a heavy tweed jacket. I arrived at the VH1 offices and was quickly taken to Jessica Paul. We had a very pleasant conversation and she thanked me for coming in. "It's such a pleasure to meet you," she said. Beyoncé had told her so many wonderful things about me, she added.

Could I trust what Jessica was telling me? I smiled. I was longing to ask her, "What wonderful things?" but instead I replied, "Beyoncé is an extraordinary performer." I was trying hard to stay on neutral ground. Then Jessica and I talked about what kind of student Beyoncé had been, and she got me to reminisce about my favorite memories as well as the worst ones.

Presently, another young woman, also named Jessica, entered the office. Jessica Number 2 would be conducting the on-air interview together with a young woman whose name I do not remember. They had been busy setting up the interviewing studio while Jessica Paul and I visited. They were now ready.

They guided me down a long hallway into a room that had a stool placed strategically in front of a black box-shaped backdrop, which enclosed the interviewee for a tight picture. Before beginning, they showed me some of the footage they'd gotten from Mathew, who had even sent Daryl's Atlanta Showcase footage. There I was, in most every frame, clearly visible. "Now we know it's you," the other woman said. "Yes, we thought that it might have been you," Jessica 2 said, "but weren't sure." She added, "You were the only one the management did not identify." Silencing my inner annoyance, I said nothing. Then we started the interview.

The questions ranged from singing to the split up of Beyoncé's parents. They asked me to describe working with the girls, how they got along, and who was the best student in my opinion. They asked me about everything imaginable about my work with the girls, my teaching, their talents. They did not ask me about Mathew's drug abuse, the physical and sexual abuse, or the lies and deceit. Not one question was asked about Celestine. That was a relief to me. I simply answered the questions they asked. Until...

They began to pry into Mathew's state of mind during the group's break-up. I preferred to side-step the issue, as their line of questioning felt inappropriate. Nevertheless, they pressed the subject.

"Mathew is not a person who tends to care what others think," I said. "He is and has always been a person who makes his decisions based on his desires alone. He has his own mind and formulates his own opinions, about everything, whether accurate or not. I can't imagine that he was sorry for firing Letoya and LaTavia – not for one minute." I concluded.

"Firing?"

"Of course. The girls were set up. LeToya and LaTavia never left the group. They asked for a personal manager, which was their right by law. They wanted someone who would look out for their financial well-being, just as anyone would do in their position."

Jessica 2's eyes lit up. Apparently this was what they had been waiting, hoping, and priming me for in our 3 ½-hour interview. I told them that I knew for sure that the girls were unfairly handled, but that it was spilt milk. I pushed to move on, saying that I was there to talk about Beyoncé, and that was an honor.

Jessica 2 and the other woman obliged. At the end of that long interview Jessica 2 said to me, "You were definitely there. Your interview has been the most in-depth and complete interview that we have ever shot, on any star." "Everyone's always so superficial," the other woman said.

On May 18, 2003, when VH1's "Beyoncé Driven" aired, I was not in one single frame of the footage, nor was there one snippet of the long interview I had given.

I finally reached Jessica Paul via telephone. After some discussion, she confessed that "management" had expressed outrage. She said that Mathew had threatened to pull the entire "Beyoncé Driven" documentary if they aired one frame of my face.

I thanked Jessica for her candor and hung up. Yet again, I felt devastated.

Several months later, my telephone rang in Berlin. This time a producer for the BBC (British Broadcasting Corporation) was reaching out, saying, "Mr. Brewer, we'd like to interview you for a documentary about Beyoncé." Once again, I was told that Beyoncé had made the request. A few weeks later, they called back. "Unfortunately, the BBC won't be able to include you in our interview about Beyoncé."

Apparently, her management was against the idea.

* * * * *

Cannes, France
May 19, 2006

At exactly 5 o'clock one late afternoon I awaited the imminent arrival of Cindy Bao, a Chinese singer from Beijing. Her ex-husband, Xiaoqiu Huang, a renowned Chinese composer and producer, had arranged everything. Fascinated with Beyoncé and her way of singing, Cindy had wanted to study with the same voice teacher, if only she could find him, or her. She had been searching unsuccessfully for the mystery teacher. My then business partner, who happened to be sitting directly across from Xiaoqiu in Beijing, learned of the wife's dilemma, jotted my telephone number down, and handed it to an astonished Cindy. Xiaoqiu phoned me at once. He and Cindy could fly into Cannes to sing for me. It would take some doing (getting the visas), he said, but "It should be no problem."

The audition took place in my suite at the Hotel Martinez, which overlooked the Mediterranean. Elegant and exacting, Cindy walked in assured. She knew what she wanted. "I want to go outside of my Beijing borders," she said through her husband, who acted as our translator. I was intrigued with this gorgeous girl. I couldn't wait to hear her sing. "We'd better get started. Dinner is scheduled for 18 o'clock," I said.

Her self-assurance melted as she began, nervously, to sing for me. Although she'd never sung in English before, her voice was ravishingly beautiful. The sound was individual, very warm and voluptuous. She sang the song "Vincent." Confident that I could help her, I accepted her invitation.

"I'd be delighted to work with you."

"Thank you very much. I am very happy," she said in heavily accented English, and without her husband's help.

After Cindy, Xiaoqiu, and I had dined together, I strolled back to the Hotel Martinez. On the way, I saw that the Palais des Festivals et des Congrès, Cannes (at the city center's convention center), was lit up, and that there were huge crowds. I didn't give it a second thought. Here in Cannes, home of the famous Cannes film festival, there was always something going on, some red-carpet event, some lit-up building, and heavy crowds were a common sight.

When I reached the hotel, I was met by even larger crowds of people, roped off and snapping photos galore. Just as I'd made my way to the hotel entrance, I heard some photographer say, "Beyoncé, turn this way!" Had I heard correctly? I had. I turned just in time to see my former student get out of a car and step onto the red carpet. While she signed autographs, I entered the hotel, consciously hiding myself in the crowd of guests and party goers. Apparently, the American film Dreamgirls had just had its French premiere at the Palais des Festivals et des Congrès and the after-party was being held at the Hotel Martinez. From what I could tell, the entire cast was there.

For a few minutes I was able to observe Beyoncé. She looked gorgeous in her powder blue chiffon halter-top gown, with what looked like a bird motif print. Her hair had been coiffed into a pullback look, with bangs and

706

a French twist pony tail. She wore triangular tear-drop earrings, trimmed in diamonds, with a stone that I didn't recognize. Her make-up was flawless and her skin glistened.

As she was being whisked away, Beyoncé and I made eye contact. In that moment, I had a sudden vision of the young, confused Beyoncé who had turned to food for solace, and I smiled at how far she'd come.

I remembered her years of worry about the stability of her parents' marriage, how she would confide in me her fears that they might divorce. Beyoncé had valiantly fought the panic voices in her head that told her that she'd lose everything, even her friends. She turned to food, comforting herself with unrestricted eating. Even after having just had a snack or dinner, she would continue to eat.

My worst memory was the day I found Beyoncé, with her head in the refrigerator, stuffing her face with whatever she could find. That particular time it was chocolate cake. From that day on I had doubled down on my efforts to teach her the importance of self-preservation, of thinking first about her own well-being. She had listened closely.

I still felt that nurturing her talent was worth every horrible day and night I'd suffered while living in her parents' house. Those self-care lessons were some of the hardest she had to learn. Now, in May 2006, at the Côte d'Azur, I was witness to the stunning results of her efforts.

Two months later, Carter Freeman, a longtime friend from Houston, then living in Munich, gave me a photo on my July birthday. I'd known Carter for years. His parents, Professor Dr. Thomas Freeman, one of the most prolific in his field of communications, and his wife, Clarice Freeman, lived on the corner just steps away from Beyoncé's childhood home on Parkwood. The picture gave me goosebumps. In it a seven-year-old Beyoncé Knowles was singing, microphone in hand, mouth wide open. She wore the same black patent leather shoes and white socks, and the dress with puffy shoulders and ruffles at the hem, that she'd worn at her audition with me in 1989. I treasured that gift, and the memory.

I felt like teaching again.

* * * * *

In 2004 I wrote a project for television called "The BRICS." A multi-generational and multi-national live action reality series about the making of the first ever multi-cultural and international girl band, it was a massive undertaking. My goal was to choose one girl from Brazil, Russia, India, and China to create a new International Supergroup, something to top what I'd done with Destiny's Child. I would train four young female singers in the Entertainment Capital of the World, Los Angeles, and guide them as professional performers and multi-platinum recording artists.

I worked hard to get my unique project up and running, and I was having success. Major television stations Globo TV (Brazil), MUZ-TV (Russia), STAR TV (India), and Shanghai TV (China), would all come on board by 2008. Before announcing the project, I'd decided to test my theory, see what worked and what didn't. To that end, I developed Master Class Berlin, 2007. In this class, I would take ten students from Hamburg, twelve from Munich, four from Hannover (Classical), and fourteen from Berlin. Traveling between cities, I would teach the lessons and prepare the singers for the monthly live performance in Berlin. Performing with a live band in a real club would give them their practical experience. My first step would be to find and audition the talent. Advertisements would hang in the underground train stations and be positioned at local bus shelters, all over Berlin.

I called the radio station Jam FM, Germany's biggest R&B/Pop station. They got on board right away, doing a special promotion to help get the word out. Even RBB television got involved. I couldn't have been more excited. God seemed to be smiling on me. Everything I touched in 2007 turned to gold. I was deeply humbled.

Then, the radio station's program director, a woman named Ina, had a great idea. She told me she'd like to interview one of my star students, on air. I swallowed hard and said, "Well, she's very busy these days, but I'll give you the direct telephone number to Mathew Knowles, Beyoncé's manager." Ina laughed.

"No, we don't want to interview Beyoncé," she answered.

Surprised, I asked "Well, who then?"

"LeToya Luckett," Ina said. They wanted to interview LeToya Luckett, whose 2006 solo album on the Capitol Records label had gone to Number One in America, selling more than 170,000 copies the first day. Now it was picking up momentum in Germany. LeToya had taken back her power, walking away from LaTavia and the Casey twins, never to look back. She'd learned.

Ina loved the album and LeToya's voice. She felt that LeToya had gotten a bum deal with the whole Destiny's Child breakup.

Pleasantly surprised, I put Ina's team in touch with Pam, who was LeToya's primary manager. The two parties started conversations. Pam immediately checked with LeToya, who, I understood, accepted the offer. After all, Jam FM was not only the biggest German R&B Soul/Pop station, but the DJ who would interview LeToya was as big as Tom Joyner in the U.S. To say it was a big deal would be an understatement. Artists would kill for the opportunity German radio was handing LeToya.

Next, Pam asked Ina for the proposed questions. Pam and I spoke frequently, and I gathered that everything was going well. They settled on a date for the interview. "I've given them the telephone number so they can reach LeToya," Pam told me.

All week long the station hyped the interview. In addition, Ina had put LeToya's single, "Torn," in rotation. Things couldn't have been more positive.

I had my radio on when the DJ announced that the big moment had come. LeToya Luckett was about to speak to Germany. Sounds of dialing the number. LeToya's phone rang, and rang, and rang. No answer. They called again. Dialing sounds. Phone ringing sounds. Same thing. The DJ made a joke, and went to station break.

You could've bought me for a peso. The whole situation was very embarrassing.

Suddenly my telephone rang. It was Tresor Pembele, who passed me on to the DJ. "What the hell is going on?" he asked me. In good German, I said, "I'm not sure. Let me call her mother." I clicked over, patching Pam in on a three-way conversation. Now we were all on the air.

A bit nervous, I asked Pam, point blank, "Where's LeToya? She's not answering her phone. The station is live, on air, trying to call her." Pam's answered stunned me, infuriated the DJ, and mystified the station's listeners. "Oh," said Pam, "she's moving today." Miss LeToya Luckett had just snubbed Germany's biggest DJ while the whole country was listening. Needless to say, LeToya was taken out of rotation.

This time I had not let her highness compromise my reputation. I would like to have apologized to Pam for outing her daughter, but this experience finally awakened me. LeToya Luckett was the one who owed the apology – to me, to her mother, to Ina, to her erstwhile fans. What is it they say? "Experience makes the best teacher!"

* * * * *

Learning that Beyoncé would be singing at O2 Arena in Berlin on Mother's Day, May 13, 2007, I decided to take my twelve-year-old student Benjamin Isakow and his mother, Irma Isakow, to the performance. It was still a bit chilly in Berlin, so before heading out the door, I took my leather jacket from the closet. Spying Carter's gift picture on the hall table, I tucked it into my pocket, set on getting Beyoncé to autograph it for me.

Benjamin Isakow had become my pupil as a ten-year-old who had stars in his eyes. Within two years he had been featured in a documentary about me and my work, and had sung before a paying public. The television loved him, as his charming personality communicated directly to the viewers' hearts. He especially loved two artists: Beyoncé and Michael Bublé. What better gift could I give my young pupil than to introduce him directly to his idol?

After Beyoncé's concert, which had thrilled Benjamin, I expected that we would have to pass inspection by Shorty-her-bodyguard. But, no. This time Papa Mathew Knowles himself escorted us to the dressing room area.

When we entered the room, her dresser was removing Beyoncé's wig and making repairs to her dress, which she had inadvertently ripped during the concert. Mama Celestine stood against the wall. Our eyes met and I greeted her respectfully. I wasn't there to see her or Mathew. I had come to talk to my student.

I intended to set the record straight. I had thought I was beyond caring, but I had every intention of explaining to Beyoncé that I had agreed to media interviews with honorable intentions. Yes, I had indeed done the VH1 interview and agreed to the BBC interview. My words and time had been wasted. To my great sorrow, her parents had erased me from her history.

Benjamin, of course, was awe-struck and nearly speechless, thrilled to be meeting a superstar. It was an emotional moment for him. Hell, it was an emotional moment for me. I could still see the twelve-year-old Beyoncé, who years earlier had been in Benjamin's place. Now, there she stood before me, the embodiment of all I had worked and hoped for her. They were calling her an icon, and I was proud. Her parents couldn't rob me of that.

Leaning in, I murmured to Beyoncé that I would like to talk with her. Suddenly Celestine interrupted our conversation. "I haven't seen your mama in years. How is she doing?" Annoyed at this mock show of interest in my mother, I said to Celestine, "Married." Turning my attention once again to Beyoncé, I saw Celestine step closer. No longer attached to the wall, she planted herself in between Beyoncé and me. Beyoncé became nervous. I was furious.

Seeing me whisper in Beyoncé's ear, Celestine had assumed the worst. To avoid a scene, I pulled my business card from my pocket in order to slip Beyoncé my contact information. I had written my telephone number on it, just in case we might have our talk in private. I had so much I wanted to say to her, to set right with her. I could see that her mother was determined to prevent a real conversation. During my entire dressing room visit Celestine never once asked how I was doing, or what I was doing. No courteous conversation. Her main goal was to butt in and distract.

Celestine's intrusion set off emotional alarm bells. A whole set of unresolved issues that I had with her and her husband flooded my mind and heart in that moment. I knew that Beyoncé would have told them that she'd seen me in 2001, 2003, and 2005, and I also knew that they would have received the information with increasing antipathy toward me.

What a career mine had become. Leading a full life of singing, performing, and teaching – in my studio, in concert and opera, on television. I had continued giving of myself to my students and my art. Still, I missed Beyoncé and indeed all the girls in Destiny's Child, and Celestine sensed it. She'd warned me. Her look said, You chose to have your career, now what the hell do you want? But I had done nothing of the sort. What I'd chosen was freedom from her. My career had never gotten in the way of my obligation to my girls, not once.

For seven years I had cautioned myself, fearing that I might not – ever – be able to talk to Beyoncé. I'd had an earnest, and appropriate, desire to redress balance in our student-teacher relationship. I cared about her. I finally recognized that Beyoncé's parents had always been self-serving. Now, in 2007, at this moment, all I wanted was to clear the air. Beyoncé's parents had gotten away with lying long enough.

I decided to take the high road. I'd say nothing. Fighting Celestine was no longer worth it. She stayed at the ready, always poised to cut off any unwanted exchange with her daughter. Suddenly, Mathew re-entered the room. Celestine gave him that look. I had seen it many a time. It broadcast danger. I hadn't come to cause a scene. It wasn't my nature. But now they both assumed the position, protecting their interest with single-minded purpose. In that instant, I knew that this was the end of the road for me and Beyoncé. And I wasn't sure if it mattered any more. I turned to Benjamin.

"Bist du bereit?" I asked. [Are you ready?]

"Uh...Yes..."

It was time to go.

Suddenly, putting both of her hands on Benjamin's shoulders, Beyoncé leaned down and in toward him so that they were at eye level. The hair on the back of my neck stood up. I'd done exactly that same thing with her at our first meeting.

"How old are you?" she asked sweetly.

Innocent of the negative energy between myself and Beyoncé's parents, Benjamin said, "I am twelve years old."

Beyoncé became emotional and glanced up at me. We said nothing, but I could see into her soul. The girl I knew and loved was still in there. I saw her. Now a superstar, she'd realized my perfect vision and her dreams. Right in front of her stood her younger self in Benjamin Isakow. He was smart, talented, and twelve, just as she had been when I took her backstage to meet her first star singer. We were having a moment.

Suddenly Celestine piped up, disturbing the mood. She asked Benjamin to sing. Under her abrupt interruption he went shy. Telling her mother not to force the young man to sing, Beyoncé blurted out that she understood how he felt. She was sensitive to this child's feelings, but she still hadn't figured out how to break free from her parents' chains.

After a moment of silence, I reached in to hug Beyoncé, nudging Mama Celestine out of the way. As I told her that I truly loved her and that I always will, a very strange energy filled the room. Beyoncé did not know what to say. My attempts to make conversation in 2001 and 2005 had elicited, at least, an automatic, polite response. Now she had no words.

Benjamin and I turned, this time really heading for the door. Celestine said, "It was good to see you, David." As she headed back to her place at the wall and the shoeprint she had left on the white paint, we had a moment, exchanging one last look. The Cheshire grin on her face spoke volumes. My stare was deafening. Fuck you.

Looking down at my clutched hand, I realized that I still carried the picture, protected in an envelope. I turned to face Beyoncé. As I stepped towards her, Celestine once again started to move in. "Will you please," I shouted. Celestine stopped dead in her tracks. Benjamin had left the room, thank God.

Beyoncé's eyes widened, and then relaxed. She didn't have to be afraid of me. As soon as I was near enough to pass the envelope to her, I raised my hand.

"What's this?" she asked.

"A gift to remind you of me," I answered.

Celestine moved in, communicating a silent fury. Beyoncé slowly opened the envelope, took out the picture, and smiled. "Oh, my God." Tickled pink, she began to reminisce with her mother.

I interrupted, saying, "Goodbye." I'd cherish the memories, but it was clear. I would never see my pupil again. And on that Celestine could depend and never worry. I turned, smiled at Benjamin and said, "Okay, let's go, buddy."

"Say hello to your mother," Celestine said.

I didn't turn. No pillar of salt for me. No thanks. I was free, peaceful. Finally.

32. An Upward Turn

Having trained Beyoncé better than most opera singers, I beamed with pride when I read Jody Rosen's review of Beyoncé's Album "B'Day" in *Entertainment Weekly*. Mr. Rosen, my favorite pop culture journalist, wrote: "Beyoncé Knowles is a storm system disguised as a singer... *you'd have to search far and wide – perhaps in the halls of the Metropolitan Opera – to find a vocalist who sings with more sheer force. [My italics added for emphasis.]* No one – not R. Kelly, not Usher, to say nothing of her rival pop divas – can match Beyoncé's genius for dragging her vocal lines against a hip-hop beat." The always knowledgeable Mr. Rosen understood what I had been doing all those years. I was tickled pink that he heard in Beyoncé's voice and singing the qualities that she and I had worked so hard for her to master.

Beyoncé's album "B'Day" might have been wonderful, but the back story surrounding its September 2006 release wasn't. Mathew was trying to ruin LeToya, and Beyoncé had apparently done nothing to refute him. Quite the contrary, Beyoncé had already called LeToya "tone deaf" and had accused her of being "lazy" and (my personal favorite) "untalented." Every source I had in the industry confirmed that Mathew had successfully had LeToya's featured performance on the BET Awards pulled. Although her new recording for Capitol had received rave reviews, LeToya was not allowed to perform on the same show with Beyoncé. Then Mathew attacked LeToya at the holy gate of the music business – radio. Was it true?

I reached out to LeToya's mother (now her daughter's professional manager), Pam Luckett. We hadn't talked in a while, and she replied in detail, clearing up a number of my questions. Pam wrote in an e-mail dated the 28th of September 2013:

I addressed the start of the solo decision in my last email to you. I will say that LeToya had no real desire to become solo. She always wanted to be with a group/friends. I had to carefully take steps to head her in that direction after she clearly saw that the Anjel group was not going to work. Even with that in her mind, she was heading to LA to act or model and perhaps do some demos (so she thought). I had made arrangements for her to go into the studio with the Noontime guys. This was with the help of Attorney Kasim Reed, who arranged our meeting with Chris Hicks in Atlanta before she left for LA. Shortly after reaching LA, Terry Ross of Noontime arranged for LeToya to go into the studio. They recorded several records, including "Torn." Then I received a very excited call from Chris Hicks to overnight some photos. Arrangements were made for us to meet with Capitol Records and the rest is history!

As far as what Mathew tried to do I am not certain. LeToya and I heard many things. But you know both of us very well to know that we hoped that these things were not true. However, both of us were told by different people and at different times certain things that were **hard not to believe**. Most were industry people that still have a working relationship with Bey, Jay-Z, Kelly, Tina and Mathew. So that we do not impair those working relationships, I know that LeToya would not want those disclosed. As we know now and then, "That no weapon formed us against will prosper." (*Isaiah 54:17)*

I must say, that I am sooo glad that you are receiving this via email, because otherwise you would be receiving a tear stained letter in the mail. I have never had the opportunity to talk about any of this. Writing is such a healer. LeToya and I have had to just keep it moving. Even interviews that she has done, we have never sat down and discussed my view. The interviews were only about what she experienced. I must say that she made me very proud in every interview because I never had to tell her to take the high road. The small details that she did not know, did not matter to me as much. But there are times when I feel that no one but God knows what I went through as well.

Much Love! Pam.

Any backlash that Beyoncé and Mathew faced (because of their attempts to undermine LeToya's career) was well deserved. Within the industry, they were objects of derision. The laughter must have been particularly hard to swallow – that is, if they took notice.

I was already consumed by disgust and concern when I landed in Mumbai on March 12, 2008, in the middle of the night. It was the last stop on a three-continent tour to gather media and television support for my multi-generational and multi-national live action reality series, and it was going well. I had started writing it in 2004 and now it was coming to pass. The plan was to identify, develop, and deliver to the world the first ever multi-cultural and international girl band, whom I called BRICS. (The BRICS was an acronym taken from the first letters of the countries Brazil, Russia, India, and China.) STAR TV in India was the last meeting and television partner to confirm. I couldn't have been more pleased. Next up was arranging the sponsors.

Enter Mathew Knowles.

Brazil's Globo had insisted on having Beyoncé's involvement. I had assured them that she wasn't available and even shared the response I'd gotten from Mathew's office, which told the representative from Brazil that Beyoncé would "never participate." No Beyoncé, no deal. And no Brazil meant no BRICS.

On the 29th of February, Lee Anne Callahan, executive vice president of artist management at Music World Entertainment had written: "Hi David, I met with Mathew and he wanted me to get back to you right away to let you know that he is currently working on a project that is similar to what you are doing. He is putting together a multi-cultural girl group for youth market and Beyoncé will be one of the producers. It is in conjunction with programming on Nickelodeon. It is in early stages so I can't give much detail but he wanted me to share the basics with you so you would know that it was already in the works before he heard of your plans. It should be officially announced in a few weeks. If you would like to call me to discuss further please do. My cell number is 917- [xxx – xxxx] or you can call me in office on Monday (our phones are down today)."

"That is bullshit," I thought to myself. Mathew hasn't ever built a girl group, and he sure as anything isn't building one now. But I was the only one in the world, besides the girls, who knew that, and they weren't talking.

Still, Globo didn't see the conflict, and to be quite honest, for rationally thinking people there wasn't a problem. Mathew's project was local, "dedicated to the U.S. market," they said. "Yours is global." Exactly, I thought, my mind on Rule No. 1 in *The 48 Laws of Power*: "Never outshine the master."

I learned that Globo believed they could sway Beyoncé's father's opinion, "somehow." They owned 75% of print media and television in Brazil and South America. Did they intend to throw money at Beyoncé? Mathew? On the 18th of October, 2008, my vision came to a crashing halt. The entire deal fell apart. All that I'd worked for was lost. Four years of work down the drain. Of course, Mathew's so called multi-cultural group never materialized, and as far as I could tell there was never an official press/announcement/release mentioning anything about collaboration with Nickelodeon in 2008. (Some deal with Nickelodeon would appear in 2012, but it wasn't clear what it was or when it came about.)

Two months later, in December 2008, on my way home to Omaha for Christmas, I stopped in New York to meet with Alan. The BRICS might have been dead, but my idea wasn't. "Rename and regroup," Alan suggested.

The result was "The Center by David Lee Brewer."

Turkey was interested.

* * * * *

Sprawled out on Shevon's table, along with a few other popular women's magazines, lay the December 2008 issue of *Elle*. I picked it up, intrigued. Beyoncé was on the cover, and like I'd not seen her before. Something about the picture was hard and defiant. Flipping through its pages, I opened to the rather lengthy article titled "The Liberation of B.," written by Will Blythe, with photos by Alexei Hay. The article's subject covered Beyoncé's new movie *Cadillac Records* and her stunning portrayal of the drug-addicted superstar, Etta James.

Will Blythe wrote: "As Tina Knowles, Beyoncé's mother and best friend, puts it, 'Etta's a little rough around the edges. And when Beyoncé came off the set, she'd be rough too, and a little snappy. Even her walk. She had said 'Mama, show me that Galveston walk.' She modeled it after our housekeeper, Janelle, who's what we call a real beer-joint woman. Smoking, swaggering.'"

"Jay-Z watched B. sauntering around the room that night and he exclaimed, 'Oh, here we go! We've got Etta in our midst.' He looked at B. and said, 'You better go get a hotel.'"

The writer continued, "Here, at long last, was a role B. had been waiting her whole life to play. And not just in the movies."

As I continued to read the article, I was surprised to read that Beyoncé said she'd wanted to be a psychologist. Not once had the subject ever come up in all our years together. Had she confused my childhood dream with her own? I had told Beyoncé many times about my childhood ambition to be a psychiatrist. She had frequently shared with me her ambitions for her future. Singing, always singing. Now Beyoncé said to the inter-

had accused her of being "lazy" and (my personal favorite) "untalented." Every source I had in the industry confirmed that Mathew had successfully had LeToya's featured performance on the BET Awards pulled. Although her new recording for Capitol had received rave reviews, LeToya was not allowed to perform on the same show with Beyoncé. Then Mathew attacked LeToya at the holy gate of the music business – radio. Was it true?

I reached out to LeToya's mother (now her daughter's professional manager), Pam Luckett. We hadn't talked in a while, and she replied in detail, clearing up a number of my questions. Pam wrote in an e-mail dated the 28th of September 2013:

I addressed the start of the solo decision in my last email to you. I will say that LeToya had no real desire to become solo. She always wanted to be with a group/friends. I had to carefully take steps to head her in that direction after she clearly saw that the Anjel group was not going to work. Even with that in her mind, she was heading to LA to act or model and perhaps do some demos (so she thought). I had made arrangements for her to go into the studio with the Noontime guys. This was with the help of Attorney Kasim Reed, who arranged our meeting with Chris Hicks in Atlanta before she left for LA. Shortly after reaching LA, Terry Ross of Noontime arranged for LeToya to go into the studio. They recorded several records, including "Torn." Then I received a very excited call from Chris Hicks to overnight some photos. Arrangements were made for us to meet with Capitol Records and the rest is history!

As far as what Mathew tried to do I am not certain. LeToya and I heard many things. But you know both of us very well to know that we hoped that these things were not true. However, both of us were told by different people and at different times certain things that were hard not to believe. Most were industry people that still have a working relationship with Bey, Jay-Z, Kelly, Tina and Mathew. So that we do not impair those working relationships, I know that LeToya would not want those disclosed. As we know now and then, "That no weapon formed us against will prosper." (*Isaiah 54:17)*

These were bald-faced lies.

It had been Celestine who had driven to the Bottoms. She was looking for her strung-out husband, and her car. *We*, meaning she and I, took my car to do it. The children certainly didn't go on that joy ride/sightseeing tour. She'd say anything to make herself look like Mother Teresa. Unbelievable.

Nevertheless, it was Beyoncé's reaction to all this talk about rough neighborhoods and hard times that set me squirming. Instead of describing her middle-class upbringing, she said "I grew up upper-class – private school. My dad had a Jaguar. We're African-American and we work together as a family, so people assume we're like the Jacksons. But I didn't have parents using me to get out of a bad situation."

Disappointment hit me like a brick. What the hell was she talking about? I asked Shevon. Not only did her parents use her to "get out of their bad situation," they were still using her.

I figured that having sold more than 100 million records, and getting used to living on $80 million + income, there were many things about her that had changed or been embellished.

Was it my student's idea to make up this fake, idyllic life? I was more than done, stick me with a roasting fork: done.

Exactly twenty-six days later, I was in a Chicago hotel suite, watching the 31st Annual Kennedy Center Honors. The show aired on CBS Television on December 30, 2008. Beyoncé had been chosen to pay tribute to the Kennedy honoree Barbra Streisand, singing her gigantic hit "The Way We Were" to perfection. Now this was the girl I knew, excellent and focused relentlessly on the performance. Her singing was exquisite. She and I had worked every phrase, smoothed out the vocal lines, cleaned up the vowels, and took every hint of R&B out of her rendition. She sounded amazing, clean, and authentically accurate, well within the framework of the style required to deliver a Streisand tribute. The Legend would go on to call Beyoncé the real deal. "She knows what she's doing."

On that December night, I switched off the TV, thinking, "At least her talent remains real."

February 22, 2009

For many years I had lived with the shame and guilt of what I had done to the young, innocent Ashley Támar Davis. I couldn't get past it. I'd given Beyoncé everything, while denying my support of another one of God's gifted souls. Peace escaped me.

Finally, on a trip to the United States with my surrogate mother and mentor, Grace Bumbry, God's grace was bestowed upon me. Grace was being honored with a life-time achievement award from the press in St. Louis, where she also received the key to the city from the mayor. I decided that I would fly up to Omaha after the ceremonies for a visit with my family. I had five days before Grace and I would head off to Chicago and then back to Europe.

I was scheduled to fly out on the wintery morning of February 22nd, but following a very strong feeling I changed the reservation for later that afternoon. Boarding the plane to Omaha in St. Louis I found myself amidst a sea of black people. My seat-mate, who immediately struck up a conversation, introduced himself as Tony Grant. It came out that all those black people constituted the cast of Tyler Perry's new play, "The Marriage Counselor."

"Oh, really! Are you guys going to Omaha to present the play?" I asked.

"Yes, we are going to be there for a couple days."

"I would love to see it," I said.

Tony offered to let me use his tickets. He didn't know anyone in Omaha, and I was delighted to be able to give my mother and step-father, George, a night out on the town.

"A former student of mine has done Tyler Perry plays in the past. Maybe you know her," I said to Tony.

"What's her name?"

"Ashley Támar Davis," I answered.

Tony smiled and immediately looked over the seats to a couple rows in front of us. "Hey Támar," he called out. My heart dropped. Could it be?

Was it really her? On the same plane? On that very day? A young woman wearing Audrey Hepburn-like sunglasses turned her head. Tony signaled to her and asked "Do you know this guy?" She looked over her glasses and then screamed. She stood up, and I stood up, and we headed towards one another for what was going to be the reunion of all reunions. But as the plane was taking off, the stewardess told us both to take our seats. My excitement was indescribable, while fear suddenly robbed me of breath.

An hour later we touched down in Omaha, I walked through the galley door to find that "Támar" was excitedly waiting for me. We hugged for what felt like ten minutes. She immediately tried calling her mother to tell her whom she had met on the plane. Overwhelmed with emotion, I had to strain to stay focused. She asked me how I had been and what I'd been up to. "I've thought of you often," she said. Nervously, I told her that I lived in Germany and was singing in opera all over the world. "That's what you always wanted to do," she said, smiling. "I'm happy for you." I asked her if she had gone to college, as she had planned to do when she was a child. (I did not share with her that in the intervening years I had heard her once, secretly, at her Sweet 16 Concert at the Liberty Baptist Church in Houston.)

Támar told me that a few years after she left Girl's Tyme, her demo CD had caught the attention of Prince ("The Artist formerly known as Prince"), who had taken her under his wing. He invited her to his Paisley Park studio in Minneapolis and offered her a production contract. However, she was intent on furthering her education, so she declined his invitation and headed for Los Angeles to study at the University of Southern California, where she finished her bachelor's degree in music performance. While there she learned to write and arrange music, singing in French, Italian, German, Swahili, and Italian.

"Wow, how exciting. I am glad that you continued your education," I said.

"Yes, I graduated totally prepared. Just as you always told us: be prepared. And Prince told me the same thing. That is why he understood when I wanted to go to college. He was in full support of the idea."

"Oh, so he wasn't disappointed?"

"No," Támar said. "He became a real friend. He even took me to nego-tiation meetings with him. We studied religions and he taught me how to really see God in all that I do. He is amazing." She told me that her second chance to meet the star came in early 2005, when at the invitation of the famed choreographer Fatima Robinson, she attended an awards show party hosted by Prince. "Can you sing for me?" Prince had asked. Támar's voice and performance blew him away, and the seed began to grow. This time she became a vocalist in Prince's band and even joined him on stage in duet. She told me that when Prince felt she was ready he gave her a solo opportunity, together with him on stage at the NAACP Image Awards. Deals were being offered from Universal Records, but it didn't feel right to Prince, who had become her mentor. Everything had to be just right to introduce his "new favorite singer" to the world.

I was so happy for Támar. Then she did something I had not expected. She thanked me. She said that because of our work together all those many years ago, she had been excellently prepared for her studies at USC.

"I still remember what I learned from you back then. You were an amazing influence."

Her voice teacher was able to pick up where I had left off, even com-menting on how well prepared she was for vocal study. My eyes welled up with tears.

"Aw," Támar said. Then she started to tear up. She hugged me again.

As our bags arrived she asked if I were coming to the show the next evening. Just then my mother walked into the airport and Támar, happy to see her again, greeted her warmly. "Hi Baby, it's been a long time. You look good," Mama said to her. I told Mama that we were going to see Támar's play, which delighted her, as she was a huge Tyler Perry fan. "I can hardly wait," Mama said.

The next evening, my parents and I arrived a bit early to Omaha's con-vention center, where "The Marriage Counselor" played. My mother warned that the traffic could be horrendous in downtown Omaha. I hadn't lived there in 28 years, since I was 17, and I figured she knew better than

I. Mama was more than right. Traffic was brutal, and there were long lines at the theater. Thank God we could go to the will-call window, because our tickets had been reserved. After we found our seats Mama and I spoke about my life in Europe and she asked me if I was dating anyone. She always wanted to know if I was dating anyone. George, her husband of thirteen-plus years questioned me about the operatic roles I had premiered. He, too, is a musician, an amateur saxophonist and an avid music lover who played in his church. George has been extremely supportive of my career.

As the lights went down for the start of the evening performance, my heart began to race. I could not believe that I was sitting in this theater, at this moment, about to watch one of "my girls" in an important stage role. The curtain went up and there she was. She was quite the actress. I felt such pride. Tony Grant, who played her husband, had the first song, and when Ashley began to sing she took my breath away. I felt transported. Her voice had developed exactly in the way I had imagined it would back in 1992/93. It was ravishingly beautiful and slender and it showed great flexibility. It was obvious that her teacher had carried on the principles of *bel canto* singing, and Támar had mastered them. She was able to employ every emotion through her voice, just as all truly fine singers can. Her technique was impeccable.

After the show, Támar called my cell phone and asked if I was coming to the hotel. "Of course," I told her. My mom, step-father, and I were already in the lobby. Within seconds Támar emerged from the elevator. She introduced my parents to the entire cast and as my mother and step-father engaged with them in excited conversations, Támar and I stepped aside for a private moment together. I told her that I had a television project that I wanted to include her in.

"Are you available in August 2009?" I asked.

"I think I am, why?" she replied.

"I have created a casting show called 'The Center.' The audience gets to look in on how a star is built from beginning through to the launch of their career. I will be shooting the pilot in Antalya, Turkey. The mock

724

candidates – all protégés of mine – will give a live performance at the end of the shooting. It will be broadcast in more than twenty countries simultaneously within the region. I would love to have you as my guest star!"

"I would be honored," she said.

"Great! You will be one of two. I have also invited my Chinese star to perform. Her name is Cindy Bao and she lives in Beijing. She is huge in China."

"Great! I look forward to meeting her." She then told me that her mother would have to travel with her, to which I replied, "No problem. I look forward to seeing Carolyn again."

The night had come to an end and I felt truly grateful. Ashley had forgiven me.

"David, what happened back in 1993 was not your fault. I know you love me, as I do you. You were my first teacher, and I am so thankful that God put me in good hands from the very beginning. As you know, that is a true stroke of good luck in our business."

I thanked her for her kind words, welling up again. We hugged once more. I promised to be in touch about Turkey and then we parted ways. Mama and I left the hotel together, with George walking slightly ahead of us. Then I stopped. I could not walk any further. I just wept; from the deepest part of my soul, I wept tears of joy. The only person on earth that I'd hurt had forgiven me. I gave God praise. Támar's and my meeting on that airplane on that day was no accident. I am forever in awe of his grace. Deep-seated peace had finally found me.

Forgiveness felt great!

* * * * *

March 1, 2009

Back at home in Berlin, I had an idea: to nominate Grace Bumbry for the United States' annual Kennedy Center arts award for her great achievements in the opera world. The Kennedy Center for the Performing

Arts in Washington D.C. annually honors the best of the best in several areas of music performance. In order to receive this honor, one has to be a real legend, as Grace surely was. I was determined that she should be a 2009 Kennedy Center Honoree.

Following my instinct, I contacted John Dow, who worked in the Public Relations department of the Kennedy Center. As Grace Bumbry's PR representative, I wanted to be sure that the award committee would pay attention to my nomination. John advised me to write a strongly worded letter to the committee. He said that because there are so many world-class American stars, my letter would have to be the letter of my life.

Every year the Kennedy Honors committee ponders their complex decisions, and I hoped that my sending along not only my letter, but also the short public relations video that I'd made for Grace's St. Louis press honor, the members of the committee that might not have been familiar with her name and work would have a good review of Grace's illustrious career. I began my letter with, "Some of you may know the name Grace Bumbry, her impressive career, her commitment to excellence, the one of a kind art of bringing characters to life through her voice and of the trailblazing historical accounts that propelled her to Stardom. She is undeniably a STAR!" ... Later I included the reason for my letter, "It is my wish that she be part of the Honorees in 2009-10." I closed by saying, "Her legacy is tremendous and her heart is gigantic. Grace Bumbry should be honored by your organization and it is my hope that you will agree with me. She is a champion and an American who has made and continues to make a difference in the world..."

Naturally, my letter was a complete run-down of all things gloriously Grace. I was careful not to leave out one single important point. Coupled with the election of Barack Obama as the nation's first black President, Grace Bumbry's nomination would be all too fitting. She is a woman of many firsts. For instance, she is the first person of color to debut at the highly revered Bayreuth Festival, Germany, altering that country's course on race relations. At age 23, she'd been the first black singer ever to sing at the Paris Opera. She'd also been the first black opera singer to sing at

726

the White House, under the Kennedy administration, at age 25. Perhaps most interesting for the committee was reminding them that Grace Bumbry had participated as one of the guest performers in the first ever Kennedy Center Honors in 1987, honoring Marian Anderson. She had sung "Vissi d'arte" from Puccini's opera *Tosca*. On that same night she was followed by Aretha Franklin, who also honored the "Lady from Philadelphia," singing the Negro spiritual "He's got the whole world in his hands," backed by the Howard University concert choir.

Six months later, on the 20th of August, we got word. In a letter addressed to Grace, but mailed to me, I read: "Dear Ms. Bumbry: On behalf of the Kennedy Center Trustees and our national Artists Committee, I am writing to invite you to receive the Kennedy Center Honors in recognition of your extraordinary contributions to the life of our country..." I was elated. The 1994 Kennedy Center honoree Aretha Franklin would do the tribute. Talk about coming full circle.

I called Grace in Munich, where she was sound asleep. "Mommie, wake up!" I said. "I've got good news." And good news it was. I started to read, pausing only to allow the weight of this incredible honor to sink in. Her teary response said it all. "The letter is signed by Michael M. Kaiser, President of the Kennedy Center Honors." I added "It's official." Oh, so proud of myself, I read the list of honorees. "Mommie, you're being awarded the Kennedy Center medallion alongside Robert DeNiro, Dave Brubeck, Mel Brooks, and Bruce Springsteen." She was deeply honored and moved. I made a joke, asking her what she was going to wear. We both laughed. "I know you," I said.

Grace was wide awake now, and we chatted for a long while. That after-midnight talk would be one for the books. I'll never forget it. Grace told me story after story about Marian Anderson, about her greatness and her deep-rooted humanity. I listened with my good ear, because "They've asked me to act as the liaison, responsible for coordinating and organizing every facet of your honor together with them," I told her. She respectfully agreed. "The letter says that the honorees are not allowed to have any say in what will happen," I added. "Everything is supposed to be a surprise."

Concluding, I said, "And yes, I've already faxed the letter to the hotel. It should have already been put under your door." I could feel her smiling through the phone.

Grace respectfully agreed to all the proposed plans for the awards ceremony and the many details leading up to it. We ended the call and I got a good night's sleep. My work began the next morning. The Kennedy Center festivities were just months away.

As part of the festivities on that December 4th weekend, in Washington, Grace and I dined with distinguished dignitaries in American government, including former Presidents and Secretaries of State. Meeting President Bill Clinton and Secretary Hillary Rodham Clinton was a real highlight. I'd never encountered more generous, gracious, and charming human beings. Meeting President and Mrs. Barack Obama, America's first black President and First Lady, remains an indescribable highlight of my entire life.

At that dinner, which turned out to be a Who's Who in politics and entertainment, I sat across from Sting, my all-time favorite pop singer. Meryl Streep sat directly behind me. The room was brimming with energy, each person more regal than the other. And boy, did I people-watch. I loved observing my favorite film director, Martin Scorsese, command the room, holding court. There were so many unbelievable moments, like talking with Aretha Franklin in the elegant hallways of the White House.

It felt as though the evening couldn't get any better. And then it did

Playwright Terrence McNally delivered a moving tribute to Grace, just before the transference of the Kennedy Center medallion to her. It touched the deepest part of my heart. I remember thinking, sitting in the honoree box on December 4th, that this must be what it feels like to walk around heaven. I can't begin to describe all that raced through this black boy's head. I'd come a long way from that sixteen-year-old Nebraska kid who dreamed of belonging to the upper echelon of music and meeting his idol one day.

It seems that I still had a lot to learn. Mathew Knowles and I were long from being done with one another.

The post-script to the "Center by David Lee Brewer" story is that Támar did appear in 2009 in the pilot on Turkish Television. She was a complete success. However, half a world away, Beyoncé's father's malignant force intervened to de-rail my Turkey project.

Once again, I would lose my TV show, which was scheduled to begin shooting in late spring of 2010. It seems that a young executive made an inquiry about me with Mathew's Music World Management. I learned that Mathew's office had said that he "couldn't speak to Mr. Brewer's ability as a teacher." At which point the young executive asked me, "So what do you do for Beyoncé again?" I hit the roof, fuming, but keeping my composure. Professionalism at all times, I thought. My prospective partners had no interest in suing Mathew Knowles. It was much easier, and more cost effective, to see me as a liability, and we split up. I would have to forge ahead, alone, to find another way.

One afternoon in April, 2011, my phone rang. A German television producer, Nikole Kraack, was calling me at my home in Berlin. Following up on clues that she had discovered on the internet, she asked me if I was the same David Lee Brewer who had been somehow involved with Destiny's Child. If so, she wanted to interview me about Beyoncé for a series called "The Queens of Pop," scheduled to air in July 2011 on *ARTE,* Europe's leader in cultural television. After some discussion I agreed, and she came to my home shortly thereafter.

Exclaiming that she could hardly believe I was right there, in Berlin, Nikole made conversation while her production team set up their equipment for the interview. I naturally assumed she wanted to discuss Beyoncé's current life with Jay-Z, her new album, "4", or perhaps Beyoncé's recent firing of her father as her manager, subjects I had definite opinions about. But, no, she wanted history.

"I was just in Houston, interviewing Mathew Knowles. He told me he was responsible for developing Beyoncé," Nikole said. "What exactly then did you do for Beyoncé?" she asked me, in German. There was that damned question again, I thought.

My strained smile told Nikole that Mathew had his facts wrong. I suggested that, contrary to his story, it had not been Mathew who developed Beyoncé's talent, it had not been Mathew's idea to create a series of summer training camps, and he certainly never left a six-figure salaried job to further his daughter's dream. No, he and his wife, Celestine, had not been keepers of the keys that unlocked the door to their superstar daughter's artistic successes. Like many parents of celebrities, Mathew and Celestine had regarded their children as possessions to be exploited. Exploit them they did, particularly their older daughter, Beyoncé. And yes, Mathew was as irresponsible as they come: a drug addict who abused his family. I paused, realizing that I was getting ahead of Nikole's interview.

She looked puzzled.

"To answer your question Nikole, I would have to return to our beginnings, even before Destiny's Child."

"Beginnings? How long were you involved in Beyoncé's life?" she asked.

"Longer than a decade," I said, "during which I gave Beyoncé four lessons a week. Furthermore, I lived in the midst of the family, at Celestine's invitation, in the apartment above their garage."

Long silence, as Nikole looked at me intently. "Wow. That changes everything, now, doesn't it?" In that moment, the entire scope of Nikole's interview expanded.

Placing her prepared questions on the floor, Nikole looked me square in the eyes and asked if I was ready. "Most definitely," I said.

This interview proved to be a turning point for my own career as a teacher and an entrepreneur. I was reassured that because Mathew had no influence on European television, he would not be able to block my appearance. During the ten-episode documentary, I was interviewed not only about Beyoncé, but also about Mariah Carey, whose voice I had used as a model in my teaching. After the documentary's successful airing, the show's producer, and the TV channel ARTE, Europe's equivalent of A&E and Biography Channels in the U.S., offered me my own casting show. This time I changed the scope to classical music. The producer and I decided to call it "Open Opera," where I would cast, of all things, the opera *Carmen*. Shooting was scheduled for 2011. (It would prove to become a great success, airing in 2012 and seen over the course of four weeks by more than 10 million viewers.)

In November 2011, propped up on my bed pillows in London, I channel surfed. Happening onto MTV Europe, I saw a familiar face. And more significantly, I also saw my intellectual property being played out before my eyes. According to the show's intro, Mathew Knowles was "building a girl group" that he called "Breaking from Above."

Even if he hadn't stolen idea, I saw the show and Mathew as fraudulent. Beyoncé's father, while touting himself an absolute authority, said to the girls "I wanna be clear. It's about *ME* evaluating all of you, the next three weeks and deciding what *I* want to do with you." Then he said, "Look, if you're ever going to get to the level of a Destiny's Child, you've gotta give me two things: Trust that I know what I'm doing and you have to give me all of the control." Concluding, he squawked, "I make the fuckin decision of what's gonna happen. It might be four of you. It might be five. I might just decide to not do it at all. Or, I could form a group in Houston…" Then Mathew mentioned that he was going to have to take one of the girls "down a notch."

Of course I was enraged, not only that he had stolen my idea, but also that he was pandering to the public, presenting the worst, cartoonish stereotype of an artistic developer. In that moment he exposed himself as an abusive narcissist.

This time I had no partners involved in my decision. I sought immediate legal advice with the London-based firm of "Bolt Burden Solicitors" and was informed by Attorney Mike Shephard that I had enough to prove that Mathew had indeed stolen my intellectual property, according to British Law. "You have a two-year window to make up your mind," Shephard said.

I called Alan in New York. He suggested that I write, put pen to paper, as it would be an efficient method of helping to prepare any potential case which may or may not arise. Once again, I found myself in Eisenach, this time in spirit. I remembered that the great German Reformist Martin Luther, whose words I had often sung in the music of Johann Sebastian Bach, had a great respect for the power of the written language. I recalled Luther's wisdom on the topic: "The best weapon to use against the devil is black ink." I copied his words onto a piece of paper, tacked it onto the wall, and began to write.

* * * * *

The first time the words "book" and "David Lee Brewer" had combined in the same sentence was in 2009, shortly after the Kennedy Center Honors. My operatic student and friend, the classical coloratura soprano turned recording artist Jolie Rocke Brown, suggested I write a book about my life and work. "It's so interesting," she said. Then, "Hey, you could call it 'Girl Group Heaven.'" I laughed it off, having never given writing a book any real thought. I did say, however, "If I did write it, it would have to encompass a lot more than my time with Beyoncé and Destiny's Child." Jolie said she agreed completely. I was so much more than the teacher behind Beyoncé's voice and Destiny's Child's success, and I had so much to say about maintaining integrity in the music profession. Little by little I found the courage to do more than put pen to paper. I dug deep. Beginning simply not only served me later, when I needed to present written evidence to my London solicitor, but more importantly, it was my principal tool for healing, for finding the way to my own truth.

During that period (ca. 2009-2011), Paul Burrell's 2001 book *A Royal Duty*, which chronicles his life and experiences with Princess Diana, inspired me in significant ways. Reading the book and then researching Burrell's journey, I read about the lawsuits and all the name calling he suffered. In the end he was exonerated of all accusations, at the Queen of England's request. Diana's family had intimated that he'd stolen her belongings, and had intentionally set out to defame her name and character. Queen Elizabeth cleared the matter up. *A Royal Duty*, which was his story, enjoyed massive success.

I was struck by the fact that Burrell's wasn't the first book to take on Princess Diana's private life, but it was the first to provide a first-hand account of this internationally known woman, and it was written to honor her. Likewise, I realized that mine would not be the first book to talk about the Knowles family, but it, too, would be written by an eyewitness – me – and that I would be honoring the internationally known Beyoncé. Like Burrell, I would be writing to tell my truth.

I leapt from my chair when I read Burrell's declaration of intent: "I never thought I would have to write this book – but then I never believed I would have to redress balance." He'd said what I felt in my heart. So, there was precedent, and I read and re-read his words as though the Universe had just sent me permission to tell my own truth.

I pondered the issues for days. What is this fascination with stars really all about? Why do we ignore behaviors that each one of us, under normal circumstances, can see are harmful and dysfunctional? Why do we buy into cookie-cutter images and fabricated stories of the rich and famous, without regard for fact? We hold famous people in highest esteem, forgiving them everything, no matter how and what they'd done to reach their successes.

These thoughts led me to research successful people who had made their millions while maintaining their moral integrity. I didn't have to look far. My fellow Nebraskan Warren Buffet, had become a billionaire while adhering to standards and practices that I approved. With Burrell and Buffet in mind, I set out on an eight-year, emotionally draining journey.

The first issue I pondered was my abhorrence of pedophilia (Charles). Could I talk about that painful topic, which affects so many? Did I have the courage to release myself from the shame that Cheryl had tried to cast upon me? I recalled Cheryl's cursing me out. She must have carried anger against me for years. The way she attacked me in New York told me so. That kind of rage is not the spontaneous reaction of a mere moment. I asked myself why people turn a deaf ear to the cries of our molested children, who suffer such shameful abuses by trusted grownups?

I engaged in lengthy discussions with myself on the question of silence, and its ramifications. I had maintained silence for many years. Why? Partly, I realized, because of my religious convictions: Turn the other cheek. Well, I had no more cheeks to turn by 2011. Truth is difficult. Fear? Of what? That no one would believe me? That's where Burrell helped me. "…I never believed I would have to redress balance." I sought professional advice from a child psychologist, a therapist, and a psychiatrist. I would leave no stone unturned on my journey to writing a book that I could be proud of.

Could I help LeToya with the truth? Did I even care to? In later years, long after the implosion of Anjel, and the damage to my reputation, LeToya admitted her own fears. While speaking to freshly graduated high school seniors at The New Olivet Baptist Church in Memphis, Tennessee, LeToya spoke earnestly. "I didn't want to sing anymore. I was depressed and saw no way out of the horrible situation I was in. One day I was on top and the next I was nobody," she recounted. I was grateful for her honest admission and hoped that her public declaration of truth gave her some relief.

My girls had known, in their younger years, that what they felt and suffered was abuse, but they had hidden and devalued themselves and their talents for a long time, apparently hoping that one day Beyoncé would smile favor upon them. I mean, who calls the girl who ruined your career and reputation her "shero" (LaTavia's word)? LaTavia did and does. Tragic, I thought.

Kelly still had no clue how to get out from under the Knowles spell and most likely couldn't even recall that she'd had the self-worth beaten out of her. Was I biting off more than I could chew? "Of course you are,"

Mama said one day, as I shared my thoughts with her. She was not only my supportive parent, she was also a proven expert in the field of human behavior. "This is your story and the minute you stop caring about protecting them you'll be able to write it. They don't love you. They never did."

Those were hard words for me to hear, but I heard them. I even felt them. Mama was right. If I was going to write a true story, one of substance, "I'm going to have to kill the desire to protect my girls."

"David, I mean this with all the love in my heart," Mama said. "Stop already with the 'my girls' bullshit."

I dropped my head.

* * * * *

Acceptance
March 28th 2011

Mathew was too high on his own ego to realize that his wife was complicit in his demise as his daughter's manager. Neither Jay-Z nor Live Nations' "conniving executives," as Mathew accused in the press, had anything to do with it. He even filed a petition to sue, which ultimately went nowhere. Did he truly not realize that only Celestine had the power to cut him off at the knees and get away with it? She had used her daughter Beyoncé masterfully, always demanding that Beyoncé "Honor thy mother and father," until the time came for the *mother* to take the *father* out of the commandment.

The press reported that Beyoncé had ordered an independent audit of her accounts, which apparently revealed that her father had indeed stolen money from her. She was devastated, but for the life of me I didn't understand why. OK, I know she thought her Daddy wouldn't steal from her. But he'd stolen from everyone else.

Beyoncé called her mother in for a private meeting, according to my sources at Music World Management. It was substantiated by the author J. Randy Taraborelli, in his 2015 book *Becoming Beyoncé: The Untold Sto-*

ry. By the end of the conversation, Mathew was toast. This time Mama Celestine would not stand in her daughter's way. She finally approved her husband's beheading. The way I heard it, Celestine played the wounded wife to the hilt, even stopping by a secretary's desk to bewail her plight, saying solemnly, "My family will never be the same." Or words to that effect. The next day Beyoncé's ax fell.

Every report I read alleged that Beyoncé had fired her father because he'd stolen from her. Mama Celestine certainly knew this. She was complicit. But the public embarrassment of a bastard child would be too much to bear. Mathew had had an affair, getting a woman named Alexsandra Wright pregnant. Celestine had been able to put a public face, a mask, on Mathew's drugs, his abusive name-calling, his lies, their hateful physical and psychological relationships, the cardboard marriage that they maintained. None of that had brought him down. His love child would. Even Celestine couldn't explain that one away. She tried to work it out, reports said, and then she found out about the second child, a little girl named Koi, who had been born in 2010. Her mother, Taqoya Branscomb, would also get an injunction for a court-ordered paternity test. It proved with 99.9% accuracy that Mathew was the father.

Days later we all heard CNN's report that the split was amicable, with both sides claiming that it was a mutual decision. "I've only parted ways with my father on a business level," the 29-year-old Beyoncé said in a statement released on Monday, March 28th. "He is my father for life and I love my dad dearly. I am grateful for everything he has taught me…I grew up watching both he and my mother manage and own their own businesses. They were hardworking entrepreneurs and I will continue to follow in their footsteps."

Mathew said in a separate statement, "The decision for Beyoncé and Music World Entertainment to part was mutual." He concluded with, "We did great things together, and I know that she will continue to conquer new territories in music and entertainment."

When I picked my jaw up off the floor, I asked myself, sarcastically, "Remind me again about the ambitious parent – you know the one – the one who dreams of being important in the world but has no special skill – the one who gets lucky and gives birth to a prodigy – *why is he or she a genius?*"

I know that others have asked themselves the same thing.

* * * * *

On February 16, 2013, I was on the telephone with Patricia "Pat" Felton, going over a few details regarding my book. As Ann Tillman's best friend, Pat was the best resource for the accuracy of details that I wanted to include in describing the terrible subject of Ann's death. It had taken me four months just to get through the chapter. Incredibly painful, it cost me emotionally to write it. Yet, still I wanted to check in with her best friend. Had I hit my mark? Pat was in tears when I finished. "You've done more than justice to her name," Pat said. Then we talked a bit about Ann's sons and how they had been cheated out of their inheritance. "No, I still haven't found a way for them to file a new claim for their money," I said. "I fear they've lost their chance," I concluded. "Hell, I never got my 2%." Then Pat asked me if I thought Beyoncé would ever tell the truth. "We will see in two hours," I answered. The premiere of Beyoncé's big documentary *Life Is but a Dream* was about to air on HBO.

Berlin, February 15, 2013

On February 15, 2013, the day before HBO premiered *Life Is but a Dream*, the British newspaper *The Guardian* had run what proved to be my favorite of all the "will she or won't she?" articles. Beyoncé had – her PR had – proclaimed that this documentary would be a no-holds-barred look at her life. On every journalist's lips – foreign or domestic – and on mine, as well, was the question "Could it be true?" Would she dare to tell the truth, and nothing but the truth, so help her God?

Written by Ruth Spencer and Katie Rogers, the *Guardian* article predicted the documentary's likely content: "Since Beyoncé is a woman who spends about 98% of her time in front of a camera – but who doesn't really tell us much about herself at all – we can make some very educated guesses about how exactly this documentary will play out. Save yourselves a $60 HBO subscription and read this outline," they wrote. This was their "outline":

Act I: Destiny's Favorite Child
Enter Tina Knowles, stage mom

"Célestine Ann Beyincé, aka Tina Knowles, aka mother of Beyoncé and her decidedly not-favorite child Solange, gained notoriety in the 1990s as a ruthless "momager" and creator of some of the worst stage costumes ever stitched...." [Ruth and Katie provide readers with a picture of the original quartet, the group I founded and assembled, in one of Celestine's/Tina's cheap creations.]

"We can guarantee Mother Knowles will be waxing poetic about her daughter's early musical genius, fashion sense, and golden voice gifted by God.

"Beyoncé will say something slightly annoying about early divahood. Something like this (taken directly from the film): "Sometimes it's overwhelming. Why did God give me my talent, my gift, my family? But I know you're not supposed to question God."

[I can't lie. The article was more than dead on, despicably delicious. Did I even need to write my story, the truth? Katie and Ruth's satirical take was off the chain. Even though Beyoncé had let me down in the past, I decided to reserve judgment until I could see the HBO special for myself. After all, she did finally fire her drug addict, whore-mongering daddy. Perhaps she was really ready to clear the air. Then Ruth and Katie slayed me with their next lines.]

Destiny's Lesser Children will speak.

"Kelly Rowland and Michelle Williams will be repurposed once again and no doubt be given a few seconds to talk about how wonderful Beyoncé is. Hopefully the documentary's producers will have learned from the Super Bowl and have the good sense to have the lesser of Destiny's Children miked correctly."

[The article continues.] "…After Beyoncé's world domination and self-satisfaction has been firmly established, we'll get a look at some of the other people in Bey's world, all of whom agree that she is the best…"

And I'll be damned if Katie and Ruth's predictions didn't come to pass. I did notice something that they had not predicted: that only Beyoncé talked in the film about Beyoncé. Once again, I was agitated. I read everything I could get my hands on about the documentary.

Beyoncé began the film talking about independence. "I'm feeling very empty because of my relationship with my dad. I'm so fragile. At this point – and I feel like – my – soul has been tarnished. Life is so unpredictable but I felt like I had to move on and not work with my dad. And I don't care if I don't sell one record. It's bigger than the record. It's bigger than my career."

Her words pierced my resolve and even though Beyoncé doesn't let her fans in on what "It" is, I know first-hand what she meant. Her powerful statements in that documentary mirror my sentiment exactly – all of them but one. When Beyoncé said "All the crazy things my father did were necessary," I lost it. I couldn't believe my ears. I saw his obsession eat away at Beyoncé as well as everyone around her. It seemed to me, taking in her words, that she believed her success made everything worthwhile.

I say: Abuse is never worthwhile.

That night, disappointed by her apparent lack of insight, I didn't sleep well at all. The next evening, tired and distracted, I fell and broke my ankle. I'd missed three steps, running to the grocery store across the street. Why had I gone down the stairs in the dark? That was 9:45 p.m. Berlin time. At 10:20 my neighbors heard my screams and called the ambulance. I was operated on that night.

With six weeks of post-op recovery to think about my continuing work on the book, I read every article I could get my hands on, cataloging them, and pulling videos down off the internet, material that supported what I knew to be true. I was gaining clarity, beginning to get hold of my emotions.

In America, a *Washington Post* journalist, Hank Stuever, said that Beyoncé's "Life is but a Dream" Documentary was a " – fleeting glimpse, which is ultimately a disappointment, given the world's desperate and ongoing interest in all things Beyoncé." A *Billboard* magazine journalist, Brad Wete, wrote: "Among media types, the verdict has been clear for nearly a decade now. Beyoncé is a boring interview. For an artist as famous as she, opportunities to pull back the curtains and let fans into her world off of the stage have been abundant."

As I continued to browse the internet, the comments of Alessandra Stanley, a journalist for *The New York Times*, raised the small hairs on the back of my neck. She nailed the documentary's coffin shut, writing, "Beyoncé: Life is but a Dream" is as contrived as "Madonna: Truth or Dare," but probably for good reason it is neither daring nor entirely truthful." Ms. Stanley's suspicions couldn't have expressed my own more accurately. I was beginning to see that I was not alone in my doubts about Beyoncé's image.

Could it be that journalists were beginning to sense what I'd known for years – that Beyoncé's 'picture perfect' childhood was a complete fabrication of the truth? That her perception of reality was, shall we say, distorted?

I'll never forget the day Beyoncé cursed her voice. If only she hadn't been born with talent, she wailed.

Beyoncé deserves every accolade she has received. In the time-honored tradition of passing musical knowledge and expertise from one generation to the next, I made the suggestions and she did the work. She helped make her talent phenomenal. It took two.

I kept writing. Hashing things out.

May 21, 2013

Physical therapy was going well. The doctors had taken the screws out of my ankle, and as soon as they did, I increased my pursuit of research that would help me to finish the book.

Still prowling around online, I read about Kelly's new release. This headline got my attention: "Kelly Rowland song "Dirty Laundry" reveals her jealousy of Beyoncé." Oh, no, I said to myself. They had it all wrong.

Kelendria Trené "Kelly" Rowland had never been jealous of Beyoncé. She was, however, envious of Beyoncé's seemingly perfect home life and the fact that Beyoncé had a father. Kelly was in desperate search of a father figure. That is, until she moved into the Knowles house and discovered what I had known for years. That household was far from idyllic. And her new father image, Mathew? What a poor excuse for a parent. Like Doris, Kelly's mother, he ruled by abuse. The lyrics to "Dirty Laundry" broke my heart as I listened to Kelly spin out an account of physical abuse at the hands of her lover. Might she be singing about her mother? I was transported back to Doris's senseless berating, and the beatings. Children are so vulnerable.

I realized that I had finally begun to gain healthy emotional distance from the Knowles chapter in my life. I was seeing that there was a limit to what any teacher can do against overwhelmingly negative parental influences.

At that time I had been teaching, for about a year, a girl who I will call my Nordic student. Incredibly talented, she was selfish as hell. Her mother was making a mess of everything, and I was frustrated by the girl's petulance. To my every suggestion she would retort, "Why do I have to do this?" Her disrespect had been my own fault. I'd done it again, gotten excited about talent. The girl even had a sister who sang and had an absolutely gorgeous voice. Still, my student told me that I was there for her, not her sister. My response was, "Been there and done that. I'm not going to ignore another sister, especially one with her talent." By September 2014 both my Nordic princess and her mother were history. I had learned that lesson.

Then almost a year later, on the 13th of May, 2014, The media reported on Solange Knowles's infamous elevator attack on Jay-Z, and Beyoncé's reaction to the brawl. My friends were shocked that I accepted the story so matter-of-factly. They hadn't known Solange, that she had grown up angry, that she did not hide her feelings. They certainly couldn't have known that Beyoncé avoided, even denied, reality at all cost. She stood in that elevator like her sister wasn't kicking the shit out of her husband.

Of course. She was Beyoncé.

The regal soprano Grace Bumbry took her place beside the other four Kennedy Center honorees to receive the President's award in December 2009. Grace and I were both entranced by the events of the whole grand evening at the White House.
Licensed by Getty Images, *Photo: Brooks Kraft*

In 2011 the TV channel ARTE, Europe's equivalent of A&E and Biography Channels in the U.S., offered me my own casting show. The director/producer of the firm SMP Signed Media Production, and I decided to call it "Open Opera," where I would cast, of all things, the opera Carmen.

Astute readers of this memoir will have noticed that the opera *Carmen* has made a frequent appearance. When, as a teenager, I agreed to attend the opera (my first) with my high school French teacher, I had no idea that

742

this would be *the* watershed moment of my life. Everything about that *Carmen*—the music, singing, characters, production—thrilled me. I seized the threads of this experience and began to weave my life's fragile fabric. Already in my student years I added the tenor role of Don José, the shamed and hapless wooer of the seductress Carmen, to my fledgling repertoire. Don José's choices bewildered me at first. In 1992 my beloved teacher and opera coach Sylvia Olden Lee helped me to dig deep into Don José's character in order to portray him onstage with all the subtleties and compassion that this tragic character evinces. Under Ms. Lee's wise guidance I learned to understand my own role in Life's cycle of love, betrayal, and forgiveness. When I earned the prestigious contract to create my own casting show for ARTE television in Europe, I naturally agreed with the choice to present the opera *Carmen*. The threads that I'd seized as a teenager had become a weaving of real strength. I realized that what I now held in my hand was the invulnerable crimson thread in life—God's unchanging grace—and that by cleaving to His truth, I was enough.
We are all enough!

Open Opera Premiere! Mai 2012
Photo: SMP Signed Media Production

33. Frosty

My ankle was all healed. British Airways flight 195 from London landed in Houston at 2:45 p.m., on the 20th of December 2014. After gathering my bags and getting through the customs nightmare, I headed for Alamo rental cars. Shortly thereafter, my publicist, Tony Coles, buzzed my cell phone.

"David, where are you?" he asked.

"Sitting in the drive-thru at Frenchy's chicken, eating a honey bun," I said.

"I can't believe it. The first thing you did was go to Frenchy's and buy a honey bun?"

"Yep," I said. "Some things don't change."

Laughing, Tony asked when we would meet to talk about the master classes, the newspaper interviews he was working on, the radio spots and the television interviews that had been confirmed, and a few other things.

"As soon as I am done here I'll head over to your place."

Approximately thirty minutes later I pulled into the parking area of Tony's I-45 North apartment complex, with enough food for two. Tony was doing a bang-up job as my publicist. I felt lucky to have such a brilliant strategist and thinker on my side. Not to mention, he'd been there to live through the Beyoncé years with me. He was exactly the right influence to offer me the moral support I needed in putting this story to bed. I had put it away, again – for the third time – insistent that I would not publish it.

Tony's dog, Boe, was always happy to see me. That dog was crazy. Without fail he'd lick me, jump on me, and hump my leg, always in that order. Inviting me in, Tony asked about my flight. I told him that I would never fly British Airways again, to which he offered to write a letter clearing up my concerns. "Don't bother!" I wouldn't waste his time. I was sure I wouldn't get a satisfactory response from the airline even though the Cabin Services Director (CSD) had personally handled my complaint.

"He offered me 15,000 miles and a bottle of Champagne, but I wasn't interested," I said. "It's the principle of the matter."

744

Changing the subject, I asked "So what's on the agenda? Any new developments?"

"Actually, yes," Tony said.

My ears stood at full attention.

"Now just hear me out before saying anything," he said.

"OK, now I am nervous," I said. "I hope what you are about to tell me isn't going to sour my day even further."

"It might, but I believe it is the right thing to do. Now listen," he said. "God gave this to me," he exclaimed. Tony knew that I always listened to what the "still small voice" said, but normally only when it spoke to me.

"What is it?" I asked him cautiously.

"I've arranged for you to go to Beyoncé's Church, St. John's Downtown."

I didn't say a word. Actually, I must have had a look of both astonishment and disgust on my face, because Tony said, "Close your mouth!" He broke into laughter. "Do you have to tear up your face like that?"

"No, but I have no intention of going to Beyoncé's church." Why would I do that? I thought to myself.

"I have written the Pastor and he is expecting you," Tony said. "I think it will be an important part of your trip here to the United States. Something tells me it is going to be interesting," Tony added.

Once again, I had nothing to say.

"Say something! What do you really think of the idea?"

"Well, I think it is crazy," I said, "but I am reserving my opinion until later. Let me digest this shit for a few minutes."

Tony seemed sure about his idea, absolutely convinced that his instincts were right. I agreed to think about it and promised that we could talk later that evening. Reiterating his point, Tony said, "Something interesting is going to happen. I don't know what it is, but it is going to be good. I can just feel it."

Changing the subject again, I asked him why he had chosen New Orleans as one of the cities for my master class series. I didn't want to go to New Orleans. In spite of its being a music place, I had never been impressed with the city. And what would I find, in the wake of Hurricane Katrina? Tony assured me that the city was functional again and that I would not be sorry about going to New Orleans. I wasn't convinced.

The conversation shifted to Toronto, Canada. I had been to many other Canadian cities in the past, but never to Toronto. I looked forward to that new experience, and we discussed some potential dates. Then Tony brought up Brooklyn. Having been born there, he always talked about Brooklyn. This time he described to me his idea to create a foundation that would support children, a potential project that really interested me.

After we had set dates, discussed itinerary, and touched on a whole lot more, Tony slipped back into Beyoncé and her damn church. All this talk about Beyoncé and her church was wearing me out. "First things first," I said to Tony. "I'm here about business, and Beyoncé isn't my business no more." I wanted to stay focused on what was important. I wanted to save time on this trip to visit family from December 21 to 29, move on to Oklahoma City on the December 29, and travel to Dallas for New Year's Eve. Then I'd spend one week in Los Angeles visiting my Aunt Lerl, Roy Brown's mother, and my cousin Hermine and her children. I hadn't seen Hermine since I was nine years old.

The next day, Sunday, I showed up to Tony's house at exactly 8:00 a.m. It was three days before Christmas, December 21, 2014. Although I was still suffering from transatlantic jet lag, I had decided to oblige his fantasy and attend Beyoncé's church's early morning service. We were late.

"The service starts at 8," Tony said.

Apologetically, I said, "Truth be told, I am not looking forward to the experience – at all." The entire night I had lain awake, imagining I would be bumping into Celestine. I didn't want to deal with her fakeness – no way, no how. Not too far along on our journey into downtown Houston we hit a traffic jam. Thank God, I thought. My prayers have been answered. I decided to exit the freeway.

"What are you doing?" Tony asked.

"I'm not going to sit in this Stau" – apologizing for speaking German, I corrected myself – "I mean traffic jam."

746

"I'm getting angry," Tony said under his breath.

Ignoring the noises coming from the passenger seat, I said, "Why don't we just go have breakfast? My treat."

If looks could kill, I would have died that instant.

Tony began yelling at me. I yelled back, all the while driving toward downtown, but doing my best not to get there any time soon. I could see it in the distance. A real argument ensued and escalated to boiling point. Tony was adamant and so was I. I wasn't going to Beyoncé's damn church, I said. "And why do they call it Beyoncé's church?" I asked. "Does she even go there?" I had changed my mind just that quickly. I was tired of Beyoncé and her damn family. I didn't want to see them, or sit where they once sat. Plus, I knew St. John's Church.

"You are getting in the way with your shit," Tony screamed.

He was right and I knew it, but I wasn't going to admit it. I had been suffering tremendously over the last six years reliving the various situations and dramas. I hadn't been able to finish the book, stopping and starting several times in the last six months alone. Deciding that I wouldn't release it after Beyoncé's "Life is But a Dream," I suffered through several bouts of depression, argued with Grace and longtime friends over their non-support of the book, lost friendships, kicked a few students out of my studio and house, senselessly attacked my editor, a longtime friend of sixteen-plus years who had been nothing but supportive, and walked away from a publishing deal with a reputable publisher in London. He wanted me to water down my story. I refused. I even switched the radio off every time I heard Beyoncé's voice. I couldn't stand the sound of it and I was pretty upset with Kelly Rowland, Letoya Luckett, and LaTavia Roberson to boot. I was deeply disappointed in their lack of caring and consideration for others. They showed me no respect or appreciation, and they had arrived in their 20s possessing, apparently, not an ounce of honor. Not one Mensch in the lot of them. The entire history of Destiny's Child, and certainly Beyoncé's history, had been altered to benefit the Knowleses and to erase me. So, no, I didn't want to go to Beyoncé's damn church, and Tony knew it.

"What is your damn problem?" Tony asked.

"I don't have a damn problem," I answered, but that was not the truth and God knew it. Suddenly, I heard his voice.

Relentless, Tony did not let up. This time when he mentioned the "still small voice," I was convinced. "Go to the church," my own still small voice said. I found myself speeding, racing towards downtown Houston, this time determined.

Getting to the church 45 minutes late for the service, Tony and I entered the building, my suitcases in tow. Leaving the bags in the fellowship hall, we proceeded upstairs to the church sanctuary. I started to tremble. I couldn't control my emotion, wanting to scream out in anguish. It felt like my soul's desire to right an injustice, but I dared not. I worked hard to put my uneasiness to the side. In spite of the not-so-good singing in that sanctuary, I stomped my feet and clapped my hands, earnestly turning my prayers into music. At the end of it all, nothing spectacular had happened.

Still Tony would not be deterred. "This day ain't done," he said. That may have been his reality, but mine was focused on taking off from Hobby Airport at 2:45. American Airlines flight number 2323 was due to land in Omaha at 6:15 p.m., and I would be on that plane, come hell or high water.

Once outside St. John's, I put my luggage back in my rental car and agreed to Tony's idea for a photo in front of the church. He fussed with the set-up, being sure that the church name stood out in the picture and composing everything just so. Several pictures later he seemed satisfied, and we proceeded to the car. He still had more than an hour before he had to be at his own church, so I started to suggest that we go to breakfast now. Suddenly, in mid-sentence, I stopped.

"Go take pictures in front of Music World Management," the still small voice said.

"Tony, where is Music World Management? Isn't it close?" I asked.

"Yes, it's right around the corner," he answered.

"I want to take pictures in front of the business I help build," I said. "Should we walk around the corner or drive?"

748

"Drive! It's cold out here," Tony answered. Temperatures had fallen in the night since my arrival, and Houstonians were frail beings in chilly weather.

Getting into the car, buckling up, and driving out of the parking lot, I started to get butterflies in my stomach. I had no idea why, but I pressed on. I made the left turn off Gray Street onto Crawford Street. One block later, at the corner of Crawford and Webster, there stood the reason for my angst and unexplained butterflies. The hustle bustle of people indicated a yard sale. Right in front of me, on the sidewalk, Mathew Knowles appeared.

Yes, there he was, not a customer looking over the merchandise, but the host of this yard sale. He was moving furniture into place, outdoors, on his property.

Astonished, I made the left turn on to Webster and exactly in that moment Mathew looked up, peering into my front windshield. He recognized me.

I wanted to stop, but my foot wouldn't move from the gas pedal to the brake. Tony was screaming, "I knew it. I knew something was going to happen!" Suddenly my "still small voice" spoke loudly. "Go back, and face your demons." I turned the corner, and this time I pulled into the driveway, determined to face my fears. Without blinking or expressing any real emotion or surprise, Mathew Knowles said, "Hey man, what are you doing here?"

"I just came from church," I replied. The next thing that came out of his mouth took me aback.

"Hey, have you heard about *all these motha fuckas* writing these *motha fuckin* books about Beyoncé?" he asked animatedly. I was one of the *motha fuckas*, but in that moment I could only reply yes with a nod of my head. I needed a minute to collect my stunned self.

"Yes, this *motha fucka* named Tony Moore has written a horrible book, full of mistakes and wrong *motha fuckin* information. He called the girls *bitches and shit*. You must remember that *motha fucker*," Mathew said, now gesticulating.

"Tony Moore? No, I'm afraid I don't remember that name."

"Sure you do. He was Ann's friend. That *punk ass bitch*," Mathew said.

Turning to Tony, I inquired if he had heard anything about a book being written by a Tony Moore.

"You must mean Kenny Moore," Tony answered.

"Yes, that's that *motha fucka*," Mathew shouted. "Tony was his real first name."

"No Mathew, I believe his first name was Brian," I said. A quick second of dismay and wonderment from Mathew followed. Seconds later he exclaimed, "Ah, yea – that's right, that *motha fucka – son of a bitch…*"

"Yes, I had heard that Brian Kenny Moore had written a book, but I thought his book was about Ann," I said.

"Yea it is but that *motha fucka* is claiming credit for discovering the girls. That *motha fucka* ain't discovered nobody – *punk ass…*"

Mathew looked OK, but he must have been high. I remembered that when he was high he talked like this – belligerently, to put it mildly. I awaited the question. I was writing a book too; surely he must have known, I thought. Whoever told him about Kenny Moore's book must have told him that I was writing one, too. I had heard that Kenny Moore outed my writing a book in the telling of his story. But no, Mathew continued with his barrage of lies, oblivious to our presence. I prepared myself for the showdown, standing flat-footed and purposeful.

"Yeah, this white *motha fucka –* his ass is good. That *motha fucka* found my *motha fuckin* cousin in the woods somewhere in Alabama, *talkin bout* what was Mathew like as a twelve-year-old – shit, I thought my *fuckin* cousin was dead," Mathew said, laughing hysterically.

"Ah, you must be referring to J. Randy Taraborrelli," I said.

"Yeah that's that *motha fucka*. He wanted to interview me but I wasn't gon talk to his ass but since that *motha fucka* dug up my no good ass cousin I thought I *betta* talk to his ass," Mathew said, scratching his acned face and rubbing his ill-shaped and aging body.

"Yes, I understand," I said. "His assistant called me, but I refused to talk to them."

"Thank you man," Mathew said. "Yeah, Beyoncé been asking *motha fuckas* not to talk to his ass," he stuttered. (Had Mathew just forgotten that he had told me that he did talk to Taraborrelli? The man was still crazy, I thought).

I had had enough. All I could do was think about getting the hell away from this delusional asshole. I told him how nice it was to see him and turned to make my exit.

"Wait, where you *goin*" he asked. "I need your telephone number."

"Excuse me?" I said.

"Your phone number. I need your phone number. I been *tryin* to find you," Mathew continued.

"Why have you been looking for me Mathew?" I asked, quite perplexed. What was going to come out of his mouth next?

"We're *gonna be makin* the Destiny's Child Movie – Uh, the Destiny's Child story for television. I'm in negotiations with HBO and a few other giants about it right now. I want to bring you on board as a consultant."

"Really," I said. And this is why you're holding a yard sale? I wanted to ask him. I was pissed off now and sure of Mathew's ruse. This mother fucker was toying with me. What was my dumb ass thinking? I continued to mask my agitation and replied "Oh, OK."

Just in that moment a man approached us dragging some metal bins. In it were books, CDs, and other household things. On the front of it someone had hung the word "Bargain." My God, was that Solange's CD, front and center, and for only 99 cents? As I reached down to pick it up, Mathew's voice interrupted me. "Your number," he repeated. "I need your number." Completely numb and a little sick to my stomach, I rattled off the long number, country code, then city code, and finally the number.

"Damn." Mathew said. "You still live in Berlin don't you?"

"Yes, I do Mathew."

"Oh, I thought you might have moved back to Houston" – again laughing nervously. "I hadn't seen your ass in years. Shit – it could be the case, right?" Mathew said.

Smiling, I answered blandly. "Yes, Mathew." Then I noticed that in his stupor Mathew had taken my number down wrong. I had to repeat it three times before he got it right, reminding him that he'd have to include the country code and city code before a call would go through.

"Ah, yeah – that's right."

"Wait a minute!" he said suddenly. "I'm *gon* call your number right now. *Motha fucka's be givin* you the wrong number *an* shit."

I was getting angrier by the minute. I swear for all that is righteous and holy, I started praying, fervently but silently. It took every ounce of strength I had not to knock the shit out of Mathew. After making several mistakes dialing the number, he finally reached my office number – he said. He had the nerve to show Tony and me that he had actually dialed the number. Pausing, as if time had stood still, he let it ring, and ring, and ring. Then he said, "OK, this you."

Once again I positioned myself to make my getaway. "It was a real treat," I said and turned towards my car. "Oh, I almost forgot," I added. "Good luck on your yard sale."

"Oh, yeah…shit, I need to clear out space for the expansion of my empire," he exclaimed proudly. "I need to get rid of this shit anyway."

Tony asked, "Have you advertised Mathew, it's Sunday and you have so much stuff. Garage sales are normally held on Saturdays aren't they?"

"Yea they do, but I'm having mine on Sunday. It's in all the papers."

I wished Mathew well on his yard sale again, still trying to make my great escape to the black Jeep Cherokee I'd rented. Mathew said that he had to get *goin* anyway. "I *gotta* lot a shit to finish before the first customers show up."

"Oh OK, well, I have got to get Tony to church and catch my flight. Take care of yourself Mathew." He reached out, hugging me good-bye. I almost lost last night's dinner. I was in such shock that it took me a moment to register that I wasn't hugging him back. To my disgust, he held on until I did. Seconds later I backed out of the driveway, mad as hell.

"Oh my God – Oh my God," Tony screamed, laughing hysterically. He couldn't stop laughing until all of a sudden he looked at me and said, "And your ass wanted to go have some eggs at Denny's." Then it was my turn to laugh.

"Do you think Mathew really called your house?" Tony asked.

"Hell no. That mother fucker ain't called my damn house. Do you remember how many times he let the phone ring before exclaiming, in all his glory, 'this you?'"

"Yes, three times," Tony answered.

"Exactly. My answering machine is programmed to answer after the first ring. Mathew did not call my house."

"I don't know, he dialed the number and even showed us!!!" Tony said, still laughing hysterically.

"Believe me; Mathew did not call my damn house. I can't believe that he stood in my face and lied to me," I said.

"Why not? He has lied in your face before," Tony answered.

With 45 minutes to go before Tony had to be sitting on the organ bench at his church, Tony screamed, "Whoa, Lawd, I'm hungry now." He laughed so hard that I thought he'd pass out. "I'm famished. I could eat a horse," he said, completely in love with himself.

Tony Coles had been right. Something did happen, but it wasn't just my meeting Mathew on the street. The picture of him needing money and selling his daughters' things (Solange's, Beyoncé's and Destiny Child's paraphernalia) had consumed my imagination. I had just been given what I needed to finish my book. A good dose of Mathew Knowles cleared up any misgivings, fears, or concerns I had about telling my story – about telling my truth.

They say that one man's trash is another man's treasure.

To hell with Mathew, I shouted, pulling into Denny's on Southmore Street.

* * * * *

My flight landed in Omaha, on time. As I made my way to baggage claim I passed the small food court, where I could see on the television that the news was on. KETV-7 News was talking about Mathew. Apparently, TMZ had heard about his little yard sale and had shown up with cameras to document what they were intimating was Beyoncé's father's fall from grace. Not a fan of yard sales, I hadn't been to one in years. That I had just witnessed the mother of all yard sales felt to me like fate.

I must have died and gone to heaven twenty times as I stood before the large airport screen watching as TMZ told America about Mathew Knowles's plight. I confess to feelings of some glee as the reporter roamed the grounds with his camera, focusing its lens on that bargain bin with Solange's CDs. Just imagine! I had watched Mathew's cronies put it into place and write 99 cents on it. TMZ showed Beyoncé's hard-earned work, spread across Music World Management's lawn, complete with price tags ranging from five to twenty dollars and more.

In his delusional state, Mathew apparently believed that no one knew that he had no clients left in the music business. Reportedly, people did not trust him and wanted nothing to do with his off-brand "guidance." I'd read that his connection to BET, and a show called "Sunday's Best," was waning. Radio One (which has stations all over America) had long since banned Mathew Knowles's artists from their air waves. And now that Beyoncé had fired him as her manager, he was unable to capitalize on her continued success, which was unrelated to him. But never you mind, Beyoncé's daddy held on tight to his little coin box, standing firm on his yard sale prices. The TMZ reporter said that Mathew would take "not a penny less than $200.00" on some giant-sized images of his daughter and her bandmates.

What a farce.

Christmas with my family and friends was great. Keeping to schedule, I visited Oklahoma City and Dallas and enjoyed Los Angeles. Now it was time to return to Houston. Tony called me in Omaha to tell me that the popular Houston show, "Great Day Houston," had agreed to an interview. They were excited about it. The interview would be live and I was supposed to talk about my master class and Beyoncé. "It's Grammy week," Tony reminded me. I was a bit anxious about it, having grown accustomed to not getting credit for anything. This was a major deal. Not only would I be claiming my role in developing Beyoncé's singing and performing talents, but I would be doing so in her hometown, where it had happened. I remembered Deborah Duncan from years ago, when she invited a young Destiny's Child for their first television appearance. Would she remember me? What would she ask me? I knew that she was a fan of Beyoncé's and Destiny's Child. Hell, all of Houston was.

When we arrived at the TV studio, Tony and I were ushered into the greenroom. Shortly thereafter, Deborah Duncan walked in. "It's good to meet you, David." She said, conversationally, that she'd talked to Tina (Celestine) the day before. I cringed, hoping like hell she hadn't noticed.

As soon as she left the greenroom I turned to Tony. "Did you hear her say that she'd talked to that bitch Celestine?"

"Of course I heard it. And we need to leave before she pulls up outside."

"I wish her ass would."

"So what do you think Celestine said about your ass?" Tony asked.

"I don't know, but I'm pissed."

"Why?" Tony asked.

"I'm tired of Celestine, shit."

"Well, you know she can't get Beyoncé on the phone. Beyoncé acknowledged Deborah Duncan the last time she acknowledged you," Tony said. "And that was last century."

We both laughed, conscious that the other guest could hear us.

Suddenly, I was being called to the set.

Tony grabbed my arm. "I don't give a damn what Deborah Duncan says to you. Don't you put those damn shoes on. If you do, I quit."

I laughed and then said, "If she asks, I must oblige." I thought Tony was going to explode.

Just as he'd suspected. Deborah Duncan got around to asking me to show her how I'd taught the girls to walk in heels, reaching down to unzip her own boots. Suddenly, I heard an audible moan coming from behind the camera. Tony had turned white. Naturally, I laughed off Deborah's joke. Although I hadn't taken seriously Tony's threat to quit, I knew that he was right. Playing into Deborah's interview shtick of putting the shoes on would've killed the reason I was there, diverted attention from my story.

Suddenly, the moment I had been dreading had arrived. "I talked to Tina yesterday," Deborah said, on camera. "She said the thing that you did, because Beyoncé was always singing the melody while the other girls were doing the harmonies, so if she kept going and going, like a machine, and she wasn't a machine, she started to lose her voice. You trained her how to keep that voice and still be able to perform."

What bullshit! I thought. Then, Smile, David. Just smile! I managed to answer Deborah, "Yes, and not just to maintain that voice, but to take it to the heights. I took what was a wonderful talent and worked to make it extraordinary."

After the interview, Tony suggested taking me out to lunch. He was happy I hadn't put those boots on. I laughed again, and told him that I wanted to go to Wendy's.

"What?" he said. "Did you say Wendy's?"

"Yes," I answered.

"That's not food!"

"Don't you blaspheme against Wendy's. The Frosty was there for me when I couldn't call a friend. I ain't never been let down by no Frosty."

Actually, there was a method to my madness. I looked forward to burying the hatchet with Celestine, once and for all.

We settled down at Wendy's, where I contemplated my Frosty in anticipation. Judging from Tony's reaction, I gathered that he was happy that Celestine had, at least, acknowledged me when she'd spoken with Deborah. I was not, but held my peace.

Celestine had inadvertently said one thing that was, however, correct. Study with me had made Beyoncé consistent, dependable. She had no idea what a great compliment she was paying her daughter's true teacher.

Opening up a picture of Celestine in Google on his telephone, Tony added, "Too bad we don't have any exploding candles."

I didn't pay Tony no mind. I was on a mission.

"I wonder what Witch Celestine is doing right now?" he asked.

756

"You remember that?" I asked, almost choking.

"How could I forget Witch Celestine and Donkey Mathew?" Tony said. "I wonder if that Donkey is still snorting all that hay and spreading his seed all over the barn?"

I just kept slurping on my Frosty, shaking my head. "You are a damn fool, Tony Coles." Then, looking at him sideways, I said, "I'm not dealing with Mathew right now. I'm concentrated on Celestine at the moment." Slurp, slurp.

"Well, you need to be eulogizing Beyoncé's ass. And throw that Frosty upside her head," Tony said. "I know you love her, and I love her too. She worked hard, and has a great work ethic but she's ungrateful. And tell me again, what did you ever do nasty to her? Oh, that's right. You're the motherfucker who moved into her house, gave her four private lessons a week, six group lessons, shoved Hamburger Helper down her throat, picked her ass up from school, helped her intellectually challenged ass with her homework, and gave her all your time, forsaking all others. And to top it off you had the nerve to not help Mathew steal all her money, while genuinely trying to help Kelly and the other girls. You're a horrible bastard, David Lee Brewer. That's what you are, unforgivable."

I laughed.

Then Tony said, "I'd be mad at your ass, too."

"So what do you think I should do then?" I asked.

"You should've cursed Beyoncé's ass down to the ground. Now here you sit having a sugar séance with ole Celestine and you need to be holding Beyoncé responsible. Eat that Frosty and say goodbye to that evil Veltone so we can go to Luby's."

I lost it, laughing out loud. "This ain't about Beyoncé." Slurp, slurp. "Why, Beyoncé is as sweet as this ice cream," I added.

"Yep, so sweet she'd never imagine bothering you with a hello, how you doing, a goodbye, or even a kiss my ass. She's so sweet that you had to talk to her through a bodyguard. She can't even remember you running in the park, or living in her house for that matter. But she can remember riding around in a Jaguar, being better than Janet Jackson."

I said nothing, determined to bury *Celestine*. Not tomorrow, but today, February 3. She'd been the thorn in my side long enough. I knew Tony was just trying to find a way in to my psyche, to make sure I was all right. I was fine. And after I'd take the last gulp of that Frosty I was going to be even better. Betrayal was no longer welcome.

"If you had it to do over, would you?" Tony asked.

"Absolutely," I answered. "I never stopped. Purpose is bigger than disappointment. God guides, our job is to follow."

"Okay, but what have you learned?"

I thought for a second and then answered. "I know that when I wake up tomorrow that I will love Beyoncé, and that's okay. I raised her."

Slurp, slurp, slurp....

"All done."

Special thanks

I would like to acknowledge all of my students, both former and current. I love and thank my mother, Fern Brewer, for her undying and unconditional support. I offer eternal gratitude to my late grandparents, Evelyn and Charles Sims, without whom I would not have become who I became.

From the place in my heart that few get to see I say thank you to my friends: my very own oracle, the unbelievably dependable and brilliant editor Sandra Hyslop; my surrogate mother and mentor Grace Bumbry; my talented publicist Tony Coles, who keeps me grounded and is a brother to me; my surrogate sister Shevon Jacob-Loftin; my ever- supportive and wonderful friends Dr. Alexander Kwasi Homenya M.D., Ricky Baker and Glen Hunter, and Marijona Kraponiene, for their selfless help and always great advice; my German mother, Gerlinde Baier; my go - to therapist Aaron Edwards; and the celebrated author Clayton Delery-Edwards.

I am grateful for the refuge to write that Sabrina Lorenz and my friends at the Clinic Lauterbacher Mühle, Seeshaupt, so generously provided. And I would also like to show heartfelt appreciation to Wiara Vogl, the author and journalist Ralf Dorweiler, psychiatrist Dr. Manuela Schade, and child psychologist Dr. Bernd Dietrich, as well as Ralf Hebig, Tino Schreiber, Evangelist Cassandra Bennett, William Volk, and the German tax office's, Dorothea Mundinac, for showing me why my book is important. And last, but certainly not least, I would like to thank Petra Senftleben for her unyielding patience and support. She will never fully understand how much of a blessing she is and was.

I thank from the bottom of my heart my manager, the television executive Yves Fernau, and my longtime collaborator and great friend, the German record industry executive Björn Teske, for their invaluable contributions to this book.

Bibliography

Barbier, Patrick (1995). Farinelli. Der Kastrat der Könige.
Düsseldorf: ECON

Blythe, Will (2008). The Liberation of B., under:
http://www.elle.com/culture/celebrities/a9721/the-liberation-of-b-271284/
Last reviewed on 12.04.2017

David, Marc (1996). Farinelli.
Munich: Limes

Duenwald, Mary (2005). The Physiology of … Facial Expressions, unter:
http://discovermagazine.com/2005/jan/physiology-of-facial-expressions/
Last reviewed on 12.04.2017

Feldenkrais, Moshe (1990). Awareness through movement.
New York: Harper Collins

Feldman, David Henry (1986). Nature's Gambit: Child Prodigies and the
Development of Human Potential.
New York: Basic Books

Foster Brown, Jamie (2002, July). Meow. Warm Whispers and Hot Se-
crets. Happenings at our 13th party party!
SISTER 2 SISTER, 8.

The transcript from the depositions of Mathew Knowles, in Harris County,
Texas, USA / 281st Judicial District Court of Harris County, Texas (2000).
Case number: 2000-13299-A; *LeToya Lucket, et al. ./. Mathew Knowles,
et al.*

Greene, Robert (2000). The 48 Laws of Power.
New York: Penguin Books

Ing, Richard (2006). Spiritual Warfare.
New Kensington: Whitaker House

Knowles, Beyoncé / Rowland, Kelly / Williams, Michelle (2002). Soul
Survivors. The Official Autobiography of Destiny's Child.
New York: Harper Collins

Mayo, Kierna (2015, July). The Life and Times of Tenie.
EBONY, 90 – 99.

Miller, Alice (2008). The Drama Of The Gifted Child.
New York: Basic Books

Nietzsche, Friedrich Wilhelm (2016). Jenseits von Gut und Böse.
Kindle Edition

Norment, Lynn (2001, September). THE UNTOLD STORY OF HOW
Tina & Mathew Knowles Created the Destiny's Child Gold Mine.
EBONY

Rogers, Katie / Spencer, Ruth (2013). Beyoncé's new HBO film: how
might Life is But a Dream play out?, under:
https://www.theguardian.com/music/2013/feb/15/beyonce-hbo-film-life-
but-a-dream
Last reviewed on 12.04.2017

Rosen, Jody (2006). B'Day, under:
http://ew.com/article/2006/09/04/bday/
Last reviewed on 12.04.2017

Taraborelli, John R. A. (2015). Becoming Beyoncé – The Untold Story.
New York: Grand Central Publishing – Hachette Book Group

The Free Library by Farlex (2001). Former Vocal Coach of Pop Group
Destiny's Child Responds to Allegations Against Former Members, under:
https://www.thefreelibrary.com/Former+Vocal+Coach+of+Pop+Group+D
estiny%27s+Child+Responds+to...-a069268184
Last reviewed on 12.04.2017

THE HOLY BIBLE (2001). Old and New Testaments. Authorized King
James Version.
Belgium: Thomas Nelson

Turner, Niki (2000, December). Farrah. The Split with Destiny's Child.
SISTER 2 SISTER, 68 – 75.

Turner, Niki (2001, May). Destiny's Child's longtime voice coach David
Brewer.
SISTER 2 SISTER, 46 – 51.

Writer unknown (2001, Februar). Article about the break up of Destiny's
Child.
VIBE

Vázquez, Luci (2002). When Destiny's Child broke through in 1997, they
had been rehearsing for that day for almost 8 years..., under:
http://www.hitquarters.com/index.php3?page=intrview/2002/February6_1
0_10_32.html
Last reviewed on 12.04.2017

William, Otis / Romanowski, Patricia (2002). Temptations.
New York: Cooper Square

Made in the USA
Middletown, DE
30 August 2024